DATE DUE

ALSO BY JOE NICK PATOSKI

Selena: Como la Flor

Stevie Ray Vaughan: Caught in the Crossfire
(coauthor Bill Crawford)

WILLIE NELSON

An Epic Life

JOE NICK PATOSKI

LITTLE, BROWN AND COMPANY

LARGE PRINT

Little, Brown and Company
Hachette Book Group USA
237 Park Avenue, New York, NY 10017
Visit our Web site at www.HachetteBookGroupUSA.com

First Large Print Edition: April 2008

The Large Print Edition is published in accord with
the standards of the N.A.V.H.

The author is grateful for permission to include the previously copyrighted material:"Night Life," copyright 1962 Sony/ATV Music Publishing LLC. All rights administered by Sony/ATV Music Publishing LLC, 8 Music Square West, Nashville, TN 37203. All rights reserved. Used by permission; "Mr. Record Man," copyright 1961 Sony/ATV Music Publishing LLC. All rights administered by Sony/ATV Music Publishing LLC, 8 Music Square West, Nashville, TN 37203. All rights reserved. Used by permission; "I Never Cared for You," copyright 1964 Sony/ATV Music Publishing LLC. All rights administered by Sony/ATV Music Publishing LLC, 8 Music Square West, Nashville, TN 37203. All rights reserved. Used by permission; "One Day at a Time," copyright 1965 Sony/ATV Music Publishing LLC. All rights administered by Sony/ATV Music Publishing LLC, 8 Music Square West, Nashville, TN 37203. All rights reserved. Used by permission; "What Would Willie Do?" copyright 2001, Tiltawhirl Music. All rights administered by Bluewater Music Services Corp., 1212 16th Avenue South, Nashville, TN 37212. All rights reserved. Used by permission.

LCCN: 2008920817
ISBN-10: 0-316-03023-6 / ISBN-13: 978-0-316-03023-6

RRD-IN

10 9 8 7 6 5 4 3 2 1

Printed in the United States of America

To the Nelsons, the Patoskis,
and families everywhere

CONTENTS

WILLIE NELSON

Somewhere in America, 2007

THE SEA OF humanity swells and roils all the way to the horizon, thousands of eyes fixed on him, thousands of hands clapping, a chorus of voices cheering and yelling, lips whistling, feet stomping, smiles everywhere, all because of him. Lone Star flags and arms thrusting skyward, hands clutching cigarette lighters and cans of beer above heads bobbing like buoys because of the music. The old man with the wild white eyebrows and wrinkled skin, his long white hair pulled back into two braids, tries to make eye contact with as many eyes as he can in ten seconds before glancing offhandedly over his shoulder at the musicians standing and sitting in place behind him. He straps on his guitar and steps to the microphone with a casualness that betrays a lifetime of going through the very same ritual night after night, year after year. He half sings, half talks five magic words that trigger a sonic roar.

Whisk-key Riv-verrr take my miiiiiind.

Abbott, 1938

EYES HAD BEEN gazing at him wherever folks tended to gather ever since he could remember. His first audience was a group of families at the Brooken Homecoming, an all-day reunion, picnic, and songfest in a shady grove by the small community eight miles southeast of Abbott, Texas. His grandmother had dressed him up in a white sailor suit with matching shorts. The stage was the back of a flatbed truck. The five-year-old boy showed little sign of nervousness other than picking his nose, as young boys are known to do. There was praying, singing, eating, visiting, more singing and more praying, and so much nose picking that when it was his turn to stand and recite the psalm his grandmother had taught him, his white sailor suit was splattered with blood redder than the boy's hair.

The boy acted like the nosebleed was no big deal. He followed the prayer with an original poem he recited while holding one nostril shut with his hand. In a voice that was small but not shy, he said:

What are you looking at me for?
I ain't got nothin' to say.
If you don't like the looks of me,
You can look some other way.

The audience clapped and cheered. The boy beamed. He'd remembered all the words. The people seemed to like him. He liked the attention, all eyes on him. He liked making them smile. The people listening felt like family. He flashed a not-so-shy grin of gratitude. From that moment forward, Willie Hugh Nelson, who earned the nickname "Booger Red" for his bloody nose, was determined to give a good show.

East of Western Grove on Pindall Ridge, 1925

MUSIC WAS IN the Nelson blood long before Texas, back in the rugged hills of north central Arkansas, where the isolated communities of settlers could hardly be described as settlements.

The rickety wooden shack on cedar blocks that passed for a one-room schoolhouse was hardly fit to be occupied. The floor sagged and creaked with every step taken. And yet, the room was packed to the rafters. Those present were just happy to be there.

Singing school was in session. Singing school was the social event of the year for many folks living in the hills, hollows, and backwoods of Searcy, Newton, Boone, and Marion counties in north central Arkansas. Sometimes the only social event of the year outside of church, a funeral, or a barn raising, singing school brought out the whole community, from babies to elders. For a week or two, the singing school students would learn music theory, how to sight-read by recognizing music notations, how to write lyrics, and how to write multiple parts to a song for harmonizing.

The Baptist and Methodist congregations, the faiths of the God-fearing white folks attending the schools, warmed up for each song by singing the words of the notes on the scale. Their voices were robust. No instrumental accompaniment was needed. When a particular song roused the gathering, they clapped hands and stomped feet, about as loose as Protestants got around Pindall, and sang with such power, the whole building would shake.

At times like that, Willie's grandparents, Alfred and Nancy Nelson, knew they were doing their job.

Alfred was a blacksmith by trade, but music was his pleasure. Nancy embraced music formally, earning a degree through mail correspondence from the Chicago School of Music. She gave lessons to children around Pindall Ridge throughout the year, and both Alfred and Nancy taught singing school in surrounding communities with names as lyrical as the music they taught: Western Grove, Union Y, Everton, Snowball, Gilbert, Morning Star, Lone Pine,

Evening Star, Harriet, Canaan, Hasty, Erby, Valley Springs, Zinc, and Eros.

Their love of teaching music came from Nancy's father, William Marion Smothers, a farmer born in Barren Creek, Marion County, Arkansas, whose people had emigrated from Carroll County, Tennessee. William had married twice, fathering eighteen children, and learned music from his parents well enough to teach it himself.

For the first 150 years of the United States, singing school masters like William Smothers, Nancy and Alfred Nelson, and others were the most influential music educators in America. Few folks in the hills and hollows and backwoods in and around Searcy, Newton, Marion, and Boone counties could read, so they used songbooks in which notes were represented by distinctive shapes: a triangle for fa, an oval for sol, a square for la, and a diamond for mi. The major scale was sung in syllables: fa sol la fa sol la mi fa. Shapes made it easy for people who couldn't read words to follow when they were cued by the teacher or in the songbooks.

Shape note singing conventions were held in churches, schoolhouses, and campgrounds, and singing sessions extended from hours into days, with voices the sole musical instruments and the audience the participants. Shape note singing was vigorous in the early twentieth century, sometimes bordering on shouts, and subtlety was not part of the curriculum in the Arkansas singing schools. Alfred Nelson led the singing in his rich bass voice, complemented by Nancy's alto. If there was a pump organ or piano where they gathered, Nancy played it while Alfred led the singing. If not, their voices led together. Either way, they made beautiful music.

Students paid their traveling teachers with shelter, food, and other necessities, and sometimes money—just enough for them to come back again when the opportunity arose, and when Alfred wasn't pounding hot steel into horseshoes, wagons, barrel staves, and fences for their neighbors back in the hills of the Boston Mountains, a vast woodland of sharp ridges and steep valleys in the southwestern part of the Ozark Mountains, a vague western extension of the Appalachian Mountains.

THE FOREBEARS of the Nelsons stopped near the Buffalo River in the mid-nineteenth century along with a few thousand others—in sufficient number to push the Cherokee nation into Oklahoma "beyond the Permanent Indian Frontier," where many settlers eventually moved, too. The ones who stayed were called Arkies or, more generically, hillbillies. Many had Cherokee blood.

Arkies were a curious mixture of self-reliance and self-denial. Most settlers were religious, and even after Prohibition ended, the counties around north central Arkansas continued to ban the sale of alcohol. At the time, moonshine stills proliferated in back hollows for those who took a nip of liquid corn or enjoyed gargling "White Mule." Few African Americans lived among them; farms were so small and farmers so poor that owning slaves was considered a luxury.

The one thing Pindall Ridge and most of north central Arkansas had going for it was water. The area's springs, caves, and sinkholes spawned gristmills, water mills, and stave mills throughout the valley. If you were near water, you could survive, and in 1882, when Franklin C. Nelson paused at a spring in an area designated Prairie Township, between the settlements of Western Grove, Pindall, and Everton, he liked what he saw. He and his wife settled the land and fifteen years later, on June 11, 1897, made it official with a homestead declaration: eighty acres — enough for a man to make something of himself and raise a family.

The Nelson homestead contained a grove of hardwoods shading a trickling stream that emerged from the pile of rocks marking the headwaters of Clear Creek, which drained into the mighty Buffalo River a few miles away. A log house would be raised a few hundred paces east of the spring, along with a barn and a smokehouse. Chickens, hogs, cows, and mules were kept nearby. Franklin came to be called Uncle Peck, and his wife, Aprilla Ann, was called Prilly. She kept a sizable garden and cultivated hollyhocks and other ornamental flowers around the home.

A small clearing was made for Uncle Peck's blacksmith shop near the path to Western Grove and Pindall by an old stagecoach stop under a towering walnut tree by the creek, one hundred yards from the spring. There, Uncle Peck mentored his son, William Alfred, in making horseshoes, wagon wheels, staves for barrels, wheels, gates, plows, gigging poles, tools, and whatever else was needed to keep the whole grand enterprise of an agrarian and industrial society going in the hills and hollows.

William Alfred, one of Uncle Peck and Prilly's seven children, married Nancy Elizabeth Smothers, in 1900. They built their own log house over a rise on the other side of the creek on a gentle slope in a hardwood grove of walnut and red oak. Nancy had five children — Clara May, born in 1902, Rosa Lusetta, born in 1903, a stillborn child in 1904, a stillborn daughter in 1909, and Ira Doyle, born July 9, 1913.

The youngest, Ira, the only boy to survive birth, was a free spirit who enjoyed playing guitar and banjo and working with his father around his blacksmith forge. He had a striking presence and rode a jenny mule to school. "He was tall and handsome and would make music," recalled Irene Young, who attended Pindall School with him through the eighth grade (anyone seeking a higher education had to go somewhere else). Irene was one of dozens of children who took music lessons from Nancy Nelson. "She had a big ol' pump organ. She'd go all around, teaching lessons at country schools. She taught at Glencoe school, Union Y school. Nobody had no money, so sometimes she took chickens for teaching." Young knew Miz Nelson was special. "She and the rest of the family was talented. They could sing. All the Nelsons and Smothers played guitars and French harp. All them Nelsons was musicians."

But music was not enough to sustain the Nelsons, and in the fading heat of the summer of 1929, a few weeks before the October day when the stock market would crash and send the economy of the United States tumbling into the Great Depression, Alfred, his wife, his son, and Mildred Turney, a niece they were raising, decided to go to Texas.

Alfred had lost his mother earlier in the year, and after his daughter Rosa Lusetta married, she and her husband, Ernest Nichols, had moved to Hill County, Texas, a place where cotton grew tall and plentiful on the blackland prairie. The living was good down there, she informed her father and mother in letters, and after their Ira came back from visiting his Texas kinfolks and declared he was ready to move, his parents were persuaded to go with him. The family needed to be closer together, Alfred reasoned. He left little behind except blacksmith customers, the land, and his father; Frank — Uncle Peck — was determined to die on the homestead.

Before they left, Ira, the youngest of Alfred and Nancy's children, married his girlfriend, Myrle Greenhaw, on September 6, 1929, in Newton County and took her along.

Like the Nelsons and just about everybody else in this part of the Ozarks, a fair number of Greenhaws were music people. Myrle's daddy, William, a noted moonshiner in the area, was an expert banjo player. Myrle's brother Carl played piano, and Myrle played guitar. The whole family sang. Myrle was a well-known flirt around Pindall, with a wild streak attributed to her mother's being three-quarters Cherokee. But if Ira was game for settling down, she was game too.

The family left the rocky outcroppings and impenetrable thickets and headed south five hundred miles, where the farm fields were like fertile river bottom. And just like that, the Nelsons were GTT. Gone To Texas.

The Nelsons were gone to Hill County, a sprawling plain that opened up to the heavens in a way not seen back in Arkansas. The sky dominated the landscape there. The Brazos, the longest river in Texas, marked the county's western border on its journey to the Gulf of Mexico. The landscape was lush with native grasses, including buffalo grass, big bluestem, and switchgrass. Post oak, live oak, pecan, and hackberry were the most common trees. An average of thirty-five inches of rain fell on the prairie every year, enough to make one or two crops, although one quickly learned that in Texas, *average* was merely an arbitrary number halfway between drought and flood.

Except for the cultivated crops, the small communities, and the railroads and highways, the land had been little altered since the time when woolly mammoths and, later, buffaloes rumbled through on seasonal migrations, eventually followed by native peoples, who set up seasonal campgrounds to take advantage of the abundant wildlife before moving on. Indians knew better than to establish permanent settlements in a location subject to tornadoes and seasonal drought. The pioneers, who began arriving from the east in the 1830s, thought otherwise.

The country's Anglo settlers considered themselves Southerners. At the beginning of the Civil War, voters in Hill County overwhelmingly approved secession from the United States by a vote of 376 to 63. But despite allegiance to the Confederacy and the county's future as farming country, Hill County was western in outlook. The outlaw John Wesley Hardin arrived in 1869 to barter cotton and hides and murdered a citizen. Other outlaws created more serious problems, especially along the Chisholm Trail, the storied cattle route up the middle of Texas to the Kansas railheads that crossed the county's northwest corner in the early 1870s.

One community's destiny became intertwined with the rest of the world's with the arrival of the railroad in 1881. The need for a watering stop inspired a town site, named for Jo Abbott, a lawyer, banker, civic leader, judge, and U.S. congressman from Hill County. The fifteen-block plat of streets and alleys— ten blocks east of the railroad, five blocks west of the railroad—was formally dedicated in April 1891, nine years after Winston Treadwell's general store opened. A hotel and a drugstore followed.

On September 15, 1896, in the middle of the cotton harvest, many locals dropped everything to join forty thousand spectators a few miles south of the town of West to watch the Crash at Crush, a publicity stunt that was the world's first planned train wreck, in which two steam locomotives intentionally crashed into each other near the Katy line. Two men and one woman were killed by flying debris, while six others were seriously injured.

The original town of Abbott burned down the next year. Seed and steel were no match for the kind of fire that occasionally swept over the plain. The town was rebuilt, only to burn down again in 1903.

IN 1910, Hill County produced more cotton than any other county or parish in the nation except Ellis County, the next county north. Sixty percent of the cropland in the county was cotton. By 1913, two hundred miles of rail crisscrossed Hill County, and with the train came Germans and Eastern European farmers—Czech immigrants in particular—who would have a major impact on the development of towns in southeastern Hill County such as Mertens, Penelope, and Abbott, and on the local culture, including the nightlife.

Seed and steel were no match for the boll weevil either. The infestation of the pernicious insect that feasted on cotton sapped Hill County's upward spiral. What the weevil didn't waste, the Great Depression destroyed. Three-quarters of the farmers in the county were working land they did not own, and with the economic downturn, the train didn't stop in Abbott anymore. Riders had to flag it down.

By 1929, Abbott was little more than a scattering of three hundred people in houses and barns, churches for Methodists, Baptists, and Disciples of Christ (the Catholic Church for the Czechs moving into town would come later), a Baptist church for the colored folks, a tabernacle for singing conventions and revivals, three cotton gins, and the three transportation routes bisecting town — Highway 81/77, the north-south border-to-border routes connecting Canada and Mexico, the Missouri-Kansas-Texas railroad, aka the Katy, which also ran north-south, and the Interurban trolley, which ran from Waco, twenty-four miles south, to Fort Worth and Dallas, sixty-three and seventy-three miles north, respectively. For those who lived there, Abbott was something to be proud of. As native son Leo Ruzicka pointed out, "Abbott is the first town in Texas, alphabetically."

Abbott, 1933

BOBBIE LEE and Willie Hugh were the first Nelsons born on Texas soil. She arrived on the first day of 1931. He came two years later a few minutes before midnight, during the last hour of April 29, 1933. Doc Simms, who delivered both Nelson children at his home, recorded the boy's birth on the first hour of April 30. He was a healthy baby with big brown eyes and flaming red hair. "He had beautiful hair," his sister, Bobbie, said. "He was like a strawberry blond, kind of like Aunt Rosa's hair." Cousin Mildred, who was thirteen years older than Bobbie Lee, named him Willie Hugh—Hugh because that was the middle name of her dear departed little brother, Wallace Hugh, and Willie because she just liked the sound of it. Bobbie called him Hughty and so did his grandmother Nancy Nelson—whom the boy knew as Mamma—when she shouted his name on the back porch at suppertime.

Three days after Willie was born, his father, Ira, and mother, Myrle, went out to play music with a band, leaving the baby in the care of his grandparents and his cousin. Ira and Myrle had been sixteen when they married—still kids in many respects but old enough to work in the fields and bear children and old enough to know better. Myrle hated Texas. All her people were back in Arkansas or moving west across Oklahoma to the Pacific Northwest. Some folks said that maybe it was Myrle's Indian blood that made her want to ramble.

But rather than stick around to fight the inevitable fight or submit to her man, like they taught in church, and continue living with Ira's parents, and as much as she loved them and her kids, Myrle couldn't be true to herself if she stayed. She left Abbott six months after giving birth to Willie and went to Oklahoma, then points west, working as a waitress, a dancer, and a card dealer in San Francisco, Oregon, and Washington, where she caught up with her kinfolk. The divorce became final when Willie Hugh was two.

Ira Nelson remained in Abbott after Myrle left, but for all practical purposes, he left his children to be raised by his parents, Alfred and Nancy. He picked up occasional work farming "on the halves"—splitting the proceeds of a crop with a landowner who provided the dirt and tools to raise a crop—and with a little determination and a lot of patience learned how to fix engines for the living it provided. But mostly he liked picking his guitar, staying out late, and hanging in honky-tonks. There wasn't much in life more fun than picking and singing. That's how he had met Myrle. His boy and his girl were like that too. It ran in the family blood.

"WHEN my father began playing beer joints and started drinking, my grandfather and grandmother gave him holy hell," Bobbie said. "One night they found a whiskey bottle in his car. That was the beginning of the end of the family thing."

Ira remarried and lived for a while in the blacksmith shop with his second wife, Lorraine, and pumped gas. Then he drifted to the oil fields of New Mexico, to Lorraine's hometown of Covington, in Hill County, and eventually found work up in Fort Worth.

"Ira didn't like to work, I don't think," said neighbor Leo Ruzicka, who used to play marbles for keeps with Ira. "I never saw him working. Living off his daddy is what it amounted to. He'd rather play music."

"Our grandfather didn't want us to visit either Mother or Daddy," Bobbie Nelson said. "They had to come see us. My grandfather totally looked out for me and Willie." Myrle came back when she could, riding the bus or catching the train, but she never stayed long. Once, she came back to tell the kids she was dying of cancer and wanted them to learn a song to remember her by, the Rex Griffin composition "The Last Letter" ("I'll be gone when you read this last letter from me").

"I remember one time she hitchhiked to come see us," Bobbie said. "It cost money to ride the bus or train. She took the bus back. We did not want her to be hitchhiking. My mother was very independent." Myrle liked moving around, and so did her boy. Willie developed a tendency to wander early on, most often heading to Jimmy Bruce's house next door. Nancy Nelson quickly figured out if she didn't want to spend all afternoon searching for a lost child, she'd have to keep Willie tethered close to home, so she put a leash on him and staked it to a post, like she did with the family cow. It didn't keep Willie from getting loose—Bobbie kept untying the leash—but it slowed him down enough for Mamma Nelson to keep an eye on him.

When they first moved to Abbott, Nancy and Alfred did farm labor for a lady until Alfred went to work for John Rejcek, a blacksmith with the biggest family in Abbott, who also led a polka band in his spare time. Alfred eventually opened his own shop, doing his smithing with a motor, a fire, an anvil, and a hammer. The kids in Abbott gravitated to his shop, where he let them help turn the forge, play marbles and dominoes, and hang out. Occasionally, he would gather them around the potbellied stove and treat them to real-life stories with a parable at the end.

Religion played a major part in the Nelson family's life, the same way it did for most other families throughout the South, where church was the all-purpose community center. Shortly after they arrived in Texas, the Nelsons joined the Abbott Methodist Church, a simple white clapboard building with a burnt-orange composite-shingle roof topped by a humble steeple that had been raised in 1899. Alfred became the church's music director, and both Alfred and Nancy taught Sunday school.

Mamma Nelson used a Methodist hymnal to teach her granddaughter to read music and play piano. "It made sense to me right away," Bobbie Lee said. The first song she played on the upright piano after her grandparents traded away a pump organ was "Jesus, Lover of My Soul."

The church was one of the most important institutions in the community, perhaps the most important institution. But church wasn't all there was to life in Abbott. And church wasn't the only place for making music.

HILLSBORO, the county seat, was a larger version of Abbott, its eight thousand residents mostly white folks and mostly Methodist and Baptist, with some colored folks who lived on the edge of town. Hillsboro was where you went to sell your eggs on the courthouse square on Saturdays and sing at singing conventions inside the gingerbread county courthouse on Sundays. If you had money, you could buy essentials at Buie Hardware, Hillsboro Dry Goods, Martin-McDonald, or Laura's Bargain Store, watch a picture show at the Ritz or the Texas, or sit in a booth and eat fried chicken at Jiggs, the Kai Kai Coffee Shop, or the Kre-Mee Cafe. If you didn't have money, you could at least stare at the new Philco radios in the window of Goodman Company or wish for a piano at Walter Piano.

"The Crossroads of Texas" had its own airport, called the Bryant Sky Ranch, several car dealerships, the Hotel Newcomb, alternately identified as "Hillsboro's Modern Fireproof Hotel" and "Hillsboro's Only Steam-Heated Hotel," a radio station,

KHBR, which broadcast at 1560 kilohertz on the radio dial from sunrise to sunset, three grocery stores, four tourist courts, a dominoes parlor, a junior college, and pretty much everything you couldn't get in Abbott.

West was different. It wasn't much bigger than Abbott, but it was nothing like it. West was where the Czechs lived. They were largely Catholic, they enjoyed their music differently, and they drank alcohol, a pastime made easier when Prohibition was repealed a little more than eight months after Willie Hugh was born. In those Central Texas counties that went "wet," Czech families typically gathered at the SPJST Hall to socialize, sing, dance, and drink their beers. SPJST, or the Slavonic Benevolent Order of the State of Texas, was a Czech organization that sold insurance, ran a rest home, and harbored social clubs; its motto was "Texans for Texans." The Czechs enjoyed their beer, but good Baptists and Methodists in Abbott and adjacent dry counties had to sneak around to indulge in such activities, which is why several beer joints were clustered across the county line on the highway to West. True Baptists, rooted in the Primitive Church and able to quote Scripture at the drop of the good book, believed dancing was sinful and pagan, nothing more than a vertical substitute for copulation.

Czechs in general were considered sinful and then some for those reasons. The Ruzickas, the first Czech family to move into Abbott in 1925, were treated like dirt when they came to town, even though Leo and Jerry Frank's daddy ran one of the three cotton gins in Abbott, a position of considerable importance.

"We were treated as outcasts," Leo Ruzicka said. "Real bad, worse than Spanish people, as bad as black. I couldn't look at a white girl." Fran Pope faced similar prejudice. "They called us Bohemians at school to make fun of us, I guess because we could speak Czech," she said. "We were always laughed at. I'd call them 'biscuit eaters.' We didn't have to eat biscuits. We had homemade bread."

"Spanish" was polite reference to the handful of Mexican immigrant families who'd wandered up from across the Rio Grande and settled on the edge of town, pretty much keeping to themselves except when it came to working in the fields. The Spanish were treated as foreigners and second-class citizens, evidenced by the lower pay offered for the same labor and the "No dogs or Mexicans" signs posted in front of more than one café. However low they were regarded by the whites in town, "meskins" didn't have it as bad as African Americans — "niggers" — the descendants of slaves brought into Texas to work the fields and do the menial labor no one else would do.

Black and Mexican children were not allowed to go to the white school. Colored children attended classes in the one-room school at the Negro church. Black and Mexican adults were not allowed to use public toilets or water fountains, or to ride in the train cars reserved for whites. If they were lucky, they could ride in the back of the train, sit in the balcony of the movie theater, and eat around the back in a café. Those who ignored the rules or, worse, intentionally violated them, such as a black man even talking to a white woman, faced harsh punishment. But the young Booger Red didn't think the Czechs or the Mexicans or the Negroes were any different from his people. The Nelsons lived across the street from two Mexican families. More than once, Willie and Bobbie walked over by the colored church near the highway to listen to what the congregation was singing. Once a year, the good folks at Abbott Methodist attended services there. Those experiences led Bobbie Lee to question segregation. "I was always asking, 'Why can't I invite these people home? What's wrong with me inviting our Mexican friends and our black friends or someone who is raggedy-looking?' "

SINGING was an important element of worship for Abbott's Christians, and it took the lead role when meetings were held at the local tabernacle, a kind of all-purpose social center for true believers. In the summer, the Baptists held revivals for two weeks, followed by the Methodists and the Disciples of Christ, with singing conventions staged throughout the warm months.

Along with instilling a love of God and Christ, the elder Nelsons infused their grandchildren with a love of music, gathering around the dining table and writing music or studying the lessons for their correspondence courses by lamplight.

Alfred Nelson could see Bobbie had a natural talent. "I built the first piano I ever had out of cardboard," she said. "We played with cardboard under the peach tree, Willie and I. We created a piano with Crayolas on a cardboard box while Mamma Nelson was doing the laundry. It was not near satisfying enough. No matter how hard I pushed on this cardboard, it didn't make a sound."

Once she learned to play a real keyboard, Bobbie said, "My grandfather got tired of 'Chopsticks' and all the things I was trying to create on my own. He told my grandmother, 'It's time for her to learn to read music, Nancy.' My grandfather wanted my grandmother to teach me to read music, and not just shape notes. We had gospel singing books, hymnals, the Stamps-Baxter songbook—the Brown Book—

that was where I learned to read music." When Mamma Nelson gave Bobbie piano lessons, her little brother would sit on the piano stool and try to learn the chords his sister was learning.

"I was so into this piano," Bobbie said. "From that moment on, I didn't have to pick as much cotton or do anything. Everyone was amazed because I was a little kid and learned really fast, as big as my fingers would go. My grandfather encouraged me. He told me, 'You know, you need to learn, you need to stay with this piano. It could really make you a living one of these days.'

"I learned to play the first song the first day. I don't know how I learned to play it that quickly that young, but I did. My grandmother and grandfather would sing this song and I'd play it. Then they would have me play something in church." When she learned a song out of the songbook, Mamma Nelson would reward her by putting a gold star on the page.

Unlike some families in Abbott, Daddy Nelson and Mamma Nelson encouraged music outside the church, too, harkening back to their Arkansas roots. "My grandfather would take me to the singing conventions they used to have in the big courtroom in the Hill County Courthouse in Hillsboro one Sunday afternoon a month," Bobbie Nelson said. "That's what got me hooked. There was a woman there playing gospel music on piano. I can still see her in my mind. She had long fingers, like my mother. Her hands were much bigger than mine. But this woman could play. I was hooked on her. And Daddy loved to sing."

Bobbie's first performance was at a singing convention in the courthouse, the same year her brother first recited a poem in front of an audience. "There was a full house, a thousand people in that courthouse on a Sunday afternoon," she said. "At the singing convention, everyone had a chance to choose a number out of the Stamps-Baxter hymn book. My grandfather always led one or two songs at the singing convention and he had me lead a song. They lifted me up on this bench, a big pew. They taught me how to conduct. I was conducting these people, singing lead on 'I'll Fly Away.'

"I don't remember being nervous," Bobbie Lee said. "My grandfather told me, 'You need to practice because you could play the piano for them and sing like Miss Martha, the preacher's wife, does.' I was anxious to do that."

When Alfred saved up enough money to buy the family a Philco radio, the box of wire and tubes brought music from far outside the church into their house.

The Philco was placed atop the marble washstand

that had been brought from Arkansas. Booger Red was exposed to recordings of songs performed by Jimmie Rodgers, the Blue Yodeler from Mississippi and the biggest record star of his time; by the Carter Family, whose harmonies provided the foundations of what would be called country music; and by Roy Acuff, Minnie Pearl, and all the entertainers on the Grand Ole Opry from Nashville. Bob Wills and His Texas Playboys filled their living room courtesy of KVOO, a powerful 50,000-watt station broadcasting from Tulsa, where Wills held forth at Cain's Academy. Ernest Tubb and his warm Texan friendliness came in every weekday from KGKO 570 in Fort Worth and held a special place in the young Nelson boy's heart. "He was my first singing hero," he said. "He was the first guy that I had a songbook of. 'Jimmie Dale,' which was about his son that died, was one of the saddest songs I ever heard." Hank Thompson had a show just down the road in Waco on WACO and later on KWTX. But it was hardly just country coming out of the radio. Boogie-woogie piano man Freddie Slack was no farther than a twist of the dial. And jazz from New Orleans drifted in late at night, thanks to the 50,000-watt clear-channel signal of WWL.

If not for the radio, the boy almost certainly would never have contemplated the superior vocal skills of a skinny young Italian crooner from Hoboken, New Jersey, named Frank Sinatra or discovered Hank Williams's spiritual alter ego, Luke the Drifter, who intoned about the wisdom of seeing things "From Life's Other Side." Neither jukeboxes nor churches considered Luke the Drifter particularly significant. The radio took Willie farther than an automobile, a bus, or the Interurban ever could.

After supper, Willie and Bobbie would mimic Cousin Mildred—"Meemee"—and Daddy and Mamma Nelson when they sat down and composed song lyrics together. Watching them made him want to write lyrics too. "You can study music always and never learn it all," Mamma Nelson liked to say.

FROM the outside looking in, the Nelsons lived in poverty. "They were pretty poor," one neighbor said. "They were hardworking people. His grandma gave piano lessons. His grandpa was always sharpening plows, designing and building machinery for tractors and hay balers, doing something." The truth was, everyone was poor back in those days. The Nelsons were just a whole lot poorer.

"If we didn't grow it, we didn't eat it," Bobbie remembered. "Ol' Reddy, our first cow, was part of the family. We kept one of her calves. We had another cow and hogs. Those were my grandfather's. I saw him butcher a hog one time and that just ended it for me. I wasn't going to help with that sort of thing. My grandmother and grandfather, they had to be their own butchers. That's one reason we didn't eat any of our chickens. Our chickens had names. We raised them from eggs. We ate the eggs and sold the eggs for money to buy our groceries. That's the way we survived."

To kids in Abbott, far removed from world events careening toward a global war, money didn't mean much, anyhow. They went crawfishing, hiking down to Dr. Blair's swimming hole while dodging water moccasins, exploring Hooker's cave south of town, or scrounging a ride to Mountain Springs, where white kids could swim—no blacks or Mexicans allowed. They rode horses when they could get hold of one and even tried to ride cows. On Saturday mornings they would observe the exotic customs of the colored folks when they came to town and ordered bologna and crackers and a strawberry soda at the grocery for a nickel, or poured peanuts into their Dr Pepper.

Kids would play marbles, pitch washers, or spin tops under the roof of the open-air tabernacle at the corner of Chestnut and Border, attend sing-ins at the church or the tabernacle, fight, or hang around school for the Thursday skate nights in the high school gymnasium, when girls from Hillsboro and West would show up. The sports-minded were doubtless inspired by the banner that hung from the gym's ceiling, "Losers Never Win, Winners Never Quit."

In summer, there were games of Hide and Seek, Annie Over, Follow the Leader, and Piggy Wants a Signal, with ghost stories told in the dark. Every Halloween, the mischief makers would drag an outhouse and leave it on the front steps of Pope's Grocery.

When all else failed, there was the sport of Foolin' Cars, as explained by Jerry Frank Ruzicka: "We'd tie a string to a purse and leave it in the road and hide behind a sign. If a car would stop, the kids would pull the string and the purse and run off. One time somebody with a running board got the purse before we could pull the string," he remembered. When the boys were feeling especially mischievous, they'd fill the purse with excrement. "You'd see a car stop and the driver pick up the purse, then go a few hundred feet before the purse went flying out the window," recalled Jimmy Graves.

There were bumblebee wars too. "The farmers would run into bumblebees and they'd come here and tell the guys at the [Abbott Cash Grocery] store," Morris Russell said. Billy Pope, the son of the owner of the grocery, was ringleader, being two years older than Morris and about five years older than Willie,

Jerry Frank, Gene Crocker, Jimmy Bruce, and Eldon Stafford. "Billy Pope had a horse and wagon and on Sundays he'd round up all the boys in town," Jerry Frank Ruzicka said. Morris remembered it like this: "We made us some paddles out of shingles. We'd drill holes in them. We'd fan them and get them stirred up. Once they get stirred up, they'll chase you. It was kinda fun to get at them. If we missed, we'd start running."

"We'd stick together," said Jerry Frank. "One time when it snowed, the train pulled into town and we snowballed that train, so the engineer turned steam on us." When no one was looking, they'd sneak off and smoke cedar bark, corn silk, coffee grounds, and grapevine like it was tobacco. "Willie and I smoked cedar bark in my dad's lumberyard," Jerry Frank said. "We wrapped newspaper around it, and man, that fire went down my throat when we drawed on it. That paper was on fire."

WHEN Willie Hugh turned six, Mamma and Daddy Nelson bought him a Stella guitar out of the Sears catalog. Daddy Nelson taught him how to make the D, A, and G chords (the basic chords in country music), gave him a chord book, and taught him the song "Show Me the Way to Go Home." "Polly Wolly

Doodle" and "She'll Be Comin' 'Round the Mountain" followed. He couldn't read music like Bobbie could. But he was already writing lyrics. The boy's gift for composing poetry attracted notice from Miss Lawrence, his first-grade teacher, who sought out Mamma Nelson to tell her how special her boy was.

Mamma and Daddy Nelson responded by giving him elocution lessons so he could speak and sing clearly and properly and by teaching him the importance of breathing. "My grandparents were great voice teachers," the boy would say many years later. "My grandmother taught deep breathing and singing from way down in the diaphragm. These were natural things we were taught growing up, the better your lungs are, the longer you can hold notes."

Darkness descended upon the family on February 24, 1940, when complications from medication taken for pneumonia unexpectedly took Alfred's life. He was fifty-six. His six-year-old grandson, Willie Hugh Nelson, was old enough to understand that his family, strong as it was, would never be the same. He was the man of the house now.

The loss of Alfred left a giant hole in all their lives. Nancy, Bobbie Lee, and Willie Hugh moved from the house on the edge of town to a smaller dwelling by the tabernacle. The house had plank floors. Its walls were made of cardboard and pages of the *Fort*

Worth Star-Telegram, the newspaper of West Texas, which provided insulated protection from cold drafts in the winter and more fodder for a boy's imagination. The cracks in the ceiling were big enough for him to stare at the stars at night.

The loss of the grandfather who raised him had a profound impact, inspiring Willie to write a flurry of heartbreak songs about losing in love, betrayal, and cheating, subjects a seven-year-old boy had not experienced himself, although he was working on it—he already had a girlfriend, Ramona Stafford. On a school trip to the State Fair of Texas in Dallas, he sat next to her and took her hand in his. They both looked straight ahead and smiled, their hands clasped together.

Nancy Nelson did her best to get by, teaching music lessons on the pump organ for a quarter or fifty cents and eventually taking a job at the Abbott school cafeteria for $18 a week. Sometimes the boy would help out, mopping floors for a dinner. It was no way to keep up with the prominent families who lived west of the tracks and the highway on the "nice" side of Abbott, but Nancy managed to instill in her family a sense of dignity and the urge to be creative.

Within a couple years of Alfred's passing, sister and brother were putting their music learning to practice. World War II was raging in the bigger world and three local boys who joined the army—Nookie Holland, Cleo Rafferty, and J. V. Kennedy—were killed in action. But music was more than a call to arms in the small wood-frame house in Abbott; it was the glue that held them together.

THE WORDS flashed on the big screen.

REPUBLIC PICTURES PRESENTS
BACK IN THE SADDLE

The letters were superimposed over black-and-white images of singing cowboy and radio star Gene Autry, riding his stallion, Champ. It was a dramatic introduction to a story about a cowboy named Gene Autry who discovers copper on his ranch only to have evil miners pollute the water supply and poison his cattle. Along with his loyal but hapless sidekick Frog Millhouse (played by Smiley Burnette), Gene retrieves the jailed son of a neighboring ranch owner and cures him of his big-city ways to fight the bad guys and prevail in a climactic gunfight. The saga concludes back at the corral, with Gene and his beloved gal, Patsy (played by his "Little Darlin'," Mary Lee), and all the ranch hands singing together.

The whole concept of good over evil had never

made so much sense. Not even the most inspiring preacher had explained the whole cosmic reason for being as fully and eloquently as Gene had. All of Willie's friends wanted to be like Gene, who grew up in Tioga, northeast of Dallas. Willie just wanted it a little bit more.

"Willie liked them ol' western movies," his friend Morris Russell said, citing films starring cowboy actors and recording artists such as Gene, Roy Rogers, Bill Boyd, Ken Maynard, and Tex Ritter. "We called them shoot-'em-ups." "We could spend the whole afternoon on Saturdays at the Ritz in Hillsboro," Bobbie said. "We loved Gene Autry and Roy Rogers, Johnny Mack Brown, Tom Mix, Sunset Carson," she said, laughing. "We'd try to reconstruct the movie. I'd try my best to be Mary Lee. Until we went back again, we were into that movie, playing all the parts. We never were bored."

When Willie was seven, he went to Hillsboro to meet his first real live cowboy-movie star. Johnny Mack Brown was no Gene or Roy, but the former football player who won the 1926 Rose Bowl for the University of Alabama Crimson Tide was certainly prolific, starring in more than 130 movies and serials. He came to Hillsboro in 1941 to do a fund-raiser for war bonds, and although "we didn't have a hell of a lot of money," Willie said, the family scraped together

$18.75 for a $25 war bond. For doing their patriotic part, young Willie got to meet handsome Johnny Mack, shake his hand, and get an autograph. He came away telling friends that Johnny Mack was "a very good guy with a strong handshake and a winning smile."

The encounter fanned the flames of his wanting to perform. "Johnny Mack, Gene, Roy, all those guys, made me want to ride my horse [or the family milk cow, the only animal the Nelsons had to ride], play the guitar, sing, shoot my gun, and win all the fights," he said. "I wanted to do that."

Willie and Bobbie fantasized about cowboys and cowgirls, horses and singing. Their play acting did not include cotton.

Few places on earth are hotter than the blackland prairie of North Central Texas in late August and early September. At least that's the way it felt when you were stooped over from sunup to sundown, trying to separate the soft white fluffs of cotton from their thorny dead plant stems with your bloody fingers while dragging a nine-yard cotton sack behind your feet. The heat was wicked, with temperatures soaring well past 100 degrees during the day and rarely dipping under 80 degrees at night.

Picking cotton under such conditions may have struck outsiders as exceptionally strenuous labor. But to poor white folks, poor black folks, and poor brown folks scattered around the southern edge of the Grand Prairie, picking cotton was one of the few sure ways to earn a few dollars in late summer. The voices of colored people were a constant across the cotton patch, and the freckle-faced redheaded kid took it all in.

"One guy would start a line over to my right and then another guy would answer him a quarter mile away on the way down the field," Willie remembered as a man. "Next thing you knew, you'd have a whole opera going on. They sounded good to me."

The boy picked cotton, baled hay, whatever it took. "It was sort of expected that I went and make the money, because we needed it," he said. "I just went out and earned wherever I could." There wasn't much choice.

"When school started in September, they'd have half a day, then let the children go to help pick cotton," explained Leo Ruzicka, who was a few years older than the red-haired boy. "We'd make seventy-five cents a hundred [$.75 per 100 pounds]. If a kid going to school could make that much, he'd help his mom and dad. All the farm kids did it. So did the town kids. I'd run, trying to get out there in the fields. Before school started, you picked all day. Bending over, or getting on your knees without knee pads, was the worst, one hundred degrees eating you up. You'd be glad when a cloud comes over you."

Willie used cardboard or a piece of tire as pads for his knees to ease the pain that came from doing stoop labor. While lifting one-hundred-pound hay bales on his friend Morris's family farm, he hurt his back. But he kept at it, and Mamma Nelson, Daddy Nelson, cousin Mildred, and sister Bobbie all picked at one time or another.

Picking made the boy wish sometimes he was anywhere else. Every time he paused to watch a car go by, headed to Waco or Dallas or Chicago or West, he'd feel the tug. "I want to go with them," he would think.

The boy had convinced himself he could do anything if he set his mind to it. When he spied a passing train, he'd stare hard at the engineer at the helm of the locomotive to see if he could attract his attention. More often than not, the engineer would turn his head in the boy's direction.

But he stayed and picked and sang, along with everybody else, accompanied by the rhythm of their labor. Besides stooping down in the field, he always had chores to do, lessons to learn, and things to do to take care of Bobbie and Mamma. In the summers, he would do farmwork at his friend Morris Russell's family place, two miles east of town, or pick up money baling hay with Morris for Rudolph Kapavik.

There was always music to work on. "His grandma would make him practice guitar every day," Jerry Frank said. "His sister was a really good piano player. I really enjoyed listening to her. She could play boogie-woogie and make that piano walk."

The Nelson place was always a reliable place to quench a thirst. "His grandmother always had a bucket of water at the door with a gourd with a handle like a dipper," said Jerry Frank. "They caught the rain off the roof and it went into a cistern. That's how they got water." Mamma Nelson used the water as a motivational tool. If Bobbie Lee or Willie Hugh was slow to rise in the morning, she'd splash them with water. The slower they got up, the more she splashed water. Bobbie Lee figured out the drill and was quick to get out of bed. Willie Hugh got wet a lot.

WILLIE Hugh passed a milestone when he got drunk on beer for the first time, at the age of nine. He'd accompanied his father, Ira, to Albert's Place, a beer joint across the county line toward West. Both sat in with Charlie Brown's band, and little Willie sang a couple numbers. When nobody was looking, he was also knocking back beer. After two bottles, he felt a buzz and somewhat dizzy. His words slurred, his eyes blurred. "I had to sleep it off in the car before my father would take me home to my grandmother, because she would have kicked the shit out of both of us," he later said.

He got drunk but did not regret it. Nancy Nelson, charged with raising him, was upset when she found out, and gave both Willie Hugh and his father a tongue-lashing. But it didn't put the fear of God in him enough to keep him from doing it again and again.

"I was going straight to hell, no doubt about it," Willie said. "It freaked her out, plus it freaked out my neighbor Miss Brissler. By then, I decided that there was no chance for me to go on to heaven, I had already fucked up more ways than God was going to put up with, and I wasn't even ten years old yet, so I had in mind, the sky's the limit from here on, I mean I can't go to hell twice."

At least when he was playing music, Willie didn't have to grapple with the question of whether or not dancing was sinful. He was too busy making the music for dancers to dance to. He may have been baptized and raised Methodist and been just as involved with the church as his sister and their grandparents, but Booger Red was what preachers would deride as a questioning Christian. He believed in Jesus Christ as the Son of God, as did most everyone around him, but also realized that in that big world beyond Abbott were millions and millions of people who followed different faiths. Jerry Frank Ruzicka remembered Willie talking about reincarnation when they were kids. It may have been a reaction to Alfred's unexpected death, which the Nelsons never got over. Whatever reincarnation was, Jerry Frank and Willie talked about it and went back to playing marbles.

As a ten-year-old, Willie joined Billy Pope, Burl and Merle McMahan, and a bunch of older town kids in building a clubhouse out of pasteboard. They played dominoes, cooked, smoked, and drank coffee in the hangout. The red-haired kid was tolerated. For his part, he liked hanging with guys old enough to have a car, if they had a car. Cars took you places. Like out of Abbott.

The urge for going was almost a birthright of growing up in Abbott. In 1941, the main highway through town, US 81/77, was rerouted one mile west. The new US 81/77 was a paved road and major thoroughfare, making Abbott seem a little sleepier, a portent of the stagnation that would impact most small towns and rural areas in Texas and America once residents began their mass exodus to nearby cities in search of opportunity.

• • •

MUSIC was an opportunity, and it took you places too.

Willie had started writing songs and now he became a performer too, strumming acoustic guitar in John Rejcek's orchestra, a family ensemble of brass instruments and drums that played polkas, waltzes, and schottisches at Czech dances. Mr. Rejcek sired sixteen children in all, but he took a shine to little Red and his musical aspirations. The night Mr. Rejcek paid the ten-year-old $6 for doing what came naturally was a revelation to Willie Hugh. It didn't take him long to realize that was as much money as he could make on a good day in the cotton fields. Only, playing music felt good and didn't leave him wasted and hurting, and strumming a guitar didn't make his fingers throb the way the thorny cotton burrs did.

The stage was where Willie was meant to be. "I felt right at home up there," he said. "That was what I wanted to do. It seemed normal for me to be on a bandstand."

He also played on the courthouse steps in Hillsboro and at Frank Clements's barbershop in Abbott, where he shined shoes and sang a song for fifty cents a pair. By his twelfth birthday, Willie had finished his first songbook. Written on manila paper by hand in cursive script that resembled a lariat, "Songs by Willie Nelson, Waco Texas" featured an index and the lyrics — some handwritten, some typed — of fifteen original songs, including "The Moon-Was-Your-Helper," "Sweethearts Forever," "I'll Wonder Alone," "Only True Love Lingers On," "You Still Belong to Me," "Long Ago," "Faded Love and Wasted Dream," "The Storm Has Just Begun," "Hangover Blues" ("You can keep yo rotgut whiskey / you can keep yo gin and rye / I'll quit waking up with headaches and a wishing I could die / Don't want no hangover blues / You can keep yo hangover blues"), "I Guess I Was Born to Be Blue," "So Hard to Say Goodby," "Teach Me to Sing a Long Song," "Whenever," "Gold Star," and "Starting Tonight." At the end of each lyric, he wrote "THE END" and "WILLIE NELSON," the *W* and *N* done with a practiced flourish. On the last page, he wrote "HOWDY PARD" in lariat script and drew small cowboy hats on the borders.

At the invitation of his friend and classmate Roy Gene Urbanovsky, he also joined the Urbanovsky family's jam sessions out at their farm near Brooken, and when Bernard Urbanovsky got married, he hired thirteen-year-old Willie to play at his wedding, along with the dance band Bernard fronted, the Czech Mates. Willie promised Mamma Nelson he'd be home by eleven, played the gig, and was paid $5 for his services.

By then the kid was old enough to have figured out that if there was money to be made in music, it was in the beer joints and dance halls, two of the few places where people spent money freely even though America was at war. He knew he was already condemned to hellfire and damnation by loitering in beer joints, and Nancy Nelson let him know she was not happy her boy worked in places like that. But she allowed it, since he went into such places out of a desire to help provide for the family.

The dens of temptation were a short bicycle ride away, clustered three miles south of town just across the line separating Hill County and McLennan County on Abest Road. The beer joints that became Willie's training ground for performing and for learning songs were Albert's, Frank Clements's place, known as the First and Last Chance, and, a few hundred yards up the hill, Margie Lundy's Nite Owl, the hardest of the honky-tonks hugging the line.

The jukeboxes in those joints helped form his musical tastes. He could feed nickels into the record machine and play the same song over and over to figure out the chords and lyrics. He wasn't the only one. Others poured nickels in for more personal reasons, which usually involved heartbreak, misery, or love lost. The honky-tonk was where you went to find somebody or to forget somebody. "I learned everything on the jukebox," Willie said, including the words and musical structure of every song.

Jukeboxes were programmed with records that would inspire beer drinking, the kind of music that amounted to white man's blues, whether it was sob songs such as Floyd Tillman's scandalous "Slipping Around," one of the first widely popular cheatin' songs, Hank Williams's "Your Cheatin' Heart," or "Walking the Floor over You," by Ernest Tubb and His Texas Troubadours ("Ernest personified what I thought someone from Texas should sound like," Willie later recalled), or "Always Late," "If You've Got the Money (I've Got the Time)," or "I Love You a Thousand Ways," by Lefty Frizzell, a hard-core honky-tonker from Corsicana, just northeast of Hill County, or anything by Bob Wills.

WILLIE Hugh, a cute red-haired fellow with big brown eyes and a ready smile, and Bobbie Lee, a slim, attractive blonde with sparkling eyes and pouting lips, were popular kids at school. Both brimmed with confidence and were happy to perform in classes, study halls, and graduation exercises. They were accustomed to winning talent shows at school and in town. They were best friends. They both sang, and she played the piano at any event that called for a piano player. "We always had an assembly at the school on Friday, and usually they would play, sing, just about every week," Morris Russell said. "Bobbie, she was good." Fran Pope liked it too. "When she played 'In the Mood' on the piano, we'd just go wild." Schoolmate Donald Reed was a fan as well. "I always thought she would be a star," he said.

Boogie-woogie was a distraction for America at war, and in war's aftermath, music was comfort food. Willie began sitting in with Charlie Brown and the Brownies, the biggest country band in West, and took a liking to Charlie's daughter Faye Dell Brown, who sang with the band. "We kind of fell for each other," said Faye Dell Brown Clements. "I really cared about him and he cared about me. I'd sing with him when we'd go on a date to watch the cowboy movies, and I'd sing with him when he came to the house. He used to pick me up Sunday mornings and we'd go to his house and just sing. He really thought we were going to travel and sing. We talked about getting married, but we were just kids."

By the time they were high school juniors, Faye Dell had broken up with Willie and was going with Jackie Clements, Willie's friend, who happened to drive a '46 Ford convertible, one of the few cars any teenager had in Abbott.

ARLYN "Bud" Fletcher was a charmer and a con, a smooth-talking hustler and, without a doubt, the handsomest man she'd ever met. Bobbie Nelson was the most popular girl in her class at Abbott High, and easily the prettiest, he thought. He was a soldier back from World War II, the son of a prominent family in the area, and his father was the county commissioner from Aquilla, near Hillsboro. He hung out in all the wrong places. She played organ in church.

Bud Fletcher was not the kind of fellow Miss Bobbie Lee Nelson could easily ignore, even if she'd wanted to. She couldn't resist his request to take her out on a date. She didn't turn around and go back when he took her to Shadowland in West, although it was not the kind of place a good Christian girl frequented.

Shadowland "had a very small room with a great jukebox," she recalled. "This jukebox had all these great songs that I'd listened to on the radio. I never went to a beer joint in my whole life until I was dating Bud. Bud knew where they were."

Bud swept Bobbie off her feet, even if she knew what she was doing was wrong in many people's eyes. "I'd been in church and playing revival meetings with ministers and evangelists. That was a very emotional thing for me. Bud asked me to dance. I'd never danced, because I was forbidden to do anything. I felt guilty. But this is Bud. And I'm dancing with Bud. I felt very awkward because he was a fabulous dancer." When she came home, she didn't tell Mamma Nelson where she'd been.

"It wasn't very long between my meeting him and marrying him," she said. Bobbie was in love, and they tied the knot on April 29, 1947. Ira Nelson and his wife, Lorraine, attended the wedding ceremony. Myrle Greenhaw Nelson had a fit when she heard about her daughter's pending marriage but was too far away and too far removed from the family to do anything about it. Despite her misgivings, Nancy Nelson gave her blessings.

The marriage was not without a tinge of scandal. Bobbie was determined to finish high school. She had one year to go and wanted badly to play basketball, her favorite sport, although no married student had attended Abbott High. With hair headed skyward in a towering beehive, the preferred style among Texas women at that time, she stayed in school, played basketball, and graduated with pride as Bobbie Fletcher. "Everybody treated me pretty much the same," she said.

Not long after the honeymoon, Bud Fletcher organized Hill County's version of Bob Wills and His Texas Playboys — Bud Fletcher and the Texans. Ira Nelson played rhythm guitar with the group and sometimes fiddled. Glen Ellison, an Abbott High School teacher and the football coach, played trombone. Whistle Watson was drummer. Joe Andrews played bass. Bobbie Nelson played piano. Willie Hugh Nelson sang and played lead guitar. Bud Fletcher was . . . Bud Fletcher.

"We were excited," Bobbie said. "Willie and I had been playing together all our lives. Willie already played with the Rejcek polka band, but he'd only played rhythm guitar. He was just starting to play lead and sing vocals when he joined Bud. Bud fronted the band, and, Lord, what a front man."

But Bud Fletcher couldn't sing worth a hoot, and he didn't really play an instrument. Sometimes he feigned playing a washtub bass fashioned with a broomstick, or thumped an upright bass. For a stretch he allegedly drummed. Mostly, though, he conducted, calling out leads, orchestrating the band, throwing out commentary, and keeping the crowd moving — doing pretty much what Bob Wills did.

"He was a salesman, not a musician," explained

Willie. He was enough of a promoter to get the band booked and draw a crowd, and enough of a con to hustle a piano or organ from a church or tent revival so the band could play a booking.

In 1947, Bud booked the band into the Avalon Club, a spacious beer joint in Waco owned by the father of a friend named Nolan Flowers, and they made enough from the cover charge at the door to pay for the sound equipment they'd rented and to pay themselves. They also performed on Mary Holliday's talent show on WACO, the radio station where Hank Thompson first became famous, and hustled dates at the Plantation and the Scenic Wonderland in Waco (though they drew so poorly at the Wonderland that they were not asked back), Bill Drake's and Scotty's in West, and Albert's, the Nite Owl, and the First and Last Chance at the county line.

"WHEN Willie was just getting started, me and Eldon Stafford would go down there to Albert's place and listen to him," Morris Russell said. "We'd eat one of ol' Black Cat's cheeseburgers down there— nobody made cheeseburgers like ol' Black Cat. He was the cook, a black guy, and famous for his cooking." Black Cat cooked the very first steak that Bobbie Nelson ever ate.

The Texans got their own fifteen-minute radio show every Saturday on KHBR 1560 AM in Hillsboro. Sandwiched between the Rhythm Wranglers and the Lone Star Playboys, the Texans would entertain the listeners in Hill County and plug any upcoming dates. The redhead who strummed the electric F-hole guitar, his newest possession, won the attention of a group of high school girls from Hillsboro and West, including Barbara Jean McDearmon, Floy Belcher, and Laura Gilmore, who formed the Willie Nelson Fan Club to support him and his playing.

Barbara Jean was Willie's biggest booster and, after he and Faye Dell Brown broke up, his girlfriend. The Willie Nelson Fan Club showed up at all Bud Fletcher and the Texans shows at the Nite Owl and even at out-of-town bookings. Barbara Jean and all the girls knew every song and danced to the requests. The fan club also showed up to cheer Willie on at school football, track, basketball, and baseball games that he participated in. To show their appreciation, they bought him a nice western suit, which he wore with pride. "I thought Barbara Jean was the greatest chick in the world," Willie said. They were sweethearts until the night Barbara Jean was driving back to Hillsboro from the Nite Owl and her car missed a turn and sailed off an overpass, and she was killed.

Her death hit him hard. But it did not stop him

from contemplating life beyond Abbott. His favorite song was "Far Away Places with Strange-Sounding Names," made popular in 1949 by Bing Crosby and later by Margaret Whiting. Willie sang it all the time, wondering what the rest of the world was like.

BUD's parents thought Bobbie Lee and her brother were no-count music gypsies leading Bud astray. Playing music was no way to make a living. They were corrupting their Bud. And "Mamma Nelson worried about us going into a beer joint and traveling so far from home, meaning the six miles to West," Bobbie said. "But she never condemned us for playing at a beer joint. She knew we were into this music. That's all we're doing. We're playing music and learning music. And she's music. Then I started having babies, she took care of my babies while we'd go to play. She was proud that we could play that well and sounded good. The minister, Brother Dunston, he was very inspirational to me. He knew I was this sweet little girl going to the beer joints. He didn't really like it. He'd tell me, 'There's one thing for sure. If you're going to play for the Devil, you have to play for God the next morning.' So I'd go play for the Devil and then I'd go play for God." Sometimes it was the same audience. "If we saw someone we knew from the night before, we didn't talk about it," she said. It was all music to her and her brother.

Bobbie was philosophical about the leap of faith. "I've always thought about the teachings of Jesus because I'd been raised in the church all my life. I lived in this church. I learned all my life you never go along with the crowd if you're a true Christian because of the decisions that you make. I thought, What would Jesus do? Maybe Jesus wants me to go play here. And I'm going to play good. And that's what I did."

BOBBIE, Bud, Willie, and the whole band idolized Bob Wills. On weekends when the Texans weren't booked, Bobbie and Bud would go to Fort Worth with Ira and Lorraine to hear the Texas Playboys live.

"Bud tried to be just like Bob Wills," Bobbie said. "He'd be talking while Willie was singing, calling out leads. I'd do 'Under the Double Eagle,' all the boogies, and the other music that we had learned. Our crowds started picking up because we were energetic. We had quite a swing band going with the trombone and piano." Bobbie tried to teach music to Bud, like Mamma Nelson had taught her. "He had great rhythm. I tried to show him the strings on the bass fiddle, help him learn how they worked, which notes to hit right. He didn't care which ones he hit. He just kept the best rhythm in the world."

Bob Wills was Willie Hugh Nelson's hero, and Bud Fletcher resembled Bob in more ways than one. So Willie was an easy mark when Bud talked him into copromoting a Bob Wills dance in a town on the Brazos River near Hillsboro. Being a promoter meant Willie helped put up some of the money to bring Wills to town and helped advertise the booking with posters, on the radio, and by word of mouth. If the show drew enough people, Willie and Bud would make more money for promoting the event than they would for the Texans' being the opening act. They hauled the family piano in the back of a borrowed pickup truck from Abbott to the gig.

The gamble paid off. Twelve hundred people showed up.

Willie was starstruck by Wills. "He would hit the bandstand at eight and never leave it for four hours," he said. "He would play continually, there was no time wasted between songs. You keep the people moving and dancing and you don't lose their attention. The more you keep the music going, the smoother the evening's going to go. His band watched him all the time, and he only had to nod or point the bow of his fiddle to cue band members to play a solo.

He was the greatest dance hall bandleader ever. That man had the magnetism or whatever a man has, which is every eye in the house glued on them all night long."

The gamble bit back after the show. According to Bobbie Nelson, the wife of the club owner had run off with the money taken at the door. The band got paid and nobody got hurt or killed, but the Nelson kids and the Fletcher boy were left holding the bag. "We kept going back to her husband," Bobbie said, but to no avail. "It kind of put the squelch on us promoting," she said. "But it didn't take Bud long to recover. He was into promoting this band." The Texans, as far as he was concerned, were the Next Big Thing.

Several other players drifted in and out of the band, including George Uptmor on steel and fiddle, guitarist Ken Frazier, Pete Nemecek on saxophone, Lawrence Ducas on violin and jazz fiddle, and Cosett Holland and Ridley Dixon on country fiddles. "We were playing whatever Bob Wills was playing," Willie said. "The fiddle players were trying to do the twin fiddles with three fiddles."

Bob Wills was an inspiring role model, and he ably demonstrated who ran his show several years later, when his Texas Playboys were finally invited to perform at the Grand Ole Opry, the cradle of country music in Nashville, Tennessee. The Opry didn't allow drums, but Wills convinced the Opry staff to compromise by letting him bring his drums and keep them behind a curtain. The ploy worked fine until Wills got particularly worked up on a song and with his bow pulled back the curtain, revealing to one and all a drum kit on the sacred stage of the Grand Ole Opry. The Opry staff went pale. The Opry audience went wild. Bob Wills and the Texas Playboys were not asked back to the program, reflecting the great divide between Tennessee and Texas when it came to music. Johnny Gimble of the Texas Playboys always said WSM, the Nashville radio station that broadcast the Grand Ole Opry, stood for "Wrong Side of the Mississippi." Every Texas musician worth their salt who'd made the pilgrimage to Nashville knew that.

More revealing were the comments Wills had uttered to producer Art Satherley during the Texas Playboys' first recording session, on September 23, 1935. In his liner notes for a Bob Wills compilation, music historian Rich Kienzle wrote:

"Satherley, expecting a string band like the many others he recorded, questioned the need for horns. Bob responded testily that they came with the package. Rehearsing 'Osage Stomp,' an adaptation of the Memphis Jug Band's 'Rukus Juice and Chitlin',' Bob maintained his usual running commentary until

Satherley stopped the band and chastised Bob for hollering. Leon McAuliffe never forgot what happened next.

" 'Is that right? Okay!' Turning to the Playboys, Bob angrily declared, 'Pack up! We're going home!'

" 'No, Bob, I don't want you to go home. I want you to make records for us!'

" 'You hired Bob Wills and the Texas Playboys and Bob Wills hollers anytime he feels like it and says whatever he wants to say! Now if you want to accept that, Mr. Satherley, we'll do it. But if you don't, we're goin' home!' "

In the eyes of Willie Nelson, Bud Fletcher was Bob Wills, and the Texans were the hottest Western Swing band this side of the Texas Playboys.

"The music was danceable even when we were little," Bobbie Nelson said. "We had a great audience when we were just very small. Our audience kept building until we'd fill these places up where we played. After a while, we had no trouble booking a job, because we'd bring the people and they danced. We knew how to get them on the floor."

Bud Fletcher and the Texans were good enough to travel.

"Bud got us a booking to play Llano [160 miles

southwest of Abbott] once," Bobbie related. "We had to take my piano, so Bud loaded it into this little-bitty Ford pickup. The piano was really too heavy for the pickup. So we had to strap the piano to the pickup. It was me, Bud, and Willie going there. We drove to Llano. It was a longer way than we thought. Willie and I had never been around. We didn't know where Llano is. We go through miles of roads with no one or anything. I'm thinking, There's not going to be anybody when we get there. Before we got there, this horse crossed the road and with the load we were carrying, we just avoided catastrophe. It was frightening. But we made it. It was like the SPJST hall in West where I used to go to dances with all my Catholic friends. There were church benches in this big hall, no tables or chairs, with this big bandstand in the middle of the floor. We had to put the piano up on the bandstand. It was really high.

"We got our equipment set up. It was four in the afternoon. We didn't think anybody would be there. We'd driven all this way, we're not going to make enough money to pay for our equipment, even. But, you know what? Just about sundown, dark, people started coming from where-I-do-not-know. They filled that place up. It was the best performance we had ever done. We played 'There's a Big Rock in the Road,' 'Blues Stay Away from Me.' It was a rocking night. We went home feeling pretty good. We drove over by Buchanan Dam and pulled over and slept by the side of the road so we could rest enough to get home. The only problem was my grandmother trying to get Willie up to go to school after we'd been up half the night," Bobbie said.

Music was just one aspect of the teenager's life. Willie Hugh was a well-rounded individual. He managed to make good grades, encouraged by teachers like Mrs. McCamey, who saw a bright kid in Willie, and Mr. McCamey, the principal, who impressed Willie with his dynamic oratory whenever he made a speech in the school gymnasium.

Sports kept him in school as much as anything. He was good enough to make all the teams and felt needed. "I felt like they had to have me over here, they had to have me over there," he said. Math, English, geography, and classroom teaching were things to be tolerated so he could compete for the Abbott Panthers as the scampering halfback for the football team, a guard for the basketball team, and shortshop on the baseball team. The kid may have been small, no taller than five foot seven, but he was a scrapper and a fighter who relished competition. "I never did think losing was a lot of fun," he said.

"The simplest thing that I learned was to believe that you could do anything you wanted to do. That was instilled in us in Abbott at the house, in the school, in the field. 'You're a Texan.' They all throw that at you. It's pride. You take that and go with it."

When he showed up a little bit drunk at a basketball tournament in 1949, his teammates covered for him, and Coach Bartlett never had a clue, even if one shot he took from the free-throw line flew all the way over the backboard.

Outside of class and sports, Willie wore the distinctive blue Future Farmers of America jacket with pride. Twice he won the FFA Sweetheart contest. During his freshman year in high school, a group of farmers donated $60 to buy him a calf. He went to Whitney to fetch it and brought it home to the pen where the milk cow was. It wasn't two minutes before the calf found an opening in the pen and ran off, never to be seen again.

He helped publish the high school annual. He and Bobbie were consistently voted class favorites, Duke and Duchess, King and Queen, and the main entertainment on Friday assemblies in the cafetorium. And he excelled in the role of Uncle Billy Babcock, the Hated Old Bachelor Next Door, in the senior class production of *Oh, Aunt Jerusha,* performed in the Abbott gym on Thursday, March 30, 1950, then held over a second night by popular demand.

Acting onstage was no big deal. Mamma Nelson

had brought up Willie not to be afraid to look a man or a lady in the eye when he talked to them. "There is, I think, a power there that you lose when you don't do that," he said.

Confidence came naturally to him. "I always instinctively felt like I was sort of in control with what was going on," he said. He realized that when he stared at trains and got the engineer to look over his way. "I started thinking along the line that if you put your mind to something, you could do those things. When you think positive about those things, you have a better chance of getting them done. If you think you can't do it, you won't do it. If you want something to happen, pretend it has already happened."

WEARING the western suit purchased by the five girls in the Willie Nelson Fan Club, he joined twenty-one other students from the Abbott High class of '50 in graduation exercises in the gymnasium and a baccalaureate service at the Methodist church. The graduates were all exceptions to the rule, Willie especially, considering the hand he was dealt growing up. Only 11 percent of the adults in Hill County could claim a high school degree. Willie Hugh was one of them. So were Mary Ann Kolar, Danny Ozyomy,

Adolph Janecka, Jean Carroll, Bobby Watson, Donald Reed, Ermalee Ellis, Lawrence Hlavaty, Helen Pettitt, Gayle Gregory, Joseph Jenecka, Mattie Row Payne, Jackie Clements, Ramona Stafford, Billy Harsler, Helen Urbanovsky, Donald Pendegrass, and Ralph McIlroy.

The year Willie completed high school, country music was redefining itself as Red Foley racked up jukebox spins with his version of "Birmingham Bounce," a song initially popularized by an Alabama cowboy known as Hardrock Gunter, while another 'Bama boy, Hank Williams, was moaning the blues with "Long Gone Lonesome Blues."

AFTER graduating, Willie started running around with Zeke Varnon, a buddy of Bud Fletcher's whose main mission in life seemed to be the pursuit of a good time.

"I met him at the Nite Owl," Willie said. "I was playing music. He'd just gotten out of the army. We started hanging out together." Zeke endeared himself to Willie by dancing with all the girls in the Willie Nelson Fan Club seated at the table by the front of the bandstand and by clowning and carrying on. Zeke and Barbara Jean McDearmon, who was Willie's sweetie when she was killed, were old friends from Hillsboro.

When Willie wasn't playing, he and Zeke liked to "drink, run around and chase the girls," Willie said. "He had done it all his life. I never knew what he was gonna do. He never knew what he was gonna do, and when he'd get drunk he was like everybody else— there was no telling what he was going to do."

Some nights, Zeke and Willie would drink to the point of passing out and wake up the next morning and start drinking again. They attempted to enter the bootlegging trade, pooling their earnings and buying nineteen half-pints over the McLennan County line and driving the haul back to Hillsboro, where half-pints went for twice the price. "We sold two bottles," Willie said, and drank or gave away the rest. "We were great bootleggers."

Zeke had a wild streak wilder than Willie's and was a natural-born con, always trying to work a scam, shave an angle, and hustle up money, with a willing Willie as his coconspirator.

"One night, another good friend of mine who'd get a little alcohol in him beat the hell out of Zeke with a ball-peen hammer and landed him in the hospital, almost killed him," Willie said with understatement. "It had to do with a woman, of course. They were the best of friends, when all of a sudden, Zeke opened the door and—bam! It wasn't the first time for him."

He was Willie's soul brother. "We always wore the same size of everything—clothes, boots, hat," Zeke said about Willie. "He used to stay all night with me on Saturday night, and he would wear my clothes on Sunday. If I stayed with him, I'd wear his clothes."

Willie followed Zeke to Tyler later in 1950, where they found work as tree trimmers for the Asplundh company for eighty cents an hour, until Willie fell from a tree and hurt his back. Out of ideas about what to do next, he followed in the footsteps of other young men his age and signed up for military service, joining the air force. He had been classified 1-A, meaning he'd likely be drafted into the armed services anyway. At least this way, he could choose which branch of the military to join. And just in case, he brought along his guitar.

He was stationed at Lackland Air Force Base in San Antonio, then transferred to Sheppard Air Force Base in Wichita Falls, Texas, Scott AFB in southwestern Illinois, just east of St. Louis, and Keesler AFB in Biloxi, Mississippi, where he went into radar mechanics.

The air force afforded him the opportunity to sing and play along with other musically inclined airmen from every corner of America, which helped him realize he was more than the best guitarist in Abbott, Texas. When he was at Sheppard AFB, Bobbie or Bud would fetch him from Wichita Falls to play with Bud Fletcher and the Texans on weekends. By the end of his hitch, he was playing six nights a week at the Airmen's Club.

But too many drinks, too many wild nights off base, one too many fights, and a bad back led to his departure from the military. Whether it was from falling out of the tree in East Texas with Zeke or from baling hay for Rudolph Kapavik alongside Morris Russell as a boy, the pain in his back came on so fiercely, he was hardly mobile. Nine months in, his rank reduced to private, he was offered an honorable medical discharge from the air force as long as he agreed not to sue the military for his back problems.

Willie returned to play with Bud Fletcher and the Texans, but the band was on its last legs. Bud's temper led to a separation and eventual divorce from Bobbie. Years later, he was killed in a tragic wreck on the highway. The girls in the Willie Nelson Fan Club had moved on to other singers. Willie traveled to Dallas to check out the city lights and to Fort Worth to see his father, Ira, and his wife, Lorraine, and their two boys, Doyle and Charles. Ira had found work as a mechanic at Frank Kent Ford, where Doyle worked in the parts department. Whenever Willie visited, they'd go hear music. "My dad knew a guy named Chester Odem, who had a band, and we'd go listen to them," he said. Drinking, playing dominoes, drinking, cruising, hell raising, and drinking with Zeke occupied most of his time. When Willie was at a loss for what to do, he and Zeke would stand on opposite sides of the highway, thumbs out, and take the first ride offered, no matter if it was to Hillsboro or to West. It was enough to get out of town and go somewhere. Anywhere.

When Zeke bought a '48 Studebaker, they had mobility to go wherever they wanted whenever they wanted, as long as they had enough money for gas. Most often, they found themselves drawn to the bright lights of Waco, the closest big city to Abbott.

Waco, 1952

THE HEART OF TEXAS was a kind nickname for the city of Waco, acknowledgment of its location in the center of the state's population, which in the wake of World War II was evenly divided between rural and urban citizens. The heart part did not suggest a soul. Ever since it was established in 1849 by Jacob de Cordova, replacing the Hueco Indian village next to abundant springs, Waco had been a tough place to live.

Waco's leaders bragged that the small city was a manufacturing, retail, and wholesale hub, as well as home to Connally Air Force Base, and the capital of the Brazos River agriculture empire. More accurately, Waco was an overgrown small town controlled by good Christian oligarchs who were joined at the hip to the administration of Baylor University, the oldest institution of higher learning on Texas soil and the world's largest Baptist institution. Drinking and dancing were not part of Waco's official history. Neither were honky-tonks.

But to a charismatic kid from Abbott with music on his mind, the city of almost one hundred thousand "wide-awake and hospitable people," according to the local chamber of commerce, looked like a wide-open situation. Any place on the Dallas Highway with enough electricity to power a 40-watt bulb was a beer joint, dive, private club, or roadhouse, with the featured entertainment a live band or a jukebox. The city's main drag, the red-bricked Austin Avenue, was an aspiring neon-lit Broadway. Storied venues such as the Melody Ranch, the Western Club, the new Terrace Club, Geneva Hall, Linden Hall, Elk Hall, and various SPJST and Knights of Columbus halls were scattered all over Waco.

Waco was devotedly Southern in outlook, western in underbelly, and closer to Jesus than most communities, or so its citizens liked to think. New people with new ideas contrary to their own were not wanted in a place where cotton was still king and African Americans were still "nigras," as far as most respectable Wacoans were concerned.

But Waco was also a weird, gothic kind of place that was home to a succession of cranks, crazies, and rugged individualists, including the gentlemen who invented Dr Pepper and Big Red, two distinctive soft drinks that endure to the present. The parade of different drummers began with William Cowper Brann, the publisher of the *Iconoclast,* an incisive, wickedly biting journal published during the late nineteenth century that boasted a circulation of one hundred thousand who ate up the opinions Brann openly shared with his readers. A consistent critic of all things Baptist, Brann was twice engaged in gunfights in the streets of Waco. He lost the second battle along with his life at the corner of 4th and Austin on April 1, 1898, shot in the back. But the God-fearing Christians were not satisfied. More than a hundred years later, the profile of his likeness etched on his tombstone was defaced, a chunk of marble near his temple chipped out, supposedly from a bullet.

The Waco that Willie Nelson came to know was more the Brann version than the Baptist. His first impressions were formed from the radio, where Hank the Hired Hand, as Hank Thompson was first called, was a daily feature on WACO, 1460 on your radio dial. The son of Bohemian immigrants, Thompson had been exposed to the same breadth and variety of music as Willie. He had his first hit record, "Whoa, Sailor!" when Booger Red was starting out with Bud Fletcher and the Texans. "He came to the gymnasium in Abbott and had braces on his teeth," Willie recalled. "He was just getting ready to go Big Time."

Thompson proceeded to heat up jukeboxes well into the 1950s with a string of singles, from "Humpty Dumpty Heart" to "Six Pack to Go," as he built a rep as the new King of Western Swing, despite Thompson's being a cultured man who'd seen the world in the navy and had attended Princeton University, which earned him derision from his musical peers. "Hank Thompson had a great band until Billy Gray left; he didn't know shit about meter," one player remarked. Bob Wills called him a pretty boy. "If Hank ever runs out of nursery songs, he's going to run out of songs," Wills once said. The comments could have easily been dismissed as jealousy; by 1954 Thompson could brag twenty-one Top 20 country hit singles. The rhinestone sparkles on his western suit spelled the word STAR for a reason. His hottest streak began with "Wild Side of Life," which would become his signature song, charting number 1 nationwide for three months in 1952.

Bands like Thompson, the Lone Star Playboys featuring the Booker Brothers and Johnny Gimble, and the Texas Swingsters starring Doyle Brink gave Willie his musical cues. Zeke Varnon was his social mentor. Zeke got Willie to start carrying a pistol, and he roomed with Zeke at the Grandy Courts in Waco. Whenever he would pawn his guitar, Zeke would repay the loan plus interest on Friday so Willie could play the instrument over the weekend before he put it back in pawn again on Monday.

Willie was riding shotgun in the old black '34 Model T Ford that they had bought together on the night Zeke drove to the Lone Oak Drive-Inn on the Dallas Highway. The hot Spanish-looking car-hop delivering hamburgers caught Willie's eye. She wasn't moving around on skates like the other car-hops, and there was a pronounced sway to her hips as she walked.

Martha Jewel Matthews was a looker, a ravishing brunette with a shapely figure, and a natural flirt. She was neither Spanish nor Mexican but rather full-blooded Cherokee. Her sharp facial features reminded Willie more than a little of his mother. She was only sixteen, but she looked old enough to buy beer and could hold her own when it came to tossing a few back. She had been around the block, married to a steel guitar player at age fourteen, only to be widowed at sixteen. She knew who Willie Nelson of Abbott was. They'd once talked at a dance he was playing in West, and they talked some more at the Sunday matinee dance at the 31 Club in Waco.

But she refused Willie's request to ride with him and Zeke. She wasn't going to get in the car with two guys who appeared to be all liquored up. She would have to be properly wooed. "I'm going to come in here one of these nights and I am going to take you home," Willie promised before they drove off. Two nights later, he pulled into the drive-in alone behind the wheel of the car he had borrowed from Bud Fletcher and drove her home.

He was smitten. "She was a beautiful girl," he said. "She had a lot of fire, I liked that. She had long black hair, and I was always a sucker for long-black-haired women."

In a matter of months, a justice of the peace at the Johnson County Courthouse in Cleburne married the couple. Willie was nineteen and ready to take on the world with his hot momma at his side.

Their marriage was fermented in beer joints and honky-tonks. He played music. She loved to dance. They moved in with Mamma Nelson in Abbott while Willie picked up day jobs in Waco and played music at night. But being young and restless, the couple told a few lies so they could put down a deposit and take a drive-away car from Dallas to the West Coast. The experience made them both feel a little bit like the outlaws Bonnie and Clyde, and they drove all the way to Eugene, Oregon, where Willie showed off his bride to his mother and her second husband, Claude Sharpenstein.

Willie enjoyed being around his mother. They'd never spent much time together when he was growing up, and this was an opportunity to catch up. He tried to plant roots in Eugene, briefly hiring on as a guitarist with Joe Massey and the Frontiersmen, a western band that appeared regularly on the Hayloft Jamboree, a barn-dance show broadcast on KUGN radio in Eugene. Myrle and Martha bonded. But Willie and Martha both missed Texas and left Eugene for Mamma Nelson, Abbott, and Waco.

Like Myrle, Martha was not a woman to be trifled with, and she proved it time and again, stuffing a biscuit in her new husband's mouth when she took umbrage at something he said at the breakfast table and, after he came home late and very drunk one too many times, tying him up with jump rope and beating him with a broom.

"I didn't do half what I should've done," she later complained.

They argued, they fought, they smoked, they drank, only to kiss and make up and dance before they fought again.

"Martha was a full-blooded Cherokee Indian," explained Willie. "And every night was like Custer's last stand."

• • •

WACO'S appeal diminished at 4:36 p.m. on May 11, 1953, when a monster black cloud dropped a tornado a half mile wide on the city. Willie and a friend watched the twister from across the Brazos. The twister killed 114 people, injured more than 1,000, damaged 850 homes, and trashed 2,000 automobiles. Most of Waco's downtown was torn apart. The city never fully recovered, not even three years later, when a very famous GI from Fort Hood named Elvis Presley started hanging out in Waco on furlough.

Willie stuck around Waco for another year. His brief tenure in the military allowed him to enroll at Baylor University for the spring and summer semesters in 1954 with his tuition paid by the GI Bill. Ostensibly, he was studying agriculture and business as a part-time student with the vague idea of going into law. He rented a house for Martha and their new baby girl on North 5th Street near Cameron Park and got a job at Ozark Leather on a saddle-making assembly line, coming home stinking of wet cowhide. He tried selling encyclopedias door-to-door, until a dog chased him back into his car. In truth, Willie was spending more time catting around with Zeke, majoring in 42 (a popular game of dominoes) while working on a PhD in honky-tonk.

San Antonio, 1954

THE NEON SIGN on the Laredo Highway blinked "AL'S COU TRY CL B." A handpainted signboard leaning on the front of the windowless building advertised "Live Band." Willie and Cosett Holland pulled over. They'd found the place they'd been looking for on the south side of San Antonio, the oldest and third-largest city in Texas, which looked more like Mexico than any part of Texas Willie had seen.

Al's Country Club was where the Mission City Playboys were playing. Willie and Cosett, who worked together in Bud Fletcher and the Texans back home, had already approached Easy Adams, the leader of the Texas Tophands, the hottest Western Swing dance band in South Texas, but Easy didn't have any work to offer.

79

"Well, then, who's the second-most popular band in San Antonio?" Willie asked. Easy Adams's answer took them to Al's. "They wanted to know if they could sit in," Dave Isbell, the bandleader, said. "I told them, 'Come on.' At the end of the night, I asked Holland if he wanted to join the band, because I was looking for a fiddle player. He said he wanted the job. Then the other guy came up to me and said, 'We're working together. We'd like to be together.' "

The band agreed to add Willie Nelson too and to give him a split of whatever money they made. Dave Isbell said Willie's timing was good. "My lead guitar player was at Lackland AFB and got transferred to Germany. Willie stepped right on in." Cosett Holland played fiddle, Johnny Bush played drums, Lucky Carajohn played piano, Carl Walker played steel, Frog Isbell played bass, and Dave Isbell led the band, much like Bud Fletcher led the Texans. Willie played lead guitar but never sang.

Willie moved Martha and his baby girl, De Lana, born in Hill County on November 11, 1953, into the back half of a rent house on Labor Street, just southeast of downtown San Antonio. Carl Walker lived with a woman in the front of the house. Cosett Holland slept on a cot in the dining room in between. When they weren't playing dances, they were checking out other dances and the nightlife of San Antonio, which was not unlike the nightlife in West and Waco. "Same music, same people, only more places to play," Willie said.

San Antonio was the biggest small town in Texas. Between its reputation as a trade center for rural folks, ranchers, and farmers across South Texas from the Wintergarden to the Rio Grande Valley, and the city's curious mix of Anglos, Mexicans, and blacks, and its distinctive Latin flavor, San Antonio was more exotic than Hill County or McLennan County. Nowhere but in San Antonio did Mexicans play polkas with as much zeal as the Germans and Bohemians did. Audiences measured music by how danceable it was. If you could do the two-step to a song, it was worth playing.

JOHNNY Bush, the Mission City Playboy who drummed and sang, wasn't that impressed by Cosett Holland. He'd heard too many hot fiddlers around his hometown Houston, like Cliff Bruner and Harry Choates. But Johnny took an immediate shine to the little red-haired cat with Cosett. There was something about the glint in his eye that suggested a fellow mischief maker, which became apparent the first time he went to visit the Nelsons at their rent house on Labor Street.

"As I drove up, Willie was running out the back door, and this iron pot was following him," Johnny said. "It was the strangest thing I've ever seen. He outran that pot. Then he turned. When he did, that pot hit the garage. He stood there with that grin and said, 'She loves me. You got a cigarette? I need a match. What time is it?' They'd be fighting one minute and be laughing about it the next."

Dave Isbell liked Martha well enough, but he encouraged her to stay home like the other women attached to members of the Mission City Playboys. "We didn't want the gals coming out," Dave said, fearing the women would chase away prospective fans. But Martha's case was special, since she was as adept with a knife as she was with a pot.

"She was beautiful. She was an Indian gal, so she was pretty mean to him when she got pissed off," explained Dave, relating how she threw a knife at Willie as he was walking out the door once and almost hit Holland. "I'm gonna find the meanest goddamn girl in the world and I'm going to marry her and I'm going to move in with you," Cosett growled at Willie.

"I already found the meanest goddamn woman in the world," Willie informed him.

Johnny Bush kept his distance. "She was hostile, it didn't matter if she was drunk or not," he said. "She liked me and my wife, Jean, all right. But she wanted Willie to get a job, she wanted some money coming in, just like all women did."

Willie preferred playing music. "If he needed money, he'd go hock his guitar," Johnny said. "If he got a gig, he couldn't play the gig because he didn't have a guitar. If his guitar was in hock, he'd hock the bumper jack he carried around with him in his green 'forty-seven Ford. The gas tank was always empty, but he could pull the choke and get the last drop of gas from the tank. He was always hustling until he could land on his feet."

The Mission City Playboys played the Walter Ranch House, the Texas Star Inn, Mugwam's, the old Al's Country Club, Charlie Walker's club, the Barn, out on the Houston highway, the Skyline in Austin, the Cherry Springs dance hall out on the Mason Highway near Fredricksburg, and clubs in Houston every once in a while.

One trip to Houston took them to ACA Studios, on Washington Avenue, a recording facility where a band could make a record by playing a song and having it recorded on audiotape. The Mission City Playboys' recordings became seven-inch 45 rpm singles released by Sarg Records, a small label in Luling, east of San Antonio. Charlie Fitch, the owner of the label, chose the tunes "Satisfied or Sorry," "No Longer Afraid," and "Let's Do It Up Brown," hoping one would become popular on the radio and on juke-boxes, a hope unrealized.

When Dave Isbell quit so he could look after his sick wife, the band morphed into the Mission City Playboys led by Carl Walker, then Johnny Bush and the Hillbilly Playboys, with "exclusive management by Willie Nelson," according to the posters printed up by Johnny's father. Willie had played long enough to know that if he was going to make money playing music, he needed a piece of the action, like managers and booking agents got. But there was precious little action to get a piece of, which made it hard to keep food on the table and Martha off his back.

Willie didn't give a shit. He was playing music and having a good time honky-tonking, and San Antonio was made for drinking, drinking songs, and drinking songwriters like himself. The city was sprinkled with icehouses, informal open-air social centers where beer drinking was a year-round pastime. The Lone Star and Pearl breweries, the biggest regional brands in the Southwest, were based in San Antone. Both breweries sponsored large Western Swing bands—Adolph Hofner's Pearl Wranglers, which featured a jazz fiddler named J. R. "Chat the Cat" Chatwell, and Lone Star's Texas Tophands, the first band Willie tried to sit in with in San Antonio, which featured fiddler Easy Adams and Big Bill Lister, at six foot seven the tallest guitar player in Texas. The Pearl Wranglers performed on 50,000-watt KABC radio every weekday at 1:15 p.m. and regularly appeared on KABC's *Parade of Stars* live show. Each band was considered the best dance band in South Texas, depending on what brand you drank, and frequently engaged in battle dances that concluded with an inebriated audience.

Adolph Hofner was San Antonio's Bob Wills, a singer and bandleader well versed in swing and blues who also played to the local Czech, German, and Mexican communities by working in popular ethnic dance numbers such as the "Paul Jones," "Herr Schmidt," "Put Your Little Foot," "Julida Polka," "El Rancho Grande," and "Jalisco."

Willie was good enough and bold enough to ask to sit in with the Wranglers and to continue to do so in case Hofner needed another musician. But before Adolph had the need, Willie found a better home thirty-five miles southeast of the Alamo in a rolling pasture between Poteet and Pleasanton, at the base of the transmitter for KBOP radio 1380. The station was licensed to broadcast during daylight hours and serve the small farming community of Pleasanton, but its 50-watt signal reached into parts of San Antonio.

Aaron Allan had just left KBOP to take a job at WOAI in San Antonio, and word reached Dave Isbell. "My sister wanted me to take that job," Dave said. "I told her I wasn't interested, so Willie stepped up and proposed he interview for the position. He lied like a dog and said he'd been a DJ before."

Willie drove to the door of Dr. Ben O. Parker, who owned the station. Dr. Parker was the dean of the Texas Chiropractic College in San Antonio, pastor of Harriman Place Christian Church, and a community leader in Pleasanton. The station had gone on the air in 1950 and was one of three owned by Dr. Parker and his wife, Mona. He was operations manager, doing the hiring and firing. Mona was the station's business manager and chief engineer — the first woman in the United States to receive her First Class Radio Operator/Engineer's license from the Federal Communications Commission.

KBOP looked like KHBR in Hillsboro, where Willie had performed with Bud Fletcher's Texans. The red-haired, brown-eyed man with the winning personality proceeded to sell himself to the Parkers — selling being a fundamental element of radio, of making music, and of going through life.

Doc Parker had Willie go into the broadcast booth and read the tongue-tangling copy he gave him.

"Pleasanton pharmacy, where your pharmaceutical needs are filled precisely and accurately . . ." He flubbed some of the lines but acted like he'd read the copy perfectly, flashing a confident smile at the end of the reading. Parker hired him for $40 a week, and Willie moved Martha and Lana into the Palm Courts, a small apartment complex in Pleasanton.

He proceeded to learn the ins and outs of radio by performing any and all duties required — signing on in the morning, playing records, reading the news, entertaining the folks at home, keeping logs, selling advertising time, recording commercials and announcements, whatever was called for. The Parkers quickly determined that signing on the station at sunrise was Willie's weak hand. "My parents would get up and wait to hear the signal come on," said Charlotte Ramsey, the Parkers' daughter. Too often they were greeted by silence. Willie was a slow riser, usually because he'd been out the night before singing and playing. The Parkers liked him so much they moved him to a later shift.

Pleasanton was close enough for Willie to listen to Aaron Allan on WOAI, the 50,000-watt station in San Antonio that carried the Grand Ole Opry on Saturday nights, Charlie Walker on KMAC, Stan Cox on KONO, and the on-air talents who performed live, like Red River Dave, the Singing Cowboy, on WOAI, Big Bill Lister on KABC, and Adolph Hofner on KTSA. Charlie Walker was a role model. An engaging, charismatic radio host whose folksy speaking manner was said to have been influenced by his habit of dipping snuff, Walker was also a performer who recorded for Decca, eventually recording the Texas two-step classic "Pick Me Up on Your Way Down." Charlie Walker worked radio, ballrooms, and recording studios with equal panache. He befriended Willie and they used their microphones to tease one another on the air.

Willie wanted to be like him and like Aaron Allan—a performer, not just a disc jockey playing the performer's song. "I can write better songs than the ones I'm playing on the radio," he would complain to Manuel Davila, who hosted the conjunto radio show in Spanish, which aired for two hours before Willie came back on the air to sign off the station at sunset. "Then do it," Davila would tell him.

Taking advantage of the electronic equipment around him, he made a recording of two of his songs in his spare time and sent the tape to Charlie Fitch, the owner of Sarg Records in Luling, who'd put out the recordings he did with Dave Isbell and the Mission City Playboys. Willie recorded on an old tape that Dr. Parker had used to record stock reports on, and in an eager, convincing voice made his pitch:

"Hello, Sarg, you probably don't remember me. My name's Willie Nelson. I cut a session with Dave Isbell down at ACA in Houston the Sarg Record label was going to release. I talked to you about a recording contract and I was supposed to send a tape over but I never got around to it till now. I work down here at KBOP in Pleasanton, Texas. I got a few minutes, I thought I'd put down a couple on tape and let you listen and see what you thought about it."

He'd been singing both songs since he was a kid. "When I've Sang My Last Hillbilly Song" was sung in a voice that almost mimicked Lefty Frizzell as he whined, "I hope and I pray you'll forgive me and remember . . ."

"The Storm Has Just Begun" was equally heartfelt, evoking sorrow in the line "when those teardrops start to flow, I realize the storm has just begun."

When he finished singing, Willie signed off.

"Well, there they are. See what you think about them. If you like them, let me know about them, will you? I work down here every day. I'm off Saturday. And if you don't like them, well, let me know that too. It won't hurt my feelings a bit. Thank you a lot, Sarg."

His voice was followed by Dr. Parker's voice reading the stock report: ". . . Seventeen and three-quarters, we have some food lockers selling . . ."

Charlie Fitch did not respond.

WILLIE Hugh Nelson wasn't making progress. Johnny Bush and the Hillbilly Playboys weren't getting many bookings. Johnny Bush allowed how he really liked Willie's guitar playing more than he liked his singing, a comment Willie never forgot. "Willie didn't really give a rat's ass what I thought, or so I believed at the time," Johnny said. "But evidently he really did. He didn't say anything directly to me, but he let me know."

Johnny became a KBOP regular. When records were playing, Willie and Johnny would compare opinions about what it took to make it. "We'd sit in that studio in Pleasanton and talk about it. We knew to make it you had to have a distinctive style so if people heard you, they knew immediately who you are. Willie already had his style, but he was covering it up."

They figured out they should take advantage of the radio station, so Johnny, Willie, and KBOP's engineer, Red Hilburn, took turns hosting their own shows back-to-back. "Red had a fifteen-minute show and I would be his guest," Johnny said. "I would have my show and have Willie as my guest. Then Willie would have his fifteen-minute show and have Red as his guest. Between the three of us, we had forty-five minutes of playing time."

In early December, Willie and Johnny pulled over in Leming, about ten miles north of Pleasanton, to talk to the lady who owned a club there called the Red Barn. She immediately recognized Willie as the disc jockey at KBOP. "Y'all have a band?" she asked.

"Yes, ma'am, a great band with fiddle and steel," Willie replied, looking her straight in the eye. Johnny Bush could scarcely believe what he was hearing. Willie was lying his ass off, but the woman was buying every word.

"I need a band for Christmas Eve and Christmas night," she told him. "What would you charge?"

"One hundred dollars a night," Willie told her without hesitating.

When they got back in the car, Johnny looked at Willie like he was crazy. "What are we going to do? We don't have a PA. We don't have a band."

"Don't worry," Willie assured him with the smile of a confidence man. "We'll think of something."

Willie found a pedal steel player named Dale Watson. They pulled off the gig, but when Willie was settling up, the club owner confronted him.

"Where's your fiddle player?"

Willie told her the fiddler was sick and couldn't make it, a better excuse than telling him the truth.

"If you don't have a fiddle player tomorrow night, you're not going to get paid."

As they walked back to Willie's car, Johnny Bush was worried. "What are we going to do? We don't have a fiddle player."

"Something will happen," Willie said with a shrug. He didn't seem worried at all.

Willie's father, Ira, had driven down from Fort Worth in a brand-new Ford to see his son, his daughter-in-law, and his baby granddaughter for the holiday, and he'd brought his fiddle with him. "Ira could only play two hoedowns on fiddle," Johnny said. "There was a popular dance called the Paul Jones where everyone would go 'round in two circles until a whistle blew and you danced with the person standing in front of you. Every time the club owner would look up at the stage, we were playing the Paul Jones while Ira fiddled. It was a great crowd and we got paid. Willie never gave anything like that a second thought. He just knew things would work out, and they did. He was fearless. He conned that lady and she didn't even know it."

Despite Willie's persuasive powers and Johnny's belief in him, the two were having a hard time making ends meet. Johnny was so desperate, he had hitched a ride to Houston on a Central Freight Line truck, looking for gigs, and went to his mother's house way out on Humble Road. "I heard this noise and went into the living room, and there was Willie on the couch, looking through the phone book."

Johnny asked what he was doing.

"I wanted to make sure I was in the right house," Willie said. "You have a job?"

Johnny told him he was broke and stranded.

"I've got a car," Willie said. So they went out looking for gigs. At the Chuck Wagon, a little-bitty joint out on North Shepherd, the club owner informed them he had an opening for Friday. "We can do it," Willie volunteered.

"How are we going to do the gig?" Johnny asked.

"Hell if I know," Willie replied.

They borrowed a beat-up Fender amplifier and a microphone from Johnny's uncle, Smilin' Jerry Jericho, and a National guitar from Johnny's dad. Johnny found a pedal steel player named Joe Brewer, who'd just been fired from Webb Pierce's band. Nobody showed. The club owner was pissed. Willie drove Johnny to San Antonio and then returned to Pleasanton.

When he got home, Martha and Lana were gone. Martha had written a message on the mint-green wall of their living room in aerosol fake snow for Christmas trees that read "You Son Of A Bitch." Johnny and his wife, Jean, came by and found Willie in the room, staring at a television with the vertical picture flipping on the screen.

After explaining what had happened, Willie asked Johnny, "What are you gonna do?"

Johnny said he was going to look for work in Houston, and once he found something, he'd send for Jean.

Willie had fewer options. Charlie Fitch from Sarg Records had never called. His frustration had grown to the point where he left a box of song lyrics in his rent house when he finally took Dr. Parker's advice to seek greener pastures.

All Martha had wanted was for her husband to provide enough to live on and to be at home. Willie wanted to be that man, but he wanted to provide by playing music. He headed to the only other place where he knew he could satisfy both urges, to where his father and his second family lived. If he could get settled in Fort Worth and pick up work, Martha might not be so mad.

Fort Worth, 1955

FROM THE NEON American flag that flew above the Tarrant County Courthouse to its sordid underbelly, Fort Worth was a toddling town full of contradictions. It was never a fort, but a camp, and not a very organized one at that; the same year a military presence was established on a bluff above the Trinity River, in 1849, Fort Worth's first Hell's Half Acre, a strip of brothels, bars, and gambling joints that serviced the troops, sprang up adjacent to the camp, attracting the likes of Butch Cassidy and the Sundance Kid. Eighty years later, another Hell's Half Acre attracted the likes of Bonnie and Clyde. What was left of that version in 1955 looked good enough to a young man from down around Waco.

Fort Worth had grown into the fourth-biggest city

in Texas, although its proximity to Dallas, thirty miles east, forever sentenced the city to second-city status, imbuing its citizens with a peculiar character. Like San Antonio, "Foat Wuth" was a hide and horns town that proudly wore its Cowtown and "Where the West Begins" reputations like a giant rodeo belt buckle.

The Stockyards on the North Side were a magnet for cowboys, ranchers, and farmers for hundreds of miles throughout West Texas, but Fort Worth's wealth also was remarkable for a place of its size. Local resident Sid Richardson, an oilman who'd struck it rich in East Texas and West Texas, was the richest man in the world, with a net worth of $1 billion, according to *Life* magazine.

The music that came out of Fort Worth reflected the city's wide-open nature. Fort Worth was the "Cradle of Western Swing," where Bob Wills and Milton Brown emerged from the Light Crust Dough-boys to create the sound that came to be known as Western Swing. Bob Dunn, who played lap steel guitar with Milton Brown's Musical Brownies, was widely recognized as the first player to super-charge the instrument, previously considered lit-tle more than a means to achieve mellowness, Hawaiian-style. Dunn played steel like a sax, riffing off the melody to lead the rest of the strings in the ensemble.

While other forms of country music found favor in Fort Worth — every pedal steel player worth his salt knew the lead to Webb Pierce's "Slowly" — Western Swing remained the preferred sound even after Milton Brown died in a car wreck on the Jacksboro Highway in 1936 with a sixteen-year-old girl by his side and Wills found a better home in Tulsa. Western Swing was really nothing more than an amalgam of popular American music — country, of course, swing, jazz, pop, Dixieland, and country blues — tailored for dancing, with a strong Texas flavor. Swing in Fort Worth wasn't just a western thing, either. It was the hometown of big-band orchestra leader Paul Whiteman and numerous other swinging big-band musicians, and it was the frequent stomping ground for the rhythm-and-blues guitar swing of T-Bone Walker.

Of all the honky-tonk, bar, and club clusters around the city, none rivaled the Jacksboro Highway, State Highway 199, which ran northwest from downtown toward rugged country and some of the biggest ranches in the state. There was something for everybody on "Jaxbeer Highway." Though gambling was illegal, several casinos set back from the road did brisk business, equipped with roulette wheels and blackjack tables that conveniently folded into cabinets in the wall and with underground tunnels for quick getaways.

The Jacksboro Highway was also a major stop for top-shelf acts riding the Chitlin' Circuit for black entertainers throughout the South, most notably semiregulars Ike and Tina Turner, Ray Charles, and Jimmy Reed, local heroes such as Ray ("Linda Lu") Sharpe, the Ron-Dels ("If You Really Want Me To I'll Go"), featuring Delbert McClinton, Bruce ("Hey Baby") Channel, and Trini Lopez and his brother Jesse, along with Candy Barr and exotic dancer colleagues such as Tammi True and Chris Colt and Her 45s.

Sandwiched between the nicer neon-lit establishments were meaner spots, many of which draped chicken wire in front of the bandstand to keep flying beer bottles from hitting the hired entertainment whenever fights broke out. They carried nicknames like the Bloody Bucket and the County Dump that were well earned. "They called it County Dump because it was right next to the county dump," said Paul English, a sometimes musician and full-time police character, the respected description of what others might call a hood, a thug, a gangster, or an underground figure. "It was on Handley Drive [on

Fort Worth's east side] all the way until it dead-
ended. We played there for nine months. They
couldn't get anybody to play there because it was too
rough. My brother and I picked up a trumpet player
who didn't want to go. I told him it wasn't rough
anymore—we carry guns. We all went out there,
and that night there were two fights and one knif-
ing." The trumpet player didn't come back.

One joint was so nasty, the only person Paul
English could persuade to take a gig with him was
his cousin Arvel Walden. A two-piece band suited
management just fine. All they needed was enough
noise to cover up the sound of dice hitting the wall
when craps games were going on in back. One night
when Arvel took the evening off, the guy who took
his place was stabbed.

The patrons of these venues included a disproportionate number of characters, due in no small part to
a protracted gangland war that erupted at the tail
end of World War II and featured a cast that earned
Fort Worth another reputation, as a little Chicago.

They worked the rackets, running backroom gambling joints, prostitutes, whorehouses, numbers, and
vending machines, and car lots were often their base,
an easy front for laundering ill-gotten gains. But they
weren't hoodlums like the hoodlums over in Dallas,
down in Houston, or on Galveston Island.

"Fort Worth gangsters had families, everybody kind of worked together, they all knew each other's family, they all needed one another, and of course the police over here were a little softer," said Richard Davis, who worked as a card dealer at Pappy Kirkwood's club. "There was more honor among thieves in Fort Worth. When those people started getting blowed up and killed, they deserved it. No one was killed without permission and it was usually for things like beating up on prostitutes or getting out of line with the law."

WILLIE Nelson came to this Fort Worth in search of someplace better than where he'd been. He put his salesmanship skills to use, picking up work selling Bibles, encyclopedias, Singer sewing machines, and Kirby vacuum cleaners, enough to bring Martha and Lana up from Waco. "Willie was a very good salesman," his sister, Bobbie, said. But Willie had bigger ambitions than making Salesman of the Month. He talked his way into selling ads for KDNT, a small 250-watt radio station at 1440 on the AM dial, broadcasting from Denton, thirty miles north of Fort Worth, and, citing his experience on KHBR back in Hillsboro and KBOP in Pleasanton, hosting a country music program.

A fellow announcer, Lee Woodward, a voice major at Arlington State College trained in classical music, noticed the redheaded kid. "He had these lively eyes behind this laid-back look that said, 'I'm not gonna give you anything unless you ask.' I thought, here was a guy straight off the farm. He sounded like it too." On Saturdays, the kid went down the hall of the radio station to run the audio board while Woodward sang with members of the North Texas State College Lab Band, which was turning out musicians capable of joining the road bands of swing stars.

Willie didn't stay at KDNT long, because he hustled another radio gig in Fort Worth with a salary higher than the $40 a week he was making, minus the expense of driving to and from Denton. KCNC was a low-wattage daytime station at 720 on the radio dial, run by a cranky fellow named Jim Speck, who gave Willie enough rope to hang himself with when he hired him. Willie Nelson's *Western Express* came after *Melody Time* at the noon hour. After *Western Express* ended at three p.m., Gordon Fitzgerald's prerecorded *Disc n' Date* and *Blues at Sundown* concluded the station's broadcasting day.

Willie called Lee Woodward not long after he settled in at KCNC station, telling him about an opening for an announcer at the Fort Worth station. Lee auditioned and won the job. "That's when I discovered the real Willie," he said.

"I saw him with his guitar in the studio booth where he did his show," Lee Woodward said. "He would play his guitar and sing along to the records he was playing. He was singing songs. Every time he did it, the phones would light up. The management figured out real quick he must be doing something right, because nobody called when we were on KDNT together. He invented this niche."

The diminutive announcer with flaming red hair read his commercials live with his guitar strapped around his neck, strumming along to the ad copy. He sang and played at the live weekend remotes with Lee Woodward and Walt Jones from the furniture department at Leonard Brothers Department Store downtown, where he interviewed salespeople from various departments who were touting the Big Specials of the Day from ten to eleven in the morning. He strummed his way through remotes from the Bomber Grill at 10th and Houston and commercials for American Auto Salvage and Clardy automobile air-conditioners, the futuristic clear, horn-shaped pipes that spewed refrigerated air into one's automobile from a compressor in the trunk, one of the precursors of the device that would ultimately tame and industrialize Texas.

Every afternoon from one to one-thirty he played children's songs, such as Tex Ritter's "Blood in the Saddle," in anticipation of nap time. No song was as popular for napping as "Red Headed Stranger," a song written by Edith Lindeman and Carl Stutzby made popular by Arthur "Guitar Boogie" Smith, a family entertainer from Charlotte, North Carolina, who blazed trails as one of country music's first television stars, with the *Arthur Smith Show,* syndicated in forty-one markets throughout the southeast.

Willie would play the song for his daughter, Lana, and say hi to her on the air. At home, she'd have him sing "Red Headed Stranger" to her at bedtime. Lana was her daddy's girl. Smitten with the Disney movie *The Alamo,* she had an imaginary husband, Jim Bowie, the legendary Tennessee adventurer and Texas folk hero who died at the Alamo, and would have a place set for him at the supper table. After Jim "died" when she was four, she developed a huge attraction to Ernest Tubb. "He was my first crush," she said. It was Daddy's fault. "He was always singing, always playing his guitar and working on something," Lana said. "I would ask him if he had any new songs and he'd sing them to me."

Willie liked clowning around the station. Lee Woodward remembered taping a commercial one Saturday afternoon while ensconced in a sound booth, when he heard a tapping noise from the other side of a curtain covering a window separating the sound booth from a larger recording room.

"I reached up and pulled the curtain open," Woodward said. "There was Willie. He'd fashioned a hangman's noose and is standing up on this stool and has the noose tied to his member. He was a funny little guy, kinda quiet, with this mischievous look about him, always coming up with something to crack you up."

Several times Lee accompanied Willie on afternoon drives in his beat-up '47 Ford two-door sedan to Jacksboro Highway to visit clubs. "We'd walk into these joints with chicken wire around the bandstand and check them out when no one was around," Lee said. "They were rough places, but Willie would act like he'd entered Valhalla. His eyes would get wide and he'd say, 'One of these days, I'm going to be playing here.' That's what he was shooting for. That's where he wanted to be."

Fort Worth was a hard city in that respect. The club business was controlled by the gangster element, the kind of folks who imparted life's lessons without a flinch. He might have been a star in the imaginations of some radio listeners, and he was getting up close and personal with music and music people, but the clubs were another matter.

Still, music was all around him. Less than a mile from the KCNC studios, in a red-brick building on a hill, a stern band director who hated jazz named G. A. Baxter was turning out a generation of high school students at I. M. Terrell High School who would reinterpret and redefine American soul and jazz music. IMT was the "colored" high school for African Americans in Fort Worth, which, like all other cities in the South, remained staunchly segregated down to the water fountains at the "Monkey Wards" (Montgomery Ward department store).

The first notable out of this parallel universe, a slight, small-framed saxophonist named Ornette Coleman, was already on the path toward recording an album for Atlantic Records titled *The Shape of Jazz to Come,* which would set jazz and the greater arts scene in New York on their collective ears for decades. In his footsteps was another saxophonist who played in a full-bodied style, named Curtis Ousley, who would achieve fame as King Curtis, the honker behind Aretha Franklin, Sam Cooke, Nat King Cole, Wilson Pickett, the Coasters, and Buddy Holly. The guitarist Cornell Dupree played behind many of the same Atlantic stars. Jazz legends Charles Moffett, John Carter, Prince Lasha, Dewey Redmond, Julius Hemphill, and Ronald Shannon Jackson all came out of the same school.

Music knew no color lines, and good music wasn't found just in Fort Worth. Thirty miles east in Dallas, Lefty Frizzell, Ray Price, Jim Reeves, Marty Robbins, and Billy Walker were recording monster country and western hits at Jim Beck's homemade studio on Ross Avenue. Don Law of Columbia Records was taking all his acts, including Carl Smith, to Beck's, who got a better sound on musicians than did the Decca studio in Nashville that Owen Bradley built. Beck, a disc jockey on KSKY, augmented the Ampex recorders in his studio with equipment he and his partner, Leo Teel, put together themselves. Audio buffs regarded him to be as forward-thinking as the engineers over at Texas Instruments who'd designed the first transistor radio in 1954, and as innovative as Les Paul, Robert Moog, and Rupert Neve would become in audio engineering technology. Had he lived, Dallas perhaps would have become the capital of country music, not Nashville. But in 1956, the fastidious Beck was cleaning his tape machines with carbon tetrachloride solvent when he passed out from the fumes and died of asphyxiation.

Studio or no studio, Dallas was a music scene unto itself, and occasionally Willie would drive over to check out the action. "There was a big difference between Dallas and Fort Worth," he said. "You noticed the change somewhere around Grand Prairie, it got a little more high-falutin'. Fort Worth was still a Cowtown and wanted to stay that way."

Willie and Joe Andrews, his old buddy from Bud Fletcher and the Texans, would sit in with Leo Teel and his band at Danceland at Corinth and Industrial, or with whoever was playing the Aragon or Bob Wills' Ranch House, a three-thousand-seat ballroom that became Dewey Groom's Longhorn Ballroom.

On Saturday nights, Willie and Joe could check out the Big D Jamboree, the country "barn dance" staged inside the wrestling ring of the Sportatorium, a tin-sided sixty-three-hundred-seat arena at the corner of Cadiz and Industrial that also hosted wrestling and gospel shows. The "Home of the Hillbillies" had been a springboard for Lefty Frizzell, Ray Price, Charlene Arthur, and Billy Walker, among others.

The Big D also played to the emerging rock-and-roll audience by featuring young rockabillies—hillbillies playing that newfangled rock and roll, which was really honky-tonk and swing music on speed. The Jamboree's stars included Ronnie Dee, the "Blond Bomber" later known as Ronnie Dawson, as well as teen heartthrob Johnny Carroll, "Groovy" Joe Poovey, Sid King & His Five Strings, the Belew Twins, and Gene Vincent, who relocated to Dallas after his biggest hit, "Be-Bop-A-Lula," and was managed by the Sportatorium's Ed McLemore.

The main drawing card every week was a major star from the Grand Ole Opry or its rival Louisiana Hayride, someone like Johnny Horton, Webb Pierce, Carl Perkins, Carl Smith, Roy Orbison, or Johnny Cash. After the broadcast, the act would go next door and play Dewey Groom's Longhorn Ballroom, the "Number One Country Dancehall in Dallas," for the rest of the night.

When he couldn't be at the Big D, Willie heard it on KRLD 1080 radio, whose nighttime signal covered most of Texas. "Johnny Hicks was the master of ceremonies, him and Hal Horton," Willie said. "At one time or another, most everybody worked on the Big D Jamboree. I wanted to be on it. 'Course I wanted to be anywhere there was a crowd or an audience or somebody that would listen. You did for the exposure, to say you played the Big D Jamboree. It was something you could use, but there wasn't a lot of money there."

The money was at joints like the Southern Club in a pasture off Greenville Avenue, Deb's out on Highway 80 on the Grand Prairie strip, and the Top Rail and the Star Lite, out on 114 toward Grapevine, where Willie would sit in with the house bands in the hope of getting work.

"The first thing I learned when he came down and sat in with me was not to play guitar when he sang," said Leo Teel, who helped build Jim Beck's studio and had recorded for Decca. "Lawsy me, he moved that meter around. I was used to playing on the one, two, three count. Willie would mess with that count. If you let him sit in, surrender your guitar 'cause he'll move that beat around. When he plays guitar, he'll wait till that last little moment to put a tag on it."

TV was broadening country music's horizons more than Elvis and his wiggling hips. The Big D Jamboree was broadcast on KRLD-TV. The Ozark Jubilee, a barn dance in Springfield, Missouri, starring Red Foley and a cast that included long tall Porter Wagoner, the mustachioed Hawkshaw Hawkins, Arlie Duff, and instrumentalist Grady Martin and His Crossroad Boys, grabbed nationwide exposure when the ABC-TV network began airing the program from eight to nine p.m. on Saturday night. Tennessee Ernie Ford hosted his own variety show on NBC-TV, while the Grand Ole Opry launched its own filmed series sponsored by Falstaff Beer.

TV brought Paul Buskirk—whom Willie had seen play at the Round Up in Dallas—into sharper focus. Buskirk played banjo weekdays at WBAP-TV, Channel 5, on a local variety program called *Jones Place*. Neal Jones's presentation of "Comedy, Humor,

Philosophy" aired from noon to 12:45 p.m. but started fifteen minutes earlier in 1955, when it was presented "in living COLOR." That allowed Willie enough time to watch and listen to Buskirk before going on the air with his *Western Express* show. A renowned stringed instrumentalist from Parkersburg, West Virginia, Buskirk was equally proficient on mandolin, guitar, and dobro, as well as banjo, and possessed a broad knowledge of all different kinds of music like no one Willie Hugh Nelson had ever met, and that included Alfred and Nancy Nelson.

Back home in the Appalachian hills, Buskirk was frequently compared to Bill Monroe. He grew up under the tutelage of the famed bluegrass duo Johnny and Jack. He followed the Callahan Brothers to Texas, where they all became radio stars as the Blue Ridge Mountain Folk, broadcasting radio shows aired in Texas and Kansas while recording for Decca, the crème de la crème of country music record labels. Buskirk had played with everyone from Roy Acuff and Chet Atkins to jazz drummer Art Blakey. He was knocking around the same country joints in Fort Worth, Dallas, Waco, and San Antonio as Willie was when they first met.

Buskirk introduced Willie to the singer in his band, a scrawny, scruffily handsome young man named Freddy Powers. He'd come from Seminole,

Texas, a hardpan, sparsely inhabited piece of flat, dry scrub. Paul told Freddy that Willie was writing some interesting pop songs and shared their interest in Western Swing and swing in general. "There was a lot of swing going on because of Bob Wills and Hank Thompson," Freddy said. "Playing the nightclubs, we had to play it all because of them. Paul turned me on to Django [Reinhardt]. He had the whole Django catalog. Swing musicians and jazz musicians considered him a hero."

Freddy could tell Paul was mentoring Willie too. If someone wanted to talk music or theory or exotic sounds, Paul loved engaging them. He'd quickly gleaned the small kid from down around Waco was hungry to learn, and Paul was glad to assist. "Paul had the connections that Willie didn't," Powers explained. "Paul helped him because he had a lot of respect for Willie."

Paul occasionally joined Willie and his guitarist Oliver English and drummer Tommy Roznosky on Willie's *Western Express* radio show on KCNC in Fort Worth. Freddy Powers visited Willie in the studio several times, often plugging the latest Paul Buskirk 45 on Lin Records, the small label out of Gainesville near the Oklahoma line. He saw what Buskirk saw, and heard what Buskirk heard. "I was pretty much impressed with his songs," Freddy said.

Paul cut a track on a song Willie had written called "Heartaches of a Fool," with Freddy singing vocals, at Jim Beck's, but the recording was never released. At least his songs were good enough for someone else to record.

In his own quiet way, Oliver English, Willie's lead guitar on the radio, was as much an influence as Paul Buskirk. He was the grandson of a champion fiddler and had worked most of the joints a musician could work in Fort Worth, including Rosa's and Stella's on East Belknap, where Freddy Powers used to sit in, the Crystal Springs Pavillion, the Casino Ballroom on Lake Worth ("a job everyone hated to play because you had to wear monkey suits"), Jimmy's Westland Club out on Highway 80 West toward Weatherford, and all the joints up and down the Jacksboro Highway and the Mansfield Highway, where the featured entertainment was "Live Band Tonight."

After the clubs closed, Oliver would sit in at the New Jim Hotel downtown, the "colored" hotel where black touring musicians stayed when they were playing in North Texas. "You had to be careful and know the right people or they'd roll you," Oliver said. "You wanted to have some black friends." The reward was getting to play with some of the finest road bands, black or white, on earth.

Oliver learned to play a little bit of everything and

a whole lot of Western Swing, usually doing four sets a night from eight until midnight, except at the Westland Club, where they went till sunrise. "We didn't make much money," he said. "Nobody did. A musician in it for the money was in the wrong business."

For Oliver, music was its own reward. "When I was at the Westland Club, from eight to twelve, we'd play country. From twelve to four in the morning, we'd play jazz. Everybody back then liked Django Reinhardt and the Hot Club of France. I idolized him when I was a little kid." Oliver turned Willie on to Django. Willie helped Oliver whenever he could. "If Willie had ten dollars, he'd give someone five if they needed it. He didn't have anything, but he'd give you half of what he had."

Willie was learning a lot and making enough at sales to move Martha and Lana out of Ira and Lorraine's house into their own rent house out toward Arlington. But he still wasn't satisfied. What Willie really wanted, Oliver realized, was to be understood and not get too distracted. If someone offered him a shot of whiskey, he'd drink it and keep drinking until the bottle was gone, which led to nights when he didn't come home. He took his first knowing drag off a marijuana cigarette behind a building on East Belknap. "I didn't realize it until then that I'd already smoked marijuana before as a kid with my cousin who had asthma," he said. "The doctor had given him some cigarettes and while we were fishing out on the creek bank, he brought out one of these asthma cigarettes, and I took a couple of puffs. That smell stayed with me for the years later when I first ran into what was really pot." A lot of musician friends smoked. "I was smoking for six months before I realized I was getting high."

But the presence of family kept him out of serious trouble. Between Martha and Lana, Ira's family, and Bobbie Lee's family, who moved to Fort Worth along with Mamma Nelson to live with Aunt Rosie and Uncle Ernest in White Settlement, there were plenty of kinfolk with an eye on him.

SISTER Bobbie thought she had lost her way. She had divorced Bud Fletcher, and after Bud's influential parents went to court early in 1955, they won custody of Randy, Freddy, and Michael Fletcher, leading Bobbie to suffer a nervous breakdown. When she recovered and regained custody of her boys, she headed to Fort Worth to find work and raise her sons. "I thought I couldn't play music anymore. It was sad," she said. She found a job in a TV repair shop and enrolled at Brantley Business College to learn secretarial skills. "I had to find a way to raise my children and make as much money as I could," she said.

When she completed secretarial school, she went to the Texas Employment Commission. "I was the only person at the employment agency who was a pianist and a stenographer," she said. The Shield Company called to ask if she would work as a stenographer in the organ department and be trained to teach the new Hammond electric organ. Bobbie needed no persuading. "I could go back into music," she said. "I played pump organ but this was a different thing. Me and my boys started going to Edge Park Methodist Church. They bought a little spinet organ from Hammond. I started playing for the church. Willie and his father and his wife went to Metropolitan Baptist Church. That's where Willie taught Sunday School until they told him he couldn't. He had to choose between playing music in bars or teaching Sunday School. He chose to play music."

Bobbie's job for Hammond Organ led to evening demonstrations at the El Chico Mexican restaurant and Wyatt's Cafeteria. "They trained me to play organs there and all the grocery stores [Buddie's], the Stock Show, Home Show, Boat Show," she said. "I was the person on the little carousel going around and around, talking to people about how easy [playing organ] is to do. I sold organs. I taught organ.

There were three teachers, and I wound up teaching the other teachers. And I'm the organist at Edge Park Methodist Church. They had their own sanctuary by this time. I sold them the big concert model."

Just as Bobbie was getting settled, her brother came down with a bad case of itchy feet. If Fort Worth was the first place where his career showed potential, it was also the first place where he learned hard lessons about making a living playing music. He'd been raised to play music. But the truth was, the few dollars he made were earned because he sold beer and sometimes provided cover for gambling. No one was paying attention to all the songs he was writing. He risked getting beat up for not smiling when he was informed there wasn't any money to pay him at the end of the night, or getting his head split open behind a beer joint just for saying something nice to a pretty young lady from the bandstand.

Even with Martha waitressing, it was still tough making ends meet. He had grown sick of old man Speck barging into the control room whenever he heard a record being played that he didn't like, knocking the tone arm off the turntable, picking up the offensive record, smashing it to pieces, and stomping out of the room. An asshole like Jim Speck was all the convincing he needed to conclude KCNC was a dead-end gig. And Martha coming down hard on him for staying out and paying no mind to her or their daughter was just bacon grease poured on the fire.

For Willie, a change of scene might make it all better.

Vancouver, Washington, 1956

MYRLE NEVER LEFT Willie's life. She came back to Texas often to visit her children as they were growing up, but never stayed long, always heading west again. Ever since his discharge from the air force, Myrle had encouraged her son to come play music in Oregon, where she'd put down roots in Eugene and married her third husband, Ken Harvey. Several times, he had obliged her.

With Myrle's help and encouragement, while Willie was working at KCNC in Fort Worth, he sent a demo tape to Grandpappy Smith, the man to see when it came to country and western music in Eugene, Oregon. Grandpappy owned the Melody Ranch dance hall and was bandleader of the Western

Valley Boys, the Melody Ranch house band, and hosted a show on KASH radio. He also had a small recording empire going on, with two record labels, Orbit Sound (for country acts) and Willamette Records, and a song publishing company, Myrtle Mountain Publishing.

The demo reel began with an introduction from Willie and the promise that if Grandpappy didn't like the songs, he had fifty more. The first song was "One Time," followed by "When I've Sang My Last Hillbilly Song," "Just a Million Years," "Maybe You'll Know," and "Born to Be Blue." Willie was still singing "The Storm Has Just Begun" when the tape ran out.

Grandpappy liked the demo well enough to book Willie at the Melody Ranch in May 1955. Grandpappy's twelve-year-old son, Leon Smith, played lead guitar behind him on the dates. Grandpappy liked Willie, but not enough to offer a recording contract or more bookings.

When Willie left Fort Worth, he didn't go to Oregon but instead headed for sunny San Diego. California was a land of opportunity, he had heard, and San Diego's climate was close to ideal, with warm days in the winter and summer nights cool enough you could sleep outside. Willie's cowboy movie heroes

Gene and Roy were in Southern California—Gene Autry was one of the biggest developers of land between Los Angeles and San Diego.

Westward movement had grown in number and desperation during the Dust Bowl drought that decimated much of North Texas and the Great Plains during the 1930s, and a quest for prosperity following World War II prompted the next great migration wave, which Willie joined. San Diego sounded good to him. He felt confident he could get work playing music and possibly score a disc jockey job; Charlie Williams, the DJ he replaced at KCNC in Fort Worth, found work on a country radio station in Los Angeles, just up the road from San Diego.

Willie hit walls from the moment he arrived. The most imposing barrier was the Musicians Union. You couldn't play music in California without joining the Musicians Union, and you couldn't join the union without paying for your membership. Without gigs, he didn't have the means to scrape together the fee, and no radio station was looking for new talent.

Broke, busted, and running out of options, he finally accepted his mother's invitation to come stay with her in Portland, Oregon. She had moved there and was tending bar at a local tavern in nearby St. Helen's. The idea of a roof over his head felt pretty good. Even better, his mother knew the lay of the local country music scene and all the good dance bands in the area. Willie hustled a job as a plumber's helper to bring home a paycheck and started looking for real work.

If there was a stereotypical character of the Northwest, it was the lumberjack, the big tough physical man of the woodlands, trained to fell as many tall trees as he could to render into timber. Many of the people who worked in the woods came from Texas, Oklahoma, Arkansas, and across the South.

But though the Pacific Northwest was about as far removed as it could be from where country music was manufactured and marketed and still be in the United States, its clubs and dance halls were jammed and jumping with customers with money to burn from the logging, railroad, shipbuilding, and shipping industries, abundant fruit orchards and grain farms, several large military bases, and general construction.

The stars performing in the dance halls and clubs were touring artists and regional talent, including T. Texas Tyler from the Lone Star state, Rusty Draper, Bud Isaacs, Rose Maddox, and a popular Pullayup, Washington, disc jockey named Buck Owens. Records were being made and played in the Northwest too. One local hero from Spokane named Charlie Ryan had scored a monster hit with his Timberline

Riders two years before Willie arrived, a bopped-up cover version of Arkie Shibley's "Hot Rod Race" song about car racing, retitled "Hot Rod Lincoln."

Portland was the largest city in the northwest, with a city population of 412,100 in 1957 and almost a million souls living in the metropolitan area. Hundreds of taverns in and beyond the city functioned as community hangouts, many featuring country music. The lush scenery, the volcanic soil that produced bountiful crops, and the bright lights of the big city had spoken to the roaming gal from Arkansas and Texas with a wild streak a mile long. Now they were speaking to her son. "Well, it rained a lot, but I didn't really mind that," he said. "I enjoyed the greenery and the fruit. It was apple country and fruit country."

Martha got waitress work at Fran's Café in Portland, and Myrle tipped Willie to a job at a radio station in Vancouver, Washington, fifteen miles from downtown Portland. Vancouver was a good town for a country music radio station. It was Portland's smaller, more rural sibling, much like Fort Worth was to Dallas, less than one-fourth the size of Oregon's largest city, although locals liked to point out that Fort Vancouver, from which Vancouver had sprung, was the oldest European settlement in the Pacific Northwest, established as a fur trading post and headquarters of the Hudson's Bay Company.

Willie's friendly, authentic drawl, his experience at KBOP, KDNT, and KCNC, and his increasingly effective ability to sell himself, as he'd learned to do peddling Bibles, encyclopedias, and vacuum cleaners, scored him a shift on KVAN AM 910. KVAN's "instant radio in Ear-O-Phonic Sound . . . first in the metropolitan Portland/Vancouver area" station already boasted an all-star cast of disc jockeys, including Shorty the Hired Hand, Cactus Ken DuBord, who fronted his own band, the Trail Riders, and Pat Mason, a promoter of Grand Ole Opry package shows, who ran Wagon Wheel Park, a big dance hall outside Camas, Washington, east of Vancouver, where touring country acts frequently played.

The station's new boy was touted as a very big deal in newspaper print ads.

A photograph depicted Willie looking suave, wearing a striped shirt and a convincing smile. Opposite the photo was a cartoon drawing of a donkey standing on its hind legs holding a guitar and looking at Willie's image, asking, "Who, Him?"

"Why, he's yer cotton-pickin', snuff-dippin', tobaccer-chewin', stump-jumpin', gravy-soppin', coffee-pot-dodgin', dumplin'-eatin', frog-giggin', hillbilly from Hill County, Texas . . .

"WILLIE NELSON!

"Just rode into town to take over his own show on

KVAN . . . an' this young fella fits right in, here at the station with the sense of humor. See that panhandled description up there? Them's his very own words! Willie's got wit, warmth and wow . . . and once you hear 'Western Express' you'll agree!

"He's no newcomer to radio though. Been entertaining folks since he was sweet 15 . . . and for the past 3½ years, he's been a big name in Ft. Worth on station KCNC. But now he's moved 'kit 'n kaboodle' to Portland. An' ya know what? He likes rain!

"You'll like him . . . an' you'll get your 'enjoys' listening to Texas Willie Nelson on 'Western Express,' 2:30 to 3:30 Monday through Saturday on KVAN.

"KVAN 910 on your dial.

"The station with the sense of humor."

Unlike at KCNC, he stuck to playing records without singing and picking along with them. He selected the music he played during his show by relying on personal taste and street sense. "I grabbed some records I wanted to play—and they were all good records—and went into the studio and surprised myself," Willie explained of his programming methodology. "No one was telling me what to do."

When he wasn't on the air, he sought out businesses and promoters throughout the greater Portland-Vancouver area to sell them airtime on his

Western Express show and other KVAN programs. He was selling Willie Nelson too.

Willie played to the image he'd created for himself, making personal appearances dressed in fringed buckskin and moccasins and wearing a holster around his hips with two pistols (the guns were plugged), an outfit influenced by the hugely popular Walt Disney version of Davy Crockett as played by fellow Texan Fess Parker.

Once he could float enough credit, he embellished the image by driving around in a red Cadillac convertible. He bought a cut proud palomino from the radio station's engineer Leo Erickson and joined the Sheriff's Posse so he could ride in parades on his steed. It sure beat the cow he used to ride in Abbott.

He was Gene Autry, a movie cowboy on the radio, living out his boyhood fantasy formed by the shoot-'em-ups at the Saturday picture show. His timing was perfect. The singing cowboys from the movies were migrating to television; the two most-watched weekly series on TV in America were the westerns *Gunsmoke* and *Wells Fargo*. In a matter of months, Willie moved into the ten a.m. to two p.m. midday shift and bragged that he was so popular, he had more listeners than any other radio personality in Portland/ Vancouver, including Arthur Godfrey, who was broadcasting from New York on the CBS radio network. His competitiveness didn't end in the sound booth. In 1957, he entered a celebrity stock car race against eighteen other local disc jockeys and radio people and won the race.

Disc jockeying, performing music, and Martha waiting tables brought in enough money for Willie, Martha, Lana, and her new sister, Susie, born during a snowstorm on January 20, 1957, to move. They rented a Mexican adobe home with a barn on farmland out Burton Road on the eastern edge of Vancouver. Martha's mother and father moved up from Waco to live with them and look after the girls. The family got a dog named Duke and Willie rode his palomino as often as he could around his spread.

He befriended Max Hall, a pump jockey at the gas station near the KVAN studios, which were located in a red-brick building above a furniture store at the corner of 7th and Main streets. Max was friendly and game enough to step into the role of a surrogate Zeke Varnon. Willie would advise Max to come visit him at the radio station when he got off work. "I've got a bottle we can share," he'd tell him. While Max watched Willie spin 45s and entertain listeners, they'd get loaded and make plans to go hear music, chase skirts, and carry on at the end of his shift. One night while hanging with Max at the gas station, Willie spied a shiny new motorcycle parked by the pumps and, wanting to try it out, hopped on, revved the engine, and sped off, promptly hitting a brand-new Plymouth.

The accident did not detract from Max's high opinion of Willie. "He was the top DJ," he said. He also recognized his wild streak. "He was a loose cannon. He was always looking for adventure." The combination brought him a lot of attention. "The ladies really liked Willie," Max said. It was no surprise, then, that his celebrity caused trouble at home, especially with that "Indian lady," as Max referred to Martha, who had quite a temper. "She was a fiery little thing," he said.

Meanwhile, Willie was performing live, picking up work with several area bands and as a solo act. "I was playing the same songs I played in Waco, and people liked them," he said. Pat Mason, the KVAN disc jockey who ran the Wagon Wheel Park dance hall outside Camas, Washington, hired Willie to play. So did Heck Harper, host of *Heck Harper's Bar 27 Corral* western show on KPTV, Channel 27, "Portland's Pioneer Station," following *American Bandstand* every weekday afternoon.

Harper was one of Portland's first local TV stars.

He played cowboy songs for the young ranch hands at home, told stories, and introduced fifteen-minute segments of cowboy movies. Willie sometimes appeared as Heck's guest, singing a cowboy song to the kiddos, and also performed on Heck's weekly country music television show, sponsored by Hollywood Ford (Heck also DJed on KGW radio, the biggest station in Portland). On weekends, Willie played dances with Heck. For one six-month stretch, he and Heck and Cactus Ken DuBord from KVAN joined Roger Crandall and his Barn Dance Boys, a Western Swing big band from Kelso, Washington, who had an extended residency at Tiny Dumont's Dancehall.

Playing music was more rewarding than being on the radio. Besides the Wagon Wheel, Tiny Dumont's, and Heck Harper's show, Willie worked Watkins Park, the Wishing Well Restaurant in St. John's, and the Dollars Corner Barn Dance. He was a featured attraction at events such as the Clark County Fair and the Rose Festival Western Jamboree and No-Cash Auto Auction staged at Bud Meadows's Pontiac, Sandy Boulevard at Lucky 13th in Portland. Texas Willie Nelson was part of an undercard with the Powder River Boys, Shorty the Hired Hand, and square dance exhibitions from Mel's Bells and Beaus, Rafferty's Rhythm Rustlers, and Faye Gerber's Barn Owls. All of them performed on a flatbed trailer at the car dealership to warm up the crowd for head-liner Jimmy Wakely, "America's foremost Western tune wrangler, In Person Direct from Hollywood."

Texas Willie developed enough of a following to attract two talented young musicians named Bobby Gibson and Buddy Fite, who showed up at the radio station and wherever he was gigging so they could sit in with him for a few songs. Willie liked the young fellows all right, although he allowed that Buddy "was a real weird guy. He would sleep with jazz music in his ear and wake up playing all kind of shit." As much as the kids loved hanging out and playing with Willie, they were too young to appreciate the side benefit of music stardom when a friend dropped off Willie at the home of a woman who was not his wife. "We didn't know that was going on," Bobby Gibson admitted.

Being on the radio and playing dances gave Willie a taste of what it was like to be the center of attention. Now he needed a record to promote his existence to the world. He used a studio at the radio station to record two songs, bringing in Buddy Fite to add his steel guitar to the magic sound of Willie Nelson. The setup was "as basic as it sounded," Willie said. The vocal, guitar, and steel were drenched in echo, about as close to a sound effect as could be coaxed out of the primitive technology.

"No Place for Me" was a sad, almost prophetic Willie original, given his residence in the Pacific Northwest. Leon Payne's "Lumberjack" was the easier local sell, opening and closing the song with the sound of a timber saw, while Payne's lyrics were loaded with logger references and the Saturday-night promise of going to Eugene. "Lumberjack" was not among Payne's finest pieces, but it reflected Willie's sense of place as much as the other song did.

Audiotapes of the recordings were mailed to Starday Records, the country label in Houston run by H. W. "Pappy" Daily and Jack Starnes, which pressed five hundred 45 rpm records. As part of their custom-record-pressing contract, Starday reserved the right to release the record on the Starday label or act as publisher of any songs, but Willie's single did not move the label to exercise either option.

It was a straight-up cash deal. Willie bought the records and sold them on the air and any other way he could. Issued in February 1957 on the Willie Nelson label, the little record with the big hole was offered to KVAN listeners for the low price of $1 with a free autographed 8 x 10 glossy photo of twenty-four-year-old Willie Nelson, country disc jockey and singing star and movie star—handsome with dark, wavy hair, soulful puppy-dog eyes, and pursed Sal Mineo lips, suitable for framing. Three thousand copies of the 45 sold.

Not everyone who ordered a record received a copy, though. As one musician who worked with Willie delicately put it, "Times were tight and sometimes you had to do things just to make ends meet." Willie had already written checks that bounced to steel player Wes Bakken and to Merle Tofte, the guitarist for the Powder River Ramblers for playing gigs with him.

WILLIE Nelson might have found contentment in the Northwest if Mae Boren Axton hadn't dropped by KVAN. Axton was helping publicize a Hank Snow tour on behalf of Snow's manager, Colonel Tom Parker, even though the Colonel was in the process of dropping Snow to focus full-time on his new act, Elvis Presley. Elvis's career, oddly enough, had been boosted by Mae Boren Axton, who'd cowritten a song called "Heartbreak Hotel" that Elvis released in January of 1956.

Willie cornered Axton on her meet-and-greet tour and tried to pick her brain in the most polite way he knew how. He put her on the air and interviewed her. She sized him up: "Very shy, very clean shaven, very clean overalls, although his outfit was pretty worn and patched." And very up to speed on Mae Boren Axton's talents, telling her, "I play every record of yours that comes to the station and I read every magazine I can find with stories that you've written."

He was an aspiring songwriter himself, he told her, and had some songs published, but he didn't know if he had the right stuff to be a top songwriter. He'd sure like her to listen to his songs.

Mae looked in his eyes and saw a young man poor from hunger but exuding sweetness. She could tell he was shy but she could also tell he was looking right at her.

"Son, I'll take the time," she said, cracking a smile.

He brought out his small Japanese reel-to-reel tape recorder and turned on the machine. Axton was sold four bars into the first song. When it ended, he turned off the machine.

"You have any more?" she asked.

He played her a song he was working on called "Family Bible," telling her at the end of the song, he'd been inspired by his grandmother and how she used to sing "Rock of Ages" and read from the Bible after supper.

"Son, I've got a plane to catch," Mae Axton said. "But I have to tell you two things. Number one, if I could write half as well as you, I would be the happiest woman in the world. And two, I don't know a thing about you or your situation, but I suggest you quit and either come to Nashville or go home to Texas if you want to make it as a songwriter. Write me. I don't have a lot of money, but I can always raise a couple hundred dollars."

A few weeks later, KVAN switched formats, abandoning hillbilly music for rock and roll, the sound Elvis and Mae Boren Axton helped make famous. Shorty the Hired Hand and Cactus Ken DuBord moved over to KKEY, the "Number One Town and Country Western Station" and the only western music station serving the Greater Portland/Vancouver area. And Willie went east.

As he was getting ready to leave town, he sought out Max Hall, the gas station attendant across the street from the station, to sell his horse to Max's uncle. Max thought Willie was leaving because he was splitting up with Martha, much as they fought with each other. But it wasn't about chasing skirts. It was about finding a bigger pond. It was time to expand his horizons.

Fort Worth Again, 1958

HIS EYES WERE on Nashville as the Northwest grew smaller in the rearview mirror. He stopped in Denver and worked a club called Hearts' Corner for six weeks before moving on to Springfield, Missouri, where he looked up Billy Walker. He knew the smooth tenor from back when Walker was a disc jockey on KWTX in Waco and a member of Hank Thompson's band and he played the Hadacol Caravan radio shows with Hank Williams. Billy had cut records for Capitol and Columbia under his own name up in Dallas at Jim Beck's, where Lefty Frizzell and Ray Price were also making records. Willie kept in touch as Billy bounced between the Big D Jamboree, the Ozark Jubilee, and the Louisiana Hayride while achieving fame for playing on the bill of Elvis

Presley's first show in Memphis and Hank Williams's last show anywhere.

Springfield was vaguely familiar territory, ninety miles north of Searcy County, where Willie's parents and grandparents hailed from. But even as he tried to stay put by taking a job washing dishes while Martha waited tables, it didn't take long to determine Springfield wasn't his kind of place. Willie auditioned for Sy Simon, the manager of the Ozark Jubilee, but Simon passed on hiring Willie. Billy Walker was still a believer. A little more than a year later, he would become the first recording artist to cover a Willie Nelson composition, "The Storm Within My Heart," during a recording session for Columbia Records on April 28, 1959. This reworked version of "The Storm Has Just Begun," which Willie wrote as a child, was released as a single and generated some radio airplay in Texas.

Unfazed by rejection, Willie hightailed it back to Fort Worth and plugged back into his family, friends, and a few dependable gigs between Cowtown and Waco. Nashville could wait.

Family life was as stable as it could be for a husband and wife bent on out-drinking, out-partying, and out-hell-raising each other. In 1958, Martha gave birth to their first son, Willie Hugh Nelson Jr., better known as Billy, in Fort Worth.

Like Willie, his sister, Bobbie Lee, was playing music for a living, using the gift their grandparents gave them. She was still raising her sons by teaching and playing the Hammond electric organ, learning and utilizing the rich-sounding instrument with rhythm and bass pedals.

Her life too was beginning to settle down. She married a gas station owner named Paul Tracy. Nancy Nelson, Mamma Nelson, was helping raise her great-grandchildren.

If the chips were down for Willie, Martha and the kids could stay with Willie's father, Ira, and his wife, Lorraine, or with Aunt Rosa and Uncle Ernest, or with Bobbie and Paul and Mamma Nelson. Willie wanted to give his wife and children a good home, but it all depended on where he could play, what he was writing, and the luck of being discovered.

He gravitated back to the honky-tonks, beer joints, and roadhouses around Fort Worth. One reliable touch for a booking was Inez Mortenson, a tough, sometimes mean barkeep, whose clubs, including Inez's 50/50 on the Jacksboro Highway out by Robert's Cutoff, seemed to relocate as often as Inez took a new husband (she had eleven in all). Husband number two, Bill Jenkins, a local underworld character, taught her the bar business in the 1940s and put the club's beer license in her name. After divorcing him,

Inez figured there was more money in beer joints than in burger joints and stuck with what she'd learned, earning a reputation for running reputable operations, as she related to the *Fort Worth Star-Telegram* forty years later: "First, you serve full drinks and you give honest change every time. Second, you greet your customers and make them feel at home and you get to know their names. You thank them for coming by and you make them want to come back and see you. And you keep control of the place so that you run it and it doesn't run you."

Inez had movie-star good looks but was unafraid to fight like a man. She had a big heart, yet she didn't back down from anybody, though she almost met her match in the smiling young man from Abbott. She did not hesitate telling Willie what she thought of his music. "Dammit, Willie, quit singing all those tear-jerking songs and play something that will get these people on the dance floor," she advised more than once. "Make them work up a thirst." As for his own thirst, Inez knew Willie drank too much whenever he could run a tab. Whenever he got drunk, Inez would 86 him. "Go on down the road and play somewhere else," she'd holler, kicking him out the door. And he would, only to come back again that night or some other night. All was forgiven until the next time.

Margie Lundy at the Nite Owl on the county line between Abbott and West booked him because she had loved Willie since he was a boy and would do anything to boost his career. He picked up work twenty miles south of the Nite Owl on Highway 81 at a new venue in Waco called the Terrace Club, a cinder-block building at 1509 Old Dallas Highway with all the essential ingredients — a stage, a bar, and a dance floor.

Johnny Gimble, the Western Swing fiddler who'd returned to his hometown of Waco after an extended run with the Texas Playboys, discovered him there. "I'd never heard of Willie, but I needed a bass player for the Saturday Night Dance up near Clifton at Lake Whitney," Johnny said. "I called ol' Bill Mounce, the drummer who used to book a lot of bands and knew every musician in the country. He called me back and said all the bass men were busy but there's a kid up in Abbott who plays guitar and is a songwriter. Willie came and played the TV show [the Bluebonnet Barn Dance on KCEN-TV, starring Clyde "Barefoot" Chesser] and the dance that night." Gimble could tell the redheaded guitarist knew his music, and what Johnny wanted was neither dense nor complicated. "I just told him to bear down on the rhythm because you're replacing the bass," he said. Willie made a fan out of the fiddler, beginning a long musical and personal friendship.

While physics engineer Jack Kilby was inventing the integrated circuit at Texas Instruments in Richardson, near Dallas, Willie was doing his own research, developing a distinctive Texas sound with his voice and instruments by playing live wherever and whenever he could, which often meant seven days a week.

Billy Todd, a booking agent for Bob Wills, and a musician, hired Willie to play for a few weeks in 1958 at his bar, Todd's Western Lounge, on Exchange Avenue just off North Main near the Fort Worth Stockyards, which catered to real cowboys. Todd's was a rough place, prone to fights and violence, but it wasn't anything Willie Hugh hadn't seen before.

"After the Nite Owl, there wasn't anything too much more exciting than that," Willie explained. "I expected it all. It wasn't a big deal when somebody got into a fight. When there was a fight, you played louder. Some people came in looking for trouble. Some people came in and found trouble. Some people drank too much. Some people danced too close to somebody's girlfriend. That shit was always going on. Usually, dancing had a lot to do with the problems. We'd play from eight to twelve and take a couple breaks along the way. You could make a living if you were making fifteen bucks a night for five or six nights a week."

Todd's turned into a reliable booking, and Willie hustled up players to work with him as the house band. One musician he shared the stage with at Todd's was a bright, young songwriter signed to a Nashville publishing house, named Roger Miller. Miller was in and out of Fort Worth, visiting his mother, and found plenty of common ground with Willie. They were both hillbillies and wrote songs and liked to play music. They drank too much, smoked too many cigarettes, and popped too many pills, as was the custom for musicians of their kind. Willie brought Roger over to sister Bobbie's home. Their impromptu appearances left Willie's nephews wide-eyed and amazed that grown people could be so crazy.

Bobbie's son Freddy Fletcher said, "They were kind of a mess. It was really my first time going, wow, these are some wild folks, these people are nuts, but I liked it. They were having fun, they were making music, and somehow making it work. I thought that was cool as hell."

Playing bars had its advantages; win over that wild bunch and you're on your way. The bad part about it was, there wasn't much money to be made. In a matter of weeks after returning to Fort Worth from Vancouver, Washington, Willie traded in the red Cadillac for cheaper transportation and some running change.

When he wasn't gigging, Willie was sitting in. "He used to sit in whenever he was in town," said Charlie Owens, the steel player in the house band at Jimmy's Westland Club on Highway 80 West, the only after-hours country venue in the county. "We got the overflow from all these other clubs. It went all night long. We played from midnight to four-thirty in the morning. It was dance music, a lot of Hank Thompson songs. Bob Wills, Ray Price, whatever was hot on the radio, we'd do."

Jam sessions broke out frequently, though they were hardly tolerated by club management. "The pedal steel was real popular then," said Owens, who played one. "Jimmy Day was playing with Ray Price, Buddy Emmons was with Ernest Tubb — they'd all come to the Westland Club and set up and kill the club. They'd get to playing jam music, and no one would get on the dance floor."

Willie was another sit-in, though he was no Day or Emmons. "To tell you the truth, he didn't impress me all that much," Charlie Owens said. "His phrasing was real odd. It was hard to work with him with that offbeat phrasing. He'd drop fifteen words in there real quick, but he was staying in meter, he wasn't breaking time. He was let go around here three or four times because people didn't enjoy dancing to his music."

Freddy Powers remembered trying to keep up with him the first time they played together. "He'd play so far behind the beat, it'd mess me and my bass player up. You had to really concentrate and look at each other, not listen to Willie."

Willie also sat in at the Tracer Club, a new-concept nightclub where each table had its own telephone, so a guy could ring up a good-looking chick at the next table or buy her a drink. The house band at the Tracer was the Ron-Dels, a white-boy blues, rock, and country band led by a soulful singer named Delbert McClinton and his buddies Ronnie Kelly and Billy Ray Sanders.

Willie picked up day jobs wherever he could. Shortly after he returned to Fort Worth from Vancouver, Willie's father found him temp work at Bailey Grain on the North Side following a fire at the grain warehouse. The burned grain had to be removed from the grain elevators. Willie filled out a W-4 form, listing his address as 1512 Sharondale on the south side of Fort Worth. One of his first tasks was to drive a cat whose fur was singed to the veterinarian and then pick it up. The rest of the time, he was down in the fifty-six-foot elevators, shoveling out the burned material. One morning, owner Frank Bailey climbed to the top of one elevator and found Willie sleeping, obviously worn out from working a gig the night before. Bailey was so frightened by what he saw — if Willie had rolled six inches in his sleep, he would have fallen into the elevator and surely died — that he fired him on the spot.

Willie hired out as a carpet installer's helper but was fired for spending too much time writing lyrics instead of rolling carpet, and he sold encyclopedias on the telephone, then followed up on prospects with in-person visits.

For a few weeks, he found steady work at the Premier service station at Main and Berry, owned by Paul Tracy, Bobbie's husband. The low-maintenance job freed him to roam the clubs at nights, and if he fell asleep at work, it was unlikely he'd get fired. Plus, if there were mechanical problems with the used car Bobbie and Paul bought him, he could get it fixed and get away with owing his brother-in-law for a while.

The pump jockeys at the Premier quickly surmised Willie had other things on his mind than rising up the ranks in the service station business. "When cars would pull into the station, it was me and Leonard Sanders filling the tank, checking the oil, and wiping the windows," said Richard Davis, who also wore the red Premier badge. "Willie was always slow getting out of his chair." Richard knew where he fit in. "Willie could come and go as he pleased, since he was kin to the owner. He never showed up on time. He used to take a car over to the grease rack, which was in a separate building from the rest of the station, and it would take forever for him to change the oil or wash the car. One day I went over there and on the sides of these Amalie oil boxes were verses that he'd written. Up in the office there'd be scraps of paper with verses written on it. If you said something he thought was lyrical, he'd write it down. He always said he was going to be a songwriter and a country music singer. You knew he was special. You just didn't know what kind of special."

Richard and his pal Leonard used Willie's talents to their advantage. "Willie said he could take any girl's name and make a song out of it," Richard said. "I was dating this girl Sharon, she was a pretty good looker, and I told him I was going to bring her up there. He came out and made up the prettiest verse you ever heard. He looked at her and put her characteristics into the line," flattering her eyes, her hair, and her smile.

Willie's way with words was a chick magnet as far as Richard was concerned. "He wasn't a handsome fellow. His hair was kinda curly, his teeth were rotten, and his complexion was terrible. But he could always attract a woman. He talks in poetry. To me, poetry makes you think about the words."

That sort of response kept Willie on the path. It was an exciting time for country music, which was on the verge of becoming America's music. Willie was part of the Texas wing of country, an amalgam of Western Swing and honky-tonk music held together by twin fiddles and a beat you could dance to. Sophisticates may have derided hillbilly as low-class white-trash fare, but it was ringing cash registers like no other music. Webb Pierce demonstrated country's commercial clout by constructing a swimming pool at his Nashville home in the shape of a guitar, built on proceeds of such hits as "Slowly," "There Stands the Glass," "More and More," "Even Tho," "In the Jailhouse Now," and, with the Wilburn Brothers, "Sparkling Brown Eyes."

The Grand Ole Opry in Nashville was the grandest of country's numerous barn dances, whose reach was amplified by the radio stations that broadcast them. Every part of Texas sported a smaller version of the bigger dances, such as the Opry and Shreveport's Louisiana Hayride. Central Texas briefly had the Blue Bonnet Barn Dance in Temple, on KCEN-TV. Paris had the Red River Jamboree, which aired throughout East Texas on KFTV-TV. Tyler boasted the Saturday Night Shindig, a little cousin to Houston's Home Town Jamboree at the City Auditorium, which morphed into the Grand Prize Jamboree, sponsored by the beer company of the same name, and aired on KNUZ-TV and KNUZ radio before switching to KPRC. The Home Town Jamboree's star was Arlie Duff, whose "Y'all Come" became the show's trademark. A slew of regional talent, including George Jones, Tex Cherry, Tommy Collins, and Hank Locklin, shared the stage with aspiring amateurs.

Willie found his place at Fort Worth's barn dance, the Cowtown Hoedown. The Hoedown was not to be confused with its bigger cousins east on Highway 80, the Big D Jamboree in Dallas and the Louisiana Hayride in Shreveport. Still, it provided a steady gig in 1958 and 1959 so he could get his act together as a player as well as a performer. Staged every Saturday night at the Majestic Theatre at 1101 Commerce Street in downtown Fort Worth, in the heart of Fort Worth's second edition of Hell's Half Acre, the Cowtown barn dance aired on country station KCUL. The two-and-a-half-hour revue was built around a guest headliner along the lines of Faron Young, Webb Pierce, the Browns, Charlie Walker, Roy Orbison,

Ray Price, Ernest Tubb, Bob Luman, or Johnny Horton, and anywhere from six to eight local stars, all supported by the house band.

With no admission charge, the ornate 1,565-seat theater, once the city's grandest movie house, with opera boxes, marble columns, and terrazzo floors, was usually packed for the Hoedown.

Just being around a lot of similarly inclined entertainers was an education, and Willie paid attention. A few of the Hoedown regulars had enjoyed success. Frankie Miller, one of the cast regulars, had written a number one song for Webb Pierce, "If You Were Me (And I Was You)," in 1955 and was on the verge of scoring a huge Top 5 country hit of his own for Starday Records in 1959 with a song he wrote called "Blackland Farmer."

Howard Crockett, a veteran of the Louisiana Hayride, was still riding high from writing Johnny Horton's 1957 breakout hit, "Honky-Tonk Man," and the durable tale "Old Slewfoot." Tony Douglas, a singer from Martins Mill with a Hank Williams lonesome moan and Louisiana Hayride exposure, was hired as a Hoedown member after receiving five encores the first time he sang there; in 1957 he recorded "Old Blue Monday," the first of many hits, for the Cowtown Hoedown label.

The Hoedown was hosted by Jack Henderson, the Hoedown's original producer, who was assisted by Dandy Don Logan from KCUL. The show was broadcast on KCUL from 8 to 10:30 p.m. and rebroadcast the following Saturday night on XEG, a powerful Mexican station within earshot of a good chunk of the Western Hemisphere. After the Hoedown concluded, the star of the night usually left the building and headed out East Belknap to play Rosa's Western Club. KCUL, whose call letters were *luck* spelled backwards, wanted to emulate the success the Louisiana Hayride had brought to KWKH, a 50,000-watt station in Shreveport, and the Big D Jamboree brought to KRLD in Dallas. The players' incentive, besides the $10 pay, was exposure to the up to fifteen hundred fans in the theater and the listeners on the radio, as well as the three-track recording studio in the theater that captured the performances on audiotape.

Willie joined the Hoedown as lead guitarist, playing alongside Doug Winnett on bass, his brother Ernie Winnett on guitar, a steel guitarist named Shady Brown, and guitarist Chuck Jennings, one of Tony Douglas's Shrimpers.

"Not that he wasn't a good singer or picker, but Willie wasn't no standout or nothing at that time," said Joe Paul Nichols, the Jacksboro teen sensation country singer, who joined the Hoedown cast in 1957. "We knew he was a songwriter and had been a DJ on the radio for a while."

Willie was popular among the players and learned from his peers. "We liked the way he sang behind the beat," said Frankie Miller, who used to run around Houston with another distinctive country voice, George Jones, when both were just starting out. "Willie was writing good songs," Miller said.

The gig was good schooling for Willie's instrumental skills. Paul Buskirk was always giving him tips and turning him on to all kinds of music until he moved to Houston. Playing the Hoedown was the next best thing, teaching him to think on his feet, improvise when necessary, and play it all—or at least look like he was playing it all.

After Jack Henderson sold the show to Ronnie and Peggy McCoy's parents, Uncle Hank Craig from KCLE in Cleburne and XEG in Mexico became the Hoedown's voice as well as the show's producer. Uncle Hank was like a grandpa to most of the cast, who were years younger than he was, and he took a special shine to Willie, representing him as his manager.

"Uncle Hank was a really sharp guy, a really good

friend, and he really liked me," Willie said. "When I would get in over my head, he would bail me out. He was a buddy."

Willie's association with Uncle Hank offered an opportunity to combine his musical skills with his salesmanship, a quality any good Texan was proud to possess. At Uncle Hank's urging, Willie went downstairs to the basement of the Majestic Theatre to the Jack Henderson Studios. Under Hank's guidance, Willie made a commercial for the Mexican radio station that Hank was involved with.

With a warm voice brimming with confidence, Willie made the pitch:

"Attention Songwriters and Poets. Here is the big break you have been waiting for—the chance to have your songs on record, recorded by professional musicians. Thousands of dollars are earned each year by songwriters who, not so long ago, were struggling unknowns waiting for their big break—to have their songs recorded and placed before the public. Now there's no need for you to wait any longer. You can have your songs recorded by professional musicians on your own record to either present to publishers, or just to play in your own home to your friends and relatives, or for your own personal enjoyment. You can actually have your own record library consisting of your own songs—songs you have written yourself. You may have a song worth thousands of dollars to you. Lots of the professional songwriters of today who are financially independent were once amateur songwriters waiting for that one big break. These people learned the hard way that success does not come to you—you have to go out and at least meet it halfway. In order for the right people to hear your songs, you have to take it to them, and there is no better way to present your song than to have it on your own record so they can listen to it played by professional musicians. So if you are a songwriter and you would like to have a professional-sounding record of your own tune, grab a pencil and paper, because I am going to give you the address. Do it now while you are thinking about it, because this could very well be the turning point in your songwriting career. And you are in for a surprise—you're in for a big surprise—when you learn how little it will cost for you to get your big break as a songwriter, and how little it will cost to have your own song recorded by professional musicians on your own sturdy, durable record that will give you many years of enjoyment. Now here's what you do: pick out two of your best tunes, or more if you like, but at least two in order to have one tune on each side of your record. Pick out the tunes you want, include the sheet music or lead sheet or a tape recording of your tunes, and send it to

Records—that's R-E-C-O-R-D-S—Records, XEG, Fort Worth, 11, Texas. And now here is the best part—the part that you are going to find hard to believe. For each tune you include, send only ten dollars. That's all. That will cover everything. That's just one ten-dollar bill for each tune you send, and this little ten dollars will cover the cost of having your song taped, cut on record by professional musicians, and mailed directly to you, postage paid. And, if you wish, your songs will be listed with your nationally known publishing company at no additional cost. So don't put it off; do it without delay, and send your songs (at least two—one for each side of your record, and more if you like) to Records, XEG, Fort Worth, 11, Texas, and enclose ten dollars for each tune you send. If you write only words to songs or poems, you may send words or lyrics to your songs or poems and one of our professional songwriters will add the music for the unbelievably low price of ten dollars. There is no longer any need to delay your future in songwriting. That address again is Records—that's R-E-C-O-R-D-S—Records, XEG, Fort Worth, 11, Texas."

XEG, the radio station across the Rio Grande that emitted the most powerful radio signal on the continent, sold time to hellfire-breathing preachers, wild disc jockeys like Wolfman Jack and the Howlin'

Rooster, and to promoters like Uncle Hank, who in turn sold gospel records, baby chickens, prayer cloths, autographed pictures of Jesus Christ, and the easy path to songwriting success to millions of listeners across the continent.

From the convincing presentation, a listener might have concluded Willie Nelson had already cracked the code to songwriting success. But he too was still looking for the turning point in his songwriting career. His persuasive powers were more effective than his songwriting talents. Listeners to XEG sent in their $10 bills and their song lyrics and Willie put music to their words "until I got tired of it," he said. There were better ways to make a living playing music, and he preferred selling his own songs instead of putting music to the words of others.

His worth was validated by Jack Rhodes, a Fort Worth disc jockey and well-known Texas country figure with his own music publishing company. Rhodes licensed the publishing on Willie's song "Too Young to Settle Down." Willie gave up half of the credits and potential royalties in the hope that Rhodes would get the song recorded by another singer, which Rhodes knew how to do. He had cowriting credits with Red Hayes on "A Satisfied Mind," which Porter Wagoner, Jean Shepard, and Red and Betty Foley had just recorded, and would share credits on "Silver

Threads and Golden Needles," and "Woman Love," which were covered by the likes of Hank Snow, Sonny James, Ferlin Husky, Jim Reeves, Porter Wagoner, and Gene Vincent. Before that, Rhodes led the Western Swing band Jack Rhodes and His Lone Star Buddies ("Mama Loves Papa and Papa Loves the Women"), formerly Jack Rhodes and His Rhythm Boys, which featured Rhodes's step-brother Leon Payne, whose loose singing style influenced Willie.

Willie wanted to be like Jack Rhodes and Leon Payne and write songs like he'd always been writing songs, only sell them and have them performed and recorded by others, and perform them himself in front of a crowd. If he had that opportunity, he was confident he'd win them over as long as he wasn't too drunk or too distracted.

The Cowtown Hoedown and Uncle Hank Craig led to Willie's first record deal. Several acts on the Hoedown had record contracts with D Records through Uncle Hank, and acting as Willie's manager, Uncle Hank signed Willie to D Records and to a publishing contract with Glad Music, Pappy Daily's song publishing firm in 1959. The agreements were little more than mere formalities, because no exchange of money was involved. But Willie finally was a recording artist. In exchange, Willie gave Uncle Hank a piece of his songwriter's publishing rights to

"Man with the Blues" and a piece of his second single, "What a Way to Live," as well as a taste of "Crying in the Night," which was later covered by Claude Gray. Selling off some or all of your potential future royalties as a songwriter was expected if you were going to be a recording artist.

Willie cut his first sides in Fort Worth at Manco Studios, a homemade one-track recording facility west of the city on White Settlement Road in River Oaks, next to E. E. Manney's house, in 1959. Manney had his own label, Bluebonnet Records, which had nowhere near the prestige of D Records. Willie brought along some Western Swing players he knew from Waco—steel guitarist Bobby Penton, Lonnie Campbell on drums, and bassist Johnny "Smitty" Smith—and recruited the Reils Sisters from the Cowtown Hoedown to sing background vocals. The Reils had recorded as the Pittypats behind J. B. Brinkley and as Johnny and the Jills behind rockabilly Ronnie Dee; their little brother Johnny would eventually enjoy success as the Nashville singer John Wesley Ryles. But on this recording, their attempt to replicate the Nashville Sound smothered Willie's vocal rather than complementing it.

Manco was the same studio where Willie had played guitar on a session earlier that year behind Homer Lee Sewell, another Cowtown Hoedown regular, from Cordell, Oklahoma. Sewell was making a single of two songs he'd written, "Whisper Your Name" b/w (backed with) "She's Mad at Me." "I found out he was a good lead man," Sewell said, "so I asked him if he wanted to play on my record." Sewell rounded up Willie, Paul East, an upright bass player named Bill Bramlett, and two fiddlers and paid Uncle Hank Craig $200 to get his recording made and released on D Records. An alternate version of "Whisper Your Name," recorded on the stage of the Majestic with Sewell on fiddle and Willie and Paul East on guitar, supported by Jack Zachary, Hank Craig's son Eddie Craig on bass, and Bill Bramlett — members of the Hoedown house band — was used as the B side of the single. "I got more airplay on that than I did with 'She's Mad at Me,' " recalled Sewell. "It had a good beat to it." Lawton Williams played the record on KCUL, and so did the disc jockeys on KTJS in Sewell's hometown, Hobart, Oklahoma. But sales were feeble, as Willie's were.

Willie sometimes wondered whether he was moving forward or just running in place. One night, Oliver English, Willie's guitar player from back on KCNC, ran into him on Exchange Street after he'd played a gig at Pappa Gray's with two Mexicans named Momolito and Moose. Willie was down.

"They don't understand my music here," he complained to Oliver.

But his old friend Johnny Bush noticed a change. Billy Walker had told Johnny that Willie was working the Terrace Club in Waco again, so Johnny and his wife drove from San Antonio to hear him. "I heard him sing a couple songs and immediately recognized I was hearing something different," Johnny said. "He didn't sound like the singer I had known." He'd dropped the Lefty Frizzell pretensions and embraced Leon Payne's freewheeling vocal style. "It was like the first time I heard George Jones sing," Johnny said. He was knocked out.

Houston, 1959

WITH MARTHA and the kids staying at her mother's in Waco, Willie decided Houston, the biggest city in Texas (pop. 932,680), was worth the 19.9 cents a gallon expense to check out the scene he'd sampled with Johnny Bush a few years earlier.

Wide open, the physical layout of "America's Industrial Frontier" and "World's Greatest Petro-Chemical Center" was perched at the edge of Galveston Bay, fifty miles from the Gulf of Mexico. Houston's hot, humid, buggy, and muggy climate was one ingredient in a strange gumbo that also included poverty, cheap guns, stoved-up passion, and redneck sensibilities fermented in alcohol; when cooked together, they fostered Houston's reputation as Murder City, USA.

Houston was Texas, all right, but in many respects,

more Southern than Fort Worth, Abbott, San Antonio, or Waco, even. It was the blackest city in Texas, with African Americans comprising more than a quarter of the population with almost as many Mexicans as San Antonio. Since the end of World War II, Houston had become a magnet for thousands of Cajuns and Creoles from southwest Louisiana and southeastern Texas as well.

Big Houston was big fun, and big business. The galaxy of homegrown country stars included Floyd Tillman, George Jones, Benny Barnes, Smilin' Jerry Jericho, Claude Gray, Sonny Burns, James O'Gwynn, Link Davis, Ted Daffan, Leon Payne, Leon Pappy Selph, and Eddie Noack. Two significant country music record companies were based in Houston — Starday Records, formed by Pappy Daily and Jack Starnes, which launched the career of George Jones, and Daily's D Records, created in the wake of Starday's move to Nashville. While dance halls, honky-tonks, and icehouses were the scene's underpinnings, its showcases were Houston's recording studios, especially Bill Quinn's Gold Star Studio in southeast Houston.

Harry Choates recorded his Cajun classic, "Jole Blon," at Gold Star. George Jones cut a string of early hits there, beginning with "Why, Baby, Why," and the Big Bopper did his rock and roll chart topper

"Chantilly Lace" at Gold Star. The bluesman Lightnin' Hopkins recorded most of his early material with Quinn, and conductor Leopold Stokowski was bringing in the Houston Symphony Orchestra to take advantage of the studio's superior acoustics.

"Quinn was always trying to get you a good sound," said Frankie Miller, who cut his biggest hit, "Blackland Farmer," at Gold Star Studio. "He wanted to get it right."

So did Willie Nelson, which is why he went to Houston.

In the spring of 1959, he showed up one afternoon at 11410 Hempstead Highway on the northwest fringe of Houston to check out the Esquire Ballroom, the spacious dance hall owned by Raymond Proske, where the house band led by Larry Butler was rehearsing new material. A waitress informed Larry that a man wanted to talk to him. After rehearsal Larry sat down at a table and drank a beer with the out-of-town musician who wanted to play some songs for Larry. Larry was game. Willie played him four compositions—"Mr. Record Man," "Crazy," "Night Life," and "Funny How Time Slips Away."

Those are good songs, Larry told him.

"Ten bucks apiece," Willie said. Larry could have the songs, publishing and everything, for $10 each. He needed the money. Larry leaned across the table.

"Don't do that," he said. "They're worth more than
ten bucks. If you need money, I'll loan it to you. You
can pay me back by joining my band and working at
the club here."

Larry fronted Willie $50, and Willie became one
of Larry Butler's Sunset Playboys, the house band at
the Esquire. Larry went one step further. Musicians
worked for union scale in Houston. As bandleader,
Larry made $25 a night and the other musicians made
$15. When owner Raymond Proske said he couldn't
afford Willie, Larry offered to add him to the band
by splitting his leader's pay with him, as long as he
showed up and did his part.

Larry Butler gave Willie hope, letting him showcase his own songs during the band's sets and closing
out the evening with Willie's original "The Party's
Over." Frankie Miller, who'd played with Willie at
the Cowtown Hoedown, was surprised to run into
him at the Esquire, "playing guitar, paying his dues,"
when Miller passed through, promoting his single.
In addition to working with Larry, Willie was playing gigs with Denny Burke, with Curley Fox and
Texas Ruby, the husband-and-wife fiddling-singing
duo who brought country music to Houston television, and with anyone who needed a guitarist who
could sing and write songs.

The gig at the Esquire and other pickup work convinced Willie that Houston was for him. With Larry Butler's help, he moved Martha, Lana, young Susie, and baby Billy into a tiny rent house in the shadows of Houston's oil and chemical refineries clustered around the Houston Ship Channel in Pasadena. He scored a shift at KRCT 650 AM in Pasadena, the Houston-area country music radio station owned by Leroy Gloger; the job didn't pay much, but he used the airtime to plug upcoming gigs.

Instead of playing for scale as a sideman, which was $12 to $15 a night, he was able to get up to $25 from front men such as Smilin' Jerry Jericho, for whom Johnny Bush was playing, in exchange for free mentions on the radio. Guitarist Lucky Carlisle frequently called on Willie to play rhythm for him, but he didn't think Willie's media status justified a higher salary.

When Lucky called, Willie asked, "What's the pay?"

"The usual, scale."

"I don't like to get out much these days for less than twenty-five," Willie replied, trying to up the ante.

"I bet you stay home a lot," Lucky said.

"Come to think of it, you're right," Willie said, wrapping up the negotiation. "I'll be there."

Paul Buskirk, Willie's mentor and friend, offered a

third job to Willie, which would fit in with his plan to make a living writing, singing, and playing music. Paul had moved from Dallas to Houston to open the Buskirk Music Studios at 108 East Bird in Pasadena while picking up recording session work on the side whenever he could. He thought Willie would make a good guitar teacher. Willie hesitated. He'd taught Sunday school, but he'd never taught music. "C'mon, brother," Paul Buskirk cajoled, pooh-poohing Willie's complaint. "Teaching music isn't hard. Just buy a beginner's book and teach what you learn from that." Willie did just that, reading a lesson a night from the Mel Bay book of beginning guitar and the next day imparting what he had learned. "It's really where Willie learned to play guitar," said Freddy Powers, Paul's friend. Between Paul's teachings and Willie's book learning, he figured out chords and styling that would have otherwise gone unappreciated.

Willie didn't know it, but his own songwriting was improving too. Houston was an inspirational setting for some of his best songs. The struggle to provide for Martha and three kids was more of a challenge than ever, but it offered plenty of material for sad songs. The long, lonely commutes on the Hempstead Highway, the Gulf Freeway, and Eastex Freeway provided close to an hour's worth of quality time to think and create every night. If a lyric came to him, he wouldn't necessarily write it down until he'd reached his destination. "If I forgot the words," he would later say, "they weren't very memorable in the first place."

The twinkling lights and pungent odors of oil and chemical refineries, paper mills, and factories turned private thoughts into poetry as he reviewed the day, the night, the people he encountered, the family he was trying to support, his wife, the other women who were attracted to him, the slices of life that crossed his mind. The songs flowed like never before. "Night Life," "Crazy," "Mr. Record Man," "I Gotta Get Drunk."

He showed his stuff to his sister on a visit to Fort Worth. "That's the first time I remember ever seeing a tape recorder," Bobbie said. "He had this little tape recorder. On his way up, he had written three songs. He was so excited. One of them was 'In God's Eyes,' one was 'It's Not for Me to Understand,' and one was 'Family Bible,' " the song he'd played for Mae Axton two years before.

His musicianship continued to improve. Paul Buskirk was turning him on to more Django Reinhardt. They discussed singing and vocal styles, agreeing Floyd Tillman was as much of a crooner as Frank Sinatra was. And when Willie found himself behind on bills, Paul bought some of his songs.

Selling songs was nothing new to Willie. Despite his three jobs, he was so broke, he didn't have a pot to piss in. Finding someone willing to pay for something that he made up was validation in his eyes. If one he sold ever became a hit and made the buyer all the money, there were more where that came from. "I knew my songs were good," Willie said.

Buskirk paid $100 for the rights to "Night Life" and $50 for "Family Bible." Willie had been enjoying a beer and barbecue with him in a Pasadena bar when he sang "Family Bible" and told him, "This is one you'll like. I'll sell it to you." Selling a song was more honorable than borrowing money, in his mind.

Buskirk led to a second buyer. Claude Gray was a spindly six foot five honky-tonk singer from Henderson, in East Texas, who worked as a DJ in nearby Kilgore before moving to Houston to sell Plymouths and Dodges for a living after he'd gotten out of the navy. The same year Willie came to Houston, Claude quit selling cars when he scored another disc jockey job at a radio station in Meridian, Mississippi.

Claude returned to Houston, though, for several recording sessions at Bill Quinn's studio, paid for by D Records and Pappy Daily. Paul Buskirk put together a studio band for Claude and between sessions sent several songs for Claude to consider covering. They were "Night Life," "The Party's Over," and

"Family Bible." Claude knew Willie from the Esquire Ballroom up north of Houston and followed Buskirk's suggestions by recording them all.

D Records issued 45 rpm singles of Claude Gray singing "My Party's Over," slightly changing the song title, and "Family Bible." Claude Gray paid $100 for a piece of "Family Bible" and another $100 for the musicians and studio time to cut that tune as well as "Night Life," "The Party's Over," and "Leave Alone." In exchange for the session work, Gray shared ownership of "Family Bible" with Paul Buskirk, who backed up Gray on the recordings, and Walt Breeland, a friend of Paul's who was a business agent for the Drivers and Helpers Union and an aspiring singer with a Jim Reeves voice, who was looking for songs. Claude signed a napkin, promising to buy "Night Life" if his version was released as a single. "Willie wanted it released," Claude said. "He would give me half the writer's [royalties]. But Pappy Daily didn't think it was country enough."

Pappy Daily's D Records was one of the main reasons Willie had come to Houston. He was signed to the label, and if he was closer to the home office, maybe he would get more attention from D Records and Glad Music, the record label and publishing company owned by Pappy Daily.

D Records was the big dog of country music in

Houston, a critical piece of the vertically integrated country-music empire Pappy was trying to build out of his H. W. Daily one-stop record wholesaler. With all the elements working, he could take what he learned with his previous label, Starday, and make his new start-up label competitive with any Nashville record label short of Decca and RCA.

Willie's first single for D Records, the surprisingly upbeat "Man with the Blues," done honky-tonk style, b/w "The Storm Has Just Begun," one of the first songs he'd ever written, were released on both D Records and Betty Records in 1959 after the sides were recorded in Fort Worth.

In Houston, Willie managed to do two more sessions for D Records at Bill Quinn's Gold Star. "What a Way to Live" and "Misery Mansion" were recorded on March 11, 1960, with the backing of Paul Buskirk on guitar, Ozzie Middleton on pedal steel, Dean Reynolds on bass, Al Hagy on drums, and Clyde Brewer and Darold Raley on fiddles. Both songs were head and shoulders above his D sessions in Fort Worth, a reflection of the musicianship behind him, the recording facility, and Willie's developing talents. He sang the vocal of "What a Way to Live" like a spirited blues, in contrast with the melodramatic sound of the backing band, and tackled "Misery Mansion" like a traditional country beer-rhymes-with-tear weeper. They were fine, though unspectacular, tunes.

A few weeks later, Willie and Paul Buskirk, Al Hagy, and Dean Reynolds returned to Gold Star, along with pianist Bob Whitford, steel guitarist Herb Remington, and vibraphonist-saxophonist Dick Shannon, to do two more originals. Something had happened between the two sessions.

"Rainy Day Blues" was a classic Texas shuffle, a popular dance rhythm that had been played with equal exuberance by white country players and black rhythm and blues artists since the 1930s. The music, projected over sad honky-tonk lyrics, showed Willie had chops as a guitarist.

"Night Life" was from another realm. Mature, deep, and thoughtful, the slow, yearning blues had been put together in his head during long drives across Houston. At Gold Star, he was surrounded by musicians who could articulate his musical thoughts. He sang the words with confident phrasing that had never been heard on any previous recording he'd done. Paul Buskirk's and Willie's guitar leads were straight out of the T-Bone Walker playbook, while Dick Shannon's bluesy saxophone was pure Texas tenor, with his vibe work adding subtle jazz atmospherics. If not for Herb Remington's low-note hokum on his steel guitar and his Hawaiian flourishes, the song could have passed for race music. No matter what style the music was or how personally Willie sang it, the lyrics were a commentary just about anyone could relate to:

> *When the evenin' sun goes down*
> *You will find me hangin' 'round*
> *Oh, the night life, it ain't no good life*
> *But it's my life . . .*
> *Life is just another scene*
> *In this old world of broken dreams*
> *Oh, the night life, it ain't no good life*
> *But it's my life.*

"It was a level above what we had been doing," Willie said of the session.

Pappy Daily hated the song. He refused to release the song as the A-side of a single because it was neither country nor commercial as far as he was concerned. If Willie wanted to write blues, he should be doing it for Don Robey over at Duke-Peacock Records, the nigger music company down on Erastus Street in the bloody Fifth Ward of Houston.

Willie thought Pappy was full of shit. "Night Life" was a great song and he knew it. So did Paul Buskirk. He knew a groove when he heard one, and he knew Willie was about to blow his top out of frustration. If Pappy wouldn't release it, Willie would, and did, with Paul's help. "Nite Life" was released on a small Houston label, Rx ("Prescription for Happy Times"), under the name of Paul Buskirk and His Little Men featuring Hugh Nelson. The single was mastered at Bill Holford's ACA Studios. A few copies were pressed and passed around as demos in the hope that someone would hear it. But only a handful of disc jockeys, including Uncle Hank Craig on XEG, played the single.

If "Night Life" wasn't his ticket to recognition, selling "Family Bible" to Claude Gray sure helped. Claude's single, also on D Records, began climbing up the charts in the early weeks of 1960, eventually nudging into the Top 10, topping out at number 7 on the national country singles chart compiled by *Billboard* magazine. Whatever royalties he'd lost by signing his rights away were balanced out by the word getting around that this Willie Nelson fella knew how to write songs. "When it went into the Top Ten, I thought, goddamn. I'd sold it for fifty dollars," Willie said. But he didn't regret it. "I just thought I would write more. I would have just as soon got fifty here, a hundred there, because it was cash in hand, and I knew plenty of guys who recorded their songs and still didn't make a quarter."

• • •

HE might have written a hit single, but he didn't have much to show for it. His gig on the radio had ended when he was fired for showing up late one too many times after way too many nights out late, so he sought out Charlie Brown, the country singer from back in West whose daughter Faye Dell had once been the light of his life. Charlie had a nightly gig at a club on Canal Street in a rough part of Houston down by the port. "I'm broke," Willie said when he found Charlie. "I've got my family with me, I need some work."

"Tell you what I'm going to do," Charlie said. "I'll give you some money. You get you something to eat, and come back and sit in, you can make a few dollars."

Willie followed Charlie's advice and stuck around for the next few nights. By the end of the week, the club owner took Charlie Brown aside. "Charlie, you're going to have to fire that guy sitting in," he told him. "He cain't sing worth a lick."

Willie had heard it all: He couldn't sing. He couldn't play. He was hard to follow. He couldn't keep a beat. He tried not to take it personally. "You know, I always thought I could sing pretty good," he told writer Michael Bane. "I guess it kind of bothered me that nobody else thought so. I was into a lot of negative thinking back then. I did a lot of bad things, got into fights with people. My head was just pointed in the wrong way."

With no income, no respect, and no options, he felt it was time again for a change of scenery. Leaving a pile of bills behind, he dropped off Martha, Lana and Susie, and baby brother, Billy, in Waco with Martha's mother, promising to send for them once he got settled, and steered his ugly green '46 Buick east.

The first stop was Meridian, Mississippi, where Claude Gray, the man who was making him famous with "Family Bible," was a DJ on the radio. Maybe Claude could help him find work. "Willie moved out to where I was and we palled around for six weeks, going to the honky-tonks and the dives," Claude said. "But I never could get a good job for Willie at the station. We were a small radio station."

Willie decided he might as well go for all the marbles.

He aimed the Buick, four payments behind, north. "Family Bible" was a hit. Word had spread in the business that Willie was the one who wrote it, even if his name wasn't on the single. It was time to show his face to the powers that be in Nashville, Tennessee.

Nashville, 1960

THE SHINING CITY on the bluff above the Cumberland River looked like the promised land to the hungry Texan who rolled into town, running on fumes. The home of the Grand Ole Opry and Music Row was where country music's stars shined brightest and where the hits were made.

But Nashville was much more than that. The state capital and the commercial hub of Middle Tennessee was built on agriculture, insurance, and religious publishing. It was also a bedrock southern city of faith. Since being established in 1772 by "42 able-bodied men and 200 souls," it had grown into a metropolis of almost a half million residents, most of whom declared their faith in Jesus Christ by attending one of 671 churches. Thomas Nelson published more Bibles than any printer in the United States, and more religious literature was printed in Nashville than anywhere on God's earth.

Nashville's reputation as a music center was initially fostered by its sizable African American community. Five years after Fisk University opened its doors in 1866 as the first institution in the south to offer a liberal arts education to students of color, the Fisk Jubilee Singers introduced slave songs to the world. They were hailed for preserving the American tradition of Negro spirituals, touring Europe for the first time in 1873.

Compared with other cities in the still-segregated southern United States, Nashville was fairly enlightened, having desegregated public parks and recreational facilities in 1956. When Willie hit town in 1960, civil rights activists were staging lunch counter sit-ins to desegregate restaurants in the city. Freedom Riders would soon be passing through on their way to Mississippi, Alabama, and Georgia, where segregationists maintained an iron grip on the political system.

Nashville's ties to country music went back to 1925, five years after the birth of radio in the United States, when the National Life and Accident Insurance Company built WSM radio (the call letters stood for "We Shield Millions") with the goal of selling insurance policies. Instead, the station known as the Air

Castle of the South became famous for selling country music. WSM's program director, George D. Hay, decided to start a weekly barn dance show, presenting a variety of music that could be broadcast on the radio, much as he did at the radio station where he was previously employed, WLS in Chicago, home of the National Barn Dance.

The first WSM Barn Dance aired on November 28, 1925, and featured championship fiddler Uncle Jimmy Thompson, who bragged he could "fiddle the taters off the vine." The show, staged in a five-hundred-seat auditorium designed for radio broadcast, found immediate acceptance, thanks to WSM's 50,000-watt clear-channel signal, which carried the program to ears throughout most of the United States and into Canada. Within two years, the show had moved to a larger venue and was renamed the Grand Ole Opry. In 1939, the NBC radio network began carrying a portion of the Saturday night show. Two locations later, in 1943, the program settled at the Ryman Auditorium in downtown Nashville, which became known as the Mother Church of Country Music. Roy Acuff was the Opry's first and by then biggest singing star. Acuff was soon joined by Minnie Pearl and Ernest Tubb.

The Grand Ole Opry that Willie Nelson witnessed when he arrived in Nashville was a friendly, folksy, and family-oriented showcase of all styles of southern, western, and mountain music, in a tightly regimented format tailored for radio broadcast on WSM and the NBC radio network and for television. Half-hour segments featured two or three Opry stars and maybe one new act, interspersed with commercials for Martha White Flour, GooGoo Clusters, RC Cola, and Prince Albert tobacco. Cast members included traditionalists Marion Worth, Ernie Ashworth, the Browns, and Dottie West, bluegrass pickers such as the Osborne Brothers, and stars like Acuff. Several performers took on hillbilly personas, including Grandpa Jones, String Bean, and Lonzo and Oscar.

Around the corner from the Ryman Auditorium on Broadway, the Ernest Tubb Record Shop hosted another live show on WSM after the Opry. WSM also aired the Friday Night Frolics, another live music show broadcast from the National Life studios of WSM on 7th and Union.

Nashville was proud of its reputation as "second in the record cutting industry," behind New York. The process of making records in Nashville was an easy-to-follow system. Songwriters were the basic building block. Song pluggers representing songwriters and song publishers pitched songs to producers, artists, and A&R (artist and repertoire) representatives at the record labels. Producers had the last say on song selection, chose the musicians for recording sessions, and, in the case of high-profile acts, ordered up arrangers, backing vocalists such as the Jordanaires and the Anita Kerr Singers, and strings and other instrumental embellishments to sweeten an artist's sound and (theoretically) broaden his or her appeal. The labels packaged and released the finished product as singles and sometimes albums, accompanied by marketing campaigns, radio promotion, and advertising to widely varying degrees. Radio played the records and, ideally, listeners rushed out and bought the records they heard, making money for everyone in the system.

Nashville's reputation as a recording center hinged largely on two recording facilities—Bradley studios, consisting of Bradley Film and Recording on 16th Avenue South and the Quonset Hut in back, assembled piece by piece by Owen Bradley, the former musical director for WSM radio, which Columbia would buy in 1962; and Studio B at RCA, Nashville's state-of-the-art facility for Nashville's state-of-the-art label, managed by guitarist Chet Atkins, the virtuoso Tennessee picker.

Nashville cemented its reputation as a songwriting center when Acuff-Rose, the city's first music publishing house, established in 1942, had its first hit in 1950 with "Tennessee Waltz," a tune so popular it ultimately became the official state song. Two other major publishing houses, Cedarwood Publishing and Tree International, opened their doors in the mid-1950s, followed by a slew of smaller publishers.

Following the signing of Elvis Presley to RCA in 1956 and his subsequent sessions at Studio B, Owen Bradley and Chet Atkins led efforts to smooth out country's rough edges with an "easy listening" touch by overdubbing vocal groups and strings and horns onto basic tracks. This "countrypolitan" sound, called the Nashville Sound, was tailor-made for smooth vocalists such as Eddy Arnold, Tennessee Ernie Ford, Jim Reeves, and Ray Price, whose appeal transcended hillbilly music.

But the Nashville Sound was just one slice of the country music pie. When Willie hit town, Texas honky-tonker Lefty Frizzell topped the charts compiled by the major music trade magazines (*Billboard, Cash Box,* and *Music Vendor,* later renamed *Record World*) with "What You Gonna Do, Leroy?" sharing the thin air with Texan Ray Price's smooth "One More Time," Louisiana's Webb Pierce's "Drifting Texas Sand," Texan Ernest Tubb's swinging "Everybody's Somebody's Fool" and "White Silver Sands," Oklahoman Johnny Bond's rockabillyesque "Hot Rod Lincoln," East Texan Johnny Horton's "North to Alaska," which was the theme of a John Wayne movie, San Antonio's Red River Dave's topical novelty "Ballad of Francis Powers," about the crash of a U-2 spy plane over Russia, and "Didn't Work Out, Did It?" a fatalistic country blues by a young singer named Shirley Collie, the wife of Texas and Los Angeles disc jockey Biff Collie, making her debut as a Liberty recording artist with three subsequent songs that channeled Julie London and Peggy Lee via Nashville, "I'd Rather Hear Lies," "Sad Song," and "Slow Rider."

Among the rising stars was Billy Walker, the one Nashville resident sold on Willie's potential. After quitting the Ozark Jubilee, Billy had gone back to Fort Worth, then to Nashville, where he was invited to join the Grand Ole Opry.

Billy was at the Clarkston Hotel coffee shop one afternoon in the summer of 1960, chitchatting after finishing *Noontime Neighbors,* a midday show on WSM radio, whose studios were next door to the Clarkston, when Willie Nelson walked in.

"Lord, what are you doing over here?" Billy asked him.

"Ain't nobody buying no songs in Texas," Willie deadpanned. "I came to see what I can do here."

Billy and his wife, Bettie, took Willie in and put him up at their house for ninety days. "I helped him get his first job, selling encyclopedias here in Nashville," Billy said. "I waited in the car while he knocked on a door, and there was this big ol' dog come around the corner about that time, and Willie took off back to the car with this ol' dog nipping at his rear end. He jumped in the car and said, 'Man, I ain't ever going to sell no encyclopedias anymore. The guitar is my bag!' "

But in order to get a break, he knew he would have to sell himself. Trying to hawk encyclopedias was one way to warm up. "You have to promote yourself—the biggest salesman for yourself has got to be you," Willie explained. "Whenever you are selling things, that's the first thing they tell you—you have to sell yourself first. After that, whatever you are selling is easier."

Other salesmen had mentored him in the art of the sell. When he sold *Encyclopedia Americanas* in Fort Worth, he was taken under wing by sales manager Bill Kelly, who had a girlfriend who worked for the phone company. "Every week there was a list of people who had just got a phone, just moved to town," Willie said. "Ninety-nine percent were young couples, seminary students, or college students, prime targets for a set of books. So when this list would come out every week, the girl would drop the list in the trash outside and Bill Kelly would go by there and get that list, and Monday morning we would start calling all of these new people who had just gotten a phone. The first thing they wanted to know was 'How the fuck did you get my phone number?' " After hawking encyclopedias, Singer sewing machines, Bibles, and Kirby vacuum cleaners — all good products that required little persuasion — selling himself as a songwriter in Nashville was no big deal.

Billy drove him around to a bunch of record and publishing companies and talked Don Pierce at Starday Records into recording a demo of Willie. But Pierce told Billy he wasn't impressed. "I knew Willie was a talented writer," Billy said. "I knew that sooner or later he would get something going with his songs, but, boy, it seems like every door was closed at that particular time." Willie tried to sell Billy "Funny How Time Slips Away," "Slow Down Old World," and four other songs for $500, but Billy's pockets were empty. "Just hang on a little while longer, something's bound to click," he encouraged him.

Billy and Bettie talked Willie into bringing up Martha and the kids, so three kids and one crying mother fretting about leaving her kinfolk rode the Greyhound to Tennessee to join Willie chasing his dreams. Willie scrounged enough to rent a trailer home for $25 a week plus heating oil. Martha hired on to waitress at the Hitching Post, the Wagon Wheel, and several other bars downtown. Willie got busy meeting folks, including Webb Pierce and Faron Young, big-name stars who liked hanging with the musicians as much as the musicians liked to hang with the stars.

Willie's reputation preceded him. "Word got around that I had written 'Family Bible,' " he said. "I spread the word myself."

He finally got his foot in the door when Billy took him to Tootsie's Orchid Lounge, the home away from home of a circle of Nashville's songwriters. Tootsie's looked and felt like a honky-tonk and was strategically located across the alley from the Ryman Auditorium and the Grand Ole Opry and across Broadway from Ernest Tubb's record shop.

"I knew it had to be the right place," Willie said. Tootsie Bess greeted them at the door and showed Willie around. "She didn't know me from Adam, but I was the new boy in town, and she was that kind of gal," he said. "She showed me where all the stars wrote their names on the wall, everything. She told me, 'You know, when I took this place over, it was nothing but a goddamned dump.' It still looked pretty much like a goddamned dump to me, but it was a better dump. It was where everybody gathered, and it was the place where Opry stars would come between songs or sets. You got to meet a whole lot of people."

Willie already knew one Tootsie's regular, Buddy Emmons, the pedal steel guitarist he'd met in Houston when Buddy played with Ernest Tubb, and Willie was playing a pickup gig with Smilin' Jerry Jericho. Buddy introduced Willie around, and he quickly fell in with the crew of songwriters and entertainers, most of whom liked to drink, smoke cigarettes, pop pills, bullshit, and create music. Among them were Mel Tillis, Roger Miller, Don Rollins, Ray Pennington, Harlan Howard, and Hank Cochran, who'd hit Nashville a year earlier.

After being introduced, Willie told Hank he'd come to Nashville to see what was happening.

"You're looking at it, I guess," Hank said, laughing.

Harlan Howard may have been the most successful of the bunch, but Willie identified with Hank. They both had grown up poor, rural, and Southern. Both had been recognized as children for having a gift for poetry, and both had put that gift to good use, writing music, adding melody to the words.

Hank was raised in Isola, Mississippi, in the gut of the Mississippi River Delta, barefoot and often without pants. He had done a fair amount of wandering, leaving home at age twelve and by age fifteen finding his way to sunny Los Angeles, where he worked in the catalog room at Sears, Roebuck on Pico Boulevard. Playing his guitar and singing a Carl Smith song and a Hank Snow song won him a watch on the "Amateur Show" portion of Squeakin' Deacon's country music radio program featuring touring Nashville stars live from the Santa Monica Ballroom. That led to his forming the Cochran Brothers with another teenager, named Eddie Cochran (no relation). By the time Hank was eighteen, the Cochran Brothers were opening shows for Lefty Frizzell in Honolulu and making records, which led them to make a pilgrimage to Memphis in search of Elvis Presley.

"He [Elvis] only had one record out and he couldn't believe what was happening to him," Hank recalled. "We said we just wanted to see what the hell was going on."

"I hear y'all are pretty good, the Cochran Brothers," Elvis told Hank and Eddie.

"Well, we think we are, but we ain't doin' nothing like you're doin'," Hank said. "In fact, we're thinking about goin' back to California where we're from and trying to get [rock and roll] started out there."

"That's a hell of an idear," Elvis reckoned.

The Cochrans returned to California but soon split up. Eddie Cochran went solo and recorded "Summertime Blues," one of the first genuine rock and roll hits in the wake of Elvis. Hank rejoined the California Hayride, starring Cottonseed Clark and Eddie Kirk, working as a solo country act. He teamed up with songwriter Harlan Howard and followed him to Nashville in 1959, where he was hired to write songs for Pamper Music, with a $50 weekly advance. Hank's engaging over-the-top personality and his ability to engage bigwigs as well as plain folks paid off in his other skill, song plugging, pitching tunes to artists and producers. He knew great songs even if they weren't his.

Hank's buddy Darrell McCall, who played bass in Patsy Cline's road band, introduced him to Patsy, who took a shine to Hank and, after much resistance, recorded a song of Hank's called "I Fall to Pieces," which reached number 1 on country and pop charts.

HANK and Willie really got to know each other at a "guitar pulling" (song swap) at Tootsie's, where songwriters showed their peers their best stuff. Willie was hardly intimidated. "I figured mine were as good as theirs," he said.

After several go-rounds, Hank asked Willie a question: "Who wrote them songs?"

"I did," Willie replied.

"Who plays them?" Hank asked.

"Nobody," Willie said, grinning. "Nobody wants 'em."

"Can you get out to my office at Pamper Music

out in Goodlettsville tomorrow?" Hank asked, knowing full well what Willie's answer would be.

Willie drove twenty miles north of Nashville to Goodlettsville the next day in his puke-green Buick. "I thought I'd had some bad-looking cars, but that one beat it all," Hank marveled. Willie sang the songs to Hank that he'd sung the night before and sang a few more. "What do you have to have?" Hank asked Willie. "Not what do you need, but what do you have to have?" Hank was making $50 a week and he had a wife and three kids, just like Willie did. "Fifty bucks," Willie said.

Hank went in to talk to Hal Smith, Ray Price's business partner, who was running the publishing house. "If we give him the fifty dollars, then we can't give you that raise," Hal protested.

"Give it to Willie," Hank said.

Hank had two dollars in his pocket. He gave Willie one dollar for gas so he could drive back to Nashville, and Hank followed there. When they arrived at Louie Dunn's Trailer Court, where Willie had rented a trailer for his family, Hank let out a loud belly laugh.

"What's so funny?" Willie asked.

"What's so funny is that me, my wife, and three kids lived in that same damn trailer when I first got here," Hank told him. It was also the very same trailer home that Roger Miller and his wife and three children had lived in when they moved from Amarillo a few years before, providing Roger with all the inspiration he needed for the lyrics of what would become his most enduring song, "King of the Road," with the simple line, "trailers for sale or rent, rooms to let fifty cents."

Martha and the children treated Hank like the Music Man. Finally there was hope, even though getting by was still a struggle. For the first three months of Martha's job at the Wagon Wheel, all she could afford to protect herself from the winter elements were a raincoat and plastic sandals.

In exchange for the weekly draw, Willie and Hank showed up every day at Pamper's office on Two Mile Pike in Goodlettsville. Hank arrived early to work the telephone, doing song-plugging research. "I'd just sit down there and call and find out who was recording and what was going on in town, and call Owen's [Bradley] office. I learned very young that the people who run the damn town is the secretaries, so I got in with all the secretaries. They'd say, 'Well, you ain't supposed to know this, but . . . ,' and I'd say, 'I don't know it.' So she'd tell me who was cutting and what they were looking for."

After plugging, Hank would meet Willie out back in the writers' house, half of the clapboard garage behind the big house, which Willie and Hank refurbished by putting up plasterboard and bringing in two desks, two chairs, and a portable tape recorder. A light bulb was installed outside on the porch to signify "Writers at Work" whenever it was lit. Susie Nelson and her sister and brother would come and play at Pamper while Daddy was at work, and when the red lightbulb was on, they would sit patiently on the porch, drinking soda until the light went off.

"Me and Willie'd meet out here and write. Just me and him, you know. That's all it takes."

Every day they'd strum guitars, sing songs, throw out lines, write lyrics, record on the reel-to-reel tape machine, and listen to songs on the recorder. Willie Hugh had been preparing all his life for a job like this, having written lyrics on scraps of paper, in notebooks, on boxes, on walls since he was a boy. Getting paid for that was a dream come true.

Pamper Music bought three hours of studio time at producer Fred Foster's studio in the Mason building next to the Clarkston Hotel downtown so they could record demo tapes of what they'd written to pitch to artists and producers. Taking turns singing and strumming their compositions, they were accompanied by a cast of musicians that included Hargus "Pig" Robbins on piano, Ray Price's steel guitarist Jimmy Day, guitarist Pete Wade, bassist Bob Moore, rhythm guitarist Ray Edenton, and pedal steel player Buddy Emmons. Hank or Willie would run through a song so the musicians could write it down on a chart before recording the demo, no do-overs.

"Musicians would cost you around ten dollars an hour," Hank said. "It depended on who you got and how hot they were. I could do a demo session for a third of what you could, because I could call certain guys and say, 'Hey, I need a little favor here. I wanna do three or four songs,' and they'd just charge me so much a song."

Hank and Willie tried collaborating, which was the way many Nashville hits were written. But Hank realized the hard way that Willie worked better alone. One morning in the writer's house in the back of Pamper, a secretary buzzed Hank. He was needed on the phone to consult a singer who was doing one of his songs in a studio. Hank stepped outside. Willie made the best of the pause by looking at the walls around him and jotting down on a piece of cardboard lyrics that became "Hello Walls."

They were getting it done, Hank said proudly. "For days I wouldn't go home because I was sleepin' on couches, hitting all the studios in town, running like a sumbitch to sessions at Starday, one at RCA, and one over at Decca. I would say, 'Man, that Willie's got a damn song you will not believe,' and they'd say,

'Well, let me hear it,' and I'd say, 'Well, Dale, I don't know, I think I . . . ,' and they'd say, 'Give me that sumbitch, and cut it.' I never would tell anybody I thought a song was good unless it was."

Willie's wife, Martha, was doing her part, telling Faron Young her husband had a song that was meant for him when the Sheriff (Faron's nickname) came into the Wagon Wheel on Broadway, where she was working. Faron was "wilder than a guinea, just like always," Hank said when he and Willie ran into him, hanging out with Webb Pierce and some musicians at Tootsie's. In the midst of some lightweight bullshitting accompanied by guitar strumming, Faron looked at Willie and asked him to sing him a song.

Willie sang "Hello Walls." Faron asked him to sing another one. Willie sang him "Congratulations," a sweetly acerbic putdown of a vindictive lover.

"Can I cut those?" Faron asked. "Hell, yeah!" Hank blurted before Willie had a chance to reply.

"Bring me a dub tomorrow," Faron instructed.

Faron had already taken a shine to the Texas kid, as had most of his posse. "Willie was down to earth and humble, Faron was loud," said Frank Oakley, a paint company representative who ran with Faron and hung at Tootsie's. "Roger Miller said Faron had a mouth as big as his heart."

Before Faron Young's version of "Hello Walls" was

released, Willie tried to sell him the song for $500. Faron, knowing full well what Willie had coming to him once the recording came out, did him a favor. He loaned him $500 instead, on the condition he not sell the song to anyone else.

The latest Faron Young single, "Hello Walls" b/w "Congratulations," was released on Capitol Records in the spring of 1961. Done as an uptempo shuffle, the song resonated. It was about a guy so sad and lonely, he starts talking to the walls and the walls talk back—pure-D honky-tonk subject matter—with a weird harmonic "hello, hello" chorus echoing off the canyons of listeners' minds. "Hello Walls" reached number 1 on the country singles chart the first week of May 1961 and stayed there for nine weeks. It remained a standard on jukeboxes for years. The song had such wide appeal that Faron's single crossed over to Top 40 radio, reaching number 12 on *Billboard*'s Hot 100 singles chart. The song would be covered by pop crooners Perry Como and Vic Dana, rockabilly Johnny Burnette, orchestra leader Lawrence Welk, and Ernest Tubb, one of Willie's first heroes. Faron's original interpretation was recognized by the music trade papers as the country and western record of the year. Willie celebrated the song's success by French-kissing Faron at Tootsie's after he received his first royalty check for the sum of $14,000.

It was huge money, considering composers earned two cents a record for sales—one penny to the writer and one penny to the song publisher.

Willie was sitting in high cotton. Songwriters like him were redefining country music, covering the subjects of drinking, sleeping around, and lust—the stuff of real people, real emotions, real problems—in creative tellings. Billy Walker recorded Willie's "Funny How Time Slips Away" on April 21, 1961, and another Willie original, "Mr. Record Man," just as Faron Young's "Hello Walls" was zooming up the charts. Walker's version of "Funny" edged onto the country singles chart, reaching number 23 that summer. The song had staying power on jukeboxes, though, and eventually was certified for selling a million copies.

Meanwhile, Hank Cochran used the same strategy for another song Willie had written, called "Crazy," as he'd used for his own composition "Walking After Midnight" by playing it for Owen Bradley, Patsy Cline's producer. The words, the melody, and whole song structure were music to Owen's ears. Patsy should record the song, Owen told Hank. Despite her reputation as the queen of sophisticated country female vocalists, she could use a hit. It had been a while since "Walking After Midnight" and "I Fall to Pieces."

Charlie Dick, Patsy's husband and manager, already knew about Willie. He'd heard "Night Life" by Paul Buskirk and His Little Men featuring Hugh Nelson on the jukebox at Tootsie's but couldn't find the single in record stores. So when he met Willie Hugh Nelson, Willie gave him a copy. Charlie went home and played the song over and over, marveling at the slow, languid rhythm and the soulful texture of the song and its jazz-influenced use of minor seventh and major seventh chords.

Patsy wasn't quite as taken with the song. "She didn't want to hear Willie Nelson's name mentioned," Charlie Dick said. Patsy didn't much cotton to songs that made her sound so wounded. So when Hank Cochran went over to Patsy's house to play "Crazy" for her, Willie waited in Hank's car. Charlie Dick had told Willie of Patsy's initial reaction to "Night Life," and Willie didn't want to ruin his chances.

"I took it in and said, 'Patsy, I think I got a hit,'" Hank related. "Whose is this?" Patsy asked. "It's Willie's," Hank said. "Where's Willie?" she asked. "He's settin' out there in the car, he's too embarrassed to come in," Hank told her. "Well, I'm going to get that little son of a bitch," Patsy declared. "She went out there and drug his ass in and had him sing it to her until she learned it," Hank said.

Patsy still wasn't convinced, living up to her reputation as hard to please. But Owen Bradley liked it enough to propose a compromise, like he always did: "You choose one song, and I'll choose one song, but I get the first pick," Owen told her. He was going to cut Patsy Cline singing "Crazy," and that was that.

"Look, Hoss, there ain't no way I can sing it like he's singing it on the demo," Patsy protested to Owen. But she did more than a credible effort of adopting Willie's unique phrasing, singing slightly behind the beat, waiting to sing until the chord hit, lingering on key words a little longer before cutting the phrase off cold while singing about the instability unrequited love brought on. The way she wrapped her voice around the opening line, "Crazy," was just like Willie had heard Floyd Tillman intone "Baby" at the beginning of "I Gotta Have My Baby Back." It wasn't that long ago that Paul Buskirk had told Willie, "Write me something like Floyd Tillman." With "Crazy" he had done that.

The instrumental part of the song was rehearsed and recorded over the course of one session. Pianist Floyd Cramer, a veteran of the Louisiana Hayride, played the signature piano notes that seemed to be walking alone in a dark alley on a rainy night. Gordon Stoker played a jazzy tick-tack bass tuned on octave lower than a normal guitar and an octave higher than a normal bass. Harold Bradley, Owen's brother, picked a subdued guitar. Owen focused on slowing Patsy down to sing the song as more of a blues than a dance tune. She was mad at Owen for making her do that, but that emotion somehow translated into hurt on the record.

Patsy did her vocal in one take. Owen Bradley invested another three-hour session on background singers and music, bringing in the Jordanaires, Elvis Presley's backing singers, to add a reassuring vocal chorus.

"I don't want four male voices covering mine up," Patsy protested to Owen.

"You just leave that to me, Patsy," he reassured her. "You'll be all right."

There was still one stumbling block. Billy Walker had placed a "hold" on the song, meaning he had first dibs on recording it, according to song publishing protocol. Hank Cochran panicked. Hank went to see Billy Walker. "Please, please, release your hold on the song," he begged. "I'll get you a hit song, I promise." Billy Walker relented for Willie's sake.

Almost overnight, "Crazy" became Patsy Cline's signature song. The record peaked at number 2 on the country charts and, like Faron Young's cover of "Hello Walls," crossed over to pop and easy-listening charts but in an even bigger way, breaking into the pop Top 10. A number one country song was good for maybe a hundred thousand copies sold. A pop chart topper could sell up to ten times that.

Patsy also covered Willie's "Funny How Time Slips Away." Billy Walker had done the first cover version and others would follow. A particularly soulful interpretation by Jimmy Elledge, an eighteen-year-old singer produced by Chet Atkins, would reach number 22 on American pop charts and was eventually certified gold for selling one million copies. Teen heartthrob Johnny Tillotson's version of "Funny" peaked at number 50 on the pop charts, while a mellow falsetto interpretation by Memphis soul balladeer Joe Hinton for Houston's Peacock Records in 1964 broke into the pop Top 20.

Willie possessed an innate understanding of a great country song—keep it short, keep it simple enough to work within the box that producers provide, and make it tug at the heart. Willie had been composing sad songs since he was a child, before he could comprehend the emotions he was writing about. Cindy Walker, a Christian woman who grew up twenty miles from Abbott and never took a drink of alcohol in her life, said she wrote "Bubbles in My Beer," a hit for Bob Wills, using her imagination. Willie possessed that gift too. But as an adult, he drew on first-hand experience for his hard luck songs about lost love, and it showed.

Willie's songs, and his adoption of Tootsie's as his home away from home, were following in the footsteps of Hank Williams, the honky-tonk spirit of country music. "It was called Mom's when Hank Williams was hot," explained singer-songwriter-picker Darrell McCall, who was a Tootsie's regular when Willie hit town. "Hank would go out the back alley behind the Ryman. Hank and the boys would have a bottle back by the rear entrance of Mom's where some cardboard boxes were stacked. Later on, some tables were put in the back room. The owners knew we wanted to pick and stay up all night. So they got to letting us go in that top room. They come up and say, 'Boys, you can stay as long as you want to, but we're going to have to close the bar down. Help yourself to the beer box. We'll be back tomorrow morning.' When they'd open back up in the morning, we'd still be picking."

The change in ownership of the humble beer joint was a mere formality. Tootsie Bess's stepson, Steve Bess, drummed with Ray Price. Her husband was a prison guard. "So nobody gave Tootsie too much trouble," Darrell McCall said. "She had a damn hat pin about [twelve inches] long. If someone got drunk in there, if someone got belligerent, it could be a picker or anybody, she'd pull out that hat pin and push them all the way out the door."

• • •

THERE were three levels of pickers in Nashville: the A team, the musicians who got most of the studio work; the demo guys, who honed their chops so they could make the A team; and the club guys, who played live or on the road.

The artists, the ones who sang the hits, liked to carouse and gamble and trade war stories; they could afford country clubs and second homes out on Old Hickory Lake. The songwriters were bent on playing their latest compositions for their peers in the hopes it might lead to an artist interested in the songs. All the pickers wanted to do was pick. Whenever they weren't on the road playing behind one of Nashville's stars or working in the studio, they were picking and playing as long as they physically could in some motel room or somebody's house.

Darrell McCall came to Nashville with another local boy from southern Ohio, named Donny Lytle, who would later change his name to Donny Young, then Johnny Paycheck. Darrell and Donny were taken in by Buddy Killen, owner of the Tree International song publishing house. Both fell into work as harmony singers in the studio, complementing the vocal talents of artists such as Faron Young, Webb Pierce, Ray Price, and George Jones.

"That was our little niche," Darrell said. "I did a 'hearts' album with George—'Heartaches by the Number,' 'Candy Heart,' 'This Ol' Heart,' then 'Keys to the Mailbox' with Freddie Hart. Faron [Young] heard me and picked me up and I started doing harmony with him in front of his band on the road and on his recordings of 'There's Not Any Like You Left' and 'Congratulations.' "

In 1960, Darrell's harmony work led to his unintended role as one of the Little Dippers, a harmony group whose recording "Forever" was in the Top 100 songs of 1960 and landed them on television's *American Bandstand*. But Darrell was all about hard-core country and fiddles and steel, which led to road work with Faron Young, Ray Price, and Webb Pierce while he was trying to develop his own career, with sporadic success. A booming baritone with considerable vocal power—he sounded operatic—he sang the title song to the motion picture *Hud* and had a Top 20 country hit in 1962 with "A Stranger Was Here," his first and biggest country hit. But when he was off the road, he ran with pickers like Buddy Emmons, Jimmy Day, Bobby Garrett, and Tommy Jackson. "We were all one little group," Darrell said. "If one of us had five bucks, we all had it. We all ate out of the same bowl of chili."

They shared illicit substances to keep it all going.

The pills were as much to stave off an appetite as to stay awake. Pickers lived hand to mouth. "We was all eating those diet pills, Roger [Miller], Buddy Spicher, all of us," Darrell said. "Buddy gave me my first Old Yeller diet pill. L.A. Turnarounds. West Coast Wagon Wheels, Black Mollies, those were the heavies. We were more into Dexedrine Spansule capsules, but mainly the Old Yellers. They were a vitamin pill for pregnant women. They were full of vitamins but they had Obedrine in them. You take two of them and you're ready to pick—I mean *pick*—in front of the president of the United States."

Darrell got to know Willie when "Hello Walls" hit for Faron Young. "He was so different," he said. "Up until that point, Faron's idols were Eddy Arnold, George Morgan, and Hank Williams. You'd hear a little of each of them up until that point. Once 'Hello Walls' hit, you heard Willie. Faron took to him right away."

Willie was the toast of Music Row. But all the time he spent with his rowdy friends and business associates, blowing his publishing royalties as fast as he could, was time away from his family. Martha did not necessarily approve, especially when she was still waiting tables and tending bar while he was out having a good time with his party pals. One night at the Wagon Wheel, Willie egged her on so bad that Martha picked up a shot glass and aimed it at her smart-mouth husband. Willie ducked and the glass hit the wall and ricocheted straight into Hank Cochran's chin. Willie took Hank to the emergency room. Ben Dorcy, a Nashville hanger-on who saw what happened, walked up to Martha and said, "You can't talk that way to my friends." Martha stared daggers into Ben's eyes, reached down and picked up a giant ashtray, and coldcocked Ben on the head, splitting his head open.

Faron Young urged Hank and Ben to file a lawsuit on Mrs. Nelson, but they just chalked it up to the price of running with Willie. The hot-headed wife was part of the package. Willie knew Martha had a right to be pissed, putting up with his crap. He was a no-good scoundrel. He drank too much. He chased women who chased him. But he wasn't about to give up those ways. Whatever his faults, he was finally being recognized and making enough money to provide for his family. Wasn't that the important thing?

WILLIE was a star songwriter, at the top of his game, but the urge to perform still burned deep inside. He played briefly behind Bobby Sykes, Marty Robbins's guitarist, who was being promoted as a solo act with several hit singles, including "A Touch of Loving" and the truckers' tune "Diesel Smoke and Dangerous Curves."

Then Frankie Miller called. Willie's pal from the Cowtown Hoedown in Fort Worth had relocated to Nashville and was working his single "Blackland Farmer" again after it had been rereleased on Starday. Booking agent Hubert Long had put together a small package show with Frankie and Hal and Ginger Willis to promote Frankie's 45. Frankie thought Willie might like to come along.

The "tour" — six people stuffed into a sedan pulling a trailer — got off to a bad start. "The first job we went to was in Bangor, Maine," Miller said. "I was playing those air bases and army bases. That was our first date. But there was a cop stop on the highway on the way, and they ended up fining everybody in the band, but we didn't have enough money to pay our fines. I left my D-twenty-eight guitar as collateral, and the justice of the peace let us go. I picked it up on the way back." Willie saw poetry in the guitar payment. "Frankie's the only one carrying anything worth something," he said. "We got to Bangor, Maine, and they were closing the joint up. A sergeant put us up in empty barracks and helped us get some cash with the Mobil credit card I had."

Willie switched from guitar to drums and back again on show dates in Syracuse, New York, and suburban New Jersey, while a player whom Willie called Skinflint played steel. "[Willie] wasn't worth much on drums but he did fine for what we had," Miller said. For Willie, the run was fulfilling. "I was getting out of town," he said. "But I don't know what Frankie was thinking."

That brief taste of the road informed Willie's thinking when Ray Price tracked him down in 1961. "He co-owned Pamper Music and called and asked if I could play bass," Willie related. "I said, 'Of course, can't everybody?' " Price's bass player, Donny Young, had quit Price's band and moved to California. Willie signed up for a hitch as a Cherokee Cowboy alongside Darrell McCall, Buddy Spicher, Steve Bess, and Pete Wade for $25 a day. Martha altered the Cherokee Cowboy suit designed by Nudie of Hollywood that had been passed on to Willie, sewing sequined music notes down the side of the slacks. Willie hit the road, riding in style on a real country music star's bus. On the way to the first gig, Jimmy Day taught him how to play bass.

Touring with Ray Price was nothing like touring with Frankie Miller or Bobby Sykes. "Anywhere we went, everybody knew Ray," Willie said.

Besides owning the publishing house that fronted Willie $50 a week, Ray Price became Willie's role model as a bandleader. He'd enjoyed a decade-long run as a recording artist and remained a big draw on the road. For two consecutive years, *Cash Box* magazine had recognized him as the top singer on the jukeboxes. He was a smooth, sophisticated crooner as uptown as Sinatra, while his band worked a beat known as the Ray Price shuffle made for western dancing. Price was discovered while attending North Texas Agriculture College in Arlington. He had been singing at a place in Arlington called Roy's House Café. "There was a small group of musicians at the barracks where I was staying when I was going to school and I guess they heard me sing, because one guy asked me to sing a couple of songs of his to a music publisher," Price said. "So I agreed to do it. The publisher [Jim Beck] heard the song and looked at me and said, 'You can come back tomorrow.' I came back the next day and there was a guy from Nashville, Tennessee, with a record contract who signed me to the Bullet label."

The record went nowhere, but Ray kept singing and landed a spot on the Big D Jamboree alongside Lefty Frizzell, whom he met at Jim Beck's studio in Dallas.

Price followed Lefty to a little town near Beaumont called Voth, where Neva Starnes, the wife of Jack Starnes, who started Starday Records with Pappy Daily in Houston, was booking bands. "We was playing dance halls, playing in Louisiana a lot, playing in Texas, anywhere she could book us. I tried to get on the Louisiana Hayride, but they didn't want me."

A Nashville publisher named Troy Martin got Ray signed to Columbia in March 1951, where he covered Lefty Frizzell's "If You're Ever Lonely" as his first single. Later that year, Martin introduced Ray to Hank Williams. Hank took him on the road and cowrote a song for Price to record, taking full credit for the song, "Weary Blues (from Waiting)," which Ray recorded with Hank's Drifting Cowboys in 1952.

They roomed together the last year of Hank Williams's life. "I learned from Hank you have to be yourself," Ray said. "When you figure that out, you got it whipped."

After Hank died on the road in Oak Hill, West Virginia, on New Year's Day of 1953 at the age of twenty-nine, Ray hired Hank's band, the Drifting Cowboys, eventually renaming them the Cherokee Cowboys. He developed the Ray Price shuffle on May 1, 1956. "It just came out at the end of a session one night," he said. "I heard it in my head, I got to talking to the musicians, got them to listen and get it down, then we recorded 'Crazy Arms.'" The $\frac{4}{4}$ rhythm became the standard for country music you could dance to.

Ray Price consistently topped the charts with "beer-drinking songs" that were cleaned up and polished by his whiskey-smooth vocals accompanied by strings, not fiddles, which rendered the music "prettier and sweeter," as Ray liked to put it.

Price had the good sense to start up Pamper Music during country's growth spurt fueled by radio. Publishing was the one safe place where it was hard to get screwed, as long as you held on to your rights and didn't sell your song for $50. Price was known for hiring some of the writers at the publishing house as Cherokee Cowboys to go out on the road as his backing band, including Willie Nelson.

"I'd heard his songs," Price said. "We knew what Willie was like. Willie had the desire. He was willing to work for it. He had the best song pitcher in the world on his side, Hank Cochran. We knew good songs. Harlan Howard out in California, I found him. Those were the songwriters we were looking for. I did quite a few of Willie's songs.

"Willie knew he had it," Ray said. "He worked at it all kinds of different ways. He was raised in the honky-tonks, just like I was. They were the only places you could get a crowd to play to in Texas. Texas, California, New Mexico, Arizona, the west — they were all honky-tonk places. Honky-tonk people are a hard crowd," Ray said. "They're drinking and dancing, they're not thinking about the music too much. They're busy polishing their belt buckles."

Willie became an important Cherokee Cowboy. He was a competent musician and fun to run with after the show. His generosity, fueled by publishing checks when they arrived, was unlike any other sideman's. He bought Ray Price's '59 Cadillac. He booked the nicest suites and would treat the other Cherokee Cowboys to booze and cigarettes. He rented a nice house for Martha, Lana, Susie, and Billy in Goodlettsville near Pamper Music. "Daddy got me a nanny," Lana recalled sweetly. "She was a woman known as Suckin' Sue who used to hang at Tootsie's. She was trying to go straight. She was nice to me."

He recruited Paul Buskirk from Houston to play with Price for a spell while trying to get his old friend Johnny Bush, from San Antonio, hired as drummer. He was being paid to write songs, but playing behind Price was a bigger thrill. Faron Young introduced Willie to friends as the composer of "Hello Walls." One night at Tootsie's, Faron cornered Willie. "Why don't you just stay here and write songs for me?" Willie said thanks but no thanks. "It won't be too many more years on the road until I'm hotter than you are," he told Faron with a wink. Faron shot back that Willie was an acquired taste like Floyd Tillman because he was so different. "Willie, you gotta make up your mind whether you're going to sing or talk," he ribbed.

As Ray Price's front man, Willie got to sing a song or three to warm up the crowd before the star of the show took the stage each night. But he wanted to *be* Ray Price, not just his sideman or his songwriter.

OFF the road, Willie and Roger Miller, another sometimes Cherokee Cowboy, were among the few songwriters who hung with the pickers as much as with other songwriters or the recording artists who could move their careers. "We'd have these jam sessions when we'd get off the road," said Darrell McCall. They were all about Ray Charles, Miles Davis, or some other jazz cat. "That's where the licks came from for Buddy [Emmons] and Jimmy [Day] both. Go back in the old Hank Williams stuff. Sammy Pruett and Don Helms, they were playing jazz. You'd have three or four steel players, two or three bass players, four guitar pickers, feeding off each other. One steel player would play till he got tired and he'd go sit down for a while, drink a beer. This would go on for days at a time."

Road work scratched Willie's girl itch. Fidelity was

not among Ray Price's rules and regulations. Women showed up at gigs and clustered around their favorite Cherokee Cowboy, not just the star. Martha, no dummy, got wise to Willie's ways. "He was always messing around with somebody and come home and tell me he hadn't done doodly shit," she said. "He'd have lipstick smeared from one end to the other." Willie always had a good excuse, but Martha knew better. She was so determined to catch him in the act that she hid in the car trunk once to spy on him. She caught him red-handed by following Ray Price and His Cherokee Cowboys to a show in Fort Smith, Arkansas. Drinking herself into a rage, she barged into his motel room and caught him fooling around with a backdoor woman. Without a second thought, she coldcocked Willie over the head with the whiskey bottle she had emptied, unleashing a torrent of epithets. She was so enraged and so drunk that when the police showed up, she went to jail. Her husband bailed her out.

Something had to give.

Los Angeles, 1961

LOS ANGELES, the third-largest city in the United States, wasn't in Willie Nelson's plans when he set out to be a hit songwriter. But L.A. pulled him in anyway in the summer of 1961, when he signed a recording contract with Liberty Records. The label was based in Los Angeles, the new center of the recording industry, where the California sound, celebrating cars, blonde girls, surfing, and teenage hedonism, was beginning to take shape. Liberty Records had started a country division, aiming to challenge Capitol Records as the dominant country record label on the West Coast.

Ken Nelson, the head of Capitol's country division, had developed a warm, close-to-the-microphone sound for country singers signed to the label, effectively smoothing out the Bakersfield Sound popularized by Buck Owens and Merle Haggard. Ken Nelson's recording of Ferlin Husky's "Gone" in Nashville in 1956 was said to be the inspiration for the Nashville Sound.

Liberty's country division chief, Joe Allison, was determined to follow in Ken Nelson's footsteps. A good ol' boy from Texas with an ear for hits, Allison was one of Hank Cochran's favorite people to pitch songs to. Hank was on the verge of wrangling a recording contract of his own, when he played Willie's demos to Allison. Allison flipped. Signing Willie would give Liberty the inside track to one of Nashville's best writers. But as great as his songs were, Allison thought Willie's singing style was almost as intriguing, beginning with his sophisticated sense of phrasing. Joe Allison understood Willie from the get-go.

Liberty's roster was nothing if not eclectic, ranging from the Ventures, the kings of instrumental surf music, surf music vocal duo Jan and Dean, balladeer Timi Yuro, the sexy and sultry "Fever" gal, Julie London, composer and singer Jackie DeShannon, to the Johnny Mann Singers, Si Zentner, "Quiet Village" composer Martin Denny, Nancy Ames, Texas-Mexican singing star Vikki Carr, the novelty act the Chipmunks, and pop vocalists Gene McDaniels and Bobby Vee. Among the country acts already on the label were Bob Wills, California swing leader Tex Williams, whose "Smoke, Smoke, Smoke (That Cigarette)" was Capitol Records' first million-seller, Little Joe Carson, Tommy Allsup, Walter Brennan, and the Crickets. Twenty-two Liberty songs reached the Top 10 on pop charts in 1961, and they had put the personnel in place to do the same with country records.

Willie's first recording session for Liberty was in Nashville on August 22, 1961, in the Quonset Hut studio built by Owen and Harold Bradley. Four guitarists were booked for the recording, including Ray Edenton, who doubled on fiddle and worked many of Chet Atkins's sessions, Texas Playboy Kelso Herston, session leader Grady Martin, the dean of session pickers, and Harold Bradley. Pig Robbins played piano, Buddy Harman drummed, Joe Zinkan played bass, and the Anita Kerr Singers sweetened up the proceedings with soothing choruses emulating the Nashville Sound.

Tracks for two Willie originals, "The Part Where I Cry" and "Touch Me," were finished.

Not satisfied with the results, Allison took Willie to Radio Recorders in West Los Angeles, near the Liberty headquarters, for a second session a month later. This time Willie joined three other stellar guitarists — session leader Billy Strange, Roy Nichols from the Maddox Brothers, and Johnny Western, who had worked with Johnny Cash and sang the "Paladin" theme to *Have Gun—Will Travel,* one of the most popular western series on television. Jim Pierce played piano, and Red Wootten and Ray Pohlman split bass duties. Roy Harte, a jazz player who founded Pacific Jazz Records and worked with hillbilly Cliffie Stone on his weekly Hometown Jamboree, handled drums. B. J. Baker led the vocal chorus that attempted to replicate the Anita Kerr Singers. The singers got lost trying to follow Willie's lead vocals until Joe Allison put up baffles between Willie and the singers so they couldn't hear one another. To stay on the beat, the singers followed Johnny Western's direction. A session player who went by the name of Russell Bridges (real name: Leon Russell) added some piano while another guitarist, named Glen Campbell, threw in some riffs.

Fourteen tracks were finished in two days: "Mr. Record Man," "Go Away," "The Waiting Time," "Three Days," "Darkness on the Face of the Earth," "Undo the Right," "Where My House Lives," "Country Willie," "How Long Is Forever," "One Step Beyond," "Funny How Time Slips Away," "Wake Me When It's Over," "Hello Walls," and "Night Life"—more than enough to make an album, several singles, and B-sides.

A third session was scheduled for Nashville in November. Liberty was still trying to figure out where Willie Nelson fit as a performer. Joe Allison gathered fiddler and guitarist Ray Edenton, pianist Pig Robbins, and drummer Buddy Harman from the earlier sessions, along with bassist Bob Moore and steel guitarist Jimmy Day at Bradley's Barn. Jimmy Day and Willie had become drinking and picking buddies as Cherokee Cowboys long enough for Willie to develop a great deal of respect for Jimmy's music and his talents on pedal steel and rhythm guitar. His ability to bend chords to cry and weep was to the pedal steel what John Coltrane's styling was to the saxophone. His steel was the hook on Ray Price's breakthrough "Crazy Arms," which prompted folks like Webb Pierce, Red Sovine, Hank Williams, Jim Reeves, Lefty Frizzell, Elvis Presley, Ray Price, Ernest Tubb, Ferlin Husky, and George Jones to seek him out for their recordings. On this recording, though, Jimmy Day's primary task was instructing the Anita Kerr Singers how to sing the steel parts so they could define the up-and-coming singer-songwriter sound as Liberty's sweeter version of the Nashville Sound.

Joe Allison also brought in a young singer from the West Coast named Shirley Collie, who was recording for Liberty, to see how she and Willie would match up. Willie already knew about Shirley and supposedly offered Joe a piece of a song if Joe would get her on his record. One thing was clear: He'd never sung with a woman with a voice like hers before, or with someone quite as pretty. Shirley was a star in her own right, a featured regular on the television shows *Country America* and CBS's *Town Hall Party,* which were taped in Los Angeles, and she'd appeared on *Divorce Court* and *The Groucho Marx Show.*

Shirley and Willie first met through Hank Cochran, who was pitching Shirley some of Willie's demos over lunch and brought her over to Radio Recorders when he was recording "Mr. Record Man." Ever the hustler, Willie told her, "I've got a song you should record." As their eyes locked, Shirley didn't hear a word. It was instant love. "I saw things in him that even give me goose bumps now," she later recalled. She also heard quite a songwriter.

Shirley and her husband, Biff, went to see Ray Price and the Cherokee Cowboys at the Harmony Park Ballroom and invited Willie over to dinner at their house the following night, an off night for the band. While there, Biff enticed Willie to record some promotional spots for KFOX in Biff's home studio. Willie liked Biff and Biff liked Willie. They were fellow Texans with plenty in common. Before Biff married Shirley, he'd been married to the ex-wife of Floyd Tillman, one of Willie's heroes.

The two couples socialized in Nashville whenever Biff came to town. But on one visit, Shirley stayed after Biff returned to the coast. Not coincidentally, Willie didn't come home for two days. He had taken a motel room at the Downtowner Motor Inn next to Shirley's room, right under Martha's nose.

Nashville's music community being smaller than a small town, word spread fast of an affair and eventually reached Martha. Shirley and Willie weren't even trying to pretend anymore. The engaging red-haired singer with the expansive smile and Patsy Cline tough-gal moves had stolen Willie's heart. She wasn't just good-looking, she could sing, she could yodel, and she could entertain. She could play bass. She was the first singer to not only grasp his vocal styling but match him note for note, keeping up with his notorious phrasing, singing harmony that fit hand in glove with his leads. They were so in sync, both could switch from lead to harmony at the nod of the head or a wink of an eye. She wrote songs too. She brought out the best in Willie Nelson, the performer.

Shirley thought he had all the right ingredients to be a star. Everyone else had yet to get the message. The first Willie Nelson single on Liberty, "The Part Where I Cry," recorded in Nashville, b/w "Mr.

Record Man," recorded in Los Angeles, was released late in 1961 to little fanfare.

"It did get airplay, which is all I wanted, really, because I knew I wasn't going to make a bunch of money," Willie said. "I didn't know anybody who was making money off of selling records."

About the only place the single made a splash was Texas, where it ginned up spins on Texas radio stations and on jukeboxes across the state, mainly for the B-side. Linking heartbreak to record retailers with poetic lines, and putting the words to a $\frac{4}{4}$ Ray Price shuffle was two-stepping dance-floor bliss. Bass, snare, and brushes pushed the beat, and Jim Pierce's earthy honky-tonk piano licks provided the sad counterpoint.

*Mr. Record Man I'm looking for a song I heard
   today
There was someone blue singing 'bout someone
   who went away
Just like me his heart was yearning for a love that
   used to be
It's a lonely song about a lonely man like me
There was something 'bout a love that didn't
   treat him right
And he'd wake from troubled sleep and cry her
   name at night*

Mr. Record Man get this record for me won't you
  please
It's a lonely song about a lonely man like me

I was driving down the highway with the radio
  turned on
And a man that I heard singing sound so blue
  and all alone
As I listen to his lonely song I wonder could it be
Could there somewhere be another lonely man
  like me

"The first time I heard Willie on the radio singing 'Mr. Record Man,' I flipped out," said his nephew Freddy Fletcher. " 'Wow, that's Uncle Willie on the radio!' I couldn't believe it. When he came and stayed at our house in Fort Worth and he took my bedroom, I thought he really was a big deal, so I went and started charging all the neighborhood kids to come and watch him sleep. When he woke up, he's got a roomful of kids there, staring at him. We thought this guy is one of the biggest things ever."

Despite only four thousand copies sold, the single became Willie's calling card. "The only way you could make any money was by personal appearances," he said. "I used the record to get gigs. You had a record, you went to the radio stations, you got them to play it, and you go to a beer joint and say, 'Hey, I got a record over here, I'll draw you a crowd,' and you put it together."

The second Willie Nelson single fared considerably better, mainly because Shirley Collie was singing on it. Their duet, "Willingly," issued as a Willie Nelson record, rose into the country Top 10 when it was released in March 1962 with "Our Chain of Love" on the flip side. Their harmonies were as sweet as the Everly Brothers', with Willie sticking to an artificially high tenor to blend in with Shirley's richer voice, which carried the song. Willie's vocal served mainly as a complementary echo. Whoever was singing the lead didn't really matter. The formula worked.

A third single, "Touch Me," sung without Shirley, was released in May 1962 and broke into the Top 10 country singles chart, rising to number 7. A sad blues done in a slow drag with the rough edges smoothed out by harmony singers and a cool instrumental arrangement, the song earned Willie a place on jukeboxes throughout the United States.

A second duet with Shirley, "You Dream About Me" b/w "Is This My Destiny?" didn't do much chartwise. But by then, Willie didn't much care, nor did Shirley. Their passionate affair was aflame. Her marriage, her home, her TV bookings, her audition for the role of Cousin Pearl Bodine in a new TV comedy called *The Beverly Hillbillies*—none of that mattered anymore. She left a good-bye note to Biff before sneaking onto Ray Price's bus while the Cherokee Cowboys headed north to Canada for an extended tour. She was chucking it all for the bass player.

She rented a car, using Biff's American Express card, and ran around with Willie for weeks, leaving Biff with a $2,000 bill. When Willie got a booking opening for Roy Orbison along with comedian Allen Kaye at the Fox Theatre in Atlanta, where the poster for the September 19, 1962, concert hyped Willie with the endorsement "Elvis Presley says he is the Greatest Singer of All Time," he and Shirley spent three days in the Georgia city, acting like kids. "We'd run around the streets and look in the windows and laugh and go back to the motel and eat pizza or Chinese food and tell each other what we wanted to do," she said.

Ray Price auditioned Shirley as a singer, but she had other ideas. She wanted to work with Willie, and as far as she was concerned, he had the potential to be bigger than Price. She was aware of Willie's reputation in Nashville as someone who didn't keep appointments and seemed to be in a daze most of the time. She wanted to straighten him out, get him a driver's license, and file his taxes, so they could write songs and play and tour together. She went back to L.A. to get a divorce, only to discover Biff was going to try to commit her to a hospital.

Willie was in love. "He came to Mom and told her that he met a woman and he loved her and that she was going to die," Lana, Willie's oldest daughter, said. "She had a life-threatening illness and she didn't have long to live. He was only repeating what he was told. Martha took boyfriends when Willie took girlfriends, partly because she was lonely, partly to get back at him. I was old enough to know. They were fighting so much, I used to pray that they would get a divorce. I thought they'd be happier because they wouldn't be fighting and screaming all the time. But that made Mom real depressed. She had a nervous breakdown. She became alcoholic. And Shirley's still got her life-threatening illness.

"She just wanted to be together and be happy and not struggle," Lana said of Martha. "Being a musician, he was struggling a lot." When success came, the marriage fell apart. "He took lovers. She took a boyfriend," Lana said. "He always had lovers. He'd come home and she'd beat the hell out of him, he'd beat the hell out of her. It was fire and water. I don't know who was right and wrong. The mother's trying to raise three kids. The husband's a good person and

222 / JOE NICK PATOSKI

really sweet and will give you the shirt off his back, although maybe he's not being as faithful as he could be, and maybe not bringing home the money, although he's really trying, he's really always trying. We always had to move when the rent came due. They were always turning the lights off."

Martha had a tough hide, but she could no longer conceal her hurt. "You know how people are strong on the outside but really fragile? That was her," Lana said. "She had an 'I'll knock you in the head' personality, but she would cry at the drop of a hat."

Martha tried to make the marriage work, but she was no match for a high-falutin' lady singer. She finally threw in the towel. She took the kids and moved to Las Vegas to get a divorce. And Shirley stayed on the road with Willie.

When they came to Las Vegas to play a gig, Willie called to get together with the kids. "We were living in a tiny apartment and we hadn't seen him in a long, long time," Lana said. "But he didn't come to get us. He sent Shirley to pick us up. Now, why anybody thought that was going to work, I don't know. But it didn't."

Shirley knocked on the door of Martha's apartment. When Martha opened it, Shirley told her sweetly, "I've come to pick up the kids." Martha looked back at Lana and in a flat voice said, "Go get me a butcher knife." Lana wouldn't do it, but Susie did. Knife in hand, Martha chased Shirley off the porch, screaming, "Don't ever come back, and you tell that fuckin' Willie Nelson he'll never see his kids again! If he wants his kids, he better be man enough to come and get them himself and don't send his fuckin' whore next time!"

Martha would soon marry Chuck Andrews, a man who worked construction for the company that was installing elevators in the new Caesar's Palace. They moved to Los Angeles, then to Albuquerque, where Martha passed off Lana's dark complexion as Italian blood. "I'm not going to have you treated like no damn Indian," she informed her daughter. Being Cherokee in the Land of the Hopi was asking for trouble.

Martha's marriage to Chuck was brief, and she took up with a man named Mickey whom she had dated in Waco before she met Willie. Mickey had gone into the army, and when he found out Martha had married Willie, he went AWOL. After he was caught, he spent two years in prison.

But family was the farthest thing from Willie Nelson's mind. He was determined to be a country star. If that cost him his marriage and his family, that was the price he would pay. After a lifetime of preparation, the first Willie Nelson album, . . . *And*

Then I Wrote, consisting of tracks Willie had recorded in Nashville and Los Angeles over the previous year, was released in 1962 in mono and stereo versions. Charlie Williams, a disc jockey on KFOX radio in Los Angeles, whom Willie had replaced at KCNC in Fort Worth eight years earlier, wrote the liner notes, comparing Willie's songwriting-vocalist talents to pop songwriters Johnny Mercer and Hoagy Carmichael.

The songs were all Willie's, except for Hank Cochran's "Undo the Right," including his big three—"Crazy," "Hello Walls," and "Funny How Time Slips Away"—as well as "Three Days," which had already been covered by Faron Young as a follow-up to "Hello Walls," reaching number 7 for Faron on the *Billboard* country singles chart. Despite the success of his songs as covered by others, the public was not responding the same way to the songwriter as performer. Still, being a Liberty Records artist got him road dates on his own.

WILLIE convinced his old bandmate Johnny Bush to join him as drummer with the idea of grooming Johnny to be a solo act. The bass chair belonged to Shirley, who could yodel and sing as well as keep the rhythm. "[The other musicians] respected me," the only woman in the band said. "I had been traveling for a long time, and they respected me and looked after me." When Shirley didn't travel, Pete Wade from the Cherokee Cowboys or Wade Ray filled in. Sometimes Wade and Willie worked as a duo with pickup bands when money was tight. When Willie could afford him, Jimmy Day came along.

Johnny Bush thought Willie was going to be bigger than Dean Martin someday, which was saying a lot, since Martin was cranking out number one pop hits like "Everybody Loves Somebody." Johnny shared that opinion with Willie on a night after a not-so-good gig when a mic stand had been left behind.

"I want to let you know I'm doing the best job that I can and tonight I really fucked up," Johnny told him. He tried to improvise a mic stand from a drum stand and duct tape, but the mic kept falling off. "I know I should have brought our mic stand, and if you don't have a mic stand, you're up the creek. If you want to eat my ass out, go ahead," Johnny said.

"Are you through?" Willie asked. "Let's have a drink. I ain't gonna eat your ass out. You already did a pretty good job of that yourself." Willie wasn't going to give Johnny shit. He liked his voice and he liked his person too much for that. He wanted to help him, not fire him.

Paul English, the brother of Oliver English, who'd played with Willie on the radio in Fort Worth, and

steel guitarist Charlie Owens were working in the
house band at Ray Chaney's place in Fort Worth a
few nights later when Willie, Johnny, Jimmy Day,
and Shirley Collie walked in to play. Paul rekindled
his friendship with Willie and renewed his appreciation for Willie's talent. "You realized he really could
sing," he said. "Shirley was a great bass player. She'd
just smile. She had this charisma. She could really
yodel too. We liked them all because they were musicians."

Paul was clearly in awe of his friend, a real genuine
Nashville recording artist. Paul took Willie's Liberty
album to a Fort Worth radio station to copy it onto
a four-track tape cartridge. That way, Paul would
have something to listen to on the new tape player he
had installed in his car to keep him company on
drives to Waco and to Houston, where Paul had call
girls. He listened over and over, enough to figure out
Willie was doing more than writing catchy country
tunes. "I was amazed, because this guy could write,"
Paul said. "I'd have people over to my house and ask
them, 'What do you think he's writing about here?'
It was deep."

Willie made other hires for his band whenever a
tour was put together. For one run, he hired fiddler
Ray Odem to complement Jimmy Day's pedal steel
and brought in his music mentor from Fort Worth

and Houston, Paul Buskirk, to add his custom-designed double-neck half mandolin and half guitar to the sound, leaving Willie to strum and sing.

The group rehearsed in Roswell, New Mexico, then gigged in Albuquerque, where they picked up a second guitarist, Dave Kirby, a Brady, Texas, native who was Big Bill Lister's nephew and a onetime Cherokee Cowboy. They worked their way to Las Vegas for an extended run at the Golden Nugget, one of the first Vegas spots to book country acts, doing six forty-minute shows between eight p.m. and two a.m. They managed to work the schedule with the help of pills, including Placidyls, aka "green meanies," the kind of downers that inspired an abuser "to run yourself to pieces," Shirley explained.

On January 12, 1963, at the end of the Vegas engagement, Willie and Shirley married at the Chapel of Love. Jimmy Day was best man. Johnny Bush was flower girl. Inside the wedding ring Willie placed on Shirley's finger was the inscription "I promise you love forever and after forever, your Willie."

His divorce from Martha Matthews wouldn't become final for several months, but that was a mere technicality. "She couldn't handle the way I was living," Willie said about Martha with regret. Going down the highway, he explained, "is just the nature of what I do."

Willie and Shirley worked the road, although they kept a mailing address in Fort Worth and stayed with his sister Bobbie and her husband, Paul Tracy, when they weren't playing bars somewhere or recording.

Paul Buskirk had gone back to Houston and Ray Odem stayed in Fort Worth, so Johnny Bush recruited Charlie Harris, a guitar player from Corpus Christi; Eddie Sweatt briefly; then Pete Burke Jr. to play bass. Burke had road experience behind Hank Thompson. The new band picked up dates on touring package shows headlined by Slim Whitman, Little Jimmy Dickens, the Wilburn Brothers, Orville Couch, Frankie Miller, and Ray Price. Ray Price told Willie that Willie's band was the worst he'd ever heard. But within a year, most of the same players were backing up Ray as the new Cherokee Cowboys. The backhanded compliment validated his determination to make it on his own.

Dallas gossip columnist Tony Zoppi noted Willie's recording artist credentials when he touted Willie's 1963 Valentine's Day engagement at the Chalet. Four months later he was headlining the Big D Jamboree, appearing alongside Sonny James and Alex Houston. On September 2, he starred on a one-hour special live from the studios of Channel 11 in Fort Worth, along with Shirley Collie, Red Foley, Uncle Syp Brassfield, and Billy Gray. They were promoting a new barn dance in Fort Worth, the Cowtown Jamboree, staged at a recently opened venue in Fort Worth called Panther Hall.

Willie and Shirley gravitated from Fort Worth back to Los Angeles, where Willie hustled appearances with his guitar-picking pal Phil Baugh on car dealer Cal Worthington's television show. He contemplated opening a West Coast office for Pamper Music and starting a booking agency with Tommy Allsup. With friends like Roger Miller, Gordon Terry, and Bob Wills living nearby, Southern California was almost like back home, only sunnier.

"We all ran around together and had a lot of fun," Tommy said. "We had a lot going on." Willie cobbled together a circuit working the Palomino in the San Fernando Valley, Phoenix, Fresno, and Northern California. Playing clubs provided plenty of opportunities to drink, smoke, and chase women, but the volatile combination could be dangerous. After a gig at J.D.'s in Phoenix one night, a jealous husband, pissed to see his wife flirting with Willie between sets, split Willie's head open with a car jack in the parking lot after the show. "Put him in the hospital, almost killed him," Tommy deadpanned. It was the price you paid when you worked the night life.

"Me and him had a booking agency, Willie Nelson Talent," Tommy said. "Liberty gave him an office where the studio was. We put on some shows out in a ballroom in Pomona with Bob Wills, Roger Miller, Glen Campbell, and Ernest Tubb. Bob loved Willie's style. Bob loved him because he was different. He'd let Willie sit in and he'd let Gordon Terry sit in. He'd hand his fiddle to Gordon and he didn't do that for anyone."

Tommy and Willie got along fine. "He'd let his hair down at times," Tommy said. "We liked to go deep-sea fishing out of Santa Monica for bonito, yellowtail, and redfish. We'd take a sackful of brownies that Shirley baked with 'that wacky 'baccy.' We had a good time."

The main reason Willie was hanging with Tommy Allsup was to record more sessions at United Studios on Sunset Boulevard. When Joe Allison left Liberty after failing to deliver hits for the label, Tommy took over as Willie's producer.

The Oklahoma guitarist had played Western Swing with Bob Wills and His Texas Playboys and rock and roll with Buddy Holly, giving up his airplane seat on the flight that killed Holly, Ritchie Valens, and the Big Bopper in the winter of 1959. Liberty hired Allsup to produce and make records as leader of Tommy Allsup and the Raiders, who did an all-instrumental album *Twistin' the Country Classics* for Liberty after being recruited by Snuff Garrett to play on a recording session for Buddy Knox, another West Texas rocker who had a number one hit, "Party Doll."

"The previous album wasn't that big of a hit," Tommy said, so Willie and Tommy met at arranger Ernie Freeman's house with Jimmy Day to strategize for the second go-round. "Willie sang Ernie some of the songs he recorded on the first session that had strings on the recording. We was trying to feel our way around. Disc jockeys loved him but he wasn't selling any records."

United was the hit factory where Bobby Vee and Johnny Burnette were cutting singles and where Tommy Allsup produced *Bob Wills Sings and Plays*. The studio players at United, paid a scale of $50 to $55 a session, were masters of the recording art. Drummer Earl Palmer knew rhythm. He was a jazz player raised in New Orleans with recording credentials including Fats Domino, Frank Sinatra, B. B. King, Barney Kessel, Professor Longhair, and Lou Rawls. Bassist Red Callender turned down offers from Duke Ellington and Louis Armstrong to pursue a freelance career that earned him session work with Armstrong, Lester Young, Billie Holiday, Dexter Gordon, Oliver Nelson, Mel Tormé, Erroll Garner, Nat King Cole, Art Tatum, Charles Mingus, and Charlie Parker, among others. Fiddler-violinist Bobby Bruce played with Henry Mancini and Lawrence Welk, as well as with Luke Wills, Bob's brother, and with Leon McAuliffe, Bob's steel man. Guitarists Glen Campbell, John Gray, and Bobby Gibbons and pianist Gene Garf augmented by Gentleman Jim Pierce and an uncredited Leon Russell were all known studio entities. Jimmy Day was Jimmy Day.

Tommy knew the best singers were the ones with distinctive voices who stuck out on any jukebox, like Hank, Sinatra, Dylan, Cash, Tubb, Odetta, Jimmie Rodgers, and Bob Wills. But "we had an agreement," Tommy said. "Willie said, 'If I don't tell you how to produce this, you won't tell me how to sing.' " Like Joe Allison, Tommy appreciated Willie's unorthodox delivery. "He sang behind the beat, but he was always in meter," he said. "That's the way jazz singers sing. If you recorded with Willie, I don't care if you knew the song backwards, you better write you out a chord chart, and read that sumbitch. He's going to be away from the lead line. That's what we'd do. If you start listening to him while he's playing, you're going to break time."

Kenny Rivercomb, Liberty's West Coast promo man, thought Willie was more of a jazz singer than a country singer and pushed Tommy to have him record the standard "Am I Blue?" Eddie Brackett, the engineer of Sinatra's "Strangers in the Night" and sessions with Barbra Streisand and Sam Cooke, told

Tommy that Willie had the most natural voice he'd heard in a studio. "I don't have any EQ [equalization of the increase or decrease of signal strength for a portion of audio frequencies] on his voice and it just cuts through like a knife. He's the easiest guy I've ever recorded. I don't have to do nothing."

When the newly wedded Shirley Nelson added her vocals, the sound took on a whole other texture. "They burned it up on 'Columbus Stockade Blues,' " Allsup marveled of the fast-paced number allegedly written by Jimmie Davis in the 1920s. The February 20, 1963, sessions were Willie's most fiery tracks yet, featuring Shirley and him speed-scatting like harmonizing jazz vocalists. "She could hang right in with him," Tommy said with respect. Willie had recorded "Columbus Stockade Blues" earlier in Nashville, but it was nothing like the two versions he did at United. One version featured flashy Merle Travis–inspired finger picking by John Gray and Tommy Allsup. The second version was pure jazz, pushed by bassist Red Callender and drummer Earl Palmer, seasoned jazz musicians who earned their keep doing recording sessions. "We did two takes on it," Tommy Allsup said. "First one, Earl played brushes. The second one he did with sticks. It was fast for a swing tune but they played their asses off on it. Red usually played bass in a business suit, and when he heard we were doing a second take, he said, 'Excuse me, gentlemen,' and removed his jacket."

Tommy Allsup produced twenty-six sides on Willie between December 1962 and November 1963, including another Nashville session at RCA Studios, where Ray Price's pedal steel guitarist Tommy Jackson replaced Jimmy Day, and two final sessions back at Bradley's Barn in Nashville with Fred Carter Jr., Jerry Kennedy, and Wayne Moss handling the guitar chores. Some of those tracks found their way onto his second album, *Here's Willie Nelson,* on which Willie's voice was complemented by a pronounced country and swing sound, although the tracks arranged by Ernie Freeman blatantly pushed him in a pop or jazz crooner direction. "Nobody could get a handle on what he was doing," said Tommy with a shrug.

The liner notes to *Here's Willie Nelson* were written by none other than Bob Wills, who observed that Willie's style was "just right for his material," suggesting he did his songs as well as the big stars like Patsy Cline, Faron Young, and Ray Price. Willie returned the favor by opening the album with "Roly Poly," written by Fred Rose, and "Right or Wrong," both from the Texas Playboys repertoire. The pop chestnut "Am I Blue?" followed, then "The Last Letter," a sadder-than-sad song written by Rex Griffin in

1937. He did other covers — Jimmy Day's "The Way You See Me," "The Things I Might Have Been," a song popularized by his fiddling pal Wade Ray, Roger Miller's "Second Fiddle," "Let Me Talk to You," by Nashville songwriters Don Dill and Danny Davis, "Feed It a Memory," written by Hank Cochran and Justin Tubb, ET's son. The strongest songs were the four he wrote — "Half a Man," "Lonely Little Mansion," "Take My Word," and "Home Motel."

The first single, "Am I Blue?" came out of the chute fast. "Man, that was busting out of Cleveland on the radio," Tommy Allsup said. "Then the Beatles came out."

The British Invasion that began in early 1964 didn't scare Tommy Allsup, but the impact of the British rock groups caused Liberty to reassess their commitment to country while prompting Willie to assess the songwriting game, country music, the music business, and all the new sounds he was hearing. He would soon be covering the Beatles' "Yesterday" in his shows.

The sessions produced two more Liberty singles, with "Half a Man" and "You Took My Happy Away" on the A-sides. "Half a Man," a very personal, cry-in-your-beer blues peaked at number 25. "Half the country stations wouldn't play 'Half a Man' because they thought it was morbid," Tommy said.

A similar fate awaited Little Joe Carson, another Liberty artist Allsup produced, who had recorded Willie's "I Gotta Get Drunk" backed by guitarists James Burton and Glen Campbell. "That record sold a hundred thousand copies off jukebox play—five times what 'Heart to Heart Talk' sold, and that was number one," Allsup said. "But Joe Carson barely made it into the charts, no higher than number thirty-five. There was a thing about Nashville at that time. They didn't use electric bass on their recordings. Disc jockeys wouldn't play a record with an electric bass. Figure that out."

Willie was having to settle for word-of-mouth buzz and for being a musician's musician, a well-kept secret only insiders were hip to. The Liberty sessions made a fan of labelmate Timi Yuro, a soulful pop balladeer who covered Willie's "Permanently Lonely" and "Are You Sure?" and recorded duets with him on "Did I Ever Love You?" and "There's a Way." "She dug the shit out of him," Tommy Allsup said. Except to her and a few others, Willie Nelson was hardly a household name.

EVEN with royalty checks coming in, he was spending money faster than he was taking it in, paying for two wives while trying to satisfy his musical habit.

Whenever he and Shirley were staying in Fort Worth, he'd make regular stops at places like the Star Lite Club out on Highway 114 on the northwestern fringe of Dallas, a ballroom known for swing dancing and frequent visits from Bob Wills. Nice as the club was, the players and the management didn't get him like Joe Allison did. "He used to come out all the time and try to sit in, and basically they didn't take him seriously; they were laughing at him," said Mark Fields, son of Sandy Lee Fields, who co-owned the club. "They thought he sang funny." But as a genuine Nashville recording artist promoting his hits "Touch Me" and "Half a Man," he fetched a cool $300 guarantee at the two-hundred-seat room, working with the house band, Lynn Echols and the Losers.

"He had on a lime-green suit and a turtleneck sweater, and his hair was combed back. He looked really nice," Echols recalled. The Losers were a swing band with a sax player, equally schooled in Bob Wills music in "Misty," "Honky-tonk," and "Stardust," and in Jimmy Reed songs you could dirty dance the North Texas Push to. They were bluesy enough to work "nigger nights," as Echols described Sundays at the Longhorn, when colored acts played for colored audiences and, according to Echols, "there were so many blacks in there you couldn't see nothin' but white teeth." Echols and his boys saw Willie as a writer first "because he wrote all those great songs for Patsy Cline and Faron Young. I wasn't as impressed with his singing talent."

Dewey Groom booked Willie at the Longhorn Ballroom in Dallas, the dance hall formerly known as Bob Wills' Ranch House. If Willie didn't draw huge crowds, Dewey liked him well enough to never short Willie on his money. He also played the Remington and the Trianon in Oklahoma City and Cain's Academy in Tulsa, storied ballrooms from the Western Swing era, and too many small joints, dives, and lounges to count.

He worked as a solo at the Southern Club in Lawton, Oklahoma, where the house band, the Southernaires, were the stars on the bandstand on weeknights. On weekends, they backed touring acts such as Lefty Frizzell, Ray Price, Ferlin Husky, and Bob Wills.

Willie arrived with the reputation of having written "Hello Walls" and "Crazy," which usually meant he was no great shakes as a singer, a guitarist, or an entertainer. That's why they called songwriters songwriters.

"Willie, he come loping out there when it come his time to come on," Carl Cooper, the steel player in the Southernaires, said. "He came out in a suit, white shirt, tie, carrying a little acoustic guitar, and we all looked and groaned, 'Oh boy, it's gonna be a long night, here comes a strummer.' First tune he calls was 'San Antonio Rose.' Every musician has always done 'San Antonio Rose' ten thousand times. That's home ground. But not the way that Willie did it. Of course, he does his own phrasing. And when he's fired up . . . we tried to follow his phrasing and everything was all messed up. Bobby Day saw that and said, 'Boys, just hold the row. This guy knows what he's doing.' We muddled through until we got used to him. After a while it was a pretty enjoyable job because he wasn't a great singer, but he certainly was an excellent phraser."

Hard to understand, hard to keep up with, and not selling records made road work a struggle. But the Internal Revenue Service had already recognized his success. Willie owed several thousand dollars in 1963, according to the tax man, which Willie did not deny. He had never paid taxes because he'd never had the money to pay them. But whenever he was hit with a bill, he paid it. The IRS found the most efficient way to collect from Willie was to lean on the venues he played and garnish his wages, even the Nite Owl near West.

He continued gigging, playing Vegas as a single, where he developed a friendship with Curtis Potter, the former teenage singing star who fronted Hank Thompson's Brazos Valley Boys, Willie's backup band for two weeks at the Golden Nugget.

He auditioned a young band from Paris, in east Texas, who called themselves the Sundowners, at an agent's office on Haskell Street in Dallas. The players already covered "Touch Me" and a few other Willie songs, but when he ran them through "Columbus Stockade Blues," the kids from Paris folded their tent. "He was at a level way above where we were," said the group's guitarist Jerry Case. "They didn't have to say anything. It was obvious we couldn't cut it."

The Sundowners went back to Paris with their tails between their legs. But Jerry Case got a second chance to play with Willie several months later. He'd nailed down a seat in the house band at the Cavalier Club in Wichita Falls, which backed up Little Joe Carson, the singer signed to Liberty who did Willie's "I Gotta Get Drunk."

When Willie played a date at the Cavalier, backed by the house band, Jerry Case was prepared. "This time I was ready for him," Jerry said. "We backed him really nice. He was really impressed that I knew his songs. A lot of his songs were off-the-wall and he could throw a basic player pretty easy with his phrasing. Some had more than two or three chords."

Willie acknowledged Jerry's talent by asking for his phone number.

"I CAN'T afford a band yet," he told Case, "but when I do get enough money, would you be interested in joining?"

Willie never called, but Case was still flattered. "Just him asking was a real compliment."

Willie opened a date in Dallas for Roger Miller at the Sportatorium, where he met promoter Gene McCoslin. Geno, as McCoslin was known, was a hustler who knew entertainment, knew the street, and knew this Willie guy was worth booking. Willie took an instant liking to Geno because he immediately recognized he wasn't just a promoter but a real character who knew how to make money. The date was the first of hundreds Willie would do for Geno.

Willie's show posters read "Liberty Recording Artist" long after Liberty Records was bought by an electronics company called Avnet and the country division was folded by the new owners. Willie had an untitled album scheduled for release in November 1963, but the record was never released due to the reorganization at Liberty.

The album in the can included his deepest, most

tortured ballad yet, "Opportunity to Cry," in which love lost leads to murder and suicide, "At the Bottom," a miserable, depressing blues Willie had written, and "River Boy," a whimsical song that reflected the popularity of Mike Fink, the King of the Keelboaters, popularized by the *Disneyland* television series in the 1950s. "I Hope So," which was credited to Shirley, sounded like something Willie could have written. Covers comprised the rest of the album — Floyd Tillman's "Cold War with You"; "Seasons of My Heart," and "Blue Must Be the Color of the Blues," both early hits for George Jones; Hank Williams's "There'll Be No Teardrops Tonight"; "Take Me As I Am (or Let Me Go)," written by Boudleaux Bryant; Hank Thompson's "Tomorrow Night"; and Sammy Cahn and Jules Styne's "I'll Walk Alone," popularized by Dinah Shore.

Liberty had turned into a hard life lesson. The sessions in Los Angeles had introduced him to his second wife and a whole new group of musician friends. Being a recording artist had made him some kind of celebrity back in Fort Worth. But neither place, he concluded, was where he needed to be. "It just wasn't time," Willie said. If he was going to be a country music star, his destiny was in Nashville.

After finishing what would be his final sessions for Liberty, Willie signed a contract on November 22,

1963, to buy a red-brick ranch-style home on seventeen acres in Ridgetop, Tennessee, a rural community north of Goodlettsville, twenty-five miles from Music Row. That very same day, President John F. Kennedy was assassinated in Dallas, putting Texas in a different light in the eyes of the rest of the world.

Ridgetop, Tennessee, 1964

RUNNING ON THE ROAD with Shirley had been fun, but the newness had worn off for him and for her within a year of their marriage in Vegas. Mailbox money from writing songs, especially from "Crazy," which was much covered and much played, was what paid the bills, and Shirley convinced Willie to focus on that. Getting off the road to write songs made sense. And Shirley was ready to settle down after an extended run of one-nighters in a station wagon. "I was brought up to be a homemaker and a housewife. I didn't have any problems adjusting."

Hank Cochran and Hal Smith of Pamper Music agreed with Shirley. If Willie holed up and focused on writing songs, he'd be more in demand. "We kept him in Ridgetop up there and wouldn't let him work dates and wouldn't let him see nobody for many months to build up a damn mystique about him, by keeping him away from everyone," Hank Cochran reasoned. "He wore overalls, slopped hogs, and just done everything up there, but he kept writing songs."

Faron Young swore he'd cover everything Willie handed him. And Willie had given in. "Nashville is the store," he concluded. "If you have something to sell, you go to the store."

Shirley threw him the first birthday party he'd had since Abbott a few months after their move to the country. "I fried chicken and made potato salad and we cleaned the basement and had over Fred Foster and Haze Jones and Hal Smith and his wife, Velma, and just scads of people," she said.

The Ridgetop farm, purchased with royalties from "Crazy" and "Hello Walls," was far enough from Nashville to qualify as a hideout. Just as the name implied, Ridgetop was a high, densely wooded ridge with thickets of hickory, oak, pine, sycamore, weeping willow, and cedar. Wherever the woodland had been cleared, the exposed red clay and sandy loam produced abundant crops of corn, tobacco, squash, apples, pears, okra, peppers, and tomatoes.

The ridge with its hollows, springs, and creeks could have been confused with Uncle Peck and Prilla's homestead on Pindall Ridge, in Arkansas, the land where Willie's people came from. Here, Willie would live the life of a gentleman farmer who happened to be a very talented songwriter, raising hogs and chickens and horses, picking and singing and writing songs.

Over the next three years, one by one, Martha sent Billy, then Susie, and finally Lana to Ridgetop to live with their father. The itinerant country music song-writer offered more stability than their mother, the itinerant waitress. For Willie, it was a second chance to raise his kids. Billy, the youngest, was the first to arrive at the Nelson farm. He was a shy boy who thought that all parents screamed at each other when they were together, that daddies were usually gone, and that families always struggled. Willie may have been an absentee father to Billy, but at least with Shirley around, the boy would have someone to look after him.

"We were sitting on the porch right after he moved in," Shirley recalled. "He was six years old. He told me he didn't want to grow up and do anything dan-gerous. He was a sweet little boy. We all got along good." Willie tried his best to make up for lost time. "He was a good dad and spent lots of time with the kids," Shirley said. "They played out in the yard, rode horses, ate together. He would tell us, 'This is the way a family should be.' And we were a family."

The thirteen-year-old Lana and her stepmother hit it off particularly well. "We were pals. My mom hated her so much, I got along with her," she said.

It was a new role for Shirley. She had performed since she was a teenager, always onstage, in the band, always playing. Now she was a homemaker and a mom, raising three kids who were the offspring of the man she loved. Shirley instinctively kept her guitar within reach and continued writing songs and working on music, but though she didn't realize it, she was effectively retired. It was a new role for Willie, too. He wanted to do his part to ensure domestic tranquillity by swearing off the road. But when a booking came along, he'd do it.

The Mullins family down Greer Road became Billy's surrogate parents. Joel Mullins was a hard-working welder who had a great love for Woody Guthrie songs and other folk music from an earlier time. His wife, Nancy, was a tireless homemaker. They both recognized Shirley was not Supermom and that Billy Nelson needed special attention. "They took Billy in," Lana said of the Mullinses. "Billy was rebelling. He was having trouble being away from Dad. Shirley tried real hard and had good intentions," Lana said. "But there was a little boy who wanted his mother or his father and he wasn't getting either one of them. He was stuck with this person he didn't even know. The Mullinses stepped up to the plate. Mrs. Mullins coddled him, hugged him, doted over him." Billy wanted attention, and when he wasn't getting it, he would make sure he was noticed by doing things like playing with matches in the closet. His daddy was concerned but rarely there to do anything about it.

Shirley tried to run the house, best she could. "She was patient," Lana said. "She didn't lose her temper like a lot of people had." But she was human. "She wasn't on the road, singing and playing. She became this instant mother. She always wanted to have kids and never could have kids," Lana said. Now Shirley had a full-blown family, but she didn't have the man she'd run away with. Ridgetop was supposed to keep Willie home.

Other country stars put down roots in Ridgetop. Opry stars Grandpa Jones, famous for his anthem "Turn Your Radio On," and the country comedian String Bean lived nearby and would entertain residents at the local nursing home with Sunday gospel sing-ins. Sheb Wooly lived in Ridgetop. Fiddler Wade Ray was Willie's next-door neighbor. Willie's kids picked blackberries at the Rays' in the summer. Hank

Cochran and Pamper Music were a few miles below the ridge in Goodlettsville.

Willie grew a beard trimmed around the edges, enhancing his country-boy image, and put on weight from Shirley's home cooking. "He liked to eat cornbread and beans and a big onion—all that heavy stuff," Shirley said. The farmer guise was genuine, Willie swore. "It was just a replay of what I wore growing up. There's nothing more comfortable than a pair of overalls."

He took kung fu classes at a martial arts studio in Goodlettsville. Kung fu helped him practice "mind over matter." He learned to break a two-inch board or a brick with his hand, which Willie said "was a good thing to know if you're ever attacked by a brick or a board." He showed Shirley enough moves for her to put the hurt on him worse than Martha had.

One night, after Shirley tried all day to get Willie on the phone, he showed up at the front door so drunk he didn't recognize her in curlers and thought he was at the wrong house. Shirley thought he wanted to go back to town and he was so drunk, she wasn't going to let him drive. When he turned to walk away, she grabbed him and threw him headfirst through the storm door, cutting his forehead deep enough to leave a scar. "He was laying there, bleeding and all, and I thought I'd killed him," Shirley said.

Willie ran off into a pasture, where he passed out. The next morning, he woke up bug-bit in the tall grass, with a crust of blood on his head. He vowed then and there he would not teach Shirley any more moves. Shirley didn't mind. She knew enough moves. "I stood my ground with him," she said. "It worked. After I threw him through the door, he stayed home a lot more."

He tried to be a better husband and a better father, chasing Mickey Newbury off the property with a gun when the young Nashville songwriter from Texas asked Willie for the hand of his teenage daughter Lana in marriage. And he tried to be in better touch with his neighbors, flagging down one of the Greer boys, Ronald, when he saw him driving a tractor hauling wood. With winter coming on, he needed firewood and introduced himself to the twelve-year-old boy. "I'm a country singer and I'm going to be famous." He went inside and fetched a copy of *Here's Willie Nelson* to give to the boy. Ronald, more attuned to rock and roll than to country, quoted him twice the usual price for a cord of wood, figuring if he really was a country music star, he could afford the higher price, although Ronald did pick out "the best wood we had." Ronald took the record Willie gave him and put it on the turntable when he got home.

He let one side play through, then tossed the record into his closet. "I felt sorry for him," Ronald said.

Ronald was clueless about the growing cadre of believers and converts in the small circle of rowdy songwriters Willie ran with in Nashville. A half hour from his country retreat were hangouts where making up rhymes, telling lies, passing around a guitar and a bottle, swapping songs, and swapping pills was called work.

The guitar pullings at the Downtowner Motor Inn were particularly serious affairs. Joe Allison told Tommy Allsup a surefire way to hear songs was to rent two rooms, one to sleep in and the other for picking, and stock the second room with a hundred bucks' worth of booze. "You'll get every songwriter in Nashville to come and hear songs before the song publisher does," Allison said.

"I remember they did an extended guitar pulling that lasted five days and five nights and Roger Miller never went to bed," Tommy Allsup said. "Willie to me was the big dog writer in Nashville. He was the guy all the songwriters would come out to see. If we was in the Downtowner, you could be sure five to ten songwriters would be in there. I never saw a reaction to another writer like there was with Willie."

Willie bought another hundred acres of pasture

down the road for his cattle and pigs, some of which he named Lester Earle and the Foggy Mountain Hogs. He'd invite Hank Cochran up to the house to sit by the fireplace and read the Bible to Hank for hours. Home was great. But it wasn't the same as playing for people.

"He had to have his little kingdom on the road," Shirley eventually figured out. "That's what made him happy." Shirley Nelson had tried to adjust and ended up blaming herself. "I loved him so much that my understanding really left," she said. "I would get calls when he was out on the road and I never did think he did anything wrong. I thought it was me. Maybe I wasn't a good enough mother because I'd never had any kids and didn't know anything about raising kids and here I was, raising three kids. I didn't know anything about running a home."

After a while, Willie's absences didn't make Shirley's heart grow fonder. Instead, she grew jealous, knowing he was prone to mess around on the road whenever a pretty young thing showed up after a gig. In her loneliness, missing the stage and the attention that came with it, Shirley became involved with men other than her husband. "That was her way with dealing with Willie being gone," Lana said. "She didn't hide having lovers, because we were friends. She felt like I would never tell. I didn't. Susie told."

Finding comfort in other partners was a repeat of the Willie and Martha saga, done partly out of need, partly to get back at their spouse.

DESPITE his initial efforts, family took a backseat to career again. After Liberty Records' country division folded in 1964, Willie talked to Chet Atkins about signing a recording contract with RCA, the top country label in Nashville. But at the last minute, he convinced himself he'd found a more willing ear in Fred Foster, a native of the mountains of western North Carolina who'd come of age in Washington, DC, hustling songs and promoting records. Foster came to Nashville to record a song with Billy Grammer, the guitarist from *The Jimmy Dean Show* with whom he'd reworked a traditional folk song in the public domain into "Gotta Travel On." Subsequent success with the made-in-Nashville recordings of "The Shag (Is Totally Cool)," by Billy Graves, and Grammer's "Bonaparte's Retreat" prompted Foster to move his small label, Monument Records, to Nashville in 1959.

A fan of eclectic artists and enduring songs, Foster struck gold as the guiding light behind Roy Orbison's biggest hit records, which burnished his reputation as a Nashville outsider, tight with neither Owen

Bradley and the Decca crew nor Chet Atkins at RCA. Wesley Rose, who'd dropped Roy Orbison from RCA before Foster signed him, ambushed Foster at a luncheon once, asking, "We want to know why you're trying to destroy Nashville. What have you got against Nashville? You're cutting all that nigger music. We had a great thing going until you showed up and messed it up. We're the country music capital of the world, and you're cutting all that crap."

Fred Foster did not have an office along Music Row but in suburban Hendersonville in a building owned by songwriter Boudleaux Bryant. His free lunches for music people, known as Foster's Follies, attracted Harlan Howard, Hank Cochran, Willie Nelson, and others from nearby Pamper Music. Willie liked to sing his latest songs for Fred, and Fred liked hearing them.

In the early summer of 1964, Fred Foster signed Willie to a three-year recording contract with the promise he could make records on his own terms and Fred would promote the product. A recording session at the Monument studio next to the Clarkston Hotel was promptly scheduled in July to figure out how to get this cool cat in a cardigan a hit. Three Willie originals were recorded—"(There'll Be) Someone Waiting for You," "King of a Lonely Castle," and "To Make a Long Story Short." Willie sang and played guitar. Bill Justis, who had had his own hit with the instrumental "Raunchy," led the session, which included old familiars Harold Bradley, Ray Edenton, Bob Moore, harmonica player Charlie McCoy, and Buddy Harman, and a pianist named Bill Pursell, who'd had his own Top 10 hit with "Our Winter Love" and also played in the Nashville Symphony and taught at Vanderbilt. The recordings were garnished with a xylophone, vibes, French horn, and trumpets.

A second session with a smaller combo of David Parker, a classical guitarist from Georgia, on guitar, Bob Moore on bass, Jack Greubel on drums, and Boots Randolph on sax, produced five more songs. One Willie composition called "I Never Cared for You" became the A-side of the single issued on Monument b/w "You Left a Long, Long Time Ago," despite a complaint from Bob Moore to Foster that Willie was singing so out of meter he was impossible to follow. "If you can't play with him, just lay out," Foster advised. "I'll overdub it." Moore had played Willie sessions before, and Foster knew the basis of the complaint was an old story in country music. "Fred Rose told me Hank Williams had the same tendency," Foster said. "During the recording of 'Cold, Cold Heart' he held the vocal two beats too long to be in meter, or cut it off two beats too quick to be in meter. If you're dancing, your foot's in the air. Rose said, 'Hank, it's not in meter. There's a two-four bar in here on "heart." On "apart" I suggest you hold it two more beats.' Hank said, 'Mr. Rose, I don't know nothing about no meter. I thought that was something on the wall to tell you how much electricity you're using. I tell you what I do know. When I get to a note I like, I'm going to hold it till I get ready to turn it loose. You'll just have to watch me.' "

David Parker's flamenco guitar lead on "I Never Cared for You" suggested a Marty Robbins gunfighter ballad, but the words were far more complex than the Anglicized corridos Marty sang. The dark love song cut straight to the bone, painting a portrait of passion, rejection, and desperation, seething and sizzling under the surface:

The sun is filled with ice and gives no warmth at all
the skies were never blue
the stars are raindrops searching for a place to fall
and I never cared for you

The single flopped nationally. Those lyrics were way too dense for mainstream country and western. Country radio programmers shared Chet Atkins's assessment of the song as "weird." If anything, the lyrical imagery he conjured was as deep as the folk-rock of Bob Dylan, the nasally singer-songwriter who'd found his voice with profound pieces of poetic commentary such as "Blowin' in the Wind" and "The Times They Are A-Changin'." Country music harbored only a few free spirits whose words compelled the listener to pay attention, notably Johnny Cash, whose compositions reflected the blue-collar, working-man foundation of America and established him as the king of folk-country music.

But the single of "I Never Cared for You" got enough airplay back home to tour Texas behind the record, which kept Willie on the road chasing guarantees. Houston was the only big city in America where the single was a radio hit. KIKK, the big country station in what was growing into the top country music market in the United States, gave the single enough spins for KILT, the powerhouse pop music station of Houston, to add the single too, crossing the record over from country. KILT was one of three Texas radio stations owned by Gordon McLendon, the Dallas radio innovator who helped invent the Top 40 format in the 1950s that became a critical component in the global explosion of rock and roll.

ONE faithful KILT listener was a statuesque blonde two years out of Galena Park High School named

Connie Koepke. She considered herself a rock and roll and soul gal, partial to Elvis, Jimmy Reed, and James Brown, as were the majority of white teenagers in urban Texas and the South. But "I Never Cared for You" was different. She liked it so much she switched over to KIKK, the country station, to hear the song more often. Connie was working the night shift in a glass factory in Houston when she heard that the singer of the song would be appearing at the 21 Club in Conroe, in the Piney Woods just north of Houston. She traded out her regular night shift to go hear him with her girlfriend Jackie.

Bassist Eddie Rager couldn't help but notice the two pretty young women seated behind a girder in the back of the club. Why didn't they come sit up front by the stage at the band's table? Connie Koepke got a close enough view of Willie Nelson to be smitten. She checked his ring finger for a wedding band but saw none. (Willie, like many musicians, knew well enough to remove his ring when he was onstage so as not to disappoint female fans and to keep his options open.) She flipped when he sang "I Never Cared for You," letting the lyrics do all the talking. He sang the song in person with even more passion than he did on the record, she thought.

During a set break, Jimmy Day asked Willie, "Anything I can get for you, boss?"

"That tall blonde over there," Willie replied.

Jimmy fetched Connie and seated her next to his boss so they could talk during set breaks.

The band made $784 for the night, not bad considering the cover charge was $2.

After the gig Connie and Jackie went to the motel and met the band and the owners of the 21 Club, Larry and Pat Butler. Somewhere toward daybreak, Willie asked Connie for her phone number. He came through Houston frequently, he told her, and he'd like to see her again. Willie may have been married to Shirley, but his eye couldn't help wandering, especially when he was rambling on the road. In this case, it confirmed he wasn't blind to beauty. She gave him her number but wasn't fooling herself. He was a musician. She'd never see him again. He gave Connie Crash Stewart's phone number. His Texas booking agent would know when Willie was coming through before anyone else did, himself included.

TOWARD the end of October 1964, Willie came to Fred Foster's office to pitch a Christmas song he'd written. "I know it's too late for anybody to do this year," Willie told Fred, "but listen anyway. Maybe someone can do it next year." The song was inspired by a legless man who got around on rollers and sold pencils and "pretty paper, pretty ribbons" on the sidewalks of Leonard's Department Store in downtown Fort Worth when Willie walked its red-brick streets.

"Good God!" Foster exclaimed at the end of the recitation. "It's not too late." He picked up the phone and called London, England, where Monument's biggest act, Roy Orbison, was living. He told Orbison he'd just heard a smash hit and was sending the tape of the song special delivery. "If you love it like I do, call me back with your key [to sing in]. I'll take care of the rest."

Willie's eyes widened when he heard what Foster was doing.

Two days later, Orbison called back. It was a go.

Less than a week later, Roy Orbison lay on a sofa in the Decca studios in London, fighting off a fever of 102 while Fred Foster and Bill Justis finished the orchestral arrangement with the symphony they'd hired. Each violinist wore experimental custom microphones around their neck that Decca engineers had designed for amplification of the strings. Once the symphony was set, Roy rose from the sofa, feverish and flu-ridden, and sang "Pretty Paper." He nailed his vocal in one take.

But by the time "Pretty Paper" was released in late November, Willie was no longer with Monument. The excitement that "I Never Cared for You" stirred up in Houston had already been forgotten. The split was over the full-page color advertisement in all the music trade publications that Fred Foster had promised Willie when he signed him. The label had planned a dual release of Willie's single "I Never Cared for You," aimed at the country market, and a single by Lloyd Price that was aimed at the rhythm and blues audience. Foster was gambling both would cross into the mainstream. Lloyd Price's ad looked fine, Willie's not so much. The colors ran and bled, rendering the lettering illegible.

"Willie got upset when he saw it and in a huff went to RCA," Fred Foster said. "Willie says he intended to sign with RCA all along, but if he did, why did he sign a three-year contract with me? I think he got drunk when he was so upset and went and signed with RCA. We only got one record out. I could have caused him problems because I had a signed contract. But rather than lose Willie as a friend, I let it go. I wanted to keep him as a friend if I couldn't keep him as an artist."

Two weeks later RCA released its first single on Willie Nelson. Even if he was no match for Roy Orbison, Willie and the label wanted to show up Fred Foster. It was his version of "Pretty Paper."

• • •

RIGHT before Thanksgiving, Willie raised his profile another notch when Ott Devine, the stage manager of the Opry responsible for extending membership invitations, issued a press release that was announced from the stage of the Ryman: Willie Nelson was joining the Grand Ole Opry. He was a solid choice, still riding the reputation of "Crazy," "Hello Walls," and "Family Bible," and now he was an RCA recording artist. He made his debut on the stage of the Ryman four nights later.

The Opry crowd was not like audiences back in Texas. "If you're playing a dance place [like in Texas]," Willie said, "you want them to hit the floor every time and dance." The Opry was a sit-down affair, restricting shows of appreciation to clapping, cheering, standing up, or dancing in place.

"I would do different songs when I played the Opera," as Willie called it, "and I would do different rhythms because I knew up-tempo things were good. Anything to get the old people tapping their feet and clapping their hands was good, and I don't mean that in a derogatory way. These folks, it was good for them, spiritually, physically, mentally, to start clapping their hands and moving. That's one of the things I learned early: Get some audience participation."

"The Grand Ole Opry was the first time I'd seen Daddy play," Lana Nelson said. "It was bigger than life. I was on the fourth row. He was there with the Glaser Brothers. He always played honky-tonks, and they wouldn't let a girl like me in. I never got to see him play till the Opry."

Joining the Opry was a smart move politically and careerwise, exposing his music to a national radio audience. He needed the exposure, even though early on, the Opry announcer once introduced him as Woody Nelson.

In spite of stars such as Flatt & Scruggs, Roy Acuff, Minnie Pearl, Hank Snow, Bill Monroe, Jean Shepard, and Porter Wagoner, the Opry cast was in sore need of new blood in 1964. Other barn dances like the Louisiana Hayride and Big D Jamboree were fading and the road was decimating the Opry's ranks. Willie's biggest song benefactor, Patsy Cline, and two other Opry cast regulars, Hawkshaw Hawkins and Cowboy Copas, died in an airplane crash ninety miles from Nashville on March 5, 1963. Singer Jack Anglin was killed in a car wreck on the way to Patsy's funeral. On March 29 that same year, another Opry cast member, whom Willie had worked with in Houston, Texas Ruby, perished in a house fire. On the last day of July of 1964, another plane crash, ten miles south of Nashville, took the lives of Gentleman Jim Reeves, one of the Opry's most popular stars, and his pianist and manager, Dean Manuel. On

December 6, two weeks after Willie joined country music's most prestigious family, twelve members were kicked out.

"Opry Drops 12 Top Stars" screamed the front-page headline of the *Nashville Tennessean* on December 6, 1964. George Morgan, Don Gibson, Johnny Wright, the Jordanaires, Faron Young, Ferlin Husky, Chet Atkins, Kitty Wells, Stonewall Jackson, Ray Price, and Justin Tubb had not fulfilled their obligation to play twenty-six dates a year, as their contracts stipulated. Minnie Pearl, saint that she was, took a leave of absence. They were all denied the use of the Grand Ole Opry on their showbills and advertising as well as exposure on the radio show and on the syndicated television series that had just started up.

It didn't take long for Willie to join the exiles. Doing the math, he realized the Opry was holding him back. Less than a year after he joined, Willie left, allegedly after asking Ott Devine if he could play with his own band on the show and Devine demurred. "Willie, a lot of the members would like that too," he said condescendingly.

"Okay," Willie said, walking away without saying anything. He just didn't come back.

"I quit the Opry because I couldn't afford it," he said. "You had to play Texas to make any money—at least I did. I'd go down there and work Friday, Saturday, and Sunday, but I couldn't work down there on Friday, Saturday, and Sunday and work the Opry too. You had to be there twenty-six weeks of the year, and if I did that, I'd miss half of the weekends in Texas, and I just couldn't do that. The prestige of working the Grand Ole Opry was nice. I loved saying I was on the Opera. But as great as it was, just because you were a member didn't mean you were going to run out there and set the woods on fire. You might have to get with three or four other members of the Opry and get on a package show and open for Grandpa Jones and several others. I didn't mind doing that, and did that. I already knew I could do pretty good in the nightclubs."

Willie liked to tell about being so miserable in Nashville that he lay down on Broadway, trying to get someone to run him over late one night but nobody would—though it sounded more like a drunken dare than attempted suicide. Nashville was actually treating him pretty good. He could swim in Webb Pierce's guitar-shaped swimming pool or putter around Old Hickory Lake on Hank Cochran's boat, listen to jazz musician Gary Burton play vibes at Boots Randolph's club in Printer's Alley, or watch fellow Texan Candy Barr do a striptease at the Rainbow. Being in Nashville meant easy access to recording studios, booking agents, song publishers, television studios, and shows like *Country Music Time,* a radio program sponsored by the United States Air Force and broadcast around the world on the Armed Forces Radio Network.

Willie's official base of operations was the house he'd bought from Bobbie and Paul Tracy in Fort Worth, which he still owned. His checks read "WN Enterprises, 2921 Morrell, WA 3-7659, Ft. Worth, 15, Texas," including one for $150 that bounced, made out to Johnny Bush for playing some road dates. The business was in Texas because that's where his audience was. "Whenever I'd run into him," Johnny Gimble said, "he'd say, 'Let's go to Texas and play some dances.' "

Performing in a bar with a bandstand brought more satisfaction than singing two tunes at the Ryman, where whiskey-drinking, pussy-chasing, backroom gambling, and carousing were officially frowned upon. Hidebound tradition couldn't match the pay or pleasure of a one-nighter, no matter how tight the space was in the station wagon pulling a trailer. Staying in motels and being able to leave behind whatever mess you made, night after night, day after day, made you feel like you were at least going somewhere as the fading memory of the last town and the last performance shrank into a vanishing point in the rearview mirror.

But to work the road successfully, Willie had to be a recording star. Now Chet Atkins, the player's player who'd risen up the ranks under Steve Soles to take the reins of the Nashville division of RCA, was his guide. Chet was the champion of the Nashville Sound, which aimed to reach a larger audience. Willie wanted to reach a bigger audience too. But in order to do so, he would have to mesh with the efficient system Chet had built.

Chet Atkins brought in the cream of session players for the November 1964 session for "Pretty Paper" and the Harlan Howard/Hank Cochran collaboration "What a Merry Christmas This Could Be." Pig Robbins played piano, Pete Drake pedal steel, and Henry Strzelecki bass, while Kenny Buttrey drummed and Jerry Reed Hubbard and Velma Smith, Hal Smith's wife, split guitar duties. The vocal chorus included Velma and Ray Stevens. Willie was leader, playing lead guitar and singing vocals. He squeezed in two of his own tunes, "Talk to Me," a plaintive midtempo ballad with echoing choruses that recalled "Hello Walls," and "Healing Hands of Time," a lush ballad with violins and viola adding to the stirring spirituality of the lyrics.

Willie returned to the studio in December with Harold Bradley, Ray Edenton, Henry Strzelecki, Buddy Harman, Floyd Cramer, Pig Robbins, and the

Anita Kerr Singers to cut two tracks in phonetic German for Chet and coproducer Wolf Kabitzsky, "Whisky Walzer" and "Little Darling," which was "Pretty Paper" *in deutsch,* as well as his version of "Don't Fence Me In," the Cole Porter cowboy song written from a poem by an engineer named Bob Fletcher. RCA wanted to tap into Germany, the third-largest record market in the world, which bought a disproportionately large amount of country music made in the USA. The single would help pave the way for a place on a package show tour of Germany starring Hank Snow with *der Country-Boy aus Texas.*

Most of the same cast returned for sessions in January and April 1965, accumulating enough tracks to make an album. Willie's debut LP for RCA, *Country Willie: His Own Songs,* was a countrypolitan effort that resurrected "Mr. Record Man," "Funny How Time Slips Away," "Hello Walls," and "Night Life." The album also introduced originals, such as the spiritual-on-the-surface, creepy-and-dark-when-you-think-about-it "Healing Hands of Time," along with "Darkness on the Face of the Earth" and two numbers that spoke of Willie's evolving personal philosophy, "My Own Peculiar Way" and "One Day at a Time." The songs were wrapped in overwrought semi-orchestral arrangements not unlike what Ernie Freeman did for his Liberty recordings.

The content was fairly sophisticated stuff aimed at the not-so-sophisticated guy in the corner of the local beer joint, alone and lonely, pouring nickels and quarters into the jukebox to hear songs that were sadder and more miserable than he was.

Sales were puny, the one exception again being Texas, where the album solidified Willie's standing as a genuine Nashville star, one sure way to sell tickets to a show.

HITCHING up with Ernest Tubb's syndicated television show, where Willie would make some 150 appearances over the course of six years from 1965 to 1971, spoke of country music's growing clout as well as his own potential as a TV personality. ET was a Nashville institution, a one-man empire who was a touring entertainer, recording artist, Grand Ole Opry star, owner of a world-famous record shop on Broadway, and host of the live midnight jamboree that followed the Grand Ole Opry Saturday-night broadcasts on WSM 650. No matter what people thought of his froggy voice or simpler-than-simple approach to music, Tubb was a role model in how to be a country star, always reminding viewers to "be better to your neighbors and you'll have better neighbors" and thanking the crowd after the last song of the dance by flipping over his guitar to reveal the message "Thanks A Lot" on the back of his instrument.

Ernest Tubb's show, "thirty minutes of the finest TV entertainment," was produced by Hal Smith, Ray Price's partner at Pamper Music and Willie's sometimes manager. Pamper's booking agency worked Tubb as well as Willie and other acts, so the exposure on the tube benefited all parties involved. Though its clout could not compare with radio's clout in the mid-1960s, TV was seen as another vehicle to sell records and tickets, largely through broadcasts of live-music variety shows such as the Big D Jamboree, and syndicated programs such as the one hosted by Porter Wagoner, with the Pretty Miss Norma Jean and, later, his new partner, Dolly Parton. Buck Owens, the Bakersfield, California, country singer, taped his program in Oklahoma City, where he learned the business and technology of television from the ground up. Perhaps the greatest sign of TV's embrace of country was Johnny Cash hosting his own network variety show during prime time.

Willie was *The Ernest Tubb Show*'s face of modern country, his cardigan wool sweaters and turtlenecks a cosmopolitan contrast to the beehive hairdos of the women singers and the cartoonish sartorial splendor of the Texas Troubadours in their sparkly western suits and western hats with the brim riding higher than the crown. They were descendants of hillbillies. Willie looked like a member of Frank Sinatra's Rat Pack. He was there for his musical talents, and his smooth, sad ballads and hit reprisals fit in with the cast of Ernest, Cal Smith, Jack Greene, Buddy Charlton, and the other Texas Troubadours, who could play as hot as any swing band or play it straight and tight like a honky-tonk band.

Willie revealed brief flashes of his developing finger-picking style on several models of acoustic Gibson guitars he played, but mostly it was the timbre of Willie's voice that left an impression. He reminded viewers at home of Ernest with his unapologetic twang of an accent, though his timbre more closely resembled Lefty Frizzell's and Leon Payne's. In that respect, he sang like no one else on TV except maybe Wade Ray, the featured fiddler on the show who also liked to move his voice in front of and behind the beat. Even when he joined the Johnson Sisters on "Crazy" and "One Day at a Time" or flirted with edgy by doing "I Never Cared for You" as if he were a folk-rocker, he used his voice like an improvised instrument, redeeming himself during the Sacred Song segment of the program when he sang songs of praise, including his own "Family Bible" and "Kneel at the Foot of Jesus."

Willie played his songs, smiled for the camera, but

offered precious little banter. Like Bob Wills, Willie preferred letting the music do his talking, which may have been why there was no *Willie Nelson Show* on television.

"Hal Smith produced [Ernest Tubb on TV]," Willie said. "Personally, I loved Ernest and all the guys in the band. I had a crush on one of the Johnson Sisters, so that helped a lot. He had a great band. But then I was watching everybody else [who had a show, like Roger Miller, Glen Campbell, and Mel Tillis] crash and burn and I knew why. Roger didn't make it because they wouldn't let him be Roger. Glen Campbell was the same thing. Once the corporate people got in there, they took over their deal. It made me not want to do TV."

His ET association influenced his second RCA album, *Country Favorites: Willie Nelson Style*. Like his second Liberty album, the recording made in mid-December 1965 had a strong Western Swing flavor. At Willie's request, he was backed up by the Texas Troubadours (Buddy Charlton, Jack Greene, Jack Drake, Cal Smith, and Leon Rhodes) along with his buddy Wade Ray, pianist Pig Robbins, and bassist James Wilkerson. The pairing made musical and commercial sense, since the Troubadours knew Willie's work from the television show and tours and were regarded as an ensemble with enough appeal to make their own records for Decca sans Ernest. With Chet Atkins once again at the controls, Willie's performing talents were showcased on covers of Lawton Williams's Texas dance-hall classic "Fraulein," Harlan Howard's "Heartaches by the Number," two Hank Cochran tunes, the Fred Rose swing number "Home in San Antone," a reprisal of "Columbus Stockade Blues" that would better have been left off compared with the fiery earlier versions he'd recorded with Shirley Collie for Liberty Records, a spirited interpretation of "My Window Faces the South," first popularized by Bob Wills, and an exquisite interpretation of Wills's trademark "San Antonio Rose." No Willie originals were included.

The counterintuitive approach paid off. Although singles were still the engine of the business, al-bums were beginning to sell on their own almost as well as they did in the pop and rock fields, where they were no longer just two singles with a bunch of filler material in between. When *Country Favorites* was released in early 1966, it stayed on the country albums chart for seventeen weeks, peaking at number 9. Trend spotters could make much of the photograph of Willie on the album cover, wearing a powder-blue fuzzy wool pullover with matching pink and white diamonds on the chest, looking very uncountry.

The way he had dressed since leaving Ray Price said a lot about where his head was at. "I had to wear those Nudie suits [with Ray]," Willie said, referring to the rhinestone suits favored by country stars. "I had a pink one with rhinestones and a blue one with rhinestones. Ray was doing that, Porter was doing that, Webb was doing that, everybody had on the Nudie suits."

He was not like them. "I personally liked to dress up, wear [business] suits," he said. His heroes had been cowboys, but *Playboy* provided the fashion cues. When The House of Lords [a Nashville clothier] came up with a bunch of clothes they wanted him to wear, he was game. "I said, 'Fuck, yeah! Free clothes! What else you got?' I enjoyed dressing up." And dressing down.

According to the official Willie Nelson souvenir program sold at Willie Nelson shows, Willie Nelson was really a farmer and a rancher who happened to dabble in entertainment. He was pictured in the program wearing dark shades and doing a variety of farm chores. One photograph showed him sitting astride his Ford 3000 tractor. "Farming is my business and songwriting is my hobby," the program quotes Willie saying. "I can make a good living working the farm, and it would bug me if I thought I had to make it writing. The pressure would get to me. Yet it is sure nice and I'm fortunate to have a hobby that is financially profitable."

He'd accumulated more land and more animals by 1966, including a four-hundred-acre produce farm where twenty-five brood sows produced eight hundred Duroc and Poland China hogs a year, along with two acres of cultivated tobacco and a two-hundred-acre ranch where his Black Angus cattle grazed on clover, fescue, and lespedeza grasses alongside a stable of horses that included three Tennessee Walkers and two palominos and a three-year-old quarterhorse named Preacher. The operation was overseen by his right-hand man, George Hughes.

In 1966, Willie repaid his long ago $500 debt to Faron Young, who'd loaned him the money rather than buy his rights to "Hello Walls," by delivering a $50,000 bull to Faron's ranch with a sign hanging around its neck that read "No Bull. Paid In Full." Faron pawned the bull to Jimmy C. Newman, another country singer and gentleman farmer who lived nearby. "It was show livestock, a Simmental bull bred in Switzerland that he bought at an auction," Jimmy C. Newman said. "It weighed three thousand pounds. I started wondering what I'd gotten myself into. I took care of that bull for a year or two, but it was so big, I wouldn't let my cows breed with him. I used him for AI [artificial insemination]."

Ridgetop also led to an extended estrangement from Ray Price over a chicken. "I had a game rooster," Ray said. "Willie said I could bring him out there to be cock of the walk with Willie's hens. The rooster didn't like the hens and he tried to kill 'em. So Shirley got upset at Willie and said, 'If you don't kill it, I'm going to kill it.' Willie called me, so I told a worker to go get him, and he didn't, so Willie killed it." Ray was pissed at Willie for years, although he eventually conceded, "The boy should have went and got it." Was Willie a good farmer? "No," Ray said. "But I ain't either, and I was raised by one. Willie tried raising hogs for a while, and they almost ate him out of house and home. Willie's a country boy. If you gotta go broke, go broke doing what you like to do."

With his bib overalls and straw hat, he was the walking embodiment of his grandfather Daddy Nelson. Bobby Bruce, the former Texas Playboy who played with Willie on his Liberty Records sessions, got a taste of Willie as Country Boy when he dropped by Ridgetop after playing Nashville on tour with pop orchestra leader Lawrence Welk. Willie picked him up and took him home and invited neighbor Wade Ray to come over with his fiddle for a jam session in the living room, aided by frequent sips of white lightning. "Willie brought out some of the most delicious homemade corn liquor I'd ever tasted," Bobby said. "Where'd you get this?" he asked Willie.

"The town sheriff," Willie beamed.

Willie showed Bobby around his house, opening the door to the bedroom he shared with Shirley, then opening the next door, where a sheep rested on a blanket piled with hay.

"That was Pamper," Willie's daughter Lana said. "Shirley raised her with a bottle and she was always trying to get into the house. One day she jumped through the plate-glass door. So after that, we let her in." Pamper wasn't the only head of livestock being treated like a pet. Shirley had given all the chickens names. One of the horses adopted a calf named Flower. "The horse tried to cut the calf off from Dad and Mr. Hughes when they were trying to load it up to go sell it in Springfield," Lana said. "We were all bawling in the truck on the way to Springfield. When we got there, Dad said, 'Forget it.' We brought her back and kept her."

Tennessee to Texas, 1965

WILLIE WAS REALLY all about picking. Proof was the souvenir program sold at his shows; if he'd really been a farmer first and foremost, like the program implied, there would have been no need for a program. Even Willie wasn't buying into his own hype. "I didn't want to sit there and raise hogs and write songs," he said. "I wanted to be out there playing, going from town to town and playing my music."

When there were gigs, he'd take Wade Ray with him to Texas and elsewhere and work with house bands or pickup bands. After they had performed for several months as a duo, Willie enlisted Johnny Bush to join him again. Johnny had been barely surviving as a Cherokee Cowboy, making $25 a night to play drums behind stars making $350 a night. Tommy Hill at Starday would throw him some spare change whenever Johnny was off the road, with demo session work at $10 a pop, but Johnny wanted some of that front-man money, so he quit the Cowboys.

He went by Ridgetop to store some stuff at Willie's.

"Why did you leave Ray Price?" Willie asked Johnny.

Johnny sucked in a deep breath and unloaded. "I want to record. I want to get something going with me. I don't want to be dependent on someone else anymore."

"Would you go with me for ten days back to Texas at thirty-five bucks a night?" Willie asked him.

Johnny knew that Texas was solid ground. Willie Nelson might be a minor celebrity in Nashville but he could pull in a thousand people at the Cotton Club in Lubbock, Big G's in Round Rock, or the Reo Palm Isle in Longview on a good night just by showing up. Johnny took the bait. It was ten bucks more than Ray Price was paying him. Texas was home for Johnny too. Between the drive from Nashville to Memphis they'd done enough catching up for Willie to make Johnny an offer. "Stay with me a year and I'll produce a session on you. You find your own musicians. You find the songs. I'll pick up the tab. I'll turn that red light on for you. Then it's up to you."

Johnny turned down George Jones's offer of $50 a day to go on the road as one of the Jones Boys to cast his lot with Willie, which meant memorizing every gas stop and all-night café along the almost seven-hundred-mile drive from Nashville to Fort Worth along Highways 70, 67, and 80 — a drive they would be making several times a month.

Johnny arrived just in time to join Wade Ray on Willie's four-song recording session in June 1966, accompanying studio pros Jerry Reed and Velma Smith on guitar, Buddy Emmons on steel, Pig Robbins on piano, Junior Huskey on bass, and a full complement of strings and backup singers. Two originals — "One in a Row," a phrase borrowed from Crash Stewart, Willie's Texas booking agent, and "The Party's Over," which Claude Gray had recorded seven years earlier in Houston as "My Party's Over" — would be the A-sides of his next two singles.

IN July, Johnny Bush and Wade Ray backed Willie on the album *Live Country Music Concert*, recorded over two nights at Panther Hall, Willie's home away from home in Fort Worth. Chet Atkins was fine with

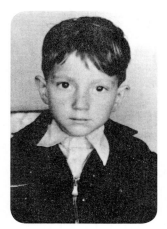

Alfred and Nancy Nelson, 1929. *(Courtesy Lana Nelson)*

Second grader Willie Hugh, 1939. *(Courtesy Lana Nelson)*

Bobbie Lee and Willie Hugh, 1946. *(Courtesy Lana Nelson)*

Shooting hoops for the Abbott High Panthers, 1948. *(Courtesy Lana Nelson)*

Willie and Bobbie (left) and Ira (right), with Bud Fletcher and the Texans, 1948. *(Courtesy Lana Nelson)*

Willie Nelson and Bobby Gibson, 1956. *(Courtesy Lana Nelson)*

Promotional photo for Texas Willie Nelson, aka Wee Willie Nelson, 1957. *(Courtesy Jurgen Koop)*

Willie, a new member of the Grand Ole Opry, 1964. *(Courtesy Jurgen Koop)*

Susie, Lana, and Billy with Daddy, 1965. *(Courtesy Lana Nelson)*

Ridgetop, Tennessee, pig farmer Willie, 1964. *(Courtesy Lana Nelson)*

Clockwise from bottom center: Willie, Jimmy Day, Johnny Bush, Ben Dorcy, Eddie Rager, and Paul English, 1966. *(Courtesy Jurgen Koop)*

Left to right: Paul English, Willie, Jimmy Day, and David Zettner, 1968. *(Courtesy Lana Nelson)*

Backstage at the Armadillo
World Headquarters, 1972.
(Burton Wilson)

Willie and Waylon,
1975. *(Scott Newton)*

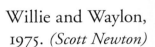

Willie and Charley Pride, 1976.
(Scott Newton)

Lana, Mother Myrle, and Willie, 1977. *(Scott Newton)*

Willie and Merle Haggard, 1980. *(Scott Newton)*

Willie and Connie Nelson, 1980. *(Scott Newton)*

Willie Nelson and Family, 1983. *(Scott Newton)*

Willie Nelson in *The Songwriter,* with Rip Torn (left) and Kris Kristofferson, 1984. *(Movie Still Archives)*

Willie receiving Indian of the Year honors, 1987. *(Pamela Moore)*

Willie with (left to right) Jody Payne, Larry Greenhill, Paul English, Grady Martin, Bee Spears, Mickey Raphael, and Bobby Arnold, 1987. *(Scott Newton)*

The two Ws, 1991.
(Scott Newton)

Willie Nelson and superstar friends at the taping of his sixtieth-birthday show, 1993. *(Scott Newton)*

Willie in the Luck
World Headquarters
saloon, 2001.
(Scott Newton)

Willie Hugh and Bobbie
Lee, 2007.
(Todd Wilson)

a live album because the cost was considerably less than a studio recording and it could be easily marketed to Willie's hard-core fans. To be on the safe side, Chet let Felton Jarvis — Elvis's producer — produce and Chip Young overdub guitar parts and add some steel guitar fills back in RCA's Nashville studio.

Willie was a Panther Hall regular, stopping in every four to six weeks to play the big room on Fort Worth's east side or the Annex across Collard Avenue, Panther Hall's own little honky-tonk that was kept darker than dark, no matter what time of day it was.

From the night Panther Hall had opened in June 1963, the building with the futuristic, eight-sided exterior that resembled a flying saucer was the country music showcase in Fort Worth and Dallas. No chicken wire was necessary to separate the bandstand from the audience. The dance floor was huge, the air-conditioning cold, and the surroundings nice, with long tables for seating. Waitresses dressed in western outfits. Even though pop tops had already been developed for beer cans in 1962, the waitresses or bartenders could still open cans quicker with a can opener (popularly known as a church key) as long as the cans were opened on the bottom, which explained why beers were served upside down.

Panther Hall was also Willie's second television home. He played Panther Hall so often, he was a semiregular on the Cowtown Jamboree, broadcast live from Panther Hall from 6:30 to 7:30 p.m. every Saturday to viewers in the Fort Worth–Dallas area to hype the show later the same night. The televised portion of Jamboree was hosted at various times by popular Fort Worth disc jockeys Bill Mack, Bo Powell, and Dale Wood. The primitive production was so notoriously horrible that "Buck Owens always seemed to take sick just before the broadcasts, only to recover in time to play the show later that night," Bill Mack noted. Hank Thompson flat out refused to appear.

But KTVT was the first nonnetwork independent channel in North Texas and an early adapter of an emerging technology called cable television. In isolated pockets all over the United States where cable was available, KTVT was often part of the channel lineup, which meant the Cowtown Jamboree Live from Panther Hall had a nationwide, albeit limited, audience. Front and center was Willie Nelson, dapper in outfits that ranged from bow ties to a brown suit with a turtleneck sweater—a marked contrast to typical country music couture.

Willie's relationship with Panther Hall had been cemented by Bo Powell, a disc jockey at KCUL, who started at Fort Worth's country music station in November 1963. "I always looked on the record to see who wrote the song," he explained. "It seems like every good song I was hearing was written by Willie Nelson." The singles and albums that Willie put out under his own name impressed him too, which is why Bo was surprised to hear Panther Hall's co-owner Corky Kuykendall complain one night, "I really like Willie Nelson, but he doesn't draw worth a shit as a headline act, and he's getting too expensive to bring in to open for somebody else."

"Tell you what," Bo Powell offered Corky. "Bring him in as a single act and give me thirty days advance. I'll bet you a pair of cowboy boots I can fill this place."

Bo had a 50,000-watt radio station to cover his bet. "It got kind of embarrassing," he said. "After a while, everything I'd play on the air would either be a Willie Nelson song or Willie Nelson singing."

By eight p.m. the night of the show, there was a line snaking outside the building all the way to Collard Avenue. Corky Kuykendall was more than happy buying Bo Powell a pair of cowboy boots. He told Willie about the bet and suggested he drop in on Bo at the station. "He's really a fan of yours and he plays the hell out of your songs." Willie showed up at KCUL with a demo of a new song. He and Bo went

to the production room at KCUL and listened to
"The Party's Over."

"What do you think?" Willie asked. Bo reckoned
it was a hit.

Willie had found another friendly ear in radio,
which in his line of work was as important as finding
a record label to put out your records. KCUL and
especially Bo Powell showcased Willie Nelson with
as many as three singles charting simultaneously on
the station's Top 30 survey. When Jack Clement at
RCA called Bo to inform him the record label was
going to record a live album on Willie at Panther
Hall, he said Willie wanted Bo to be master of ceremonies.

"I'll do it on a stretcher if I have to," Bo said.

Bo Powell's booming voice introduced Willie Nelson with all the flair of a wrestling announcer. The
live music concert recording that followed validated
Willie Nelson as a songwriter and a performer as he
covered his own songs and songs of other composers.
The material suggested he had eclipsed his earlier
goals of being the next Ray Price or Ernest Tubb and
was striving to be an even more distinctive voice.

The recording replicated the heart of the Willie
Nelson Show. "Wade Ray was a ripping swing fiddle
player and with the house band would just destroy
the audience," Johnny said. "Wade would call me up

and I'd sing for a while so the audience would dance their ass off. Then we'd get the house band off the stage, Wade would go to bass and I would go to drums, and we'd call Willie up."

Johnny would invite the audience to move in closer. Most of Willie's songs were too blue or circumspect for a Ray Price shuffle. Instead of two-stepping, the crowd stood and watched as if he were a folk singer or sat at the long tables, drinking whiskey out of brown bags. Either way, Willie made them listen.

"It had a lot to do with me singing my own songs and performing as a songwriter," Willie said. "I felt it was important that they understood what I was saying. A loud band behind me would interfere with what I was trying to say. If they can't understand my lyrics, which were a little different to begin with, or some of the chord progressions which were different, too much production would be confusing."

The stripped-down ensemble with Willie playing guitar covered the Beatles' "Yesterday" with its "weird changes" that the three had rehearsed back in Ridgetop. Willie's fealty to Bob Wills's philosophy of presentation by never giving the audience time to catch their breath was underscored by three medleys of originals. The first strung together "Mr. Record Man," "Hello Walls," and "One Day at a Time." The second medley of "The Last Letter" and "Half a

Man" emphasized sad themes. The third medley of "Opportunity to Cry" and "Permanently Lonely" was even sadder.

Unlike Wills's music, most of the album's material was not dance tunes but songs that told a story. One in particular, "I Just Can't Let You Say Goodbye," bordered on psycho-creepy. Willie had read about a crime of passion in the newspaper and used his imagination to take it one step further. Delivered in an up-tempo Latin rhythm, it was told from the perspective of a man so distraught over his breakup and so upset by the bad things his lover is saying to him that he gets pissed off and strangles her to death. Country music was a hotbed of twisted tales. Next to songs such as "I'm Gonna Kill You" (". . . and forever shut your cheatin' bedroom eyes/ . . . and cut you up in a box half your size"), a collaboration between Jimmy Velvet and Wynn Stewart, or the ditty by Willie's old D Records labelmate from Houston, Eddie Noack, "You Think I'm Psycho, Don't You, Mama?" Willie's happy downers were rather tame by comparison.

The cover of *Live Country Music Concert* depicted a clean-cut, clear-eyed, confident young man in a dark suit, white shirt, and skinny tie, hair slicked back, face beaming as he sang while playing a Fender Jazzmaster electric guitar, with the banner "Cowtown Jamboree, Panther Hall, Fort Worth, Texas" hanging behind him. A deep thinker hunkered beneath his urbane, country-club-sophisticate exterior, someone who was in fact the polar opposite of the image he was projecting. On the back of the album cover was another photograph of Willie as a sharp-dressed man in a suit and tie, with the words "None To Compare To Willie Nelson" imposed over the picture.

The album enjoyed decent sales in Texas and lousy sales almost everywhere else. What the bean counters couldn't see was a very small number of younger fans more attuned to rock than country who were getting hip to Willie's trip. And the live album was validation for Willie because it showcased his work with his own band. "I wanted to record with my band so I could reproduce every night what I was doing in the studio, but no one would let me do that," he said. "I recorded with studio musicians and made really good records, but there was no fucking chance of doing them on the road because those guys didn't travel."

That's what people came to hear—the sound that they bought on the record. But using your road band in the studio was a foreign concept in Nashville. Precious few artists got away with making records with the band they played with on tour, the notable exceptions being Hank Williams, Little Jimmy Dickens, and Bob Wills. Except for the live album, Willie would have to learn to live within the system and "just play the song and forget it."

RATHER than chafe against the system, he was trying to be more accepting of it for what it was. His attitude was informed by a growing interest in personal fulfillment. Wade Ray, Willie's Ridgetop neighbor and his steadiest road companion, turned Willie on to a spiritual organization known as Astara. The group embraced a lot of the ideas and thinking that Johnny Bush and Willie had read in Kahlil Gilbran's *The Prophet* and in the writings of the psychic Edgar Cayce. Concepts such as reincarnation, an afterlife, and astral traveling were nothing new to them. "*The Prophet* made sense to us," Johnny Bush said. "If you're going to do anything, like be a baker, make that bread as if you're making it for the person you love the most."

Astara took that kind of thinking one step beyond. Wade and his wife, Grace, were avid followers of the discipline that Willie later described as a "mystery school," leading him to spend time in libraries reading about religion in general and specific religions around the world. He became as well versed in the concept of reincarnation as he was in the Bible. Going through this world and getting it right the first time was a tough go, he concluded. He arrived at this way of thinking by taking note of the millions of people who suffered, starved to death, or were massacred. "You wonder why a just and loving God would let things like that happen. I figured that there was more to it than what we see. I knew there was something else at work, calling the shots. Then I learned about the law of karma, that you live more than one time until you get it right, and if you want to come back one more time and show off, that's okay too. I started thinking and believing that, and the more I saw, the more I knew it made sense. It was like going to school: Pass your lessons in the first grade and you advance to the second grade. If you don't, you repeat first grade again to learn what you missed the first time."

Johnny began to look at Willie as more than a friend and a benevolent bandleader. He was a teacher and a spiritual guide who gave good advice, but always with caveat "Take it or leave it. It worked for me. It may not work for you."

Johnny had never forgotten a sit-down he had had with Willie a few years earlier while preparing for a run on the road with Jimmy Day, Paul Buskirk, and Dave Kirby. Johnny fretted over his ability to hold his own with the other musicians in the band and had confessed to Willie that he might not be cut out for the job playing in the band. "What the fuck are you talking about?" Willie told Johnny with fire in his eyes. "You're a negative thinker, do you know that?"

"I always thought I was a realist," Johnny replied. "Weren't you at the rehearsal today?"

"You're not Gene Krupa," Willie acknowledged. "But you're a good drummer and you're going to get better. Your main problem is you're a negative thinker and you've got to stop it. Set your sights high, and even if you don't hit as high, look how much better off you are than when you started." Johnny took Willie's advice to heart. His faith in Willie remained strong after that.

For all his vocal disgust toward negativity, Willie could bring it on himself at times. Rayovac flashlight batteries put together gigantic Country & Western Road Show package tours with twenty acts that would tour coast-to-coast for a year. The head of the company, Art Anderson, was such a big Willie Nelson fan that he let Willie choose many of the acts for the 1966 tour, which included Webb Pierce, Carl Smith, and Ray Price. At one of the first shows in Key Biscayne, Florida, Art Anderson showed up along with Fort Worth disc jockey Bo Powell to visit with Willie. Sideman Johnny Bush was thrilled to be on the tour because he was starving on Willie's schedule of ten to twelve dates a month.

"I heard this familiar monotone saying, 'Well, as far as I'm concerned, you can take your Rayovac batteries and stick them up your ass,'" Johnny Bush said. "Then I heard Art saying, 'If that's the way you feel about it, then that's the way I feel about it.' The next day I asked Willie, What was that all about?" Willie said Art had been bugging him for a while and he was tired of listening to him.

"Willie, this is three hundred shows. Is there any way this can be . . . ?" Johnny asked.

"Not as far as I'm concerned," Willie said, cutting Johnny off. He knew what he wanted. Willie went back to playing dates on his own while Johnny Bush and the rest of the band tried to survive on their meager pay. That was the price for following Willie.

After Wade Ray declared he'd had enough of the road, citing health problems, Jimmy Day, Willie's other loyal sideman, took over bass. James Clayton Day had become a compass for Willie Hugh Nelson. The baby-faced kid from Shreveport with a blond bouffant was a sideman among sidemen, a support player admired by his peers for his musicianship but largely unknown. He began playing lap steel guitar in honky-tonks at the age of sixteen. He came up with Floyd Cramer on the Louisiana Hayride, playing steel behind Webb Pierce, Red Sovine, Hank Williams, Jim Reeves, Lefty Frizzell, and Elvis Presley, ultimately electing not to follow Elvis to New York and the fame and fortune beyond because, he said, "I didn't want to play rock and roll."

His chosen instrument, the steel guitar, was the most evocatively country of all instruments in the modern country music ensemble. He was the unnamed codeveloper of the Sho-Bud pedal steel guitar manufactured by his friend Buddy Emmons and mentor Shot Jackson, setting the standard on Ray Price's groundbreaking country dance hit "Crazy Arms" and playing the ride on a string of hits for the next seven years while anchoring Ray Price's Cherokee Cowboys as well as picking up work with Jim Reeves and Ernest Tubb, playing steel, rhythm and lead guitar, and bass.

He left the Cherokee Cowboys when Willie did, backed Willie and Johnny Bush for spells, moved with Willie and Shirley to Fort Worth briefly, and later returned to the Cherokee Cowboys along with Johnny Bush. After that, he moved on to back Ferlin Husky and George Jones before rejoining Willie in 1966.

Although Jimmy was hired to play bass, Willie recognized him as the steel guitar virtuoso he was. He could bend chords with his slide bar and slow down a tempo until the notes did a slow-motion moan for mercy. The sonic wail was the perfect complement to Willie's sad songs. The purposeful tempo and the half-spoken lyrics drew falling teardrops into the beer glass just as Jimmy's steel echoed the melody of a haunted voice on his instrumental rides.

Jimmy Day was a purist to the point of being a mess otherwise, prone to drink or pill up so he could stay up a little longer and play a little more. He was mulish to a fault and would often be sent to stand in the corner for a while. Willie and Jimmy were close enough in temperament that they argued and fought verbally and sometimes physically. During one tour while riding on a bus, Willie ordered the driver to pull over, and he took Jimmy outside and whipped his ass. Jimmy might have been a fuckup who deserved being beaten up every now and then, but Willie always apologized and took him back into the band because Jimmy Day was that good a musician.

"Nobody but me and Willie could get along with Jimmy," Johnny Bush said. "And it wasn't easy for me."

"You'd hear the stories about Jimmy drinking or pilling or smoking pot, getting crazy, pissing people off, and he'd be gone. Then all of a sudden, he'd be back," one well-acquainted musician said.

Willie, as the musicians who played with him

learned, could sometimes be as bad a drunk as Jimmy. He was not to be trifled with when he was drinking, demonstrating a proclivity to punch holes in walls, in doors, and windows when he got shit-faced. Friends would blame it on his Indian blood. In truth, he had no one to blame but himself. A charter member of the "-ine" generation that knew their benzedrine from their methedrine and morphine, Willie satisfied his nicotine fix by smoking two to three packs of Chesterfields, Camels, Lucky Strikes, or Kools a day. He could keep up with the pickers and pop his fair share of white crosses, Mexican Blackbirds, and Black Mollies when needed. He had heard about LSD and other psychedelic drugs the hippies were doing and had smoked marijuana too. But he wasn't buying in just yet.

One night he worked Schroeder Hall, a storied Texas dance hall in the country near Victoria, Texas, where he'd enlisted Johnny Bush to round up bassist Eddie Sweatt and a drummer. Willie pulled up to the dance hall in his car next to a tree where Johnny and Eddie were standing around smoking a joint of marijuana. Johnny offered him a hit, but Willie waved it off. "I can't smoke that shit, man," Willie told Johnny. "It gives me a headache." Whiskey and cigarettes were his drugs of choice.

Keeping a band together was headache enough.

On one run, Willie took Jimmy Day off bass and put him back on steel, recruited Buddy White to play guitar and Sonny Hicks to drum, and moved Johnny Bush to bass. But Buddy White had a bad habit of playing over Willie's guitar leads, so Willie had Johnny bounce him from the band. Years later, when Buddy showed up at a gig and asked Willie why he fired him, Willie wiggled off the line by telling him truthfully, "I didn't fire you. Johnny did."

FOR all the musical chairs, Willie Nelson's revolving supporting cast turned into a real band when Paul English signed on late in 1966. Paul was a striking presence, a skinny man with high cheekbones, jet-black hair, and a wicked goatee, who dressed sharp in suits and ties and alligator shoes and was so street-wise he could intimidate a stranger just by looking at him. Willie had worked with Paul for a few weeks back in Fort Worth in 1955 when he was on the radio on KCNC and Paul's brother, Oliver, considered one of the best country and jazz guitarists in Fort Worth, backed Willie on his thirty-minute daily *Western Express* program. Willie might not have paid much, but he knew how to pick 'em. "There are people called musicians," Cowtown jazz piano mainstay John Case said. "And there are those who're master

musicians. Oliver English was a master musician."
When the drummer Tommy Roznosky didn't show
for the radio program, Oliver's little brother Paul, a
trumpet player by training, was recruited to fill in.

Paul listened to the show every day while he worked
at his shop tooling saddles and other leather goods,
and not just because his brother was playing. He
loved the introduction by the "snuff-dippin', coffee-
pot-dodgin' hillbilly from Hill County" and the
whole persona he projected. He was surprised when
he actually saw the impish face behind the voice in
the KCNC studio. "Listening to him, I thought he
was an old man," Paul said. "But he wasn't much
older than me. It was a good radio show."

The idea of playing drums for the first time did
not daunt Paul. "They had a snare drum, and my
older brother said, 'Just start going one and two and
three and four.' That's all I could do." Paul dug the
experience enough to skip work and back up Willie
and Oliver on the radio for three weeks for free.
"Someone gave me a bass Salvation Army drum, and
I hooked a pedal up to it and sat on a Coke box and
managed to hook some bongo drums to the bass
drum," Paul said. "They told me to just keep patting
my foot. They kind of counted out every song for
me, just one, two, three, four."

When Willie hustled a gig at Major's Place, a dim-lit, low-ceilinged lounge at 4010 Hemphill on the south side, he suggested that Oliver bring along Paul so he could get paid for his drumming—$8 a night, three nights a week for six weeks. "The money wasn't that great," Paul admitted. "But I loved playing, and I got to play in front of the girls. The girls loved musicians."

Three weeks into the engagement, the club was sold and Major's took on new management, a common occurrence in the club business, ending their run. But Willie's friendship with the English brothers endured. He hung with Oliver and Paul and did business with them, purchasing an automobile from the small car lot they operated at 2222 Main near the Stockyards. "We didn't have one good enough to sell him, so we went out and found a 'forty-seven Buick convertible, one owner, black with red leather upholstery," Paul said. "I paid $165 plus the $22 tax and sold it to Willie for $175 on time for $25 down. I lost money on the deal."

The friendship endured even as Willie pulled up stakes and left Fort Worth with stars in his eyes. Paul kept his day and night jobs. The leatherwork Paul and his cousin Arvel Walden were doing was so good, they could fetch $45 for a saddle when everyone else was getting $15. The used-car lot Paul ran with his brother Oliver provided some nice running change too. Mainly, though, both were covers for Paul's real profession of running numbers, running whores, and smuggling whatever the marketplace demanded.

But Paul never gave up his love of playing music. He caught on with a guitarist named Billy Wade at a Jacksboro Highway joint, then joined Oliver and their cousin Arvel and an insurance salesman known as Good Time Charlie Taylor, the Texas Fireball. Paul was one of Good Time Charlie's Famous Rock & Roll Cowboys. The band's show poster identified his handsome floating head, replete with Sal Mineo curl and pencil-thin mustache, as the "Bip Bob Drummer."

As a teenager, Paul had run with a gang of hoodlums called the Peroxide Gang, "because we all peroxided our hair," Paul said, and became adept at wielding a gun and a knife. "I was headed straight for the penitentiary when I was young because we would hold contests to see how many burglaries you could pull during the daylight hours." After getting thrown in jail and serving time in Ellis County for breaking and entering, a crime that in this case he did not commit, he made a choice to play the rackets instead of thieving. Racketeers were fined if caught and rarely did time.

He learned to drill and rob pinball machines that paid cash prizes. He pimped prostitutes and operated backroom card games and telephone banks for betting. He became close to some of Fort Worth's most storied gangsters, including Tincy Eggleston, Cecil Green, and Herbert "The Cat" Noble, named for surviving nine attempts on his life, only to get blown to pieces opening his mailbox one day. "Herb used to send his wife out to start his car. They were all knocked off around me," English recalled to reporter John Moulder. "There were as many as five blown up in a weekend." He made the "Ten Most Unwanted List" in the *Fort Worth Press* frequently, and after being run out of Fort Worth, he relocated to Arlington, White Settlement, and Hurst, only to be run out of those communities by local police. At one point, Paul was pulling down $3,000 a week while dodging hit men working on contract.

"I was a good street hustler," he explained, "because I treated it as a business."

He kept up with Willie's songwriting career, his road work with Ray Price, his joining the Grand Ole Opry, and his records. Paul had been living in Houston, working girls and fading the Fort Worth heat while picking up gigs with Paul Buskirk when they reconnected. Whenever Willie played Gilley's in Pasadena, Dancetown, U.S.A., or other Houston venues, Willie would spend the night at Paul's. "I had girls at my house, working girls, but they weren't working for me," Paul explained. "A couple of girls Willie knew lived downstairs. Willie would come over and we'd stay up all night talking." Willie stopped over one night in 1966 and asked Paul if he had a phone number for Tommy Roznosky, who used to play drums with Willie and Paul's brother Oliver on KCNC back in the 1950s.

"Why?" Paul asked.

"I need a drummer," Willie told him. It was time for Johnny Bush to step out from behind his kit and showcase his powerful tenor voice.

"I can play better than him," Paul said about Tommy Roznosky, stretching the truth just a tad. "Or at least as well. Don't call him. I'll go with you."

Willie acted surprised. "Well, you wouldn't work for thirty bucks a night, would you?"

It was a loaded question. Willie knew Paul wouldn't be crazy enough to do road work for that kind of pay, not when Paul was making thousands a week as a pimp.

"For you I would," Paul said. "You got a deal."

What Willie didn't tell Paul was that he could use someone with Paul's powers of not-so-gentle persuasion. Collecting money was the hardest part of the gig. If Willie was going to be a promoter and go into strange towns on his own, rent a gym or municipal space and four-wall a gig, bringing in sound, lights, and a cigar box to collect money from strangers, he needed protection. Paul was that person. He believed a person's word was better than a contract, and anyone who broke that word deserved to be tied up with barbed wire in the woods and left to die.

The gig was supposed to be temporary for Paul. But eleven years after they first gigged together, the arrangement turned permanent. Willie became Paul's life. He gave up the rackets for the road. It was his first honest job since he had tooled leather. Playing in a band was a chance to go legitimate and do what he loved, and playing with Willie was downright inspirational. "I was really hostile," Paul said. "If somebody was to say something wrong to me, they would have a fight. I finally learned from Willie to turn around and say, 'Thank you very much.' And they'd stand there with a guilty look on their faces and say, 'What did I just say?'"

Willie had used that trick when Biff Collie's daddy tracked him down at the Roundup Club in Bandera, Texas, after Biff's wife, Shirley, ran off with Willie. The seventy-year-old Pop Collie cornered Willie in the back of the club and after introducing himself informed Willie he was about to beat the shit out of him.

"Well, whatever will make you feel good, you go right ahead, Mr. Collie," Willie told him with a smile. Flummoxed at the invitation, Pop Collie just walked away. Biff Collie heard about it and fully understood. "I can't think of anybody I would rather have had steal my wife than Willie Nelson," he said.

"Characters believe that violence breeds violence, but Willie is given to a lot of tolerance," explained Paul. "I'm sure I've changed his attitude toward a lot of things and he's changed mine."

One thing Willie full well understood was Paul's value watching his back. "The club business was rough," Willie said. "So you went in with a you-motherfucker-you-better-pay-me attitude from the start. When I was with Ray Price, he'd always say, 'You guys hurry up, let's go. Let's not give that sum-bitch any excuse not to pay us.' Every day he would say that. And he was right. They were just looking for an excuse not to pay you."

Paul wouldn't let that happen. He put a premium on loyalty and friendship. If anyone tried to fuck with Willie, they'd have to fuck with him first. And if they fucked with Paul, Paul liked to point out, "three or four people would be looking for them."

Johnny Bush took time to teach Paul some drumming basics, including the kind of beat Willie preferred. "Willie was hard to play with," Paul said. "I would sit at the table and listen to what John was doing. I had a really hard time learning to play with

Willie." Willie offered better advice. "Don't count," he told Paul. "Just feel it." He was baptized by fire, playing twenty-eight consecutive dates in Texas. After Paul had completed four months of road work, watching, listening, and doing, Willie told John he thought Paul had figured out the groove well enough to do the whole set.

Of all Willie's friendships over the years, none was tighter. If not for Paul, Willie Nelson would've most likely wound up dead, toothless, or selling Kirby vacuum cleaners. Willie had a smart mouth and didn't mind using it, especially when he was right. Paul was at home in dark alleyways and dim-lit clubs and knew the unwritten code. He understood the ritual of the honky-tonk, how folks liked to take their fill of Pearl, Lone Star, Jax, and Southern Select with a heaping helping of good ol' country music, and how that combination inspired dancin', lovin', and sometimes even feudin' and fightin' with fists and bottles. And whenever a boiling point was reached where guns and knives were displayed, Paul knew how to keep the peace.

If the situation merited Willie calling a club owner or promoter a "cheap-ass motherfucker," "shithead," or "asshole" to make his point, Paul's presence would prevent them from having Willie's ass handed to him on a platter for flapping his lip. If Paul happened upon Willie being beaten to a pulp in a back room at the end of a gig, as happened several times, he wouldn't hesitate to pull out one of the three heaters he carried. That's what guns were for, never mind the blood stains on the floor.

"You see, I have a good reputation," explained Paul. "A character means exactly what he says. A character has got to have a lot of character. I never drank, didn't smoke until I was thirty-four, have never had a needle stuck in my arm outside a hospital. All that wasn't done where I came from. A character has to treat everybody right. When you call a friend a friend, you have to treat him as a friend. It's respect. Being a character means respect."

BUSH, Day, Nelson, English. The band needed a name and Johnny Bush was quick on the draw. "I was watching television in Nashville and a television ad came on for a breath mint. The announcer said, 'It eliminated the offenders, be it garlic, onions . . .' " Willie loved the name the Offenders, but some promoters did not, so in the spirit of stamping out negative thoughts, they tried the Chosen Few at Paul's suggestion to fit their self-image as outsiders. But when announced from the stage, "Willie Nelson and the Chosen Few" sounded a little "too Asian," as in the Chosin Fu. So they went with the Record Men in honor of Willie's first single for Liberty Records, "Mr. Record Man."

They traveled in a 1947 Grumman Flxible Flyer bus that originally belonged to Faron Young before he sold it to a movie company and the movie company sold it to Houston oil well firefighter Red Adair, who sold it to Willie for $4,000. The Flex had seen better days and required constant mechanical repair. Willie Nelson and the Record Men drove it hard, doing between five hundred and eight hundred miles between dates booked by W. E. ("Lucky") Moeller or Crash Stewart. Johnny, Paul, and Willie took turns behind the wheel, running up the odometer until the road bit back.

Johnny Bush had been taking care of the band's business, collecting the money and paying the players and the bills. Paul inherited the job in San Diego after John, Jimmy Day, and Doyle Nelson, Willie's stepbrother and extra driver, showed up drunk and bloodied from a wild time in Tijuana. Johnny was so trashed, Paul had to take him to the emergency room. On his way out, Johnny gave Paul instructions on how to collect the money for the band at the end of the gig.

"That's how I figured out the business," Paul said wryly. There wasn't much to figure out. Paul had been schooled in repossessing autos after missed payments and righting wrongs without calling a lawyer or the cops. Getting money after a show was no different. "I wasn't a really nice person when it came to collecting. I'd put my briefcase on the desk in the club office whenever it came time to settle up after a gig," without mentioning the briefcase contained a pistol, Paul said. "They knew I meant business. In New Mexico, I had to chase down the guy to get our money. There was a forklift outside the club, so I got the forklift and raised his Thunderbird up on the lift, took the key out of the car, and wrote him a note, 'Come see me.' He did.

"I've never had a club that didn't pay me," Paul later told reporter John Moulder. "No, I had one," he said, correcting himself. It was in Florida, shortly after he joined up with Willie. The owner offered $750 instead of the guaranteed $900. Willie said, "All or nothing." Paul's gun was on the bus, and the owner had his own security detail. "I ran to the bus to get my pistol and they shut the steel doors in front of the club. I tried to kick the doors open but couldn't. They had cops working for them anyway."

The best defense was a good offense, especially a firearm. On an off-night at a bar in Phoenix, Doyle Nelson sought out Paul. "Two guys I was playing pool with lost their bets to me and won't pay up," Doyle reported.

Paul got up from his table and walked into the pool room.

"Hey, you lost this bet, why don't you pay it?" Paul said, confronting the two men with his piercing eyes and threatening countenance.

"We were just playing for a quarter," one protested.

"Pay him the quarter," Paul said, seething. "Anybody who won't pay on a bet is a rotten motherfucker." Making a bet was like signing a contract as far as Paul was concerned, and these two were not men of honor.

A fight erupted, with Paul ending up on top of one guy, pounding his head with his fists. The other came up behind Paul and used his pool stick as a garrote around his neck, pulling him back. Paul swung his right arm up. In his hand was his "bidness," whose snub-nosed barrel was inserted into the guy's nostril. The gun was cocked and ready when Willie walked in. "Paul will whip any one of you guys, and I'll take the other," he said with perfect timing. The fight was over.

Despite his commitment to Willie, Paul says he harbored no delusions. "I never figured it would amount to anything," he said. "I was just along for the ride and for what it was at that time. We were having a real good time." On Christmas Day 1966 they found themselves at a Holiday Inn hundreds of miles from home. "We went out and got shaving cream and toilet paper and decorated the Holiday Inn and took pictures," Paul said. "It was being with best friends."

Willie's next hire was David Zettner, a bass and pedal steel player with George Chambers' Country Gentlemen out of San Antonio, the showcase dance-hall band of South Texas. Adding David allowed Willie to move Jimmy Day to pedal steel full-time. David was multitalented, a painter in addition to being a musician, and a sensitive, soulful cat. His tenure with the Offenders/Record Men/Willie Nelson Show was cut short in 1968 when he was drafted into the military to fight a war in Vietnam. Just before he left, his friend Bee Spears, who replaced David in the Country Gentlemen back in San Antonio, showed up in Houston with a couple ounces of manicured Mexican *mota*.

The band had developed an appreciation for good weed, Willie included, once Paul put his connections to characters trafficking in high-quality marijuana to use. While the band gathered on the bus to check out the farewell gift from David's San Antonio buddy, the conversation drifted to David's pending departure. Who would they get to play bass? Willie asked Paul about a bass player they knew from California.

"Naw," Paul said. "We can't afford him. Besides, he's married and has three kids."

Jimmy Day glanced his glazed eyes toward the tall, gawky friend of David's who brought the dope. "Why not him? He can't play worth a shit but we can teach him what we want him to play and he gets high."

Why not? Bee Spears may have been a stringbean of a nineteen-year-old and half crazy with a healthy appetite for illicit substances, but he was good enough to replace David Zettner in the Country Gentlemen and came from good stock. His daddy, Sam, a fiddle player with the Texas Tophands, raised his family across the road from John T. Floore's Country Store and dance hall in the Hill Country town of Helotes, outside San Antonio.

"Can he play?" Willie asked David.

"Naw," David said, twisting his face into a wise-ass grin, plainly high as a Georgia pine. "But he's a fast learner," he said, exhaling smoke.

From that day forward, George Chambers would always turn just a tad testy whenever Willie Nelson's name came up; the Country Gentlemen wasn't Willie's farm team.

Bee's first gig with Willie Nelson and the Record

Men was the Nashville Room in the basement of the Taft Hotel in New York City. "I was scared to death," Bee said. "There was a very steep learning curve, but Jimmy helped a lot and I snapped real quick that Willie plays bass lines on his guitar, so I started playing low." The New York gig was followed by twenty-eight gigs in twenty-eight nights.

The 1947 Flex eventually gave out at the end of the tour, forcing them to switch to a black Lincoln Continental with a matching black trailer that Paul bought from Leroy Van Dyke. The Continental gave out a few months later, prompting the band to switch to a turquoise Mercury Marquis station wagon that Billy Gray sold them.

The musicians got by on $100 a week if they were lucky, plus whatever bar tab they could run up wherever they were playing. But that didn't stop them from looking sharp like the professional musicians they were, resplendent for a few hours every night in their shiny blue outfits or Nehru jackets with turtlenecks. Other bands wore uniforms. Willie Nelson and the Record Men styled.

"We dressed hipper than most of Nashville," Paul English said. "That's what I liked about Willie—we weren't conformists." When Paul first went to work for the band, they were wearing frilly shirts, maroon brocade tuxedo-like coats, bulldog ties, and black pants. When cleaning all the coordinated outfits at the same time became a pain in the ass, Willie gave them each $100 during a layover in Los Angeles and encouraged them to go out and buy something different.

Paul and Willie were walking past the display window of Sy Devore's in Hollywood, when Willie spied a cape.

"You have to have that!" he said.

Paul's trimmed beard and sharp-edged sideburns had always prompted comments that he looked like the devil, which he took as a compliment, since he always said, "The devil was the prettiest angel in heaven." A cape would enhance the image.

The effect was immediate. People treated him differently when he wore the cape. At Panther Hall, he took the image one step further, placing dry ice around his drum kit, creating the effect of smoke. "When I got off the stage, there were fifteen girls waiting for me, wanting my autograph," Paul said.

Willie Nelson and the Record Men stood out on any package show bill. They were road dogs of the highest—and most offbeat—standing.

And they were always evolving. David Zettner's flat feet earned a medical discharge from the military after he'd been away from the band for a year, and he picked up the bass again and Bee moved to play behind Johnny Bush, who was touring as a single act on the Willie Nelson Show. "David and I would get together and he'd play guitar and I'd play bass," Bee said. "The older guys taught the younger guys how to play, one on one. They'd tell you, 'Sorry, son, that shit ain't gonna fly.' They taught you feel. We were learning cool tunes, all kinds of jazz—Brubeck, "Blue Rondo Ala Turk" in nine/eight time, odd beats like seven/four, five/four. Country guys jammed jazz. We didn't jam to 'Stand by Your Man.'"

A THOUSAND miles west, another iconoclast was making a name for himself. He was the embodiment of macho, a ladies' man who favored black leather to match his slicked-back greasy pompadour, and had a cigarette constantly dangling from his lip and a bad-ass biker vibe. His husky voice matched the image.

Waylon Jennings was a fellow Texan who was even more outside the box than Willie was. Like Willie, he had been a disc jockey, first in Lubbock, Texas, near where he grew up, and at KCKY in Phoenix. When they met at the Adams Hotel in Phoenix, Willie, newly signed to RCA, was doing a one-nighter at the Riverside Ballroom. Waylon, on the verge of being signed to RCA by Chet Atkins, was enjoying a very sweet setup at JD's, a giant nightclub in Phoenix near the campus of Arizona State University, with two dance floors and two bands. A different rock-and-roll band was booked downstairs every week for the college crowd. Upstairs, Waylon Jennings and his Waylors played their unique brand of country and western music mixed with rock and roll in front of more than a thousand customers a night six nights a week, each band member taking home a $1,200 weekly guarantee.

Waylon and Willie compared notes about their recording deals. Waylon was still signed to A&M Records in Los Angeles, which put out an album and a single of "Just to Satisfy You" with a version of the Ian and Sylvia folk song "Four Strong Winds" on the flip side, which was a local hit. Willie hadn't gotten over how Monument Records had treated him. Waylon told Willie he was thinking of moving to Nashville. Willie half-jokingly offered to take over Waylon's gig at JD's if he left.

"He asked me what I thought about him going to Nashville, and when he told me what he was making, I told him he'd better stay where he was at," Willie said. "I knew what I'd have to do out there to make the equivalent of what he was making. You have to gross a whole lot of money to come out with that kind of net income, and on the road, that's not even a guarantee. But Waylon knew what he wanted to do."

Waylon already had quite a story to tell. He'd gotten into the music business as a protégé of West Texas rock-and-roller Buddy Holly, who'd produced sessions on him in Clovis, New Mexico. Along with Tommy Allsup, Waylon was part of Buddy's band on the Winter Dance Party tour. Scheduled to fly out with Buddy in a private plane after a show in Clear Lake, Iowa, on February 3, 1959, Waylon gave up his seat to J. P. Richardson—the Big Bopper—who had the hit "Chantilly Lace" and was feeling ill, while Tommy Allsup let Mexican American rocker Ritchie Valens, who was promoting his hit "La Bamba," have his seat. Richardson, Valens, and Holly were killed when the plane crashed shortly after takeoff in a snowstorm. Waylon possessed a rich, vibrant voice and projected a magnetic presence onstage. He also was writing some splendid songs. He was a country boy through and through, but he played with a rock and roll swagger. Plenty of Buddy Holly had rubbed off on him.

Bobby Bare, one of the most popular singer-songwriters in the emerging folk-country subgenre, heard Waylon's version of "Four Strong Winds" and recorded the song himself, charting number 3 as a country single. At Bare's urging—"He's the best thing since Elvis," Bare told RCA's chief, Chet Atkins—Atkins signed Waylon to RCA and Waylon immediately moved to Nashville. Willie did not take over Waylon's residency at JD's.

RCA's executives knew where they thought Waylon should be slotted, titling his debut *Folk-Country*. But the more records Waylon made and the more he understood how the system worked, the less he appreciated what RCA thought was best for him. As his record sales increased, his complaints grew louder. The Nashville Sound was cramping his style.

The two W's from Texas were soul brothers. "We both liked each other, respected each other's music and ideas, but our music wasn't that similar," admitted Willie. "It was the fact we both were pretty independent and insisted on doing it the way we wanted to do it that made us closer friends. It got to be fun to play games with the studios and with the record company and record with other artists from different companies at four in the morning that RCA didn't know anything about and all of a sudden come out with a record and we're all on it—that was fun."

He was referring to "Poor Old Ugly Gladys Jones," a joke song written by country comedian Don Bowman and Waylon that Waylon, Don, Bobby Bare, Jerry Reed, Willie, and others cut at RCA when nobody was looking.

Willie kept plugging away in the studio. In March 1966, the overwhelmed Chet Atkins farmed out Willie to staff producer Felton Jarvis, who had just started producing Elvis Presley, for four tracks. "I had about thirty-five artists and had hired some people to help me produce," explained Chet. "There was a lot of mediocre stuff. But that's the way we did it. Make a bunch of records and throw them out."

Felton had a lighter touch, and Willie was nowhere near as intimidated by Felton as he was by Chet. When it came to picking guitar, no one was as good as Chet, so Willie often deferred to Chet's judgment at his own expense. Felton accommodated Willie's request to bring in Jimmy Day and Johnny Bush from his road band to join Jerry Reed, Velma Smith, Junior Huskey, and Jerry Smith in Studio B. The tracks became most of the album *Make Way for Willie Nelson,* one very mixed bag of music. Willie covered old standards like Hank Williams's "Mansion on the Hill," Cy Coben's schmaltzy "Make Way for a Better Man," Frankie Brown's "Born to Lose," and the ballad "What Now My Love?" as if he meant every word he sang. His own "One in a Row," recorded in June with Johnny Bush and Wade Ray, was released as a single and worked its way into the Top 20, peaking at number 19 on the country singles chart in September, Willie's first significant chart single since he was with Liberty Records. The album followed suit, entering the Top 10 and stalling at number 9 on the country albums chart in early 1967.

Album sales were a pittance from a performer's standpoint. Unless you were someone huge like Johnny Cash, Buck Owens, or Merle Haggard, you couldn't move enough units to get out of debt to your record label. For several years, Willie lived well off songwriter royalties from "Hello Walls," "Crazy," and "Funny How Time Slips Away," but those had slowed to a trickle. Although Willie owned land, a tractor, and hogs, he was tight on cash, and whenever he had money, he spent it. His eye was on the road. Playing live gave him the greatest personal satisfaction. He didn't feel whole unless he was on a stage in front of a crowd. And in order to do that, he had to have a single or an album to promote. "Nashville recording artist" was his calling card.

Chet Atkins produced the next album of all-Willie originals, *The Party's Over and Other Great Willie Nelson Songs*. Jimmy Day and Johnny Bush returned to the studio to play steel and drums along with Grady Martin, the studio legend who'd been recording with Ray Price for years under Don Law's tutelage until Law retired in 1967, Junior Huskey, Jerry Smith, Jerry Reed, and three violins, a viola, and a cello.

The material, which included "A Moment Isn't Very Long," "No Tomorrow in Sight," "Hold Me Tighter" (cowritten with Hank Cochran), and "A Long Story Short (She's Gone)," cowritten with Fred Foster, was solid. But except for "The Party's Over," a redo of the codified last call in a nightclub or bar with the phrase "turn out the lights," it was not Willie's most stellar work. "The Party's Over" reached number 24 on the country singles chart. A follow-up single, "Blackjack County Chain," written by Willie's friend Red Lane, was released later that year with Floyd Tillman's "Some Other World" on the flip. It was climbing the country singles chart at number 21 when radio stations started banning the record for its grisly content. The song tells the tale of a Negro chain-gang convict who wins his freedom by killing a sheriff with "thirty-five pounds of Blackjack County chain" to gain his freedom. Red Lane had originally offered the song to a rising young talent named Charley Pride, who was black. Pride, anticipating the potential controversy, wisely turned down the offer.

Charley Pride entered Willie's life through the Willie Nelson Show package tour featuring Marty Robbins, Lefty Frizzell, and Bob Wills, with Tag Lambert and Hank Cochran and Jeannie Seely. "That was me and Crash Stewart's production," Willie said. "Nobody knew who in the hell I was, but we called it the Willie Nelson Show featuring Bob Wills, Marty Robbins, and the others." There was a method to the madness. "Most of the audience didn't know who I was but they knew who all those other folks were," explained Willie, "and after the show, they knew who I was too."

One night, Marty tried to hip Willie to a new singer who wanted to get on the tour. "His name is Charley Pride," Marty told him, "and he only wants two hundred fifty a night, and his manager Jack Johnson is coming with him and they'll share a room." Willie knew who Marty was talking about. Crash Stewart had already been working on Willie, telling him, "He isn't just a country singer, he's a *black* country singer."

"Never heard of him," Willie said.

After Crash played him Charley's single "Snakes Crawl at Night," Willie turned more receptive.

"Don't you worry about taking him into Dallas, Fort Worth, San Antonio, all those places?" Crash wondered. "What do you think's going to happen?"

"I don't know," Willie said, sensing another opportunity to stir up some shit for the sake of stirring up shit. "Let's go see."

Charley Pride's first night on the Willie Nelson Show was in Dallas. Johnny Bush was fronting Willie's band and sang two songs before he started introducing the stars of the show. When he'd met Charley backstage, Johnny realized his announcing chores would be a little trickier than normal. Country music was white folks' music, never mind that Charley had grown up in Mississippi. No black man had ever been identified as a country music singer before; his label had wisely omitted sending out a publicity photograph to accompany his singles. Most country fans didn't much cotton to the idea of a colored country singer. They were still chafing at new civil rights laws being enforced by the federal government, particularly in the South, where segregation was still embraced.

Johnny Bush gave Charley Pride a straight-up introduction: "Ladies and gentleman, here he is, the new singing sensation with the hit 'The Snakes Crawl at Night.' Let's give a big Big D welcome to Country Charley Pride!"

The crowd cheered. The record was hot and many in the audience were familiar with it. Then Charley Pride came out from behind the curtain. The clapping stopped. Beads of sweat were visible on Charley Pride's brow as he stepped to the microphone. "Ladies and gentlemen," he said, "I know I look funny to y'all standing up here. Don't let this permanent tan fool you. I'm a country singer and I hope you enjoy hearing it as much as I enjoy singing it. My favorite country singers are Ray Price, Jim Reeves, and Connie Smith."

Afterwards at a jam at Dewey Groom's Longhorn Ballroom, Willie encountered resistance from the owner. "Dewey didn't want Charley on the bandstand," Willie said. "So I got up on the stage and introduced Charley, had him come up on the stage. When he got there, I laid a big kiss on him, right on the mouth. Then he started singing and they loved it. Dewey didn't know and didn't understand the way it was supposed to be," Willie said. Later that night, everyone went to Willie's motel room and jammed. "The next morning I wished I would've had a camera," Willie said. Charley Pride and Dewey Groom had both passed out on the same bed.

Willie never did think Charley's race was a problem. "Music crosses concrete blocks; it goes right through everything," he said. "I always felt that if they hear this guy and he's good, the audiences didn't care if he's red, black, blue, yellow, striped. I know they don't mean it [racial epithets], I know if they hear him, [even the worst racist] will say, 'OK, well let this nigger in.' "

Willie took it upon himself to advocate on behalf of this outsider's outsider and show the country music world that black folks wouldn't bite or poison the purity of their music. He went out of his way to call

Charley "Supernigger" in public places, neutralizing the power of the verbal insult. "I loved doing that and he loved it because it scared a lot of people and pissed off more people—it was shock value," Willie said. "I'd yell at him from across the airport and we would always kiss when we'd see each other, so the rumors continue. I know that all the other guys out there who said the same thing under their breath, they just didn't know."

Resistance broke down, venue by venue. Corky Kuykendall, the co-owner of Panther Hall, showed up at Will Rogers Auditorium when the package show came through Fort Worth. He wanted some of the acts to come join Tony Douglas at Panther Hall afterwards. Willie, Johnny Bush, Jimmy Day, Jeannie Seely, and Charley Pride rode over in Willie's car. When they arrived at Panther Hall, Corky Kuykendall pulled Willie aside. "Who's that? I don't want a nigger on the show," he told him. Johnny Bush tried to intervene, telling him, "Corky, you don't understand. This guy is dynamite."

"It's Tony's show," Corky said, washing his hands of the responsibility, "and Tony won't allow no niggers on his show."

They ignored Corky. Jimmy did his guitar playing. Jeannie went up and sang two songs. Johnny Bush sang just one song before introducing Country

Charley Pride. Charley and Johnny started singing "Crazy Arms" and the house roared.

There was one downside to Willie's boosting Charley's rapid ascent. "I closed the show," Willie said. "I thought I had put myself in there in a pretty good spot. But all of a sudden I was following Charley Pride. The crowd was screaming and yelling for Charley halfway through my set."

Giving breaks to people like Charley Pride separated Willie from other entertainers. He seemed to go out of his way to lend a hand whenever he could. Willie delivered on his promise to produce Johnny Bush, sort of. He'd made the same promise to Jimmy Day, so, in the spirit of compromise, Willie Nelson produced two artists in one three-hour session. "That pissed me off," Johnny Bush said. "Jimmy Day had no aspiration of becoming a singer. He was a steel player—a great steel player, one of my best friends. Well, half a session is better than no session."

Paul, Jimmy Day, and Johnny Bush drove all night from Texas to make the recording session at Little Victor studio, the smaller studio in the RCA building where Elvis Presley recorded. Johnny sang an original composition, "Sound of a Heartache" b/w "A Moment Isn't Very Long," a Willie Nelson song. "My thinking was, if they saw Willie Nelson as songwriter, disc jockeys would play it," Johnny said.

The single was first issued on the New Star label owned by Pamper Music. After doing enough tracks to release an album, Willie and investors Paul English and Jack Fletcher, another Fort Worth character, sold Johnny Bush's recordings to Pete Drake, the steel player who co-owned a small label, Stop Records, with Texan Tommy Hill. "I was charting higher than Willie was charting," Johnny said. "Willie was proud. His thing was, 'Anybody in my show who can do something that people like is only going to help my show.'"

Willie bumped up Johnny to $50 a day plus a $10 per diem. But after a show in Longview, a few days later, he knocked on Johnny's motel room door and sat down on the bed. "What do you think?" he asked Johnny.

"What do you mean?" Johnny asked back.

"Are you ready to go out on your own?"

"No, not yet," Johnny said. "I like it where I am."

"Want to stay another year?" Willie asked. "I'll give you a hundred a day if you stay another year. We're drawing good crowds. You're doing a good job and I'm proud of what you're doing." Willie did not hide his pride in Johnny's success. One night, after introducing him onstage, he heard a fan yell out, "Aw, to hell with Johnny Bush." Willie shifted his gaze in the direction of where the voice had come from, his eyes narrowing. "No. Not to hell with Johnny Bush," he growled to the fan.

WILLIE made two recording sessions in August 1967. The first session produced the A-side of his next single, "Truth Number One," a spacy, philosophical tune written by Aaron Allan, the disc jockey Willie had replaced at KBOP some thirteen years before. Willie liked the song because it fit in with his interest in Astara and metaphysics. True to form, hardly anyone else understood what he was singing about except maybe the hippies out in San Francisco, who were dropping out of society to take drugs and grow their hair long and listen to weird rock music, and they weren't country fans. The single went nowhere.

The second session was for a concept album Chet was producing on Willie that played to his identity and fan base—an album of songs all about Texas. The cover of *Texas in My Soul* featured the drawn likeness of a smiling Willie in front of the Alamo, and the futuristic Tower of the Americas, the symbol of the HemisFair '68 world's fair, staged in San Antonio.

The tunes were topically to the point. "Dallas," a honky-tonk tune coauthored by Dewey Groom of the Longhorn Ballroom, was the first song since

"Big D" to make that city sound appealing, with references to Love Field airport, the North Central Expressway, and some of the prettiest women in the world, at a time when the city was still regarded negatively as the city where President John F. Kennedy had been assassinated. Jerry Blanton's "San Antonio" featured the first use of the term "homeboy" in a country song. "Streets of Laredo" was his version of the western gunfighter ballad made famous by his occasional touring pal Marty Robbins. "Who Put All My Ex's in Texas" was a catchy tune coauthored by a young country talent named Eddie Rabbitt. Willie put his vocals on the gloriously overwrought Cindy Walker–Glenn Paxton composition "Hill Country Theme," more popularly known as a symphony-suitable instrumental. Redos of Ernest Tubb's classics "Waltz Across Texas" and "There's a Little Bit of Everything in Texas," and "Texas in My Soul," cowritten by ET and popularized by Hank Penny and Tex Williams, were payback for all the good ET did for Willie. "Beautiful Texas" was a composition attributed to W. Lee ("Pass the Biscuits, Pappy") O'Daniel, the Fort Worth showman who took over the Light Crust Doughboys Western Swing band after running off Bob Wills and Milton Brown, and used another band, the Hillbilly Boys, and a platform of the Ten Commandments and the Golden

Rule to become governor of Texas. Respects were also paid to the epitome of Texas patriotism with a reading of "The Travis Letter" that segued into "Remember the Alamo."

Grady Martin picked his nylon strings in a way that rubbed off on Willie, with Chet Atkins's electric and Jimmy Day's glistening steel chiming in. Funnyman songwriter-performer Ray Stevens, who had already worked several Willie sessions, added vibes and organ. Johnny Bush drummed. Chet informed Willie after the sessions that he didn't want Johnny Bush or Jimmy Day back in the studio. They may have been Willie's guys but they were road pickers, not studio musicians or Chet's guys, and Chet was producer, CEO, and had the last word.

Johnny Bush didn't give a shit what Chet Atkins wanted, because he was doing better as a recording artist for Stop One, hitting number 4 on the country charts with the Nelson-Cochran composition "Undo the Right" in November, then Willie's releases of "In My Own Peculiar Way," "Permanently Lonely," "I'm Still Not Over You," and "San Antonio." It was time to fly on his own. On Johnny's last night with the Record Men in December 1968 at Panther Hall, Willie gave Johnny a plaque of gratitude during the Cowtown Jamboree TV show on Channel 11. What the audience at home did not see was the inscription on the back: "No matter how big you are, you'll always be Willie Mac Big Shit John to us."

Willie's gamble (and Paul English's and Jack Fletcher's) on Johnny Bush paid off. But Chet Atkins wasn't willing to gamble on Willie the same way. For the next album, he kept the studio arrangement intentionally spare, limiting the recording to Willie, Grady Martin, and his own acoustic guitar, with Junior Huskey on bass. Violas, violins, and the Anita Kerr Singers were added afterwards, effectively burying Willie's vocals in the mix.

The ballad-heavy *Good Times* included "Little Things," cowritten with Shirley Nelson, which was released as the first single and reached number 22 on *Billboard*'s country singles chart. Shirley shared writing credits on two other tunes on the album, "Pages" and "She's Still Gone." The second single, "Good Times," barely charted, reaching number 44.

The album cover, which had absolutely nothing to do with the songs inside, pictured Willie in golf clothes on a putting green, his arms around a pretty girl, showing her how to putt. If the Nashville Sound defined modern country music, golf was the new horseshoes. Consumers didn't follow the logic. The record stalled at number 29 on the country albums chart. "She's Still Gone" wound up as the B-side to "Johnny One Time," a pensive ballad written by Dallas Frazier and A. L. Owens that nudged onto the country singles chart, reaching number 36, only to become Brenda Lee's first country hit in a decade when she covered the song several months later.

The next single, "Bring Me Sunshine," a swinging upbeat number written by Sylvia Dee and Arthur Kent, featured Willie doing an impressive imitation of a Vegas lounge singer. Unexpectedly, the single generated enough radio airplay and sales to chart at number 13 on the *Billboard* country singles chart, Willie's best showing yet for RCA, even though that translated into sales well under fifty thousand copies. Its relative success once again validated Chet Atkins's Nashville Sound method of recording.

But chart action took a backseat to friends in need, as far as Willie was concerned. He wanted to save everyone around him. He was so upset about David Zettner getting drafted that he felt compelled to write an antiwar song called "Jimmy's Road." "I never thought he needed to be in a war," Willie said of David. "He was far removed from a soldier who wanted to go out and kill somebody or hurt somebody. Being out there wasn't right." Paul English agreed. "David had never held a gun before," he said. "He was a pacifist."

Willie's altruism prompted him to hire Paul English's big brother Oliver, his guitarist on KCNC radio in Fort Worth back in 1955. Oliver had lost the index finger of his left hand in a gun accident, and Jimmy Day was off with the Cherokee Cowboys again, so Willie offered Oliver the pedal steel guitar chair on the Willie Nelson Show. "I thought I could hang on to that steel bar," Oliver said. "I'd shot off my finger and the doctors had put it back on, but it was all messed up when they put it back on. I couldn't use it at all. I couldn't hang on to that bar. I couldn't hit a lick. I'd just sit up there onstage." Oliver stuck with the Record Men for nine months before quitting out of frustration. "Willie knew I couldn't play when he offered me the job," he said.

Willie didn't care. The friendships he formed on the highway were deeper than his other relationships, with his family and his wife. The road was his chosen path, and it was more fun traveling it with spiritual brothers. One town, one night, another town, the next, always leaving them wanting more. And if you left a mess, it didn't matter because you were already gone. "We didn't know any better," Paul English said. "We were having fun."

Coast-to-Coast,
Border-to-Border, 1967

TEXAS WAS THE SWEET SPOT, where there was money to be made, and Fort Worth and Dallas offered the most dependable paydays. "They'd come in a lot to where I played, the Stagecoach Inn, because we played Western Swing music," said Charlie Owens, the Fort Worth steel guitarist. Paul had played behind Ray Chaney, the owner of the Stagecoach in the early 1960s. Once he joined up with Willie, whenever they were gigging around North Texas, Paul would persuade Chaney to let Willie and him play a Sunday matinee as a two-piece for the door. "That was Paul's idea," Charlie Owens said. "But they'd make ends meet. Paul's a pretty good promoter. He kept telling Willie, 'You got it. You're going to make it.' He just had to get known. And playing free is a good way to get known.

We all knew he could write songs after 'Crazy' and 'Hello Walls,' " Charlie said.

Willie was a known entity in the Metroplex, as civic leaders identified the growing sprawl of the Dallas–Fort Worth area. His reputation swelled considerably through his budding friendship with Don Meredith, the quarterback of the Dallas Cowboys, the biggest celebrities in all of Texas. Don was a handsome good ol' boy from Mount Vernon in northeast Texas who had played college football at Southern Methodist University in Dallas, graduating the same year that the National Football League franchise came to town. He was a local hero first, then a national hero as the Cowboys became known as America's Team. Off the field, Dandy Don burnished his partying credentials in area clubs and demonstrated his affection for country music in public by jumping up on the stage of the Sportatorium and singing along with Willie, Wade Ray, Thumbs Carlisle from Ernest Tubb's Texas Troubadours, Roger Miller, David Houston, Tillman Franks, the Cedar Grove Three, and the Big D Jamboree Band, even though Don couldn't sing worth a hoot.

Before the Cowboys' National Football League Championship game against the Green Bay Packers in the dramatic Ice Bowl of January 1967, the quarterback demonstrated better vocals in the locker room by singing Willie's "One Day at a Time" to demonstrate how he approached every game. If Willie Nelson wasn't a household name in Nashville circles, his friendship with Dandy Don elevated him to celebrity status back home in Texas.

Willie's frequent appearances in Texas were still largely subsidized by his publishing royalties. The checks that arrived in the mailbox quarterly were enough for Willie and Hank Cochran to buy out Ray Price's share of Pamper Music in 1967. But within months, Willie turned around and sold his piece of Pamper to Hank, telling him, "I don't want to be a song publisher." Two years later, Hank and Hal Smith flipped Pamper to Tree International for $1.6 million, but Willie didn't lose any sleep. Money was almost beside the point as far as he was concerned.

On the larger stage, Johnny Cash had been elevated to American legend status, thanks to his television show and his association with folk poet Bob Dylan, who'd recorded his 1966 album *Blonde on Blonde* in Nashville, using many of the same players Willie used on his debut sessions for RCA, including Henry Strzelecki, Charlie McCoy, Jerry Kennedy, and Pig Robbins. Pete Drake, Kenny Buttrey, and Charlie McCoy played on Dylan's follow-up album, *John Wesley Hardin,* released in 1968, with many of the same musicians appearing on 1969's *Nashville Skyline,* which included Dylan's duet with Johnny Cash on "Girl from the North Country," despite the fact that neither voice was particularly suited for harmonizing.

Nashville's response was to promote a slew of smooth singing vocalists such as Don Gibson, whose "Sweet Dreams" fit the invented folk-country genre, Roger Miller, George Hamilton IV, who covered New York folkie Tom Rush's "She Got the Urge for Going," the iconoclast's iconoclast, Bobby Bare, the Glaser Brothers, and a new singer-songwriter, who'd started out as a studio janitor, named Kris Kristofferson. Even Willie's friend and labelmate Waylon Jennings got in on the act, covering the Beatles' "Norwegian Wood" and Jimmy Webb's ambitiously overwrought song suite "MacArthur Park."

Both Willie and Waylon were coming to the realization that they were fellow travelers and partners in crime. Though their music was decidedly different, they had more in common than just being country boys from Texas who thought outside the box. "They thought I was rock and roll," Waylon explained about the suits' impression of his artistry. "They thought [Willie] was on another planet."

WILLIE took advantage of his status as an RCA recording artist to road test different guitars. If a musician had a record deal and worked dates, manufacturers would loan or give instruments to him. For a long time Willie played Fender Telecasters, Jaguars, and Jazzmasters, along with an occasional Gibson and a custom double-neck guitar. His guitar of choice changed for good after the Baldwin company sent a representative to a gig at the Pan American Ballroom in El Campo, southeast of Houston, to give Willie and Johnny Bush its new Model 801CP Electric Classical Guitar with a Prismatone stereo pickup and a Baldwin amplifier. The Baldwin was a big axe similar to a Gibson, and the first gut-string electric. Willie took it out on a run and liked the way it played in a big room. But the neck was so poorly constructed, it eventually fell apart. David Zettner and Jimmy Day took it to Shot Jackson in Nashville to get it fixed. The luthier was unable to salvage the guitar, but he had another instrument that might interest Willie—a new Martin N-20 made of Brazilian rosewood with a blond top. Shot told Willie he'd sell him the Martin for $750, which was little more than what it cost Shot. Willie told Shot he'd buy it, but only if Shot could install the ceramic pickup from the Baldwin into the Martin. Shot salvaged the pickup and put it into the body of the Martin acoustic, effectively electrifying the instrument. The jury-rigged instrument fit Willie like a glove. It had the tone of a wooden instrument but with the pickup could project its sound in the biggest dance hall. Willie named the guitar Trigger.

The Martin guitar changed Willie Nelson's sound, giving it an earthy folk texture. But you couldn't tell by the records he was making. Vibes, trumpets, violins, a cello, saxophones, and a trombone embellished *My Own Peculiar Way* to the point of once again drowning out Willie's voice and the sound of his guitar. Worse, the production did little to change the public's perception of Willie Nelson as a recording artist. The recent success of the single "Bring Me Sunshine" was an anomaly. Chet Atkins brought in Danny Davis, a producer, arranger, trumpet player, and leader of his own instrumental group, the Nashville Brass, to fluff up four tracks.

Willie had already recorded the title song on his debut album for Liberty seven years earlier, on his Panther Hall concert recording, and it had been covered by pop crooner Perry Como. Five other tracks—"I Let My Mind Wander," "I Just Don't Understand," "The Local Memory," "I Just Dropped By," and "The Message"—were Willie originals, along with a Hank Cochran collaboration, "Any Old Arms Won't Do." He did five covers—John Hartford's "Natural to Be Gone," Marty Robbins's "I Walk Alone," by the esteemed thumb picker Merle

Travis, Don Baird's "It Will Come to Pass," and Dallas Frazier's "Love Has a Mind of Its Own"—but to no avail. The album reached number 39 on the country album charts. The single of "Natural to Be Gone" b/w "Jimmy's Road," the protest song Willie wrote for David Zettner, didn't even chart.

Chet Atkins and RCA were losing faith. A year passed before the November 1969 sessions for *Both Sides Now*. Producer Felton Jarvis let Willie record on his own terms and bring along Billy English, Paul's nineteen-year-old brother, on drums, young David Zettner on guitar and bass, Shirley Nelson on vocals (her last collaboration with her husband), and Jimmy Day on bass and steel.

Billy English joined Willie by drumming for Billy Stack, a Fort Worth singer with a Roy Orbison voice whom Willie, Paul, and Jack Fletcher were backing to launch as a solo act like they had with Johnny Bush. Session player Norbert Putnam led one session and added his bass. James Isbell, the brother of Dave Isbell, who'd fronted the Mission City Playboys that Willie played with thirteen years earlier, played bongos to convey the folkie vibe Willie was going after. He covered Joni Mitchell on the title track, New York folk singer Fred Neil's "Everybody's Talkin'," made popular by the film *Midnight Cowboy*, Shirley Nelson's "Once More with Feeling," and the old folk-country chestnuts "Crazy Arms" (if Ray Price's classic was old enough to be classified as folk), "Pins and Needles (in My Heart)," a Fred Rose original written under his Floyd Jenkins pseudonym, "Wabash Cannonball," and the honky-tonk standard "One Has My Name." He also introduced a new original—a slice of the wild side of life on the road called "Bloody Merry Morning"—and threw in his underappreciated original "I Gotta Get Drunk" and another Hank Cochran collaboration, "Who Do I Know in Dallas?" that had nothing whatsoever to do with folk music. The cover featured a photograph of Willie standing in the woods on his land, dressed in a double-breasted suit, a cigarette in his hand, looking pensive. "Once More with Feeling" was released as a single, reaching number 42 on the country singles chart.

The "Billy Stack as the Next Johnny Bush" promotion cratered when Stack returned to Fort Worth due to marital troubles. But Billy English stuck around. "I'd been coming out playing guitar and David would switch off to trumpet, but Willie couldn't afford the bigger band," Billy English said. But he stayed with Willie long enough to play the Palomino in Los Angeles, Atlanta, and more than a hundred other cities. "I know we played New York," Billy said, "because the electric windows on the Mercury Marquis got stuck and it was wintertime." On one run in the Mercury Marquis, Willie Nelson and the Record Men covered fifteen thousand miles in eighteen days, playing nine gigs, including one in Stamford, Connecticut, after playing Los Angeles, making the thirty-two-hundred-mile drive in sixty-nine hours.

The long drives left plenty of time to contemplate the grind, smoke cigarettes, drink beer or whiskey, pop pills, listen to the radio, shoot the shit, tell jokes, cuss the electric windows when they got stuck, or do whatever it took to get on down the road.

Late one evening in that darkest time between midnight and dawn, on the way from one show to the next, Willie and Paul were going over gigs past and gigs to come. Willie was lying down in the back of the station wagon. Paul was in the backseat. At one point, Willie propped himself up on his elbows until his eyes made contact with Paul's eyes, illuminated by the flickering lights of passing cars.

"One of these days," he said to Paul in a soft voice, "I'm going to make it up to you."

WILLIE'S promise to Paul reflected his growing feeling that recordwise, he was spinning his wheels and going nowhere. His next two albums, *Laying My*

Burdens Down and *Willie Nelson and Family,* were familiar stories: a new cast of studio players (guitarists Pete Wade and Chip Young, Norbert Putnam on bass, David Briggs on piano, and Jerry Carrigan on drums); good cover songs (solid versions of "Sunday Morning Coming Down" by Kris Kristofferson, Hank Williams's "I'm So Lonesome I Could Cry," Merle Haggard's "Today I Started Loving You Again," and folk-rocker James Taylor's hit "Fire and Rain"); good originals (a stirring gospel tune, "Kneel at the Feet of Jesus," and the weeper "I'm a Memory," which reached number 28 on the country singles chart); interesting concepts (a collection of downer blues and the Ridgetop gang posing for an album cover); and lousy sales.

Willie had become a problem to the suits at RCA. Waylon was enough of a pain in the ass. In addition to doing more and more of the songs he wanted to do rather than what the producer chose, Waylon wanted to produce himself and was demanding control of where the records were made, the song selection, and the artwork that decorated the album cover. Waylon gave RCA plenty of reasons to compromise, namely impressive record sales and box-office receipts. Handling Willie was like selling fine art that no one wanted to buy. "Honestly, I always thought I could sing pretty good, and it bothered me that nobody else thought so," Willie told Carleton Stowers. "The more I thought about it, the more negative I got. I got into fights with the recording company and all kind of bad things." It was a delicate balancing act. He knew in his head what he wanted his music to sound like, but it never came out that way on record. And yet he needed to have a record so he could sell himself. Chet Atkins and Felton Jarvis were supposed to know what record buyers wanted—that's why they were producers, or so Willie thought. So if they were so smart, why couldn't they get him a hit?

His unconventional manner of singing, his painfully sad songs, and his preference to play songs for a listening audience rather than a dancing crowd, not only made it hard for the RCA boys to understand him, but it sometimes cost him bookings. Management at Cain's Academy in Tulsa sent him a letter informing him, "We no longer need your services." But other venues rarely frequented by Nashville recording artists, such as Hillbilly Heaven in Upstate New York, at the dead end of a lonely road in the woods by the Canadian border, and the Horseshoe Tavern in Toronto, where Canada's biggest country star, Stompin' Tom Connors, would open the show, welcomed him with open arms.

The relentless road work made his brief stops at home almost pleasurable, despite the fact that his once-fiery romance with Shirley seemed cooler and cooler each time he came back. By 1969, Ridgetop had grown into one big happy family—some by birth, others through friendship. The lettering on the mailbox identified the tenants as "Willie Nelson and Many Others." It might have been called Nashville's first hippie commune, only hippies didn't exist in Tennessee and no one knew what a commune was.

Once he had discovered how easy it was to accumulate things whenever he was flush with cash, Willie began developing contempt for material goods. He'd go out of his way to break something just to show he didn't care, his don't-give-a-damn attitude usually expressed when he was shit-faced. Fans offered drinks so often, he started carrying a collapsible cup in his back pocket. And when he got real loaded, he turned mean.

"Willie was a bad drunk," Paul English stated flatly. "When he got really liquored-up, he'd want to drive. I'd have to take the keys from him. He didn't know what he was doing, he was so drunk."

No small part of it was the friends he kept. He was wild, all right, but Hank Cochran, Roger Miller, and Zeke Varnon were wilder. He could pop pills, drink whiskey, and pick for a few days straight, but he could never keep up with Jimmy Day, who could stay up for weeks. Compared with them, Willie was kind of straight-laced.

"Ridgetop was wild as hell," Bee Spears said. "People in rural Tennessee—as long as you mind your business, they'll leave you alone. Willie showed me this house to live in, but I'm not sure if anyone knew who owned it. It didn't have any electricity. The shower was a piece of garden hose that ran into a big can that had holes punched in it. It was a mess. It was Peyton Place. That's what happens with whiskey and amphetamines."

Whatever problems were caused by liquor and pills, women, friends, or family, or any combination thereof, they tended to disappear on the lost highway in the land of one-nighters. If Shirley was harping too much, the bills were piling up, or someone was bugging him, there was always the road. The moving landscape allowed him to reinvent himself nightly.

Playing a package show in Dallas, he was buttonholed by Morgan Choat, a North Texas disc jockey. "Willie went onstage in pink pants," observed Choat, an avowed country traditionalist. "Everyone else was wearing western clothes. After the show, I asked, 'Willie, what in the world's going on?'"

Willie leaned into his ear and whispered confidentially, "Morgan, I'm changing my style."

Crash Stewart, the San Antonio hustler with a car

lot and finance company on General McMullen Road who booked Willie's Texas dates, worked up a promotional flyer for the band that hyped Willie Nelson and the Record Men as "The Singin'est, The Playin'est, The Sellin'est Band from Nashville, Tennessee." In Texas, they were from Tennessee. In Tennessee, they were from Texas.

For every choice booking, such as sharing the bill with Hank Thompson at the University of Texas in Austin or headlining the Longhorn Ballroom in Dallas, where he was advertised as "writer-singer Willie Nelson," or being one of the four featured performers of the annual Texas Prison Rodeo in Huntsville in October (Jerry Lee Lewis, Conway Twitty, and Faron Young headlined the other shows), there were an equal number of shit-hole gigs quickly forgotten.

The cost of barnstorming may have sometimes required four grown men to share a single motel room, but you couldn't help feeling like a millionaire, standing behind a microphone and hearing the applause and cheers of people who paid money to come see you. Willie had seen too many friends, like Roger Miller, Johnny Cash, and now Waylon Jennings, pull down the big bucks and live the high life. For a few weeks, Willie was so convinced he was destined for the same success, he tried flying to gigs in an Aero Commander. Then the bills for operating the plane arrived in the mail.

The preferred mode of transportation became an Open Road camper. He may have owed Paul English $5,250 in back pay, and more than once Paul and Carlene English had to cover his utility bills, but he was a country music singing star in the eyes of those around him. Jimmy Day was semipermanently passed out in the back of the camper until Willie ran him off again, opening the door for the return of Bee Spears, the teenage bass player and pot dealer who'd gone back to San Antonio to play in a Mexican jazz ensemble. With Bee's return, David Zettner moved over to steel. The band had a history, a cool sharp-dressed look, and a sound that was out of the mainstream but clearly with a depth worth paying attention to.

IN July of 1969, Willie's daughters, Lana and Susie, their cousins Freddy and Mike Fletcher, and Willie's steel player David Zettner experienced their first rock festival. The delegation from Ridgetop drove to Atlanta to join 150,000 people like them at the Atlanta Pop Festival at the Atlanta International Raceway. The hippie phenomenon going on in California, which they had heard on records, seen on TV, and read about, was right there in front of their faces.

Atlanta Pop featured several new acts ushering in a new post-Beatles era for rock. A four-piece group from England called Led Zeppelin would sell tens of millions of albums and concert tickets by doing a revved-up version of American blues music. Two growling soul shouters, an Englishman named Joe Cocker and a sassy woman from Port Arthur, Texas, by way of Austin and San Francisco named Janis Joplin, reinterpreted rhythm and blues for young white audiences. Creedence Clearwater Revival, a band from the suburbs of northern California, rode a string of swampy Southern-sounding hit singles to displace the Beatles as the most popular band in the world. Two big band ensembles, Blood, Sweat & Tears and the Chicago Transit Authority, were in the process of creating a new genre known as jazz-rock. Also on the bill at Atlanta Pop were influential jazz pianist Dave Brubeck, the Los Angeles boogie band Canned Heat, Chuck Berry, the father of modern rock and roll, the pioneering power trio Grand Funk Railroad, Bob Dylan's organist Al Kooper, a gypsy rock-and-soul ensemble known as Delaney & Bonnie & Friends, and a blues-rocking albino kid who grew up just down the road from Janis Joplin named Johnny Winter.

Lana came back from the trip to Georgia blown away by the coolness of the entire event. "I wished all these people could hear Dad's music," she said. "If they liked Blood, Sweat, and Tears, I knew they'd like him." The way Willie thought, the way he approached life, and the community of family and friends he'd created at Ridgetop would have fit right in at Atlanta Pop or at Woodstock, the rock festival in Upstate New York staged six weeks after Atlanta Pop.

ONE morning in late November 1969, Shirley Nelson was sorting through the mail in the kitchen when Lana heard a piercing scream. "There's a hospital bill and a baby!" Shirley shrieked. She had opened an envelope and pulled out a bill from a Houston hospital for the birth of Paula Carlene, daughter of Connie Koepke and Willie Nelson, delivered on Halloween.

Shirley flipped out and started throwing things, but Willie wasn't there to hit. She shrieked again and reached for a bottle of pills, gobbling them down impulsively. Lana realized what she had done and dragged her into her car so she could drive Shirley to the hospital to get her stomach pumped, even though Lana didn't have a driver's license. "I felt so sorry for her," Lana said. "I wanted to help her but I didn't know what I wanted to do. All I could do is support her and be there for her."

When Willie returned from his tour, Shirley cornered him in the backyard with a gun in her hand. After he tried talking to her, she decided not to use it, although she did fire several shots later while they were riding in the car.

The knot between Willie and Shirley had unraveled. In reality, it had been loosening ever since she'd settled at Ridgetop to raise Willie's kids. Shirley was bored and jealous, knowing he was catting around away from home, just like he'd done with her when they fell in love behind Martha's and Biff's backs. She'd taken lovers out of need and out of spite, knowing he was taking lovers. He was taking lovers on the road because he could.

Whenever he was headed for a gig in the eastern half of Texas, he'd give Connie Koepke a call. Once Connie had discovered he was married, she put the relationship on ice for almost two years before the flame was rekindled. It was some kind of crazy love, and the affair intensified until Connie discovered she was pregnant. She told Willie she wanted to keep the baby and raise the child herself. Willie offered to help out financially, as if he were sitting on a bundle of cash. Connie rented an apartment in Houston for herself and the baby she was expecting, with her parents' support.

Shirley and Willie tried to patch things up. Willie promised he'd stay out of Houston. Shirley promised she'd take the straight-and-narrow path and quit pilling and seeing other men. The promises didn't hold. Willie tracked Shirley to the apartment of her back-door man in Nashville and confronted him. Shirley continued finding lipstick on Willie's collars and smelling perfume on his clothes.

"At one point he bugged a phone to find out who it was," recalled Lana. "He came home once and she was gone. He asked where she was. I said I didn't know. Susie said she was over at Larry's house. After dad got the taped phone conversation, he told her she had to leave."

Willie and the kids moved into an apartment. When Shirley finally departed, going back to her family in Missouri, Willie and the kids moved back into the house, along with a stripper Willie knew named Helen and her kids. Two weeks of another new family led Lana to run off and get married at the age of sixteen, the same age as Martha when she married Willie, the same age as his mom and dad when they married, and the same age as Bobbie when she married Bud Fletcher.

Susie, now a precocious thirteen-year-old, called

and talked to Connie and asked if she could come to visit her and the new baby, Paula Carlene. Connie welcomed Susie and they all got along fine. A few weeks later, Willie called Connie before he played Houston and ended up staying overnight with Connie and Paula Carlene. The next morning, he asked Connie to come with him to Ridgetop. Shirley was gone. So was Helen the stripper, who had been marched away by Carlene English, Paul's wife.

The band helped her load her belongings into the Open Road camper, and Connie and Paula Carlene arrived at Ridgetop in the summer of 1970. The next day, Willie kissed her good-bye and hit the road again.

Lana took an immediate liking to Connie. "She was about ten years older than me, so I could relate," Lana said. "She was pretty and she loved my dad. She wasn't a musician, she didn't have her own career etched out, and she brought us a baby, my little sister — she was real cute."

Connie bonded with the kids' aunt Bobbie, who had moved from Austin with her boys, Mike, Freddy, and Randy. Bobbie felt like the sister Connie never had. Willie's mother, Myrle, and her husband, Ken "Kilowatt" Harvey, an electrician from Washington state, moved in on the other side of Willie from his father, Ira, and his wife, Lorraine, who tended the seven-hundred-acre plot west of the house. Daughter Susie moved into a trailer by Pop and Lorraine's place. Wade Ray and Jimmy Day lived close enough to borrow a cup of sugar or a guitar pick. David Zettner resided in the basement of the Nelson house, where Willie went to write when he needed to get away from everyone and record songs on a two-track tape machine. Bee Spears stayed in a rickety house and later a trailer. Paul and Carlene English had moved up from Fort Worth in 1968, followed by Jack Fletcher, who was working with Paul and helping drive the band. Lana moved into another trailer nearby with her husband, Steve Warren, and their new baby boy, Nelson Ray. Even Martha Nelson, Willie's first wife, came back, moving in with Lana and Steve to look after baby Nelson.

Myrle was happy to demonstrate where Willie's wild streak came from. "She was a tough woman," Freddy Fletcher, her grandson, said. "I was in high school at Ridgetop, and she called me and said, 'I think somebody's trying to break in the house and I'm about to blow his fucking brains out.' I went to her place and she's got some vodka and a pistol on the table, just waiting. I saw a lot of Willie in Mother Harvey — Myrle. She was no bullshit. She had been down the road. She knew I was knee-deep in music and we were probably smoking a little pot here and there, but she didn't put up with anything that was out of bounds."

Myrle and Lorraine didn't get along much. Everyone else was more or less on the same wavelength, with one exception. Shortly after Nelson was born, Lana and Steve had a hellacious fight. Lana called Willie and Connie, crying. Steve had hit her. Willie went ballistic and drove down the road, where he confronted Steve and punched him out, advising him never to lay a hand on his daughter again or he'd kill him.

"Don't hit me, Willie, don't hit me," Steve begged while lying on the floor. "I got anxiety, I got anxiety."

Willie went home. Lana called to say Steve had left and that Martha, the baby, and she would come over directly.

An hour later, Steve returned to Willie's house accompanied by his brothers, who were armed with rifles. They started shooting at the house, just as Lana, baby Nelson, and Martha walked in the back door, unaware they were in the middle of a shoot-out. Connie and the kids lay low on the living room floor. As Steve and his brothers made a second pass, Martha stood up and started yelling about kicking Steve's sorry ass, until Connie pulled her down to the floor again. She introduced herself to Martha, whom she'd never met.

Willie jumped up from where he was hiding in the yard, returning fire with a single shotgun blast, joined by Paul firing his M-1 rifle from the side of the house, aiming under the bumper as Steve's car peeled away.

Steve returned a few minutes later, just as Paul predicted, because "his pride was hurt." This time Willie used Paul's M-1 rifle, while Paul produced his snub nose .38 pistol and they both returned fire. Steve stopped the car and yelled out his surrender.

"Whatever I've done, let me cool it out," he said with his hands held up.

Steve came back the next day and apologized, promising not to hit Lana again. Paul told him he was glad he kept driving after his tire was shot out; otherwise he would have had to aim to kill rather than shoot to miss. Steve told Paul he was glad he'd missed, too.

The incident brought the family closer, much to Lana's amazement and embarrassment. "There was Myrle and Ken and Pop and Lorraine and Connie and Martha all under one roof, along with Jack Fletcher and his ex-wife. It was quite a tribe. I almost got my father killed and caused quite a bit of trouble," Lana said.

Fussing and feuding was one thing, but no one messed with family.

Connie tried hard to be an accommodating partner, considering what she'd walked into. One night, Willie brought home songwriters Hank Cochran and Red Lane, along with two women she did not know or care to know. They all were roaring drunk and itching to play music. Connie cooked them dinner and cleaned up the dishes, but she was perplexed when the party didn't end but rather continued into the next day.

Susie came into the bedroom in the morning to tell Connie that Red Lane and his girlfriend had kicked Susie out of her room because they wanted the bed. Connie dutifully got up and cooked everyone breakfast, again without the girlfriends so much as offering to help. When she went out on the porch and asked Hank how he wanted his eggs and he said, "Who said I wanted eggs?" in a gruff tone, she blew her top.

"That was the trigger," Connie said. "That and Red Lane and his girlfriend kicking Susie out of her room." Connie let loose a string of expletives and went around the house, telling everyone to get out and get out now. Willie pulled her aside and told her, "You can't do that, we can't do that, it'll hurt their feelings." He had a better plan. He told her to get Paula and Susie and Billy in the car and leave. Once the visitors figured out they weren't there, they'd leave, too. "That was Willie's way of dealing with it—we'll get out, and then they'll have to get out," Connie said. "And that's what we did."

The ruse worked. Connie had a healthy dislike of Hank from that time on but tolerated him.

Usually she enjoyed the friends Willie brought home for picking sessions. "That was the fun stuff. You never knew who would show up." But Willie would just as likely be holed up in one of the suites at the Spence Manor across the street from BMI in Nashville, where the "store" was and where the other songwriters were hanging, and play until he couldn't.

"**WHEN** I came to Nashville, the people I hung out with were serious songwriters, none of whom were successful yet," said Kris Kristofferson. "Willie was the hero of the soulful set—the people who were in the business because they loved the soul of country music. They loved Willie, John [Cash], and Roger Miller, the singer-songwriters. The closest I got to Willie was Jimmy Day. He used to hang out with us. We'd sit around at these jam sessions, sing Willie songs. I went out to his place in Ridgetop, hung out with Jimmy Day, but I never did meet Willie."

Still, Kris was a fan.

"When Johnny Cash had his TV show, Mickey

Newbury and I were talking to Linda Ronstadt's manager, telling him about Willie, how he was like a jazz singer. 'You're really missing a bet if you don't pick up on him,' " Kris told the manager. Kris knew Willie had it, for all the wrong reasons as far as the Nashville establishment was concerned. "Ray Price came out to talk to me on the road once. He said performing was going to ruin my songwriting like it did Willie."

In November of 1970, Willie recorded a new song he and Hank Cochran had written called "What Can You Do to Me Now?" The lyrics were prophetic. Two weeks before Christmas, Willie bought Connie a new Mercury Cougar, the first new car she'd ever had. On her way back from the grocery, one of the first trips she'd taken in her new ride, she stopped at the mailbox to fetch the mail. As soon as she stepped out of the car, the vehicle started rolling down the hill. She tried jumping back in but couldn't engage the brake. The car headed into the woods and rolled over, stopping just before a steep drop-off. Connie's arm was cut from broken glass, but otherwise she was fine.

When the wrecker arrived to tow the car out, the front seats were missing. Someone had stolen them, someone, evidently, who knew that a brand-new car had crashed in the middle of nowhere.

Then, two days before Christmas, as a light snow dusted the Cumberland Valley, Willie was in Nashville at a pre-Christmas party at Lucky Moeller's, when he got a phone call.

"Hey, Willie, your house is on fire. The house is melting." It was Randy Fletcher, one of his nephews.

"Well, pull the car in the garage, let them have it," Willie said calmly. If his possessions were going up in flames, he could at least collect more insurance money.

Connie had been alone in the house that night with Paula Carlene when Randy stopped by, waking her from a nap. She went to check on Paula Carlene so she could show her off to Randy when she saw smoke scaling up the wall by Paula's bed. The wiring that Willie's stepfather, Ken "Kilowatt" Harvey, had rigged in the basement had caught fire. "He had wired the whole house," Lana said. "When you'd sit on the toilet, you'd get shocked. When you swam too close to the underwater light in the swimming pool you'd feel little shock waves."

Connie grabbed Paula Carlene and ran out of the house. Randy called the fire department and Willie. Willie was on the scene in less than thirty minutes. While he'd meant what he said about driving the car into the garage, he forgot about some other valuables that needed fetching. While the volunteer fire department was dousing the flames, Willie leapt over the fire hoses and dashed into the house, ignoring repeated warnings. He emerged from the smoldering ruins with his guitar, Trigger, and a plastic trash bag containing his stash of fine Colombian Gold marijuana. A few days later, Pop Nelson — his father, Ira — found in the debris a footlocker containing the first demos Willie had recorded in Nashville in 1961 and files of song lyrics and memorabilia.

The night of the fire, the family moved into the two-bedroom trailer Willie kept at Pop's place, where Susie was living. Susie fashioned a Christmas tree out of one of Willie's boots with an evergreen limb stuck in it. They spent Christmas Eve at musician and songwriter Dottie West's home, where Dottie took Connie aside for some woman-to-woman advice. It could've been worse, she told her: "You've got everything," Dottie said. "You didn't lose anything but stuff. I've been through a fire. I'm older than you and lived longer and I've come to realize what's really important. You've got your family, everybody's healthy. That was just stuff. And you get to get new stuff!" The way Dottie put it made Connie think starting over wouldn't be so hard.

"I had so much respect for her as a person," Connie said. "Forget the singer part — she got me through a really hard time."

After Christmas, with their house burned to cinders and the wrecked Cougar in the body shop, Willie and Connie took Lana, Susie, and Billy to Austin to visit Willie's sister. Bobbie Nelson had moved back from Ridgetop a few months earlier to work the piano bar circuit there. Bobbie had made a lot of friends in Austin after she moved there from Fort Worth in 1965 to play the Hammond organ at the El Chico Mexican restaurant at Hancock Center, Austin's first shopping mall. This time around, she was working places like the 40 Acres Club, the Stephen F. Austin Hotel, the Scotch Mist Lounge by Seton Hospital, the Howard Johnson Motor Lodge at I-35 and 183, and Norman Eaton's Polonaise Room private club next to the state capitol, making fans of prominent doctors, lawyers, politicians, and lobbyists, a budding young pianist named Marcia Ball, and perhaps the most popular person in all Texas—University of Texas football coach Darrell K Royal. By extension, Willie was already wired in.

Lost Valley, 1971

NOTHING LIKE A FIRE to cleanse the soul. Texas felt better than ever, especially after Crash Stewart called with an offer Willie couldn't pass up. Crash had found temporary shelter for Willie and Many Others at the Lost Valley Dude Ranch in the Hill Country near the town of Bandera, west of San Antonio. The property was in bankruptcy, and Crash arranged it so they could stay through the summer while the house in Ridgetop was being rebuilt.

Willie was game. "I was already working most of my dates in Texas," he reasoned. "Going back and forth was wearing me out."

The improvised family moved in, putting the Olympic pool, the guest cabanas, and golf course to good use. Willie, Connie, Susie, Billy, Paula Carlene,

Aunt Bobbie's son Freddy, and David Zettner lived in the ranch foreman's house. For a while singer Johnny Darnell and his wife, Sam, joined them. Paul and Carlene English and their son, Darrell Wayne, moved into the house across the way. Bee Spears and his wife had the house on the other side of them. Since they were living on the cheap, they cooked communally and were happiest whenever Connie prepared her Hungarian stew.

It was at Lost Valley that Willie really became one with the game about which he used to razz Paul and Bee for "chasing that little white ball around a cow pasture." He played seventy-two holes of golf the first day, with chemical and herbal inspiration. Before the week was over, Paul knew his buddy was hooked when rain started pouring down in the middle of a round and Willie told Paul to go on, he was going to finish his round.

They approached the game creatively, such as the time everyone on the course was high on psychedelics and played golf backwards, from the putting green to the teebox. Bee had brought up some LSD he'd scored in San Antonio called Goofy Grape. Almost everyone at Lost Valley dropped a hit. The next morning, Willie was at Bee's door, asking, "You got any more of that Purple Jesus?"

"LSD, THC, STP, NAACP, we were doing the

whole alphabet," said Billy Cooper, a recent addition to the Many Others. "We'd go, Let's try two of these or this and see what happens."

When they weren't doing dope, playing golf, playing cards, or playing chess, a pursuit that Paul English picked up as a teenager in jail, they were playing music. One dependable gig was down the road at John T. Floore's Country Store in Helotes, where Bee Spears and David Zettner had come of age and where country music and Western Swing ruled. The store was actually a bar and indoor dance floor with a giant outside patio for big dances. Mr. Floore was a cantankerous cuss known for his tamales and his old-fashioned ways—men removed their hats inside his place or faced expulsion.

Willie Nelson and band played for the door at Floore's, gradually increasing their earnings from $500 to $1,500 a night as attendance grew from 100 to 150 to 300. The uncertainty of their income was tempered by the satisfaction in knowing they controlled the deal. "I'm tired of hearing the club owners bitch about losing money," Willie said. "If I take the door, they can't bitch."

Larry Trader and Billy Ray Cooper were among the first to show up at Floore's and hang at Lost Valley. B.C., as Cooper was called, and Trader were veterans of the same kind of off-the-books, under-the-table rackets in San Antonio as the "businesses" Paul English used to run in Fort Worth and in Houston.

Larry Trader was one tough hombre. Over the ten years B.C. had known him, he figured he'd seen Larry get seriously cut or shot up at least five times. And Larry was Willie Nelson's friend for life. They'd met in the mid-1960s when Larry was Ray Price's bagman, collecting the performance fee after shows. After doing a show in Denton, Texas, opening for Price, Willie sensed he was about to get stiffed by the club owner and complained to Ray. "We gotta leave town tonight and I think this guy's screwing with us. Do you know anybody we can send in to count money for us so we don't get screwed?" Price told him he did. A black Cadillac rolled up to the venue and out stepped an imposing gentleman wearing a suit and tie and carrying a violin case. "He didn't look like no fiddle player, either," observed Willie. After introducing himself, Larry stayed after the show long enough to make sure Willie Nelson got paid in full.

When Trader took B.C. to Lost Valley to meet Willie, B.C. saw him in a different light. "He was this great little guy who didn't say anything," B.C. marveled, as if he'd met a mystic. Trader ended up taking Willie to a string of honky-tonks in the Alamo City so he could show off the country music star to his pals. B.C. went back to his place out on Babcock Road on the northern edge of San Antonio, where his daddy, Brother George W. Cooper, had a broadcasting studio in the back of their home.

Brother Cooper was a radio preacher. His sermons were broadcast on XEG, XERF, XELO, and other radio stations in Mexico whose powerful signals reaching across North America helped build a profitable mail-order business selling Bibles, sermons, religious tracts, and greeting cards for all occasions to millions of listeners at home.

Billy ran an ambulance business after a brief stint as a used-car salesman. He prided himself on his driving skills. In all his years of racing ambulance services to wrecks, he'd never had an accident. He was not so proud of his salesmanship, which he claimed was so persuasive, "people would practically beg you to sell them a piece of shit."

Willie took a shine to Billy Ray in no small part out of admiration for his daddy, the radio preacher. Brother Cooper reminded Willie of his own experiences as a pitchman on XEG back when he was at the Cowtown Hoedown in Fort Worth.

Whenever Willie Nelson and his Lost Valley Boys worked John T. Floore's, which was just about every week, Willie would go over to B.C.'s after the show with a few band members and friends, where they'd sit on the floor, drink beer, do dope, and listen to Willie Nelson sing and play guitar until the sun came up.

One morning after an all-nighter at his place, B.C. pointed Willie toward the Austin Highway so he could drive home. "Instead, he took Fredericksburg Road, picked up an Indian hitchhiker who had a joint, and ended up at his house," Billy said. In the spirit of wanting to help out Willie, the owner of Cooper's Ambulance Service offered his services. "Anytime you need a driver, I'm there for you."

TEXAS was solid ground; anywhere else, not so much. Bookings were hard to come by once he crossed the Sabine River into Louisiana or crossed the Red River toward Oklahoma. Whenever the band was out on the road and money was tight, Connie Nelson and Carlene English would gather pennies and put them in rolls so they could buy groceries.

Willie's musician friend Darrell McCall followed him to Texas at the behest of Crash Stewart, who had worldwide *and* outer space rights to book McCall. Darrell was sick of Nashville and longed for the crowds he remembered playing in front of in Texas. "They were into fiddles and steel," he said. "That's why I wanted to go to Texas, to play in those dance halls, the same places I played with Faron and Ray. I always said you'll never get rich working 'em, but you'll work all your life till you're ninety years old. I had enough of a name that Crash Stewart had a market for me."

Another of Willie's protégés, Johnny Bush, had signed with RCA Records. At the annual Disc Jockey Convention, Johnny met Jerry Bradley, the label's A&R chief and second in command to Chet Atkins. Jerry told Johnny, "All you gotta do now is write that hit song." With Harlan Howard, Hank Cochran, Willie Nelson, Dallas Frazier, Red Lane, and loads of other writers knocking at his door, Jerry Bradley hardly needed Johnny Bush to write a hit. But Johnny took up the challenge. While he was driving to a date in Texarkana, a phrase stuck in his head: "Bathing my memory'd mind in the wetness of its soul." Johnny thought it sounded like a Willie Nelson song. By the time he returned from the date, he'd finished the words to "Whiskey River."

Johnny called Willie at Lost Valley and sang it to him over the phone. "What do you think?" he asked.

"Sounds like you got something there," Willie told him.

"Good, I'll put it with your publishing company,"

Johnny told him. "But I've only got one verse and a chorus."

"Well, you've already said everything you need to say," Willie reassured him. "Sing it all the way through and sing it again."

That's what Johnny did.

When it was finally issued by RCA in 1972, "Whiskey River" by Johnny Bush reached number 14 on the *Billboard* country singles chart. But it stayed at number 1 across Texas for weeks and then years, eventually working its way into Willie Nelson's repertoire.

Willie's history of helping others brought rewards that transcended money. By bringing his personal and musical family to Lost Valley, he got to experience the soft bloom of springtime in the Texas Hill Country. The sight of bluebonnets painting hillsides laced with creeks and rivers and of armadillos rooting in the caliche soil, the soothing sensation of soft Gulf breezes warming the skin, accompanied by cold bottles of Lone Star and Pearl to slake thirsts, and the sweet, stinky smell of burning marijuana flower tops did a number on his head. From his temporary perch among the scrub oaks and the live oaks and the artesian springs and clear-running streams flanked by limestone banks came revelations. Willie's Texas network hadn't failed him. His audience hadn't forgotten him. The fire had been a good thing.

"I was raised in Texas beer joints, so I went back to my old beer joints," he later said. "I was home again. I knew all the club owners. I met a lot of my old waitresses that took care of me. I was back in my element."

He worked with promoters such as Buddy Western of Milano, who was gifted in the art of promoting concerts that were known in the business as "phone deals." A promoter would go into a town with three or four helpers, rent motel rooms, and start working the phones, calling every business in town in search of a concert sponsor, ideally an organization, like a volunteer fire department. The deal Buddy Western offered to such organizations was simple: "I'm going to raise money for you with a music benefit and I'll give you twenty percent of the total take." The organization took care of ticket sales (in most cases, ending up giving tickets away and absorbing the loss), and Western would hire acts like Ernest Tubb for a $1,000 guarantee or thereabouts and pad the bill with local talent willing to play for cheap or free.

One phone deal for Houston firefighters at the Music Hall downtown was headlined by Conway Twitty, but Conway was a no-show, the MC informed the full house, much to their disappointment. Filling in was one of the undercard acts, Willie Nelson and the Record Men. The crowd was clearly restless, especially once a smiling Willie took the stage with his band. The sight of Paul English dressed in black, mustache and goatee and cape draped around his shoulders telegraphing the Devil, prompted a few fans to start booing, according to one fan. "Willie was unruffled by the response. He kept smiling, didn't say a word, and started singing his best-known compositions—'Funny How Time Slips Away,' 'Hello Walls,' and 'Night Life.' By the time he got to 'Crazy,' the audience was eating out of the palm of his hand."

Whenever Johnny Bush found himself on the same show with Willie and being billed as the headliner, he made sure Willie went on last out of respect. "Willie's the man," Johnny would say. "He knows it, I know it. What you see today, he's not going to stay like this." Bush talked like he was some kind of psychic.

Instead of searching for ways to please Chet Atkins and RCA, Willie was prompted by the respite in Texas to embark on his most ambitious writing project ever. His composing skills had long ago transcended the simplicity of Merle Haggard's "Okie from Muskogee" and other popular country hits of

the day. Willie was writing deep and writing prolifically. Bee Spears said that whenever he was cleaning
up the bus or the camper they traveled in, some of
the pieces of paper he picked up had lyrics on them.
"When he wants to write, he wants it right now and
writes on whatever he's got to write on," Bee said.

All the playing and touring and recording mixed
with the new drugs he was experimenting with were
pushing new ideas and new concepts to the surface.
That much became clear to David Zettner the afternoon he returned to the Holiday Inn in Nashville,
where he was sharing a room with Willie on a trip
back to Nashville for a recording session. David had
gone out catting around the day before when Willie
nicely asked him to get lost because he had some
writing to do. David returned the next day to a dark-
ened room with Willie passed out under a pile of
notebook paper and more paper scattered over both
beds and the floor. Zettner picked up a page and
squinted. The pages were covered with scribbled lyrics. Willie had been in a writing frenzy. Seven songs
in one night.

Willie shrugged it off. He was due in the studio
the next day and needed to finish the album that had
been kicking around in his head. "In my mind, it
was one big picture anyway, one long song," he said.

"The creative juices were flowing. I was open, writing a lot of good stuff."

Yesterday's Wine was a whole concept, a concept far bolder (and riskier) than Chet Atkins's idea of a concept, an album of songs all about Texas. Willie's concept was about "imperfect man" contemplating his own mortality.

It was such a far-out idea that when it came time to record in early May of 1971, Felton Jarvis had no choice but to let the tapes roll. Willie and David Zettner were joined by guitarist Dave Kirby, who'd toured with Willie back in the early 1960s, Pete Wade, another fellow traveler from the Ray Price days, and Chip Young, the ghost guitarist on *Live Country Music Concert*. Weldon Myrick played steel, Junior Huskey bass, Pig Robbins piano, Jerry Carrigan drums, Bobby Thompson banjo, Charlie McCoy harmonica, and Norman Keith and Buddy Spicher fiddle. Hillbillies were scratching their heads before the music even began.

A godlike voice from on high opens the album, asking the question: "You do know why you're here?"

"Yes," replies a human voice. "There is great confusion on earth, and the power that is has concluded the following: Perfect man has visited earth already, and his voice was heard; the voice of imperfect man must now be manifest. And I have been selected as the most likely candidate."

"Yes," God agrees. "The time is April, and therefore you, a Taurus, must go. To be born under the same sign twice adds strength, and this strength, combined with wisdom and love, is the key."

Yesterday's Wine revealed Willie as a deep thinker who put his philosophy on the table in three-minute melodic chunks for all to ponder:

> *Explain to me again, O Lord, why I'm here*
> *I don't know, I don't know*
> *The setting for the stage is still not done*
> *Where's the show? Where's the show?*

"It scared a lot of people," admitted Willie. "RCA's reaction was 'Who's gonna play this?' They started thinking about AM radio. My whole idea was playing the album all the way through. It was a spiritual album." And definitely too strange for *Hee Haw*.

Yesterday's Wine marked the beginning of the end of Willie's relationship with RCA. The label pressed up the standard ten thousand copies and let nature take its course. Promotion behind Willie Nelson's albums had historically been nonexistent. Nothing had changed and the situation would remain the same for the three RCA albums that followed, *Willie Nelson and Family* (featuring a photograph of the extended family at Ridgetop on the cover), *The Willie Way*, and *The Words Don't Fit the Picture*.

He'd made fourteen albums for RCA with not much to show. Chet Atkins tried but never sold Willie as a recording artist, other than reissuing his version of "Pretty Paper" as a Christmas single every year. Chet may have been a picker's picker. But as a producer and label chief, he stuck to formula.

It wasn't just that *Yesterday's Wine* was too weird for RCA. "Willie was way too weird for Chet," observed Cowboy Jack Clement, who came from Memphis to Nashville as Chet's first assistant about the same time as Willie arrived in Nashville. Chet Atkins had kept country music alive when rock and roll took over the sales bins. The Nashville Sound he helped create kept churning out product with enough hits to justify his position. But there was no way he was going to have hits on all the acts he produced, and Willie was proof. (Then again, Chet likened Dolly Parton's vocal talents to those of a "screech owl.")

"The thing with Willie is he had to go and show them what he was gonna do, and he didn't know what he was gonna do when he got in the studio," Hank Cochran said in his defense.

Once the house in Ridgetop was rebuilt and ready to be reoccupied, Willie and Connie and the kids spent three months back in Tennessee, long enough for Willie to record and release his final album for RCA, *The Words Don't Fit the Picture*, notable for the first recorded version of "Good Hearted Woman," a song Willie had written with Waylon Jennings.

The song came out of a late-night poker game at the Fort Worther Motel on Jacksboro Highway in Fort Worth. Billy Gray, Willie, and Waylon had been playing poker all night. Toward the end of the game, Waylon said, "Willie, I've got this song I want you to help me write." Connie Nelson was a witness. "Willie had been drinking and Waylon was doing his thing [making trips to the bathroom to snort cocaine]," she said. "The only part Willie came up with was 'Through teardrops and laughter we're gonna walk through this world hand in hand.' Waylon said, 'That's it! That's what's missing' and gave Willie half the song." Waylon asked Connie to write down the lyrics because they were so out of it, "none of us is going to remember this tomorrow," he told her.

The album cover of *The Words Don't Fit the Picture* was meant to be a joke. A photograph depicted Willie wearing bubble aviator shades with his hair hanging over his ears, holding a guitar case covered with bumper stickers while standing in front of producer Felton Jarvis's Rolls-Royce, flanked by Connie in a black gown and white fur hat and Felton dressed as the chauffeur.

It didn't matter if record buyers got the joke or not. The record didn't matter anymore. Neither did Ridgetop. Willie and Connie had been back just long enough to realize that nothing about Nashville and the music business felt right anymore. Willie Nelson and Many Others were GTT — Gone to Texas.

By leaving, Willie was doing what dozens of Texans in Tennessee wished they could do but never did. Losing the immediate connection to the business of music was career suicide, in the eyes of many. No one left and succeeded. Bakersfield was its own scene, thanks to Buck Owens and Merle Haggard, and Jim Halsey was doing all right building a small management/recording empire in Tulsa. A smattering of country records were being made in Memphis, Muscle Shoals, Alabama, Los Angeles, and Houston. But Willie was crazy to think he could move to Central Texas and stay in the game. Still, everyone was secretly rooting for him.

He had put down a deposit on an apartment lease in Houston, but a festival near Austin and some friendly persuasion changed his plans.

Staged over a three-day weekend on March 17, 18,

and 19, in 1972 on a seven-thousand-acre ranch thirty miles west of Austin, the Dripping Springs Reunion attempted to replicate the festive spirit of Woodstock, only with country acts. Governor Preston Smith and former senator Ralph Yarborough showed up, along with a few thousand fans, for the Friday bluegrass lineup of Jimmy Martin, Earl Scruggs, Bill Monroe, Lester Flatt, Jim and Jessie, Charlie Rich, Buck Owens, and the Light Crust Doughboys. Around ten thousand fans attended on Saturday, March 18, to hear the stars and legends, such as Tex Ritter, Roy Acuff and his Smokey Mountain Boys, Hank Snow, Charlie Walker, Roger Miller, Sonny James, Dottie West, and Austin yodeler Kenneth Threadgill, whose first venture into the recording studio was bankrolled by Kris Kristofferson.

The crowd count was lower for the Sunday concert, which starred Merle Haggard and Bonnie Owens, Tom T. Hall, Waylon Jennings, Kris Kristofferson, and Willie. What few fans there were glommed onto Willie, Waylon, and Kris — they represented a new kind of country that didn't make them sound like old fart rednecks. Willie responded by playing his songwriting hits and some rocked-up country and joining Waylon to sing "Good Hearted Woman." Promoters who had predicted a turnout of sixty thousand fans were claiming losses in excess of

$140,000. Bob Woltering, the executive editor of *Music City News*, the Nashville trade paper owned by Faron Young, which printed programs for the event, reported fewer than three thousand copies sold. A county fair drew bigger crowds.

The payoff came after the show. The picking session at the home of Darrell K Royal following the close of the Dripping Springs Reunion made up for it all, at least for those who wrangled an invite from Coach. "Coach" was the name everyone used when referring to Royal, the University of Texas football coach who loved homespun music almost as much as he loved football, maybe even more. Willie, Kris, Rita, Red Lane, Red Steagall, Kenneth Threadgill, and Charlie Rich passed the guitar around Royal's living room while Coach, supported by his wife, Edith, kept a tight rein on the gathering, whistling loudly to warn talkers who weren't paying attention to the music to either cool it or cut out. Waylon and Willie sang "Good Hearted Woman." Rita Coolidge joined Mr. and Mrs. Charlie Rich on "Life Has Its Little Ups and Downs." Mr. Threadgill yodeled.

Shortly after the Reunion, Paul, Willie, and Bee went back to Nashville to RCA's studios to record their final sessions, laying down tracks late at night for another concept album. The songs—"Phases, Stages, Circles, Cycles, and Scenes," "Pretend I Never

Happened," "Sister's Coming Home," "Down at the Corner Beerjoint," "I'm Falling in Love Again," "Who'll Buy My Memories?," "No Love Around," "Come On Home," and a cover of the old hillbilly stomper "Mountain Dew"—were all part of a story floating around Willie's mind.

"Willie was into that Astara thing," Bee Spears said. "He was really expanding his way of thinking." The pot and the acid and whatever else came along helped.

"Mountain Dew" b/w "Phases, Stages, Circles, Cycles, and Scenes," the last single for RCA, did not chart. The last album for RCA, *The Willie Way*, stalled at number 34.

SHIRLEY Collie Nelson finally agreed to a divorce. With her real and imaginary illnesses, her depression aggravated by leaving her career behind, and her being totally pissed at Willie for shacking up with other women and having a child with Connie, she concluded their marriage was done.

Connie dropped Paula Carlene with her parents in Houston and she and Willie flew to Las Vegas and got married at the Chapel of the Bells, with the minister's wife as witness. Steve Wynn, the owner of the

Golden Nugget, where Willie frequently played, provided the hospitality.

The Dripping Springs Reunion had strengthened the bond between Willie and Kris Kristofferson. A few months earlier, Willie and Paul English had showed up at Kris's Philharmonic Hall concert in New York, and Kris had put Willie onstage. "I had to introduce him to the crowd; they didn't know who he was," Kris said. "He stole the show."

After Dripping Springs and getting married, Willie rounded up a carload of pals to drive to Durango, Mexico, to watch Kris make a movie with Bob Dylan for filmmaker Sam Peckinpah called *Pat Garrett and Billy the Kid*. Willie ended up serenading the cast and crew all day long at Peckinpah's house, gladly accommodating Dylan's requests to hear more and more. "Dylan was a little shy, scared to death," observed Willie. "They had him jumpin' and runnin' on them horses, and he ain't no cowboy." "Willie was so much fun to be around," Kris said. "We were close friends and we were both bucking the system." It wasn't just them, either. Willie's wife, Connie, and Kris's girlfriend and duet partner, Rita Coolidge, shared a wild streak and became running buddies too.

Austin, 1972

THE HIPPIE CHICK didn't hesitate when the Open Road camper pulled over to offer her a ride just outside of Kerrville. The woman looked old enough to vote, but barely. She was certainly not the down-and-out variety of hitchhiker who once populated the sides of highways. She was a genuine Texas hippie chick — straight, long hair below her shoulders, no makeup, tight tank top, no bra, denim cut-off shorts, sandals, stash bag, macramé belt, redolent of patchouli oil, the whole package sunbaked and radiating an I-don't-give-a-shit attitude. She just wanted a ride to Austin.

The men in the camper required no discussion among themselves before pulling over to fetch the young woman with her thumb pointing east.

To the hippie chick, the men in the Open Road

camper appeared to be older guys in their thirties and forties who looked sorta like bikers but sorta not, a rough bunch showing signs of wear and tear maybe, but with a modicum of cool, although they sure weren't hippies like she was. And yet, the aroma of righteous weed wafting from inside the camper got her attention before she even stepped inside.

A high time was had by all on the ride through the Hill Country. The country singer and his band and the hippie chick got along just fine. She was dropped off in the caliche dirt parking lot of a body shop near the corner of South First Street and Barton Springs in South Austin, just across the Colorado River from downtown, at the Armadillo World Headquarters, an old National Guard Armory that had been transformed into a hippie concert hall, beer garden, and cultural center.

Like the Avalon and the Fillmore in the San Francisco Bay Area, the Armadillo was all about the music and a shared tolerance for marijuana and psychedelic drugs. But unlike San Franciscans and hippies just about anywhere else, Texas hippies also embraced Lone Star and Pearl Beer and country music as a part of their twisted heritage. The Armadillo had already brought in a parade of talent that would otherwise have bypassed Texas, including Ry Cooder, Little Feat, Captain Beefheart, Taj Mahal, Dr. John the

Night Tripper, and Frank Zappa. But there was a definite twang to many of the touring acts, such as the Flying Burrito Brothers, the New Riders of the Purple Sage, Bill Monroe, and especially Commander Cody and His Lost Planet Airmen. They were younger musicians raised on rock and roll but inspired by the country music their parents grew up with, a movement defined by the seminal 1968 album *Sweetheart of the Rodeo* by the California folk-rock band the Byrds. This version of country was considered safe by hippies rather than the antithesis of the counterculture, which is how most mainstream country was regarded by the young hipsters.

The Armadillo and a smaller club in West Lake Hills, west of town, called the Soap Creek Saloon, where Doug Sahm ruled the roost, were the touchstones of the Austin version of the country-rock culture, where long hair, blue jeans, cowboy hats, boots, good pot, cold beer, and cheap tequila fit together naturally. If a line had been drawn in the sand, hippies and cowboys in Austin were hopping over it.

Willie had been noticing a few longhairs showing up whenever he played Big G's in Round Rock, some of them asking to hear chestnuts like "Night Life," "Fraulein," and "San Antonio Rose." He'd been touring all over the world trying to find his audience, and here they were, looking for him. When he started hanging out in the clubs in Austin, he realized hippies who dug cool music were everywhere. He also noticed a style, or lack thereof.

"It became apparent the audiences were dressing down," he said. "At the [Grand Ole] Opry, everybody dressed up, wore suits and ties. At the Armadillo and places like that, nobody dressed up. I felt out of place being dressed up."

He adapted quickly, letting his hair grow long, growing a beard, dressing onstage in blue jeans, tennis shoes, and T-shirts, with a bandanna around his neck or head. It was no big deal to Willie. "I'd already done that," he said, pointing out that jeans, casual shoes, T-shirts, and bandannas had been standard issue in Abbott, like they were everywhere else in Texas when he was growing up. Hippies were the new adapters.

In the summer of 1972, Willie and Connie found an apartment on Riverside Drive between Congress Avenue and Interstate 35 for Paula Carlene, Billy, Susie, and Shasta, the German shepherd they brought from Ridgetop. There was a nice view of Town Lake, which ran through the center of Austin and was in the process of being beautified per the wishes of Ladybird Johnson, the former First Lady and wife of President Lyndon B. Johnson, who'd returned to

Austin and his nearby LBJ Ranch, west of Johnson City, following the end of his presidency in 1969.

After Connie became pregnant again in the fall, with daughter Amy Lee, they moved to Lake Austin Estates off Cuernavaca Drive in the hills west of the city. Willie's family lived in a duplex, and Paul and Carlene English and their son, Darrell Wayne, lived in another nearby. The Lost Valley Country Club in Bandera was being re-created in suburban west Austin.

As the 1960s faded into the 1970s, the 251,808 residents of the capital city of Texas led a wonderfully simple, sheltered, semi-idyllic existence. Set on the banks of a river that had been dammed into a string of narrow lakes where the Hill Country descended into the coastal plains and prairies, Austin was easily the most beautiful city in a state often dismissed by out-of-staters as plug ugly. Its older neighborhoods were lush with oak and pecan trees. A natural spring less than a mile from downtown functioned as the city's main public pool. Several lakes were within a thirty-minute drive of Congress Avenue.

Education and government were Austin's economic engines. Culture was pretty much limited to football, politics, and music, along with whatever the University of Texas brought in. The population was 10 percent African American and 12 percent Mexican American and included fifty thousand college students. Local cuisine boiled down to the three basic food groups of Texas cooking: Southern-style, westernized comfort food, such as chicken-fried steak, fried potatoes, fried okra, and fried everything else; barbecue smoked meats cooked and prepared all kinds of ways—most of them exceptional—by the local Anglo, Mexican, and African American populations; and Mexican, or Tex-Mex, food rooted in the Mexican American east side of Austin at institutions like Cisco's and Carmen's on East 6th, El Mat on the brown-white borderline of the Interregional (Interstate 35) Expressway, and Matt's El Rancho on East 1st Street, two blocks from Congress Avenue and home of the Bob Armstrong Dip, named for the Texas land commissioner, who was a frequent customer. Former president Lyndon Johnson's family preferred El Patio, north of the University of Texas campus on Guadalupe, one of several Mexican eateries established in Texas by Lebanese Mexicans, where instead of the usual complimentary basket of tortilla chips, saltine crackers were served with the salsa.

The nightlife was refreshingly provincial. Scholz Garten, the city's oldest bar, established by August Scholz in 1866 and still the home of the Saengerrunde

German singing club, defined the local style. Scholz's attracted politicos from the capitol two blocks away, thirsty for a beer. (Liquor by the drink in Texas was restricted to private clubs, although you could bring in your own bottle as long as it was in a brown bag.) On hot summer nights, college students, attorneys, blue-collar folks, kids, and dogs gathered at the picnic tables out back under a string of yellow light bulbs beneath ancient oak trees to drink pitchers of Lone Star or Pearl and bullshit the evening away until midnight (one a.m. on Saturday nights), when all bars were required to shut down.

Austin didn't have the deep musical past of Dallas, Houston, Fort Worth, or San Antonio, since its population was historically smaller than even Waco's. There were some local stars among the country bands that worked the area during the forties and fifties, among them Cotton Collins, who wrote and performed an elegant fiddle-dance instrumental "Westphalia Waltz," which paid tribute to Central Texas's German heritage. Collins fiddled with perhaps the best-known musician in Austin, Kenneth Threadgill, a disciple of Jimmie Rodgers, the Blue Yodeler. Mr. Threadgill hosted folk music hootenannies at his North Lamar gas station beer joint in the mid-1960s, which were popular with a cabal of University of Texas students, including a future rock and blues singer named Janis Joplin and her friends Powell St. John and Travis Rivers—all three would enjoy careers in music in San Francisco during that city's hippie heyday in the late 1960s.

Two Austin acts made it onto the national charts in the 1950s—Ray Campi, a young rockabilly crooner and bassist, and the Slades, a doo-wop group that included the blind pianist Bobby Doyle. By the mid-1960s, a small but very hip rock and roll scene spawned the 13th Floor Elevators, a pioneering psychedelic band led by a screaming Travis High School dropout named Roky Erickson that had a national Top 40 hit, "You're Gonna Miss Me," distinguished by an electric jug, long before psychedelic became part of the music vocabulary. The Elevators and like-minded rock bands worked rooms such as the Old New Orleans, the Jade Room, and Mother Earth around the UT campus.

Austin was also a steady payday for the Top 40 and soul cover bands tapping into the lucrative fraternity and sorority party circuit around the University of Texas, a scene controlled by booking agent Charlie Hatchett that included young players such as Don Henley, who would later be the linchpin of a popular band known as the Eagles, and country rocker Rusty Weir.

The hippest venue in Austin during the 1960s had

been the Vulcan Gas Company on Congress Avenue, a local smaller version of San Francisco's Fillmore Ballroom, run by a hippie collective headed by Houston White. Famous for its posters, most created by Gilbert Shelton, who also drew underground comics, including the Fabulous Furry Freak Brothers, the Vulcan featured local bands such as Shiva's Headband, while occasionally bringing in touring blues, rock, and folk acts that otherwise would not have passed through Texas, including the Velvet Underground from New York, the California country-rock group Poco, and Chicago urban blues giant Muddy Waters.

A small clutch of white kids enamored of the blues were drawn to East 11th and East 12th, the main streets of what was left of Austin's tiny version of Harlem before segregation laws were lifted. They frequented juke joints like the Victory Lounge, the IL, Charlie's Playhouse, Ernie's Chicken Shack, and Marie's Tea Room Number 2, to soak up the music of Erbie Bowser, Hosea Hargrove, Blues Boy Hubbard, T. D. Bell, and barrelhouse pianist Robert Shaw. The white blues kids had their own playhouse, the One Knite, a self-declared dive that permanently reeked of vomit with a coffin for an entrance, a half block from the police station and one block west of I-35 — the racial border of the city. Mexicans lived east of I-35 and south of 7th Street to the river; blacks lived east of I-35 and north of 7th to Airport Boulevard and Highway 183.

Mexican Americans had their own music clubs along East 6th Street and ballrooms on the edge of town, where conjunto and Tejano were the preferred sounds and Johnny Degollado (El Montopolis Kid) and Ruben Ramos and the Mexican Revolution were the local stars.

The so-called folk music clubs in Austin, such as the Saxon Club on 34th Street at I-35 and the Chequered Flag on Guadalupe Street, south of campus, were not as tradition bound as the scene at Threadgill's. These rooms featured sincere singer-songwriters playing acoustic guitars, many of whom had taken to wearing cowboy hats and boots and jeans, a look adopted by newcomers like Jerry Jeff Walker (né Ron Crosby), a New York folkie who'd played in the band Circus Maximus and had written a hit song about a New Orleans street dancer called "Mr. Bojangles," another singer-songwriter from Houston, Guy Clark, who'd been covered by Walker, and a lanky Fort Worth kid with high cheekbones and a taste for liquor named Townes Van Zandt, considered by his peers the purest songwriter of all.

Four Austin performers were capable of drawing a thousand crazed hippies and college students at the drop of a cowboy hat: Michael Murphey, a flaxen-haired singer-songwriter from Dallas, who had the two best-selling albums in Austin, *Geronimo's Cadillac* and *Cosmic Cowboy Souvenir;* B. W. Stevenson, another Dallas folkie, whose husky voice powered several national hits, notably "My Maria," which reached number 1 on *Billboard*'s adult contemporary chart; Willis Alan Ramsey, a singer-songwriter-guitarist who also came out of Dallas, whose debut album showcasing exquisite ballads informed by country music was released on Leon Russell's Shelter Records, gaining him instant cachet with a hip audience; and Jerry Jeff Walker and the Lost Gonzo Band, whose live recording *Viva Terlingua!* made in the old dance hall in the Hill Country hamlet of Luckenbach (pop. 3) with hay bales for baffles, set the standard for Texas-style country-rock. Jerry Jeff himself was the culture's icon, the out-of-control Gonzo "Scamp," prone to extended bouts of extreme drunkenness, especially when under the additional influence of a new drug on the scene called cocaine. He became something of a role model for throwing televisions into swimming pools and wrecking hotel rooms with more vigor than a British rock band. "With Murphey I generally knew where he was coming from," said Herb Steiner, the pedal steel guitarist who played with both stars. "Jerry Jeff was an unguided missile."

Shortly after meeting Walker, Willie Nelson experienced that unpredictability firsthand at a guitar pulling late one night in Bastrop, east of Austin. A very loaded Jerry Jeff kept trying to grab Willie's guitar Trigger and play it, which irritated Willie to no end, finally prompting him to grab it from Jerry Jeff and pound him with his fists until Jerry Jeff was crumpled on the floor. As he picked himself up, he looked up at Willie and slurred, "I remember now. You're the same son of a bitch that knocked me down last night for the same reason."

Whenever Jerry Jeff wanted audiences to hear his lyrics, he worked Castle Creek, the former Chequered Flag, a listening room one block from the state capitol that booked singer-songwriters such as Guy Clark, Townes Van Zandt, Rusty Weir, and B. W. Stevenson. At Walker's request, a friend from Florida named Jimmy Buffett started sitting in between sets in the three-hundred-seat room until he earned his own gig. Castle Creek provided inspiration for a song he wrote called "(Wasting Away in) Margaritaville," which would be his calling card when he played in stadiums to tens of thousands of wannabe islanders in floral-print shirts.

• • •

As the home of the University of Texas, Austin experienced its share of student unrest in the 1960s and sported a flourishing hippie culture associated with the folk, rock, blues, and psychedelic scenes. No matter how many hippies started dressing cowboy, they were still regarded with suspicion, if not hostility, in most country music establishments. But at least Austin was a whole lot looser and more tolerant than the rest of Texas, where kicking a hippie's ass was considered entertainment. Austin had more places than the rest of Texas combined that welcomed or at least tolerated hippies, which embellished the city's reputation as an oasis of peace and love in a desert of angry assholes spoiling for a fight. That image was enhanced by Travis County sheriff Raymond Frank, who openly declared he wouldn't bust folks for personal use of marijuana.

One of the few hippies able to cross the cultural divide and venture into the country bars and get away with it was a San Angelo native named Bobby Earl Smith, a Law School student and semi-longhair who played bass in Freda and the Firedogs, a band of like-minded college students who might not have been real country people but dug country anyhow.

Freda was a dark-haired Cajun pianist named Marcia Ball who sang lead and played piano. Her instrumental foil was John X. Reed, a lean Panhandle towhead who played lead guitar with a pronounced rockabilly twang and echo. The Firedogs attracted a mélange of students, bikers, Mexican families, hippies, and rednecks, who jammed into Split Rail, a no-cover bar and drive-in on Lamar Boulevard, just south of Town Lake, every Sunday night to hear a repertoire that mixed Loretta's "Don't Come Home Drinking," Tammy's "Stand by Your Man," and Merle's "Today I Started Loving You Again" with Texas-style rock and roll (Buddy's "Peggy Sue") and a few credible originals. But the Firedogs were regarded as too hippie to be booked into Austin's country joints such as Big G's in Round Rock, Big Gil's on South Congress, where the nightly pay for bands was $45 and a case of beer, or the Broken Spoke on South Lamar.

Townsend Miller, a skinny stockbroker by day who wrote the country music column in the *Austin American-Statesman,* had taken note. He frequently wrote that his two favorite singers were Waylon Jennings and Marcia Ball (aka Freda). More than once he urged the owners of the Broken Spoke to take a chance and book the Firedogs or a band called Greezy Wheels.

The Firedogs got their chance at a benefit at the

Broken Spoke for UT Law School grad Lloyd Doggett in his bid to be elected to the Texas House of Representatives. The Broken Spoke was so packed that owner James White asked the band to come back and play his place on a regular Friday night.

Townsend Miller's mention of Greezy Wheels referred to one of the house bands at the Armadillo World Headquarters that were engaged in a similar musical experiment, borrowing bits and pieces of country and gospel and playing it like it was something brandnew for the hippie crowd. Greezy Wheels was led by Reverend Cleve Hattersley, another New York refugee with a bombastic stage presence that was part preacher man and part hippie Godfather, and featured Sweet Mary Egan, an enigmatic fiddler who could whip both the crowd and herself into a dervish on her signature rendition of "Orange Blossom Special." Their song list included an extended jam version of the traditional spiritual "Will the Circle Be Unbroken?" and their big crowd pleaser "Country Music and Friends," with the sing-along refrain celebrating "cocaine, country music, and good ol' Lone Star Beer."

WHEN Willie called Waylon to tell him "something is going on down here," he was referring to bands like Greezy Wheels and Freda and the Firedogs. Something told Willie that he could tap into their audiences. They might be a little younger than he was and they might be a little crazier about drugs than he was. But they were Texas kids like he was who loved music almost as much as he did.

Willie tested those waters by asking Sweet Mary Egan to sit in with him, Bee Spears, and Paul English at a benefit concert for Sissy Farenthold, the liberal Democratic candidate for governor at Woolridge Park, between the library and the Travis County Courthouse. Greezy Wheels was on the bill, as was the Conqueroo, the eclectic folk-rock-blues-jazz de facto house band of the recently defunct Vulcan Gas Company; the Storm, one of the white blues bands from the One Knite, featuring Jimmie Vaughan on guitar and Lewis Cowdrey on harmonica; an organic and splendidly sloppy blues-and-rock bar band called Lee Ann and the Bizarros; and, incongruously, the New York folk musician Phil Ochs, who was just passing through.

Sweet Mary played with Willie, Paul, and Bee like she'd worked with them for years, her presence warming the crowd of long-haired groovers and Democratic Party officials to the "straight" country musician. The ensemble showcased Willie playing his best compositions back-to-back as "Crazy" melted into "Hello Walls," then "Me and Paul," before he grabbed the crowd with "Night Life," a blues everyone could recognize and relate to. The small crowd signaled their approval with applause. When Greezy Wheels and the Conqueroo played, they resumed their free-form hippie dancing.

A few days later, Willie and Paul went to the Armadillo World Headquarters, the place where the band had dropped off the hippie chick from Kerrville, looking for Eddie Wilson. A gregarious ex-Marine and ex–beer lobbyist, Eddie was the Armadillo's head honcho, the closest thing to a leader of the stridently leaderless collective. The Armadillo technically functioned as a business, but those who worked there sure weren't in it for the money. They were in it for the music, the beer, the dope, the camaraderie, and whatever else the counterculture movement symbolized.

Two years earlier, Eddie had crossed over from beer-drinking yahoo to manager of Shiva's Headband, a homegrown hippie band that had a contract with Capitol Records. Shiva's performed psychedelic music driven by electric fiddle and guitar and was prone to play twenty-minute versions of every song. After the Vulcan closed, they needed a new place to play. Eddie Wilson found the Armadillo for them and rounded up some friends to help open the place in August of 1970.

Unlike most of his Armadillo brethren, Eddie was hip to Willie Nelson. He had gone on a dope run to San Francisco, to where many Austin hippies migrated, trying to make contact with the Grateful Dead and move a few pounds of Mexican weed in order to help pay the Armadillo's rent. He was staying with a homesick Texan who was playing over and over Willie's *Live Country Music Concert* album recorded at Panther Hall in Fort Worth. When the friend mentioned Willie had moved from Nashville to Austin, Eddie was determined to find him. A week after his return, Wilson was standing in the cabaret in the back of the club, when he turned around saw Willie and Paul in front of him.

"I've been looking for you," Eddie said to Willie, introducing himself.

"You just found me," Willie said, grinning.

"I want you to play here."

"I want to play here."

A handshake sealed the deal.

Willie had met some unusual folks in the nightclub business. This group might have been the most unusual of all. They made him feel right at home. Several customers at other tables left their pitchers of beer to come and say hello. As Willie and Paul graciously accepted the welcomes, Eddie Wilson noticed a trait he hadn't seen in other music people who'd played the 'Dillo: As long as someone was speaking to him, Willie didn't break eye contact. "It's a quality I'd seen in only two other people—[former Texas governor] Ann Richards when being talked to by children, and Muhammad Ali when he's talking to girls," Eddie said.

A date and terms were agreed upon. Willie would get half the door, no guarantee. It was the same deal the Armadillo worked with Dallas bluesman Freddie King and he was packing fifteen hundred hippie fans into the building every few months while he continued to work the chicken-shack circuit in the rest of Texas.

Micael Priest, one of the Armadillo's in-house poster artists, whipped up a poster depicting an old cow-boy crying into his mug of beer, with a jukebox playing "Hello Walls" in the background and a small picture of Willie hanging on the wall up in the corner.

The Armadillo had booked some weird stuff in its two years of existence. Willie Nelson might be the weirdest booking yet. Eddie Wilson hedged his bet by asking Greezy Wheels to open for Willie and accept a $100 fee even though the band had played to a full house as headliners a few weeks before. After some debate over whether the regular crowd would pay a higher price, Eddie and Bobby Hedderman set the cover charge at the increased price of $2.

Willie helped promote the booking a few nights before by dropping by Mother Earth, the rock and roll club on North Lamar at 9th Street, where Michael Murphey, Austin's cosmic cowboy, was holding forth.

On the evening of August 12, 1972, the day the last U.S. troops departed Vietnam, Willie Nelson took the stage of the Armadillo World Headquarters in front of 450 paying customers. Although the air temperature outside had peaked at ninety-six degrees a few hours earlier, the 'Dillo felt hotter than Laredo, since it lacked air-conditioning. At least half the crowd had come for Greezy Wheels, but there were at least a hundred hard-core Willie Nelson fans who'd never stepped inside the big building with its murals of strange characters, like Big Rikki, the Guacamole Queen, Shiva's Headband, and Freddie King playing guitar while an armadillo popped out of his heart. Pantsuits mixed with bell-bottoms. Beehive hairdos contrasted with long and stringy hairdon'ts. Beer flowed from the taps. A cloud of smoke hung under the ceiling.

Backstage, Willie posed calmly for photographer Burton Wilson, who was archiving the musicians and staff of the Armadillo before Willie took the stage with Bee and Paul. He was thirty-nine years old. He'd been a scrapper for ten years, a Nashville recording star for ten years after that, and he still felt like he was getting his first wind. He was clean-shaven and his hair barely covered his ears. But as he scanned the audience, making eye contact, the expression on his face telegraphed to the crowd that he might look like an old redneck shit-kicker, but deep inside, he was one of them.

Bassman Bee Spears stood to one side. "Willie passed me off as an Indian," Bee said. "I had a head-band and moccasins if we were going into a place where we knew we'd get some shit. I wasn't making a fuckin' statement; I'm a redneck too." Paul English, Willie's Man in Black, sat on a drum stool on a riser behind them, sticks in hand, black cape with red lining draped over his shoulders.

Willie rolled out the medley of hits like he did at Woolridge Park—"Crazy," "Hello Walls," "Funny How Time Slips Away," and "Night Life." Applause greeted recognition of each song. Sticking to the Bob Wills formula of presentation, he played one song after another without pause, keeping the songs short and sweet, save for a couple of solos to show the audience he could play some serious guitar.

Paul, who was now up to seven capes in his wardrobe, was in ecstasy. He drummed so hard that at one point, he fell back off his stool. "The cape I was wearing was velvet, and it was around my throat, and

I got up and all of a sudden fell back because it was choking me to death," he explained. "I was sweating profusely and didn't have much oxygen, and I just went down."

After the show, the band, fans, family, and friends retreated across Town Lake to the Crest Hotel, where writers Edwin "Bud" Shrake and Gary "Jap" Cartwright had rented a suite. A guitar pulling ensued, starring Willie Hugh Nelson with UT football coach Darrell K Royal as producer. Even though he'd rented the suite, Cartwright was threatened with expulsion by Coach when he continued talking while Willie played. "Leave or listen," Royal ordered curtly. Jap shut up and stayed, paying attention to Willie and his songs. "I don't remember having to quiet Bud Shrake," Coach said. "He was an educated listener. Gary was not as informed as Bud."

Willie might have taken a leap of faith by abandoning the Nashville establishment for the fringes of a counterculture in the making, but on that hot night in August, he knew it was the right call.

FOR all the great music being made, Willie was the only one who could work both sides of the aisle — the Armadillo one week, Big G's the next — and be completely at home in both environments, although each side had a very different reaction to Willie's new shaggy look.

Lana Nelson noticed the change when she left Ridgetop and her husband, Steve, and brought her two children to join the rest of the family in Austin late in the fall of 1972. "Dad picked me up at the airport," she said. "He was wearing shorts and sandals and had real long hair and a beard and an earring. He didn't look anything like he looked when he left. He looked like everybody that I had seen at the Atlanta Pop Festival. This was a total different look but I thought it was cool. Everyone in Austin was that way."

Hippies hurled insults at Merle Haggard for his composition celebrating middle American values, "Okie from Muskogee," not knowing the song was actually a parody and that Merle was a political liberal who enjoyed smoking pot as much as they did. In Austin, folks like Merle didn't have to hide it. Willie sure didn't. He signaled to the hippies he belonged by the clothes he wore, the facial hair he grew, and his open embrace of illicit drugs.

Lana saw what was happening. "I kept thinking, 'They're catching up. This is it. Get ready.'"

In November 1972, Townsend Miller reported in the *Austin American-Statesman* that Willie was enjoying chart success as the songwriter of Waylon's hit single "Pretend I Never Happened" and as the performer of the single "Mountain Dew" b/w "Phases and Stages." He was the toast of the town, the new hot act at the Armadillo and enough of an insider to play a private gig for UT football coach Royal, Coach's pal Ford dealer Bill McMorris, and the entire University of Texas Longhorn football team. Willie and Coach had become best friends, playing golf, pitching washers, and eating Mexican food together at least three times a week.

The exotic, very local blend of music and culture taking shape was growing sufficiently significant for an Austin radio station to switch to a progressive country music format. Willie had accompanied Eddie Wilson and a local radio announcer named Joe Gracey to urge the owners of KOKE-FM in Austin to devote at least a portion of their broadcast day to a mix of country and rock and roll recording artists, including Willie, Waylon, and Johnny Cash, local stars like Doug Sahm, Jerry Jeff Walker, Michael Murphey, Willis Alan Ramsey, and B. W. Stevenson, along with the Rolling Stones, Creedence Clearwater Revival, the Band, the Byrds, Bob Dylan, and the Allman Brothers. "I was all over the concept of Texas artists on a radio station, and I'd loved the Byrds' *Sweetheart of the Rodeo*," Joe Gracey said. "So the idea was very obvious to me, to do country music in a new Texas, young, hip way. And Willie was the greatest Texas country artist there was."

The owners initially resisted, but they eventually came around, allotting nine a.m. to midnight for the format, following the Spanish-language morning show hosted by José Jaime Garcia. It was like Willie had his own station. Joe Gracey, who also wrote the weekly rock music column for the *Austin American-Statesman,* did his part by describing Willie in one of his columns as "the Dylan of country music" and wearing out the grooves of *Shotgun Willie* on KRMH-FM, the local album rock station he worked for before joining the KOKE-FM staff as Ol' Blue Eyes.

"Willie did a lot for KOKE," Joe Gracey said, citing the jingle he recorded for the station to the tune of "Mr. Record Man" ("I was driving down the highway with KOKE-FM turned on"). "He was always up at the station," Gracey said. "He'd play the New Year's Eve shows that were done live in the studio and drop in or call in on a whim. You could tell he was a radio guy. He realized that some DJs do it for the love of music and the love of performers. He really paid us back for anything we did for him."

Radio was one means of shoring up support. Beer was another.

"After I got to Austin in 1973 to work for Lone

Star Beer, Willie called me," said Jerry Retzloff, a native of San Antonio, where Lone Star Beer was brewed. "You've got a problem with your beer because the kids won't drink what their father drinks," Willie told him. "That's what's happening with me with the music. They're not listening to my music because I'm country and their mothers and fathers listened to country. So I'm doing a little crossover deal. They won't drink your beer because Mom and Pop drink your beer and they won't listen to my music for the same reason."

It made sense to Jerry. "Willie wanted to be associated with beer because he wanted his audience to be beer," he said. "He didn't want his crowd to get drunk, and that's why he liked the Armadillo so much, because when you smoke dope and you drink beer and you reach that moderate level, you pass out if you do too much. You were really the best customer."

Jerry and Willie worked out a handshake deal. "Lone Star wouldn't pay him for anything, but I would buy ads to help promote concerts—make posters and do stuff for him like that," Jerry said. "He'd drink Lone Star, which he already did anyway. Heineken had started giving the New Riders of the Purple Sage free beer backstage and they started carrying it onstage, and Heineken started getting a movement going. I convinced the people at Lone Star to do the music thing as well."

Sales of Lone Star Beer in Austin increased 46 percent in one year. The brass in San Antonio listened when a few folks at the Armadillo, including Eddie Wilson and Woody Roberts, spun off an ad agency called TYNA-TACI (shorthand for Thought You'd Never Ask, The Austin Consultants Inc.) and pitched an ad campaign to Lone Star revolving around their traditional longneck bottles, which were losing favor among consumers, who preferred throwaway cans and throwaway bottles.

As a beer man, Jerry Retzloff understood the difference drinking beer out of longnecks made. "There was a taste factor," he said. "When you put a lid on a can, you shoot CO_2 across it and then you put the lid on, and what that does is put excess CO_2 in the can. The bottle is just the opposite. It lets CO_2 impure air out. I learned this from real beer people."

The "Long Live Longnecks" campaign began with Kinky Friedman and the Lost Gonzo Band singing the praises of Lone Star in radio commercials. The Armadillo's chief poster artist, Jim Franklin, developed a series of posters incorporating Armadillos and Lone Star longnecks. T-shirts bearing the Lone Star Beer logo were more sought after than those with the Zig-Zag rolling papers logo. Within a year, more Lone Star was being sold at the Armadillo World Headquarters than in any other retail outlet except the Astrodome in Houston.

Meanwhile, Austin-style progressive country developed its own sense of fashion — T-shirts, blue jeans, and cutoff blue jeans shorts in the summer, duck-billed gimme caps (as in "Gimme a cap") for men, and scarves and bandannas for women. Manny Gammage, the famous Austin hatter whose Texas Hatters shop was on South Lamar Boulevard, got into the act by developing an upscale cosmic cowboy look with his High Roller hat worn by Willie Nelson, disc jockey Sammy Allred, and Ronnie Van Zant, the lead singer for the southern rock band Lynyrd Skynyrd. Fancy-ass, pointy-toed cowboy boots became the favored manly footwear among hippies who could afford it. Charlie Dunn, the boot maker for Capitol Saddlery near the state capitol, became "the man to see" for handmade custom cowboy boots after Jerry Jeff Walker lionized him in a song.

AUSTIN was meant to be. Willie didn't need to consult Astara or reread Gibran to feel the vibes. Sister Bobbie was finding steady work at Lakeway, a posh country club community on the shores of Lake Travis, and several of her old piano bar haunts. For the first time since Fort Worth, Bobbie and Hughty were both enjoying careers in music in the same town.

Even if he failed—and he didn't think like that or put up with those who believed failing was an option—he could at least afford to. The living was easy in Austin. It didn't take much to get by. Garage apartments in Hyde Park and Old West Austin rented for well under $100 a month. A six-pack of Texas Pride went for ninety-nine cents. An ounce of good commercial marijuana sold for $10. LSD and peyote were plentiful (it was a UT-Austin student who first synthesized mescaline from peyote). The weather was warm, the winters mild, and good times were no farther than Barton Springs, Lake Austin, and Lake Travis.

The new culture welded the hedonistic attributes of the hippie lifestyle (drugs and sex, especially) onto the body of a Texas redneck. Real rednecks and hippie rednecks both loved pickups and both liked to drive while drinking, a longneck held between their legs (totally legal in the eyes of Texas law as long they weren't drunk). Both liked hanging in clubs and hearing music, and both liked getting high and howling at the moon just for the hell of it.

With Paul watching his back, Bee at his side, Jimmy Day reentering the picture, and friends and family all around him, Willie was sitting in the catbird's seat.

Billy Ray Cooper—B.C.—came up from San Antonio and moved in with Willie and Connie and their brood to split shifts driving the band's Open Road camper with Jack Fletcher. B.C. quickly discovered that his former career driving ambulances might be a safer line of work.

Jack was behind the wheel of the Open Road on their way back to Lost Valley after a show in Llano in the Hill Country. The road was full of twists and tight curves and the camper had clearly seen better days ("You could stick your finger through the plywood," B.C. said). Willie and Paul were in the back, playing poker, when Jack suddenly shouted, "Will, the brakes are going! What are we going to do?"

"Deal the cards," Willie shouted back. Somehow the Open Road limped back home.

B.C. became Willie's personal driver when Willie bought an old Mercedes sedan from Bill McMorris, the Austin car dealer he met through Darrell K Royal. McMorris also got the band a Blazer to haul their gear, which Bee Spears drove.

"If we could pay expenses and everybody got a hundred bucks after a gig, everything was fine," B.C. said.

Tim O'Connor signed on shortly after he met Willie one night at the door of Castle Creek, the Austin club he was comanaging. "He walked in and asked for me and introduced himself. I said, 'Sir, I know who you are.' He said he wanted to play my joint, so I asked him what he was drinking," Tim said. They went back to a little office couch, where there was a cooler with some beer "and we became friends right there." Over the course of a few weeks, Tim informed his partner, Doug Moyes, "You can have the club. I'm going with Willie."

Tim knew enough about the club and concert business to think he could help Willie upgrade his show. He began to travel with the band and demand better sound and better treatment wherever Willie was booked. At Gilley's in Pasadena near Houston, a regular stop for Willie for years, Tim got crosswise with Sherwood Cryer, who owned the massive honky-tonk, when he informed Sherwood that Willie was canceling unless a decent sound system was brought in to accommodate Willie's new and improved show, and better security was provided to protect the band from the often rowdy crowd. "That was not something you said to Sherwood, especially not at Gilley's, and you sure as hell didn't do it when they didn't know who the hell you are and had never seen you before," explained Tim. "Plus, Willie wanted the gig." Sherwood provided better sound but security was nonexistent. "Cowboys kept walking up on the stage while Willie was playing, which didn't bother Willie but really bothered me," said Tim, who bitched about it loudly to anyone within range of his voice. It was raining as Willie and Tim walked out to Willie's red Mercedes for the drive home. Tim was carrying Willie's guitar and still complaining about the sound and the cowboys climbing onstage. "Goddamnit, what do you want me to be?" he fumed to Willie after Willie treated it like no big deal. "Willie turned around and his eyes turned black, the way they do when he is angry," Tim recalled. "He said, 'I'll tell you three things I never want you to be—cold, wet, or hungry.' "

There was dead silence on the drive back to Austin. As they got out of the vehicle, Tim told Willie, "I'll follow you to hell. I'll carry your guitar case to wherever."

Willie called Tim the next day. "You did a really good job," he told him, "but I think you are a little bit ahead of us. Why don't you lay back a little until we get caught up?" It was a polite firing, but Tim never went away.

LEON Russell entered Willie's life after Connie Nelson had gone to the town of Big Spring, in West

Texas to pick up a brand-new Pontiac Grand Prix that a car dealer loaned Willie. The dearth of radio stations in West Texas led her to The Record Shop, a storied music retailer in Big Spring, to buy some music for the drive back to Austin. Leon's third solo album, *Carney*, was playing on the sound system when she walked in. She bought an eight-track tape of the album and played it over and over during the six-hour drive, and played it again for Willie. He knew who Leon Russell was. Daughter Susie had turned him on to *Mad Dogs and Englishmen*, the album and film documentary of the music revue that starred Joe Cocker and featured Leon, who used the revue as the launching pad for his own rock stardom.

Willie and Connie drove to Houston to see him in concert and Willie was blown away. Leon's songs, his voice, his musicianship, and most of all his presence were unlike anyone he'd heard. Leon was an Okie through and through with a pronounced drawl and a definite twang to his sound; he had more than a little Southern gospel preacher man in his presentation. But he was a rocker, not a hillbilly. Leon's piano had been a signature on such classics as Jan and Dean's "Surf City," Bobby Boris Pickett's "Monster Mash," and the Beach Boys' "California Girls" and "Pet Sounds." As Russell Bridges, he helped arrange some of Willie's first tracks for Liberty Records in the early 1960s and later played behind Frank Sinatra and the Rolling Stones. Now he was electrifying crowds and selling records under his own name.

Willie could relate. Leon had been run through the business wringer like Willie had, only in Los Angeles instead of Nashville, and had returned to Tulsa, Oklahoma, just like Willie had come back to Texas. But Leon had already created his own musical universe back home with his own musicians, his own recording studios in an old church and at his house, his own custom record label, Shelter Records, the Sheltervision video production company, and his own distinctive sound, all on his terms. Leon had no reason to leave Tulsa except to tour. But he was curious enough about what was going down four hundred miles south in Austin to check it out. People there were buying huge numbers of Shelter Records albums by Freddie King, Willis Alan Ramsey, and Leon Russell.

Willie was introduced to Leon by Jim Franklin, the artist at the Armadillo World Headquarters who elevated the armadillo into a Texas hippie icon. (Both hippies and armadillos were maligned and picked on, as trail boss Eddie Wilson pointed out to Chet Flippo of *Rolling Stone,* the influential rock music magazine published in San Francisco. "Armadillos like to sleep all day and roam at night. They share their homes with others. People think they're smelly and ugly and they keep their noses in the grass. They're paranoid. But they've got one characteristic that nobody can knock; they survive like a sonuvabitch.")

Franklin was in Tulsa, painting a mural in Leon's swimming pool when he heard Willie was booked at the Armadillo. He asked Leon if he'd heard of Willie. "The only thing I know of Willie Nelson is 'The sun is filled with ice and gives no warmth at all and the sky was never blue and I never cared for you,'" said Leon, quoting from "I Never Cared for You." "That's a strange lyric for a country song," he reckoned.

Leon couldn't make Willie's Armadillo debut, but Franklin did go, and Willie told him, "I'd sure like to meet Leon." Franklin gave him Leon's private phone number and Willie flew to Albuquerque the next day to watch him perform.

They hit it off. Two weeks later at four a.m., Leon woke up Franklin in Tulsa. "Let's drive to Austin," Leon said. "The Grateful Dead are playing there and I've never seen them." After seeing the San Francisco band, the standard-bearers of extended improvisations fueled by psychedelic drugs, perform at the Municipal Auditorium, Jim took Leon across the street to the Armadillo World Headquarters. "I got him settled in with some of the ladies there to spend at least one night on our side of the world," Franklin said. "The next day we went over to Willie's apartment on Riverside Drive. Doug Sahm came by and we all sat in Willie's living room, Doug, Willie, and Leon playing songs for each other. Paul English sat on the couch, which inspired Leon to write 'You Look Like the Devil.' "

That evening, the Armadillo World Headquarters staff hastily put together a Thanksgiving jam with Jerry Garcia and Phil Lesh from the Grateful Dead, Leon Russell, and Doug Sahm. The jam turned out to be mostly semicountry noodling, as Jerry Garcia stuck to pedal steel guitar and let Doug Sahm play guitar and lead the ensemble, but it marked another watershed of bringing together music people from different realms. And Willie was paying attention.

LEON invited Willie and Connie to Tulsa for a long weekend, where they stayed in his home and hung out in Leon's tricked-out recording studio.

Waylon had taught Willie how to fight for what he wanted. Leon showed Willie how to build his own music empire. Willie was clearly in awe. Leon had tapped into the kind of audience that frequented the Armadillo World Headquarters long before Willie had, and he knew how to rock the crowd. Other than covering the Beatles back in the 1960s, Willie had paid little attention to rock and roll. Leon changed his way of thinking. Okies, for all practical purposes, were like Texans, only they lived on the north side of the Red River. The red-brick streets of Tulsa, where Bob Wills achieved his greatest success, could have easily been mistaken for the red-brick streets of Fort Worth, where Bob Wills began.

Willie's fluid yet efficient approach to performing and recording was pretty much the same as the way Leon looked at his craft and profession. The difference was that Willie played music he'd grown up with. He sounded like where he came from.

Jerry Wexler recognized that distinction. He'd built a career discovering artists like Willie. Gerald Wexler was a record producer and executive at Atlantic Records, the storied rhythm and blues and pop label. A native New Yorker, he was the son of Polish immigrants with a twist—his mother hung out in largely African American Harlem and wrote for the *Daily Worker,* published by the Communist Party USA. He came into the music business as a writer for the trade journal *Billboard* and developed a reputation for having an ear for original sound.

As a talent scout and producer for Atlantic, a small independent label based in New York, Wexler produced a phenomenal string of hit records—Ray Charles's "I Got a Woman," which changed the course of modern R&B upon its release in 1954; Aretha Franklin's "I Never Loved a Man (the Way I Love You)" and "Respect," which defined soul music in the mid-1960s; Wilson Pickett's searing "In the Midnight Hour"; as well as hits on Chuck Willis, Dusty Springfield, Professor Longhair, the Drifters, and Solomon Burke, to name a few. He had enough clout to persuade Ahmet and Neshui Ertegun, the brothers who owned the company, to let him start a country division in Nashville in 1972. He may have been a New York Jew, but Jerry was all about the South. The Erteguns didn't know much about country music, but they gave Jerry the green light based on his track record.

"There wasn't a living ass at Atlantic Records that knew country music or was interested in it," Jerry said. "They wouldn't know George Jones from Hank Jones. But I'd always been interested in country music. I turned on Paul Ackerman, my editor at *Billboard* and an inductee of the Country Music Hall of Fame, to country music when I gave him seven LPs released by RCA Victor on Jimmie Rodgers."

Nashville was close enough to Wexler's beloved Muscle Shoals, Alabama, where he had recorded many of Atlantic's biggest R&B hits, and not that far from Memphis, the site of other historic sessions involving Wexler. A country division would complement Wexler's recent purchase of the recording contract of another Texas character, named Doug Sahm, who'd generated some chart action in the mid-1960s with two Tex-Mex pop hits, "She's About a Mover" and "Mendocino," and rode the psychedelic wave in San Francisco during the Summer of Love before returning to Texas and settling in Austin. Jerry Wexler knew Doug Sahm was really a country boy at heart—the San Antonio native was a child prodigy on steel guitar and was once photographed with his instrument, sitting in the lap of Hank Williams.

Doug Sahm was one of the keys to making Wexler's country concept for Atlantic work. He was an outsider with an equal appreciation of roots music and pop hits. Willie Nelson became the other key, an insider and an outsider at the same time. Willie knew how to put together a great song. He had been given little credit for his ability to perform great music and yet had the same kind of regional audience and Austin sensibility as Sir Doug did. So what if the Atlantic country division had a Nashville mailing address? Wexler was really gambling that the Austin sound was the next big thing.

Rick Sanjek, Atlantic Nashville's head of A&R, had taken Jerry Wexler to Harlan Howard's house, where he was having his annual pickers' party during the 1972 Country Music Association Awards week. "Ray Price, Conway Twitty, I can't remember who all was there," Wexler said. "But there's Willie with his Martin, Scotch tape fluttering off the strings, an earring, and a pigtail down to his butt, without a contract. He was in bad order with the Nashville establishment because he had the pigtail and was rolling fat ones with the *yerba buena*." Wexler, who had a longtime appreciation of the *yerba* himself, was a willing listener when Willie proceeded to sing an album's worth of songs beginning with "Bloody Mary Morning." The songs were part of another concept he'd put together about a marital breakup told by the man on one side and the woman on the other.

After Willie finished singing, the little bearded man sauntered up to introduce himself. "I'm Jerry Wexler," he said to Willie. "I'm starting a country division at Atlantic. I'd love to have the album you just sang. I've been looking for you a long time." Wexler's ear for distinctive sounds and voices picked up on something about Willie; Willie was ready for Jerry Wexler.

So was Neil Reshen, another new person in Willie's life. At the recommendation of Waylon Jennings and Waylon's drummer and right-hand man Richie Albright, Willie had hired Neil Reshen as his business manager. "Richie told me about him," Willie said. "I asked Waylon about him. He said I needed a Maddog Jew, so I said okay."

Both men agreed that having a pitbull to fend off the wolves would help them fight for what they wanted. Waylon had been fighting RCA for artistic control, and Neil was the right man to get it. He represented himself as a manager after briefly working as business manager of *Creem,* the irreverent rock music magazine published out of suburban Detroit. "We manage the unmanageable" was his motto, according to music writer Ed Ward, a *Creem* contributor. "At one point, he'd paid to have his open-heart surgery videotaped, a very expensive proposition at the time, 'to prove that I have a fuckin' heart,' " Ward later wrote.

Reshen's first music entertainment client was the jazz trumpet player Miles Davis, a notoriously difficult artist but a very successful one. Neil found his second client, Waylon Jennings, bass ackwards. "There was a Jersey radio station I listened to as a kid that had a show called *Hometown Frolic* that played an hour of country songs every day," Neil explained in his thick New York accent. "I was fascinated by country. I remember the day they broke into the program to say Hank Williams died. When I got into the business, I went to the Taft Hotel one night because Waylon Jennings was playing there. I talked to him, but he said, 'I don't really need a manager, and I don't need a New York manager, and I probably don't need a Jewish manager.' But I stayed on him and went to see him in Nashville when he was sick with hepatitis [in 1972]. RCA was fucking him over. So he let me represent him. I proceeded to get into an argument with Jerry Bradley, who was taking over from Chet Atkins, about recording at RCA. Waylon wanted to record where he wanted to record, not where he had to record."

Reshen stayed in Bradley's face and in Chet Atkins's face. His real aim was to get Waylon off RCA and onto Columbia Records in New York, where he already had a relationship with label chief Clive Davis, but RCA let Waylon and his fourth wife, Jessi Colter, have their own custom label, WGJ. Waylon started producing himself at Chips Moman's studio in the back of Waylon's office. The result was an unprecedented string of hit singles and albums.

By getting RCA to agree to let Waylon do his music on his terms, Neil Reshen changed the art of the deal in Nashville, effectively breaking the feudal system where the label owned the artist, and the studio and the producer controlled the creative process. "Waylon's got a better deal than I do," Chet Atkins complained to Neil. "I don't know if I like that." The manager was not sympathetic. "RCA forgot that they were a record company," he said. "They thought that they were a brick-and-mortar company that was going to make money on renting out their space to a captive audience. Even if you were good, you hated going into that studio. I kept saying to them that if Waylon could sell a million records, that would beat the income from all the sessions you're going to do in the next two years. They didn't believe me until they saw the money come in."

Willie was introduced to Neil Reshen by Waylon at the Nashville airport. Willie needed help with a tax audit. After resolving the situation, Neil offered to negotiate a more generous deal when Willie's contract with RCA expired.

Willie was open to the proposition.

"Neil really upset Nashville because they weren't used to having to deal with people from out of town," Willie said. "It was fun. They had so many buttons he could push. It opened their eyes to what was really going on, whether they wanted to be a part of it or just let it happen in the back door. They might as well jump in and get some money. Those guys from New York knew how to get it."

Willie had been locked into a contract that amounted to indentured servitude. The artist received 4½ percent of 90 percent of sales minus their recording costs and promotional budget, an arrangement that put Willie deeper in the red each time he made an album. Chet Atkins, Felton Jarvis, and Jerry Bradley all tried to produce hits on Willie, believing he had talent. But they were all so locked into a formula that drowned out his voice in the wash of strings and the soothing vocal choruses that defined the Nashville Sound that they were clueless.

"Chet liked me," Willie said. "He liked my writing, my singing. He didn't care that much for my guitar playing, but at that point, I didn't either. But whatever happened in Nashville, no matter how much I liked it, no matter how much Chet liked it, if it got to New York, when it would come time to promote and spend money, if it came out of Nashville, it didn't get the the budget. They wanted to get the same treatment from New York as the New Yorkers were getting, but that didn't ever happen really."

Three of his albums, *Country Willie—His Own Songs, Make Way for Willie,* and *The Party's Over,* made it to the number 9 position on *Billboard*'s country album chart, but that had been five years ago. No single RCA release ever matched what he'd done at Liberty Records. His singles and albums weren't making a noise anywhere but in Texas.

Neil Reshen and Jerry Wexler hammered out a deal for Willie to record for Atlantic Records that involved relatively little money (the advance was well under $100,000) and loads of creative freedom accompanied by promises of promotion. From a New York perspective, it was no great shakes. But compared with a Nashville boilerplate, Willie's Atlantic agreement was revolutionary.

Atlantic, like many other medium-size labels flush with cash, such as Warner Brothers, ABC, and Elektra, wanted to get in on the Nashville action in anticipation of a country music growth spurt. Wexler made the hires, including recruitment of Russ Sanjek to run the Nashville office. Sanjek in turn let his son, Rick, run A&R. Russ Sanjek had done some huge favors for Jerry Wexler, and Jerry owed him. The Sanjeks quickly built a roster around country talent David Rogers, who had the first album released under the Atlantic Nashville imprint, Texas honky-tonker and old Willie running buddy Darrell McCall, Henson Cargill, Terry Stafford, Marty Brown, Johnny Paycheck's front man Don Adams, Wynn Stewart, and Bobby Austin. Willie Nelson and Doug Sahm were the wild cards.

The first week of February 1973, Willie rounded up Bee Spears, Jimmy Day, Paul English, and his sister, Bobbie, and went to New York City. Over the course of a single week, under the guidance of Atlantic producer Arif Mardin, they would record two albums—a gospel album that testified to Willie's faith, and a secular album of his latest batch of songs, along with a few choice covers.

The gospel album, *The Troublemaker*, included selections that had been constants in Willie's life, such as "Uncloudy Day," "Precious Memories," "Whispering Hope," "Will the Circle Be Unbroken?" and a new song called "The Troublemaker" about a spiritual man whose "hair was much too long" and his motley group of friends who had "nothing but rebellion on their minds" going "from town to town, stirring up the young folks, 'til they're nothing but a disrespectful mob."

Just as Wexler had loaded up Doug's album *Doug Sahm and Band* with such "friends" as Bob Dylan, Dr. John, Garth Hudson, and Rick Danko, Wexler and Mardin embellished Willie's sessions with Doug Sahm, his keyboard sidekick Augie Meyers, guitar virtuosos David Bromberg, Steve Burgh, and Al Bruno, pianist Jeff Gutcheon, fiddlers Johnny Gimble and J. R. Chatwell, singers Dee Moeller and Sammi Smith, Waylon, Jessi Colter, and Larry Gatlin, along with the Memphis Horns brass section. Dylan, Kris Kristofferson, Leon Russell, and George Jones were all rumored additions but didn't show.

Willie brought along Sister Bobbie to play piano on the gospel album. If anyone knew spirituals like he did, she was the one. The session marked the first time Bobbie took a ride on an airplane. "I was playing piano at Lakeway and at another club, called Paper Tiger," she said. "So I hired people to take my place, other pianists who would help me keep my job until I got back." She didn't want to lose her day job. "The piano bar was like a paid practice session for me," she said. "I had all this music, all this knowledge, and was learning new music, the things you think the audience would like. Different crowds wanted different things. It was a learning experience, just like working at Hammond organ, where I had access to all the sheet music you could ever want, like liturgical music that I had grown up with, different from the music I'd learned in beer joints."

Willie's wife, Connie, photographer David Gahr, Neil Reshen's assistant Sam Uretsky, and *Creem* magazine writer Ed Ward joined the all-star cast singing the chorus to "Shall We Gather at the River?"

Wexler had also invited Chet Flippo from *Rolling Stone*. Chet was impressed.

"I witnessed what I would later recognize as Wexler teaching Willie that he could largely control his own music destiny—that it was in his power to do so if he would dare try to do it," he later wrote in his *Nashville Skyline* column for cmt.com. "Willie's Outlaw movement, as far as I could tell, began in that

New York studio when Wexler completed Willie's musical training. It was something he would never have heard in a Nashville studio."

The recording of the second album was sloppy and chaotic, technically and artistically uneven, with horns and strings occasionally bumping up against the musical core of Bee Spears, Paul English, Bobbie Nelson, Jimmy Day, and Willie, although not in a Chet Atkins/Nashville Sound kind of way. The mood was relaxed, helped along by the casual attitude toward smoking weed in the studio, in marked contrast to the house rules at RCA's Studio B.

In the bathroom of his hotel room between sessions, Willie grabbed a sanitary napkin wrapper and jotted down lyrics for a song about his nickname, earned when he shot at Lana's husband in defense of Lana back in Ridgetop, Tennessee.

"Shotgun Willie" opened the secular album in a lazy lope that was more blues shuffle than Ray Price shuffle—Willie laconically singing the opening lines, "Shotgun Willie sits around in his underwear / biting on a bullet and pulling out all his hair / Shotgun Willie's got all of his family here," with the observation "you can't make a record if you ain't got nothing to say" punctuated by a blast of Memphis horns, not the crying moan of pedal steel. Willie plucked out the lead guitar riffs on his gut-string acoustic rather than let a Nashville session picker do it for him. The song was a throwaway in some respects, but Willie liked it and wanted to record it, no matter what its hit potential might be. Jerry Wexler had opened his eyes to what could be. Mr. Record Man was no longer trying to replicate "Crazy" and "Hello Walls." He was writing what he was thinking, like a singer-songwriter. The times they were a-changing.

The song's lack of commercial appeal, sealed by Willie's shout-out to dance hall czar John T. Floore, a former member of the Ku Klux Klan who "sold sheets on the family plan," was Willie's creative declaration of independence. (Floore returned the compliment by erecting a permanent sign in front of his country store reading "Willie Nelson Every Sat. Nite.") More traditional territory was covered with Willie's version of "Whiskey River," the honky-tonk anthem penned by his colleague Johnny Bush and high-lighted by Sister Bobbie's barroom piano and Jimmy Day's steel, and "Sad Songs and Waltzes" and "The Local Memory," especially the lyrics of "Sad Songs" ("I'd like to get even . . . with you 'cause you're leavin' "), which revealed a lot of the real him. The music was more country than what was being played on the radio but somehow different. If there were slips and flubs, they stayed in. During one passage, the pedal steel inexplicably drops out because Jimmy Day had passed out and fallen off his stool.

Doug Sahm made his presence known. His shared respect for Bob Wills and for Western Swing music in general shined through on "Bubbles in My Beer," where Sahm's bandmates backed up Willie along with Johnny Gimble and Jimmy Day; on "Stay All Night (Stay a Little Longer)," which was perhaps the best snapshot of Willie's performing prowess, with Johnny Gimble and J. R. Chatwell on twin fiddles and Arif Mardin playing piano; and on the Western Swing romp of John Philip Sousa's traditional march "Under the Double Eagle."

The two Bob Wills covers were the only two tracks on the album with Wexler credited as coproducer. Wexler heard a lot of Bob Wills in both Doug and Willie and had it in his mind to do a *Willie Sings Bob* album. But despite Sahm and Nelson being two of the biggest reasons Austin was generating buzz as a music town, their shared affinity for blues and hard-core country, and their common appreciation of good weed, they ruled separate domains—Sahm played to more of a rock and roll hippie/hipster crowd at Soap Creek Saloon out in the cedar brakes west of Austin, a hundred yards from the hilltop mansion he rented, while Willie was more closely aligned with the country crowd and with singer-songwriter folkies—although they often attracted the same audience.

The stronger bond was between Willie and Leon Russell, who contributed two songs to the New York sessions, though "Me and My Cricket" didn't make the final cut. Willie closed the secular album with just him and his guitar Trigger doing Leon's "A Song for You," a sincere, stripped-down interpretation of the emotional ballad already covered by several pop crooners. Another track that didn't make *Shotgun Willie* was Floyd Tillman's "I Gotta Have Something I Ain't Got," which Willie belted out in a vocal that careened around a blues shuffle fortified by saxophones, trumpets, and trombones.

After the last track, "Devil in a Sleeping Bag," was finished, Arif Mardin brought out a bottle of Chateau Bonnet wine. Willie had set a studio record of recording thirty-three tracks in a single week at Atlantic. One of the few lessons learned over Willie's years of recording for RCA in Nashville was to work fast, since artists typically had three-hour blocks in which to record. Willie might have cultivated a laid-back, laconic image, but he watched the clock. Even with Arif Mardin's acknowledgment of the feat, Willie didn't have much time to celebrate. He had a gig back home at Big G's in Round Rock the very next day.

Willie returned to Texas liking *The Troublemaker* so much, he proposed it as the first Atlantic release. The Atlantic promotion team in Nashville, hungry for hits that could be promoted through radio airplay, nixed the idea. If Willie was the flagship of Atlantic's country division, he needed a better introduction to the marketplace than church music.

He returned to New York three months later, using the pending release of *Shotgun Willie* as the excuse for Paul, temporary bassist Jackie Deaton, new boy Mickey Raphael on harmonica, and him to blow away the audience during a weeklong engagement at Max's Kansas City, the punk rock club in New York that Waylon had already electrified. Ian Dove of the *New York Times* observed, "Calling him a country performer is unnecessary straight-jacketing because his range is wide," and wrote that while he was better known as a songwriter, his singing was "without frill or filigree, very direct and with a lot of heart."

In Austin, *Shotgun Willie* created a buzz that left Willis Alan Ramsey's debut, Jerry Jeff Walker's epic *Viva Terlingua!*, and Michael Murphey's *Cosmic Cowboy Souvenir* eating dust. The album went into heavy rotation on progressive-country KOKE-FM, on the album rock station KRMH-FM, and on country-rock radio programs that were springing up on the left end of the FM dial across Texas.

Nationally, the album climbed to number 41 on the *Billboard* country album chart, falling well short of the level Willie typically achieved with his RCA recordings. Atlantic radio man Nick Hunter fought with Neil Reshen over releasing the title track as the first single. Nick wanted "Stay All Night" as the first single. Neil took the long view. "If it isn't a hit, it's not a hit," he told Hunter. "I want to establish the name 'Shotgun Willie.' "

They were both right. The single "Shotgun Willie" peaked on the *Billboard* country chart at number 60, a solid failure. "Stay All Night," the better single, rose as high as number 22 before stalling. The moniker "Shotgun Willie" lingered for a couple years until a better nickname came along, even though plain ol' "Willie" was working just fine.

More important, the Family Band, as it was becoming known, was gelling behind him, especially after he added his sister to the show. "Willie had a gig in Houston and said, 'Why don't you come with me and play this gig?' " Bobbie recalled. They looked at each other after the Houston show and asked each other the same question: "Why have we not been doing this?"

"Well, we knew why," Bobbie said with a soft chuckle. "We didn't have that many jobs and we weren't famous, so I was still trying to hold down my piano bar jobs. Finally, when we had enough jobs, I gave notice."

Sister Bobbie fit right in with Willie Nelson and Family and with real family too, marrying Jack Fletcher, Paul English's character friend from Fort Worth, who was driving and working as a jack-of-all-trades for Willie.

Several months earlier, a Dallas harmonica player named Mickey Raphael had joined up. Mickey Raphael had first encountered Willie Nelson in 1972 at a concert on the campus of Southern Methodist University in Dallas that was being broadcast live on KERA, the local PBS television station.

"Willie was late," Mickey said. "That old Open Road camper rolled into the back of the venue, and out came Willie and Paul. They had driven from God knows where. Willie was decked in an old straw hat, leather shirt, big Elvis glasses, and Paul was wearing a black cape. I'm thinking, 'Who are these assholes showing up an hour and a half late?'" But when the two-piece ensemble played, the performance "fucking blew me away," Mickey said. "So I started taking this shit a little more seriously."

Weeks later, Mickey got a call from Coach Darrell K Royal, inviting him to a picking session. Coach had heard Mickey play behind B. W. Stevenson and Jerry Jeff Walker in Austin and was sufficiently

impressed to invite him to join Willie Nelson and
Charley Pride in a Dallas motel room after a football
game at the Cotton Bowl.

Mickey managed to hold his own at the picking
session, even though he didn't know squat about
country music. "I'd play along with these Hank Williams songs I didn't know but was starting to learn,
trying to follow Willie's playing," he said. He was a
Jewish hippie city boy from Dallas. Country people,
he said, "were rednecks who'd whip my ass." Still,
Willie liked Mickey's playing. "If you hear we're in
town, come and join us," he offered.

Willie called Mickey to join him at a fireman's
association benefit in Lancaster, just south of Dallas.
Afterwards, he asked him to accompany Paul and
him to play Max's Kansas City in New York. It was
baptism by fire. "During a song the first night, Willie turns to me and says, 'Take it,' " Mickey said of
the Max's gig. "I was like, 'Take it?' I was the only
one playing—I'm it. '*You* take it.' "

Every time Willie scored another booking in Texas,
he invited Mickey to come along. "I would drive my
own car to the joints and would stay in my car until
they got there, because they were bad-ass joints,"
Mickey said. "Paul or Willie would walk me in."

Mickey didn't know it, but he was filling a void
left by Jimmy Day, who had wandered off the reser-

vation again. During a three-night stand at Castle Creek in Austin, Jimmy was so drunk and doped up, he was playing with his volume knob turned up to ten inside the intimate listening room. Willie was nowhere near as wasted as Jimmy but drunk enough to be a whole lot madder. Finally Willie stopped the music in the middle of a song and turned to Jimmy. "Do you see the name on the fucking marquee? It says Willie Nelson, not the fucking Jimmy Day Show! Shut up!" Jimmy hung his head, and his wife, Sheryl, started screaming at Jimmy. During a break, Willie and Jimmy went out in the alley and duked it out. Willie came back. Jimmy didn't. "The World's Greatest Steel Guitarist" was no longer part of the Willie Nelson Show. His departure from the band became official when Paul shot Jimmy in the hip after Jimmy's extended taunting of Paul in an inebriated state.

With Jimmy gone, Mickey's harmonica added an earthier, rootsy quality to Willie's sound and quickly became as much of a signature as Jimmy's steel once was. After a show at Big G's in Round Rock, Mickey told Willie they were headed places, which led him to wonder aloud how much longer the band would have to play dumps like Big G's.

"Hopefully a long time," Willie replied without missing a beat.

• • •

JODY Payne joined the Family Band later that year. He had been working in the bands of Merle Haggard and Sammi Smith (to whom he was married at the time) when Willie invited him to add his Kentucky-bred thumb-picking guitar to Willie's expanding band of gypsies. A child prodigy taught by family friends Ike Everly and Merle Travis and mentored by Charlie Monroe, Bill Monroe's brother, Jody had solid credentials as a soul man as well as a bluegrass picker, having worked rhythm and blues recording sessions at King Records in Cincinnati and Motown Records in Detroit. A self-described "Telecaster-playing fool," he showed up at a Texas concert to play second guitar and sing a song or two at Willie's request. Willie thought Jody could be groomed to be his own front man, just as Willie had groomed Johnny Bush, Ray Price had groomed Willie and Johnny Paycheck and others, and Hank Williams had groomed Ray Price.

Jody was a strong, silent presence onstage. A handsome man with a bigger mane of blond hair than even Michael Murphey, he let his guitar do the talking. "My role was to try and put something down for Willie to walk on [with his guitar], try to lay it down for him and sing a little harmony to support his vocals," he explained.

Mickey and Jody had hired on despite the band's feast-or-famine lifestyle. When Willie asked Paul how much Mickey was being paid and Paul replied, "Nothing," Willie ordered, "Double his salary." Sister Bobbie Nelson was just thrilled to be playing with her brother.

Despite business manager Neil Reshen's gruff presence and steamroller attitude, Willie took an immediate shine to Neil's gopher, a kid named Mark Rothbaum whom he'd met at the Holiday Inn in Nashville when Neil brought him along for a meeting. Mark was a Long Island native who'd played lacrosse at the University of Cincinnati and went to work for Neil at the urging of Neil's client Miles Davis.

"Miles was playing a date at Central Park in New York City, and my sister was working for the Parks Department," Mark said. "Through that, I met Miles. He was an affable, funny, endearing man who contradicted the image he was portraying. He could bring a smile to your face. There wasn't anyone I'd rather hang out with. He took a liking to me and asked Neil Reshen, who managed Miles, to let me work for him. I was a flunky, really."

When Mark wasn't hanging with Miles, who was sick and rarely toured, or helping out with Waylon, who was becoming Neil's highest-priority client, he found himself in Texas more and more. "I got to talk with Willie directly when I met him," Mark said. "It was just him and me. He couldn't have been nicer. He showed me how to do laundry on the road, how to wash your jeans in a motel room."

Mark's impressions were informed by Miles's respect for Willie. "Miles listened to Willie and appreciated his genius—his choices of silence, and his odd phrasing, and his waiting until the last minute and then waiting another second before hitting his note," Mark said. "If you were sticking to a pattern, Willie was frustrating. But if you were playing outside of the rules, you appreciated how accomplished a musician he was."

Orange to El Paso, Dalhart to Brownsville, 1973

DESPITE TEPID SALES outside Texas, *Shotgun Willie* opened doors for Willie across the Lone Star state, and opened Willie's mind to act on his impulses. He had enough money left over from the Atlantic advance to buy a forty-four-acre ranch on Fitzhugh Road, west of Austin, and had garnered enough local support that he started to believe he could do anything he wanted. When he couldn't get the Dripping Springs Reunion out of his head, a bee buzzing around his bonnet told him a reunion of his own with all his favorite pickers sure would be fun. One afternoon in the late spring of 1973 he was sitting in the barn of his ranch, smoking a joint with Tim O'Connor, who'd rejoined his family. Out of the blue Willie said, "I think I'm gonna have a picnic."

439

"Really?" Tim said, exhaling.

"Yeah, I think so. What do you think? The Fourth of July?"

"Willie, it's June first!" Tim said with a reality check.

"That should be plenty of time, don't you think?" Willie smiled.

He wasn't kidding.

He started calling up friends and seeing who wanted to come and work for nothing. He borrowed $5,000 from Joe Jamail, the Houston lawyer who was Coach Royal's good friend, and enlisted his old promoter buddies Gene McCoslin from Dallas, Larry Trader from San Antonio, and Tom Gresham from Waco to sell the picnic in their respective territories. He enlisted Eddie Wilson, Bobby Hedderman, and the gang from the Armadillo World Headquarters to take care of Austin ticket sales and do the staging, since the hippies there knew how to put on concerts.

Gene McCoslin thought up a creative way to pay everybody without incurring the heavy losses that promoters of the Dripping Springs Reunion had taken the year before. "The artists have all agreed to put all the money into a pile and everybody get his cut," McCoslin explained with a straight face to the *Dallas Morning News*.

Geno was a half-crazed, very wily, very charismatic Dallas nightclub owner who'd earned Willie's loyalty by steadily booking him into whatever joint or club he happened to be running, including his current venue, the Western Place, where he also booked Willie's protégé Johnny Bush and his Bandoleros as headliners. "He recognized talent, and he recognized money," said Willie.

With considerable experience operating clubs along the Harry Hines strip in the sleazier part of northwest Dallas, Geno spoke the language of old-school entertainment, where gambling, drugs, and prostitutes all figured in the income stream. In the same way Crash Stewart once booked Texas dates for Willie while Lucky Moeller booked his dates everywhere else, Willie allowed Geno to informally operate on his behalf in Texas while Neil Reshen represented Willie in the rest of the world. There was more than a little used-car Dixie mafia in Geno, who never hesitated to display whatever firearm he happened to be packing. Unlike Willie, Geno had absolutely no crossover appeal to hippies. Guns intimidated the folks who ran the Armadillo World Headquarters but did not impress. "He was a thug," Eddie Wilson of the Armadillo groused.

Jerry Retzloff of Lone Star Beer did not dispute that assessment. "We had so many run-ins with Geno in Dallas when he was a retailer there. He pulled a gun on my district manager up there. He pulled a gun on everybody. His elevator would go up and down so quick." But Jerry quickly gleaned that Geno was someone you had to deal with because he was part of the Willie package. "When you're friends, Willie don't draw no boundaries and he never forgets you," he said. Even Geno, or especially Geno.

The Armadillo's attorney, Mike Tolleson, and his accountant friend from college, Randy McCall, set up a budget for the picnic, managed the checkbook, and controlled ticket sales in Austin. Bobby Hedderman and the Armadillo stage crew did most of the site prep and stage production, hiring Showco Productions, the Dallas company regarded as the best in the business for concert sound.

The first Willie Nelson Fourth of July Picnic was staged in 1973 in an open field charitably described as a natural amphitheater on Burt Hurlbut's seven-thousand-acre ranch near Dripping Springs, forty miles west of Austin, the same site as the Dripping Springs Reunion held the year before. The lineup was a mix of progressive and traditional country featuring Willie's expanding band of fellow renegades, including Waylon Jennings, Kris Kristofferson and wife and duet partner, Rita Coolidge; singer Sammi Smith, who had become Willie's frequent duet partner; a hot Texas songwriter who wrote for Waylon named Billy Joe Shaver; two other budding songwriters named John Prine and Lee Clayton; Willie's new hero, Leon Russell, country-folk singer Tom T. Hall; old buddies Hank Cochran, Johnny Bush, and Ray Price; old-guard stars like Loretta Lynn, Ernest Tubb, Larry Gatlin, and Charlie Rich; and George Chambers and His Country Gentlemen, the country dance band from San Antonio that Willie raided for David Zettner and Bee Spears. Austin was represented by the Geezinslaws, Asleep at the Wheel, Jerry Jeff Walker, and Doug Sahm and his Tex-Mex Trip. Bob Dylan was a rumored guest but never showed.

Willie gave away three hundred tickets to the good people of his hometown, Abbott. Admission for everyone else was $5.50, $6 at the door, with tickets sold at all Pant Place locations in Dallas, L&M Western stores in San Antonio, and the Armadillo in Austin. Country music stations across Texas, including KKYX and KVET, advertised the picnic, as did XERF in Mexico. Super Roper Radio KOKE-FM, the new progressive-country radio station in Austin, hyped the event around the clock.

The demand was certainly there. Willie was promoting *Shotgun Willie,* and Waylon was fresh out of the chute with his smokingest, hard-rockingest album yet, *Honky-tonk Heroes,* almost every song written by the hard-bitten crazy-ass cowboy primitive from Waco, Billy Joe Shaver.

Billy Joe and Willie were Texas country boys with once-upon-a-time dreams of writing songs for a living—Willie's realized, Billy Joe's not quite yet—and a similar history. "We met in 'fifty-six out on the highway," Billy Joe recalled. "A guy named Johnny Dallas [real name: Joe Poovey] introduced us. He was a friend of mine and he liked my songs. Willie wrote on a little matchbox, 'Good luck with your songs in Nashville.' I used to admire him so much. I'd see him at the Terrace Club, the Nite Owl, he'd play up and down that road [the Dallas Highway between West and Waco], little-bitty jobs that didn't pay no money. If I was in a bar where he was in there singing and someone was talking, I'd take them outside and whip their ass."

They had palled around Nashville after Billy Joe moved there in 1966. "Willie would always say, 'If you can help yourself with my name, go ahead,' but he didn't really help," Billy Joe said. "He'd just get me drunk." That changed the year before at the Dripping Springs Reunion in a trailer behind the stage. Billy Joe was singing "Willie the Wandering

Gypsy and Me" when Waylon came in, higher than a kite.

"Who wrote that song, Hoss?" Waylon asked Billy Joe.

"I did," Billy Joe said.

"You got any more of them cowboy songs?" Waylon asked him.

"I've got a whole sackful," Billy Joe said, smiling sheepishly.

"You come up to Nashville and I'll record a whole album of your songs," Waylon promised him. Billy Joe did not forget. For six months, he chased after Waylon in Nashville. "Finally, I had had it," Billy Joe said. "He was recording in the big studio at RCA full of wannabes, hangers-on, and bikers all over the place. I was determined to get to him one way or another." Waylon's people thought the hulking big boy from Texas was a nuisance. Captain Midnight, a disc jockey friend of Waylon's, handed him a folded $100 bill and told him, "Waylon said for you to take this and vamoose."

"Well, you just tell him to stick that up his ass," Billy Joe replied, fuming.

Waylon stormed out of the control room all pissed off, with a couple bikers on each side of him, all three headed to the restroom. Billy Joe followed.

"Whatchoo want, Hoss?" Waylon glowered while standing at a urinal, giving Billy Joe the nastiest look he could conjure.

"I tell you what I want," Billy Joe said, standing toe to toe with him, clutching his guitar in one hand. "I've got these songs here. You told me you was gonna do this album."

"I tell you what I'm gonna do," Waylon said, clearly irritated. "I'm gonna whip your ass in front of everybody." The bikers moved in, ready for a stomping, but Waylon pulled them back and moved in himself. "He started coming towards me and I figured, if he's going to take a shot, I'm going to take a shot too, 'cause I used to box," Billy Joe said.

Waylon grabbed him by his funny bone and said, "Come on with me, Hoss. I'm going to let you play one song. I'm going to have you do that 'Willie the Wandering Gypsy and Me.' If I stop you in the middle of the song, you're going to have to get out that door and that's the end of it. I don't ever want to see you again."

Billy Joe played the song without being stopped. Then he did "Ain't No God in Mexico."

"That's pretty good," Waylon allowed. "You got another one?"

"Old Five and Dimers" came next.

By the time Billy Joe got to "Honky-tonk Heroes"

Waylon slapped his knee. "I know what I gotta do," he told Billy Joe. "He called his whole band in and recorded the mess," Billy Joe said.

A "MESS" was an accurate description of Billy Joe's appearance at Willie's musical summer holiday picnic. He claimed he'd been bitten by a black widow spider but more likely had ingested some psychotropic substance.

The morning of the picnic, cars and trucks were backed up on Farm to Market Road and Ranch Road in northern Hays and western Travis County. "I spent the day of the show out on the road leading into the area, trying to direct traffic," Mike Tolleson said. "I was standing in the middle of three lines of cars going off in each direction as far as you could see. It was total gridlock."

The crowd count ranged from twenty thousand to sixty thousand. No one knew for sure because the $6 ticket price failed to discourage thrift-conscious brothers and sisters from tearing down fences and storming the gates. Advance ticket sales had been tepid. With Willie's associates as copromoters, the volatile chemistry of rednecks on pills, speed, beer, pot, and maybe even some acid, and hippies on their usual botaña platter of herbal stimulants and psychedelics warmed by hundred-degree heat, spontaneous combustion was guaranteed. Fights broke out over the sight of hippie chicks going topless on the shoulders of their boyfriends, and horn dogs thinking they were hippie chick magnets. The power failed. Brains were fried. The whole shebang sizzled like spit on a frying pan.

The rednecks and the hippies did not lie down together in the soft grass like lions and lambs, much less stand on concrete next to one another amicably enough like they did at the Armadillo. Meanness trumped good vibes in the audience. Pistol-packing yahoos cruised the parking areas looking for trouble. Fists flew with the intensity of hand-to-hand military combat. The fragile alliance between Willie's family and the Armadillo World Headquarters' collective frayed.

"The whole day from the time I tried to get Willie to help me convince [powerful state legislator] Jumbo Atwell to move his RV is just an unpleasant blur," said Bobby Hedderman from the Armadillo, who was trying to manage the chaos on the stage, including territorial fights for small patches of shade. "I pretty much gave up after that."

Brother George W. Cooper, the Bible-thumping, hellfire-invoking radio preacher heard on KDRY and XERF in Mexico (and daddy of Willie's personal driver, B.C.), married Paul English and his fiancée, Diane Huddleston, onstage that afternoon. Waylon Jennings was best man. Sammi Smith was matron of honor. "My nephew got married a while back and it cost me sixty bucks to go to his wedding," Paul explained to the *Daily Texan*. "I didn't want my friends to have to rent a tux and drive one hundred miles. Since most of my friends are in the entertainment business, they'll be at Dripping Springs anyway."

Rather than honeymoon, Paul surveyed the battlefield with $100 bills hanging out of his pockets and a bone-handle skinning knife hanging from his hip with a pistol stuffed into a sock. The message he telegraphed was plain. "Touch the money, I'll cut your hand off." Nobody tried.

In the midst of the craziness, bands played music. Waylon electrified the crowd with a set that rocked up his country songs with lots of twang and thunder, staking a claim to both the rock and the country legacies that this thing called progressive country was built upon. Ernest Tubb and His Texas Troubadours performed a set of traditional Texas-style country music by which all Texas country music could be judged, even though most of the crowd failed to appreciate it. In a disjointed daze, Billy Joe Shaver previewed many of his original songs that were about to make Waylon even more famous. Backstage, a very young Stevie Ray Vaughan was photographed hanging out with Charlie Rich, the Silver-Haired Fox and master of mellow crooning.

Stevie played guitar with Marc Benno and the Nightcrawlers, who'd been added to the bill shortly before the event in a perfectly Willie way. Marc was a Dallas cat who'd partnered with Leon Russell as the Asylum Choir in Los Angeles, which sputtered to an end just as Leon's solo career took off. Marc knew his way around a studio, played lead guitar on the Doors' "L.A. Woman," and had written the hit "Nice Feeling" for Rita Coolidge. On a back-to-his-Texas-blues-roots kick with funds provided by A&M Records, he had hired an Austin blues-rock outfit called the Nightcrawlers, which featured a singing drummer with a smoky voice named Doyle Bramhall and Stevie Vaughan on guitar. The main reason Marc Benno got added to the picnic, though, was that he lived across the street from Willie.

"It was on Redbud Trail in Westlake Hills," Marc said. "People kept telling me there was a guy across the street who wanted to meet me. I went over to his house with a big garbage bag full of Oaxacan tops and there were these guys playing on the floor. It was Kris Kristofferson, Waylon Jennings, and Willie.

Willie played for about thirty minutes, we talked and played, and he put our band on the bill."

Marc Benno and the Nightcrawlers had to be shoved off the stage so Willie could close out the picnic. "When we came on, we were so into playing that we could not be controlled," admitted Marc. "I don't know how long we were playing. We had a ride going and Stevie's burning. But the power went off. The lights went out, everything went dead. I heard Willie was the one who personally pulled the power plug."

It was ten p.m.

"You guys don't know when to quit," one cowboy onstage informed Doyle Bramhall as he reared back to punch him out. Doyle responded with a swing of his own, a full Budweiser can clutched in his fist. The beer can exploded on contact. "He proceeded to beat the shit out of that cowboy," Marc Benno related. The Nightcrawlers left the stage with their heads held high, their testosterone raging, the blues cat having whipped the yahoo, at least this time.

The Willie Nelson Fourth of July Picnic wound down at two a.m. on July 5, with Willie Nelson and Leon Russell commanding the stage. It was a triumphant moment, with Leon working the crowd like a holy-roller preacher and Willie staying with him. The aftermath was not a pretty one. Ticket receipts that actually made it to the site covered production costs. Otherwise, no one knew for sure how much was taken in and how much was skimmed off along the way.

"Randy and I met with Willie afterwards and gave him the financial report," said Mike Tolleson, who was in charge of the accounting. "We had just enough money to pay all performers the allotted amount, production costs as budgeted, and a small fee for the Armadillo production staff. But there was no money left over to pay Willie. He was not too happy about that, but we also knew that the money from Dallas, San Antonio, and Houston was in somebody's pocket close to Willie."

Lana Nelson, Willie's eldest daughter, saw the Willie Nelson Fourth of July Picnic as the somewhat twisted realization of what she'd witnessed four years before at the Atlanta Pop Festival. "I didn't see Dad as a country player and Grand Ole Opry star. That was what he had to do to get out there, but I knew there wasn't a slot for him. You can't put him in one slot. He wore the Grand Ole Opry hat just to get his music out. At the picnic, I saw another hat. It was Atlanta Pop all over again, but here."

Her dad gave all the credit to Leon: "Leon had as much to do with making that picnic a success as anything. He brought in a whole different crowd, the rock 'n' roll crowd. It's something that it needed. It's something everybody wanted. It was all about everybody coming together to listen to music—country, rock, blues, gospel, jazz—everything."

DESPITE some heated arguments at the picnic, Willie's business collaboration with the Armadillo World Headquarters continued with another promotion. The Armadillo Country Music Revue was an ambitious mini-tour road show starring Willie and Michael Murphey that would travel to San Antonio, Dallas, Midland, Corpus Christi, and Amarillo. Willie Nelson and Michael Murphey were a can't-miss combination in Austin, as far as the tour organizers at the Armadillo World Headquarters were concerned. Putting them together on the same bill would spread the fever throughout the rest of the state. Only the rest of Texas hadn't gotten the word yet. Advance ticket sales were nonexistent in every city and those few who did show up came largely to sing along to "I Just Want to Be a Cosmic Cowboy."

"Willie was tough as shit, calm, and quickly resigned to the tiny audiences," Eddie Wilson said. It wasn't the first time Willie had been in a situation like this. But Michael Murphey was devastated. By the time the tour concluded back in Austin, he was too sick to perform at the homecoming show at the

Armadillo, and Jerry Jeff Walker filled in for him in front of a sold-out house.

MURPHEY got over his disappointment and agreed to do one more Armadillo Country Music Revue show with Willie at the Armadillo—one that would be videotaped and broadcast on television. Music on television was a relatively new concept. Films from the 1950s such as *The Girl Can't Help It* and *Rock, Baby, Rock It* featured performances by rock and roll acts, and Elvis and English bands from the 1960s like the Beatles and the Dave Clark Five starred in movies as themselves. But except for a handful of concert films such as *The T.A.M.I. Show* and pay-per-view live concerts by the Beatles and the Rolling Stones in the 1960s, music concerts on film or television didn't have much mass appeal.

But by 1973, the response to the films *Woodstock, Sympathy for the Devil,* and *The Concert for Bangladesh* and television programs such as NBC's *Midnight Special* made music on video something to be taken seriously. Austin embraced the idea wholeheartedly. Concerts at the Armadillo World Headquarters were being videotaped by a visionary crew from Taylorvision in the nearby small town of Taylor, Leon Russell's Sheltervision was videotaping music in clubs all over town, and Austin's city government had funded a community access television channel and was offering video equipment and free training to anyone who asked.

The Armadillo Country Music Revue, starring Willie Nelson and Michael Murphey, along with Billy Joe Shaver, Greezy Wheels, D. K. Little, and Diamond Rio, was broadcast live late in 1973 on KLRN-TV, the San Antonio and Austin Public Broadcasting System affiliate, with radio stations in both cities simulcasting the concert.

"We saw this as a pilot for a series of shows [taped at the Armadillo that] we were trying to get off the ground," explained the Armadillo's Mike Tolleson, who coordinated the video shoot. "I was searching out every bit of video equipment in town and found that KLRN had a mobile video van. So I talked Bill Arhos into taping a show at the Armadillo for a TV/radio simulcast. We put the talent and show together, KLRN provided the TV crew and truck, then edited it and aired it. The director/producer of the show was Bruce Scafe. Bill was executive producer role on his end and I was on our end." Ratings were negligible. The audience for a locally televised music concert was out in the clubs instead of at home watching television.

But the TV concert did get Bill Arhos $13,000 in

funding to further his idea of a music concert television series based in Austin. Another pilot would be videotaped at the television station's new state-of-the-art Studio 6-A on the campus of the University of Texas, a setting that made more sense, since the lighting and sound could be controlled. But Arhos stuck with the best talent the Armadillo Country Music Revue had to offer—Willie Nelson—along with singer B. W. Stevenson, who would be edited out of the pilot due to technical glitches and a small turnout for his taping. Arhos described Willie's performance as so "seamless," it required only three edits. The pilot birthed *Austin City Limits,* the longest-running music program on television. The Armadillo's people quickly peeled away. "I saw this as a sterile version of what we thought should happen at the Armadillo," Mike Tolleson said. "But KLRN had the money and gear and we did not. Bill called me to talk about talent for their pilot and first season of shows. We tried to negotiate a deal whereby we would be consultants regarding talent, but it didn't work out past the pilot, since we felt so proprietary about the whole concept and we asked for too much participation."

The fragile Willie-Armadillo alliance broke up for good when Willie came around to book another Armadillo gig following the TV taping. Bobby Hedderman, who was still steamed about how he and the Armadillo staff were treated by some of Willie's people at the Fourth of July Picnic, objected. "I'd love to have you do a show, but you have got to control your friends," he said. "I can't have them pushing around the staff and packing heat in the building." As far as the 'Dillo crowd was concerned, nothing remotely close to good vibrations came from wild men on dope brandishing pistols.

Willie shot a glare at Bobby and smiled at the other Armadillo people in the room. "They don't all carry guns," he said matter-of-factly, conveniently ignoring the fact he had carried a .357 magnum himself until a Dallas cop talked him out of it. Bobby informed Willie that the Armadillo was not a saloon and that weapons weren't welcome in a place built on hippie ideals — Willie needed to put the brakes on his boys. Willie said he couldn't be responsible for all his people's actions. Mike Tolleson and Carlotta Pankratz, the Armadillo staffers who'd brought Willie into the office, counseled Bobby to be a little more understanding of Willie and his background. After all, he was bringing big crowds to the Armadillo. As Willie departed, he told Bobby to call Neil Reshen on Monday to work out the details for his next gig.

When Bobby called Neil on Monday, he got an earful. "Willie says, 'Fuck you,'" Neil snarled over the phone. "If his friends aren't good enough for you, then neither is he."

"Well, he's probably right," Bobby replied, relieved he wouldn't have to deal with that bunch again, no matter how much it cost the Armadillo.

A week after the breakup, Townsend Miller reported in the *Austin American-Statesman* that Willie was looking to open a club of his own with Leon Russell.

OCTOBER was traditionally the month for the automotive industry's unveiling of Detroit's latest models for the coming year at car dealerships across the nation. Every new-car dealer staged promotions to pull in prospective buyers. Austin's Bill McMorris was no different. He hired Willie Nelson and band to play on a flatbed trailer at his Ford dealership downtown on West 6th Street at the corner of Wood Street to show off the new 1974 models.

Most of the folks who wandered in were more interested in the free hot dogs and Dr Peppers and the new LTDs, Mustangs, Capris, Broncos, Fairlanes, Mavericks, Falcons, and F-100 pickups than they were in Willie. He ran through his usual set, getting a few claps of recognition when he played the triad of his early songwriting hits and sang a few songs familiar to Texas country fans, like "Mr. Record Man" and "The Party's Over" and some material from *Shotgun Willie*. But when the band got to "Bloody Mary Morning," a song that Willie had recorded as a single for RCA and would record again soon as part of his *Phases and Stages* song cycle, people couldn't help but pay attention.

The song had all the trappings of a country and western hoedown, upbeat and danceable with lyrics celebrating booze for breakfast after partying all night. But when it came time for the instrumental break so the musicians could play their improvised leads, the going got weird. As if on cue, the whole band launched into a jam, the music shifting organically into a fluid flow that recalled the Grateful Dead and the Allman Brothers Band. With the bass and drums pushing the rhythm, the playing stretched out and intensified over the next fifteen minutes while Willie and band demonstrated that country music pickers could play just as far-out as any rock and rollers. They fed off the small crowd who had bunched around the flatbed trailer, cheering them on. The new Fords could wait.

A **WEEK** later, the movers and shakers of the country music industry in Nashville got the same message loud and clear, times two, at the annual Disc Jockey Convention in October 1973. Neil Reshen booked a special show at Nashville's Sheraton Hotel starring his two country clients. "They did these breakfast shows during the convention," Neil Reshen recounted, "but none of my people were awake at that hour unless they were still up from the night before. So we rented the Sheraton. I put Sammi Smith and Bobby Bare and a whole bunch of other people on the bill, and Willie and Waylon kept playing all night. It was a real changing of the guard." This was no polite thank-you-and-play-your-hit-single-and-leave affair. These were two greasy, long-haired wildcats out of control as Waylon and Willie tried to one-up each other, playing louder, longer, and more hard-charging. No rock concert that had passed through Nashville had had this kind of sweaty intensity. At the Disc Jockey Convention, no less.

"It's not a secret that a lot of people view Texas as a lot more friendly than Tennessee," explained Kinky Friedman, the self-proclaimed singing Texas Jewboy and new Willie acolyte, to the *Nashville Tennessean*. "The music industry in Nashville is still based on a repressive establishment system. There are some people who want to be outsiders."

Music Row was on notice: The Outlaws, true music rebels faithful to the tenets laid down by Hank

Williams and Bob Wills and Jimmie Rodgers, were a force to be reckoned with. Waylon lived up to his reputation as a contrarian by blowing off his greaser "country longhair" pompadour—a look that blared "outlaw"—for a beard and a fluffy, shampooed Beatle bob that conveyed the hipness of a boutique shop owner in suburbia (at least Jessi Colter liked it). But it was just a look. His sound was greasier than ever, due in no small part to the addition of two of Willie's boys to his band.

Bee Spears had left Willie's band to work for Waylon for the money and the chance to play more rock and roll. Willie went without a bass player for a stretch before hiring Larry Patton from Johnny Bush and the Bandoleros as a fill-in, then Jackie Deaton, another San Antonio four-stringer. He eventually enticed Chris Ethridge, a bass player from Mississippi who had been part of the storied California country-rock band the Flying Burrito Brothers.

Mickey Raphael had joined Bee Spears in Waylon's band for a couple months until his old boss called.

"Didn't you used to work for me?" Willie asked Mickey.

Mickey returned to Texas the next day. Bee Spears was not far behind.

• • •

WILLIE'S conquest of Texas worked on the domino theory. Once Austin fell, Houston was the next city to go cosmic cowboy, even though it was a tougher sell. Individuals who claimed to be affiliated with the Ku Klux Klan had bombed the transmitter of KPFT-FM, the left-leaning listener-supported radio station in Houston—twice—so Willie headlined a fund-raiser at Hofheinz Arena on the campus of the University of Houston to keep the station on the air. He was joined by a picnic-worthy lineup of Michael Murphey, Jerry Jeff Walker, Asleep at the Wheel, Kinky Friedman, and Sir Doug Sahm with Freda and the Firedogs, who stole the arena show by mixing up hillbilly, rock, and Tex-Mex.

Willie attempted to bring his musical movement back home with the Abbott Homecoming, staged in Willie's hometown on November 11, 1973, to coincide with the high school's homecoming football weekend. He announced his intentions in a press conference, promising to give any profit to the Abbott PTA. But some residents were not eager to embrace Abbott's prodigal son. He had a hard time finding a site. "The man who bought the store from Billy Pope offered his land north of town," Willie's boyhood friend Morris Russell reported. "But people were giving the landlord a hard time because all these hippies were going to show up. People just got in an uproar. One guy told me, 'There's going to be a hippie in every barn.' " Not coincidentally, the advertising for the event used old promotional photos that depicted Abbott's favorite native son as a clean-cut and clean-shaven smooth operator.

There was hardly a hippie in every barn, but ten thousand fans did show up, along with most of the three hundred citizens of Abbott for a twelve-hour music marathon starring their favorite son and a bunch of his buddies, including Johnny Bush, Waylon Jennings (though Waylon didn't perform, due to a curfew), Michael Murphey, Jerry Jeff Walker, Billy Joe Shaver, Sammi Smith, Kinky Friedman, and Kenneth Threadgill and His Velvet Cowpasture. Sammy Allred, Willie's disc jockey friend from Austin who was one-half of the satirical Geezinslaws, was designated MC and carried out his duties in a very stoned state after Willie handed him the list of bands and instructed him to let everyone play as long as they wanted.

Many of the acts, including Willie, Jerry Jeff, Asleep at the Wheel, and Waylon, had driven six hundred miles overnight from Terlingua, a mining ghost town west of Big Bend National Park in extreme southwest Texas, where they'd just played a country-rock festival. The festival had been inspired by the Terlingua International Chili Cookoff, an event that had grown out of a pissing match between New York journalist H. Allen Smith and Dallas scribe Frank X. Tolbert over who made the best bowl of chili, an original Texas concoction of beef, corn flour, and spices. The Terlingua chili cookoff attracted several thousand chiliheads to the middle of nowhere on the first Saturday every November. The music festival, which had nothing to do with chili, drew about sixty curious and determined fans and a crazed film crew under the direction of Nick Ray, the director of *Rebel Without a Cause.*

The Abbott Homecoming lost nowhere near as much money as the Terlingua event did, but Geno McCoslin blamed the Abbott losses on the local PTA anyway. If there had been any profit, it had been taken long before the cash reached the PTA.

Despite the financial baths at outdoor concerts and less-thanstellar record sales beyond the state line, Dallas newspaperman John Anders declared Willie to be the Godfather of Texas Country music. When Willie did a four-night stand at 57 Doors, North Texas's first progressive-country nightclub not coincidentally owned by Geno McCoslin, *Dallas Morning News* reviewer Dave McNeely compared one of the performances to Bob Wills and His Texas Playboys. Willie Nelson and Family closed out a very good year at Dallas's cavernous Market Hall, sharing the New Year's Eve bill with Leon Russell and Kinky Friedman. The $5,000 guarantee Willie and band received was the most money they'd ever made for a single show.

Music was an all-night, every-night proposition, and Willie was up for the challenge. Willie and band played a four-night run at Castle Creek in Austin, the listening room a block from the state capitol, while Commander Cody and His Lost Planet Airmen, the young band of rockers doing Western Swing and boogie, recorded a live album at the Armadillo, where the crowd was so loud, the audio was later inserted into live recordings by other bands. Willie sat in with Freda and the Firedogs at Aqua Fest, Austin's annual August celebration at Fiesta Gardens, and double-billed with the band at a fund-raiser for Symphony Square and at a voter registration benefit in Dallas. He played an unadvertised, sold-out gig with the Family Band at Soap Creek Saloon, where he'd been hanging out and partying with his pals, and split the box-office receipts evenly with the club, even though he could've taken it all. "At the end of the night David Anderson [one of the new additions to Willie's family] took all the money and divided it up among everyone, even the employees," Soap Creek co-owner Carlyne Majer said. "The employees had their rent paid for a month, grocery money, and money to do things with. It was a gift that he played—he wanted to play Soap Creek. It had nothing to do with money."

Ira Nelson had a hard time believing what his son had started in Austin until he saw it for himself. Willie Hugh had hair flowing over his ears, neck, and collar, an earring, a beard, and Lord knows what else. Ira couldn't help but ask, "What's happened to you? The last time I saw you, your hair was short and you had on a suit."

"That's right, Pop," Willie said. "And the last time you saw me, I was poor and hungry, and now I'm fat and happy."

"I got to grow me some hair," Ira said with a chuckle.

He did just that when he and Lorraine moved down to Austin to run Willie's Pool Hall, an old U-Tote-M convenience store at 2712 South Lamar Boulevard that had been refashioned into a beer joint. A hangout for his buddies and a touchstone for tourists, it provided a decent income for Ira and Lorraine.

The pool hall was home away from home for Zeke Varnon, Willie's longtime partner in crime from Hillsboro and Waco, who played dominoes out front and slept in the back. "Just mention Zeke's name and you'll hear sirens," joshed Sammy Allred, the wild

KVET disc jockey who was a regular. Sammy marveled at Willie's sense of timing around the old pool hall. "He was a genius at knowin' when to hang out. He knew just how often to come by to keep the rumors going — 'Hey, Willie's comin' in.' 'Willie was here.'"

When tourists grew impatient waiting for Willie, they posed for pictures with "Mom and Pop" Nelson and went away happy.

News of the pool hall reached all the way to Washington state, where Willie's birth mother, Myrle, was living again. "Myrle got tired of everybody calling Lorraine Willie's mom, so she decided that she's gonna let the world know that Lorraine was not Willie's mom," Willie's nephew Freddy Fletcher said. "And you don't tell Myrle no." Myrle was so ticked, she telephoned media people to tell them she was Willie's mother and damn proud of it.

THE VIBE that Willie had created down in Texas convinced Atlantic Records to record a second Willie album, *Phases and Stages,* an ambitious song cycle in the tradition of *Yesterday's Wine,* only more overt. The theme was a marital breakup told from the viewpoint of both the husband and the wife. Willie used his first marriage for inspiration, as he had been doing for years, and drew upon Lana's bad marriage to Steve as well. Family was an underlying theme of the album. "Sister's Coming Home" was about Lana. "It's Not Supposed to Be That Way" was inspired by Susie's first experiences with dating.

Willie had been road testing and massaging the song cycle at picking sessions and guitar pullings in Nashville and Austin for several years, and the title song had been issued as a single for RCA when nobody was looking or listening. All the folks who counted, from Coach Royal to Jerry Wexler (especially), gave him their thumbs-up on the material, so it was worth a shot. As the buzz for *Shotgun Willie* faded in the fall of 1973, a November recording session was set up in a small town of trailer parks and shotgun shacks tucked away in the northeast corner of Alabama.

"For *Phases and Stages,* I wanted Willie to come to Muscle Shoals," Jerry Wexler said. The fact that *Shotgun Willie* was done at Atlantic's New York studio had pleased the Erteguns and the Atlantic brass. Jerry wanted this one on his turf—Muscle Shoals, Alabama, 130 miles south of Nashville, about as close as Jerry wanted to get to Music Row, where he had been producing soul and rhythm and blues hits by African American artists largely backed by a studio band of white boys who happened to play very funky. Wexler came to Muscle Shoals from Memphis and the Stax studios and had already rung up a string of million sellers, including the Staple Singers' "I'll Take You There" and Wilson Pickett's "Mustang Sally" and "Land of 1000 Dances."

Jerry recruited Conway Twitty's pedal steel man John Hughey (Jimmy Day being on the outs with Willie and family) and the earthiest of all Nashville session guitarists, Fred Carter Jr., whose credits included the Band, Bob Dylan, Simon & Garfunkel, and Muddy Waters. Willie brought along his boys, plus Johnny Gimble, the swing fiddler who'd worked the *Shotgun Willie* sessions. Guitarist/dobroist Pete Carr, keyboardist Barry Beckett, David Hood, and Roger Hawkins came with the house.

Eleven tracks were recorded and mixed in two days before Thanksgiving, nothing out of the ordinary for someone conditioned to watching the clock. But a few weeks later, Rick Sanjek, the head of A&R at Atlantic Nashville, convinced Willie he could do it better, leaving Jerry Wexler out of the loop. So they went to Fred Carter's Nugget Studios in Goodlettsville, just down the road from Ridgetop. Willie brought his road band of Mickey Raphael, Bobbie Nelson, Paul English, and Bee Spears to join Grady

Martin, and they cut the whole album all over again in another two days, with the exception of "Pretend I Never Happened."

"It was nowhere near as slick as Jerry's production, but it was Willie," said Nick Hunter, Atlantic Nashville's radio guy. Rick Sanjek took Hunter with him to New York for a meeting with Jerry Wexler. "The Muscle Shoals tracks were too R&B," Sanjek insisted to Jerry. Country radio would never buy it. On his own, Sanjek told Wexler, he had remixed the album to give it more of a country flavor. This new mix was the one to use. Sanjek avoided telling Wexler they'd rerecorded the entire album. Calling it a new mix was easier to explain.

Jerry went ballistic nonetheless. "After I listened, the red rage started in my heels, up my backbone, up to my neck," he said. "It was the most horrible piece of shit you ever heard. Suddenly, I slapped myself: What the fuck is a country mix? There is no such thing. A mix is a mix."

"This was the one that closed Atlantic Nashville," Nick Hunter said of the meeting.

Jerry Wexler ran Rick Sanjek out of his office. Within weeks, he fired him. "Rick was my representative of the Nashville aristocracy," Jerry later said. "I took him on because he was the son of a very dear friend of mine. Big mistake. He came down from Yale with a ten-gallon hat and a big buckle and he tells me, 'You gotta know how to talk to these people.' "

Wexler authorized Tom Dowd, Atlantic's chief engineer, to do the final mix of *Phases and Stages,* which was released in March 1974. The album was promoted as something new and completely different, using the phrase "When Willie Nelson tells you the same old story, it's not the same old story anymore."

For all the emphasis on concept, many of the songs on *Phases and Stages* stood out on their own. Three songs — "Pick Up the Tempo," "Heaven or Hell," and "It's Not Supposed to Be That Way" — also appeared on Waylon's pivotal album *This Time,* released in July 1974, which was not coincidentally coproduced by Willie Nelson, a cross-promotion that built the Waylon and Willie brand.

"I Still Can't Believe That You're Gone" was arguably Willie's saddest composition to date, written in the aftermath of Carlene English's suicide, which no one saw coming. A few hours earlier she had been laughing with Connie Nelson, her neighbor down the street and her soul sister since Connie had met Willie. She departed, complaining of a headache. Paul said he had taken a sleeping pill, as he usually did, and slept through the incident. Their son, Darrell Wayne, discovered her body the next morning.

She had left a brief note to Paul to take care of their son and to Darrell Wayne, telling him to be good and to finish school. Carlene hadn't exhibited signs of being suicidal, but suicide ran in her family. Her father took his own life years before. Paul was devastated and wasted away, dropping from 190 to 120 pounds as he sank into depression. Willie did all he could do to help his best friend and his best friend's son, including writing the song.

The single reached number 51 on the country singles chart. "Bloody Mary Morning," a flat-out countrified run through the jungle, with a flurry of picking and rhythm under a contemporary Texas storyline rife with drinking and fooling around, did much better, reaching number 17. "Sister's Coming Home," released as a single at Willie's request, barely charted at all, checking in at number 93.

Another single that wasn't on the album almost broke out. "After the Fire Is Gone," a Loretta Lynn composition made popular by Conway Twitty and Loretta a few years earlier, was redone by Willie and Tracy Nelson (no relation), a Wisconsin girl with a bluesy Big Mamma voice who led the San Francisco band Mother Earth (which included Austin folkie Powell St. John) and had relocated to Nashville, where she was signed to Atlantic. Her producer, Bob Johnston, heard Tracy sing the tune at a showcase at the Exit/In in Nashville. Leaving the club, he told an Atlantic associate, "I just heard the greatest song in the world and we've got to get Willie to do a duet for Tracy's album."

It was the first time Willie had charted with a duet since his first single with Shirley Collie, "Willingly," was issued on Liberty late in 1961. His plaintive whine was the perfect complement for Tracy Nelson's brassy voice. For the B-side, Tracy added her vocal to the existing track of "Whiskey River" from the *Shotgun Willie* sessions. "After the Fire Is Gone" peaked at number 17 on the *Billboard* country singles chart. The recording earned the two Nelsons a Grammy Award nomination for Best Country Duo in 1974.

The single might have climbed higher or actually won a Grammy if Atlantic Nashville hadn't shut down on September 6, 1974. "We weren't doing too well," Jerry admitted. "My partners and the chief financial officer made the decision to close the Nashville office because it was running behind in start-up money." Wexler protested feebly, telling the Ertegun brothers, "You can't do this. We've got Willie Nelson now." The response was "Willie who? Go ahead and close it."

There were plenty of reasons to reassess Atlantic's Nashville venture. Country may have been changing, but if anything, it was veering away from the roots sounds that appealed to Jerry Wexler. Country was hell-bent on becoming the sound of America's suburbs, a trend signaled by the March relocation of the Grand Ole Opry from the Ryman Auditorium to a new development on the northeastern fringe of Nashville called Opryland; soon-to-be-disgraced President Richard M. Nixon yo-yoed with Opry star Roy Acuff onstage at the last Ryman show.

Jerry Wexler's instincts had served him well, but in this case, hanging out with cool musicians and getting high and having a gas without bringing in a Top 10 hit proved a fatal flaw. His attempt at making Atlantic Nashville as much a Texas label as a Tennessee operation had failed. Jerry had flown Austin-by-way-of-Lubbock blue-collar rocker D. K. Little to Los Angeles in an attempt to cut a deal; once the plane landed, D.K. didn't leave the terminal before catching the next flight home. Jerry had persuaded Ray Wylie Hubbard, whose song "(Up Against the Wall) Redneck Mother" had become the cosmic cowboy national anthem, to record in Muscle Shoals under Wexler's direction with Bob Johnston producing. But Ray Wylie and His Cowboy Twinkies turned around and left Alabama after one day in the studio with Johnston. Marcia Ball, the singer, pianist, and front person for Freda and the Firedogs, the one band

Wexler actually got to do a demo, hesitated signing any deal long enough for Wexler to pull the offer from the table.

"Whenever I ask who I should sign, nobody seems to know," Jerry complained to *Rolling Stone.* "Is it a mirage down there?"

Austin music people had a built-in distrust of old record pros like Jerry Wexler who made their living dropping in on similar scenes and cherry-picking the best and brightest to shape them into recording stars. Austin musicians were not into making money, or so they postured. In truth, for all the curiosity about Austin, labels weren't signing up acts because the potential wasn't there. Jim Dickinson, a Memphis producer and musician, contended Austin music was not so much about art but rather a celebration of amateurism. Jerry Wexler may have been cool for a record man, blowing weed with Willie, Sir Doug, and the Firedogs, and partying as hard as the kids. But without hits, Jerry Wexler and Atlantic Records were nothing. Most start-up labels with sufficient financing worked on a five-to-seven-year plan. Atlantic Nashville lasted a year and a half.

Two months before the axe fell, Jerry Wexler had bankrolled a Willie Nelson live album at the Texas

Opry House, Willie's new performing home in Austin. The crowd who'd crammed into the Texas Opry House asshole-to-elbow was very drunk, very high, and very sweaty, no matter how well the air-conditioning was supposedly working. They packed the big room to see the star of the Willie Nelson Fourth of July Picnic and to be part of the live album being recorded over the two-night stand on June 29 and 30, 1974. The recording documented Willie Nelson and Family at the top of their game, throwing out great balls of sonic fire into the sea of fans. The band—Paul English, Bee Spears, Mickey Raphael, and Sister Bobbie—augmented by Jimmy Day, back in good graces again, and Johnny Gimble, Mr. Dependable on the fiddle, was tighter than ever. Willie's voice had matured and lost some of the flat nasal twang of the RCA years, gaining depth and tone. His guitar playing was virtuous. Everyone cooked.

The show opened the same way all Willie shows opened—with five strums of the guitar followed by the plea:

Whisk-key Riv-verrr take my miiiind. Don't let her
   mem-ree torture meeeee
Whis-key Riv-verrr don't run dry. You're all I got,
   take care of meeee

The band joined in, with Mickey wailing blues riffs on his harmonica followed by Bobbie plinking out honky-tonk piano straight from the beer joint. Another midtempo blues original, "Me and Paul," Willie's tribute to his friend for life, followed, telling the story of a bond formed by hard times on the road. While the song was never regarded as a hit when it appeared on both *Yesterday's Wine* and *Shotgun Willie,* it was Willie's way of explaining in less than three minutes what Paul's friendship meant to him.

His voice, his guitar, Mickey's harmonica, and Johnny Gimble's swing fiddling were the hooks to the medley of "Funny How Time Slips Away," "Crazy," "Night Life," and "Stay All Night (Stay a Little Longer)," the Bob Wills swing number that was transformed into a rockin' toe tapper.

He then launched into "Bloody Mary Morning," expanding the song into an extended jam that ultimately spilled over into "Take Me Back to Tulsa," another Bob Wills classic that had been covered by Asleep at the Wheel. The breadth of the songs and the band's feel for them left a strong impression. This was no run-of-the-mill country band. This family could really play.

"The Party's Over" had become a standard for sports fans across America thanks to Willie's old Dallas Cowboy buddy, Don Meredith, who after retiring from playing football became one of the three announcers on ABC's *Monday Night Football,* the highest-rated sports program on television. Whenever the outcome of the game being televised was assured, Dandy Don would sing in his croaking voice "Turn out the lights, the party's over" to millions of viewers.

Willie altered the opening lines of the old honky-tonk standard "Truck Driving Man" from "Pulled into a roadhouse in Texas" to "Pulled into a whorehouse in Texas" just because he could, endearing him to the young audience in front of him. He was outlaw and proud and they ate it up.

He mixed originals such as "Sister's Comin' Home" and "Good Hearted Woman," which would become a hit duet with Waylon, with classics like "She Thinks I Still Care" and a cover of Leon Russell's "You Look Like the Devil."

During the day between the two concerts that were recorded by Atlantic, Willie and Family recorded an improvised instrumental riff they called "Willie's After Hours." The jazzy slow blues featured Jimmy Day's drenched-in-reverb steel out front accompanied by Willie's cool guitar, which summoned simultaneous visions of Wes Montgomery and Django Reinhardt, and Bobbie's stellar piano and organ riffs, some so fat and funky on the Hammond B-3, they could've been lifted from a Ray Charles recording.

JERRY Wexler had chosen the Texas Opry House to make a live record for good reason. The room was the kind of club Willie had been wanting to open ever since his split from the Armadillo. He quit looking when he met Wallace Selman.

Wally had arrived in Austin a year after Willie did, in 1973. A fast-talking, thick-drawling hustler with an innate appreciation of the con, he came from Crockett, in the Piney Woods of East Texas, and had done well in the restaurant-supply business in Houston, where he met Bronson Evans, who ran a chain of nightclubs called the Abbey Inn located near singles' apartment complexes. Together, they moved to Austin and opened up a joint in an old carriage shop on 6th Street downtown between San Jacinto and Trinity streets called the River City Inn.

First developed in Houston in 1918, refrigerated air, commonly known as AC, became prevalent in homes, automobiles, businesses, and institutions across the state by the 1960s. But to hippies running the Armadillo on a shoestring budget, air-conditioning was a luxury, which created an opportunity for Wally

Selman and his business partners. "We got to thinking, with all the music going on in this town, why don't we do a place with air-conditioning and tables and chairs where people can sit down and enjoy a mixed drink?"

Austin was primed for a place like that. Voters had just passed an ordinance extending drinking hours from midnight and one a.m. on Saturday to two a.m. nightly. Two years before, Texas had dropped the legal minimum age for drinking alcohol from twenty-one to eighteen.

Dude McCandless, the owner of two large motor inns in Austin and several other choice properties throughout the city, had shown Wally the convention center ballroom of the Terrace Motor Inn just off South Congress Avenue. The Terrace had seen better days since it was built as a luxury motor inn resort in 1957, mainly because highway traffic had shifted to the Interregional Expressway—Interstate 35. But the convention center was big enough and cool enough for Wally to sign a lease with Dude.

Wally and Bronson Evans headed a partnership that included Wallace's cousin Ricky Spence and a character from Dallas whom Bronson knew named Buddy Wages. Wallace would handle the booking, the PR, and the bands. Bronson would do the books and take care of the bills while continuing to run the

River City Inn with his wife. Ricky and Buddy were in charge of the bar, which, unlike the Armadillo, served mixed drinks. The main room, which was filled with long tables like a Texas dance hall, could hold two thousand customers on a good night. A smaller adjacent room could hold six hundred.

The Texas Opry House opened in early 1974 with Doug Sahm, Freda and the Firedogs, Alvin Crow, and free beer, drawing an overflow crowd the first night. "We gave away thirty kegs of beer and sold fifty-five hundred dollars' worth of liquor," Wally said. Two weeks later, the Eagles, the country-rock band from Los Angeles that was just beginning to break nationally with their second album and a single called "Tequila Sunrise," played the room to another sold-out crowd at $5 a ticket. Wally paid the Eagles $6,300 for the performance. A cabana by the pool became the Texas Opry House Annex, featuring live music seven nights a week for a $1 cover charge.

Before the Texas Opry opened, Willie's protégé Tim O'Connor had paid Wally and Bronson a visit. "Will and I are opening a club called Nightlife," Tim informed them, suggesting they might not want to go through with their plans. "When he left, my partners were freaking out," Wally said. "We'd signed the lease but hadn't done a show."

Wally Selman had already met Willie through

Townsend Miller, the country music columnist for the *Austin American-Statesman,* who consistently hit at least five clubs in a single night. "Willie and Coach Royal were the two figures in Texas you knew existed but weren't sure they weren't figments of the imagination because you'd never see them up close," Wally said. "Willie was playing on a stool and during a break came and sat with us, and we were knocking back tequila shots and having a good time. Townsend said, 'Tell him what you're doing, Wally.'" Willie gave him his phone number and told him to call when the room got up and running.

But Wally's partners were still nervous about Willie Nelson's Nightlife and urged Wally to ask Willie if he'd consider being a partner. Willie showed up at the almost-open Texas Opry after playing golf with Coach Royal, and Wally tendered the offer.

"Why don't we do this?" Willie proposed while sucking on a joint. "Instead of me worrying about you stealing from me, why don't I just give you my word? I'll call this my home. I'll play here. I'll bring my friends here, and we won't worry about any partnership."

Guns were not an issue at the Texas Opry House and there was a whole lot more cocaine floating around backstage than at the Armadillo. ("You can hear it on some live versions of 'Bloody Mary Morning,' " Mickey Raphael wisecracked.) The room put an upscale face on Austin's rootsy music scene. Willie demonstrated his approval by performing a string of four-hour shows. He didn't need to tell the Armadillo people to fuck off (Neil Reshen had already done it for him). Although the cover for shows at the Opry was sometimes twice what the Armadillo was charging, fans could vote with their pocketbooks.

The Annex became Willie's hangout and unofficial office. "He'd sit in with Milton Chesley Carroll or someone like that and take over the stage for two hours, all for a one-dollar cover charge," Wally said. He packed the big room consistently and told his friends. *Rolling Stone* devoted three pages to the Texas Opry House, citing wannabe outlaw David Allan Coe's cussing out the crowd as proof country music and its audience had changed. "Booking agencies knew who we were," bragged Wally.

Everyone was getting in on the act, including the former Donny Young and Donny Lytle, whom Willie Nelson replaced in Ray Price's Cherokee Cowboys in 1961. Now known as Johnny Paycheck, he grew his hair, embraced marijuana, scored a monster country and pop hit written by David Allan Coe called "Take This Job and Shove It," and ultimately lived up to his outlaw reputation by serving two years in prison for shooting a man who allegedly questioned why he called himself Johnny Paycheck instead of Donny Lytle.

Of all the stars coming to the Texas Opry House on Willie's word, Wally Selman was the most pumped about Waylon Jennings. "Waylon's rider called for Coors Beer, and at that time the closest place you could get Coors Beer was up in North Texas," Wally said, ignoring the fact that Waylon himself did not drink alcohol. "I was crazy about Waylon's music, so I drove to Plano myself. I pulled into the Opry parking lot and there was that big ol' black bus that had that big ol' eagle painted on the back and everything. The hair on the back of my neck stood up. I went on the bus and said, 'Here's your beer.' "

Waylon came out of the back room, looked at Wally, and grunted, "Hey, Hoss, is this Opry your place?"

"Yes, sir," Wally said, puffing up his chest.

"You working with that short-ass Willie?" Waylon asked him. Wally nodded tentatively. "You tell that little bastard I ain't goin' in there and playing one goddamn song if he doesn't pay me my money for the picnic. Goddamn right, Hoss. Go tell him. Find him."

"Well, I don't know anything about that," Wally protested.

"He does," Waylon insisted. "Go tell him what I said."

Wallace went looking for Willie and found him sitting alone in his Mercedes in the parking lot.

"He knew something was going on, because he was sitting low in that Mercedes," related Wally.

"What are y'all doin'?" Willie asked Wallace off-handedly.

"I just come off the bus with Waylon."

"What does he got to say?"

"Nothin' much. We was just talking."

"What did he say?"

"He told me to tell you to pay him his goddamn money or he wasn't playing and that you were a short motherfucker," Wally said.

"Well, you tell him I told you, 'Fuck him!' " Willie turned on the ignition and hit the accelerator, his tires peeling as he sped away.

Wally had a sold-out house, but his featured attraction and his featured attraction's special guest were having a Mexican stand-off. B.C., Willie's driver, suggested Wally find Willie's wife.

Connie Nelson went on Waylon's bus and read him the riot act for being so chicken shit.

"Willie's upset," she told him. "What's going on?"

"I don't trust him," Waylon informed her. "He's

got Gene McCoslin working for him and I'm not going on until I get my money."

"Waylon, for God's sake, this is Willie. He'll give you the money from his pocket before he'll let you leave here. But don't tell him that—that's a slap in his face," she said.

Waylon cooled down. Connie walked off the bus and told Wally everything was okay. The show went on without incident. Waylon rocked. Willie sat in. They acted like brothers onstage. The crowd went beserk, and Wally Selman developed a strong liking for Connie Nelson. Fans may have thought Willie and Waylon were blood brothers, but Wally learned, as others would, they were on separate paths.

The Texas Opry was more Waylon's style than the Armadillo was. Waylon didn't smoke pot or drink beer. But he did cocaine—piles of the sparkling white powder, so much coke that when he played poker with friends in Austin, he kept excusing himself and going to the bathroom, though everyone knew what he was doing in there.

"Why don't you just do your coke out here?" a buddy asked him.

"Because I want you to be able to say, 'On October nineteenth, 1974, I never saw Waylon take coke,' " Waylon said.

The Texas Opry House was the setting for Waylon's hugely popular single "Bob Wills Is Still the King," a live recording that came on the heels of "This Time," Waylon's first number one country single ever. The album of the same name was charting in the Top 5. Many misinterpreted the song to be a put-down of Willie for the line "It don't matter who's in Austin/ Bob Wills is still the King." Waylon's song simply put the whole movement in perspective: Both he and Willie were sons of Bob Wills, who put Texas music on the map.

The old school met the new school at the Opry. Bee Spears remembers looking back at Paul English working his brushes onstage and leaning so far forward that Bee could see a gun sticking out of his hip pocket.

"You expecting trouble, Paul?" Bee asked him.

"You can never tell," Paul replied with a wicked grin.

Paul was preaching peace and love, carrying a business card that read "So long as we love, we serve. So long as we are loved by others, we are indispensable; and no man is useless while he has a friend." But just in case, he still packed heat. That preferred method of security may have offended hippies, but someone had to collect the money, and if there were going to be questions raised at the settlement, a chrome .45 caliber pistol was a persuasive means of getting them answered.

When Willie scored a gig in California a few years later to play for the HBO cable television channel that paid $79,000 for a single show, Paul insisted the band be paid in cash before going onstage, no matter how good the check looked. "No money, no Willie," he declared. His demand may have struck the corporate types who were paying Willie as offensive, but the method worked. "He's my friend who watches over me," Willie said of Paul. Paul felt the same about Willie.

Waylon Jennings corroborated the realities of the business of music in the 1970s during an impromptu talk to a class at the University of Texas. He concluded by citing the last tour with Buddy Holly in February of 1959, on which Waylon and Tommy Allsup were Holly's backing band, to explain what he'd learned over his career. The tour bus had arrived in Moorhead, Minnesota, after an overnight drive from Clear Lake, Iowa, but Buddy, the Big Bopper, and Ritchie Valens were not there waiting for them, even though they were supposed to have flown in the night before on a private plane Buddy had chartered (Waylon and Allsup gave up their seats on the plane to the Big Bopper and Valens). "We knew something was wrong," Waylon related. "The weather was bad, and we got the word that the plane had crashed. The promoter talked us into doing the gig anyway. We just wanted to go home. But we did the show. After the gig, the promoter said he wouldn't pay us, and the reason he gave for not paying us was that Buddy wasn't there." In other words, the music business was full of sharks and assholes lacking sympathy, much less ethics. Waylon paused, then told the room full of college students, "That's what you need to know about the music business."

THE SECOND Willie Nelson Fourth of July Picnic, expanded to three days, was held at the Texas Motor Speedway, an auto racetrack near the towns of Bryan and College Station, ninety miles northeast of Austin, over the July Fourth weekend of 1974. Tim O'Connor and Larry Moeller, Lucky's son, shared production duties, constructing a wide stage out of telephone poles and sliding barn doors so one band could be setting up on one side of the stage while another was performing. Tim was also in charge of security and hired bouncers from Austin nightclubs to protect the performers and the stage.

Leon Russell headlined again. Floyd Tillman was revived to perform with Freda and the Firedogs as

Willie's oldest old friend on the show. Jerry Jeff Walker and the Lost Gonzo Band, the Dirt Band, Doug Kershaw, Sir Doug Sahm, Greezy Wheels, featuring Sweet Mary Egan on fiddle, B. W. Stevenson, Michael Murphey, and Steve Fromholz all played on the raceway's treeless infield, along with a few close personal friends of Willie. Musicians showed up bearing notes from Willie that said they could play the picnic. Tim took them at their word and would later consult Willie with the list of acts, which often led Willie to ask, "Who is that?"

"I don't know, you sent them to me," Tim would tell him. So they made a rule. "If you don't know them, and I don't know them, we'll pay them five hundred," Willie decided.

The rednecks and hippies went wild together at the picnic, partaking of beer, whiskey, marijuana, acid, meth, white crosses, uppers, downers, peyote, and, increasingly, the by now ever-present cocaine.

A few arrests were made before the picnic got under way for racing RVs around the racetrack. There was a ruckus when Willy Nelson, the cousin and manager of former teen sensation Ricky Nelson, whose musical memoir "Garden Party" was a huge hit, tried to get backstage and was attacked by a security goon under the influence who thought anyone trying to pass himself off as Willie Nelson deserved to get beat up.

Sixteen cars in the racetrack infield caught fire and burned, sending an apocalyptic black cloud into the sky that persisted for days after the event. Leon Russell got sloppy drunk and delivered a half-ass performance. Police and sheriffs enforced the Texas Mass Gathering Act curfew of eleven p.m. each night. Wolfman Jack and a crew from NBC Television's *Midnight Special* music series had several confrontations with security guards. Still, the crowd, estimated to be anywhere from twenty thousand to seventy-five thousand, was large enough to prompt some folks to conclude this Texas thing had legs.

Tim O'Connor had to flash a gun to collect the money from the picnic's other business partner, a judge in Brazos County, so he could pay Leon Russell his $10,000 guarantee. When it came time to settle at the end of the event, the judge remembered O'Connor's strong-arm tactic and slowly peeled off fifty $1 bills for Tim's work, telling him, "Get out of Brazos County and don't come back."

WILLIE didn't spend a whole lot of time crying over a picnic gone bad or over losing his deal with Atlantic Records. From the front porch of his ranch, life looked pretty good. The move to Texas that was supposed to mark the end of his career had revived it instead. His blood family and his musical family were living around him. Musicians were streaming into Austin in droves in search of the scene he helped build. The national media were taking note of the scene boiling up in Texas and its ringleader who had been anointed in Austin as Godfather and was regarded as almost as big a deal in Dallas and Houston. What was there not to like?

The Willie effect was directly responsible for the much-publicized relocation of the band Asleep at the Wheel from northern California to Texas at the end of the summer of 1974. Choice slots on picnics, numerous shared bills with Willie, and a history at the Armadillo through their friends Commander Cody and His Lost Planet Airmen made the move a no-brainer.

"We were already known," the pianist Floyd Domino said. "We were on the radio in Austin. Townsend Miller wrote us up. We were in. We were nobodies out in Berkeley. I've never been a strong melody player, I just keyed off the chords, but in Texas, people would come up and say, 'I like how you solo.' 'You solo like Al Stricklin.' 'You play out on the edge like Jimmy Day.' We were a natural fit down here."

The Wheel played a week at the Armadillo, living in the parking lot on their bus. "We were booked to play six nights at the Western Place in Dallas, but after two nights, Geno McCoslin, the owner, said, 'You're not playing. Willie's playing,'" Floyd said. Geno wanted to kick them off the bill. They'd drawn twelve paying customers the first night and not many more the second, no matter how well they played Western Swing and sounded like Bob Wills. When Willie showed up, the Wheel told him they'd been bumped from the bill. Willie told Geno in no uncertain terms, "They don't play, I don't play."

"Geno immediately starts kissing our ass," Floyd said. "Geno was a real standup guy. Our road manager, Baggett, was a black belt in karate, and Geno put his gun on the table when they were settling up. Baggett asked him, 'Is that faster than my hand?' We got paid, no problem."

The Wheel's introduction to characters like Geno was instructive. Geno was having a small war with a vending machine distributor over pool tables in the club. At one point, he removed the pool tables and put them on the sidewalk and said, 'Come get your fucking pool tables.' The next week on Saturday night the place was packed, when three Doberman Pinschers were set loose in the club as retaliation, clearing out the place. "That's the kind of people we were dealing with," Ray Benson, Asleep at the Wheel's leader, concluded. Geno attracted trouble, yet Willie always did business with him. Did Geno have something on him? Or was this loyalty of the most extraordinary degree? Ray Benson developed a theory: "The more you fucked up, the more Willie liked you."

Ray had already learned a lot about the business from Willie when they met on the road in Greenville, South Carolina, early in 1972. Asleep at the Wheel was backing up Connie Smith, Stoney Edwards, Freddy Hart, Vickie Lee, and the rest of a package show that Willie was joining. "We were really excited because we knew who Willie Nelson was," Ray said. "They pulled up in that Open Road mobile home with Bee and Paul. The first thing Willie asked us was whether we'd been paid. It was the fourth show that week and no one had been paid. Otis Woody, the promoter, told everybody not to worry, that we'd be paid on the next date." Ray got to drinking Jack Daniel's and talking about dope with Paul English and Bee Spears, when Willie interrupted the conversation. "Come on, boys, we're going home," he said without further discussion. "Willie saw that the promoter didn't have the money, wasn't going to pay him, so he said 'fuck you' and went home," Ray said. "That's how I met Willie Nelson."

Ray Benson realized he was witnessing the start of

something big at Geno's new Dallas club, 57 Doors. "The room was a dump, but the gigs were amazing. We played Thursday, Friday, and Saturday, starting at nine, four alternating sets. On Thursday, there were forty people in the club. By Saturday it was packed. These strippers came in who just worshipped Willie Nelson. They would say, 'You speak to me.' People were fanatically devoted to Willie. Waylon Jennings was supposed to be the star—he was sexy, the women loved him. Willie was goofy, a hippie like all the rest of us."

He was also a certified rabble-rouser. Things started turning ugly at the Texas Opry House after Willie's endorsement of the Opry at the expense of the Armadillo helped ignite bidding wars over several acts, including Willie, Waylon, Boz Scaggs, and Ray Charles. "I wrote a column in the *Statesman* knocking the Opry people for stealing Ray Charles," said Joe Gracey, the paper's rock and roll columnist and the KOKE-FM disc jockey. "They threatened to kill me," he claimed. "They put out a hit on me with some thug in San Marcos."

Gracey's worry over the threat was short-lived. Despite the crowds, the Texas Opry House folded less than a year after it opened. Bronson Evans hadn't paid rent in two months and suddenly disappeared with no forwarding address. Wally Selman faced tax evasion charges for failing to withhold income tax on the Opry's employees. "The beer license people was on me, the liquor license people was on me, they pulled my license. The whole house of cards fell. They come out and put tape on the doors. The IRS locked the doors and they didn't give me no key."

Wally went to Willie for help. He found him in a booth at the Opry Annex, which remained open.

"I need some money or I'm going to jail," Wally pleaded.

"You know what we used to do in Fort Worth when a place we played had financial trouble?" Willie asked him.

Wally shook his head.

"We'd go somewhere else and play."

Wally's heart sank.

"We'll help," Willie said, laughing, once he knew he had made Wally squirm. Willie and band played five nights at the Opry Annex club to pay off debts and make sure neither Wally Selman nor anyone else had to go to jail for having too good a time. Waylon joined the shows, asking only that Wally pay for his rooms at the Holiday Inn on Town Lake, where he liked to stay.

Wallace Selman paid the taxes, stayed out of jail, and went to Houston and opened another Texas Opry House.

And Willie Nelson got a new record label.

On his way out the door, Jerry Wexler had left a gift for Willie—the release from his contract, along with the promise he could keep the signing bonuses and the masters he'd recorded for the label. "We got more to leave than we did to come to Atlantic," Neil Reshen bragged. He was free to negotiate a deal with anyone except RCA—no way would Willie go back there. RCA represented everything wrong about the business in Nashville.

Columbia Records had been a suitable prospective home for Waylon two years earlier before he ended up with a new contract with RCA. Columbia might be even more perfect for Willie. The label was one of the oldest in American recorded music and had a history of iconoclastic artists, including Johnny Cash, the original Nashville rebel, folk-rocker Bob Dylan, folk-popper Paul Simon, and jazz trumpet master Miles Davis, another Neil Reshen client. Even more important, the label was flush with cash.

"I was sitting on the porch swing with Willie at his place on Fitzhugh Road and he was talking with his accountant on the phone," Jerry Retzloff of Lone Star Beer said. When he hung up, Willie turned to Jerry and said, "I made a million dollars for the first time last year." He credited Neil Reshen. "New York Jews, you have to have them," Willie told Jerry. "If

you don't have a New York Jew in the record business, you ain't gonna make it. I got a New York Jew.
I don't like it, but I got him."

He actually got more than one. Mark Rothbaum,
the kid learning the business by working for Neil,
was assuming more of the day-to-day responsibilities
for Willie. "Willie was almost forgotten by Neil,"
Mark said. "It seemed to me that Neil thought Waylon was the greatest living artist and that's where his
attention was. I respected Waylon's talent and his
ability. Willie was just so much more of a human
being. When I saw the album cover of *Willie Nelson
and Family* with everybody around that circle, I
wanted to be one of them — part of a different family than the one I grew up with. It was safe haven. I
wanted to make their lives a little easier, make things
flow better."

Mark loved Willie, adored Connie, and found Paul
to be "the most honest person I knew," recalling Bob
Dylan's observation that "to live outside the law, you
must be honest." And he became tighter than tight
with Mickey Raphael. Both were nice Jewish boys
with the same MSR initials whose fathers were in the
furniture business. Both were taking a lot of heat
from their families for casting their lot with a Texas
country musician instead of striving to become a

doctor, lawyer, or accountant. And neither gave much of a shit.

"I want him," Bruce Lundvall, the CEO of Columbia Records, told Neil Reshen late in 1974 when informed of Willie's availability. Lundvall loved Willie's writing and loved his voice, and signing him would be a poke in the eye of Jerry Wexler and Atlantic Records, who had stolen Aretha Franklin from Columbia and made her a star. Turnabout was fair play.

Bruce Lundvall called Billy Sherrill, the record producer who for all practical purposes ran Columbia's country division in Nashville, based upon the slick, made-for-radio product he was cranking out on George Jones, Tammy Wynette, Johnny Paycheck, David Allan Coe, and the rest of the roster. Billy Sherrill's blessing was important to Lundvall, but Billy wasn't biting.

"What?" Sherrill said to Lundvall when he was told Columbia was signing Willie. "We don't need him. He's old."

"He's a genius," Bruce said, reminding Billy that he worked for him.

"Yeah, you're right," Billy shrugged.

Bruce Lundvall could afford to gamble. Willie fit in as a prestige act for the label, an outsider appreciated mostly by insiders, who, if nothing else, made Columbia cool. The New York office could handle him if Nashville couldn't. There was little risk in the deal. The investment was less than $100,000, pocket change compared with what the company was advancing to rock royalty such as Blood, Sweat & Tears, Santana, and Aerosmith. The advance for the first album was $60,000 plus another $17,000 each for the rights to *The Troublemaker* and *To Lefty from Willie,* albums that had been made on Atlantic's coin.

"We did a signing party at Marty's, a club that used to be Toots Shor, right next door to the CBS building," Bruce Lundvall said. "Very few people showed. People in New York didn't know who he was. What was going on down in Texas hadn't reached here yet. Willie and I got drunk and had a great time talking."

Garland to Hollywood, 1975

IN JANUARY 1975, while driving back to Texas from their first ski trip ever to Steamboat Springs, Colorado, Willie informed Connie he had to deliver an album to Columbia soon and didn't have a clue what to do. He needed songs. According to the contract Neil Reshen had hammered out with Columbia Records, giving him artistic control for the first time in his career, Willie knew he could go in and do whatever he wanted, and the label would take it. Connie pulled out a pad of paper while they were talking about songs. She brought up "Red Headed Stranger" and how that and similar songs might make a nice story album, like a cowboy movie on record.

The ideas started flying back and forth. Willie could write some songs like that and find some others that fit in. The ideas were flowing without his even trying. When they drove over a rise and saw Denver at night, he came up with the line "The bright lights of Denver were shining like diamonds." "It was the weirdest feeling," Connie said. "The whole drive we didn't even get sleepy because we were so excited. By the time we got back to Austin, he pretty much had the whole thing done," she said. "He just sat down with his guitar and the tape recorder at the ranch on Fitzhugh Road and filled it all in."

The idea was not without risk. If it didn't sell, there would be no second Columbia album. A Willie Nelson concept album would be industry shorthand for commercial death. But he didn't second-guess himself. He simply pushed all his chips to the center of the table.

This bet was cowboy mythic, based on the song made popular by Arthur "Guitar Boogie" Smith, the Charlotte, North Carolina, singer and pioneering country music television star in the early 1950s. It was the same song that Willie used to sing on his radio program on KCNC in Fort Worth when it was nap time for the children listening at home and that he sang to Lana, Susie, and Billy at bedtime, and to Paula and Amy years later.

Trying to imagine what happened to the Red

Headed Stranger, he wrote "Time of the Preacher" in the same spirit as his package show fellow traveler Marty Robbins's "El Paso City," which was a follow-up to his hit "El Paso." A gothic western storyline began to take shape about a preacher man who killed his wife, then drifted from town to town, condemned to pull his dead lover's horse behind him. He resuscitated "Blue Eyes Crying in the Rain," a forgotten country music ballad written thirty years earlier by Fred Rose that had been previously covered by Gene Autry and Elvis Presley; "Can I Sleep in Your Arms?" one of Hank Cochran's saddest, straight-to-the-heart compositions; and Eddy Arnold's "I Couldn't Believe It Was True," the most downbeat song Eddy ever made popular. Billy Callery, a young songwriter who found Willie in Austin, brought him "Hands on the Wheel." "Just As I Am," one of the least judgmental numbers in the hymnal, added a spiritual component.

The ideas would be articulated at Autumn Sound, a new recording studio in a light tan one-story stone building in an industrial park in Garland, a suburb beyond the northeastern city limits of Dallas. Autumn's studio, a quiet room with cypress wood paneling, featured the first twenty-four-track studio console in Texas and came equipped with a Bösendorfer concert grand piano, a ninety-two-key instrument made in Vienna with four extra bass notes that retailed for $25,000.

Mickey Raphael found Autumn Sound. Western Swing banjo virtuoso Marvin "Smokey" Montgomery of the Light Crust Doughboys had introduced the nineteen-year-old harmonica player to studio engineer Phil York at Sumet-Bernet Studios in Dallas when both were just starting out. Mickey was hungry to do recording work, so whenever Phil was doing a session, he'd call Mickey to come and hang out in the studio's coffee room. "I'd leave the control room door open so he could play along with whatever was being recorded," Phil said. During a break, Phil would ask a recording artist to get him a cup of coffee in the hope he'd hear Mickey playing and perhaps be inspired to invite him into the session. The ploy actually worked on several occasions, with Mickey picking up a few bucks while gaining valuable recording experience.

When Autumn Sound opened in October 1974, Phil York was recruited to use the studio as a freelance engineer and bring in some of the artists he'd already been working with. He could earn more than twice what he was pulling down at Sumet-Bernet. But no one followed Phil. Desperate for business, he cajoled the owners into giving Willie Nelson a free day in the studio to road test the room, no strings attached.

"I heard he was looking for a studio in Texas to make a concept album," Phil said. "He wasn't happy with what they did with his recordings after he left the studio, overdubbing his singing with chirpy background singers, speeding the track up to give it more pep because producers thought he was laying back too much. He'd be driving down the highway and hear his song on the radio for the first time and discover they'd screwed it up. I told Mickey to come on in, have a good time, bring the beer and whatever, the studio was theirs, no charge."

Willie liked the proposition. You couldn't beat free. The band showed up on a cold January day and recorded five songs, including "A Maiden's Prayer" and "Bonaparte's Retreat." Bobbie fell in love with the Bösendorfer piano. Paul English dug the drummer's booth. The whole band felt comfortable in the room.

"Thanks, Phil," Willie said on his way out the door after the freebie session wound down. "Mix it and send it to me down in Austin."

"You mean I get to mix it myself?" Phil asked.

"Yep. Send it down to me."

Phil did as instructed. A week and a half after the freebie session, Mickey called Phil. Willie wanted to record his concept album at Autumn.

A full week was blocked out at the studio. The band hauled in their equipment and set up. Willie proceeded to play the cassette of the album he'd made at the ranch on Fitzhugh Road. No one had heard the songs before. The whole room burst out laughing over Willie's semi-solo rendition of "Hands on the Wheel."

Phil York: "As Willie sang the lyrics 'There's a man, and a boy, catching whales, spinning tales, of the lady that they both enjoy . . . ,' you'd hear this dog in the cabin with him, howling. He'd start over, and as soon as he got to 'catching whales, spinning tales,' the dog started barking. This happened three or four times. Then you heard Willie letting out a long sigh, then yelling, 'Goddamnit! Shut up!' Then you heard his wife coming in, saying 'Poor puppy, get away from that mean man' right there on the tape. We just roared. That set the tone of the session."

Willie kept it loose. His real and musical families clogged the studio hallways throughout the run. Bobbie didn't show up for the first day, so Bucky Meadows, whom Willie added to the sessions, subbed on piano (and subbed very well before switching to guitar after Bobbie arrived). Willie also invited Paul's brother Billy English, who was playing drums with the Austin dance band Country Music Revue, to join in.

With one exception, Phil York was the neutral recording engineer. He had noted what he described as "Willie's penetrating voice" and EQed the edges out for a mellower vocal bottom. When Willie came into the control room to hear the playback of the song, he glared at Phil. "What the hell did you do to my voice? You ruined it!" Phil quickly undid the EQ on the playback and Willie nodded approvingly. Phil tried adding some reverb to his voice as well but Willie nixed that, too. "That's what Nashville did to me," Willie instructed. "Take it off."

Phil did as he was told. "My job was to get the sound Willie wanted to get," he said. "He was the producer. I was the engineer."

"Time of the Preacher," the first track in the studio and the first track on the album, was knocked off in several takes. "I didn't know this album was anything special," said Phil York. "I knew it wasn't the Nashville cookie-cutter formula. I remember thinking, What's he going to do with this? Nashville isn't going to buy it, it wasn't cut there, and it isn't their sound."

The third song was the chestnut written by Fred

Rose, cofounder of the Nashville powerhouse song publisher Acuff-Rose, "Blue Eyes Crying in the Rain."

"Just play what you feel," Willie instructed the band on the first run-through without the tapes rolling. Bucky Meadows responded by playing tricky jazz licks on his big Gibson. Bee Spears did a rave-up of jazz bassist Jaco Pastorius. Paul and Billy swung the brushes.

"That wasn't exactly what I had in mind," Willie said after the run-through. "This is more of a solitude-sounding kind of song. I tell you what, put your instruments down and let me play it solo. Just play along only if you feel like you can add something to it."

Bucky walked out of the room, followed by Billy and Paul. Bee and Mickey stuck around, adding minimal fills. "It was all about Willie," Mickey Raphael said. "We learned to lay back."

Willie knew what he wanted. He did one song at a time until he got it right, then moved on to the next. Phil York was used to saving money in the studio by starting the tape only when he knew the musicians were recording a keeper. After several starts and stops, he noticed Willie whispering to Paul in the main room, and Paul came into the control room to repeat this message from Willie: "Phil, stop stopping the tape machine. Let the damn tape roll."

"I didn't get what was going on until about a third of the way through the damn record," Bee Spears said. But he never doubted Willie. "I learned a long time ago not to second-guess him."

The cost for five days of recording and a day of mixing was under $4,000. The $60,000 advance from Columbia that Neil Reshen had negotiated was nonrecoupable, meaning whatever Willie didn't spend from the advance, he was able to keep. Enough was left over to upgrade the band bus and band equipment and still have some running change.

Phil York came away from the sessions a believer. Bobby Earl Smith, the singer-bassist for Freda and the Firedogs, and Joe Gracey, the most popular disc jockey on progressive-country KOKE-FM in Austin and an aspiring engineer, called Phil, needing a dub of a song he'd recorded called "Muleshoe." Phil told Bobby Earl and Joe to come up and get a dub and listen to these tapes he had.

"I've never heard anything like it," Phil told them when they arrived while he was rewinding tape to sequence the songs correctly. Bobby Earl was stunned. " 'Blue Eyes Crying in the Rain' actually had lyrics. I'd been hooked on the Shot Jackson/ Buddy Emmons instrumental version on the album *Sho-Budding Again* and thought it was the prettiest melody ever, and here was Willie, singing the words," he said. "We knew we'd just heard something like never before."

Gracey was not so impressed. "I thought it was a career-ending mistake, because it was too stark and too off-the-wall. I thought he had just taken a really hard road."

Willie tracked down Hank Cochran, who was hanging out on his boat in Fort Lauderdale, Florida, and asked him to fly to Dallas that day to hear what he'd just done.

"Here I are," Hank announced after he arrived at the motel where the band was staying.

Willie played him the entire recording and asked Hank what he thought.

"Truthfully, I don't have the slightest damn idea," Hank told him. "But I love it, I like it, and I guess that's all that matters. Because what else is there? I don't know what to compare it to, which is great. And thank you for putting one of my songs in it. And I'll tell you one thing: If you do put it out—and I know you will—and my song is on it, I'll spend all the money on the other side, promoting it. I'll make damn sure it's promoted."

Stripped-down, spare, and clocking in at just thirty-four minutes, *Red Headed Stranger* was a dark, violent telling masked in graceful melodies, effectively capturing the same harsh Old West reality that the writer Cormac McCarthy would soon bring to his novels. But Bruce Lundvall, Columbia Records' president, didn't hear a hit, or an album, when Neil Reshen brought an acetate of the recording, along with a leather-clad Waylon Jennings, to a listening session in New York. Lundvall thought Neil was pulling his leg. The ink on the contract wasn't dry, Lundvall thought to himself. And what the hell is Waylon Jennings doing here? He's on RCA.

Lundvall diplomatically commented that the recording might be a real collectors' record, it was so unusual. Spare and simple was nice for a demo, but four days in the studio and you're done — that was ridiculous. No one of Willie's stature was making albums for less than $250,000.

Waylon practically jumped up on Bruce Lundvall's desk.

"You tin-eared, tone-deaf son of a bitch!" he fumed. "See, that's where you're wrong. You ain't got a goddamn clue what Willie Nelson's music is about." Waylon glared menacingly at the CEO, fist clenched and ready to coldcock his Yankee ass onto the rug. "He doesn't need a producer, he doesn't need Jerry Wexler. This is what he's all about! That's why I'm here. To tell you that."

Waylon stomped out, with Neil Reshen following behind.

Bruce Lundvall honestly thought there wasn't much to the album. "You can hear the drum pedal squeaking through the whole album," he said, though the performance by Waylon made him wonder. Maybe Billy Sherrill down in Nashville should sweeten up the recording with some strings or background singers. Lundvall overnighted an acetate to Nashville and spent the weekend listening to what Neil had delivered.

"Did he make this in his living room?" Billy asked when Bruce called Monday morning. "It's a piece of shit! It sounds like he did this for about two bucks. It's not produced."

"I think that's the whole idea," said Bruce, who was starting to feel defensive.

Willie knew he was upping the risk by making a record so inexpensively. "There weren't a lot of people who made money off the recording," he admitted. "It's a lot better if you've got a million dollars, and that way you can spend half of that on studio time and the rest of it on musicians, and a few well-placed dollar bills in this guy's pocket. Then everybody gets fat off of somebody's album. But it doesn't mean that ten good songs were cut."

The reaction in the rest of Columbia's Nashville office was similar to Billy Sherrill's. "Ron Bledsoe, who was running Columbia Nashville, Dan Beck,

Mary Ann McCready, and I all sat and listened to the record," said Nick Hunter, who had been hired by Neil Reshen. "They were disappointed. They had seen Willie's high-energy shows, and this record just laid there."

The live show was dynamite. With Jody Payne being primed as a solo act with the release of the single "Three Dollar Bill," a second drummer, Rex Ludwick, had been brought in to augment Paul. After Carlene English's death, "Paul got sick," Willie said. "He needed help back there. Some days he just couldn't get there, so I hired Rex. When Paul got better and came back, I kept Rex." After rolling with Waylon Jennings for almost a year, including playing on Waylon's *Honky-tonk Heroes,* then moving on to work with singer-songwriter Guy Clark for a spell, Bee Spears came back too. But Willie wanted to keep Chris Ethridge, so the band expanded into a two-bassist, two-drummer ensemble that packed a wallop. "Whiskey River" had been transformed from a honky-tonk anthem done as a Ray Price shuffle into a crunching rocker. Willie Nelson and Family were no longer tethered to the traditions of Ray Price, Faron Young, and Ernest Tubb. Their new peers were Southern rock bands like the Allman Brothers of Macon, Georgia, who also carried two guitars and two drums, the Charlie Daniels Band of rural Tennessee, the Marshall Tucker Band of South Carolina, and whatever ensemble Leon Russell had going up in Tulsa. "When it worked, it was like thunder, or a train rolling down the track," Bee Spears marveled. "It was smokin'." "It sounded great if you had the right chemical mixture in your body," observed Willie. "It was a really hard-core, heavy metal, rock kind of country."

People had noticed, including Columbia Nashville's Ron Bledsoe, who was wondering, where was *that* band on the recording?

Even Willie's friends were questioning his wisdom. "Willie, that album isn't going to sell shit," Joe Jamail told him flat out.

Bruce Lundvall played the recording at an executive meeting in the New York office, announcing to everyone around the table, "This is the first album by Willie Nelson on Columbia. It's probably not commercial and might not be made for country radio, but I want you to live with it. It's going to be a collector's item because it's so special."

Bruce was ready to suck it in. Jerry Wexler might not have had a hit on Willie, but Columbia would stick with him until he did. He was worth the investment. Bruce Lundvall's instincts were validated by national media coverage of Willie's picnic at Liberty

Hill. As the Bee Gees dominated the national pop charts in 1975 with the disco hit "Jive Talking," the Third Annual Fourth of July Picnic drew seventy thousand true believers to a five-hundred-acre treeless pasture on the banks of the South San Gabriel River near Liberty Hill, a picturesque small town in the Hill Country, thirty miles northwest of Austin. The picnic starred Willie, Kris and Rita, Billy Swan, the Charlie Daniels Band, Doug Sahm and His Tex-Mex Trip, singer-songwriter Alex Harvey, Johnny Bush, Delbert McClinton, Floyd Tillman, and the Pointer Sisters, a trio of retro-dressing, very good-looking African American females from San Francisco whose cool harmonies had been championed by the Armadillo World Headquarters.

Fifty thousand advance tickets priced at $5.50 were sold, and another ten to twenty thousand were sold at the gate for $7.50. The Texas Senate declared Willie Nelson Day. Music press was flown in from around the world to take note of the cultural phenomenon in progress, signifying Willie, as it were.

To live up to its image as a giant-size wild and woolly outlaw concert, traffic backed up for miles on Farm to Market Road 1869, the main route into the site, and Paul English drew down on a guy he caught hopping the fence, inserting the barrels of two pistols into his mouth before running him off. Otherwise, it was basically a whole lot of roaring, musically and personally.

The accounting system Paul and Neil Reshen had devised was primitive at best. Paul, Neil, and Willie had a plywood box built with a hole in it and had Lana sit inside. "They threw the money in the box and I counted it and handed it to the Purolator armored-car man," she explained. But the heat and lack of ventilation made her pass out. "Dad came in with Neil Reshen and Paul," she said. "Paul was still scuffed up by the altercation. I was sopping wet. They picked me up and told me to get out. They shoved the money into the plywood box with a padlock on it for three hours until it got full enough to give it to the Purolator man."

No matter how much came in, it wasn't enough to pay for the cost of throwing the picnic, just like Dripping Springs and Bryan–College Station. Unlike with the Bryan and Dripping Springs picnics, Geno McCoslin and friends did not bother applying for a Texas Mass Gatherings Act permit, passed by the Texas Legislature in 1971 to prevent any more hippie conventions like the Texas International Pop Festival staged in 1969. Why bother, when the penalty was a misdemeanor punishable by ninety days in jail and/or a $1,000 fine? They were thinking like characters.

The show ran all the way to five a.m. the next day, but only ten arrests were made and thirty-five traffic violations issued, relatively tame by previous standards, with no clashes between factions in the audience. Williamson County sheriff August Bosshard ignored enforcing the Texas Mass Gatherings Act and reported "no violence, no affrays, and no complaints about the crowd's behavior from locals. Those people who were down there, if they want to swear there were more than five thousand people there for more than twelve hours, they can file a complaint. I'm not going to."

Along with sunburns, heat strokes, overdoses, bug bites, and more music than a mortal could keep up with, the picnic served notice that Willie and Texas were happening on their own terms.

The picnic conveniently coincided with Columbia's release of the first single from Willie's new album. Nick Hunter hatched a plan to send white label copies of the album to the program directors of the fifty-four country radio stations that reported their charts to the music trade magazines. The PDs would know if there were hits on the album.

Columbia's radio people were leaning toward "Remember Me" as the first single. The disc jockeys thought otherwise. Joe Ladd of KIKK in Houston, the top market for country record sales, was dead certain: "Blue Eyes Crying in the Rain" was a smash. It had all the right ingredients to move up the charts, never mind that the song was written by Fred Rose for Roy Acuff thirty years ago and there were no drums on the track.

Willie had been building goodwill with radio people since 1961. For once, he'd given them a song they could pay him back with for all the generosity and good hang time. Airplay was strong the day the single of the beautiful lullaby was released, thirty years after the song was written.

The single struck a particular chord with Bruce Lundvall. "I remembered hearing 'Blue Eyes Crying in the Rain' when I was ten years old," he said. "I knew the original by heart because I'd always hear it on *Hometown Frolic* on WAAT in Newark, the only country radio in the New York/New Jersey area. I was a country fan before I was a jazz fan."

The single finally reached number 1 on the country singles chart the first week of October as it began crossing over onto the pop charts, peaking at number 21 a few weeks later. But Willie was still being second-guessed. The appeal of the record escaped country legend Charlie Louvin. One night on Bill Mack's *Midnight Cowboy* program on WBAP-AM, a truckers' show broadcast from Fort Worth that could be heard throughout half the nation, one-half of the

Louvin Brothers voiced his opinion: "I can't understand it. That thing wouldn't have even made a good
demo."

Willie discovered that despite all of the doubts, he
was a pretty good producer. "Chet Atkins was a better guitar player than me," he said. "Grady Martin
was a better guitar player than me. I thought they
knew the answers in the studio. Come to find out,
they didn't know any better than I did." He had
made an album against all odds and at one-tenth the
usual expense.

"Columbia wanted to pay for the sessions, so I
called Phil York in Garland and told him to send me
the bill," said Nick Hunter. "I sent it over to the
accountant. She called me back really nice. Could
I get all the bills together so she could send just
one check all at once? I said, 'That's it.' She started
laughing."

The *Red Headed Stranger* album officially debuted
in Houston at a Halloween party with a live performance by Willie and band at the Shepherd Drive-In
movie theater, an unlikely venue for an album debut,
much less a concert. The Halloween night show was
promoted by Dar Jamail, Joe Jamail's eighteen-year-
old son. Even stranger, Paul Simon, the folk-rock
singer who was once half of the duo Simon & Garfunkel, showed up to sit in with Willie Nelson and

Family. Columbia's CEO Bruce Lundvall had come to Houston to see Paul perform in concert at an arena and go to Willie's drive-in show. Willie urged Lundvall to bring Paul over. "He knew Willie's songs but he didn't really know who Willie was," Poodie Locke, a Willie roadie, said. "He was sitting on the steps with Steve [Koepke] and me and he'd ask, 'Did Willie write that?' We'd nod. Willie called him up, hadn't even met him, just handed him his guitar."

The first real concert date supporting the album was scheduled for Ebbets Field, a small room in Denver. Willie asked Nick Hunter not to bring Hank Cochran to the Denver gig as planned. He wanted to stay focused. Hank would get him sidelined. Ebbets Field was chosen because Chuck Morris owned the room and Willie had committed to a national tour promoted by Barry Fey and Morris and Feyline Concerts, which controlled the mountain states territory for concerts, much like Bill Graham owned northern California and Ron Delsener dominated New York City and the Tri-State area. It was a big leap for both parties. Feyline specialized in rock acts that could fill hockey arenas. Other than Waylon, country acts weren't working those kinds of venues. Fey and Morris thought Willie had the potential once they witnessed a few shows in Texas. Willie saw the potential too. After a career represented by booking agents from Texas and Nashville, going with Barry Fey and Chuck Morris was a step up.

"It is my time," he explained to another friend.

For the first time ever, Willie had the wherewithal to hire a full-time road crew. Before then, "He'd sit out in his Mercedes, smoking pot, watching people arrive in the parking lot," Wally Selman of the Texas Opry House recalled. "We'd be talking until it was time to go inside and he'd get his stuff from the U-Haul trailer and everyone would carry their stuff in."

Mickey Raphael called Poodie Locke, who was the only roadie in Austin worth a shit besides Bobby "Flaco" Lemons and Travis Potter. Poodie had worked with Mickey when Mickey was with B. W. Stevenson and had twice turned down offers to join Willie to stay with B. W. "Buckwheat was such a mess, somebody had to watch him," Poodie reasoned. "I couldn't leave him. He was drinking two bottles of Jack Daniel's a day." But Poodie did leave when Mickey called a third time.

Poodie went to Paul English's, where he was introduced to Paul's son, Darrell Wayne, Connie Nelson's brother Steve Koepke, and Willie's son, Billy, aka Wild Bill—the road crew of record—and shown the battered green Blazer wagon that Austin car dealer Bill McMorris had loaned to the band. Paul handed Poodie $1,000 and instructions for where to meet him in Los Angeles, where the band was going to showcase the album. Flush with running change and aided by two ounces of weed and an eight ball of coke, Poodie drove west, hauling the guts of the Willie Nelson and his Family Band road show to the big time.

Word about Willie and his new album had L.A. primed and ready. Bob Dylan, Paul McCartney, and most of the West Coast staff of Columbia Records turned out for the label-sponsored showcase at the Troubadour Club on Santa Monica Boulevard, a musical launching pad since 1957. The acoustic-friendly club, which could hardly accommodate two hundred customers, was an ideal setting for a song cycle that demanded paying attention to. The heavy-weights in attendance validated Willie with record buyers. More important, Columbia staff finally got what the album was about.

Other dates were added quickly. The Palomino in the San Fernando Valley of Los Angeles for the country fans, two nights at Jay's Silver Cloud in Algodones, New Mexico, near Albuquerque. "Two-thirds of the bar was for regular customers. The other third was padded for the drunk Indians," Poodie Locke said about the rough start. "Until we got to play in front of Carl Perkins and the Tennessee Three at the

Jackson Coliseum in Jackson, Tennessee, we were making five hundred a gig," Poodie said. Then the going got good, and kept on going. "It was supposed to be for two weeks. We were out for six months."

None of the crew had a title. Everyone did everything and found their place amid the chaos Willie enjoyed creating. A job description was beside the point, Willie said, "except Bee—he plays bass." They were pickers, gypsies, pirates, vagabonds, wanderers, and carneys, each addicted to "having a new reality every day," as the front man liked to say.

The band, which had been flying to gigs out of Texas for the past year, and the crew, who had been in the old Blazer, began riding in old Porter Wagoner's bus. Nice as it was to have everyone in one vehicle, it was already too small. Selling records put them on a steep learning curve. "Willie didn't know shit about sound checks, so we'd leave [for a gig] when Willie wanted to leave," Poodie Locke said. "We were touring with Poco [on Willie's first major arena tour, opening for the West Coast country-rock band] when Timmy Schmidt, Chris Hillman, and Sneaky Pete were playing with them. They'd do two sound checks. I'd go in myself and set up in the dark behind them. We blew them away every show, six shows in a row. They got all these bad reviews. Dennis Wall, their road manager, called me in Atlanta. He said, 'We really love you guys, but you guys are too unprofessional. We don't think you're going to make it.' "

Getting kicked off the Poco tour was a backhanded compliment. Within a year they would be headlining the Omni Arena in Atlanta for three nights running with the future President of the United States of America, Jimmy Carter, among the Willie-ites.

After the album passed the five-hundred-thousand-units-sold mark (it was certified gold in March 1976), Bruce Lundvall sent Waylon a gold record with the note, "This is from that tin-eared tone-deaf son-of-a-bitch. You were right. Here's your album." The album soon eclipsed one million in sales and was certified double platinum, signifying sales of two million units, in 1986. Willie took a cue from Lundvall's graciousness by sending a framed platinum album to his friend Joe Jamail, who had told Willie the album was shit. Beneath the platinum record was a message from Willie. "You're right, lawyer."

RED HEADED STRANGER empowered Willie to do as he damn well pleased and still have an audience eager to listen. He performed with the Dallas Symphony Orchestra at their new Summertop tent venue on the grounds of Northpark Mall for the symphony's summer series. Willie didn't have sheet music to give symphony musicians, so he urged them to come see him play at Dewey Groom's Longhorn Ballroom on Industrial Boulevard. Some did and afterwards told Willie to play whatever he wanted.

Columbia gave him his own custom label, Lone Star, which allowed him to sign Billy C, the songwriter Billy Callery, who wrote "Hands on the Wheel" for *Red Headed Stranger* and "Jaded Lover" for Jerry Jeff Walker; Austin songwriter Milton Chesley Carroll, a regular at the Texas Opry Annex; and fiddler Johnny Gimble, Steve Fromholz, the Geezinslaws, Family Band guitarists Jody Payne and Bucky Meadows, and Darrell McCall. Signing them all was payback for helping him along the way.

AFTER *Red Headed Stranger,* Willie returned to Autumn Sound just before Christmas in 1975 for *The Sound in Your Mind.* He didn't have a concept in mind this time other than "do some songs we already do that people like to hear when we're on the road."

The road band was joined in the studio by Tommy "Wolf" Morrell, Willie's favorite steel man after Jimmy Day, and extended family who crowded the studio hallways. Steve Fromholz was there because Willie was doing one of his songs. Willie called him into the studio to demonstrate how to sing the diminished minors in "I'd Have to Be Crazy." Steve, who had a few Lone Stars in his belly, sat where Willie had been sitting, while Willie stood next to him singing. In the middle of the song, Steve started singing along, totally into the groove, his hearty vocals picked up by Willie's microphone. Phil York recorded three takes. The keeper was the version with Fromholz singing in the background. It became the first single off the album, reaching number 11 on the country singles chart.

He covered the old pop standard "That Lucky Old Sun," a song of weariness and reflection, and the rugged chestnut "Amazing Grace." He reprised "Healing Hands of Time," did his show medley "Funny How Time Slips Away," "Crazy," and "Night Life," and paid tribute to Lefty Frizzell with "If You've Got the Money (I've Got the Time)." Willie's version was distinguished by Mickey Raphael's improvised harmonica riffs. "I didn't have any harmonica people [in country] to copy other than Charlie McCoy, and if he didn't play on it, I had to wing it," Mickey said. He winged it just right. The Lefty rave-up was the second single from the album and also went all the way to number 1 on the country singles chart. The album wasn't the surprise that *Red Headed Stranger* was, but musically it was a little more complex and adventurous, in the spirit of the road show. *Billboard* magazine cited it as the country album of the year.

While recording the album, Phil York received a call from Columbia Records in Nashville, wanting the two-inch tape of *Red Headed Stranger* to do a remix for the Country Music Association Awards show on television. "Willie's the producer, not me," Phil said, "and he's sitting here right next to me. You talk to him."

Phil handed the phone to Willie. "I was hearing his side of the conversation: 'You want to do what? Fuck you!' He wouldn't let them have it. He didn't want them to jack with his sound."

Willie liked making records and putting them out, and now that he was selling so many of them, he could make a record singing the Yellow Pages if he wanted. Thinking positive all those years was reaping rewards. A reporter approached him outside Autumn Sound to ask a few questions, including the zinger "What did it take to become a star?"

"I know the answer to that one real well," Willie replied. "You get some record label to invest a bunch of money in you. They've got to make you a star to get it back."

Whatever country music was, it was having an identity crisis, and Willie was the outsider that the powers that be could neither rein in nor figure out.

Artistically, he and Waylon represented the antidote to an industry that deemed Olivia Newton-John, an innocuous, saccharine-sweet pop singer by way of Australia, worthy of Female Vocalist of the Year honors, and an equally innocuous American folk singer who called himself John Denver, the Country Music Association's Entertainer of the Year. During a tour of Waylon's new studio, an engineer eagerly pointed out to a visiting journalist that the facility was so state of the art, "we could record the Eagles here," referring to the California rock band. Hank Williams was just a memory in Nashville.

On August 8, 1975, music critic John Rockwell wrote in the *New York Times* that Willie was "the acknowledged leader of country music's 'left wing,' working to cleanse Nashville of stale excesses by bringing it up to the present and its own folkish roots." *Newsweek* simply identified him as "The King of Country Music." His likeness was on the cover of the *Rolling Stone*. His red bandanna and battered guitar were instantly recognizable symbols.

But the real proof of success was in the bank account. He signed a multimillion-dollar, multiyear contract with Caesar's Palace, averaging between $25,000 and $100,000 per concert and indulging in such excesses as the lighting director Budrock's arranging to have Bee fly on a wire above Willie's

head during "Angel Flying Too Close to the Ground."
He was getting a $1.43 royalty per album sold, all the
money going to Willie Nelson Music, the publishing
company owned by Willie Nelson and Paul English,
who earned his 20 percent slice by getting back the
publishing rights to many of the songs Willie had
sold years before.

The move to Texas had been a godsend, he told
Robert Hilburn of the *Los Angeles Times*. "The bottom line to me is positive and negative," he said. "I
began to change my life so that I could emphasize
the positive things. There were positive things in
Nashville, but there were also all the negative ones. I
figured there'd be less negative influences in Texas.
I'd be among friends and in familiar territory. The
rest was up to me."

Worrying, he told anyone who'd ask, was bad for
your health. He had a deal with Paul. "I'll worry one
day, you worry the next."

Willie got the Texas Opry House up and running
again late in 1975. He partnered with Tim O'Connor
as Southern Commotion, Inc., taking out a scrap of
paper and writing "Tim O'Connor President, Southern Commotion. Paul English, Vice, Willie Nelson,
Secretary/Treasurer," but then scratching it out, telling Tim, "We don't need one of those." Despite an
asking price of $1.6 million, they put down $10,000

530 / JOE NICK PATOSKI

to secure the fourteen-and-a-half-acre tract, and took over 218 apartments, three swimming pools, the fifty-four-thousand-square-foot Opry building, the parking lot, and the old motel office.

"Dude McCandless had an unsecured promissory note with Farm and Home Savings and Loan in Nevada, Missouri," Tim said. "He was starting to refuse to pay it, so the savings and loan wanted to get it off the books and get it secured. We got it by paying the ten-thousand-dollar note. Willie's name was enough for them."

The spread was renamed the Austin Opry House, which prompted Wally Selman to sue the new operators in federal court. Wally still owned the name "Texas Opry House," and he insisted "Austin Opry House" infringed on that. "Yeah, let's sue each other," Tim challenged him. "We will get some notoriety out of it." The court ruled "opry" was in the public domain.

Willie put Tim in charge of operations at the Opry complex, but overseeing the concert hall and managing the surrounding apartment complex, known as the Willie Hilton, the Willie Arms, and Heartbreak Hotel, was a headache. "A band would show up with a note signed by Willie that read, 'Tim, take care of these guys,'" Tim O' Connor said. So Tim would put them into an apartment, even though they didn't have any money for rent. Half of Austin's gypsy music community moved in, among them Farmer Dave "Slappy" Gilstrap, Lucinda Williams and her beau, Clyde Woodward, gossip columnist Margaret Moser and her husband, photographer Ken Hoge, the freshly divorced Crow brothers—Alvin and Rick—jazz player and entrepreneur Mike Mordecai and his cohort Paul Pearcy, as well as columnist Townsend Miller, Poodie Locke, Willie's stage manager, and enough dope dealers, topless dancers, and trust-fund brats to make life interesting.

The Backstage Club, formerly the registration desk and lobby of the Terrace and the Annex, morphed into the third location of Soap Creek Saloon. A small recording studio and a rehearsal hall fronted an alleyway identified by a street sign as Music Lane. The whole operation was a slapdash venture worlds away from the slickness of Nashville's Music Row. There wasn't much business to be done in Austin beyond Willie, but no one seemed to care. Everybody was busy having too much fun. Whenever taxes were owed, Tim would call and say, "I need you to come play three or four days," and Willie would.

The gospel of Texas music was spreading. KAFM, a Dallas FM station, started airing records by Willie, Waylon, and the boys mixed in with the Allman Brothers, Poco, and Pure Prairie League on January

17, 1975, debuting at six a.m. with Willie singing "Phases and stages . . ." Another Dallas–Fort Worth station, KAMC-FM, had been featuring progressive country on Sundays for several years and was slowly working the sound into the station's regular music programming. A California station south of the San Francisco Bay, KFAT-FM, was around-the-clock progressive country. A new glossy magazine out of Dallas called *Texas Music* appeared, complementing the free handout *Buddy: The Original Texas Music Magazine* and *Picking Up the Tempo,* a literary journal published in Austin that took seriously country music and the culture emerging from the music.

Geno McCoslin took over the reins of the rickety Dallas Sportatorium, the post–Dust Bowl vintage wrestling arena that was the former home of the Big D Jamboree. The "new and improved" Sportatorium opened with Willie Nelson as headliner. Sam Cutler, an intimidating pistol-packing hard-ass who'd run tours for the Rolling Stones and the Grateful Dead, had been hired as Willie's tour coordinator but couldn't find the Sportatorium on opening night. When the band arrived in a station wagon, they were refused entry by the fire department. The place was oversold and no one was going in until someone came out. Meanwhile, Geno was being chased by angry ticket holders. He had called Dallas Pipe and Drape to put "Men" and "Women" signs over the exits. During the show, customers who thought they were going to the restroom found themselves outside. If they wanted back in, they had to buy another ticket.

Sam Cutler came and went as fast as other out-of-town hustlers like producers Jack Clement and Al Kooper, who left Austin as quickly as they arrived once they assessed the financial realities of the scene. Willie planted more roots, opening a business office in Oak Hill, west of Austin, staffing it with Larry Moeller, son of his old Nashville booker Lucky Moeller, his daughter Lana, and accountant Cookie DeShay.

He'd spent the previous thirty years making time to talk to fans after a show, autographing every piece of paper thrust his way, posing for photographs with his arms around strangers and a smile on his face, employing a "Welcome All Comers" policy with his fans that was paying off in spades. But now the fans were coming like never before. And he was supposed to shoo them away? After wiring his ranch on Fitzhugh Road with fencing and electronic surveillance, he complained to Larry Trader, "This fence isn't keeping people out. It's keeping me in."

Still, there were times when even Willie had had it with promoting his career. "We were out in Denver, it was freezing, and we were supposed to do a short

promotion tour to Phoenix for *Red Headed Stranger*,"
radio promo man Nick Hunter said. "Willie kept
saying he didn't want to do it. I woke up the next
morning and went to go get Willie, but he was gone.
He left a note at the front desk: 'Dear Nick, It's not
supposed to be that way.' "

Connie Nelson was reaching her limit too. She
loved seeing her girls don their Donny and Marie
Osmond wigs and join the Family Band onstage to
sing "I'm a Little Bit Country, A Little Bit Rock and
Roll" and have Uncle Kris and Uncle Waylon and
Aunt Rita and Aunt Jessi as their doting relatives.
Paula developed such a crush on Leon Russell that
she named her Bozo the Clown doll "Little Leon."
But the public life, the strangers coming over at all
hours, fans hopping the fence, fans wanting to touch
Willie, were wearing Connie down. It was either hire
a guard or move.

At one point, Willie proposed moving the family
to Abbott, but Connie told her husband, "You can't
do that to our kids. You're famous now and you're
gonna put our two little girls in Abbott and they are
going to be Willie Nelson's kids. That's not fair to
them. You might as well put Christmas lights on
both of them, light them up, and let them go everywhere. I didn't want my girls to be treated better
because of Willie, or treated worse because of him."

Connie had enjoyed a conventional childhood and wanted the same for their daughters.

It was crazy at home, or what passed for a home now, because the ranch on Fitzhugh Road was well known to a rapidly expanding fan base. An ambitious picker buzzed the squawk box at the gate and auditioned for the speakerphone and security camera. One night Willie and Connie were awakened by someone singing in the backyard. They snuck out of their room to the upstairs porch, from where they spotted Jerry Jeff Walker sloppy drunk and singing. They snuck back to their room and he eventually left.

"It was spinning out of control," Connie complained. Willie's son, Billy, eighteen years old and a roadie for the band, was a particular thorn in her side and hungry for attention. "Billy would come in the middle of the night and throw things through the window. One time Willie and I and the girls went away and there were windows broken in the kids' room. I was devastated and scared, and knowing Willie was about to leave town again, I started asking questions and found out Billy's truck had been seen nearby, so I told Willie. He didn't want to believe it. I told him this happens when he's gone but asked him not to say anything to Billy." Connie had "screamers" with Billy one-on-one and told him their differences had nothing to do with his dad. They were between her and him. Connie finally threw in the towel. "We needed to let Billy figure out who he is, and we needed to be out of this situation."

Connie moved with Paula Carlene and Amy Lee to Conifer, Colorado, in the summer of 1976, and a year later to a 122-acre spread in Evergreen, forty miles west of Denver, with a three-story, twelve-room chalet and three other houses, a teepee, horses, red Ferrari in the garage, and all the trappings of the good life in the Rockies. Connie knew her husband too well. If they were to spend time together as a family, it would be away from the craziness. "He just can't or won't say no to anybody," Connie said. "He likes people and he'll put everybody above him first. When Kris wants privacy, he'll take it. But I've seen Will so tired to the point where he can't go any further and someone will call and he'll say, 'Sure.' And from somewhere, he'll get enough energy to do it. I think the main reason is because he doesn't ever want anybody to think that because he's successful, it's changed him. I've heard him say it enough times that I know it's true."

Willie put it in a slightly different light. "I was conducting business with all manner of characters, and it just got a little bit out of hand," he said. "People don't bother me, but I can't say that for the people who have to be around me all the time. They get bummed out sometimes."

Lana wasn't pleased that Connie took her dad to Colorado. "I took it personally that someone would move him away from his family. No matter if there was this other stuff, the fact that he moved somewhere else was hard to take. I didn't think it was right. I knew where Connie was coming from, but I thought my kids and me got the short end of the deal. His parents, his sister, and everybody else were here because of him. When he moved, we started wondering, what are we doing here?"

Connie said she wasn't trying to take Willie away from Lana and Susie (Billy was a different matter). "What I was looking for was—when he was home, for God's sake, let's have family time," she said. "Give us a chance, when you're off the road, to be a family. I was thinking, Willie needs this as much as I do, but that's probably not true. Willie's more 'of the people,' and that's by choice."

Connie and the girls got addicted to snow skiing in the winter. Willie stayed hooked on the road, sometimes flying from Austin to Colorado in his private jet to have dinner with his wife and children, sing "Old Blue" and "Red Headed Stranger" to the girls before bed, or, in the summer, mow the lawn with his John Deere tractor before jetting off for a concert and flying back to his Texas spread at the end of the night. "I tried to be like other people," he said. "I tried to come home and watch TV. That just wasn't me."

He was busy going faster, and getting harder to keep up with. "He was a superstar, and everybody wanted a piece of him," Ray Benson said. "He would try to set the rules—like never answer your phone in the hotel room—but it was overwhelming. It was getting harder and harder to be close to him, and one of the things about Willie is the proximity effect. If you get next to him and talk to him, you have more influence than anybody else."

The craziness Connie and the girls were escaping reared its ugly head in a field on the eight-hundred-acre Sterling Kelly ranch near the south central Texas town of Gonzales, fifty miles southeast of Austin, for the bicentennial edition of the Willie Nelson Fourth of July Picnic. At least 150,000 fans were predicted to show up to hear a lineup of Texas progressive-country stars Jerry Jeff Walker, Rusty Weir, Kinky Friedman, and Doug Sahm, and Nashville giants George Jones, Bobby Bare, Roger Miller, and the dynamic duos of Waylon Jennings and Jessi Colter, Kris Kristofferson and Rita Coolidge, and Leon and Mary Russell.

A local ad hoc group called Citizens for Law, Order and Decency (CLOD) threatened lawsuits and ultimately persuaded Gonzales County commissioners to deny a three-day permit citing the potential for "immorality, drunkenness, narcotics abuse and nudity." CLOD's head, James Darnell, said, "To allow this invasion is to invite the anti-American, anti-Christian hippie subculture right into our homes."

Geno McCoslin ignored the permit denial and paid the fine after the fact. He was too busy planning a three-day around-the-clock music festival in his office in a rented house in Gonzales. Willie sent two roadies in his Mercedes to check on Geno. They found him in his office with an ounce of blow on his desk next to a bottle of whiskey, looking sharp in sunglasses, doing a telephone interview with WLS radio in Chicago. Asked what someone from Chicago should bring if they were picnicking in Gonzales, Geno croaked, "Ten dollars, ten dollars."

On the day of the picnic, Geno was selling tickets on one highway and Neil Reshen was selling tickets on the other highway. Despite the protests by vocal locals, the fourth Willie Nelson Fourth of July Picnic drew close to eighty thousand fans who paid $10 to sit and fry on the treeless plain in thunderstorms and hundred-degree heat. Liberty Hill had been manageable. Gonzales got out of hand, turning into a Texas version of Altamont, the free concert the Rolling Stones staged in northern California in 1969,

where there were four accidental deaths and one killing. Security guards kept the crowd off the stage by
rapping knuckles with two-by-fours.

After heavy rains halted the concert on the second
day, the overhead tarp covering the stage sagged with
so much water that on Sunday morning, Paul English
resolved the situation by whipping out his pistol and
shooting a hole in the canvas to drain the water. "The
supports holding up the canvas had bent in," said
Flaco Lemons, who'd been hired to do sound at the
picnic. "It was a sky swimming pool and was going
to go at any time." The crowd roared its approval of
Paul's shot. Paul's show of arms inspired others to
display their weaponry. "Everybody was carrying
guns, the crew, everybody," Flaco Lemons said. "I
was at a meeting a few days before the picnic started,
and we were told we couldn't wear our guns on the
outside, so everybody had their guns in their boots.
After Paul pulled out his pistol and shot the canvas,
it was pretty much open season for everybody else to
pull out their pistols. Everybody had been working
there for a week — we were all toast."

A twenty-six-year-old man from Pasadena, Texas,
drowned in a nearby stock pond. The Bandidos
motorcycle gang made a show of force. A woman was
raped. A man's clothing caught fire while he was
sleeping. George Jones did his crossover, sorta, though

his nervousness showed throughout his performance and a roaring encore. Floyd Tillman, Asleep at the Wheel, Kris and Rita, Waylon, Jessi, Bare, Coe, Weir, Hubbard, Shaver, Fromholz, B. W. Stevenson, and Linda Hargrove performed. Jerry Jeff Walker sang "This Land Is Your Land." Willie sat in with Doug Sahm at three a.m. and with Leon Russell at eight a.m. but Willie Nelson and Family never got around to doing their own set. "I was up all night promoting it with radio stations in San Antonio and just barely made it to get to Waylon's set to close it," he said after the fact. "So I got to sit in but never did do my show."

By show's end, the whereabouts of the box-office receipts was a bone of contention. Dar Jamail had ferried some of the advance sales in a Brink's armored truck to a Houston bank, but promoters were $200,000 short of meeting expenses. It didn't help that Geno had gone ballistic. "He had a bag of coke and a knife in one hand, a pistol in the other, ready to snort and shoot," a friend said. "Stick your head out the window and I'll blow it off," he dared all comers.

Billboard disapproved. "If Nelson ever again tries one, some of the money should be diverted back into sensible, efficient organization and control," Gerry Wood wrote in the trade magazine. "Otherwise he should hold his party in his backyard and invite over a few neighbors for a hot dog and a song. Confusion and callousness perpetrated in the name of Nelson only result in Nelson getting a bad name—and that's something this generous, kind, loving and talented man does not deserve."

What the *Billboard* writer did not realize was the same thing the Armadillo World Headquarters folks didn't realize when they complained to Willie about his friends toting weapons backstage. Loyalty trumped efficiency. People like McCoslin, who promoted Gonzales, had helped out Willie way back when. He didn't forget them. Thieves and gypsies needed work too. "I know they're stealing from me," Willie reasoned to one intimate. "But at least I know who they are. They have families to feed too. I could clear them out and get a whole new set, and then I wouldn't know who they are."

Willie had a history of embracing scalawags, and the thieves were not to be fucked with. "There was no way to fit in with those folks," complained Mark Rothbaum, Willie's liaison with New York manager Neil Reshen. "You couldn't be friends with them. Willie could be friends with them because he could laugh it off, he was amused by it. I didn't have standing. I wouldn't challenge the Genos, the Tom Greshams, and the Larry Traders, because I would lose. Willie would coach me, prompt me, and when he didn't trust somebody, would say to me, 'I really want you to look at this hard.' It could have been a total fucking gangster who just machine-gunned someone a week before. Willie would do it as a kind of sport, send a limo and deliver me to the wolves, just for the fun of it. He knew I was tough. I didn't have a ton of common sense but I had a lot of initiative."

The reporter from *Billboard* would have done better to look at the whole affair as Willie's version of a good time. "Willie liked chaos. He liked anarchy. He didn't like order, and he didn't like manicures," Mark Rothbaum explained. "He wanted things to be wild and to be crazy and to have volcanic eruptions. With every phone call would come another catastrophe, calamity, hysterical situation. I guess he fed off it."

A month and a half after Gonzales, Gene McCoslin resurfaced in an article written by John Anders of the *Dallas Morning News* in which the Gonzales picnic was described as Willie's "greatest fiasco." Geno told Anders, "We don't make any money on it. We have to stay in jerkwater towns. I was put in jail twice for just trying to do my job. I've got a wife and kids. I don't need this hassle. But if Willie asks me to, I will." Geno reported that Willie was crushed by the bad rap he was getting (which Geno was partly responsible for). "Willie Nelson has never made any money off any of the picnics. In fact, they've cost him a fortune. But he always pays his acts and he pays them well. The only reason he gives the picnic is that he believes the people of Texas want it. He's sick of the hassle, but he plans on doing it next year anyway."

Anders went on to quote an unidentified friend—could it have been Geno?—stating Willie's biggest flaw was "he just can't say no. He's a notorious easy touch for people needing money, and people who need favors. He gets into trouble sometimes because he overextends himself. He is by no means a wealthy man, but if somebody tells him they're low on funds, or need his talents, he doesn't know how to say no."

Wally Selman, one of Willie's promoter friends through the Texas Opry House in Austin, learned about Geno the hard way. "Willie had like a mafia in Texas," Wally said. "He had an arrangement with his manager and booker that his old cronies, promoters, and burnouts could handle Texas for him. He had divided it up into territories. Geno had Dallas, Tom Gresham had Waco, Trader had San Antonio. I knew where mine was." But when Wally booked a Willie date in Fort Worth, Geno got in his face.

"What the fuck are you in Fort Worth for, man? Fort Worth is my territory," Geno raged.

"No, Dallas is your territory," Wally countered. "Fort Worth is another city."

"Bad things are going to happen to you," Geno threatened. "You ain't ever going to work again. I'm going to kill you."

Wally was sufficiently rattled to fly to Albuquerque, where Willie was playing.

"Are y'all having a range war?" Willie asked when Wally stepped on the bus.

"Well, yeah," Wally told him. "Geno's saying he's going to kill me for promoting your date in Fort Worth."

Willie looked as if he'd heard it before. "Well, you get back on that plane and tell Geno that Will said, 'Quit that!' "

It worked.

After settling their differences (Fort Worth wasn't territory worth fighting over), Geno and Wally were playing cards and drinking beer one night, when Geno leaned across the table and hissed into Wally's ear, "Do you steal from Will?"

Wally flinched and shook his head no, wondering if this was a test or something.

"Goddamn!" Geno exclaimed. "Why not? Willie expects you to take a little." It was the unwritten Code of Willie, a philosophy of show business built on Darwinism steeped in four decades of honky-tonk music dipped in sweat and puke and sperm and 100 percent of the door.

WALLY and the other Texas promoters were close enough to Willie to learn the important need-to-know stuff about him — particularly what pissed him off and how altruistic he could be toward those around him, including cons like himself, the only people he really trusted to promote his shows.

Wally promoted a Willie show in Galveston on the same night that Galveston Ball High School happened to be playing in the nearby Houston Astrodome in the regional playoffs for the Texas 4A high school football championship in November 1976, which effectively depopulated Galveston Island. The show bombed. Afterwards, Willie and Wally sat on separate beds in Wally's room at the Flagship Hotel, counting the meager take. They usually worked a split after paying expenses. This time, there wasn't enough to pay for the overhead.

"Willie, I can't take any out," Wally told Willie, tossing him the money bag.

"No, take what you spent," Willie insisted, tossing the bag back. "We'll make it up another time." He'd seen gigs like this before. Taking a hit was part of business.

Wally shook his head. "I can't do it, no, Will." He threw the bag to Willie.

Willie fixed his eyes on Wally and spoke slowly. "I'm going to throw this bag to you one time. If you throw it back, I'm going to keep it."

"Pitch it here," Wally told him.

Willie's affinity for rogues underscored a worldview that everyone was equal as far as he was concerned. Before a concert at the Forum in Los Angeles, an assistant to the promoter informed him that steak and lobster were waiting for him backstage.

"That's for everybody, right?" Willie said.

"No, we got hamburgers for the guys," the assistant replied. Willie was getting the star treatment.

"Well," Willie said, grinning at the aspiring promoter, "I guess I'm eating a hamburger."

Poorly attended shows and debacles such as the Fourth of July Picnic at Gonzales were becoming anomalies next to skyrocketing record sales and concert grosses. The band added a second show bus that was tricked out with CB radios, sleeping bunks, televisions, stereos, showers, and all the accessories to stay on the road for months. There was solid product to tour behind, and Willie saw no roadblocks ahead.

The Troublemaker, the gospel album recorded in New York in 1973 for Atlantic Records, was finally released by Columbia in 1976. The collection, composed of spiritual songs he'd grown up with in church and the original by Bruce Belland and David Somerville about Jesus as shit-stirrer, was a new and completely different kind of concept album as far as fans were concerned. But another album that hadn't been conceptualized by Willie was making a far louder noise.

Jerry Bradley had been running RCA Records in Nashville in the wake of Chet Atkins's departure from the label, allowing Owen Bradley's fortunate son to step out from under the guitar master's shadow. Jerry had the family name but didn't necessarily have the family touch as producer, and Waylon was pissed as ever at the label. "I'd go over to a meeting and Waylon would have an ad that RCA had run on the back of his door," Jerry said. "You shut the door and him and his crew would be throwing knives at it."

Waylon was still the label's biggest gun in Nashville. "He was selling two hundred fifty to three hundred fifty thousand albums," Jerry Bradley said. "We were trying to get him into the million category. All of a sudden, Willie had *Red Headed Stranger*. He sold a million. Jessi Colter, Waylon's wife, had the single 'I'm Not Lisa' out on Capitol, and I guess she sold a million. We thought we had the better talent and we were trying desperately to get something going. We looked around—*I* looked around, wasn't no 'we' to it—to see what was happening. We had a lot of artists who were doing fifty to sixty thousand albums. Back then one hundred thousand albums was a success story. You didn't have but about twenty-five thousand bucks in an album. But nothing was happening. We were in a rebuilding stage. So I got on the phone and called business affairs in New York and said, 'Don't we have the right to put out an album on Waylon and Willie? Cain't I go down to the vault and just put 'em out?' And they said, yes, I did have the right.

"Neil Reshen came to the office, playing the part he had to play. If I wanted to go right, he wanted to go left. I told Neil, 'I got this idea, here's what I want to do.' He said, 'I don't think we want to do that.'

"I said, 'What'd y'all make last year? Three or four million dollars?'

"He said, 'That's close.'

"I said, 'I made fifty thousand. I've got the right to put this thing out. And you know what? If I put this thing out, I might make fifty thousand next year. This is insurance on my job for one more year.' "

Reshen relented and Bradley went to work. "Nobody had any interest in it except me. I picked all the songs," Jerry said. He chose well, pulling "Yesterday's Wine" and "Me and Paul" from Willie's *Yesterday's Wine* album and "Healing Hands of Time" and "You Left a Long, Long Time Ago" from else-where in Willie's catalog. Jessi Colter delivered two new songs of her own and a Waylon and Jessi duet of "Suspicious Minds," popularized by Elvis. Jerry added two songs sung by Tompall Glaser, another RCA recording artist and songwriter with a contrary streak, "Put Another Log on the Fire" and "T for Texas," the old Jimmie Rodgers yodel from the 1930s. He cobbled them together with Waylon's sentimental "My Heroes Have Always Been Cowboys" and two Waylon and Willie duets, "Good Hearted Woman," the old Waylon track that Willie overdubbed his vocal to, and "Heaven or Hell."

Willie had suggested a new, live version of "Good Hearted Woman" in exchange for an advance from RCA. "I just bought a club down here in Austin and I need two hundred and fifty thousand," he told Jerry. "Could you advance me two fifty and let me have the B-side to the next single?"

"You got it," Jerry Bradley said. Willie and Waylon's live version of "Good Hearted Woman," recorded at Geno McCoslin's Western Place in Dallas, was added to the album.

Jerry got busy trying to capture a feel for what he was putting together. "I picked up on the vibe that they were a bunch of outlaws hanging around Nash-ville going up against the big corporate structure," he said. "I had about fourteen volumes of *The Wild, Wild West,* these Time Warner books sold on television, in my office and I was thumbing through one and found this 'Wanted' poster. I took it down to Herb Burnette at Pinwheel Studios and told Herb I wanted to make an album cover and I wanted to put Waylon's picture in the middle, just a little bit bigger than the ones of Jessi, Tompall, and Willie underneath. I gave him their pictures. I said, 'Put bullet holes in it and that parchment brown paper.' Herb made it up.

"I had to take it over to Waylon's one night. He and all his buddies were all meeting at his office. My kid was with me. I took it and handed the cover mock-up to Waylon. He looked at it and said, 'That's all right to me,' and he started passing it around the room. This one didn't like it, that one didn't like it. I had a hard time hiding my expressions. I was beginning to boil a little bit but I didn't say anything and Waylon said, 'Bring it back up here.' He said to me, 'This is your idea, do whatever the hell you want.' I said thank you and walked out the door.

"*Rolling Stone* was killing Waylon. They didn't have any interest in Waylon, 'cause if we could've got *Rolling Stone* to accept Waylon, he'd've been right up there with Willie and Jessi. They loved Willie and Jessi; they waddn't that thrilled with Waylon's music.

[Bradley was stretching the truth; *Rolling Stone* loved Waylon too.] So I called Chet Flippo and said, 'I got this album of things put together out of the vault. I'd like for you to write the liner notes. I'll give you a thousand dollars.' Back then, liner notes were going for about a hundred. He said he'd be glad to. I sent him a copy of the tape. He wrote back and said he loved it. I called Chet. 'Can I use your signature?' I called Herb to get him to handwrite Chet's signature. It gave a very personal endorsement from a big writer at *Rolling Stone* that he liked the album."

Sales were projected at anywhere between three hundred and five hundred thousand units, a hit by any standard. "The way they were doing deals back then was, you do a single, and if something happened, you'd do an album," Jerry Bradley said. "This one didn't cost anything. All it cost was three new sides on Waylon plus the album cover."

Jerry leaned heavily on Willie to help promote the album. "Waylon was doing a lot of things to piss off a lot of people," he said. "Willie looked rebellious but he was very kind and generous and knew when to turn the corporate charm on. He kinda eased around a room when Waylon was bouncing off the wall. Willie was never anything but gracious when we communicated. He didn't care at all. It was another gig to him."

Wanted: The Outlaws was released on January 12, 1976, to great fanfare. "We had a big party up at Rockefeller Center in the Rainbow Room the night after the Super Bowl," Jerry Bradley said. "We had Jane Pauley and all these news press people coming out. Waylon and Willie had played a Super Bowl party the night before, and we had this big party and all this press and we couldn't find them. When they finally showed up, you've never seen so many flash-bulbs going off in your life." The attention bugged Waylon, who told Joe Galante, RCA's sales and mar-keting guru, "If you don't get those photographers to quit flashing those pictures, I'm going to kick your ass out the window."

The album shot to number 1 on the country album charts for six consecutive weeks and became a pop hit too. "We knew we had something, but we never knew it was going to be the first RIAA [Recording Industry Association of America]-certified million-selling country album," Jerry Bradley admitted. "I'm kinda like the old boy who took a beating but came out ahead."

SEVEN Willie Nelson albums and six singles charted in *Billboard* in 1976. A single that Jerry Bradley put together with Waylon and Willie called "Luckenbach, Texas (Back to the Basics of Love)," released in May 1977, would become a number 1 country single and a Top 20 pop 45. Set in the tiny Hill Country village made famous four years earlier when Jerry Jeff Walker recorded *Viva Terlingua!* there, the wistful love song was pure Nashville confection. Songwriters Bobby Emmons and Chips Moman had never set foot in Luckenbach, Texas, nor had Waylon. (Willie, on the other hand, knew Luckenbach well.) But the fantasy they conjured sold over a million copies, spurring a parade of cars, pickups, motorcycles, and tour buses to make pilgrimages to the hamlet.

With and without Waylon, Willie was becoming a one-name brand with a common touch that suggested he was still just plain folks. He won his first Grammy Award, sponsored by the National Academy for the Recording Arts and Sciences, for best male vocalist in country music. He was recording wherever and whenever he liked, and as often as possible, as if it would all disappear tomorrow. During one twenty-four-hour session, he and Leon Russell recorded more than three hundred songs, just to see if they could. If management wanted him to hold back and avoid overexposure, he wasn't paying attention. He was a picker doing what pickers were supposed to do.

He was also doing his best to bring together the

Austin and Nashville factions of country. The Country Music Association staged a party at Soap Creek Saloon in Austin starring Willie, Charley Pride, and old-timers Pee Wee King and Floyd Tillman, effectively uniting the two country cultures in the pursuit of a good time. Murray Olderman reported for the NEA wire service, "The chic drink is beer—Lone Star—and the smoke hangs hazily under the ceiling in a cloud layer, much of it sweet smelling."

Willie's career was so superheated, he could afford to put the Fourth of July Picnic into cold storage for 1977 and do two nights at his Austin Opry House with Waylon instead, then take the show to Tulsa to play to sixty thousand. The Texas picnic needed a rest. So did some of the Family. At least two hundred close personal friends were showing up backstage at gigs, each and every one of them Willie Nelson fans, most of them seized with the simple urge to get close to Willie. Those who got closest included a most unusual collection of celebrities, coke dealers, pot dealers, used-car salesmen, Texas pols, lawmen, criminals, hookers, Dallas Cowboys, preachers, con artists, churchgoing Christians, friends whom he grew up with and newcomers who'd just discovered him. A disproportionate number of weirdos materialized along with them, including psychic surgeons, who could pull guts out of your stomach without even cutting into you, *curanderos,* shamans, and healers. True to form, Willie made time for them all, lingering after the show until every autograph was signed.

Willie did a little of this and that of the offerings brought to him. Mainly, though, he smoked pot. It was a fair trade for the three-pack-a-day cigarette habit. "I was getting some benefit from pot and no benefit at all from cigarettes," he said. "So I took my last pack of cigarettes, rolled up twenty joints, and put them back and put them in my pocket. Every time I wanted a cigarette, I had a joint."

He quit drinking heavily too, a good thing because he was a lousy drunk, as the women in his life knew too well. "I was never much of a beer drinker. I really didn't like it," he said. "I drank to get drunk. Beer was a slow way to get there."

"He'd hit the window, hit the wall, hit the door," his daughter Lana said. "Our houses had big holes. He was driving up the ridge [in Tennessee] one day and got mad at [his ex-wife] Shirley and punched out the windshield in the car while we were moving. He realized there might have been an anger-management problem. Pot slows you down so much that by the time you want to react, the situation is over. By the time he moved to Austin, smoking pot was a daily thing. I don't recall any more punching holes in the wall."

Connie witnessed the same dark side. "One time we were at a motel and he didn't have his key, and he was, by God, going to kick the door down," she said. "This was after drinking whiskey, and I told him, 'Stay there.' And I ran the full length of the parking lot and got another key and ran back before he kicked the door down. I can't tell you how many doors Will has kicked down; sometimes he even had the key in his pocket. He knew he was bad on alcohol."

"The first week he played Castle Creek, he got so drunk he broke the microphone and thought I'd turned off the sound and he walked off and quit," Tim O'Connor said. "The next day he said, 'I will never play here again. I can't believe you turned off the sound.'"

Pot tamped down the rage and helped him mellow down easy.

When he quit smoking marijuana for several months on doctor's orders due to a bout of pneumonia, "he was a bastard to be around," Mickey Raphael said. "I was so much hoping he'd get a joint."

"To be the kind of person he wants to be, he has to take the edge off," Johnny Bush added.

"I don't advocate it for everybody," Willie was quick to tell Johnny and anyone else who'd ask. But marijuana worked for him.

"You know why Hitler didn't drink?" he once joked to Johnny. "Because it made him mean."

POT and booze were small potatoes compared with the by-now established high of choice—cocaine, the most expensive, most insidious stimulant on the black market. By the 1970s coke was a party drug that appealed to all social strata and sensibilities in America; at $100 a gram, it was a perverted symbol of status, excess, and allure.

Flurries of coke backstage had become part of the show wherever Willie went, including two establishments he became associated with—Willie Nelson's Nightlife, a dance hall on FM 1960 in the booming northern suburbs of Houston to which he lent his name as a favor for his old friends Larry and Pat Butler, and at Whiskey River, on Lover's Lane and Greenville Road in Dallas, a club where he was given a small piece of the action in exchange for playing there and partying there. His name, his reputation, and the presence of cocaine drew the attention of the authorities.

He and Paul, along with singer Ray Price, testified in front of a federal grand jury in Dallas investigating narcotics trafficking, specifically cocaine and heroin, in June 1976. When Willie was asked about particular individuals' use of coke, Willie pled ignorance.

"I don't know anything about it," he told the prosecutor. "I wasn't involved."

"If you don't answer, you're in contempt," the prosecutor barked.

"You're in contempt!" Willie shot back. "I'm telling you I don't know anything about it. And I don't!" Willie, Paul, and Ray Price escaped indictments and distanced themselves from those who were charged, including car dealer Joe Hicks, to whom Willie had loaned $60,000. But the heat came close enough. Willie didn't like the feeling of sweatin' like Ray Price at a bus auction — much as he loved to tell the story of Ray Price getting his bus repossessed with a considerable amount of marijuana stashed on board and having to place the high bid on the bus at the auction to retrieve his dope.

While everyone else was still rolling bills and snorting lines, Willie stepped back and took a hard look. Cocaine didn't do much for him personally. Still, practically everyone around him persisted in chasing lines in copious quantities, band and crew included, and tales abounded of situations such as sitting in a hotel room in Los Angeles when Dennis Hopper opened a Halliburton suitcase with pink cocaine flown in from Peru on one side and primo red buds on the other, while friendly dealers of unknown origin materialized backstage with vials of flake and powder wanting to share.

The cold hard truth was that coke was eating up his boys' paychecks like it was eating up all of Waylon's money. If someone wanted to be paid in coke instead of greenbacks, it had been no big deal. That had to change.

"Willie knew a bad drug when he took one," Ray Benson observed. "He didn't avoid using, although he started saying white powder ruined his pot high."

"I was just hearing the rhythms going too many different ways," Willie said. "The speed and the weed didn't mix, especially when you're up there trying to get a feel going, get the dynamics going. Nobody's thinking that way. They were just playing. I could handle the weed, but I couldn't handle the speed. I didn't want to be around people who were doing it, even my band. I didn't want in on that vibe. I could see all the negativity in the speed."

A new road rule — the only rule of the road — was mandated. Cocaine was off-limits. Smoke all the pot you wanted, swallow uppers or downers if you needed 'em. But coke and $1,000-a-week habits had to stop or the Law would stop it for them. "No Snow,

No Show" was no longer the operative phrase. "You're Wired, You're Fired" was the new code of the road. T-shirts were printed for the band identifying them as the "No Blow Blues Band."

Word traveled fast about Willie putting on the brakes. He never fired anyone (if someone needed to be fired, there were other ways to make them go away), but this was serious. The band and crew, being the band and the crew, found a way to get around the new rule when they needed to satisfy their urge to inhale something by doing methamphetamine, which was referred to on the buses as "loophole."

"It was out of control, but hell, everybody was out of control," Bee Spears said. "Willie was talking about cocaine, so we found a loophole. But everybody did it. It was everywhere. There wasn't a goddamn record company meeting that didn't start without a frickin' line nine inches long."

Three Family members would eventually depart from the Family due partly to their inability to rein in their habits. "It took a while, but reality eventually set in," Bee said. "People started getting popped for it, people started dying, you'd pull an all-nighter and you didn't bounce back, you'd be sick for three or four days, so it wasn't cool, it wasn't worth it."

Larry Trader, one of Willie's favorite thieves, felt compelled to explain Willie to the readers of his hometown *San Antonio Express-News* in a three-part series. Trader began by stating the obvious: "There are many misconceptions about Willie Nelson. The biggest one is drugs. . . . Let me tell you why. Willie has been connected to drugs," said Trader, referring to Willie's and Paul's grand jury testimony. "He's constantly on the highway, playing hundreds of shows. He shakes lots of hands and gives a lot of autographs. Every now and then he's introduced to a guy who's supposed to be someone important. Will has no way of knowing if the guy is a doctor, a lawyer or what. If he gives the guy his mailing address and later the guy is busted over drug charges, then Willie is linked to the case because his name and address are found on the guy."

Trader went on to vouch for Willie's religious fervor and how when a pastor at his church in Abbott asked him during a service where he thought Jesus was at the moment, Willie replied "at the Armadillo," because the people in church didn't need Jesus near as bad as people in honky-tonks did.

Trader also wrote about Willie breaking Sinatra's attendance record in Las Vegas and how the hotel owners couldn't understand why he lingered to sign autographs for all the fans until there was no one left. Willie's response: "I've worked 35 years to have people ask me for autographs and I'm not about to turn them down now."

"You're Wired, You're Fired" sounded good, but new characters were always showing up, ready to ignore the edict, like the character who started running with Bo and Scooter Franks, Willie's T-shirt salesmen. "He turned into a drug head, made his teeth fall out and shit," one roadie said. Step on either bus and you were taking your chances. "People got on there and they'd come back and speak in different languages," said Poodie Locke, acknowledging the collective urge to go wild on a nightly basis.

As with drugs, Willie had to readjust his loose approach to concert security. Billy "B.C." Cooper or Trader or Paul by his side wasn't quite cutting it. Enter the Hell's Angels. Despite an unsavory reputation burnished at Altamont, where Angels working security beat a man to death, Angels worked for cheap and were fiercely loyal.

"We brought these two guys, Deacon and Boo-Boo, with Waylon," Neil Reshen said. "We'd get more as we needed them. They didn't really want to get paid that much and they were good people as far as we were concerned—I mean, I know they weren't good people, but they suited the purposes we wanted, because the last thing you want to do is get into fights. Only an idiot would fight with the Hell's Angels. Anybody who tries to fight with the Hell's Angels is going to get his ass kicked."

Along with Waylon, Willie had been embraced by the Angels, who showed up in force at shows in northern California. One Hell's Angels associate ("You know I couldn't be part of any club") named Peter Sheridan adopted Willie. A Nordic blond behemoth, Sheridan had run with Hunter Thompson when he was writing the articles for *Rolling Stone* magazine that were later released as the book *Fear and Loathing on the Campaign Trail*. Thompson referred to Sheridan as "Chief Boo Hoo," and he wreaked havoc and initiated several fistfights on presidential candidate Edwin Muskie's *Sunshine Special* campaign train in Florida after Thompson handed him his press credentials. When he showed up on Neil Reshen's lawn and later on Willie's doorstep, offering his intimidating presence, Family life got interesting. Ostensibly, Peter was his chauffeur, but more often than not he was passed out in the back while Willie drove the Mercedes. He was Willie's kind of people, guaranteeing never a dull moment in the tradition of Ben Dorcy back in Nashville, and

Gene McCoslin, Larry Trader, Tom Gresham, and Billy Cooper in Texas.

More than anything, Peter wanted to be a Texan. In exchange for the honorary status and privilege of running with the Texas outlaw, he provided very visible muscle. He could get out of hand, like the time at the Whitehall Hotel in Houston when he started throwing dinner rolls across the dining room at strangers enjoying their meals, or threatened to pound Austin guitarist John X Reed into ground chuck, mistaking him for Austin writer Jan Reid, who wrote the book *The Improbable Rise of Redneck Rock,* which pissed off several members of Willie's Family. "He could spot a weakness in someone and burn right through them," Ray Benson marveled. "He'd move in and mow people down."

"He scared me to death," admitted Connie Nelson, recalling when she first met Peter. He was "bad energy" in her eyes. But he turned out to be a near and dear friend as well as her protector. "I never felt for one minute that he was doing it for the money," she said. "It was a sense of purpose and pride that he was able to do that." Connie saw his gentle side when he picked up her daughter Paula at the ranch and took her outside to show her fireflies: "He was so big and she was so little, and there he was out there her, catching fireflies. He really became a trusted part of the family."

As a reward, Willie bought him a brand-new Harley-Davidson motorcycle. Peter was riding the Harley in California when a woman ran a red light at an intersection and slammed into the motorcycle, killing him. But he left a legacy. Through the Angels connection, Larry Gorham came into the Family in 1978.

"At the time I was around, country music was appealing to more than just country-western fans," L.G. said. "I was hanging around with [bassist] Chris Ethridge when they'd come to the Bay Area and every now and then fly to gigs. It became more and more and then I was on the bus." Sometimes he was driving it, spelling main driver Gates Moore.

The stocky, muscular figure became generally known as Willie's personal bodyguard, although he described it more diplomatically as filling a hole. "I do security, a little public relations, just help a lot of people out. You have to do it with finesse and make sure he's safeguarded but not get between him and his fans like a wall. If he doesn't want to see somebody or talk to somebody, he'll just turn around and walk away quick as you can wink your eye. He doesn't want to block anybody or discourage anybody. Those people were our paychecks."

• • •

WILLIE Nelson and Family had been touring in two very crowded '76 Silver Eagle buses—almost "store-bought" compared with Porter Wagoner's hand-me-down—twelve people to a bus, when Gates Moore hired on, along with the bus he had been driving for Bonnie Raitt and Delbert McClinton when they were opening for Willie. "The buses were rough," Gates Moore said, "but the boys were rough, so they didn't mind." The Eagle that Gates drove was nicer because he kept his ride meticulous, patiently picking up the beer cans and bottles that were knee-deep in the aisle every morning before the craziness started again a few hours later.

Willie had the back room of one of the buses, but he was hardly sealed off from the rest of the entourage. "There was a round table back there, and it really was a round table—his knights would all sit around him," said Gates, who assumed the role of gatekeeper to go with his driving gig.

"It was his practice to greet people inside at his table rather than greet them outside, so I would take small groups of people inside to the back of the bus, where they would meet him and get his autograph, and then I would usher them out and usher the next group in," said the Gator, as he was known on the

CB radio. "It took forever. We wouldn't leave a venue until five o'clock in the morning. But anyone who needed to be greeted got in."

The rolling party was straight out of the Wild West, with booze, dope, and women part of the hedonistic revue. And everyone still carried guns. "I had a sawed-off shotgun and a .forty-five automatic in a holster in the seat," Gates Moore said. Before a show at the Soledad prison in California, guards contacted Gates in advance, knowing the band's reputation. "Look, man, we don't care what you got, but we don't want you carrying it in there, because we don't want any of them [the inmates] to get ahold of it," Gates was told. "So if you got any drugs or guns, we will hold it for you here at the guard station." Gates rounded up the weapons and put them in a pillowcase, and collected another pillowcase full of dope. The stash was held in one of the guard turrets until the show was over, when band and crew got it all back.

The buses got fancier the bigger Willie got. When Paul, the "road boss," got his back room on the crew bus done up in mahogany paneling, Willie went to Gates and asked, "How soon can you build me a bus, all mahogany-niggered from front to back?" Gates got it done soon enough to become the designated driver of the Willie bus. "I think his intention was for his bus to just be him alone," Gates said, but on the maiden voyage of the new bus, dubbed Honeysuckle Rose, Bobbie approached Gates and said, "I don't know what to do — I don't know where to ride." Gates asked Willie, and from that day on, Bobbie rode with her brother.

While the "Willie Express" gained momentum, Willie's hired mad dog, Neil Reshen, was putting more and more of his time and energy into Waylon, no matter how the receipts were stacking up. Neil and Waylon were both different kinds of animals than Willie. Waylon was fixated on maintaining control in the studio. Long periods of time locked in a room were good for him and good for those around him. Working the old Chet Atkins system of three hours and you're out or Willie's way of no more than two or three takes per track was not Waylon's style.

Waylon came perilously close to wiping out his career during the last week of August 1977, when agents from the Drug Enforcement Administration stormed Waylon's Nashville office and arrested him for cocaine possession. A package from Neil Reshen's office sent via World Courier Inc. had been intercepted before it reached Waylon's studio. Waylon's cocaine habit was hardly news around the music community, where a blizzard had been blowing for the past three years just like it had been blowing in

Los Angeles, New York, Austin, and all over America. Coke wasn't addictive, so the story went.

Waylon later said he was personally snorting about a quarter ounce of coke a day, easily a $500-a-day habit. But Waylon dodged the bullet—he was never convicted nor did time. The sender of the package, Mark Rothbaum, Neil Reshen's gopher, took the fall for him and went to jail for shipping the cocaine.

It was a rude awakening. The Outlaws weren't bulletproof. The real world had intruded on the fantasy.

Willie fired Neil Reshen. So did Waylon. So did Miles Davis. For Willie, letting Mark go to jail was merely the tipping point. Neil was the kind of guy who demanded respect even if he didn't earn it, just as he demanded attention for Willie and Waylon. But an unexpected $71,000 bill from the tax man put Neil's head squarely on the chopping block. Willie thought Neil had paid those taxes for him, but obviously he had not.

Willie had fired Neil several times previously, once for the tax problem, once for his negativity. He cut the cord for good when Mark went to jail. "That never did sit right with me," Willie said. "I liked Mark. I admired him. I respected him. I knew he was sharp, young, and had a lot of guts."

Mark's former boss, Neil Reshen, knew the clock had run out on his relationship with Willie. "Our management philosophy was to make their deals and try to keep them going, doing their own work," Reshen said diplomatically. "Willie liked that for the first ten years and then he decided that he would become a businessman as well."

Paul English, Willie's closest friend and financial adviser, felt it had been past time for a change. "Neil did a good job up to the point that he couldn't do it anymore," he said. In 1972, "when Neil came in, I hadn't filed income tax for six years because I wasn't making enough money to fool with it. Willie hadn't filed in three years. Neil negotiated with the IRS for Willie and for me—they settled with me for six thousand for the entire six years. Then he did a good job for three or four years. I don't think he had the ability to respect the relationship we had at that time. Something else had taken over. We came to find out he wasn't a CPA, nor was he a CPA attorney. You're not supposed to be able to negotiate with the IRS unless you are a CPA attorney, but he did it successfully."

Mark Rothbaum made the best out of his jail time. He ran the prison newspaper, maintained a garden, and worked out religiously. Willie kept him hired while he was inside, stayed in touch, and played a benefit at the prison on Mark's behalf. "The warden was a big fan of Willie's," Mark said. "He let me use the telephone. A lot of the promoters came to see me, and that was that." His sentence was reduced from years to months.

Upon Mark's release, Willie asked him to open an office to look after his interests. "Mark was honest," Willie said. "I wanted him out there to represent me without having a title. I didn't want a manager. I just wanted Mark to be out there." Miles did the same. Waylon came around a year later. "Waylon was a funny guy," Mark said, affirming again that he had a different relationship with Waylon than with Willie. "If he was nasty to you—not mad at you—you'd see him the next day and he'd go, 'How ya doin,' Hoss? Boy, I must have eaten something last night, I didn't feel well.' That's as good an apology as you were gonna get from Waylon. If you understood Waylon-speak, it was good enough."

Willie was more direct. "Mark's a friend you can go to and say, 'Can you do this?'" he said of their relationship. "He's a friend who'll call me and say, 'Hey, I think you ought to do this.' And I can either do it or not do it, and he will either say okay or argue with me a little bit. You can't buy a guy like that."

• • •

BACK in Austin, Willie was testing Columbia Records' definition of artistic control. Lefty Frizzell's death in 1975 had inspired Willie to do an album of nothing but Lefty songs dedicated to his favorite honky-tonk singer. The suits at Columbia were less than thrilled when they first heard about the idea, especially since the label had dropped Lefty three years earlier. But two years later, after Willie's version of "If You've Got the Money" from the album *The Sound in Your Mind* shot straight to number 1 on the country singles chart in the summer of 1976, Columbia brass came around and released the Lefty tribute. Even then, label personnel tried to get him to title the album *Songs for a Friend,* figuring record buyers didn't know Lefty Frizzell from Johnny Wright. But Willie held his ground, and *To Lefty from Willie* was released in 1977, featuring ten of his favorite Lefty songs, including "I Love You a Thousand Ways," which reached number 9 on the country singles chart that summer, "Always Late (with Your Kisses)," "Mom and Dad Waltz," and "Railroad Lady," Lefty's last single before he died, written by Jerry Jeff Walker and Jimmy Buffett. The album charted as high as number 91 on *Billboard*'s album chart, a testament to Willie's star power more than Lefty's legacy.

But the mixed results of the Lefty album demonstrated the downside of artistic control. Folding the Columbia/Lone Star custom-label arrangement belied Columbia's discomfort. Columbia preferred focusing on Willie, not on his friends. A second version of Lone Star Records appeared as an independent label in June 1978, this time distributed by Mercury Records. The new Lone Star was put together by Joel Katz, Willie's Atlanta attorney, and run by Katz's friend Guerry Massey. Larry Trader, Willie's pal, was Lone Star's vice president. For this go-round, Willie signed Ray Wylie Hubbard and His Cowboy Twinkies, Larry G. Hudson, Don Bowman, the comedian who issued the single "Willon and Waylee," the Geezinslaw Brothers, Steve Fromholz, and the young country swing band Cooder Browne. Willie released a single, "Will You Remember Mine," on Lone Star, and *Face of a Fighter,* an album of slow, sad songs that were compiled from old Nashville demos.

The second version of Lone Star Records lasted ten months before it was shut down. Record labels were a nice conceit, but Willie had enough business on his hands. For every well-intentioned idea that went bust like Lone Star Records came ten more wild new ideas. That had been Willie's MO for most of his life, but few people had paid attention before.

Now he was being taken seriously. He'd done the Old West bit, church gospel, and old-school honky-tonk. His RCA catalog had been recycled. Moving forward, he opted to look back and reminisce by reviving the old songs he'd grown up with and make an album out of that. At the Spence Manor in Nashville, he mentioned what he'd been thinking to Rick Blackburn, who was running Columbia's Nashville office. Rick was hardly convinced.

"You're crazy! You're nuts!" he told Willie. "You're a great writer. Go write. You're coming off 'Luckenbach, Texas.'"

Rick Blackburn's words went in one of Willie's ears and out the other. Willie was listening to his muse. "Why be predictable?" he asked Rick. "Great songs are great songs, no matter when they're written. My audience right now is young. They'll think these are new songs, or a lot of folks will. At the same time, we'll get the sentiment of the older audience who grew up with all those songs, who don't necessarily know me as an artist. I think we'll be able to bridge that gap."

"I still think you're crazy," muttered Blackburn.

Willie had a good feeling about the idea. The year before, he and Connie had secured a six-month lease on an apartment on the beach in Malibu so they and their girls could be near Kris Kristofferson and Rita

Coolidge and their daughter, Casey. Willie seemed to be spending half his time in Los Angeles, singing, playing, recording, doing TV, and sniffing around movies, so having a place there made sense. While jogging along the beach, enjoying his new exercise regimen, Willie was recognized by his upstairs neighbor. The neighbor, Booker T. Jones, was a music guy too, and knew Willie's music and a lot about him through Kris and Rita, who was the sister of Booker T.'s wife, Priscilla Coolidge.

Booker T. may have been black and Willie white, and Willie may have been country while Booker T. was all about soul stylistically, but they came from the same geographic region and were both raised in musical households where gospel music and pop songs from hymnals and songbooks by the piano filled the rooms. Both had experienced the pleasure of being paid to play music at a young age and both retained an encyclopedic knowledge of the songs of their youth. Each was in California exploring musical genres other than the ones he was associated with.

"We had a lot of common influences," Booker T. said. "Ray Charles was a big influence of mine and he was a big influence on Willie. I had heard Bob Wills and his Texas country jazz. Willie just loved jazz."

As the front man of Booker T. & the MG's, Booker T. was one of the cooks in the kitchen who created Southern-style soul music in the 1960s. The MG's were the house band at Stax Records, aka Soulsville, U.S.A., in Memphis and backed up Eddie Floyd, Otis Redding, Aretha Franklin, Rufus and Carla Thomas, Wilson Pickett, Sam & Dave, Johnny Taylor, the Staple Singers, and Albert King on their biggest hit records, while the MG's scored instrumental hits of their own such as "Green Onions" and "Hip Hug-Her." An accomplished arranger and producer and coauthor of Albert King's signature blues piece "Born Under a Bad Sign," Booker was all about groove.

"He didn't have to worry about me disturbing him when I was making music because he was making music on his own down there," Booker T. said. "We were the only ones in the complex who socialized, I think." They discovered a shared appreciation for the Great American Songbook, the informal name given to the great melodic pop standards of the middle twentieth century that practically every musician coming of age in that era learned sooner or later — songs such as "Georgia on My Mind," written by Hoagy Carmichael, the eternal "Stardust," also written by Hoagy, in 1927, "Moonlight in Vermont," popularized by vocalist Margaret Whiting,

"All of Me," a hit for both Louis Armstrong and Paul Whiteman in 1932, and the Irving Berlin classic "Blue Skies." "When I got out of high school, I was playing high school proms and high school dances around Memphis with bandleaders to make extra money," Booker T. said. "Those were the songs we played— 'Tenderly,' 'Stardust.' "

Booker T. went downstairs and jammed with Willie with guitars a few times. Then Willie went upstairs and jammed with Booker T. "I had keyboards up there," he said. One night Willie said, "We ought to record some of these." They went over songs, and the ones that felt good made the list Willie was compiling. "They were all songs I heard all the time on the radio," Willie said. "We had sheet music, and Bobbie played them on the piano and I'd figured them out on guitar. Those were hard songs to play. They weren't your normal country and western tunes. They had a lot of good chords in them, and it took some time to learn them."

When Willie got a list of ten songs, "he invited me to go into the studio with him," Booker T. recounted. "We knew what we wanted to do. Willie had a free hand with Columbia pretty much to do whatever he wanted to do, so he chose me as a producer, we got the money and started recording."

Working with Booker T. made sense to Willie. "I

was just singing songs that I liked. Luckily I found a guy who knew how to produce them, arrange them, and record them. I needed him there to make sure they were musically correct and to write the strings and arrangements," he said.

Booker felt a synergy developing. "You know how it is when you're with somebody and you don't talk about it a lot? We had a lot of unspoken understanding about bringing this music to the foreground in a soulful country way and we were just enjoying it, too," he said. "I had some music in my mind, the sounds, and I knew some of the members of his band pretty well. I knew Chris Ethridge. They fell in pretty easy." Mickey, Bee, Jody, Paul, and Rex knew their way around a recording situation too and dug the country-soul-southern thing. "The songs naturally fell in," Booker T. said. "It was pretty informal."

They gathered in Brian Ahern's house, tucked away in the Hollywood Hills. A Canadian producer married to the singer Emmylou Harris, Ahern built his Enactron Truck Studio to move around the country and record in any location. In this instance, the wires and cords ran from the recording console in the truck parked in the driveway through the front door of the Ahern residence.

Creature comforts extended to a full kitchen and a swimming pool, but little time was spent partying.

The band rehearsed songs until they got it right, rolled tape, and recorded, devoting no more than a few takes for each song before moving on to the next. Most of the musicians were set up in the living room. Mickey Raphael recorded his parts in the same tiled bathroom shower he had played in on Emmylou Harris's albums, for the "great natural reverb," he said. In less than a week, they had an album.

"I shaped the sound first and gave it something everybody can access by featuring his guitars and his voice and having the right colors underneath for the songs," Booker T. said. "I wanted the recording to reflect southern soul, so I played on the songs. We started off with 'Georgia' and 'Stardust,' and I played them the way I played them when I was working clubs as a boy. My vibe was pretty mellow. We were enjoying working the whole thing out. It was a pleasurable experience. It wasn't really work. We got the first two songs on the first day, and listening to the tapes on the way home, I realized it was something I loved. That was the most important thing to me.

"Willie saw me as a musician and gave me all the latitude as a producer to do what I wanted with it. He did his part and left. I was mostly an arranger. The producer part was organizing the logistics and doing the work of making a record—making sure the tape was happening, making sure the sound was coordinated with the engineer mastering. I tried some other piano overdubs, overdubbing some strings on some songs, some horn arrangements, having a big ensemble playing on 'Georgia.' The middle part of it I left to Willie."

Booker T. Jones finally understood what Willie was dealing with when he delivered the finished product to Columbia Nashville. "I realized what we did was somewhat unorthodox. I don't know if [the suits in Nashville] thought it was commercial. I'm not sure what they thought. But they didn't print many copies when the record was released."

The front cover of *Stardust,* a painting of the Pleiades constellation in a starlit sky by Susanna Clark, the wife of Texas singer-songwriter Guy Clark, conveyed an ethereal mood reflecting the songs inside. The inner cover was a photograph of a smiling Willie wearing a blue parka "borrowed" from Steve Wynn, Mr. Las Vegas, and a top hat and a beaded "WN" hatband presented to him by the Sioux Nation, with the Spring Mountains near Las Vegas in the background.

By the time *Stardust* was released in April 1978, "Mammas, Don't Let Your Babies Grow Up to Be Cowboys," his duet with Waylon, had rocketed to number 1 on the country charts and crossed over to Top 40. "Mammas" was on the new compilation that

RCA's Jerry Bradley had orchestrated to follow *Wanted: The Outlaws,* once again pairing the two Ws but this time leaving out Jessi Colter and Tompall Glaser. The title *Waylon & Willie* and the album cover, done up to look like a tooled-leather picture frame with their smiling faces painted over a landscape with a silhouetted cowboy on horseback in the background, said it all: Inside the cardboard package was a polyvinyl disc twelve inches in diameter containing audio performances by the country duo of country duos, the baddest-assed of all the bad-ass Texas outlaws, Big Chief and Little Willie. Several other singles spun from the album, including Willie's "If You Can't Touch Her at All," a number 5 country single, and Waylon's "Wurlitzer Prize," a sentimental slice of life about a lovesick guy pouring his coins into the jukebox to hear sad songs. The album stayed atop the country album chart for three months, eventually going double platinum, signifying sales of two million units. Willie's guitar was absent from the recording, but nobody seemed to notice.

No sooner had "Mammas" started descending from the top of the charts than "Georgia on My Mind" from *Stardust* ascended to number 1 country and number 5 pop. Whatever Columbia's initial hesitation about *Stardust* may have been, the label ended up printing more and more copies. Willie had been right. The songs sounded new to his younger fans. When he roadtested "Stardust" at the Austin Opry House, the kids responded as if Willie had written it. As for the old-timers, "the same people who danced to 'Bubbles in My Beer' danced to 'Stardust,' " he observed. The buzz grew exponentially and never stopped. "I didn't realize how many records it sold until we got a platinum record," Booker T. Jones said.

STARDUST put Willie on a whole other level of celebrity. He was flying to his gigs on a Lear jet, making runs to Vegas, to Colorado, back to Texas, often on the same day, because he could. He was a bold-faced name in newspaper gossip columns, celebrating his birthday with comedian Richard Pryor and club-hopping with James Caan, as if he were a movie star, which he was intent on becoming.

He and Connie renewed their wedding vows at the home of Las Vegas impresario Steve Wynn on June 10, 1978. Steve was best man and his wife, Elaine, was matron of honor. Country pop superstar Kenny Rogers and his wife, Marianne, were witnesses.

Even though Willie and Waylon could both pull down $200,000 playing a stadium concert, they continued to book into the Golden Nugget with Steve

Wynn for weeklong runs at $20,000 a week, ten shows a week, along with all the perks that went with it, mainly because it was Wynn and Vegas. Waylon especially appreciated the town's proximity to Phoenix, where he would take Jessi to stay with her mother, a Pentecostal preacher, until he couldn't take her religious fervor anymore.

Willie liked hanging with Wynn. They rode horses together on Steve's ranch. "I was a roper in those days, a header," Steve said. "Whenever Willie came to Vegas we'd go to the desert and ride. Willie can ride. He's comfortable on a horse. I used to rope with Spider; he'd ride Chicaro. Spider was blazing fast. Spider had a great personality. You could call him like you call a dog. I promised Willie if I was ever done with Spider I'd let him have him. When I was done roping, I gave Spider to Willie, and he lived out his days on Willie's ranch in Evergreen, Colorado."

Four weeks after renewing his vows with Connie, Willie spent the Fourth of July weekend at the Cotton Bowl in Dallas as part of the Texxas World Jam with Waylon, then throwing an indoor picnic at the Austin Opry. They were trendsetters at the top of their game, topping the charts with hit after hit while making aviator sunglasses, leather vests, long hair under cowboy hats, and cowboy boots fashionable. The whole Family was in on the act. Before a Hollywood Bowl concert starring Willie and Waylon, flamboyant rock and roll entertainer Little Richard spied Paul English walking into the venue. "Nice cape, man," Little Richard told him, paying a compliment. "I dig that!" His road gang, now led by a wiry ex-paratrooper called T Snake, could be found registered at hotels under the name Fast Eddie and the Electric Japs.

Willie had reached the pinnacle of celebrity. Two weeks after the release of *Stardust,* he had performed at the White House for President Jimmy Carter. Jimmy regarded Willie so highly that he invited him back for a private performance in September. While the president was away at Camp David, trying to broker a Middle East peace agreement, Willie played a show on the White House lawn for NASCAR, singing a duet with First Lady Rosalynn Carter. That night, before retiring to the Lincoln Bedroom, where he and Connie spent the night, he climbed on the roof of the White House and smoked a joint with one of the Carter boys.

The larger his stature grew, the more driven he became. Four albums (*Stardust, Red Headed Stranger, Wanted: The Outlaws,* and *Waylon & Willie*) had been certified platinum, signifying one million copies sold, the highest achievement in the business. For most artists, one platinum album would make a career. Four was unprecedented for anyone associated with country music. Rather than rest on those laurels, he stepped up his recording pace. *Willie Nelson and Family Live,* a two-disc set of his live show recorded at Lake Tahoe, was the first record to capture the dynamic of the Family Band in concert, with the two-bass, two-drum setup cranking out extended jams.

Even his old material, recycled and reissued, was charting. Record labels he'd never heard of—Creative Sounds, Double Barrel, Allegiance, Back-Trac, Eclipse Music Group, Hallmark, Sunset, Potomac, Delta, Tudor, Aura, Merit, Sierra, Ditto, That's Country, Ronco, Soundsational, Quicksilver—were putting out product bearing his name. Most spelled it right, which was all Willie said he cared about. He might not have had a piece of the action, and not all the releases might have been legal. But every one was promoting Willie Nelson, something he'd been doing all his life.

Every other project was turning into a buddy concept. Booker T. Jones was added to the Family Band for *Willie Nelson Sings Kristofferson,* along with Jerry Reed, the talented Nashville guitarist who played on numerous RCA sessions with Willie in the 1960s, and Albert Lee from Emmylou Harris's band. When Booker joined the Family Band for a *Stardust* tour,

Bobbie Nelson dropped out. Booker T. also produced and played on a Christmas album, *Pretty Paper,* easily Willie's most soulful Christmas sessions yet.

Willie finally got around to making an album with Leon Russell, whom he had once described as a "genius," by tapping into the Great American Songbook again as well as the hymnal and the Nashville hit parade circa 1956 for the double album *Willie and Leon: One for the Road.* The dynamic-duo recording was almost an afterthought. Leon had lost a couple steps, mojo-wise. Too cheap and too petty to keep a steady band together and too reclusive to bother winning over new fans even as he was riding on the coattails of Williemania, Leon had faded ever so slightly. Like with Waylon Jennings, Johnny Bush, and Ray Price, when Leon wasn't looking, his impish little redheaded friend snuck past on his way to superstardom. It didn't matter. They sounded like a duo who'd been playing together all their lives in some sleazy roadhouse on their rendition of "Heartbreak Hotel," the song Elvis made famous that was written by Mae Boren Axton, the songwriter who had advised Texas Willie Nelson in Vancouver, Washington, to go to Nashville to be a star. Willie and Leon's version reached number 1 on the country singles chart in June 1979.

Their two bands merged into a single unit for a

forty-five-date tour promoting the album and the single. Bobbie Nelson chose to stay home again while Leon played piano with Willie, even though her piano was tuned and set up for her to play every night.

STANDING toe-to-toe with Leon, taking the W&W brand around the world, reviving pop songs with Booker T., playing in front of thousands of wild-ass fans night after night, smoking dope on the roof of the White House—no whim went unrealized. So he took it in stride when he found himself riding horses in Utah with a big movie star, although Connie admitted to being intimidated. The views around the Double R Ranch in Utah were dreamy; Hollywood westerns never had backdrops like this—majestic mountains with jagged peaks, verdant valleys with swift-running rivers, pristine wilderness in every direction. Doing all that alongside Robert Redford made it all the dreamier as far as Connie Nelson was concerned. But there they were, several weeks after the actor made famous for his role as the Sundance Kid extended an invitation to come visit, hang out, take in the view.

The actor and the musician had met a few weeks before at a Nashville fund-raiser at producer Billy

Sherrill's mansion. "We flew back the next day to L.A. on the same plane, sitting next to each other, talking about this and that," Willie said. Somewhere along the way, Redford asked Willie if he'd ever thought about acting.

"Yeah," Willie admitted. "You must like my conversation."

While riding on a trail on his ranch, the movie star asked Connie Nelson if she thought Willie would be interested in being in a movie with him. "Yes!" Connie blurted without consulting her husband. She was starstruck, but so was Willie. Then again, Robert Redford was starstruck too, bearing witness to one of the great Hollywood truisms: The only people movie stars look up to are music stars. It's one thing to perform in front of cameras on a set and have millions watch the filmed performance in movie theaters; musicians put it all on the line night after night in front of thousands, no reshooting or do-overs allowed.

The ranch vacation was followed by a call from producer-director Sydney Pollack. Did Willie want to be in Redford's movie *Electric Horseman*? Willie realized Redford knew exactly what he was doing when he was talking to him on the plane and to Connie at the ranch. "He was checking me out to see if it was something I'd want to do," he said.

Willie had had a few experiences with films beyond absorbing movies at the Saturday picture shows as a kid. He sang "Time of the Preacher" in *Renaldo and Clara,* the unreleased film documentary commissioned by Bob Dylan, and had hung out on the movie set of *Pat Garrett and Billy the Kid* in Mexico.

Willie didn't bother preparing for the role. Redford had told him acting in movies was like having a conversation. "You don't have to go to school for that," Willie said. He played Wendell Hickson, sidekick and manager of Robert Redford's character, Norman "Sonny" Steele, a washed-up drunk of a rodeo cowboy consigned to hawking Ranch Breakfast sugar-coated cereal on TV. Leading lady Jane Fonda was in the role of Alice "Hallie" Martin, a TV reporter and city girl who falls in love with Sonny, with actress and native Texan Valerie Perrine playing Charlotta Steele, Redford's wife.

Redford and Fonda had drawn accolades for their roles in 1967's *Barefoot in the Park.* Their star power and chemistry all but guaranteed success for the film. Redford did all his own horseback riding in the film rather than let a stunt double do it for him. "We did some of it in Utah and around Las Vegas," Willie said. "We roped a horse. I had a lot of fun. It was an easy gig to do."

In addition to reading lines, Willie contributed the

song "My Heroes Have Always Been Cowboys" to the movie soundtrack along with a new version of "Mammas, Don't Let Your Babies Grow Up to Be Cowboys." With the movie promoting the single, "My Heroes" reached number 1 on the country charts in January 1980, less than a month after the movie premiere in New York.

While the plot of the comedic-romantic western was predictable, *Electric Horseman* was nonetheless nominated for an Oscar in the Best Sound category, more a tribute to Willie than to Redford's and Fonda's appeal.

Sydney Pollack was mightily impressed with Willie's work, especially the way he delivered the memorable line "I'm gonna get myself a bottle of tequila and one of those Keno girls who can suck the chrome off a trailer hitch, and kick back," a line he cribbed from the Bud Shrake and Dan Jenkins novel *Limo.* Pollack urged him to continue movie work, but Willie needed no persuading. His childhood fantasy of being like Gene Autry, Roy Rogers, and Johnny Mack Brown at the picture show was being realized.

"He felt so comfortable with Redford, it wasn't scary anymore," Connie Nelson said of Willie's cinematic debut. "He realized he could do it and do it well." He hadn't talked about making movies before

Robert Redford called, she said. "But Willie's got that little side that he keeps to himself always, and I think that was probably in that little pocket. It was just one of the things he didn't want to say much about in case it didn't happen. After Redford talked to him about it, it blew the doors open."

By the time *Electric Horseman* was released, *Honeysuckle Rose,* a vehicle for Willie as Star, was already in preproduction. Again, Willie didn't prepare other than to just be himself. "There was no acting there," he said.

For the remake of Ingrid Bergman's *Intermezzo,* directed by Jerry Schatzberg, about cheating with other women, Willie played a character named Buck Bonham, a country singer torn between his wife and his best friend's daughter. He was surrounded by an all-star cast, including Dyan Cannon in the role of his long-suffering wife, Viv; Slim Pickens as Buck's sidekick, Garland Ramsey; and Amy Irving as Lily Ramsey, Garland's daughter and the Other Woman; along with Lane Smith, Mickey Rooney Jr., Emmylou Harris, Priscilla Pointer (Amy Irving's mother), and Willie's band in the role of his band. Emmylou Harris's cameo was a consolation prize. The female folk-country singer was originally chosen to play Willie's love interest, but pregnancy forced her to bow out and give up the part to Amy Irving.

With a title inspired by the jazz standard written by pianist Fats Waller and Andy Razaf in 1928, *Honeysuckle Rose* depicted the twenty-year career of a made-up character who was eerily similar to Willie Nelson, down to the friction between his home life and life on the road and the ending with the moral "Don't buy into material trappings and deal with success on your own terms."

Filming was done mostly in and around Austin. A free concert was staged near Ranch Road 2222 and Loop 360, west of the city, to replicate a real Willie concert. When the film wrapped, Slim Pickens declared that Willie plays Willie Nelson "better than anybody."

Willie did not disagree. "Acting is like singing," he reckoned, "except there's no melody. There's a lot of one-liners in movies, every now and then a zinger or two, with conversation in between. In a song, you have to condense the whole story in two minutes or less." The experience led him to write a movie script with his tour assistant David Anderson called "The Man Who Owes Everyone," but like most scripts, it did not advance beyond the development stage.

At Sydney Pollack's urging, Willie did his first serious songwriting since becoming a one-name superstar. "Sydney Pollack, Jerry Schatzberg, and I were flying in some private plane from L.A. to New

York, talking about the movie and music for the movie," Willie said.

"I'd like you to write a song for the film," Sydney told him.

"What do you want it to say?" Willie asked.

"Make it about being on the road," Sydney replied.

The words rolled out of Willie's mouth: "On the road again / Can't wait to get on the road again / making music with my friends / I just can't wait to get on the road again."

Pollack gave Willie a puzzled look.

"Obviously he wasn't impressed," Willie said, "because he couldn't hear it like I did, didn't hear the rhythm, didn't hear anything except all those words." But Willie had the makings of a song. "I knew how he wanted it and I knew how easy it was gonna be. When he said the words 'on the road,' it all opened up. There it was. It was a no-brainer, a slam-dunk. It was the easiest song I ever wrote. I'd been doing it for years and years. I just hadn't written a song about it yet."

The melody didn't come until several weeks later. When it did, a classic took shape.

"On the Road Again" was an off-the-cuff ditty that captured the romance of wanderlust in a way that transcended mere movie filler. It became an anthem for America on the move and one of his most enduring compositions ever. Nominated for an Oscar in the Best Music, Original Song category, the song proved so potent that when the film aired on television, the title had changed from *Honeysuckle Rose* to *On the Road Again*.

He was used to being onstage every night and clearly relished his role as the object of female fans' affection. Movie stardom generated even more interest from women, including Hollywood starlets working in the same movie. Amy Irving, whose role in *Honeysuckle Rose* consisted largely of mooning at Willie with pining eyes, was winning Willie's heart.

Honeysuckle Rose was an eerie reflection of his real life. His friendship on the set with Amy Irving turned into something more—much more than the usual "Willie or Won't He?" encounters he had with woman admirers. Balancing time spent with his buddies and his blood family was a fact of life. Both would always be there, with Willie managing to juggle both and somehow keep everybody happy. But just as Willie's touring bus was christened Honeysuckle Rose, the line between reality and movies was blurring.

The make-believe world made the sadness in his real life a little easier to accept. His father, Ira Doyle (Pop) Nelson, passed away on December 5, 1978, at the age of sixty-five due to lung cancer. Eleven months later, on November 9, 1979, Nancy Nelson — Mamma Nelson, the grandmother who raised him and who was the glue who held their family together — died.

"There is an extremely strong sense of family, especially within the immediate family that we grew up with," said Freddy Fletcher, Nancy's great-grandson. "Willie's oldest kids, Susie, Billy, and Lana, we all kind of grew up through some hard times — I remember for one Thanksgiving we split a can of soup — so everybody took care of each other, especially if they needed it. I'm glad that I got to grow up like that. You really appreciate the worth of things and how lucky you are." And Mamma Nelson's death underscored what they'd all been through.

As his birth family passed on, his real family — the one he had cultivated on the road — grew larger. Kenny Koepke, the younger brother of Connie Nelson and crew member Steve Koepke, joined up in 1979. He'd been living in Denver, working at a Record Warehouse retail store when Willie called. "Why don't you quit your day job and come work for me?" Willie said. "I need you to drive my Mercedes to Miami." Kenny arrived in time for a sold-out concert with hometown boys the Bee Gees, the Kings of Disco, opening the show, and started doing whatever needed to be done, from loading in and loading out to setting up the back line and breaking it down and making sure everything was where it needed to be.

"I didn't know what I'd gotten into," Kenny said. "I didn't think I was naive, but I really was. I had to learn the hard way. I watched Poodie a lot."

Despite the band members' reputation as pirates, Poodie was nothing but encouraging, and Paul oversaw the crew without having to resort to intimidation. "If something was wrong, he'd come up and put his arm around you and let you know you'd done wrong and how you could do it right. He never raised his voice. You just wanted to do right by everybody," Kenny said. Tunin' Tom Hawkins, a friend of lighting director Buddy Prewitt, was hired to tune Bobbie Nelson's piano for three nights and ended up being sole caretaker of Willie's guitar Trigger. Tom treated the battered Martin differently from the rest of the band's guitars. "He's with me, always," Tunin' Tom said. "It's got an extra hole. It's been beat like Noah's Ark in the desert. It's gone — no it's not, it's beautiful, just like Willie. Willie keeps it together. We don't ask questions. Things work. It's not allowed to go out of tune. I've got to be able to read the weather, factor in whether the gig is indoors or outdoors. Bobbie's Steinway B is the same. It's his guitar, that's her piano. It's her Trigger."

The touring band was rolling with five buses, including the one that new sponsor Jose Cuervo tequila was taking on the road, and two trucks carrying equipment and lighting gear. But Willie himself traveled light, carrying a little bag containing his hairbrush.

The Hill, 1979

I**T WAS FRANK** Oakley's idea to open the Willie
Nelson General Store in Nashville, Tennessee.
Back when Willie was making records for RCA,
having your own souvenir shop near Music Row was
a status symbol, the surest sign you were country royalty. A store in Nashville featuring all things Willie
was almost beside the point now, but Willie understood the value of playing to his old fans as well as the
new ones. So when Frank came to Austin in 1979 at
the suggestion of Frank's running buddy Faron Young
to pitch Willie shot glasses, Willie bandannas, and
Willie braids to sell at Willie Nelson's Country Store,
Willie was ready to give his blessing with one stipula-
tion. Frank had to change the name.

"I don't want to be country," he told Frank. "I want
to be a general."

He had his own record label and his own concert hall. Why not his own store? Come to think of it, why stop there? Why not create his own reality?

The Pedernales Country Club was a bankrupt golf course resort near the village of Spicewood, twenty-nine miles west of downtown Austin, where the Pedernales River flowed into Lake Travis, the most popular recreation destination in the Austin metropolitan area. Willie had bid on a smaller piece of the club in 1977 but his offer was rejected when a competing bidder stepped in. The winning bidder's development plans went south in no time and Willie ended up with more land at a better price, paying $250,000 to buy the club out of bankruptcy in 1979. Besides his ranch, his place in Malibu, the ranch in Colorado where Connie and their kids found refuge, and the Austin Opry House and adjoining apartment complex, his domain now extended to a golf course, ninety-three undeveloped lots, and three houses in Briarcliff, the community adjacent to the golf course, each lot appraised at $6,000, fourteen condominium units in the Ledge Resort section, and, ultimately, 688 acres after donating 20 acres to the nearby Lake Travis Independent School District.

Most celebrities of a similar stature would have made the club their private hideaway. Willie saw it more as a place where all his friends and family could get together. It was the perfect place to throw the next Willie Nelson Fourth of July Picnic.

Despite the familiar threat of a court injunction filed by wary neighbors to stop the event, the sixth Willie Nelson Fourth of July Picnic was held at Willie's new headquarters on Independence Day 1979. A rambunctious crowd of twenty thousand gathered around the number 7 tee box on the golf course, where the stage had been erected.

The new site was not the only change. Unlike previous picnics, this one was actually scheduled to run under twelve hours. A press release stated that "although the Texas tradition will not fall under the [Texas Mass Gatherings] act, extreme precautions and preparations have been made to comply with the regulations and to help insure proper personnel to create a relaxed atmosphere for both the surrounding residents and, of course, the picnicgoers themselves." Tickets were $10.50, $12.50 at the gate.

Headlining were the host, his long-ago Nashville mentor, Ernest Tubb, and his new partner, Leon Russell, celebrating the release of his belated collaboration with Willie, *One for the Road*. The undercard included Ray Wylie Hubbard, Sammy Allred and the Geezinslaws, comedian Don Bowman, and country-folk troubadours Steve Fromholz, Bobby Bare, the Cooder Browne Band, and Larry G. Hudson.

The picnic kicked off at high noon—"very high noon" is how James Albrecht described it to readers of *Country Style* magazine—with Johnny Gimble leading the crowd in "God Bless America." A new act, Debbie Allen from Memphis, Tennessee, envisioned as the leading lady of Willie Nelson's first starring vehicle (working title: *Sad Songs and Waltzes*), was introduced by the forty-six-year-old Godfather himself.

University of Texas football great Earl Campbell, UT coaching legend Darrell K Royal, and actor Jan-Michael Vincent hung out backstage. Although Bobby Bare remarked, "I've been to two of Willie's picnics and can only remember one of them," this one was almost civil. Drug overdoses were down, gate crashers minimal. "I didn't hear of no stabbings," said Buster Doss, the Nashville promoter relocated to Austin who managed the band Cooder Browne. "This might be the closest thing to what Willie wanted when he started having picnics."

The show concluded with Willie singing duets with Ernest Tubb and Leon Russell before the red headed stranger left the scene in a helicopter headed to Vegas.

He held another picnic at the same site the following July in the midst of one of the hottest summers on record in Texas, where the string of hundred-degree days seemed endless. The day after his first major motion picture, *Honeysuckle Rose,* premiered in Austin, anywhere from thirty thousand to ninety thousand fans, depending on who was doing the estimating, showed up for the picnic at the Pedernales Country Club to hear Willie, Merle Haggard, Asleep at the Wheel, Ray Price, Johnny Paycheck, and other close personal friends—although one of the headliners, the Charlie Daniels Band, had to cancel when they landed at the wrong airport. Willie sang "Crazy Arms" with Ray Price, and "Waltz Across Texas." For the first time ever, the picnic made a profit, going $62,000 into the black.

No one had time to appreciate it. The warp speed at which Willie was moving was epitomized by a three-week stretch beginning August 14, when he sang the national anthem at the Democratic National Convention in New York and hung out backstage with President Jimmy Carter, who told him he'd been playing his new tape all day long for the past two days. The bourbon Willie sipped backstage, which was supplied by Democratic National Committee chair John C. White, may have been to blame for mangling a few lines of *The Star-Spangled Banner,* such as "bright stars and broad stripes through the perilous fight," and "from the land of the free." But nobody questioned the flubs. With his red, white, and blue macramé guitar strap, Willie was the paragon of patriotism.

A few days later, he was at the federal correctional institution at Big Spring, Texas, playing a show for the men in white, most of them incarcerated for drug convictions. One of them was Dr. John Marcus Young, a radiologist from Athens, Texas, who'd been sentenced in January to three years' time for unlawful possession and dispensing "narcotic controlled substances" such as amphetamines, barbiturates, sedatives, diet pills, and painkillers over the previous five years to a number of people, including Willie and Connie, Waylon and Jessi, Steve Fromholz, Sammi Smith, Johnny Rodriguez, *Playboy* playmate Kelli Murphy, and Dallas party girl Priscilla Davis, who obtained thirty-two hundred Percodan pills over four months. The prison date was payback for all the good times Dr. John had shared with his friends.

On September 1, he made the cover of *People,* the weekly magazine devoted to celebrity. The cover photograph of a smiling Willie in headband with Connie and the girls made life in Colorado look sweet. The headline on the cover read "His third marriage and new Hollywood stardom mellow music's outlaw."

Willie was *People*-worthy thanks in no small part to the popularity of a movie called *Urban Cowboy,* released in 1980. An indirect extension of the Willie effect, the film was a triumph of marketing country as cool to the noncountry masses.

The movie was based on a 1978 *Esquire* magazine article by Aaron Latham titled "The Ballad of the Urban Cowboy: America's Search for True Grit," a blue-collar love story set in Gilley's, a ratty tin-sided mega-roadhouse in the shadow of Houston's oil refineries. The drama of the article centered on Gilley's mechanical bull, the contraption upon which city boys (and female lead character Sissy) emulated rodeo cowboys in proving their manhood by riding the bucking mechanical bovine without getting thrown.

John Travolta was the movie's male lead. The poster boy of the disco dance movement through his starring role in the film *Saturday Night Fever* was dancing kicker-style this time around, and the whole nation was two-stepping and line dancing along with him.

Moneywise, everything came together for various enterprises tied to Texas progressive-country music with *Urban Cowboy*. Jerry Retzloff of Lone Star Beer reported, "At the Houston rodeo [the largest in the nation, drawing crowds of up to sixty thousand to the Astrodome for performances], I sold forty-eight thousand dollars' worth of stuff at the Lone Star booth I ran. People were buying anything Lone Star."

In terms of soulfulness, *Urban Cowboy* was progressive-country gone wrong, a new variation of a music style twisted into a look, a fad, and a trend. Designer jeans, popularized by the New York socialite and good ol' gal Gloria Vanderbilt, became the "It" segment of the rag trade. Peacock feathers to decorate cowboy hats became scarce. Gilley's was glorified into a tourist trap, selling more merchandise than beer.

The whole *Urban Cowboy* fad was proof that Texas progressive-country was big enough to be caricatured, and Austin had become a caricature of its former self. Between 1970 and 1980, the metro area population grew by 46 percent, with some of that growth directly attributed to Willie. The city could no longer boast of having the lowest cost of living of any major American city. A real-estate boom that made millionaires out of speculators who would flip property and double their money without even trying ended that. Several funky threadbare music institutions fell victim to the growth spurt. The Armadillo World Headquarters closed its doors on New Year's Eve 1980 when landlord M. K. Hage, the brother-in-law of Houston lawyer and Willie patron Joe Jamail, decided to sell the land so a high-rise office building could be erected. KOKE-FM changed its format and image from Super Roper Radio, featuring progressive-country music emphasizing local heroes, to a mainstream country format sold as Silver Country Stereo, with a logo that resembled a razor blade to chop up cocaine. The Split Rail honky-tonk was knocked down and paved over for a Wendy's fast-food franchise. The original location of the Soap Creek Saloon turned into a strip shopping center. By virtue of buying the old Terrace Motor Inn complex in South Austin and the old Pedernales Country Club, Willie was a participant in the boom.

The Pedernales Country Club, aka Briarcliff, Spicewood, Willie World, and the Hill, had become the base of operations for Willie Nelson and Many Others, a perfect complement to the Willie Hilton in South Austin. Willie commissioned a fifty-four-hundred-square-foot log cabin to be built on the highest hill for his own private aerie. Friends and family could reside in its condominiums, relax on its tennis courts and in its sauna and swimming pool, dip a line into the water at the nearby fishing camp, and, most of all, play on Willie's very own nine-hole golf course. "I've always wanted a golf course where I could set the pars," he said shortly after the purchase.

The golf course served a secondary function as Willie's own Betty Ford Clinic for those who needed to clean up from drugs or alcohol. "Nobody used to play golf except Willie, Paul, Bee, and Budrock," Poodie Locke, the Family Band's stage manager, said. "Golf saved our lives. It got us out of the hotel room and our nose out of the bag."

Ray Benson of Asleep at the Wheel bought into the program. "The golf course kept everyone out of the bars and out of trouble. Dennis Hopper got straight by coming to Pedernales and playing golf with us. It was a form of rehab. The main reason we all played was Willie had that course and you didn't have to wear a golf shirt or join a country club to play it. We could smoke dope [considered a mild drug, if a drug at all] and hang. And if you were hanging out with Willie, it was always exciting. Willie's a magnet for shit to happen. He's like the pied piper."

"He can hit a golf ball when he's blitzed," marveled Steve Wynn, the Las Vegas mogul who had a private course of his own too. "He smokes that preop catatonic shit. You got to have a lifetime of training to keep up with him."

Singer Don Cherry, a longtime friend and golfing partner, liked to tell the story of interrupting a round of golf with Willie to talk to his psychiatrist before returning in time to tee up on the last hole. Don was furious about his wife after talking to the shrink and stepped up to the tee box and addressed the ball, muttering, "God, I wish that was her head." He proceeded to hit the shot of his life straight down the middle of the fairway. Willie teed up next and crushed his shot, which went even longer and straighter than Don's. He turned to Don and wisecracked, "I never liked her either."

On his own course, Willie made the rules, as noted on the back of the golf course's scorecard: "Replace divots, smooth footprints in bunkers, brush backtrail with branches, park car under brush, and have the office tell your spouse you're in a conference. . . . No more than twelve in your foursome. . . . No bikinis, mini-skirts, skimpy see-through, or sexually exploitive attire. Except on women."

The golf course was the centerpiece of Willie's World. The only element missing was a recording studio. So he built one.

"I thought how nice it would be to have a studio so you could go in anytime you wanted to," Willie said. "I just liked to pick up the guitar, record, and play, even when there's nobody else around. When I bought the golf course, the restaurant area was there, and it just so happened it was a great place to put in a studio. I loved the idea of going in and recording whenever you want to, to have that freedom, especially if you record as much as I do."

Willie brought in Chips Moman, the Memphis

record producer by way of Nashville, to design and install a new studio in the old country club's clubhouse. Chips brought along Larry Greenhill with him to help get the forty-eight-track facility up and running. But after several months of frenzied recording in the most tricked-out recording studio in Texas, Chips decided to go back to Nashville, about the same time Willie got a hankering to record more music. He rounded up the only two people left, Larry Greenhill and Bobby Arnold, who was the studio's security guard.

"Do you want to engineer our record?" Willie asked them.

"Sure," they said, nodding their heads in unison.

Although he didn't know anything about engineering, Bobby figured between the two of them, they could make one half-decent engineer. "Larry knew how to work the equipment, and I kind of knew music, and we'd run around and learn how to do this stuff," Bobby Arnold said. "It was country music—people bought cassettes. What do they care about fidelity? They want to hear Willie's voice and guitar and Mickey Raphael." They winged their way through the project.

The first album they engineered, *Tougher Than Leather*, went gold. Also known as *Stranger Jr.* for its western theme and concept, it tells the tale of an old gunfighter and the woman who was the wife of the man he shot, and their reincarnation as a modern cowboy and cowgirl. David Zettner, who remained part of the Family though he hadn't toured with the band in years, designed the cover. After several years of nothing but duets, soundtracks and covers of old songs, *Tougher Than Leather* was a welcome collection of (almost) all-new Willie songs, including the jaunty two-stepper "Little Old Fashioned Karma" that fused the metaphysical with dance-hall fundamentals, and one very significant cover song, a straight-ahead rendering of "Beer Barrel Polka," reaching back into the repertoire of songs he heard as a boy, and doing this one so authentically that he passed for Czech.

For the next eight years, Bobby Arnold and Larry Greenhill witnessed one of the most prolific runs in modern recording history in one of the strangest settings for making records. "We didn't do much when Willie wasn't there except play golf, go sailing, play pool, play chess, play music—everything was play," Bobby related. "When Willie showed up, it was the usual Willie chaos. You were on call twenty-four hours a day. You know how recording is—it consumes your life, and then it leaves. Recording was on the 'golf-thirty' schedule [meaning after dark]. At the end of that, you'd play pool until the wee hours of the morning, and then you'd go to bed. Then you golfed, then you played music, then you played pool, played chess, then you went to bed."

Golf and gambling were as much a part of the recording process as the actual studio work. The score wasn't important. Willie and Coach Royal, who lived five minutes away, were speed players able to play thirty-six holes in half a day. "The cool thing was at the end of almost every day, we would always stop at the ninth hole and watch the sunset," Bobby said. A lot of the time Willie would review studio tapes in his golf cart. "At the end of every night, two things would happen," Bobby Arnold said. "I would always give him a cassette of what had been recorded, and Willie would always say, 'Thank you for recording my record.' Always."

The core recording band was Willie's road band, including recently added Nashville studio guitar pro Grady Martin and—if they were around the premises—close personal music friends such as fiddler Johnny Gimble, drummer Johnny Bush, pedal steel guitarist Jimmy Day, and bassist/pedal steel guitarist David Zettner, who lived at Willie World but was just as likely to be painting murals, the back of Willie's bus, or designing album covers or posters. Watching Willie work with David Zettner and Jimmy Day brought it all into focus for Bobby Arnold.

"The basic idea of Willie recording was that it was just us," Bobby said. "You would give him a cassette, and he's golfing and listening to it, and he comes back and says 'yea' or 'nay' or 'change this' or 'leave it like it is.' He wasn't specific about what he wanted—he just wanted it done."

He was more motivated to record efficiently than perfectly. "We had to capture it on the first take," Bobby said. "It might have had errors but it was still great. We were doing five and six albums a year when other people were doing an album every year or year and a half."

"I run a session like I do a show," Willie explained. "I know what I'm gonna do before I get there, we go in and do it, and we leave." His attitude was informed by his Nashville experiences. "If you got three hours in a studio, you were real lucky," he said. "During those three hours you'd better get three songs because there was another band getting set up to come in. It was just three-hour sessions, one right after the other, twenty-four hours a day in Nashville. If you went in there and spent too much time on one song, you lost that feel."

Still, Willie was hardly set in his ways. His most successful album since *Stardust, Always on My Mind* was a Chips Moman production cut in Nashville and at Pedernales in 1981 before Chips left, combining

Willie, Mickey, and Grady Martin with Chips's favorite studio players—Reggie Young, Mike Leach, Bobby Wood, and Bobby Emmons. Chips gave Willie a clean, almost sterile sound as he covered a range of pop and soul standards while revisiting two of his own songs, "Permanently Lonely" and "The Party's Over." If the album was recorded using the same assembly-line formula that led him to leave Nashville, it didn't bother Willie or his fans. The title track charted number 1 as a country single and number 2 on *Billboard*'s Hot 100 pop chart, while the album reached number 1 country and number 5 on the Top 200 albums chart, Willie's best pop-chart action ever.

Johnny Christopher, one of the guitarists Chips brought into the sessions, wrote "Always on My Mind" ten years earlier with Nashville songwriters Mark James and Wayne Carson Thompson. Brenda Lee and Elvis Presley covered the song, but neither version came close to Willie's.

Willie also sang a duet with Waylon on "Whiter Shade of Pale," an organ-heavy dirge that was a 1960s hit for the British rock band Procol Harum, with both singers stretching their vocal range as they'd never done before, leaving George and Tammy and Kenny and Dolly eating their dust. They were still the best vocal duo in country music. Willie did a fine cover of the Chips Moman–Dan Penn composition "Do Right Woman, Do Right Man" but sounded like he'd phoned in his reading of Simon & Garfunkel's folk-pop smash "Bridge over Troubled Water." Two other tracks were spun off as singles and reached number 2 on the country singles charts—"Let It Be Me," a tune written by French songwriters that had been frequently covered since it debuted in the States in 1957, most prominently by the Everly Brothers, and "Last Thing I Needed First Thing This Morning," a leaving song cowritten by Gary P. Nunn of the Lost Gonzo Band.

Recording most of *Always on My Mind* marked the midpoint of the transition to use exclusively the studio that Chips Moman built west of Austin. Why record anywhere else? The condos, the golf course, and other amenities made Pedernales Studio headquarters for a string of musical reunions. In five years Willie made *San Antonio Rose* with Ray Price, *Old Friends* with Roger Miller, *Funny How Time Slips Away* and *In the Jailhouse Now* with Webb Pierce, *Brand on My Heart* with Hank Snow, *Take It to the Limit* with Waylon, and *Music from Songwriter* with Kris Kristofferson (another Booker T. Jones coproduction).

Paying back those who had helped him was a bigger priority than worrying about putting out too many albums. Besides, he loved singing duets. "I think I have the Guinness record for more duets than anybody," Willie said. "I always sang with other people, enjoyed singing with other guys, and thought there was safety in numbers. Something out there with me and Waylon's name on it would have twice the value as just the one of us. The same thing applied with Sammi Smith, Toby Keith, whoever. I'd seen it work before with Red Foley, Ernest Tubb, Conway, and Loretta."

His recording partnerships were not limited to stars. "Willie came out and was playing the same place I was in Reno," said Freddy Powers, who'd met him in Fort Worth in 1955 with Paul Buskirk. "He was doing the big room. I was in the lounge. When he'd come over, the room would jam up. We started talking about Paul Buskirk, Johnny Gimble, players like that."

"Hell, let's get them all together and make a Django album," Willie suggested.

A month later, they were in Gilley's Recording Studio in Houston, a side benefit of the *Urban Cowboy* boom for club owner Sherwood Cryer, along with Bob Moore, who'd done several sessions with Willie in the 1960s, and Dean Reynolds, who played bass on Willie's original recording of "Night Life" in Houston.

Somewhere over the Rainbow was in the tradition of *Stardust* in referencing titles from the Great American Songbook, such as "Won't You Ride in My Little Red Wagon?," "I'm Gonna Sit Right Down and Write Myself a Letter," and "Twinkle, Twinkle, Little Star." But unlike the Booker T. sessions, the emphasis shifted to the other players and away from him, as he let Freddy sing lead on many tracks, and Buskirk and Gimble have the honors on the instrumental breaks. He was playing cool jazz with the cats who taught him how to play it. Sales were hardly comparable to *Stardust,* but it was personally satisfying and another way of repaying debts to all the musicians involved. Merle Haggard loved the recording so much he sought out Freddy Powers and hired him for his band. Powers moved into a houseboat on Lake Shasta and started writing songs with Merle, beginning a collaboration that lasted more than twenty years.

The same musicians got together for a Django Reinhardt tribute for a studio taping of *Austin City Limits.* Willie had starred at the Armadillo taping that led to the series pilot, starred in the pilot, headlined the first season, performed the whole *Red Headed Stranger* album the second season, and taped a show with one of his mentors, Floyd Tillman, and friends. Doing Django on ACL was hardly a stretch.

His jazz obsession dovetailed into another project with Jackie King, the swing guitarist who'd recently moved back to San Antonio from California to set up the Southwest Guitar Conservatory. They partnered on *Angel Eyes,* an album released only in Japan, that covered old cowboy songs ("Tumbling Tumbleweeds"), rhythmic swing ("Gypsy"), and Western Swing ("My Window Faces the South"). Willie knew Jackie from when Jackie played behind a variety of stylists, including blues shouter Big Joe Turner and honky-tonkers George Jones and Roger Miller, before joining the Billy Gray Band and relocating to San Francisco, where he backed up Sonny Stitt and Chet Baker and other jazz acts, formed the jazz-fusion band Shades of Joy, and did session work for Mercury Records.

The duet album with Merle Haggard, *Pancho and Lefty,* was special. Merle was a blue-collar brother and a fellow traveler from even before Willie met Waylon. Straight out of Bakersfield, Merle was salt of the earth like Willie was, had associated with more than his fair share of characters, and was one himself. He'd done time in prison, liked pot, and liked to talk about the paranormal; he was a big fan of Art Bell's *Coast to Coast* radio show, broadcast in the wee hours of the morning. His people came from Newton County, Arkansas, the next county over from

Searcy County, where the Nelsons and Greenhaws came from. Merle was also the first modern country star to honor Bob Wills by teaching himself fiddle and recording the album *A Tribute to the Best Damn Fiddle Player in the World* long before Asleep at the Wheel and Alvin Crow came along.

Having Merle record at the Pedernales studio was both a treat and an honor. "We're going to make lemonade out of horse shit," Willie declared before getting down to business. Willie and producer Chips Moman augmented Mickey and Grady with Mike Leech, Reggie Young, Johnny Christopher, Gene Crisman, Bobbie Emmons, Bobby Wood, and Johnny Gimble. The production was considerably lighter and less hands-on than previous Chips projects.

Merle and Willie recorded at least twenty-three tracks that were album worthy. "But they didn't have *the* song," said Lana Nelson, a sharp cookie at twenty-nine who was managing the studio for her father. "Chips [who had returned to produce the album] was done. George [Fowler, Lana's husband at the time] and I went home, went through our albums, and found Emmylou Harris's cut of 'Pancho and Lefty.' We played it and said, 'That's it.' We knew it."

In the wee hours of the morning, Lana called Daddy and told him the album wasn't finished yet. He had one more song to do. The writer of the song was Townes Van Zandt, the poet laureate of the down-and-outer school of Austin songwriters who lived for their craft and frequented songwriter joints like Spellman's, emmajoes, Chicago House, the Cactus Café on the UT campus, and the Alamo Lounge.

Townes came from a well-heeled family in Fort Worth and lived in Clarksville, a small old west Austin neighborhood settled by freed slaves who worked for the rich folks in the mansions of the Pease-Enfield neighborhood nearby. Drink and drugs were his indulgences. Songs were the reason he lived. Having Willie cover one of his songs was the break of his life; "Pancho and Lefty" already was one of his biggest crowd pleasers on the folk circuit he traveled from L.A. to New York and Europe, but even more so around Texas and especially in Austin.

Merle was sleeping on his bus in the parking lot outside the studio when Willie knocked on the door. It was four in the morning. "Haggard, I've found this great song," Willie said. "Come into the studio with me." The band was already running through the instrumental. Merle suggested that Willie do the track and he'd come in sometime in the morning and finish it, but Willie was persistent. "You need to come in with me. Now."

Merle shuffled into the studio, bleary-eyed and

more than a little spaced out. Willie handed him the lyrics he'd scribbled on a brown paper bag. Merle ran through the vocals with Willie as they both got a feel for the song about a Mexican bandit and his inscrutable friend, both of them living outside the law. The tape rolled. Merle nailed his vocal in one take and went back to his bus to sleep.

The next morning, he found Willie on the golf course and asked if he could do another vocal of the song they'd recorded a few hours earlier.

Willie laughed and shook his head. "Hell, the tape's already on the way to New York."

The single of "Pancho and Lefty" reached number 1 on the country singles chart in July 1983. The album went platinum.

DOING covers came more easily than writing a new song. "I used to not write unless I was hungry," Willie explained. "That's what motivated me back then, to get money to pay the rent. Writing is sometimes a painful experience. You have to dig it out of yourself and stay with it. A lot of the time what you're talking about is not that pleasant a subject. Country songs are usually about love that didn't make it or one thing or another that's negative. In order to go through those things in your mind, you have to build up your nerve and jump into it." Well-fed, loved, satisfied, and content, he was having too good a time making music with his friends to write sad songs like he used to.

Willie was taking a more expansive view, as he testified to the audience tuned to WHN, New York City's only country radio station. During an interview with Lee Arnold, he said, "I believe that music, not only country music, is the great communicator. It crosses all boundaries. There is zero difference between the people from Fort Worth, Texas, and the people from Tokyo, Japan. We all laugh at the same things and cry at the same things." He'd just toured Japan with Jackie King to promote *Angel Eyes* after using Jackie to play behind him and Ray Charles on his *On the Road Again* television concert broadcast from the Austin Opry House.

The *Sentimental Journey* album reunited Willie with his Django pals from *Somewhere over the Rainbow*. "There was no list of songs," said Bobby Arnold. "They'd sit around and say, 'Anybody know this one?' and of course they'd know it, and they'd do it two times and it's done. They'd just wing it."

While Willie's preferences changed from record to record, he always used a U 87 microphone for vocals and a KM 84 microphone on the guitar amp. Headphones for Coach Darrell Royal, the retired University of Texas football coach, were always placed next to Willie's. Coach showed up so frequently for the recordings, he had his own chair. Willie did not have to tell him about studio etiquette. "He knows that I know to sit and not make any noise in a recording studio," Darrell said. "Around my chair you could hear a mouse piss on cotton."

A loose-knit staff kept the operations going when Willie was on tour, making a movie, or otherwise occupied. Larry Trader was the golf pro—he married his wife, Linda, on the seventh tee and was frequently Willie's partner in taking on all comers in a golf scramble. Larry Greenhill and Bobby Arnold were the studio guys. Lana Nelson and Jody Fischer took care of business; Jody was Willie's personal assistant. "Jody was a servant," Bobby Arnold said. "Everything she did was about Willie. She was the most underestimated person out there."

"When he opened that studio, he needed someone to manage it," explained Lana Nelson. "He didn't really want to make money on the studio because he didn't want to rent it out a lot. He wanted access to it. He needed to bring in some money, but it would irritate him if he wanted to record and there was a session scheduled. He needed someone to balance it all out. It never really balanced, of course. It wouldn't have been one of our projects if it had balanced—you'd have known something was up. Jody and I would always make sure there was a pot of beans and corn-bread on the stove and tomatoes and onions and milk and buttermilk and coffee, especially if Dad was there."

Every day was a new adventure. "We responded to things as they came up," explained Bobby Arnold. "One morning we woke up and Greenhill told us we were going to be recording a movie soundtrack that day, and we needed nine TV monitors. We didn't know where to get them or how to hook them up, but you can bet that we had them working by the time they needed them. Willie would keep you on your toes—you wouldn't get bored."

Making music was a family affair more than ever. Lana Nelson directed the video for "Little Old Fash-ioned Karma" from *Tougher Than Leather,* taking a small cast and crew for a ride on Honeysuckle Rose to the South Texas town of Brackettville for location shooting. The town and Fort Clark, a U.S. military outpost on the Indian frontier, were built around Las Moras Springs, one of the largest in Texas. After the shoot, the cast and crew went to the springs, which had been developed into a swimming hole and resort.

"As soon as the bus pulled in, people started show-ing up," Bobby Arnold said. "Willie stood on the bus, looking out at the crowd, and said, 'I'm trying to decide if I'm going to go swimming.' When he stepped off the bus, the crowd moved in closer. It took twenty minutes to get from the bus to the water, all eyes on him. The first thing he does is a flip off the diving board, his pigtails flying. Willie crawls up onto this floating dock, and talks to everyone in the pool, answering every question they had," Bobby Arnold said.

Play remained an integral part of work. Everyone was expected to hold up his or her part of the bargain. "Willie, Trader, Coach, and me were playing golf and it was getting to be golf-thirty, we were recording later that night," Bobby Arnold related. "I said, 'Willie, I got to go in and get ready for the session.' And he looked at me and his eyes got really black like they do when he's mad. He said, 'When I say golf, we golf.' So I kept golfing. He got mad at me for trying to go to work."

The parade of personalities walking through the doors of Pedernales Studio was straight out of the pages of *People*. Dolly Parton and Dom DeLuise came to Pedernales when they were doing the film *Best Little Whorehouse in Texas*. Kenny Rogers stopped by. Roger Miller flitted in and out several times, often stoned out of his gourd. Webb Pierce, Faron Young, Merle Haggard, Kris Kristofferson, George Jones, Ray Price, Chet Atkins, James Burton, Hoyt Axton, and Emmylou Harris all came through, along with rockers such as Aerosmith and Bon Jovi. Ray Charles recorded several sessions, including the one that produced the Willie-Ray hit duet "Seven Spanish Angels."

Mickey Raphael brought Louisiana songwriter Bobby Charles to Pedernales for some sessions, and Bobby brought along Neil Young, Rufus Thibodeaux, and Ben Keith; the recording session that ensued planted the seed for Farm Aid as well as introduced Mickey to heroin. "I brought Richard Manuel [of the Band] with me to get him out of L.A. because he was strung out," Mickey said. "When I went to the studio, I took Richard's shit from him so he wouldn't get into it. I remembered I had his junk with me in my pocket and wondered what the stuff smelled like. So I snorted a little. I didn't know what to expect. We were doing the first song with Webb Pierce. All I remember is putting the harmonica to my mouth, and the song is over. Finally, it wore off and I remember Richard playing piano. I didn't know who Webb Pierce was. All I knew was these were old country guys, Willie's old country partners, and Willie wanted to help them out. Now I realize they were icons and that Willie idolized Webb Pierce. I had no idea. I didn't realize how cool Webb was."

Webb was a legend, but so was just about every

other character who showed up at the studio. It got to the point that recording was virtually a revolving door exercise. Unbeknownst to Hank Snow, he was one of four duet partners recording with Willie in a single day (Faron Young, Webb Pierce, and Roger Miller were the others). On his way out of the studios, Snow innocently asked, "Do you boys always cut this fast?"

One of those old-timers, Faron Young, who put Willie on the map in Nashville when he recorded "Hello Walls" in 1960, brought Fred Foster, another familiar from Willie's Nashville days, back into Willie's life. Fred had lost Monument Records and his wealth by investing in a bank that failed. Just when he needed money and validation most, Willie called. He wanted him to produce an album on Faron Young and him.

"Faron was cold," recounted Foster. "He hadn't sold a record in years. So we went to Austin, and Willie said, 'You set it up the way it oughta be.' I said, 'You do three of Faron's hits, Faron does three of yours, and then let's have a couple new ones.' The album was real country. I don't put a label on Willie, but Faron's real country. We're down to the place where we have to have a new country song. I called a few people. They weren't encouraging. Willie said, 'I can try to write one.' 'That'd be helpful,' I told him.

He woke me the next morning at five thirty, and we drove up to the Y store for breakfast. We were getting ready to play golf. I asked him if he wrote anything. He had. We played golf, but I kept wondering what this song was, because I know what he's capable of. After we golfed, he got out his guitar and sang, 'Forgiving you is easy but forgetting seems to take the longest time . . ."

Whether it was Foster's easygoing style or a case of duct-taping the old Nashville formula to the New Austin sensibility, the song became a number one country hit.

THE UNLIKELIEST duet at Pedernales Studio was the one with Latin crooner Julio Iglesias, who entered Willie's life while he and Connie were listening to the radio after midnight when they were in London. The next day, Connie went to the Virgin Records superstore and brought Julio's latest album back for Willie to hear.

"I'd like to sing a song with him," Willie told her after listening.

He called Mark Rothbaum, who tracked Julio down. One of the most popular singers in the world, Julio was recording his first all-English album in Los Angeles with producer Richard Perry to tap into the

U.S. market, one of the few countries he'd yet to conquer. Julio told Mark he was cutting a song that just might be right for Willie and him to do together. The Albert Hammond and Hal David composition "To All the Girls I've Loved Before" had been written in 1976 for Frank Sinatra, but Frank had never recorded it. Julio finished the instrumental track and brought it with him to Austin. By that time, Willie Nelson had realized that the guy whose voice he liked so much that he wanted to sing with him was the most popular singer in the Latin world, bigger than he was in the Anglo world, and had already scored one number one pop hit in English, "Begin the Beguine."

Coach Darrell Royal drove up in his golf cart, having caught wind of the news that Julio Iglesias was coming to do a song with Willie. Coach asked Willie what they were going to record.

"Hell, I don't know, he's bringing it with him," Willie said.

"How do you know you want to do it?" Coach wondered.

"Coach, have you heard about all the records that son of a bitch has been selling in Europe?" Willie answered.

Julio made quite an impression on Coach and everybody else at Pedernales when he arrived in a limousine accompanied by composers Hal David and Albert Hammond and producer Richard Perry.

"The guy gets out of his limo and he's got white shoes, white socks, a white suit, all immaculate," Coach said. "Willie greeted him and I could see the shocked look on Iglesias's face: 'What in the hell have I got myself into?' "

"It was like a Spanish Mafia," marveled Bobby Arnold at Julio's crew. It was pretty intense, with all the people, the language barrier, and the status of Julio Iglesias."

The two stars got along fine. Mark Rothbaum had advised Willie not to smoke weed in the studio around Julio because he was a lawyer as well as a singing star. Willie sized up Julio before whipping out some bombers and passing them around.

Once the tape rolled, Coach sat down in his usual chair right behind Willie, near Julio, keeping quiet. "Willie would let me come in," Coach said, "but Julio kept looking back at me and wondering what in the hell I was doing sitting there. They went through 'To All the Girls I've Loved Before' twice. Julio said, 'Weellie, may I suggest: The wind is blo-o-o-wing, blo-o-o-wing.' Willie nodded okay and cut it a third time. Julio, with those white socks, white shoes, white shirt, white slacks, dropped on his hands and knees on the floor and gave Willie a big bow. He damn sure did. He knew they'd nailed it. That was the one they released."

Julio's and Willie's voices were drenched in a shimmering wash of synthesizer strings and riding a sweet, almost syrupy melody. They made beautiful music together.

"To All the Girls I've Loved Before" was released as a single in March 1984 and shot straight to the top of the pop charts, introducing Julio to a whole other English-speaking audience and validating Willie among Latin fans beyond Tejano circles, where he was already venerated. The duo no one could have predicted performed the song at the Country Music Association Awards, where they were nominated for Best Duo of the Year in 1984, even though the song was about as far as you could get from outlaw or even *Stardust*.

Ray Charles was the mirror opposite of Julio Iglesias in his approach to recording at Willie's. He showed up at the studio a few weeks after Julio with his assistant and no one else to hang out before recording. The studio engineers accompanied Ray and some of Willie's band to Willie's cabin on the Hill, where they sat down to dinner and chatted the evening away without talking about work.

"They became good friends," Bobby Arnold said. "That dinner led to their HBO special." After dinner, the two musical giants discovered their mutual love of chess. "We played a lot," Willie said. "He kicked my ass more than once and enjoyed it, I guess, better than anybody. We was playing down here one time, we'd done a show together and he was staying over at a hotel. I went over to visit him and he invited me to play chess. I said, 'Sure.' And I kind of thought to myself, Okay, I'll play chess. The hallway was nice and bright and everything. We walked into where the table was and sat down. Not a light on anywhere. Then Ray brought out his chess set. All the pieces were the same color. It was a Braille chess set where he could feel the pieces and play. And he kicked my ass really bad. Of course in the dark, it's hard to play. I made him promise me the next time we'd turn on some lights.

"We talked a little bit about music whenever it came time to decide what we wanted to do together. Whenever anyone asked him what he wanted to do, he'd say, 'Whatever Willie wants to do.' And whatever I wanted to do, he would do it. But it was mutual."

Music built friendships. "I can't think of any time there wasn't any chemistry," Bobby Arnold said. "People would adjust to Willie. Willie didn't adjust." Except when he was playing chess with Ray Charles.

• • •

WILLIE'S endless quest to partner with as many singers as humanly possible culminated in the all-star
duet album *Half Nelson,* a compilation of his various
collaborations issued in 1985. He also carved out time
to produce and duet with Timi Yuro, the onetime
teen balladeer who was Willie's labelmate at Liberty
Records in the early 1960s. *Timi Yuro Sings Willie
Nelson* featured two duets on a recording that would
be her final album due to throat problems that eventually led to her death from cancer.

He and his best-known duet partner, Waylon Jennings, were so consumed with their respective careers,
they became less the pair than the press portrayed
them to be. "They had such a mutual respect for each
other and their music, it was like a brother bond,
literally," Connie Nelson said. "There was always a
little bit of—not jealousy—but Willie would make
him feel inferior in some ways, and I think it was
because of the cocaine." Long after "You're Wired,
You're Fired" came down, Waylon was still chasing
white lines. Bee Spears acknowledged the tension.
"They truly liked each other," he said. "Things got
crossways between them a little bit, but that happens
with artists because every goddamn one of them has
a frigging ego as big as this damn bus."

Mark Rothbaum compared their dynamic to the leads in the 1954 film *La Strada,* directed by Federico Fellini. "Waylon is Anthony Quinn as Zampano, the carnival strongman. Willie's Richard Baseheart is Il Matto, the Fool, the acrobat, who knew everything the strongman didn't know and would get under Zampano's skin by being funny and kind and sweet. Just like Zampano, Waylon would say, 'That red-headed sumbitch,' but there was affection when he said it. That was their relationship; it was almost as a Fellini film."

Mickey Raphael drew a similar comparison. "Willie was like a loose cannon and Waylon was always worrying," he said. "He never trusted Willie businesswise." "Willie tended to get the best of the argument," added Kris Kristofferson. "Willie's not slow. You don't want to get in a battle of wits with him."

Willie and Waylon were close enough to not have to say anything to each other to be understood, and close enough to fight, especially whenever Willie was punching Waylon's buttons. "I was in an elevator with them at a taping of *Austin City Limits* when they got in a fight," publicist Evelyn Shriver recalled. "The night before at a concert, Waylon played first but was supposed to join Willie at the end of his set. Instead, he was on his bus on his way out of town. Willie hadn't forgotten it. Waylon said, 'I figured with you there, you'd be all right. You didn't need me. The crowd would forget me.'

" 'And they soon did,' " Willie replied, enjoying the dig.

They were still arguing when the taping began.

Wally Selman of the defunct Texas Opry House was riding on the road with Waylon when he observed the testy Waylon-Willie dynamic up close before an arena show in Albuquerque. Waylon was scheduled to open and was already bent out of shape when Willie stepped onto Waylon's bus.

"I don't understand one goddamn thing," Waylon muttered. "Why the fuck am I opening for you? How come you didn't open for me?"

Willie smiled an inscrutable smile and nonchalantly said, "Okay. You close."

Waylon looked him in the eyes, then sputtered, "Well, fuck you, Willie!"

Waylon knew he didn't want to follow Willie. "Willie sure knew how to punch Waylon's buttons," Wally said. "At a birthday party at Willie's, Waylon was being Waylon and kept going to the bathroom. Whenever Waylon would leave, Willie would say, 'Don't anybody sit in that chair over there. It'll make you real nervous.' " Sure enough, when Waylon returned from the bathroom, he plopped into the chair and fidgeted.

Floyd Domino, the pianist with Asleep at the Wheel who was hired to play in Waylon Jennings's band in 1983, observed a similar strain in the Waylon-Willie dynamic. "You could tell Waylon was bothered by Willie's success, although he said he didn't care. He'd tell audiences, 'I don't care if I'm not number one. I'll be number two.' The crowd didn't even know what he was talking about. I saw Willie on some cooking show on TV and the host said Waylon was mad at him. Willie laughed and said, 'What's he mad about today?' Waylon cared. Willie didn't."

Waylon's musicians were almost contemptuous of Willie and Family. "Waylon's band had no respect for Willie's band," Floyd said. "People underestimate the ability of what all those people do in that [Willie's] band. At Caesar's Palace in Vegas, we backed Willie up because contractually he had to do forty-five minutes, and it was Waylon's gig. Willie didn't bring his band. He didn't want to do the gig. On 'Good Hearted Woman,' everyone had to decide, do we go where we think Willie may be leading the beat, or is he going to land right? Where is the beat? They were all looking at me. I was counting to myself, 'One, two, three, four, one, two . . . oh, shit.' They instantly had more respect."

Floyd's sense of timing and talent garnered an

invitation to play on the album *Me and the Drummer* for Willie's Luck Records, where he joined Jimmy Day, Johnny Bush, Paul English, and David Zettner from Willie's 1960s band, the Offenders. "The problem I have in the studio with Willie is there is so much quiet and so much space," Floyd said. "I don't know how Bee [Spears] does it, falling on the beat is easier said than done. Usually, the beat's subdivided. But take a ballad and all you're landing on is downbeats. That's hard, man. There's a lot of space. You can be very constrained, where you hold back, like touching a hot stove."

The last of a string of Waylon-Willie collaborations, *Take It to the Limit,* which was released in 1983, the same year as *Tougher Than Leather,* reflected the growing distance. The effort sounded half-hearted, as if they were recording together only because it was good business, and it clocked in at a mere thirty-four minutes. The redo of "Blackjack County Chain," Willie's once-banned single, was a standout compared with perfunctory readings of David Allan Coe's "Would You Lay with Me (in a Field of Stone)?" made famous by a preteen Tanya Tucker, "Why Baby, Why," George Jones's first hit record, and the redo of Willie's "Till I Gain Control Again," a song Waylon, hell-bent on snorting up his profits, would have been wise to take to heart.

Willie's world was crazy enough whether or not Waylon was in it. When the Family Band was off the road, some members got as far away as they could. Mickey Raphael had moved to Los Angeles in 1977 to get away from the craziness in Austin and get closer to the record business. Bee Spears and Jody Payne lived near Nashville. "There were too many people around Pedernales to be the family like it was in Bandera," Bee said. Apparently there were limits to Willie's chaos theory. His traveling music caravan had grown from a carny show into a corporate behemoth, with five buses, two tractor trailers, and the Franks brothers, the official Willie Nelson merchandisers, trailing behind in a van and trailer. Accountants brought to Willie's attention that close to $100,000 a year was being spent to stock beer in two cattle troughs for the several hundred close personal friends who'd materialize backstage, more than the cost of diesel fuel to keep the band's gypsy caravan running.

Innocents were swept into the vortex of excess time after time, even those who should have known better. Billy English, Paul's little brother, stepped into the crazy world of Willie Nelson in March 1984 when he was hired as Paul's drum tech. Billy had worked with Willie for a year and a half in the late 1960s and recorded *Both Sides Now* as a nineteen-year-old at the

RCA studios, and six years later he appeared on the recording of *Red Headed Stranger* in Garland. That, and being Paul's brother, qualified Billy as family.

For Billy, joining Willie was a literal leap of faith. He was leaving the fifteen-piece horn band led by Christian television evangelist Kenneth Copeland to join a whole other family of musicians who weren't exactly Bible students. Billy eventually became Willie's second percussionist and substitute bass and guitar player. Along the way he strayed from the tenets of the ministry and fell off the wagon, drinking, drugging, and carousing his way through the road along with the rest of the gang. "I took it all the way to intensive care," Billy said. "I wasn't a man of moderation when it came to drugs and alcohol until I woke up in the ICU one morning. My brother said it was God tapping me on the shoulder, saying, 'Pull over.' I was thirty-nine years old, a three-hundred-fifty-three-pound maniac. I'd stay up for a week at a time. I was a maniac. I was crazy. I got on my knees and repented. Fear of death is very strong motivation."

Red Headed Stranger, Stardust, Wanted: The Outlaws, Waylon & Willie, Always on My Mind, and the movies had the cumulative effect of ceremonial recognition by every kind of organization capable of bestowing honors. Willie was recognized as the Man of the Year by the music industry chapter of the United Jewish Appeal and the Indian of the Year at the American Indian Exposition. The Indian recognition was part of an annual powwow in Anadarko, Oklahoma, that drew thousands of Indians in their tribal regalia from all across the country. After a full day of festivities Willie was summoned to the center of the Caddo County Fairgrounds arena and given a headdress, which he donned respectfully. Without any advance warning, the announcer intoned, "And now, Willie Nelson will lead the Chosen People in the dance." Drums started beating. Willie started moving instinctively to the beat and danced a round dance, moving one foot on the beat of the drum, joined by the other foot on the next beat. As he danced, he was followed by several thousand Native Americans circling the arena several times. "I know he was a little flustered," said Carolyn McBride of the *Anadarko Daily News*. But he pulled it off. Jew of the Year and Indian of the Year—he must be doing something right.

But no matter how big he seemed, he stuck to his unspoken rule, staying until the last autograph was signed, being gracious to the people who made him who he was. Now and then a few of those fans found their way to the Pedernales, a few of whom were more fanatical than normal. Usually the staff dealt with the uninvited visitors patiently, hearing them out when they insisted Willie had to hear their song, or nodding agreeably if the person claimed they were Willie's love child. The more aggressive ones were referred to Larry Trader, whose gruff manner could intimidate without his saying a word.

The staff served as a buffer that way. If the visitors got to Willie, more often than not he'd accommodate their request. "I've seen Willie stop and write a check so many times," Bobby Arnold said, shaking his head. "You could always tell when Willie was coming to town because the cars would start showing up—a promoter would want something, somebody wanted a duet sang, somebody was always wanting. Geno would show up. Tom Gresham always had some business to do."

Despite a relentless touring schedule, recording sessions, movies to make, and places to stay in Austin, the Pedernales, Colorado, Malibu, and Maui, Willie was going home with increasing frequency. Even though Mamma and Daddy Nelson and his father, Ira, had passed, he found comfort in Abbott. Old friends would often see his Mercedes parked next to the church, where he would sometimes go to write. The house he'd grown up in had been torn down, part of it moved to the colored part of town by the highway, so he bought the next best thing,

Doc Simms's place, the home of the doctor who delivered him.

It was no surprise, then, that when Abbott, Texas, celebrated its centennial year in 1981, Willie Nelson was featured prominently in literature promoting the town, often along with his sister, Bobbie. He played a fund-raiser for the centennial and raised several thousand dollars for the celebration and a highway billboard promoting Abbott. At the conclusion of the centennial observance, the dual billboards by Interstate 35 that noted the anniversary were painted over to read "The Home of Willie Nelson." A local entrepreneur, Donald Holland, opened a souvenir shop in a reconverted trailer underneath the billboards selling Willie Nelson and Abbott T-shirts and knick-knacks.

Willie was not impressed. The billboard blew his cover in the one place where he could still be Willie Hugh. He didn't like the sign and figured since he'd played the benefit that raised money to put it up, he could take it down. One evening following a poker game with his buddy Zeke Varnon, Willie, Zeke, and J. D. Howell, another pal, who used to run a couple of clubs over in Malone, drove to the gas station, filled up a gas can, and put it in the back of Zeke's pickup.

Abbott's sole police car pulled into the station and

the officer behind the wheel asked, "Hey, Willie, what are you doing?"

"We're gonna go down here and burn this sign," Willie told him.

"Okay, have fun!" the officer said, driving away.

"We threw the gasoline on the sign and it burned for two minutes and went out," Willie said. "We tried again and again, but it had been treated with some chemical and wouldn't burn, so we left."

Around daybreak Willie's boyhood friend Jimmy Bruce was driving across town and noticed a fire. It was the billboard, which had started burning again. The one fire truck in Abbott extinguished the blaze, and a local kid who was considered a troublemaker was arrested under suspicion of arson. Willie called the police to settle the situation. "Let the guy go," he told the chief. "I was the one who burned the fuckin' sign." He was not charged.

Mayor L. A. Hykel's take on Willie reflected the conflicted feelings some folks in town had toward their most famous native son. "Of course we'd like to see him come down and visit a little more," the mayor said, adding, "Some say they wish he'd shave so when he does come they can recognize him."

He raised his hometown profile considerably when he appeared in criminal court as a character witness for Margie Lundy, the owner of the Nite Owl beer joint south of Abbott. Margie had been charged with murder in the shooting death of her brother-in-law, Louis Dickson Jr., which Margie claimed was in self-defense. Willie testified to judge and jury she was the "kindest, most good-hearted person I have ever known. She's number one in my book. I've never heard anyone say anything bad about Margie." Prosecutor Pat Murphy tried to cast the witness in a cloud of doubt. "I love some of his music," he said during the trial. "But he leaves a lot to be desired as a witness. He's well known for his appearance and a past that has been checkered in some fashion by drinking and drugs."

The jury believed Willie, not the prosecutor. Margie Lundy was acquitted.

After the trial Margie retired from the bar business after a long career of serving beer, hosting musicians such as Bob Wills, Ernest Tubb, Merle Haggard, and Johnny Gimble, and keeping the peace in her honky-tonk.

HONEYSUCKLE ROSE, which opened in theaters across America three weeks after Willie's 1980 Fourth of July Picnic at the Pedernales Country Club, had confirmed Willie's cinematic career had legs. He responded by making movies like he made records.

Over the next five years, he did a cameo before being killed off in *Thief,* a 1981 hard-boiled drama about a safecracker working for the Mafia written by Michael Mann that starred James Caan, Tuesday Weld, Dennis Farina, Robert Prosky, and James Belushi; played the role of Red Loon, an American political prisoner in Siberia in the 1920s in the 1982 made-for-television true story *Coming out of the Ice;* and played an outlaw who'd seen better days as the lead in the 1982 film *Barbarosa,* a stark western set in Mexico that also starred Gary Busey and Gilbert Roland. Coproduced and written by Bill Wittliff, an Austin screenwriter who was working with Willie to make a movie based on *Red Headed Stranger, Barbarosa* was filmed on the banks of the Rio Grande in the desert west of Big Bend National Park for $13 million. Gary Busey's character is a farmer forced to take up the life of a gunslinger, a trade he learns from Willie's character, Barbarosa. While making the movie, Willie played a gig to raise funds to buy a resuscitator for the Big Bend regional hospital.

Country music again provided the backdrop for *Songwriter,* the 1984 Willie and Kris buddy movie that, like *Honeysuckle Rose,* was inspired by his real life. Willie assumed the role of Doc Jenkins, a songwriter turned music mogul. When he gets into a bad "bidness" deal, he seeks out his former singing partner, Blackie Buck, played by Kris Kristofferson, to help him.

"The character I was playing was originally written for Waylon," Kris said. "We had a real good director, Alan Rudolph, who was open to creative stuff right on the set. We would make up whole scenes. He got the joke. He would allow us the freedom to try something, then make a suggestion so we would do it better. There's a scene where I wake up in bed with an eye mask on. He said, 'Walk over to the mirror and look at yourself with the eye mask still on.' I went over and did it. And when I did it, I thought of my crew chief when I was working in the Gulf of Mexico [flying helicopters to offshore oil rigs]. Every morning, he'd look in the mirror and say, 'You goodlookin' thing, don't you never die.' I said that with the eye mask on. Alan Rudolph said, 'Perfect.'"

Joining Willie and Kris was Lesley Ann Warren, playing the up-and-coming singer who becomes his coconspirator. Rip Torn based his seedy bad guy character Dino McLeish on Geno McCoslin. Musicians Mickey Raphael, Bee Spears, Jody Payne, Paul English, Bobbie Nelson, Johnny Gimble, Grady Martin, and Jackie King, and associates Poodie Locke, Gates Moore, Larry Trader, Larry Gorham, B. C. Cooper, and Steve Fromholz, all had parts. So did KVET disc jockey Sammy Allred. "There was a scene where I was playing the part of a disc jockey and Willie asks if I take payola," Sammy said. "I say, 'You bet!' "

Mickey Raphael actually got some speaking lines, acknowledgment of his tall, dark, and handsome stature and his Hollywood proclivities. Los Angeles had become his new home base when he wasn't on the road, which led to album and movie work, including three albums with Emmylou Harris, the underrated soundtrack for the film *Blue Collar,* scored by Jack Nitzsche and also featuring Captain Beefheart and Ry Cooder, and a five-year relationship with the actress Ali McGraw.

Willie's love affair with the camera extended to the HBO special with Ray Charles and to participating in Michael Jackson's *We Are the World* superstar recording session for Jackson's USA for Africa project in 1985, which was filmed. He and Kenny Rogers were the voices of country music on the project orchestrated by Jackson, who at the time ruled the airwaves as the King of Pop.

He also appeared in the 1983 historical documentary about the California motorcycle gang, *Hell's Angels Forever,* alongside head Angel Sonny Barger and musicians Jerry Garcia, Bo Diddley, and Johnny Paycheck; did a cameo on *Pryor's Place,* comedian Richard Pryor's 1984 kiddie television series; and was in the cast of 1986's *The Last Days of Frank and Jesse James* alongside Kristofferson, Marcia Cross, and June Carter Cash, with David Allan Coe playing a bit part. He had his own bit part in the Roger Corman B movie *Amazon,* playing the Good Wizard who leads the Amazons before he is killed off, and he sang the title song in the 1988 HBO movie of Dan Jenkins's *Baja Oklahoma,* starring his friend Lesley Ann Warren. He played opposite Delta Burke and Jack Elam in the 1988 Burt Kennedy–directed TV western movie *Where the Hell's That Gold!* which was filmed in southern Colorado; was a credible bad guy in the 1988 CBS network film *Texas Guns,* also directed by Burt Kennedy; and did two made-for-television movies playing a lovable safecracker pursued by Kris Kristofferson and Rip Torn's Texas Ranger characters in *Pair of Aces* and *Another Pair of Aces,* written by Austin writers Bud Shrake and Jap Cartwright, which aired in 1990 and 1991, respectively.

As long as movies didn't interfere with his main line of work, he was always good to go for a turn in front of the camera. "Making movies never took over thirty or forty days and sometimes only seven or eight days to do the bit parts," Willie said. "It never got in the way of the music. It was just something to do that was a lot of fun."

"I don't think he took movies seriously," his financial adviser Mark Rothbaum said. "He's Willie. I don't think he's particularly thrilled to sit around and wait all day [which is the case with most films]. He does it on his off times. Willie didn't want to do *Wag the Dog*, so I said, 'Fine.' He was going to be the band in it, and I had asked for the bigger role of Johnny Gray, and they said okay. I got them Haggard for the band instead. So everything's set, and Willie says, 'I don't want to do it.' So I say, 'Great! Do you mind if I offer Cash the role? It's too good of a role to give up.' So he says to me, 'I said I didn't want to do it, I didn't say I wasn't going to do it.' He was so loved on that set.

"He's the best third guy in the business," Rothbaum believed. "If you are a director and producer, and you have a role that you need a third fella for, get Willie. He is the best guy on a set, especially with temperamental artists, because the crew loves him, the actors love him, it's a party, the bus becomes a great place. He's just like Dean Martin."

Movie money helped underwrite construction of a second studio, the twenty-four-track Arlyn Studios, adjacent to the main room of the Austin Opry House, operated by his nephew, Freddy Fletcher.

The studios led to a glut of Willie product, which worried Mark Rothbaum. "I had to adopt a mind-set that [all the albums were] good for his career, when privately I knew it wasn't. At the same time, there were people at the record companies who earned money through billing, so four records at once from their hottest artist may not be good long-term, but these record executives weren't there for the long term. They were going to be there until they made their money and could retire, which is in fact what happened. They would welcome [more records], even though they too did not believe it was best for his long-term career."

No one spoke up about Willie being overexposed other than Colonel Tom Parker, who had opined that no way would he let Willie play as much as he was playing—not if the Colonel were running the show—and Bruce Lundvall of Columbia Records. "I had to tell him to stop," Bruce said. "There were too many Willie Nelson records. I told him he'd lose his special attraction. He wouldn't listen, but he was such a sweet man."

Bruce Lundvall remained friends with Willie after Bruce left the label in 1982 to run Elektra Records. He knew signing him in 1975 was one of the wisest career moves he'd ever made. "People like Willie and Norah Jones [another Texan who Lundvall would sign to Blue Note Records, twenty-six years later] are completely and utterly unique. When you find one, man, you don't ask questions. I learned that from John Hammond. He was my mentor. He couldn't spot a hit record but he could spot a unique artist every time. You don't even need to see the lyrics. That was Willie."

From the outside looking in, he had it all. In August 1983, Willie was featured on the cover of *Life* magazine, sitting on a fence post, guitar in hand, headband holding back his hair, surrounded by Connie and his daughters Amy and Paula Carlene on their beautiful Colorado spread next to the headline "Where C&W's Top Star Hides Away with His Family."

The *Life* cover was ironic in two respects. It wrongly suggested Willie actually stayed in one place for more than a few nights. And it ignored what many around him knew too well. Amy Irving remained in Willie's life.

Connie Nelson had hoped the relationship between her husband and his leading lady in *Honeysuckle Rose* had been an impulsive fling tied to moviemaking. What Connie didn't know was that Amy Irving had broken up with Willie instead of the other way around. He'd arranged to throw a party for Amy in New York in February of 1982 following her short but successful run as the female lead in *Amadeus* on Broadway, her first project after *Honeysuckle Rose*. But when he showed up at the party, she treated him like a country bumpkin rather than her lover. He walked out of the party and around the corner into an alley where he wept openly.

But their affair was on again. When Connie got a call tipping her off that Willie was shacking up with Amy in condo number one at the Pedernales Country Club in 1983, she flew from Colorado to Texas to confront Willie and to tell Amy Irving to keep her paws off her husband. She showed up well past midnight, very drunk and very pissed, and tried to punch out Willie when he opened the door naked. She broke her hand instead. Even as she struggled with him, Connie hollered at Amy to come downstairs so she could whip her ass, but Amy stayed upstairs. "I all but stalked her—literally—just to keep her at a distance," Connie said.

Somehow Willie and Connie talked it out and patched things up, but Willie and Amy kept coming back to each other.

In February 1985 Willie went into Pedernales Studio to make an album with his longtime bud Roger Miller. Mary Miller and Connie Nelson were close friends and came to the sessions too. But when the recording was finished, Willie informed Connie he wasn't going back to Colorado with her. He wanted to stay in Texas, he said, and he wanted to see Amy Irving again.

However, Amy blew off Willie one last time and married movie producer Steven Spielberg, her long-time fiancé. Connie moved the girls back to West Lake Hills, west of Austin, to try to be closer to him, but the flame that lit their marriage was flickering. The return was not the happiest homecoming. Paula was at an age when being pulled from her high school was as upsetting as it had been to Susie when the family moved from Tennessee back to Texas. And the Nelson girls' reputation preceded them. "Paula got into drugs at Westlake High," Connie said. "The drug crowd could have cared less if Willie was famous or not. They cared if she could get them pot. Paula fit in good."

Paula knew the drill too well. "They weren't interested in me," she acknowledged. "It was just because I was Willie Nelson's daughter."

Willie Nelson's mother may have had similar feelings, knowing people were interested in her only because of her famous son, but it didn't bother Myrle Harvey. She enjoyed letting the world know who she was. There was more than a little of Willie in her, as was revealed in a handwritten note on lined note-book paper that she had composed:

I fully realize that no wealth or position, can endure unless built upon truth and justice.

Therefore I will engage in no transaction which does not benefit all whom it affects.

I will succeed by attracting to my self the forces I wish to use. And the cooperation of other people. I will endorse others to serve me, because of my willingness to serve others.

I will eliminate hatred, envy, jealousy, selfishness, and cynicism by developing love for all humanity because I know that or negative attitude to record? Others, can bring me, success. I will cause others to believe in me. Because I will believe in them, and in my self.

I will sign my home to this formula, commit it to a memory, repeat it long once a day with full faith that's will gradually in chance. My troubles on actions as that I will become a self reliant and successful person.

Myrle M Harvey Rt 8, Box 291 d.,
Yakima WA 98908

On December 11, 1983, Myrle departed this earth in Yakima, taken by lung cancer, the same disease that took ex-husband Ira Nelson. She had been living in eastern Washington state for nine years after moving from Eugene, Oregon, with her third husband, Ken Harvey. The sassy gal and gypsy rambler who taught her daughter and son a few things about moving down the highway was gone. Willie Nelson and Family tried to make the funeral service, but their flight was delayed due to bad weather. By the time three black stretch limousines pulled into the Terrace Heights Memorial Park cemetery, the crowds had departed. It was pitch-black dark. The only people left were the grave diggers, waiting to do their business after her son and his family said good-bye.

IF Willie's life sometimes seemed too large to believe, his friends only magnified the myth. Houston lawyer Joe Jamail was representing the Pennzoil oil company in a high-stakes lawsuit against petro-rival Texaco, and the night before presenting his final argument in court, Joe was interrupted by Willie and Coach. They'd been golfing at Willie's course, as usual, when Willie suggested flying over to Houston to cheer up Joe. He had a jet at his disposal. Why not use it? So instead of spending the evening preparing his presentation, the lawyer welcomed the coach and the musician, and three regular guys who happened to be the best at what they did spent the evening telling lies, knocking back drinks, and listening to the musician play music until two in the morning.

"Obviously it hurt Joe because he didn't get anything out of it," Coach joshed, because the initial judgment—in favor of Jamail's client—exceeded $10 billion, the largest jury verdict in history. The figure was ultimately reduced to $3 billion, but the lawyer did very well for himself, earning $335 million for his troubles. He'd already won one case using Willie as an argument. "Some guy was really hurt in a car wreck, and [Joe] used the lyrics to 'Half a Man' to convince the jury to come up with hundreds of thousands of dollars that [the guy's] insurance didn't want to pay," Willie said. "Joe didn't mind borrowing a few words."

WILLIE'S drawing power remained strong, enticing thirty thousand fans to pay $18 for an all-day admission to the 1984 version of the Willie Nelson Fourth of July Picnic, staged at South Park Meadows, an eleven-acre open-air concert venue with no seating (read: a big ol' pasture) in deep south Austin. After he had held "picnics" in stadiums in New Jersey, Syracuse, and Atlanta the previous year, it was time to come back to Texas. It was a classic progressive-country bill with Waylon, Jessi, Kris, and Leon headlining, joined by Joe Ely, the Lubbock songster and rocker who'd relocated to Austin, Extreme Outlaw David Allan Coe, San Antonio country singer Moe

Bandy, semi-reformed Austin icon Jerry Jeff Walker, whose career had been revived when his wife, Susan, a onetime state political operative, took over as his manager, actor Gary Busey, who, like too many music biopic lead actors thought he was really a rock star after he did *The Buddy Holly Story,* pal Johnny Bush, ol' Faron Young, and Austin folkie Steve Fromholz.

Unlike previous picnics, this one was promoted by Pace Concerts, the dominant concert promoter in the southwest that had been staging Willie's big New Year's Eve bashes in Houston. "Now Louis Messina [of Pace] can worry about losing half the money," Willie joked. The outlaw vibe lingered, but the suits were running the show now.

A year later, it rained throughout most of the 1985 picnic at South Park Meadows, holding the crowd count to fifteen thousand, despite one of the strongest lineups ever: Neil Young at his first picnic; the Highwaymen, an old-lions-of-country supergroup consisting of Willie, Kris, Waylon, and Cash; several stars with two first names — David Allan, Jerry Jeff, Ray Wiley, and Billy Joe; the Nashville greats — June Carter Cash, Faron Young, Johnny Bush, and Hank Snow; and several Austin FOWs — Geezinslaws, Fromholz, Rattlesnake Annie, and Jubal Clark, the self-styled Gypsy Cowboy who opened the festivities. Clearly, the vibe surrounding picnics past had faded.

No matter how good the music was, sitting in a field full of stickers and ticks surrounded by drunks and dopeheads had lost its charm among a significant number of Willie's old fans.

The picnic was no longer the only way to experience Willie Nelson — movies, television appearances, touring, and the continuous barrage of new albums made him more accessible than ever. Of all the multimedia projects, the most surprising was the 1985 film *Red Headed Stranger,* on which he bet some of his own money. After six years of hemming and hawing, he bought back the film rights to the movie from Robert Redford, who at one time fancied playing the Stranger himself.

As with his music career, Willie had learned enough about how the movie business worked to think he wanted to promote the show as well as star in it. He and writer-director Bill Witliff shared the title of producers. They put together a group of investors headed by Don Tyson, the president of the biggest poultry processor in America, to get the movie made. Concert promoter Barry Fey and Willie's right-hand man on the road, David Anderson, were associate producers. Tim O'Connor unloaded what ownership he had left in the Austin Opry complex to add money to the producer's pot. Caroline Mugar, a friend and fan of some means from Boston, added $500,000 to the pot to get the movie finished. She later would become the executive director of a Willie project called Farm Aid.

The movie stuck to the same script as Willie's album, with the addition of a Texas Ranger character named El Viejo that had been created by scriptwriter Michael Mann for his hit television series *Miami Vice*. Willie played the Stranger, the Reverend Julian Shay. Dallas native Morgan Fairchild played his wife, Raysha, and Katharine Ross of *The Graduate* and *Butch Cassidy* fame played Laurie, the Stranger's love interest. Character actor R. G. Armstrong played the sheriff. Also in the cast were Austin actor Sonny Carl Davis; Paul English and Bee Spears from Willie's band; Elberta Hunter; Bill Richardson, who went on to fame making *Invasion of the Space Preachers;* Austin power attorney Joe K. Longley; and the thieves of the Pedernales, including Billy Cooper, Bo Franks, Ralph (the Midget) Franzetti, Jody Fischer, several dozen other family friends, and Jubal Clark, one of the most talented songwriters you'd never heard of, who got a speaking role as the third horse thief:

JUBAL: Get me some spurs!
(No one answers.)
The STRANGER, emerging from the shadows:
    Get Jubal some spurs!

All the THIEVES suddenly run around, yelling:
Get Jubal some spurs! Get Jubal some spurs!

The day after filming Jubal's scene, Willie spied him on the set.

"How do you like the way I shot you in the ass off that horse?" Willie asked him, reveling in the joys of being a movie cowboy.

"Willie, if you were a little taller and aimed a little higher, you wouldn't have shot me in the ass," Jubal said.

Willie sold the finished film to Shep Gordon, a movie producer who had been manager of the rock personality Alice Cooper. Shep paid enough up front to give the investors their money back plus a 25 percent profit. Willie had risen to the challenge, but the experience involved enough heavy lifting to convince him he had better things to do with his time than produce films. "Making movies is a slower process than making music," he said with understatement. "The payoff depends on who you are doing the movie with and if you are enjoying it."

But movie ownership had its perquisites. Willie got to keep the movie set as his own personal western town, which he named Luck, Texas, complete with facades of a church, horse stables, hardware store, and saloon. The saloon was eventually refashioned into the Luck World Headquarters, where Willie tended bar, cooked breakfast for the boys, played chess and pool, and picked music the old-fashioned way, sitting around, singing, and playing guitars.

Weddings were held in Luck. Cowboy gunfights were filmed in Luck. Whenever Willie had to do interviews or photo shoots, like the one he did with Annie Leibovitz, Luck was the place. The town motto—"When you're here, you're in Luck. When you're not here, you're out of luck"—said it all.

Outside the bubbles of the Pedernales Country Club and the adjacent Luck, a good part of the nation was reeling from a real-estate bust, with falling prices, rising bankruptcies, and vanishing buyers. The downturn was caused by corrupt savings and loan executives, who cost taxpayers billions of dollars by loaning easy money to speculators.

The earlier boom had jacked up housing prices in Austin, and the subsequent bust offered some real steals and bargains as the overheated economy cooled, but the breather didn't last long. City boosters had seen past the old-school wisdom of trying to attract heavy industry by offering tax breaks. Instead, two critical semigovernmental high-technology research bodies discovered Austin, like Willie had eleven years earlier. Austin won out over three other finalists (San Diego, Raleigh, and Atlanta) as the location for the

Microelectronics and Computer Technology Corporation, a consortium of twelve American technology companies that banded together to stave off competition from Japan and advance supercomputer research, bringing a new wave of best and brightest minds to town led by Admiral Bobby Inman. Another fourteen-company consortium, called Sematech, formed in Austin in 1986 to advance semiconductor (computer chip) research.

As Austin ascended to global-city status and the rest of Texas was embracing its new reputation as America on Steroids (San Antonio, Dallas, and Houston consistently ranked in the top ten of America's Fattest Cities), Willie was polishing his altruistic credentials.

Giving was always part of his philosophy. When the offering plate was passed around Abbott Methodist on Sunday mornings after the sermon, he felt responsible, like everyone else did, and wanted to drop something in the plate, even if he had nothing to give. Alfred and Nancy had taught him to do right, especially when someone less fortunate needed help. Mamma Nelson would have been proud of him and Bobbie becoming the people they were—two of the closest siblings on earth doing what they were raised to do, and doing it better and with more grace than almost anyone else. The urge to help others stayed with him. He remembered the other side of this life too well.

The desire to help took Willie to the end zone of a college football stadium in Champaign, Illinois. It was harvest time—September 22, 1985, to be exact—the time of the year when crops came in all across America, and those who prepared, planted, and nurtured them hoped to reap the rewards for the previous nine months of toil and gamble.

Willie was standing on an improvised stage between John Mellencamp and Neil Young with Illinois governor Jim Thompson to his side, looking over a crowd of eighty thousand gathered to honor the American family farmer at a fourteen-hour marathon concert dubbed Farm Aid.

Real farmers needed help, at least the ones who were still hanging in. Most of the tillable soil in America was owned by corporations. Harvesting was done on a mass scale with machinery and cheap labor. Family farmers were pretty much a memory when Willie put his mind to honoring them. The aim was to raise awareness for American farmers the same way money had been raised for AIDS through the Live Aid concerts in London and Philadelphia two months before. During his Live Aid set in Philadelphia, Bob

Dylan had weighed in with the comment "The American family farmer could use a hand too." Willie had heard the sentiment loud and clear.

Farmers were to Dylan what Gene Autry was to Willie, mostly an idealized fantasy of Americana Lost. To Willie, farmers were the folks he grew up with and who shaped his worldview. An idea grew in his head after he talked to Dylan. The more he talked to the kids he'd grown up with in Abbott who were still farming in Hill County, the more he wanted to do something on their behalf.

At a gig Willie played in Springfield, the capital of Illinois, he brought the subject up to a visitor on the bus, Governor Jim Thompson. "Every time we'd play the state fair, Big Jim would come on the bus and we'd have a beer and a bowl of chili and talk about things," Willie said. "This particular year, I'd heard the farmers were having problems and asked him if he knew anything about it."

Farmers were having a bad year, Governor Thompson told him, going into detail about the upcoming federal farm bill, soft markets, price supports, parity, drought, fuel costs, and other agricultural issues.

"That's when we started talking about doing Farm Aid," Willie said. "I knew [the government wasn't] doing the right thing. There was no good farm bill. All of us out here know that we need a good farm bill to save the farmer, and there's no good farm bill right now to protect the farmer from the big corporations. That pissed me off. I thought one Farm Aid one time with me and the governor there, how could they argue with that?"

Twenty-one days later he was at Champaign, taking the stage with Neil Young at ten a.m. to open the show with a song about farmers "trying to make a stand." A stream of superstars followed throughout the day, including Bob Dylan, B. B. King, the Beach Boys, Billy Joel, Loretta Lynn, Bonnie Raitt, Rickie Lee Jones, Waylon Jennings, John Denver, Roger Miller, Tom Petty, Lou Reed, John Fogarty, Randy Newman, Roy Orbison, Charley Pride, Kris Kristofferson, Van Halen, Merle Haggard, and George Jones. In all, more than fifty acts volunteered their services. June Carter and Johnny Cash reworked "Old McDonald Had a Farm" to tie into the day's theme. Charlie Daniels wrote and performed a new song called "American Farmer." The event raised $7 million for family farmers, which was disbursed through the nonprofit organization Willie had formed.

"No one knew what the fuck he was talking about at the first Farm Aid," said Floyd Domino, who was playing piano for Waylon Jennings at the time. "But because it was Willie, everybody figured it was for a good cause." The ones who really got it—John Mellencamp, Neil Young, and, later on, Dave Matthews—were artists representing a broad spectrum of music that shared the common trait of integrity, which people were happy to pay good money to witness.

Months later, Willie was still speaking out. Farm Aid was no feel-good one-off. It had turned into a crusade. If not for music, his involvement with Future Farmers of America in high school would have eventually led him down the agrarian path. The least he could do for all the folks back home was help.

Willie became Farm Aid's voice. He testified in front of a panel of U.S. senators in Washington, DC, telling them, "The farmers in this country are dropping out—they're dropping like flies." Back at the ranch, personal secretary Jody Fischer, who was supposed to be handling the business end of Pedernales Studio, became a crisis-hotline counselor, fielding calls from farmers and their families who wanted to talk to Willie, saying such things as "I need help," "I'm going to kill myself," and "My husband's in the barn with a gun."

"I was really discouraged because I saw us losing more and more farmers every week," Willie explained in a radio interview. "And we had about eight million small-family farmers. Now, we're down to less than two million, still losing three to four hundred every week. So I've been watching that happen and it was very discouraging. The bills passed to help the farmer were not helping the farmer. The Freedom to Farm bill was laughingly called the Freedom to Fail bill by small farmers."

In the summer of 1986, Texas's sesquicentennial year, Willie combined his picnic and Farm Aid, staging the July Fourth event at Manor Downs, a quarterhorse track east of Austin owned by Frances Carr, the comanager of Stevie Ray Vaughan, and former girlfriend and business partner of Sam Cutler, the one-time road manager for the Grateful Dead, the Rolling Stones, and (briefly) Willie Nelson. SRV joined an eclectic Farm Aid on the Fourth lineup that included the Beach Boys, Los Lobos, X, Rick James, Julio Iglesias, Waylon, George Jones, Little Joe Hernandez, Steve Earle, illusionist the Amazing Kreskin, and seventy other acts, who performed a nineteen-hour marathon in front of forty thousand fans and a nationwide audience watching on the VH-1 cable channel, raising $1.3 million for small family farmers.

The day before Farm Aid II, Willie attended Richard and Cathy Anderson's wedding in the Luck, Texas, western town, along with actor Dennis Hopper and the funk singer Rick James of "Superfreak" fame as marriage witnesses. Richard managed the club at Pedernales. Marrying the couple was Dr. Robert Shelton, the president of the Austin Theological Seminary, who liked to preach a sermon he called "The Gospel According to Willie." Richard and Cathy's dog Cinnamon was best man. Willie blessed the event by singing "Amazing Grace" to the couple. He would sing the same song at Bill and Melinda Gates's wedding on the island of Lanai in Hawaii on January 1, 1994, at the request of the founder of the Microsoft Corporation — the richest man in the world — for which he was paid $1,000,000.

The World, 1986

B Y 1986, WILLIE was demonstrating that he was indeed human and fallible. He had been putting out so many records that sales began to wane, and no longer was every album guaranteed to turn gold. His transition from outlaw to grand old man had been signified by formation of the Highwaymen — the country music singer-songwriter supergroup of Johnny Cash, Waylon, Kris, and Willie. The strength-in-numbers collaboration aimed to bolster the careers of four giants old enough to be regarded as legends but who were no longer considered suitable for contemporary country radio.

The idea had originated with Johnny Cash, the man in black who was Nashville's biggest outlaw of the 1960s and briefly Waylon's roommate when both were between marriages. "One night, Johnny said to

Willie, 'You know, you've made a record with everybody in the world except me. We should do one together,' " said Kris Kristofferson. Cash was putting on a Christmas show in Montreux, Switzerland, in 1984 for a TV special and suggested a recording session in Nashville before the concert. "Willie told me it would be to my advantage to be there because I could pitch them songs," Kris said. Waylon was dealt in too.

Producer Chips Moman brought a song to the session written by Jimmy Webb called "The Highwayman" that Chips thought the four should record. "Next thing you know, we brought in some of our stuff and we had enough for an album," Kris said. "It was really accidental."

The camaraderie in person and onstage at Montreux transcended their professional status. They genuinely liked one another. "You have to realize each one of these guys was my hero when I came to town, and to be up on the same stage with them was like a dream," said Kris Kristofferson. "I could have never imagined that back in the days when they wouldn't let me sing my own demos, that I was able to sing right along with Johnny Cash, whether he liked it or not. Considering there were four people up there who had gone their own way, had always been individuals and never followers, it's pretty amazing that we got along so well.

"We were being interviewed right before we went on *The Tonight Show* and they were asking about how we got started," Kris said. The Christmas show in Montreux was cited. The interviewer asked John why he chose Montreux. Before John could answer, Waylon piped up, "Because that's where the Baby Jesus was born."

For all their individual talent, the four began to jell as a group, with Willie often showing the way offstage. "Those guys didn't sign autographs like Willie did," Larry Gorham, Willie's bodyguard, remembered. "So when Willie stood out there and signed after shows, they had to too, otherwise they'd look bad."

The album led to a collaborative moviemaking adventure in 1986, a made-for-TV remake of the movie *Stagecoach,* which was being filmed near Albuquerque. All the spouses came along for the shoot except Willie's. "It was going to be a big get-together for all the wives, and we were looking forward to it, but Paula was having major drug behavior problems, and I was worried sick," Connie said. She had gone through all of Paula's belongings after suspecting something was up. A month before the New Mexico shoot with Willie, Connie found cocaine.

"I told Willie I couldn't go," Connie said. "Paula needed help; this was her life. I couldn't leave my daughter doing coke. I couldn't go have fun, wondering if she's going to come back on the weekends." Connie told Willie she was putting Paula in a rehab facility at the recommendation of Thomas "Hollywood" Henderson, the former Dallas Cowboy football player who was a drug counselor in Austin.

"You wouldn't really?" Willie said.

"She's going," Connie said emphatically.

Willie went on to Albuquerque. Connie took Paula to Del Mar, California, near San Diego to begin treatment. With the help of a school counselor, Paula was able to continue her studies and graduate from Westlake High School, taking correspondence courses while she was cleaning up. Paula Carlene was the first Nelson offspring to earn a high school diploma. Billy had quit in the sixth grade, and Susie and Lana had dropped out in high school. Willie had told Connie the kids didn't have to finish school, but Connie dug in her heels when it came to Paula Carlene. "Yes, she does," Connie told Willie. "Not just for what she'll learn in school, but how to get along with other people."

Kris Kristofferson said the remake of *Stagecoach* "wasn't a very good film." But it was a lot of fun making, he said. Before shooting a scene where Mary Crosby's character was giving birth, Willie snuck in a rabbit. With cameras rolling, Willie pulled out the rabbit instead of a baby during the birth scene. The

Johnny-Willie dynamic provided plenty of amusement on the set. "We were calling [Johnny and Willie] MacArthur and Truman," Kristofferson said, "because one wouldn't come out of his bus until the other came out. There could have been outrageous egos and there weren't. It was mutual respect."

For Willie, the movie was memorable for another reason.

"That's where he got mixed up with the makeup girl," Connie Nelson said. "He was the only one who didn't have a spouse there, and she was, by God, going to find a star. That was the deal; Waylon told me that."

"The makeup girl" was Ann Marie D'Angelo, who applied makeup to all the lead actors every morning and helped remove it every evening. True to her nature, Annie didn't mind giving Willie a little shit when she put on his face in the morning. She knew who he was—she used to water-ski with friends on the Colorado River on the California-Arizona border while listening to Willie and Waylon tapes—but she wasn't buying into his bullshit. Willie took a shine to her and her feisty spirit. She had a mouth and knew how to use it. She also knew how to flatter and fuss over him. Everyone else on the set seemed to have someone they were with. They fell together naturally.

Her Sicilian features vaguely suggested Amy Irving, first wife Martha, and mother Myrle, but Annie really was like no one before. She'd grown up in the Lakewood section of Los Angeles, the middle of five children, and through a cousin who owned the old Desilu Studios learned to do makeup, earning a credit in the comedy *Bachelor Party,* starring Tom Hanks. After *Stagecoach* wrapped, she did makeup on the B movies *The Rosary Murders* and *Gleaming the Cube* and served as makeup supervisor on the film *Hot Pursuit.* But as much as she loved the travel and the camaraderie of a film shoot, her career track veered into the ditch when she met Willie.

When Connie caught wind of Willie's wandering, she put her foot down. This time, though, Willie wasn't listening. So she removed his belongings from their West Lake Hills home and dumped them in the cabin on the Hill at the Pedernales Country Club. Connie and Amy moved to Del Mar, where Paula Carlene was undergoing treatment for drug abuse and for being Willie Nelson's daughter.

"My senior year of high school I had had enough," Paula said. "Not just of school work but of the whole Willie Nelson [thing]. . . . I just didn't want to be there. I was feeling a lot of pressure. I was hanging out with the wrong crowd. I went to rehab in San Diego and loved it. I was seventeen and I didn't have to go to school. I didn't miss partying. I didn't miss the Willie crowd."

Paula did so well she was asked to be a counselor, partly due to her celebrity ties. "Once I became a counselor, they told everybody. That was a selling point to the parents—Willie Nelson's daughter was a counselor. I did a lot of speaking, I told my story a lot. Same thing. It's hard to be anonymous anywhere, but I'm not blaming anybody."

Her own counselor's husband helped Paula to see the positives of her privileged life. "You know what it is about your dad?" he told her. "The everyday working man and woman sees your dad at an award show in jeans and a T-shirt with long hair and braids, and everyone wants to vicariously live through him." It turned Paula's head around. "He wasn't fish food," she realized. "I was always trying to protect him from people around him all the time. I would drag him through a crowd—'Come on!' We went out to dinner, we couldn't have a dinner. People would come up, form a line."

THE WILLIE NELSON Fourth of July Picnic kept moving almost as much as Willie. Giant likenesses of Willie Nelson, Zeke Varnon, and Carl Cornelius on billboards welcomed twenty-five thousand fans to

Carl's Corner truck stop, the site of the 1987 version of Willie's picnic. Carl's, about fifteen miles northeast of Abbott on Interstate 35E, just north of the I-35 split, was the perfect choice for a picnic dedicated to America's Truckers. The truck stop was its own incorporated city run by Carl Cornelius, a longtime buddy of Zeke Varnon's, Willie's hell-raising friend. Carl's sold gas and diesel fuel and served comfort food to truckers like most truck stops did, with added features no other truck stop could claim: a topless bar that served liquor, statues of three dancing frogs on the roof that had been designed by Texas imagineer Bob "Daddy-O" Wade, and a hostess named Treasure Chest who used her sultry voice on Channel 19 on the CB radio to invite truckers to pull over at the Carl's exit for "a piece . . . of watermelon."

The one-day affair was low key, drawing fewer than twenty thousand, despite a lineup of Kris, Shaver, Coe, Merle, Jerry Jeff, Emmylou, Roger Miller, and Asleep at the Wheel, along with pianist Bruce Hornsby, neo-honky-tonker Dwight Yoakum, blues powerhouse the Fabulous Thunderbirds, Eric Johnson, Joe Ely, Delbert McClinton, Joe Walsh, and the Nitty Gritty Dirt Band. The celebrities on hand were local—McLennan County district attorney Vic Feazell and Texas attorney general Jim Mattox.

The picnic also marked the publication of *Heart-worn Memories,* a very personal memoir written by Willie's second daughter, Susie. The book was therapy for Susie, who grew up with her father gone a lot. Like her sister, her mother, grandmother, grandfather, and aunt, Susie married at sixteen. She was a teenage mother and a divorcee at nineteen, and a victim of domestic violence, having been beaten by her second husband, who died in a car crash. Like her famous father, Susie had the show-business bug, studying ballet at the Juilliard School in New York, performing in the lead role in a road-show version of the Broadway musical *Annie Get Your Gun,* and recording a single of "Heartworn Memories" with stepmother Shirley Nelson.

Almost two months later, on August 30, 1987, Farm Aid III was staged in Lincoln, Nebraska, in the heart of the farm belt. A citizen petition drive persuaded University of Nebraska officials to host the event, which starred Emmylou Harris, Arlo Guthrie, the Fabulous Thunderbirds, John Mellencamp, Neil Young, and Willie. According to several press reports, folk-pop singer John Denver unexpectedly stole the show, putting on a performance that had seventy thousand fans roaring. The result was $1.6 million more raised for small family farmers.

• • •

WHATEVER money was lost on good causes, there was always Vegas to pump up the checking account. Beginning in the early 1960s, Willie found Nevada gambling casinos his most dependable paydays. He initially worked Reno and Lake Tahoe, especially Harrah's, where owner Bill Harrah told him straight up, "Mr. Nelson, I don't really agree with your wardrobe, but you sure bring in the dough."

Willie's first regular Las Vegas gig was at the Horseshoe Casino, run by Benny Binion, whose history with Willie went back to the 1950s. Benny was a true believer.

"He's got magic, that son of a bitch," he told the writer Bud Shrake. "I never seen nothing like him and Billy Graham. They can just capture you. He was the same kind of a person he is now. You could already look at him and tell that this guy's going to be on his way. You see a guy that can attract people."

Benny didn't hold on to Willie long. He was too good a drawing card.

"Every time we played Vegas, the dealers would get a little upset because the players were leaving the tables to watch the show," Willie said. "I just played the show. We were playing six shows a night back-to-back, forty minutes on and twenty minutes off, so I didn't give a shit what they were doing out there. I was trying to get through the night."

Willie moved on to the new Caesar's Palace, where the casino draw at the hotel jumped from an average $15,000 an hour to $75,000 an hour when Willie performed during the 1979 National Finals Rodeo.

Willie got so big that even Frank Sinatra opened for him at Golden Nugget's newly refurbished Theatre Ballroom cabaret in 1984. The double-bill had been engineered by Steve Wynn, who was on his way to becoming the biggest casino operator of all. Wynn proposed the billing to Frank Sinatra during a visit at his home in Palm Springs, California. "I took two CDs, *Stardust* and the soundtrack from *Electric Horseman,* over to the Tamarisk Country Club in Palm Springs, where Frank lived on the seventeenth hole. Frank had a couple of homes on the golf course, and one was the screening room where the stereo was. Frank was wearing a gray sweater and open-collar shirt and leaned his butt up against the back of the couch as I played him 'Georgia,' 'Moonlight in Vermont,' and 'My Heroes Have Always Been Cowboys.' "

"That cat can sing," Frank said. "That cat's a blues singer. He can sing my stuff but I don't know if I can sing his." The deal was on.

At the grand opening, Frank Sinatra, Willie Nelson's opening act, sang three numbers before walking off the stage with a very pale look on his face. "He felt something happen in his throat," Steve Wynn said. "Something popped." Years earlier, Sinatra had had a small vein in his throat break, and evidently it had happened again, Wynn said. "He flew back to Palm Springs that night and spent the next three days in the hospital. He was forbidden to talk for another week." Others suspected he pulled out because he didn't like opening for anyone.

Willie played the rest of the opening week solo. Frank's entourage, including Jilly Rizzo, stuck around and partied with Willie's band and crew. "Frank loved Willie's music," said Willie's stage manager, Poodie Locke, pointing out that Sinatra had contemplated an album of Willie Nelson covers back in the 1960s. "But he couldn't handle us [the crew]. We're wearing Wranglers and we've got titty dancers backstage. It wasn't his version of classy."

Besides the fat guarantees, Las Vegas spoke to Willie's affinity for gambling. He'd been placing bets on games his entire life and had mastered the art of the bluff. He was good enough and wealthy enough to take on the professional gambler Tom Preston, better known as Amarillo Slim, in a high-stakes game of dominoes on Fremont Street in downtown Las Vegas. In his autobiography, *Amarillo Slim in a World of Fat People,* Slim claimed Steve Wynn bet $50,000 and a new Jeep Renegade on Willie, but Wynn said he wasn't at the match and, besides, didn't bet on dominoes. "I wouldn't know how to handicap two domino players. Why would I lose money? When it comes to bullshitters, Slim is Mount Everest," Wynn said. No one, including Willie, disputed Slim's claim that Willie bet $300,000 on himself and that Slim won the best-four-out-of-seven match.

"He cheated," Willie said of Amarillo Slim twenty years after the fact. Benny Binion, who was there, had told him so, Willie said. "He had a guy looking over your shoulder, tipping off your hand," Benny said to Willie, fingering the man who was sending him over. Willie was hardly surprised. "I knew he was going to do it. But I thought, well, maybe I could beat him anyway. 'Course I didn't."

Willie wrote a blurb for Slim's book anyway, saying, "Every one of Slim's tall tales about his gambling exploits had me in stitches, except, of course, the time that country cowboy took me for a pretty penny playing dominoes. I would never make another bet with Slim, but I'd bet everything that Slim's memoir is the best I've ever read."

In November 1987 Willie shared top billing with Hank Williams Jr. for a concert at Thomas & Mack Center in Las Vegas celebrating Benny Binion's eighty-third birthday. Benny sat onstage next to Moe

Dalitz, another Vegas pioneer, while Steve Wynn served as master of ceremonies.

Vegas was the favored destination for unusual Nelson family reunions. In 1979, Myrle Harvey, Willie's mom, had made an unannounced appearance as part of her one-woman campaign to let the world know she was her son's mother. "She showed up in Vegas when Willie's playing Caesar's Palace and made her grand entrance when the band was playing 'Redneck Mother,' just walked onto the stage," her grandson Freddy Fletcher said. "She did the same thing in Houston for a New Year's Eve show at the Summit, just to let everybody know, this is Willie's mom; that other woman is not his mother. No one on the crew was going to tell her no. Nobody could stop her, not even Willie."

Second ex-wife Shirley, who disappeared for ten years after she secured her divorce from Willie, resurfaced at a gig in Vegas to join Willie singing "Amazing Grace." Seeing her ex-husband reassured Shirley. "I was so afraid that the one I knew so long ago wouldn't be there," she said. "I didn't think I had the courage to see him the way he looks now, beard and all. But he's still the same heart, the same man who's so full of love, the same sensitivity."

"There is no such thing as an ex-wife," Willie liked to say. Martha, who had remarried and was living in

China Springs, west of Waco, already knew that. Willie paid for a new trailer for her to live in and was still taking care of her taxes.

PERSONAL affairs led to the cancellation of both the Fourth of July Picnic and Farm Aid in 1988. Willie was busy working for Nebraska senator Bob Kerrey's outsider campaign for president, promoting the autobiography he'd written with Austin writer and golfing partner Bud Shrake, and working out the final details of the divorce from Connie. The affair with Annie D'Angelo was ongoing, but when Connie put her foot down over the continuing public displays of affection that seemed to always get back to her, Willie still wouldn't listen. The parting had been amicable but still difficult to accept for both, especially in the wake of Kris Kristofferson and Rita Coolidge's divorce. Staying faithful was a promise he no longer felt compelled to say he would try to fulfill. Connie stayed in touch and continued to call him "my best friend."

Being married to him was a whole other deal. At least they weren't alone. Divorces outnumbered marriages in Texas in 1987.

Willie had written a poem to Connie in cursive script just after *Stardust:*

Home is where I'll go when it's all over
Rome (sic) is what I'll do until I die.
But as long as I'm with you I'll be in
   clover
And life will be the sweeter lulabye (sic)

The song "Angel Flying Too Close to the Ground" was also written about her, many believed.

If you had not fallen,
then I would not have found you . . .

ONSTAGE, he was unwittingly stirring up his most political and potentially most damaging shit storm yet. One of his new acting friends, Peter Coyote, had talked Willie, Kris Kristofferson, Joni Mitchell, and Robin Williams into playing a benefit fund-raiser for Leonard Peltier, an American Indian activist convicted of killing two FBI agents on an Indian reservation in South Dakota. The following July, representatives of an organization called Friends of the Police picketed the Willie Nelson concert in Warwick, Rhode Island, to protest Willie's support of a cop killer. Back in Texas, another dustup erupted in Waco almost simultaneously, tied to the failure of the Leroy Bank the year before, leaving six hundred depositors in the small town of Leroy, northeast of Waco, broke and without recourse. A fund-raiser concert had been proposed for the grand opening of the new Ferrell Special Events Center at Baylor University in Waco, starring Willie Nelson. But when the event was announced, the Texas Rangers and other law-enforcement agencies in the state threatened to picket, having caught wind of the protests in Rhode Island. A big stink was raised, and Baylor withdrew the invitation to Willie.

Baylor University president Herbert H. Reynolds insisted that canceling Willie's appearance at the opening of the center had nothing to do with benefit concerts for Indian activists accused of killing FBI agents or songs like "Whiskey River" and "I Gotta Get Drunk" or his lifestyle. "His singing—I know people enjoy it. I know he's popular," the Baptist University president intoned before lowering the hammer with a big *But*. "It is our hope that he will use his influence in the future to strengthen the moral fiber of our nation." In Reynolds's opinion, Willie Nelson had fallen short. The real reason Willie had been axed from the grand opening, Reynolds declared, was out of "concern for the health and well-being of the American people." Reynolds evidently did not mean Native American people or citizens whose town bank had failed.

The Baylor University president's statements rang hollow in the ears of the good people of Leroy, Texas. C. A. Anderson, president of the Leroy Bank depositors' association, was confused. "Their explanation didn't explain," he told the *Waco Tribune-Herald*. "It wasn't a reason at all. Usually Christians want to help each other. To sympathize with us and refuse to help in any way is another matter." Willie was just as confused. "I couldn't figure what the hell Baylor wanted me for to open their building," he said. "They didn't like me all that much before."

Willie resolved to apologize to policemen everywhere, playing a benefit in Springfield, Massachusetts, following the Rhode Island date and splitting proceeds between the American Indian Movement and the Policeman's Memorial Fund. He also raised money for Leroy Bank depositors at a separate concert at the Heart O' Texas Coliseum in Waco.

Willie understood why the police would be upset about him playing for Leonard Peltier. "I didn't intend to offend anybody," he said. "This was a benefit for an Indian in prison. It seemed like an okay thing to do. I didn't know what he'd been charged with [killing two FBI agents], but I don't think that would've mattered. A lot of people thought that he was innocent. That was reason enough to go do it." Willie telephoned William Sessions, the director of the Federal Bureau of Investigation, late in 1987, and attempted to explain himself to his fellow Texan. He ended up donating more money to police organizations and moved on.

"Willie went out on the road right after the Peltier benefit," Kris Kristofferson said. "And his base of crowd was pretty conservative. He took more heat than anyone did." Willie was used to being criticized for his convictions and celebrity. The University of Texas had denied Willie permission to perform during the opening ceremonies of the Special Olympics for disabled children on the UT campus five years before, citing Willie's potential for attracting "undesirables" to a family event, even though Special Olympics staff had extended an invitation specifically to Willie.

Usually, it was water off a duck's back to him. But sometimes Willie bit back. When the U.S. Forest Service held an auction for logging rights to two tracts of land in the Winema National Forest in southern Oregon that the service had designated Willy and Nelson, attorney Joel Katz fired off a nasty brief accusing the Forest Service of "desecrating invaluable cultural and burial sites and destroying pristine old-growth forests." The lumber sale went through but without Willie's name attached.

Lawsuits, protests, and divorces were distractions

from what mattered most—the music. It had been three years since his last number one single, "Living in the Promised Land," for Columbia Records, which had been bought by Sony Music. Although he had put out several fine recordings after *Half Nelson*—*Me and Paul, Partners, The Promised Land, Island in the Sea,* and *What a Wonderful World* that followed the smooth groove he found with *Stardust,* Willie wanted more, so he asked Fred Foster to produce *A Horse Called Music,* his thirty-first album for Columbia/CBS/Sony. "I Never Cared for You" and "Mr. Record Man" were resuscitated for the 1989 release and Willie wrote an incisive new song called "Is the Better Part Over?" But the producer brought the hit, a song written by rising Nashville talent Beth Nielsen Chapman.

"I ran into her in a parking lot and I told her I was looking for songs for Willie," Fred Foster said. Three songs were on his desk the following day, all solid and good but not Willie material, Fred related to her. She protested, "I think they're perfect for him."

"Tell you what," Fred said. "He's your favorite singer, right? Would you agree he's had an interesting life?" She nodded twice. "Go home, put yourself in his shoes, and write about that life."

The next day, he got a call from Beth's husband. "What did you do to my wife?" Ernest Nielsen wanted to know. "She's locked herself in her writing room and won't come out. If I get near the door she screams, 'Get away!'" Two mornings later, Beth called Fred herself. She had the song, although she told him, "You probably won't like it."

Fred liked it enough to see if Willie would like it. He would play it for him along with her other songs, as Beth requested. He flew to Texas and was driving around Willie World with Willie listening to music in the cassette player in his Mercedes where no one could bother them. Willie agreed the earlier songs she'd written were good, but not for him.

"That's what I tried to tell her," Fred said, pushing the cassette of the song she'd written for Willie into the player.

"I'll do this," Willie blurted one verse into the song. "Do you think she'd sing this with me?"

Beth Nielsen Chapman sang with Willie on the recording, his first number one country single in three years.

But he didn't have time to bask in any glory because he was already on to Farm Aid IV, staged in Indianapolis on April 4, 1990. The rock group Guns N' Roses was the buzz band among the sixty acts on the bill, but a child dying of AIDS named Ryan White stole the show when Elton John dedicated "Candle in the Wind" to him. Dwight Yoakum, Lou Reed, Bonnie Raitt, Don Henley, and Jackson Browne also performed in front of a gathering of forty-five thousand, helping raise $1.2 million for family farmers.

The Fourth of July Picnic that year moved to Austin's Zilker Park and starred the Highwaymen, with Billy Joe and Eddy Shaver as the opening acts, a lean bill that drew fifteen thousand fans who paid $7 advance and $9 at the gate. Twenty-eight thousand dollars were raised at the picnic for Carl's Corner, Willie's favorite truck stop, which had been damaged by an extensive fire.

The name brand was leading to more endorsements. He'd gotten sponsorship deals before, drinking all the Lone Star Beer the band and crew cared to drink, wearing all the New Balance shoes everyone needed, and drinking all the Jose Cuervo Gold tequila they could drink, meaning a case of the Mexican liquor was always on the bus. At the height of the *Urban Cowboy* craze, 575,000 pairs of Willie designer jeans were sold by Mr. Fine of Dallas. But the three-year $11 million agreement to be the spokesperson for Wrangler Jeans changed how the advertising world perceived him. The endorsement led to Arrow Shirt endorsements (Willie donated that fee to Farm Aid), television commercials for the Gap clothing stores, and a Super Bowl commercial for H&R Block tax consultants, uttering the priceless line "My face is burning, my face is burning!" when being shaved at the barber shop.

Not all branding came to pass, such as Willie's Chili, but he was always game to listen to another pitch. So was his Family. That was their nature because they were still gypsies at heart. After Willie scored his Wrangler deal, Paul made his own pitch to the sponsors in his gently persuasive way. There were twenty-two Family members besides Will, he reminded the Wrangler brass, and what was to stop them from all showing up at gigs wearing Levi's? Wouldn't it be better if they all wore Wranglers? "I got ten thousand dollars a year and all the Wranglers I could wear," Bee Spears crowed.

Then the good times quit rolling.

The Valley, 1991

AT HIGH NOON on a Wednesday, the next to the last day of January 1991, a crowd had gathered on the steps of the quaint Hays County Courthouse in San Marcos, twenty-nine miles south of Austin. They had come for an old-fashioned auction. Most were realtors, bankers, and speculators, many of whom had registered as buyers and carried cashier's checks in case they had a winning bid. There were also forty farmers, many of them members of the activist American Agriculture Movement, who had driven from across Texas and elsewhere in the United States and immediately made their presence known. The object of everyone's interest was the forty-four-acre ranch on Fitzhugh Road that belonged to Willie Nelson, a prime piece of property that would easily fetch more than the minimum asking bid of $203,840.

The farmers insisted that shouldn't happen. A cattle rancher and oats farmer named Sonya Brumbloe from Midlothian, one county north of Hill County, was one of the first to speak up: "Maggots, buzzards, things that would only eat off the dead, you don't prey on the wounded," she said disapprovingly, looking around herself. When the wife of a retired businessman from Austin told her Willie Nelson would benefit from her husband's buying his ranch, Brumbloe raged, "He's my friend, and you are spitting on him." Bob Thornton, a wheat and milo farmer from Anna, northeast of Dallas, said Willie was being persecuted by the Internal Revenue Service, just like Saddam Hussein was gassing hundreds of thousands of his own Iraqi people to tamp down unrest.

Before the bidding began, Wayne Cryts, a farmer from Missouri, addressed the gathering while IRS officials glowered in his direction. "The farmers who are here today have come to show our support of Willie Nelson," Cryts said. "He has stood up for American farmers and because of him he has given hope to hundreds of thousands of farmers and their families. Willie had raised money to feed farmers and their children, even when they lost everything they had and had nowhere to turn. We believe if the IRS will back off and give Willie Nelson a chance that he has the talent to raise the money he needs. This would be in the interest of all U.S. taxpayers and anyone who bids on his property."

A realtor who'd been prepared to pay twice the asking price turned to Bob Thornton and said, "I see what you are all trying to do." No way would he bid on the ranch after that speech. No way any of the other prospective buyers would either.

John Ahrens, an Arkansas attorney who specialized in helping farmers stay out of bankruptcy, offered the only bid, $203,840, the bare-ass minimum.

Ahrens explained to writer Bill Minutaglio that during the 1980s Willie was "the only voice to be heard that farmers are worth saving. He was so faithful standing with us when people were saying, 'Why the heck are you supporting them?,' saying that we should export the farmers and keep the grain. Willie Nelson gave us great hope there was at least somebody out there who cared. The decision makers who would never care were reminded of the problem. And he got involved in other things that most people don't, including congressional issues and legislation. We know how sad it is, how cold it is to be alone and not even your friends come to the auction of your home and land. We went, initially, with just the simple mission of standing there."

After the auction, the farmers drove out to Willie World on the Pedernales, where John Ahrens informed Willie the ranch had been bought for "safekeeping." Behind the scenes, Willie's business adviser, Mark Rothbaum, his attorney, Joel Katz, and Buddy Lee, the former wrestler and promoter once married to wrestling star the Fabulous Moolah, who was Willie's booking agent of record ("You could take his jobs to the bank," Paul English had said), were gathering funds to complete the transaction.

How Willie Nelson almost lost everything was quite a tale.

Two months before on one of those warm November days that made Central Texas feel close to perfect with the air temperature climbing into the 70s, Willie was indulging in a round of golf. His concert grosses had dropped off from $14.5 million in the tall cotton days to $3.3 million in 1990, but between the shows and records, he was making plenty. As long as he could play music and play golf, all was right in his world.

Play on the fairway was interrupted by a dozen IRS agents and federal marshals who materialized out of nowhere to greet him with the news, "You're under arrest." Willie calmly advised the buddies around him to refrain from inflicting physical harm on the lawmen. He led the revenuers to his clubhouse office, where he opened the safe for their inspection. Much to the agents' disappointment, the cupboard was bare. If there was a stash of cash, jewels, or valuables, it wasn't in the safe. He offered to show the agents the saloon in Luck, where all the bad art his fans gave him wound up on the walls, but the feds demurred. They wanted his Chagalls. Only Willie didn't have any Chagalls.

Their reaction suggested the IRS was convinced Willie and his gypsy pirates had ferreted away their treasure in secret, faraway places. Whether it was for the show of cameras they'd brought along or out of pure ignorance, when they found so little of precious value at Willie World, they carted off his framed gold record and platinum records, recording tapes from the studio, photographs from Lana's office, and his golf carts—anything the agents could put a price tag on—and padlocked the recording studio and pro shop. Other assets and holdings were seized in Hawaii, Washington state, California, and Alabama. The Willie Nelson General Store and Museum in Nashville, Tennessee, was chained until Frank and

Jeanie Oakley convinced tax agents they really were the owners.

The raid was the cherry on the top of a long, drawn-out pissing match between Willie and the feds. What began as a tax bill of $1.6 million, presented in October 1984 for the period between 1972 and 1978, and a second bill of $9.4 million for 1979 to 1983, had dropped to a charge of $6.5 million the previous May, when a U.S. tax court ordered Willie to pay up. But by the time of the raid five months later, penalties and interest had ballooned the debt to $16.7 million.

The initial $1.6 million tab tied to the latest go-round led Willie to file a lawsuit against Neil Reshen for $12.7 million for alleged mismanagement of his finances. Reshen countersued, and the case was settled out of court, with the court documents sealed.

"What happened, basically, in broad strokes, is that from 1974 to 1977, extensions were filed but no taxes were paid, so the IRS put a lien on Willie's properties," explained Mark Rothbaum. After Neil Reshen had been given his walking papers in 1978, Austin attorney Terry Bray introduced Willie to Dallas representatives of the Price Waterhouse accounting firm, which took over Willie's books.

While Willie was in the middle of a two-week engagement at Caesar's Palace in Las Vegas, Mark Rothbaum called a meeting with Willie and Paul and accountants from Price Waterhouse. A creative tax deferment revolving around forward contracts in federal mortgage securities with First Western Government Securities and a cattle-feeding operation in Texas was proposed. Similar shelters were being set up to reduce taxes of other clients in high tax brackets. Willie and Connie signed the agreement and for two years participated in the tax shelter.

Unfortunately, the cattle-feeding operation coincided with the collapse of Texas's economy and lost $1.6 million, and the IRS ultimately disallowed Willie's deductions for both ventures on his tax returns for 1980, 1981, and 1982, when tens of millions were pouring in.

"Price Waterhouse had given him two great investments where you put up the money and you get credited for investing something like fourteen times as much as you put in," said Neil Reshen, Willie's former manager. "It was a leverage deal. You put in $10,000 and get credited for investing $140,000. Willie got Price Waterhouse to get him in on two of these investment deals. The IRS disallowed those investments that were supposed to wipe out [taxes owed]. So Willie was suddenly down ten to twelve times what he had owed the IRS. You put in a couple hundred thousand dollars in what you think is a secure profit-sharing investment that's been recommended by the biggest accounting firm in the country, you have nothing to worry about until somebody kicks you out of bed and says you just lost all your money."

Willie's lawyers asked for more time for the $45 million lawsuit he'd filed earlier in 1990 against Price Waterhouse in Dallas, accusing them of recommending bad tax shelters, to go through the courts, but the clock ran out on the IRS's patience. "He never hired us as investment advisers," a spokesman for the Dallas office of Price Waterhouse curtly responded. They were just accountants.

The IRS had cited him almost every year since the late 1960s for failure to pay sufficient income and payroll taxes, although the debt never exceeded $8,000 and Willie always paid the bill. Early on, paying taxes had been theoretical, since his income was too small to tax. The IRS always let him know when he was making enough.

It was a rude awakening, at least for most people. On the surface, Willie seemed unruffled. He could have declared bankruptcy and made the problem far more manageable, but that would have been too easy.

Johnny Gimble sat next to Willie during a break while working a gig and asked, "This IRS thing. You worried?"

"Naw," Willie responded. "Are you?"

Gimble nodded somberly.

"I guess I should be too," said Willie.

But he wasn't. He was still trying to laugh it all off. He told the writer Bill Minutaglio, "I want everybody to know I'm all right. I still double-bogey a lot." He confided to Ed Bradley of CBS News that he was more worried about the IRS than he was about what he owed. "I wonder what kind of guy is running that place to let a guy like me get that far in debt."

Waylon viewed Willie's shrug-and-yawn reaction as the same ol' same ol'. "If anybody doesn't give a shit, it's him," Waylon said. "He's gonna be all right because he's an original free spirit." But almost $17 million?

"That's not a lot if you say it real fast," Willie told Waylon with a glint in his eye. He was circumspect about his situation. "There were enough reasons for them to come down on me," he said. "They needed headlines to put the fear of God in everybody."

On the other hand, Willie didn't need more trouble. He had plenty of hassles to deal with. He was divorced from Connie (ironically, Amy Irving had divorced Steven Spielberg in 1989 and received $100 million in the settlement). Their daughter Paula was in rehab. His first wife, Martha, had passed away, as had Connie's mother. Connie's brother was sick and dying from AIDS. No way was this irritant going to get to him.

Willie Nelson became the punch line for jokes told by comedians on late-night television as his troubles worked their way into the public eye. According to the hype, Willie's lavish lifestyle and white-trash ways had caught up with him. But he'd given up his Lear Jet long ago. "It was fun for a while, then it got old," he said. "It was very expensive. Then when I missed two dates because of the weather, I said this ain't working. Anything is better than flying. There's no security. You're flying into weather. At least if you're on the road, you can dodge the weather. But if you're in a plane on the runway in Austin and you've got a gig in Kansas City and the weather in Kansas City is not good, they won't let you leave Austin. You end up sitting in Austin and missing the gig in Kansas City. I don't blame the guys who fly wherever they want anytime. But if you're going to do one-nighters, it's not a good idea. If you hadn't ever had a plane and wanted one, you got one. And you realized it was like having a boat." There were always reasons to pour more money into it.

On the day Honeysuckle Rose rolled up to the IRS

regional office in Austin so Willie could begin negotiations with the taxing authority, he was besieged by
employees asking for autographs or for Willie to pose
for a photograph with them. On the second day of
negotiations, he was shunned. A memo had been
issued: No IRS employee was to speak to or request
an autograph from Willie Nelson while he was in the
building. On the third day, Willie arrived early,
stepped off the bus, and plopped down in a folding
chair outside the bus, where he read the newspaper
until employees drifted outside on their breaks to
hang with him in the parking lot.

The IRS held several auctions of seized property to
recoup some of the $16.7 million owed. The first auc-
tion in January was held at the former Pedernales
Country Club. The recording studio was sold to a
consortium headed by Willie's nephew Freddy
Fletcher. A friend from whom the band leased their
buses bought the studio's Bösendorfer piano for
$18,500 and gave it back. Willie's fishing camp just
down the road from the Pedernales Country Club
sold for $86,100. Frank and Jeanie Oakley, who ran
the Willie Nelson General Store in Nashville, bought
several framed gold records and some Indian head-
dresses for the souvenir shop and museum. No bid
for the golf course and the rest of the Pedernales
Country Club was high enough to be accepted.

Ex-wife Connie Nelson was allowed to keep the family ranch in Colorado. Willie managed to hold on to the home in Abbott where he was born, his vacation home on the Hawaii island of Maui, two buses, band equipment, some of the condos, and his beloved battered Martin guitar, Trigger.

Following the auction of his ranch in San Marcos, a third auction was held in March back at the golf course. Coach Darrell K Royal, with the backing of his business partner, Jim Bob Moffett, the developer of Barton Creek Resort and designated bad guy in Austin's environmental wars, purchased the country club and golf course for $117,350, only to have the IRS buy it back. Higher-ups at the IRS didn't like hearing Coach was holding it for Willie and refunded Coach's money plus 6 percent interest, insisting they belatedly received higher offers. The golf course and country club were sold again in May for $230,000, still well under the IRS minimum asking price of $575,478.16. The buyer this time was James Noryian of Investors International, an Austin investment group. Asked if he intended to sell the club back to Willie, as Coach said he'd intended to do, Noryian replied, "Absolutely not."

For eight months, band and crew were put on hold as his advisers tried to sift through the mess. For the first time ever, doubt crept into the Family.

But for a gambler wise to the fact that his luck should've run out a long time ago, Willie's reaction was succinct and shrewd. If he was broke, he vowed to do what he always did—play the clubs. He figured he could play every club he knew on the right side of I-35 from Laredo all the way to Canada, then turn around and head south, playing all the clubs on the other side of the highway for the rest of his life.

A partial solution to Willie's tax problems was being hatched by his lawyers and him. Twenty-five audio tracks that had been seized from Pedernales Studio were being assembled into a two-disc record album. The tracks, valued at $2 million, would be sold on television with all profits going straight to the IRS, compliments of its coproducer WN Music. The arrangement marked the first time the Internal Revenue Service partnered in a record deal.

"The whole thing was very unique and very complicated," Austin attorney Mike Tolleson explained. "Willie and Larry [Trader, the album's executive producer] called me to come out and talk about setting up a record company to handle sales of the recordings. [Producer] Bob Johnston wanted to be involved as the guy to pull out the old recordings for record release. There was need for mixing and mastering. There were questions about Sony's rights and ownership of the masters. There was the question of IRS's rights to the masters under their lien."

Nashville publicist Evelyn Shriver was hired to generate interest in the album. "Willie was in a very vulnerable position. People were throwing money at Willie onstage and he couldn't deal with that. He said, 'If people feel so strongly they want to help me, then let them buy this record and make this music for sale. That way they don't have to feel like they need to throw me tens and twenties.' That was the whole theory behind it."

Shriver observed that although Willie appeared unflappable on the outside, "I could tell it devastated him. His whole life was under scrutiny by the IRS."

IRS Tapes: Who'll Buy My Memories? released by Sony Special Products, was one of Willie's most profound artistic expressions on record. It was just him and his guitar, singing twenty-five of some of the saddest songs he'd ever written, beginning with the prophetic "Who'll Buy My Memories?" followed by "Jimmy's Road," his protest song about the senselessness of war (written twenty-one years earlier but timed perfectly with an ongoing war in Iraq). A string of classics followed—"I Still Can't Believe You're Gone," "Yesterday's Wine," "It's Not Supposed to Be That Way," "I'd Rather You Didn't Love Me," "Country

Willie," "Permanently Lonely," "Home Motel," "Lonely Mansion," "Summer of Roses/December Day," "Remember the Good Times," "Wake Me When It's Over," and the philosophical chestnut he wrote with Hank Cochran, "What Can You Do to Me Now?"

The recording was sparer than *Red Headed Stranger*. Of all the sessions he was involved in from 1981 to 1989, the one that became *The IRS Tapes* was engineer Bobby Arnold's favorite. "It was in December 1984 [when it was recorded] and Willie sat down in the studio with Coach Royal, Lana, Larry, and Jody, on this cold, cold day. It was just Willie, his voice, and his guitar. I'll never forget that. It was like a private concert.

"When it was released, Sony Records had to pay Willie a bunch of money for the recording and Willie gave it away to everybody who was involved in it. So out of nowhere I get a check for several thousand dollars right around the time we were having our first child. He said, 'This is money used to produce this album. You are the people who produced this album — here's your money.'"

Good-time Willie had the blues, and it showed on the album. He had the gift of writing words in lyrical rhyme set to melody in three-minute chunks that revealed his emotions. They were songs of hurting, pain, breaking up, and love lost, haunted memories of lonely nights on the Jacksboro and Hempstead highways, of struggling to stay one step ahead of whatever threatened to pull him down, of trying to please strangers in beer joints when headed nowhere but down while an angry wife and crying kids waited for him at home, if he managed to make it home.

The packaging was as spare as the music, in marked contrast to most "As sold on TV" albums. The cover was a photograph of Willie sporting a cowboy hat, white beard, and a smile, his long red tresses falling on an open jacket revealing a black high-neck T-shirt with white letters that spelled "Shit Happens."

He wrote a note in his loopy cursive script, little changed over the course of fifty years:

Thanks for adding these songs to your collection. These are all original songs from thru the years with just me and my guitar. I hope you enjoy them. Thanks again for being my fan and friend.

Love
Willie Nelson

On the opposite side of the centerfold, song titles were imposed on a black-and-white photograph of

Willie in jeans and boots, sitting down, leaning against a cedar post topped by a rusty bucket, looking pensive perhaps, but not necessarily worried.

On the back cover, the recordings were identified as coming from "The Willie Nelson/Internal Revenue Service Tape Library."

Mike Tolleson, a lawyer from the old Armadillo World Headquarters, had introduced Willie to the Television Group, a business with extensive experience in television production and time buys. TVG paid Willie (meaning the IRS) an advance to market the tapes, along with a second album, *The Hungry Years,* of Willie's earliest recordings. A telemarketing operation was set up in Nashville with a bank of operators to process credit cards, and a fulfillment center to process and ship orders. A television commercial was produced and legal clearances were negotiated.

Four months of saturation advertising on television, mostly late at night, generated sales of 160,000 copies, far short of the four million figure that was needed to erase Willie's debt. But Willie feigned hope. "You got to be positive," he said. "It's not unheard of. I could sell three million albums. I've done it before." The problem was *The IRS Tapes* wasn't *Stardust* or *Red Headed Stranger*. The album was eventually released through traditional distribution channels and retail stores. But the idea of salvation through album sales pretty much fell apart when the Television Group got into its own financial straits and declared bankruptcy.

"I spent many hours, days, and weeks dealing with the aftermath of that, including processing all the orders that had come in but were now in the pipeline waiting for fulfillment," attorney Mike Tolleson said. "There was inventory in Nashville, orders unfulfilled due to lack of payment to the fulfillment house, money tied up in bankruptcy, and Willie customers wanting their records. Meanwhile, the IRS wanted answers, and the TVG business had claims and creditors lining up." Eventually, customers either got their record or got their money back.

The album and the auctions of Willie's properties generated about $3.6 million, with Willie reportedly promising to pay another $5.4 million in the coming years, on top of the nearly $8 million he had already paid for the periods in question. A settlement with Price Waterhouse was reached out of the public eye. According to several sources, the balance Willie owed the feds was taken care of as one of the conditions of the settlement.

In spite of his relatively straightforward attempt to resolve his debt, a perception lingered that Willie was a tax dodger. "None of that was true," Mark Rothbaum said. "Willie had the option of bankruptcy and chose not to use it. He wasn't so much stubborn as honest, and he no more believed in setting aside his tax obligations than he did his personal bills. He wasn't going to choose to use that as an option. So we fought the hard fight, and it was very creative and stressful, and at the same time, it took up so much of our time that music was really all we had."

The debt was officially settled in 1993. Evelyn Shriver was on the conference call that made it official. "I'd ended up working with quite a few people in that department [at the IRS] and they were all crying. Those people loved Willie too. Everybody's heart broke for him in that situation. When it came to a resolution everybody could live with, they cried. They were happy because it was over."

"His stubbornness got him in trouble, but it also got him out of it," Willie's cohort Kinky Friedman believed. "He has made the point to me that one of the things he has prided himself in since he was a child was getting into trouble and then getting himself out of it. He's done it his whole fucking life, and this was trouble. He didn't do it the easy way and plead bankruptcy—he did it the cowboy way. But in the end, the IRS loved Willie."

The publicity the IRS received could not be quantified. Just as Willie once persuaded a generation of grown men in white belts and white shoes to grow their hair over their ears, try marijuana, and think like an outlaw, he was now a walking billboard reminding the public to pay their taxes on time. More than ten years after the fact, his tax troubles were still fodder for public commentary as New York hip-hopper Ludacris affirmed in his 2004 recording "Large Amounts," shouting out Willie's name as a warning not to mess with "that IRS man."

WILLIE had stayed on the recording track throughout his IRS troubles, issuing another Waylon collaboration, *Clean Shirt,* on Sony/Columbia in 1991, produced by Bob Montgomery. The album with songs such as "Old Age and Treachery," "Tryin' to Outrun the Wind," and "Two Old Sidewinders," felt like two men of a certain age looking back. The effort was cathartic with "I Could Write a Book About You," which pretty well summed up their brotherly dynamic.

Besides being the year that his material possessions were auctioned off, 1991 marked two other life-changing events.

On September 16 — Diez y Seis de Septiembre — a major Mexican holiday observed throughout Texas, Father Albert Achilles Taliaferro, the founder of St.

Alcuin Montessori School in Dallas, married Annie D'Angelo and Willie Nelson, an event marked by Annie clutching a pacifier rather than a bouquet at the altar and by a parade of paparazzi chasing the couple. The marriage made formal a relationship that had already given Annie and Willie two sons, Lukas Autry, born on Christmas Day 1989, named for Willie's cowboy hero Gene Autry ("Gene was one of the first people to hold Luke," Willie said proudly), and, the following year, Jacob Micah, named for the Sheriff Micah character in television's *The Rifleman* series.

Father Taliaferro was an Episcopal priest, an enlightened educator, and an instructor in the Rosicrucian mystical order, a group of believers dating from the sixteenth century who mixed Christianity with alchemy. Willie had listened to tape recordings of A. A. Taliaferro on his bus for years and considered him a wise man for teachings that centered around a favorite saying, "Don't just sit there and vibrate. Do something!" Father Taliaferro was instrumental in inspiring Annie to advocate on behalf of the Montessori system of education and provided spiritual advice to Willie during a very trying time in his life.

Three months later, on Christmas Day, at the old family homestead in Ridgetop, Tennessee, neighbor

Ronald Greer went to check on his friend Billy Nelson, who lived in a cabin back in the woods on the family land. Greer found him hanged with a cord.

Billy's suicide was a horrible end to a troubled life.

Ridgetop was the first place where Billy had felt at home as a boy, even if his mother was in Waco and his father was mostly on the road, leaving Shirley Nelson and his older sisters to raise him. Married once and having recorded a gospel album once, he insisted on being Billy Nelson, not Willie Hugh Nelson Jr. But Billy never emerged from his father's shadow. Try as he might, he was never able to be anyone other than his famous father's son. He had the sensitivity (and deep, soulful eyes) of his father, and his wild streak too—friends didn't call him Wild Bill for nothing—but those attributes never translated into a happy life.

Too often his father had had to bail him out of trouble. His condo at the Pedernales Country Club had been burned down as revenge for a dope deal gone sour, and when it was rebuilt, the $50,000 he was given to get back on his feet disappeared in a matter of weeks. He had been in and out of rehab. Billy had been hurting for money again that December. Because of his own tax problems, his father wasn't in a position to bail him out. Willie had visited Billy at Ridgetop, trying to get him to move back to Texas again, but Billy said he wanted to stay with his friends.

Willie Hugh Nelson Jr., thirty-three, was buried the Saturday after Christmas in 1991.

Afterwards, Willie Hugh Nelson Sr. headed to Hawaii to sort out the aftermath. But before he left, Frank Oakley, the proprietor of the Willie Nelson General Store, called and asked him about the New Year's Eve date he was scheduled to play in Branson, Missouri, as a preview show for the coming tourist season. Willie told Frank he'd call back in an hour. Ten minutes later he was on the line. "Let's go picking," Willie told Frank. "It's foolish for me to sit on a beach somewhere. I should get to working again. There's nothing I can do about what happened."

He played the New Year's Eve show in Branson but did not share his grief with the audience. He stuck around for two hours after the show, signing each and every autograph thrust in his direction.

Publicist Bonnie Garner attempted to ease the pain a few days later by explaining in a press release that Willie was a firm believer in reincarnation. But no words—nothing—could erase the deep sadness of a parent losing a child, regardless of the circumstances. In this case, the hurt seared deeper and was shared with precious few.

One was Coach Darrell K Royal. "Willie's more than an acquaintance," explained Coach. "He and I have been together in some pretty emotional situations. When I lost two of my children, Willie was right there. I tried to do the same after Billy. I never brought up the subject much. I just shook his hand and was there for him. But he knew why I was there, just like I knew why he'd come to my house [after the deaths of Coach's kids]. We've been together through some emotional times. That's the reason I like 'Healing Hands of Time' so much."

Billy had appeared troubled to others around Willie. "Anytime Willie was in Nashville, Billy was around," observed Evelyn Shriver. "But, you know, so often celebrities have such fucked-up kids, particularly musicians when they're on the road all the time. They have various lives, various family groups. Willie's family is his fans, his crew, those old guys he plays cards with. Bringing women into those situations is difficult. Who has withstood the test of time longer than the wives? His friends."

Asked several years later about his biggest disappointment in life, Willie replied, "Losing Billy." He retreated to the only comfort zone he knew, the stage.

When May rolled around, Willie began a 144-show, six-month engagement in Branson, Missouri (pop. 3,706), the tourist town in the Ozarks that had evolved into a new model for country music, where fans came to the artists instead of the artists going to the fans. More than twenty theaters operated in Branson, each featuring entertainers associated with country music, many who'd seen better days (Moe Bandy, Mickey Gilley), a few who historically operated on the periphery (Shoji Tabuchi, Boxcar Willie, Chisai Childs), with almost everyone packing the house twice a day with tour busloads of middle-aged, Middle American, middle-of-the-road country music fans.

Willie's one-man chamber of commerce welcome committee to Branson was Mel Tillis, the stuttering singer and songwriter who arrived in Nashville about the same time Willie did and who had a theater in Branson. Mel spoke of the theater glowingly when he visited Willie on the road, bringing along a bottle of tequila, an ounce of pot, and a mouthful of good bullshit. Over the course of the evening, Willie grew amenable to the idea of the Mel Tillis Theater becoming Willie Nelson's Ozark Theater, Gift Shop, and Museum, featuring Willie Nelson. (Mel was building a bigger theater for himself.)

Frank and Jeanie Oakley were enlisted to oversee the theater's merchandise while continuing to run the Willie Nelson General Store in Nashville. A good part of the museum that was in the back of the Willie Nelson General Store (including many items Frank purchased at the IRS auction) was moved to Branson.

Willie might have thought Branson was the solution to his heartache and his finances, but the minute he arrived for the extended engagement, he knew he'd made a mistake. He was used to moving. It was the natural state of life. "Everything else in the universe is moving," he said. "Why shouldn't we? Even the heart is moving the blood around. I just like to keep moving. It feels good to me." In Branson, he was playing a stage that never moved, just like the people who came to Branson. The town of theaters didn't much move either. Traffic was in a semipermanent state of gridlock, gummed up by congestion and road construction as the town boomed into a major RV and motor-coach destination.

"Branson at that time was being bandied about as the new Mecca of country music," publicist Evelyn Shriver said. "Mel talked him into it. He was making money hand over fist and you didn't have to travel. But Branson wasn't finished yet. Willie was living in a motel that wasn't finished. You couldn't figure out where the office was to find out who was in what room. You couldn't get out from the motel because roads weren't finished. The traffic was a nightmare.

It was like being in the middle of Fan Fair every day of your life. There was trash everywhere."

Willie insisted on doing it his way, refusing to take breaks like most Branson performers did, mainly so they could sell more merchandise. Most acts did forty-five-minute sets followed by hourlong autograph sessions. Willie did his typical two-hour shows, then signed autographs until there was no one left. Playing two shows a day without a break and staying to sign autographs meant long days and weary nights.

"[Branson] was a nightmare," Mickey Raphael said. "We were stuck in one spot. The traffic was horrible. Artistically it sucked. It didn't sell that well. You have to schedule the bus tours that come to Branson months in advance. That was the darkest period, just being stuck there."

"He signed that agreement with Mel Tillis without even calling Mark [Rothbaum, his business adviser]," Ray Benson said of the Branson mess. Mark wanted no part of it, but it was too late. "Branson became a subject I could not discuss with Willie," Mark Rothbaum explained. "The first real substantive conversation Willie and I had happened after I told Willie, 'If you are going to be there, enjoy the Ozarks,'" Mark said. "I bought him sleeping bags and a tent. Willie pitched the tent in his motel room and put the sleeping bags in the tent. When I went to visit him, the tent was set up in his motel room."

"What are you doing? Why don't you go camping?" Mark asked.

"You see this tent pitched here?" Willie said. "Next is a campfire."

Willie was not a happy camper. "Get me out of here," he begged Mark.

Willie may have been a sucker to take Mel Tillis's theater, but so was Merle Haggard, who bit on Willie's offer to play three days a week, so Willie cut back to four days a week, two shows a day, giving him more time to play golf or play benefits for H. Ross Perot, the feisty Dallas billionaire businessman who was running as a third-party candidate for president of the United States. "Crazy" was adopted as Perot's campaign theme song. As Ethan Smith of *Entertainment Weekly* noted, "The tune was meant to allude, facetiously, to the Establishment's view of the pint-size libertarian. The song actually reflected with uncanny accuracy on the wisdom of waging a $1 million-a-day, no-chance campaign out of sheer orneriness."

Willie was GTT the day his contract expired, his residency with Merle Haggard replaced by Loretta Lynn and Charley Pride. He didn't think twice. All he had to do was compare and contrast. Which was

it going to be? Farm Aid, which drew fifty thousand
fans to Texas Stadium in Irving, the home of the
Dallas Cowboys football team, in March to hear
Willie, Paul Simon, the Highwaymen, Lynyrd Sky-
nyrd, Little Village, Asleep at the Wheel, the Texas
Tornados, and Little Joe y La Familia? Or Shoji
Tabuchi, Boxcar Willie, Jim Stafford, Kenny Rogers,
Ray Stevens, Moe Bandy, and Andy Williams, each
in his own theater, two shows a day, forever and
ever?

Band and crew were champing at the bit. "We just
weren't geared for sitting still that long," roadie Kenny
Koepke said. "After Branson, everybody was so ready
for the road, no one was complaining about anything. It was real smooth after that."

One upside to Branson was the friendship he made
with theater owner Johnny Herrington. The former
and future mayor of Springhill, Louisiana, in the Piney
Woods of northwestern Louisiana, served as Willie's
proxy to buy back the Pedernales Country Club and
Golf Course. Herrington went with Willie to Austin
to negotiate with James Noryian, who'd bought the
course from the IRS, agreeing on a price of $350,000.
Willie promised to pay Herrington back within three
years. Noryian realized a tidy $120,000 profit for hold-
ing on to the property for less than a year.

Willie raised his higher-than-ever pot-smoking

profile when he was named cochair of the board of advisers to the National Organization for the Reform of Marijuana Laws.

His embrace of weed led him to Gatewood Galbraith, a Lexington, Kentucky, attorney running for governor in 1991 on a pro-pot platform. With a campaign that was so broke that his phones had been cut off, Galbraith had sent out a plea for funding via satellite television. "The next day, I was coming back from practicing law in eastern Kentucky and there was a note on the door of my office that said Willie Nelson was trying to get in touch with me."

Willie flew Gatewood down to Texas and put him up in Doc Simms's former residence in Abbott, and for three days the music guy and the gubernatorial candidate ran together. "We rode around Texas in his pickup truck, played poker with his poker-playing buddies, hit all the night spots," Gatewood said. He was awed by Willie's humility and by his cool. While riding along a fairway, Gatewood turned to him and said, "Willie, I appreciate you spending all this time with me. You're an international superstar, you could be hanging out with kings and queens and other superstars and you're spending all this time with me."

"Well, hell, Gatewood," Willie said with a smile. "You smoke pot, play golf, and like to look at women. Who else would I want to be spending time with?"

Willie did a Hemp Aid benefit concert for Galbraith in Louisville, posed with him for the cover of *High Times* magazine, and rode on the campaign trail in Galbraith's Hempmobile. "It was a stock Mercedes station wagon with a diesel engine in it," explained Gatewood. "Rudolf Diesel designed his patented engine to run on seed oil. I was one of the few people way back then who actually knew what hemp oil was. My campaign had gotten several hundred pounds of sterilized hemp seed from China. We took it up to a seed oil company and they distilled it using the hexane method, which creates some of the clearest, cleanest oil. We decided to illustrate it by driving across the state in a cavalcade of about two hundred cars. Later on, we got a freestanding diesel engine that we set up on a platform at our public meetings."

Gatewood Galbraith captured 5.3 percent of the vote in Kentucky's Democratic Party gubernatorial primary. When he ran again in 1995, he captured 9 percent of the vote in the primary. He ran for governor in the general election in 1999 on the Reform Party ticket and received 15 percent of the vote. Each time, Willie played benefits for him. In 2007, he ran again in the Kentucky Democratic Party primary, garnering 6 percent of the vote. It didn't matter if he won. Willie liked him for what he believed in. Plus, the publicity was good for them both.

"Willie brought a presence and strength of character and commitment to my campaigns," Gatewood said. "He's educable. The ability to stay young is the continuing ability to unlearn old lies. Willie puts his money and his being where his mouth is. It's doing what you think is right."

Willie cast his lot with marijuana in other ways, endorsing a new line of hemp clothes called the Willie Nelson Hemp Collection that was grown in China and made in Macao. But his hangs with Gatewood Galbraith left a deeper impression. Why stop at hemp oil? Why not grow all kinds of crops for fuel?

Or, in the meantime, smoke it?

In the early hours of May 10, 1994, after Willie had spent a night of poker with Carl Cornelius and friends in Hill County, two highway patrolmen shined their flashlight into a Mercedes pulled over to the side of the frontage road of Interstate 35 near Hewitt, just south of Waco. They saw a bearded man curled up in the backseat. Willie had been driving back to Austin when he decided to take a nap on the shoulder rather than fall asleep at the wheel. They patrolmen also discovered the remnants of a marijuana cigarette in the ashtray.

"What's that?" said the voice behind the flashlight.

"A joint," a very sleepy, very startled Willie replied.

"Any more in the vehicle?"

"Under the seat."

"You're under arrest for possession of marijuana. You have the right to remain silent . . ."

Willie Nelson was released from McLennan County Jail in Waco a few hours later on $500 bail. He faced six months in jail and a $2,000 fine if convicted of the Class B misdemeanor.

Months later, he passed up a chance to perform at the Grammy Awards to fight for his constitutional rights at a court hearing. Attorney Joseph Turner, a noted criminal defense lawyer in Austin, pointed out discrepancies in the two officers' versions of where the marijuana was found. During the search, police twice switched off a microphone that was part of the patrol car's video recording system. Willie told the court, "It is becoming apparent in this country that we are losing our rights one after another." County Court at Law Judge Mike Gassaway agreed that the police had had no business searching Willie's car. The evidence was thrown out and the case was dropped entirely.

Sergeant Mike Cooper, one of the arresting officers, had already been fired for sexual harassment in an unrelated incident. Willie claimed celebrity discrimination. "He was not a fan," he said of the arresting officer. "I do think that once he found out who I was, he thought this might be good for his career."

Four months after the case was dismissed, Willie played a dance for a Sheriff's Association of Texas training conference in Waco. McLennan County sheriff Jack Harwell, a longtime friend and occasional golfing pal, vouched for Willie's credibility and his upstanding role in the community. "Anything that Mr. Nelson tells me, I'd believe," the sheriff said. "I'd go to the bank on it."

Willie felt the same way about the sheriff and his colleagues. But he took the opportunity to call for the legalization of marijuana. "I think it should be taxed and regulated like your cigarettes," he declared after the bust went away. If he was worried about being harassed, he didn't show it.

Willie had spent most of his adult life banishing worry, negativity, and bad vibes from his thinking. Worrying was a Waylon thing, as publicist Evelyn Shriver learned the hard way shortly after she'd been hired to represent the Highwaymen. Cash, Kris, Waylon, and Willie had managed to sell enough albums and tickets to stretch the concept to three albums and several tours over a ten-year span, even if it wasn't always peace and love between them.

Waylon wanted to fire Evelyn because she was from Willie's camp. She didn't take it personally. "He was pissed off about everything—the business, country music, not being on the radio," she said. "Waylon's legend will certainly outlive him being an asshole, but he was not the larger-than-life figure that Willie was when he didn't live here. Waylon was in town and around the business. He should have left earlier and then it would have been okay."

Evelyn knew Waylon and Willie's history: Waylon was the groundbreaker who fought to use his own band when Willie was wearing a tie and a suit and trying to do it the Nashville way. It was Waylon who ranted and raved about taking control of his own career. But that was a long time ago.

"Waylon was bitter about the fact Willie's star eclipsed everybody because of the movies," she said. "Willie became somebody everybody knew more because of TV appearances with Julio Iglesias than from 'Whiskey River.' ["To All The Girls I've Loved Before" was sung on *The Tonight Show,* starring Johnny Carson, three times in three years.] If you were outside country music, you didn't know 'Whiskey River.' You would see this when the Highwaymen would tour in Australia, Japan, or Europe," she said. "Everybody knows the Man in Black, everybody knows the guy with braids. Kris was a movie star. They thought Waylon was the roadie. His music wasn't international. His stardom wasn't international. Waylon resented everybody. There was big jealousy over Willie from Waylon, truthfully. When that second Highwaymen project came about, Capitol hired me. Waylon wrote them a letter saying he didn't want me hired because I was biased towards Willie. They wrote him back saying I was hired. I was copied on all these letters and I felt awful.

"I didn't know Waylon well," she said. "We were doing something at the Opry House in Austin, so I got Waylon to go into one of those tiny dressing rooms and he's just towering above me in all that black leather. I said, 'Waylon, I know you're not happy about me being hired.' He said, 'No. It's not you. I think the world of you. It's that goddamn Mark [Rothbaum, who was still Willie's manager after he and Waylon had parted ways]. He's always fixing things to favor Willie, putting everything off balance.'

"Forget Mark," Evelyn told Waylon. "Do you think Willie would let me push things for him over you, or Johnny Cash or Kristofferson? Don't you think Willie would fire my ass in a second if I shortchanged any of you to slant things for him?"

Waylon knew Willie well enough to know that that was true. He was okay with Evelyn after that.

The New World, 1993

BEING INDUCTED into the Country Music Hall of Fame usually meant either the best days of your career were behind you or you were dead. Willie was gracious in accepting the honor bestowed him in 1993 but didn't spend much time looking back. Nostalgia was for other people. He had more music to make.

Mark Rothbaum had approached record producer Don Was in search of someone who could orchestrate an album for Willie that would do what the song "Don't Give Up" did for Kate Bush and what the album *So* did for British rocker Peter Gabriel — reenergize their careers. Willie had already worked with Was. While touring with the Highwaymen in Europe, Sony asked Willie to do Elvis's "Blue Hawaii" for the film *Honeymoon in Vegas*. Don Was flew to

Dublin, where he recorded the song with Reggie Young and the Highwaymen band backing Willie up. Don Was also recorded Willie singing "Across the Borderline," a song written by John Hiatt, Ry Cooder, and Jim Dickinson, on which Kris Kristofferson sang the backing vocals. The two recordings were the seed of *Across the Borderline,* an album where Bob Dylan sang with Willie on "Heartland," the song they'd written together, Paul Simon produced the track "Graceland" and played lead on "American Tune"—songs that Simon had written—and Sinéad O'Connor sang Kate Bush's part on "Don't Give Up."

The collaborations worked. *Across the Borderline* was the first Willie Nelson album to enter the pop album charts since 1985, largely on the legs of "Still Is Still Moving," an updated, more ethereal version of "On the Road Again," which became another Willie theme.

The album also marked the end of Willie's eighteen-year association with Columbia/CBS/Sony. Sales had diminished since the glory days spanning *Red Headed Stranger* to *Always on My Mind,* dropping from millions of units to hundreds of thousands to even tens of thousands for some albums. A new management team had been installed in the Sony Nashville office in 1994. Sony Nashville president

Roy Wunsch, who had told Mark Rothbaum in no uncertain terms he was going to pick up the option and re-sign Willie, was fired. Allen Butler, Wunsch's replacement, dropped Willie and several other legacy artists from the label's roster.

Willie greeted the news with a shrug and a yawn. He was never shy about his willingness to record whenever he had the itch. He had a studio. He needed a label less than a label needed him. After his release from Sony, he recorded the album *Six Hours at Pedernales* with Curtis Potter, his friend from Hank Thompson's Brazos Valley Boys, who'd run with him in Vegas in the early 1960s, for the small independent Stop One Records. "Turn Me Loose and Let Me Swing" from the album was a number one video on CMT cable television for three weeks in 1995.

During the same period, he recorded a session with his friend Rattlesnake Annie, appeared on a recording by San Antonio swing fiddler J. R. "Chat the Cat" Chatwell, and cameoed with German country singer Tom Astor on his album *Meilen Steine* with the song "Two Stories Wide." He offered up his version of "What a Wonderful World" for the *Put On Your Green Shoes* all-star album dedicated to healing the planet. He added swinging vocals and guitar to the avant-garde versions of Hank Williams's "I'm So Lonesome I Could Cry" and the Eddy Arnold standard "I'm Sending You a Big Bouquet of Roses" inter-preted by Blue Note jazz trumpeter Jack Walrath for Walrath's *Master of Suspense* album. And he engaged in a mellow exercise in crooning titled "Augusta" with his longtime friend Don Cherry, the Singing Golfer from Wichita Falls made rich by writing the Mr. Clean jingle. Officially, he was touring behind an album released under his own name, *Healing Hands of Time,* a countrypolitan collection of his ballads backed by a lush string section, which was his first album for his new label, Liberty Records, for whom he had recorded thirty years before. The album cover, a photograph of Willie dressed for the occa-sion in a tuxedo, was telling. The outlaw outsider had come full circle and was dressing like he did when he was recording for RCA in the 1960s.

He promoted a creatively marketed box set of three unreleased albums. One was *Sugar Moon,* an album of swing classics and pop standards made with Freddy Powers, Merle's onetime songwriting partner, and Merle's band the Strangers, notable for covers of Louis Armstrong's "Struttin' with Some Barbecue" and "Rosetta," the Earl "Fatha" Hines swing compo-sition popularized by Bob Wills and His Texas Play-boys. He had also recorded a tribute album to Hank Williams with Larry Butler, the singer and guitarist who took him in at the Esquire Ballroom in Houston almost forty years before, and Jimmy Day, who played steel guitar and was well versed in "snap rhythm," the sonic technique that kept the beat because Hank didn't use drums. Also in the set was the unreleased 1974 live album recorded at the Texas Opry House for Atlantic Records, plus outtakes from the *Shotgun Willie* sessions in New York in 1973.

The compilation was put together by Rhino Records and sold on the QVC Home Shopping Channel in 1993. A year later, it was rereleased by Rhino in stores as *A Classic and Unreleased Collection*.

Willie toured Australia, New Zealand, Singapore, and China with the Highwaymen and performed by himself in front of forty thousand at the 1996 edition of Farm Aid in Williams-Brice Stadium in Columbia, South Carolina, while touring around the country in his new forty-five-foot Prevost bus, Honeysuckle III. Slow ticket sales the following year forced Farm Aid, now an annual affair held in different locations across the country, to relocate from Dallas to suburban Tinley Park near Chicago three weeks before the event. He'd been at it long enough to know it was no big deal. Not every benefit was going to raise $1 million. Not every show could be a sellout. Not every record was destined to go gold.

• • •

IN a stroke of good timing, Randall Jamail, the son of Willie's Houston lawyer friend Joe Jamail, started his own record company shortly after Willie was dropped by Sony. Two of Justice Records' first signings were Willie Nelson and Waylon Jennings.

The Justice Records deal allowed Willie to continue a second recording career, working with Kimmie Rhodes, the country singer-songwriter-author-playwright who lived down the road from the Hill. They met through Willie's daughter Lana, who'd given her dad a demo tape of Kimmie's song "I Just Drove By."

Kimmie had been helping Lana and Jody Fischer, Willie's office assistant, organize a celebrity golf tournament, when Coach Royal drove up in a golf cart. "He comes scooting up, saying someone had played the song for Willie, and how everyone crowded around him had tears in their eyes," Kimmie said. "Coach liked my song too."

Willie liked her band too, since Kimmie was using Bucky Meadows, David Zettner, and Freddy Fletcher—Willie's "south of the big-time players," as she called the musicians who occasionally showed up on Willie's albums.

One afternoon, Kimmie went searching for Billy

Joe Shaver at the Pedernales studio. "He was going to play me this song," Kimmie said. "We were sitting in the back part of the studio off the kitchen. We were encouraged to hang out in those days. Willie liked people being around. Billy Joe played me a song and I played him a song. We ended up playing songs when Willie walked in and said to me, 'Play me that song of yours.' I played 'I Just Drove By' for him."

"Play another one," he requested.

She played him "Just One Love."

"Well, let's just go in there and record those right now," Willie said without hesitation.

Kimmie's eyes got big as she followed Willie into the studio. "There was this humongous session going on with Grady Martin, Buddy Emmons, Jody Payne, Ray Edenton, Pete Wade, Chip Young, Bobbie Nelson, Mike Leach, Buddy Harman, Freddy Fletcher, Grandpa Jones (Willie's old neighbor from Ridgetop, Tennessee) on banjo, and Grandpa's daughter Lisa Jones on hammered dulcimer. They had a session going and they'd been on dinner break. I ended up spending the whole week with Willie doing background vocals."

"I loved doing 'Four Walls,' " Kimmie said. "We played it over a speaker instead of using headphones and stood in front of a microphone and sang. We decided neither of us liked headphones. We were doing harmonies on the chords. I'd sung with him before live, but it was the first time I'd recorded it with him.

"We'd work all night. Sometimes Willie would go off. For a couple nights, when Willie wasn't around, Grady would get Willie's guitar Trigger and go in and redo some of the solos. Grady had been like a three-year-old, parading around with Willie's guitar, holding it up, yelling, 'The damn thing's playing itself!' It was sounding so amazing. We were ready to pack up and leave [the second night], when Willie came back in about three in the morning. Willie heard Grady had played all these solos, taking Willie's solos off, so when Grady left, Willie went back in and rerecorded the solos. He ended up leaving some of Grady's solos on there.

"We mixed it and sequenced it. Willie kept writing on his pad and drawing while we were listening to the playback. Grady and I were dancing to the playback. All of a sudden, Willie whirled around in the chair and said, 'I think this should be the title cut.' He'd drawn a cover that said 'Just One Love' and drawn a little record on it that read 'by Kimmie Rhodes and Willie Nelson.' It was something like a kid would do.

"He's the easiest person I've ever worked with,"

Kimmie said. "I'm a real natural harmony singer and so is he. You don't find that a lot. We have the same gospel background. The church is where we learned music. I was a child singer in a gospel band with my father and my brother. He's the same animal.

"In the studio, he'd ask, 'What do you think?' meaning 'How was it?' We were just people having a lot of fun making music together for the first time. He's not real anal in the studio. He doesn't take it to a realm of getting nit-picky or what we call fly-fucking. He's not a fly-fucker. He just makes music. Willie likes to play music more than any musician I have ever known in my life."

"Just One Love," produced by Grady Martin and released on Justice Records, was the first of more than one hundred tracks Kimmie recorded with Willie. He could survive outside the mainstream again, take on a permanent duet partner, or do anything he wanted to do in the confines of the studio. Making music remained the driving force.

He continued making albums for mainstream record companies too, most notably the atmospheric *Teatro,* released by Island Records in 1998. Producer Daniel Lanois put a vaguely flamenco, drum-heavy twist to the album, recorded over four days in a Mexican movie theater with Emmylou Harris. Along the way, he harmonized with the Beach Boys on their 1996 release *Stars and Stripes Vol. 1,* singing a cover of their 1964 ballad "The Warmth of the Sun."

THE CORE band and core family tightened around him. Only the strong had survived, and it felt better than good. Bobby "Flaco" Lemons signed on with Willie's crew in 1996, joining Poodie, Tunin' Tom, Kenny Koepke, and the rest of a gang of familiars he'd known in Austin since the time he did sound for Plum Nelly, one of the most promising progressive-country acts circulating around Austin when Willie hit town. Flaco had been working for Jerry Jeff Walker, who'd hired him at the fourth Willie Nelson Fourth of July Picnic in Gonzales; at one time, Jerry Jeff was living in his car in Flaco's front yard. After Jerry's wife, Susan, took over his career and had it running like a well-oiled machine, Flaco moved on to do sound for Joe Ely, Darden Smith, Jimmie Dale Gilmore, and Rosie Flores, and spent three years doing time for smuggling marijuana, before walking into his best gig yet — running the soundboard for Willie. "It was supposed to be for three days, which turned into ten days, and then turned into 'See if we can keep this guy,' " Flaco said two thousand gigs later.

Jimmy Day returned to the outer orbit of the family inner circle after an extended exile, showing up backstage at a Willie Nelson performance at Bass Concert Hall on the University of Texas campus in Austin. Paul welcomed Jimmy back by hugging his neck without breaking it, prompting tears of gratitude from Jimmy, although Paul he was still pissed at Jimmy for insulting him after his wife, Carlene, killed herself. Willie suggested Jimmy take the stage alone and play one of his surefire showstoppers, "Greensleeves." Half the hall, it seemed, was crying along with him. Willie took a tolerant view of Jimmy Day. "You had to take him as he was, accept him as he was, and hope he was better than the last time you saw him," he said. "And sometimes he was."

By the dawn of the first decade of the twenty-first century, Austin had grown into a city of more than half a million inhabitants and another half million residing beyond its city limits. It was known as a Creative City, one of the few cities its size that continued to attract young, educated people from around the world to seek their fortune. The appeal was largely attributed to dozens of small design shops devoted to computer gaming and graphics and several giant-size computer companies, including Freescale Semiconductor, Advanced Micro Devices, Motorola, Samsung, IBM, and the homegrown Dell Computers.

Instead of practicing in garages and recording for small independent labels, young people were pulling twenty-hour shifts creating software and video games. But Austin's high-tech community would not have flourished without Austin's alternative scene, which was as much a magnet as the companies themselves.

The city council declared Austin "The Live Music Capital of the World" based on the vibrant club scene that Willie helped jump-start, and it posted signs on the jetways and played Austin artists on the sound system at the airport to remind arrivals this wasn't Dallas.

A healthy film community grew out of the Austin Film Society at the University of Texas and the work of three young directors—Rick Linklater, who blazed the trail with his 1991 slice of low-motivation Bohemian Austin, *Slacker,* and captured stoner culture in *Dazed and Confused;* Robert Rodriguez, whose *El Mariachi* artsy shoot-'em-up was filmed in the border town of Ciudad Acuña, Coahuila, across the Rio Grande from Del Rio, Texas, for less than $7,000 and launched a career in gore films (*From Dusk till Dawn* and *Sin City*) and kids' movies (the *Spy Kids* franchise); and Mike Judge, a bass player from a Dallas blues band who created two twisted and stupid cartoon characters called Beavis and Butt-Head for MTV before making the geek cult film *Office Space* and launching the animated Fox TV series *King of the Hill,* celebrating modern Texas redneck suburbia. A study commissioned by the city pegged the economic impact of film and visual media on Austin at $359 million annually. Music's impact was almost twice that, worth $660 million a year.

Alternative Austin went mainstream. Whole Foods Market, a natural grocery chain founded by three small organic-food-store owners shortly after *Red Headed Stranger* charted, had grown into the world's-largest retailer of natural and organic food, with more than two hundred stores across the United States and the United Kingdom. Austin being Austin, competition sprang up in the form of HEB Central Market, an upscale supersize gourmet market emphasizing natural foods that was an offshoot of the San Antonio–based HEB grocery chain, arguably the finest regional chain of supermarkets in the nation.

Prosperity came at a price. A good part of Austin's funky, earthy charm had been bulldozed to make way for progress. Real estate was the priciest in Texas. The city's crown jewel, Barton Springs, still attracted several hundred thousand locals and visitors with its clear, cool, 68-degree water, but its water quality had been degraded by pollution tied to development upstream. Where the Broken Spoke, the honky-tonk on South Lamar, once marked the southern edge of town, urban sprawl extended twenty-five miles, all the way out to Willie World on the Pedernales. At the same time, the Spoke was now regarded as a historic treasure. Owner James White, who erected a new exterior roof at considerable expense to keep the rain off the existing low ceiling without compromising the earthy ambience, opened a small museum and "tourist trap" in the club, while reminding visitors the club had the best chicken-fried steaks in South Austin but didn't serve no "Pierre" water.

By 2001, *Austin City Limits* had aired nationally on the Public Broadcasting System for twenty-five years, becoming the longest-running music series on television by featuring a mix of Austin-based and national roots–oriented music acts. The companion *Austin City Limits* music festival would be first staged in the fall of 2002 in Austin's Zilker Park, showcasing the kind of music aired on the television series and attracting close to seventy-five thousand fans every September.

The biggest made-in-Austin alternative creation was the South by Southwest music, film, and interactive conferences staged over ten days every March since 1987. By 2001, SXSW, which began as an "outsiders as insiders" music conference for those who had been shut out of the music industry, had blossomed into the largest music convention in the world, drawing industry people from more than forty countries, as well as movie, high-tech, and alternative-media types. Still, the conference remained faithful to the same sensibilities that brought Willie Nelson to Austin by presenting more than two thousand bands and solo acts in Austin's clubs and music venues over five days and nights.

At the beginning of the new millennium, Willie's friend Ann Richards was the most famous ex-governor in Texas, if not the country. The current governor, the Connecticut-born George W. Bush, was running for president of the United States as a Texan, following in the footsteps of his father, George H. W. Bush.

And Willie was pretty much the same old guy that Waylon had described years ago. "He'll give you everything, say yes to anybody, and trust events will turn out fine." For all the hurt, emotional scars, and financial challenges he had endured, he hadn't changed that much. More often than not, his instincts had proved right. What Willie started almost thirty years earlier when he walked onto the stage of the Armadillo World Headquarters and introduced himself was still in play.

At the request of his daughter Amy, Willie and

David Zettner ushered in the new century by making a record of children's songs in the little studio that Willie had built in the back of the Luck World Headquarters saloon. As a child, Amy Nelson had loved Kermit the Frog's song "Rainbow Connection." As an adult, she suggested to her father that he record it. The song had been written by pop songwriter Paul Williams as a protest anthem directed at the South African government's apartheid system of racial segregation. But when Kermit the Frog, the star puppet character in *The Muppet Movie,* recorded a version of "Rainbow Connection" as an anti-anti-amphibian piece, the meaning expanded to include all forms of discrimination.

Willie finally got around to recording "Rainbow Connection" with David while Amy was visiting Pedernales from her home in Nashville. The result was so pleasing that they figured, why stop with one song? Willie played guitar and sang. David played rhythm guitar, pedal steel, and bass. Matt Hubbard, a computer-savvy in-law married to Lana's daughter who had been hanging at Luck, contributed bongos, harmonica, and keyboards, and scored engineering and production credit, even though it was a Willie and David collaboration and Amy's idea.

As they fiddle-farted their way through "Ol' Blue," "Won't You Ride in My Little Red Wagon?" "I'm

Looking over a Four-Leaf Clover," and the Lonzo and Oscar classic "I'm My Own Grandpa," Gabe Rhodes, a neighbor with his own recording studio and a part-time picking partner of David's, dropped by to add more guitar. Amy, who was forming the irreverent duo Folk Uke (semi-hit single: "Shit Makes the Flowers Grow") with Arlo Guthrie's daughter Cathie, added her vocals.

The children's album veered into adult territory when they recorded "Playin' Dominos and Shootin' Dice," about a "guitar picker [who] lived a life of wine and liquor," written by the 1950s rockabilly Ramblin' Jimmie Dolan; Mickey Newbury's 1960s slice of psychedelia popularized by Kenny Rogers and the First Edition called "Just Dropped In (to See What Condition My Condition Was In)"; and "The Thirty-third of August," a stark, contemplative self-examination of one person's life that could've been an outtake from *Yesterday's Wine*.

Surreal material aside (care for some windowpane acid, kids?), Willie and David intentionally underproduced *Rainbow Connection,* letting their musicianship and deep familiarity with each other carry the recordings. Making a cool album on his terms with one of his favorite playing partners was just as satisfying as, or even more satisfying than, a Don Was or Daniel Lanois production. The tab for the album was less than what *Red Headed Stranger* cost. They sold it to Island Music for $500,000, with Willie splitting the proceeds with David Zettner, Matt Hubbard, and Amy Nelson.

THE NEW century was treating Willie all right. "Crazy" was voted the Number One Jukebox Single of All Time, according to National Public Radio; *Johnny Bush Sings Bob Wills,* one of the tapes confiscated by the IRS back in 1990, was finally released as an album by the Texas Music Group; and Willie earned his black belt in tae kwon do from Master Oh, his instructor in Austin.

And married life was suiting him just fine. Annie D'Angelo Nelson, mother of Lukas and Micah, became her husband's right-hand man and was instrumental in founding the Tierra Vista Montessori School of Spicewood in 1995, for which Willie donated twenty acres of Pedernales land and played several benefits. She loved the peace and quiet of the cabin on the Hill, which had been expanded considerably since her arrival, and seeing the Pedernales River winding through Hill Country at sunrise and sunset.

Her direct, outspoken manner ("my Sicilian shows sometimes," she admitted) earned her the reputation as a hard-ass. On their first encounter, she turned off business manager Mark Rothbaum by dissing the venue Willie was playing in New York, the same room Bruce Springsteen and Neil Young had recently worked. "Have you ever been there?" Mark asked her. "I've been told about it," she replied.

Annie's abrasiveness put the old guard around Luck, Texas, and Pedernales Studio on notice. As Willie's wife, she was in charge, not them. Hell on wheels, she would send sidemen, sidekicks, running buddies, and golfing pals scurrying whenever she showed up. Willie World regulars had a code for Annie:

"When you see the White Rover, you know the party is over."

But Willie loved her, and since Willie was the reason everyone was there, she was tolerated as part of the package, even if she could kill a buzz without saying a word. And the ol' boys liked her a whole lot more when she moved with Lukas and Micah to the Hawaiian island of Maui to get away from Willie World, just as Connie had fled the ranch on Fitzhugh Road with their girls for Colorado.

The permanent move was good for all parties concerned. "The boys needed to be in school more full-time," Annie said. "We decided on Maui because it is a place where it really doesn't matter who you are or what you do as long as you contribute like family and respect the host culture." Whenever Willie had a hankering to be with family, he had an island paradise to go home to. Maybe it was all those years with Jimmy Day and his florid steel guitar or the fact that Kris Kristofferson had discovered Maui in the early 1970s and lived there permanently, but Hawaii spoke to him. His chosen path limited time spent on Maui to two or three months over the course of a year. Despite a history of broken marriages and scattered offspring, blood family still gave Willie the greatest comfort outside of music—all members of his family, ex-wives included.

That much was evident in a corner booth of the Saxon Pub in Austin one Sunday afternoon before Christmas in 2006. He'd driven in overnight from Shreveport, Louisiana, where he'd been making a *Dukes of Hazzard* movie with Jessica Simpson, and before that he'd been in Nashville, where he'd recorded with contemporary-country heartthrob Kenny Chesney. He'd come to the Saxon to hear his daughter Paula Carlene, who'd moved back to Texas and was fronting her own band. Mentored by a number of independent music people in Austin, including blues impresario Clifford Antone and singers Lou Ann Barton, Marcia Ball, and Toni Price, Paula Nelson had released an album of her own songs. In one called "Alone," she wished she could have her dad alone to herself just once. "He belongs to the world and it's hard to share with the world," Paula explained. "That's where the song came from. It used to hurt my feelings at the world that I couldn't be with him and have him to myself."

The back booths of the club doubled for a family reunion setting as Susie, Amy, Lana, and ex-wife Connie visited with Willie and caught up with one another. When Willie took the stage to join Paula, the packed club went wild, like it usually did, and the band kicked into overdrive.

Playing music with his kids was a special pleasure. Willie had joined Susie in the studio on her sole recording, a single titled "Once upon a Time" for Delta Records, a small independent label based in Nacogdoches, Texas. His teenage sons, Lukas and Micah, were now eighteen and seventeen, old enough and capable enough to tour with the Family Band, playing guitar and percussion respectively, beginning in the summer of 2004, when they jammed with Billy Gibbons of ZZ Top on the stage of the Greek Theatre in Los Angeles. The boys moved from being part of a Hawaiian reggae jam band called the Harmonic Tribe to becoming half of a four-piece rock band named 40 Points, which was the first signing to a new version of Pedernales Records that Willie had formed in partnership with Nashville record producer James Stroud, his financial manager Mark Roth-baum, and his nephew Freddy Fletcher of Pedernales Studio. But the boys didn't need a manager. Their mother would look out for their interests.

Ever since the IRS troubles, recording at Peder-nales Studio was no longer a spur-of-the-moment matter. Freddy Fletcher ran Pedernales Studio as a business and sold block time to outside acts, mean-ing Uncle Willie no longer had unfettered access to record whenever the urge struck. So he asked Joe Gracey to build him a small studio in the pantry in the back of the Luck World Headquarters. The saloon was still Willie's official hangout and his designated setting for doing interviews, tapings, or formal visit-ing. Its walls were plastered with Willie photographs, posters, and other memorabilia. Willie played bar-keep, cooking breakfast or serving up drinks while doing interviews. Tables with chessboards and check-erboards were strategically placed in the middle of the room. Upstairs was a gym with speed bags, punching bags, and kickboxing gear.

Music broke out in the Luck headquarters at the drop of a hat. All that had been missing was a means to capture it. Joe Gracey heard Willie loud and clear. "He wanted a place he could just walk into and jam with all the musicians he cared to have in that one little room, and record it all," he said. Digital technology conveniently converged with Willie's yearnings. Gracey put together a system with eight inputs, eight preamps, and eight microphones rigged into a Macintosh computer, along with various pieces of hardware and software. Within a matter of days, Willie was sitting on a stool in front of a microphone in a room with wood walls and a high ceiling, singing "One Day at a Time," a reflective gospel song with secular appeal.

"He can go in there and record anytime he wants," Gracey said. "It's spontaneous. He's sitting down there picking anyway. He can just record what he's doing now. He's got his chessboard to play chess with Coach Royal, the bar, kitchen, cappuccino machine, the big giant-screen TV, the woodstove. And next to it is the recording-studio room, where some days he'll cut a hit and some days all someone will do is add another Zig-Zag pack to the wall. It's Willie's clubhouse."

Joe Gracey engineered *Picture in a Frame,* the 2003 album of duets with Willie and Kimmie Rhodes, released on Kimmie's Sunbird Records label, in the Luck saloon studio with Willie, David Zettner on an upright bass, and Gabe Rhodes on guitar. "We didn't need to go to Pedernales and do all that," Joe said.

"While some artists are singers only, and some

bands have a sound but no idea how to record it, Willie seems to plan it all out, knowing what he wants before going in," Joe Gracey said. "He understands the old-style producer situation, but he doesn't need guidance. I've seen him be more flexible than you would expect, like he was at those Fred Foster sessions when he recorded *Horse Called Music*. Fred did all the tracks and Willie just sang over them."

Gracey brought out the polkaholic in Willie, which he'd hinted at when he did "Beer Barrel Polka" on the *Tougher Than Leather* album in 1983. With Gracey at the controls, Willie joined polka legend Jimmy Sturr through the miracle of electronic recording, adding his vocals to "Just Because," "On the Road Again," "Yellow Rose of Texas," and "Waltz Across Texas" for Sturr's *Gone Polka* album; "All Night Long," "Tavern in the Town," and "Big Ball's in Cowtown" for Sturr's *Polka! All Night Long* album; "Blueberry Hill," "Unchained Melody," and "I Walk the Line" for Sturr's *Shake, Rattle and Polka!* album; and "Since I Met You Baby," "Singin' the Blues," and "Bye Bye Love" on Sturr's *Rock 'N Polka* album.

"He reminds me of ET," Joe Gracey said of Willie, invoking Ernest Tubb. "They have the same work ethic and they just get out there and play." Willie also followed ET's lead in his desire to help others out once he was in a position to do so. Gracey observed the respect and deference Willie showed to Ray Price when they recorded the Grammy-nominated *Run That by Me One More Time* album. "Willie assumed the role of session leader, but they'd work it out together." There was little planning or preproduction, and a whole lot of "Let's try this" and "Remember this one?" That project took all of two days.

Gracey was working the audio console years before at Pedernales Studio for the recording of *Spirit,* the 1996 album that marked a dramatic shift in the live sound of Willie Nelson and Family.

The Family Band was on a tour break while Willie and Bobbie were going to do an acoustic brother-and-sister show at the Greer Garson Theatre in Santa Fe. Jody Payne joined the bill when he called Willie and told him about a new downsized guitar he'd gotten. "How 'bout if I go with you?" he proposed. Jody climbed aboard Honeysuckle Rose in Columbus, Ohio, and played the new instrument all the way to Santa Fe. "It was really, really a different thing for me," Jody said.

After the performance in Santa Fe, the three of them went back to Austin, where Willie summoned Joe Gracey so the three, along with fiddler Johnny Gimble, could record. "We played all that afternoon," remembered Jody. "I left the next morning."

"Willie totally controlled the whole record," Joe

Gracey said. "He loves to record and he hates turning it into a chore. He's not into splicing and dicing. When it came time for sequencing *Spirit,* he turned it all over to me and said, 'Finish it.' He didn't review the mixes every day. He sent me to master the tapes in Nashville. Willie likes me because (a) I love voices, and (b) I mix them loud."

Willie liked the atmosphere of *Spirit* so much he decided to downsize the Family Band on their next run on the road as well, taking only Bobbie, Jody, and Mickey as his band, with Paul coming along to collect the money. But after being drowned out by a loud crowd at Tramp's in New York, Willie suggested expanding the quartet. "Let's get Paul some drums," he said, still wanting to keep the groove spare. Paul called his brother Billy to come back on the road as drum tech.

"I had been setting up a full kit for Paul prior to that," Billy English said. "The tour to promote *Spirit* was eighteen shows, and after nine shows, Paul called while I was producing a CD on a friend up in Colorado Springs and said Willie wanted me and Bee to come out for the last part of this tour." But Willie gave Billy specific orders: "Get rid of the timbals and all the loud, heavy percussion and go to the subtle stuff—triangles, wind chimes, salt shakers, things like that. We're going to have just one snare drum, not a kit." Paul wasn't too happy with the simple setup at first, but the more shows they played, the more he embraced the tamped-down ambience.

The Willie Nelson wall of sound was now infused with subtlety. For the first time in years, Willie's voice and guitar were front and center. Bobbie's piano was as distinctive a complement to Willie's voice and guitar as Mickey's harmonica. "It was totally different from what we had with the two drummers and two bass players," Jody said. "That was a rompin', stompin' band, don't get me wrong. This was the same amount of energy, only not overpowering."

Willie wanted the lighting the same way, dropping the lighting truck driver and lighting crew, leaving only Budrock the lighting director to do the job. The road caravan dropped to three buses and one tractor-trailer.

Later, Willie added jazz guitarist Jackie King in the wake of Grady Martin's death in 2001, much to the displeasure of the regular band. "Willie asked him to come out and play two songs," complained Mickey Raphael. "He never left. Willie liked his playing, but every song he'd play all over it." It didn't help that Jackie thought of himself as a virtuoso and insisted on bringing along his wife on tour. The band cheered when Willie informed them Jackie was leaving. In Jackie's absence, Willie's guitar led the way again.

By now, it had become obvious there were two kinds of albums—Mark albums and Willie albums. Mark albums were projects put together by Mark Rothbaum as a means of maintaining a high profile for Willie and keeping his career fresh. Willie and Rob Thomas, Willie and Ryan Adams, Willie produced by James Stroud in Nashville, Willie with Wynton Marsalis's jazz band—those were Mark albums.

The strategy frequently worked. Willie's collaboration with jazz trumpeter Wynton Marsalis and his quintet showed the upside of taking creative risks. Mark initiated negotiations with Wynton Marsalis and his people (Mark's history with Miles Davis opened doors in the jazz community), and four nights were booked in the Allen Room at Lincoln Center in New York, where Willie spent two days rehearsing before performing with the tapes rolling. It did not hurt that Willie's jazz sense had been informed by New Orleans jazz as well as Django Reinhardt's gypsy swing. Not only was Willie in musical sync with Louis Armstrong, Wynton's primary influence, he comported himself much like Armstrong did, appealing to audiences far more diverse than the music scene he emerged from and serving as an ambassador of good vibes as well as good music. Satchmo and Willie were American originals who made music that sounded like comfort food.

Sometimes, though, the strategy didn't work. *The Great Divide,* released in 2002, was in the tradition of Carlos Santana's *Supernatural,* using the same producer, Matt Serletic, and bringing in the same guest vocalist, Rob Thomas of Matchbox Twenty, whose masculine, emotive voice returned Santana to the charts with the single "Smooth." Thomas's self-penned collaboration with Willie, "Maria (Shut Up and Kiss Me)," did not repeat Santana's hit-single success (maybe it was the disco whistle in the background), but it did get Willie airplay on some non-country radio stations and legitimized Willie with a certain segment of a younger generation previously unfamiliar with his work. "He's the America we would like to get back to," Rob Thomas said of Willie, as if he'd gone away.

The rest of that album was a strange brew, matching Willie with redneck hip-hopper Kid Rock on "Last Stand in the Open Country," one of the first protest songs against urban sprawl, with L.A. pop-rocker Sheryl Crow on "Be There for You," with Texas pop-country singer Lee Ann Womack on

"Mendocino County Line," with the bluesy singer-songwriter Bonnie Raitt on "You Remain," and with rhythm and blues smoothie Brian McKnight on the ballad "Don't Fade Away." The album achieved the intended effect of winning converts, although among the faithful the project did little more than affirm Willie's willingness to try anything.

Songbird, another Mark album, which Willie made with alt-country rocker Ryan Adams and his band the Cardinals, released in 2006, was a critical and commercial dud despite Willie's inspired cover of Leonard Cohen's "Hallelujah." One fan in Salt Lake City mailed his copy of the CD to Willie's fan club, accompanied by a note that read, "Tell that producer not to set foot in Utah."

Milk Cow Blues, a blues album released in 2000, was a Willie-Mark hybrid. Willie and his nephew Freddy Fletcher came up with the idea, putting together a backing ensemble that largely consisted of the house band at Antone's nightclub in Austin, including guitarists Derek O'Brien and Jimmie Vaughan, bassist Jon Blondell, keyboardist Riley Osbourn, and drummer George Rains. Mark's role was rounding up blues superstars to join Willie in duets—B. B. King on "Night Life" and "The Thrill Is Gone," Francine Reed on "Milk Cow Blues" and "Funny How Time Slips Away," Keb' Mo' on "Outskirts of Town," Jonny Lang on "Rainy Day Blues" and "Ain't Nobody's Business," Susan Tedeschi on "Crazy" and "Kansas City," Kenny Wayne Shepherd on "Texas Flood," and Doctor John on "Fool's Paradise" and "Black Night."

The 2005 reggae album *Countryman,* another Willie album produced by Don Was, was inspired by Willie's and Jamaican Rastas' shared appreciation of marijuana and reggae's backbeat. Ten years in the making, the album featured two Jimmy Cliff classics, "The Harder They Come" and "Sitting in Limbo," and a handful of Willie's 1960s vintage weepers such as "One in a Row," "Darkness on the Face of the Earth," "Undo the Right," and "I've Just Destroyed the World" (written with Ray Price), with Jamaican-style beats and sound effects such as stretching out the steel guitar with reverb. The project matched Willie with another unexpectedly compatible duet partner in Toots Hibbert, the soulful lead singer of Toots and the Maytals, who joined him for a reading of Johnny Cash's "I'm a Worried Man."

His 2006 tribute to songwriter Cindy Walker, produced by his old friend Fred Foster, was one of Willie's most heartfelt recordings ever, songwriter to songwriter. Cindy was born in Mart, twenty miles southeast of Willie's hometown of Abbott fifteen years before he was. She was successfully composing songs as a teenager ("Casa de Mañana," the theme song for Billy Rose's lavish supper club in Fort Worth in 1936) before going to California, where she was discovered by Bing Crosby, who did her song "Lone Star Trail." She went on to write hits like "In the Misty Moonlight," covered by Dean Martin, "Blue Canadian Rockies," covered by Gene Autry, "You Don't Know Me," cowritten and covered by Eddy Arnold and covered by Ray Charles, "Distant Drums," covered by Jim Reeves, and "Dream Baby," made famous by Roy Orbison.

Cindy wrote prolifically for Bob Wills, including such hits as "You're from Texas," "What Makes Bob Holler," "Cherokee Maiden," "When You Leave Amarillo," "Bubbles in My Beer," and all thirty-nine tunes for the eight films Wills did for Columbia Pictures in the early 1940s. A spinster whose love for Wills was said to be unrequited (although she did coauthor "Sugar Moon" with Bob), Cindy lived most of her adult life with her mother in the Texas town of Mexia.

"Willie and I had talked about an album of Cindy Walker songs years ago because he respected her writing so much," Fred Foster said of the "Swingin' Cowgirl from Texas," regarded as country's finest female composer. "It never got done. Other things got in the way. One day Cindy called. She said she had a song she wanted to get to Willie Nelson. She sent it to me and I sent it to Willie. He said to hold the song; let's do a whole album of her songs. She liked to have fainted when I told her that he wanted her to send a bunch of songs. She sent sixty-two songs." Willie and Fred winnowed them down to thirteen songs for the album.

For *You Don't Know Me: The Songs of Cindy Walker,* Fred recorded instrumental tracks with a scratch vocalist focusing on the interplay between fiddler Johnny Gimble and steel guitarist Buddy Emmons, who both had deep histories with Willie. Willie came in and did vocals, once with forty-six close personal friends with him in the control room.

Cindy liked what she heard. "I've had many fine recordings. But Willie's are the only ones I've believed," she told Fred.

A week after the album was released, in March 2006, Cindy Walker died at the age of eighty-seven.

DAYS after three commercial jets were hijacked and crashed into the World Trade Center in New York and the Pentagon in Washington, DC, killing more than three thousand people, a group of entertainers gathered in a studio for a somber, emotionally charged performance and fund-raising telethon broadcast nationally as "America: A Tribute to Heroes." The studio setting was stark. There were no announcers, voice-overs, crawlers at the bottom of the screen identifying the performers, no audience. The players simply played, letting their music speak for them.

Bruce Springsteen opened the program with a spiritual benediction, "My City of Ruins." Billy Joel did "New York State of Mind." Dave Matthews sang a plaintive "Everyday." Tom Petty played a defiant "Won't Back Down." Alicia Keys intoned "Someday We'll All Be Free." Neil Young did John Lennon's "Imagine." U2 performed "Walk On." Paul Simon reprised "Bridge over Troubled Water." Celine Dion achieved a serviceable impression of Kate Smith on "God Bless America." Hip-hop giant Wyclef Jean covered Bob Marley's "Redemption Song," and Eddie Vedder of Pearl Jam sang a wrenching version of "The Long Road." But it was Willie who led the gathering in the closing number, "America the Beautiful." He was the voice, and the face, of the nation.

He was still country at heart. Willie had returned to the country Top 10 singles chart in 2002 for the first time in twelve years by singing a duet with Toby Keith on "Whiskey for My Men, Beer for My Horses," a nostalgic Old West story about chasing down bad guys that held the number one position on the *Billboard* country chart for six weeks. Toby, a young heartthrob from Oklahoma, sold Willie on the collaboration by telling him the song title. Toby Keith followed up the single with a patriotic song supporting the U.S. invasion of Iraq in March 2003, "Courtesy of the Red, White and Blue"; Willie followed with the quiet recording of an antiwar hymn he wrote on Christmas Day 2003 "after watching three hours of bombs on Christmas Day." Willie told his friend Frank Oakley he didn't write "What Happened to Peace on Earth?" as a Democrat or Republican but as a Christian. The recording was released quietly as a free download on the Internet rather than on a mainstream record label. He was wary of being "Dixie-Chicked" for his antiwar stance. Several months earlier, on the eve of the U.S. invasion of Iraq, the multiplatinum Texas country act the Dixie Chicks had been blacklisted from country radio playlists after lead singer Natalie Maines from Lubbock told an audience in London, "We're ashamed the president of the United States is from Texas."

Despite their opposing politics, Toby and Willie's mutual admiration was genuine. Toby recorded a hilarious tribute song called "Weed with Willie" in which he swore he'd never smoke Willie's potent pot again. "Beer for My Horses" began an extended professional relationship with Toby's producer James Stroud.

Stroud produced the 2004 album *It Will Always Be,* a Mark album that was the kind of classic Nashville assembly-line production Willie had so famously rejected thirty years before. The music tracks were laid down in Nashville with studio musicians based there. He did the vocal tracks back at Pedernales, just like he had recorded with Fred Foster. "I had a lot of faith in James and the Nashville musicians," Willie said. "Whether I could add the feel or not without the musicians, that was a challenge. I think maybe next time we'll try it the other way, just to see if there's a difference. But I thought James got the best musicians possible to do this album and help me put together what I think are some good songs."

His celebrity remained viable enough to endorse more products. Old Whiskey River Kentucky Bourbon was promoted with T-shirts and cowboy hats and free recipes for such mixed-bourbon drinks as Red Headed Stranger, Wet Willie, Silly Willie, On the Road Again, and Naked Willie, which was a double shot of Old Whiskey River. Willie's version of ZZ Top's "She Loves My Automobile," a classic Texas rhythm and blues shuffle in the sophisticated style of T-Bone Walker, was the theme song for a Red Bull energy drink television commercial. He became spokesman for the Texas Roadhouse restaurant chain in exchange for a small taste of company ownership.

The more things changed, the more they seemed to stay the same. In April 2002 a reporter for the *Montgomery Bulletin,* Rhonda Bell, who'd followed Willie since his Houston days in the late 1950s, caught a show and noted several changes and some reassuring consistencies in Willie and Family. "The groupies are getting a lot older," she wrote. "The band and crew are not even looking at them, they just want to go home to their families. I look at my old friend and I see a lot more lines on his face behind that smile and sparkle in his eye. Willie looks tired. It's 2:30 in the morning and Willie is still shaking hands, taking pictures, and even autographing blue-jeaned butts. He is still giving his all to his fans."

He also stayed close to old friends, phoning them, visiting with them, recording with them whenever possible. Johnny Bush was in awe that "Whiskey River" remained an integral part of Willie's stage show more than thirty-five years after Johnny had written it. "To have one of the greatest songwriters ever, right up there with Hank Williams and Leon Payne, choose to cover my song at his shows is beyond flattery," Johnny said. At last count, Willie had recorded twenty-seven different versions. To coincide with the publication of Johnny's book *Whiskey River*

(Take My Mind), a gritty recollection of Texas honky-tonk life extending back to the Mission City Play-boys, when he met Willie, Johnny recorded an album of songs titled *Kashmere Gardens Mud* that Johnny was exposed to growing up on the poor side of Houston. Willie joined Johnny to duet on "Pancho and Lefty" and a stirring "Send Me the Pillow That You Dream On."

Helping Johnny Bush underscored the fact that Willie enjoyed saying yes. "If you can get to him, nine times out of ten, he'll tell you yeah, no matter what it is you're asking," his personal assistant David Anderson said. Over the years, David had cultivated a furrowed-brow facial expression intended to run people off without having to say anything. It was part of being Willie's gatekeeper and knowing his boss was an easy touch.

"It is pure selfishness to not allow every Tom, Dick, and Harry to pitch a benefit," David said. "We get paid by the day, and if it's a benefit, we don't get paid. Plus, one guy can only do so much." Willie did all he could, saying yes to raising money for the Montessori school his boys had attended in Hawaii, to putting his name behind the Willie Nelson short-wave radio channel, to promoting a video series of shoot-'em-ups staged in Luck starring Willie and his buddies, and even to an arts scholarship foundation that David Anderson put together with his boyfriend. If the ideas didn't pan out, it mattered little. He'd do anything for his friends.

Friendship kept Paul English and Willie together all these years, Willie said. "The kind you can't buy, that's not for sale. You know it when you see it. Paul is probably the best friend I got."

Paul returned the compliment. "Willie is the main relationship I have had in my life," he said. "It started fifty-one years ago. He's a great entertainer and a great writer, and I am proud of him for that. Mainly, though, he's my friend. He sometimes says I'm his best friend. I really appreciate him saying that, because I know he means it, and I love him. He could get a far better drummer than me for half the price. The entertainment business is mentally tougher than the other businesses I've worked in. It takes more loyalty, and you don't get that much in the business unless it's Willie. I've been disappointed by a lot of people, but mainly because they can't measure up to Willie.

"Family is more than just blood, especially for me," Paul said. "We've been through so much together—the death of a father, the death of a son, the death of my wife, Carlene. When Carlene died, I went from one

769 / Joe Nick Patoski

eighty [pounds] to one thirty, and I was mean. I would have really liked to die, but he was there for me."

Those around Willie learned to tolerate his eccentricities. It was standard operating procedure on Willie's bus to wait until he'd mentioned something a second or third time before taking him seriously. Otherwise, they'd be running around, trying to carry out orders all day, only to have the boss say, "What did you do that for?"

Mark Rothbaum spoke to him at least five times a day and otherwise looked after Willie's interests, especially whenever Willie said yes. "Willie can't say no," Mark said. He cited the time Brian Ahern, the producer and husband of singer Emmylou Harris, had persuaded Willie to buy the Enactron Truck Studio, which recorded *Stardust*. When Ahern arrived one day before the scheduled signing of papers, Rothbaum was waiting for him in Willie's hotel room ready to kill the deal. "When he saw me, he knew it wasn't going to happen," Rothbaum said. The last thing Willie needed was another studio.

Another time, Doug Holloway brought Willie a deal for a Willie Nelson credit card, and Willie signed an agreement with him before Mark intervened.

"That's a very smart deal you made," Mark told Willie.

"Really?"

"Yeah, it's genius."

"How can that be genius?"

"Well, think about it: A third of all credit cards go into receivership, so a third of your fans will go bankrupt, and they will have to look at your picture on that credit card. Every time they see your picture, they will think, That prick is making money off of me. You'll be making money off of their credit card, so what you won't have a career. You'll be making money and that's the important thing. It's a smart deal."

Willie asked Mark to get him out of the agreement.

As much as he seemed to defy aging, seven decades of physically contorting his fingers into chords and holding picks to strum strings first caught up with him in 2003. Willie developed carpal tunnel syndrome, a repetitive-motion injury to his wrist that ultimately required surgery. For months Budrock had noticed Willie shaking his wrist during performances. In Las Vegas, Willie quit twenty minutes into a show for the first time and told the band, "Let's go home. I can't do this anymore." He tried herbal and alternative methods of healing before finally giving in to Mark Rothbaum's plea for surgery. The

Willie Nelson Show was put on hold for four months while Willie healed. With his arm in a sling, he had to have helpers roll him his joints and was so itchy for the road, he was sleeping on his bus instead of in his cabin. On his first string of dates back out, Joey Floyd, who played Willie's son in the film *Honeysuckle Rose* and had grown up to play guitar with Toby Keith, sat in with the band to spell Willie.

The surgery forced him to give up signing every autograph request thrust in his direction. Honeysuckle Rose left the building within minutes after the show was over. "We have to do it that way because he feels guilty," explained driver Gates Moore. "He always felt like the meet-and-greet was part of his job, and I have stood beside him in the freezing fucking cold with a flashlight for hours and hours when people who hadn't even been to the show were getting in line, but he wouldn't quit. His hands were black from the markers, but he would not quit." Those hours of signing were important to Willie. "I think that's what made him," Gates said. "At his shows, you can't find a person who won't pull a picture of him and Willie out of his wallet and say, 'Yeah, I know Willie. I'm in the family.'" Will spent his seventy-first birthday healing from surgery and listening to Leon Russell play at Poodie's Hilltop, the closest honky-tonk to the Hill, Luck, Texas, and the

Pedernales Country Club. Leon had "backed off," according to Willie, and settled into playing small clubs. Playing Poodie's was just another gig, even though the audience was special.

Poodie Locke, Willie's stage manager, was the only roadie in show business with his own beer joint, custom logo, and line of barbecue sauce (labels designed by David Zettner). Among the memorabilia at the Hilltop was a framed jock strap signed by Earl Campbell, the Heisman Trophy All-American running back for the University of Texas football team.

Willie filmed three television specials between 2002 and 2004 under the title *Willie Nelson & Friends* for the USA Network. He invited a host of friends, including Norah Jones, Ray Price, Keith Richards, Toby Keith, Emmylou Harris, Ryan Adams, Jon Bon Jovi, Sheryl Crow, the Dixie Chicks, Vince Gill, Patty Griffin, John Hiatt, Dave Matthews, Brian McKnight, Aaron Neville, Richie Sambora, Rob Thomas, Hank Williams III, and Lee Ann Womack, to join him at the Ryman Auditorium in Nashville, the former Mother Church of Country Music, for the "Stars & Guitars" edition.

"Live & Kickin'," filmed at the Beacon Theater in New York, featured ZZ Top, Elvis Costello, Eric Clapton, Ray Charles, Sheryl Crow, Norah Jones, Diana Krall, Lyle Lovett, Shelby Lynne, Dolly Parton, Paul Simon, Shania Twain, and former president Bill Clinton.

The third edition, "Outlaws & Angels," at the Wiltern Theatre in Los Angeles, was headlined by Bob Dylan, Keith Richards, rock rapper Kid Rock, and soul stylist Al Green, along with Jerry Lee Lewis, Merle Haggard, and Lucinda Williams. Ray Charles had to cancel due to illness.

In June 2004, Brother Ray passed away. At least he and Willie had time to say their good-byes. "We did a song together in the studio in April, 'It Was a Very Good Year' [a song about aging and looking back]," Willie said. "We had some fun. I was at his birthday party. He and Quincy Jones and two, three, of us sat around and talked and had a drink and ate cake. Right after that I went to the Apollo Theater in Harlem for the anniversary of the theater, and Ray got a tribute that night. So I sang 'I Can't Stop Loving You.'"

At Ray's funeral, one of the few Willie has attended, Willie performed Ray's signature piece, "Georgia on My Mind," the official state song of Georgia; he could hardly get through the performance as his voice intermittently cracked with emotion, sounding spent and very blue. B. B. King broke up too when he played during the service. Days later, Willie embarked on a tour of minor league baseball parks with Bob Dylan, one of his few peers in the song-writing craft.

Less than a month after a tsunami in South Asia killed more than two hundred thousand people in 2004, he headlined an Austin benefit with Natalie Maines of the Dixie Chicks, Joe Ely, Alejandro Escovedo, and Patty Griffin that was recorded as a CD and a DVD titled *Tsunami Relief: From Austin to South Asia*.

His name stayed in the public eye, even as the medium that brought him to the dance shunned him. Mark Rothbaum utilized multiple means to get Willie across, including movies, television, National Public Radio, and radio stations with AAA (adult album alternative) formats. He no longer invested money promoting his records on country radio because country radio wouldn't play him. "That ship has sailed," Rothbaum said. "There is no country music radio. It's all this soft rock crap. Just because you have a pedal steel doesn't make you country."

Paradise, 2004

H E WAS A MUSICIAN but more than a musician. He was a songwriter whom some saw as a philosopher. He was a picker who knew how to rouse a crowd. He was a New Age good ol' boy, a hillbilly Dalai Lama, as Kinky Friedman liked to call him. He was that rare high-profile person who was whatever anyone wanted him to be.

"I see him as full of Christ-like character," recording engineer Bobby Arnold said somberly. "I think he just realizes he's blessed in so many ways, and it makes him incredibly generous. There's a spirituality that is Jesus-like. He tries to make people's lives better. No one else can touch a broken heart with words the way he can." Tim O'Connor compared him to a messiah. Tim's daughter had unexpectedly died dur-

ing Will and Tim's Austin Opry adventure, and Tim
went to the Hill to ask Willie to cosign a $50,000
loan so he could retreat to a ranch in Montana. "If
you don't want to do that, I completely understand,"
Tim told him. "But you have my word that I will
repay you. I'll even give you the title to the property."

"Wait a minute," Willie said, excusing himself to
go to the bedroom. He returned bearing a $50,000
check that someone had written him.

"I've always hated banks, haven't you?" he said,
endorsing the back of the check and handing it to
Tim. The favor prompted Tim several years later to
take over a benefit concert in Crawford, Nebraska,
gone bad. The promoter of the "phone deal" benefit
starring Willie Nelson had left town with the money
two weeks before the show. Tim stepped in to produce the concert, taking a five-figure bath for his
troubles because he didn't want the locals to think
poorly of Willie.

Whether Willie was in the room or far away, he
made those around him feel good. When Jody Fischer
checked into the Christopher House hospice for cancer patients in Austin, she was unknowingly placed
in the Willie Nelson Room to conclude her life, much
of it spent in service to Willie. She died peacefully.
Whenever Merle Haggard felt Willie's intense gaze,

he turned into a different person. "You'd see Haggard come onto the bus like a caged animal, with that frantic, frenetic look in his eyes, being really uptight with a lot of people," publicist Evelyn Shriver said. "Then you'd see him sit across from Willie and you'd watch him physically change. When he makes that eye contact with Willie, all of a sudden, everything's okay. I've seen it with so many people that go on the bus. He has that ability to melt your heart and make you feel important."

Kris Kristofferson was also under Willie's influence. "I swear to God, being around Willie is like being around Buddha," he said. "He gives off these positive attitudes. Next thing you know, you're acting like him. Things that ruffle the rest of us don't ruffle him. He's got almost an Asian calm about him. I don't think things are going to bowl him over. It probably comes from all those years of scrambling and laughing at it."

Willie walked the walk.

"His creative door is wide open," Floyd Domino said. "There's nothing repressed. There's nothing you can't talk or write about, whether he feels it or observes it, he understands it. He's got this transcendence where he understands it, whether he's lived it or can feel it. Mickey told me about the band meeting this guy at a truck stop in Fort Worth on their way home.

He never had a break and he wanted to get his songs recorded. 'Come on down to the studio,' Willie said. So the guy got on the bus, rode to Pedernales, and recorded with the band."

"He takes things in stride," said Frank Oakley, who'd known him since 1961, when Faron Young introduced them. "He always says everything's going to work out like it's supposed to."

"The most important thing is to breathe," Willie liked to say. "Inhale and exhale and everything else will fall together."

The Holy Willie effect was so pervasive it was parodied, riffing off "WWJD?"—What Would Jesus Do?—a popular 1990s catchphrase invoked by people of certain Christian faiths when faced with a moral dilemma. Austin singer-songwriter Bruce Robinson put his spin on the rhetorical with the single "What Would Willie Do?"

> *I was lost in trouble and strife, I heard a voice*
> *   and it changed my life*
> *And now it's a brand new day, and I ain't*
> *   afraid to say*
> *You're not alone when you're down and out*
> *And I think you know who I'm talking about*
> *When I don't know how I'll get through*
> *I ask myself what would Willie do*

*What would Willie do, when it's all gone
    wrong
The answer's in the words of a sad country song
When you don't know how to get through,
You better ask yourself, "What would Willie
    do?"
Long ago, you came unto us,
His words were simple but they went right
    through us
And the whole world sang along
But then they didn't want to hear his songs
He was gone and we thought we'd lost him
But he just grew his hair and he moved to
    Austin
And all of the people smiled
They came to hear him sing from miles
And like a miracle all the rednecks and hippies
From New York City down to Mississippi
Stood together and raised a brew
When your skies are gray, "What would Willie
    do?"
You know sometimes I wonder when I ain't
    gettin' nowhere
What would old Willie do when things get too
    much to bear
And I see him sittin' on his lonely old bus
And he's got his problems just like any of us*

And I bet he'd just take a deep breath and he'd
  let 'em all go
And then he'd take another deep breath and
  he'd let 'em all go
And then he'd take another deep breath
And he'd hold it . . .

And then I bet he'd feel hungry in a way that
  seems strange
Yes hungry for all the things he just can't change
Like the time he passed out in his own bedroom
And his ex-wife sewed him up in the sheet and
  she beat him with a broom
And he forgave her and you think that that's
  rough,
Then the IRS came and they took away all his
  stuff
They took his golf course and his recording
  studio
And he just went on out and did another show
So when it's all comin' down on you
You better ask yourself, "What would Willie
  do?"
What would Willie do, he travels far with
  nothin'
But a song and an old guitar
And a tour bus and some semi trucks

And 30 crewmen and a little bit of luck
He loves all the people, the ugly and the randy
If you don't believe it take a look at the family
And they'll tell you that it's true
So when your skies are gray, "What would
  Willie do?"
What would Willie do, he'd take a little time
And talk to old Rooster as they drive on down
  the line
There's millions down that road
And with a word he's gonna lighten their load
He loves all the people no matter their races
Hell, he even made a hit country song with
  Julio Iglesias
And that ain't easy to do
So when it's all too much, "What would
  Willie—"
When the game gets rough, "What would
  Willie—"
When they call your bluff, "What would Willie
  do?"

Bumper stickers appeared around Austin that read "Matthew, Mark, Luke and Willie."

And when the pilgrims had questions, Willie had answers.

While hanging with Willie, Ray Wylie Hubbard

once suddenly realized he'd forgotten a gig. "It's two-twenty and I'm supposed to be in San Antonio at three," he told Willie. "What do I do?"

"Call and tell them you lied," Willie said automatically, suggesting he'd been in a similar situation before.

Advice was sometimes offered even if not requested, according to Billy Joe Shaver. "Willie's always had this charisma, this aura thing around him," he said. "He doesn't realize it but he's always good to be around. When you leave, you feel good. The longer you stay around, the better you feel. I got into drugs and women in Nashville. My family was suffering. I had to leave to save my life. I went down to Houston and went cold turkey. I didn't know they had these places where you could get relief from drugs. Jesus Christ is all I had. I dropped to a hundred fifty pounds. All I could drink was a diet root beer. That's all I could keep down. Willie called me up and said, 'Come on over and play with us.' He always knew when I was down."

Willie didn't quibble with the praise or portrayals. If anything, he played up to them. As he'd aged, as his hair grew longer, his beard became scruffier, and his nature more iconoclastic, he looked wiser. He could quote the Bible, Edward Cayce, the Dalai Lama, and Roger Miller with equal ease, and he left the distinct impression that he hovered above the fray, laughing and singing, articulating a simple message: Whatever Happens Happens.

His point of view explained his ability to keep his sunny side up when others around him gave him plenty of reasons to cry in his beer. Waylon's various ailments, including a quadruple heart bypass, diabetes, emphysema, and carpal tunnel syndrome, took him down for good in 2002. Floyd Tillman passed a year earlier after having a last go-round on record with Willie issued by Heart of Texas Records, a classic country label based in Brady. Geno McCoslin blew his brains out; he'd been diagnosed as bipolar. Jimmy Day went in 1999 from a heart attack following treatment for stomach cancer. David Zettner was taken by a brain aneurysm in 2006. Billy and Bettie Walker were killed in a car wreck on their way back to Nashville, also in 2006. Larry Trader was felled by a stroke and then a heart attack in 2007. (Willie went to the hospital to comfort him, talking to him and telling him jokes for a good twenty minutes before it was brought to his attention that Trader was already dead.) Grady, Bucky, Webb, Faron, Cash, Martha, Billy—all gone. Dee Herrera, the Brown Mexican Bear whose family ran Dallas's oldest family Mexican restaurant and who showed up for Willie gigs armed with margaritas, was buried in shorts and a

Billy Joe Shaver T-shirt, with a Willie Nelson back-stage pass attached to a lanyard around his neck and a yellow rose in his hand.

Willie was philosophical about loss. "You know, there are a lot of younger people than you and I already gone on," he said with a soft sigh. "It has nothing to do with age. There are those huge disasters that happen on the planet when twenty thousand people get wiped out and there are no age preferences there. We're all headed that way."

His response was to choogle along and stay one step ahead of the game. He was still driven. People tended to forget his passion for moving forward and his competitive streak. "We were in Sydney in the rooftop pool a half hour before showtime, seeing who could stay underwater the longest," said Mark Rothbaum. "Connie was standing at the side of the pool, looking at her watch, telling us we were going to be late to the show. Willie shouted, 'Shut up! Time us!'"

He operated by different rules. One morning, Willie was walking to his bus in a hotel parking lot with Coach Royal, when Coach told him that he'd left a gift from a fan in his hotel room.

"Willie, you forgot your thing there," Coach told him.

Willie kept walking. He later explained himself to Coach. "After they give it, and I receive it, the transaction is over. They enjoyed giving it to me and I enjoyed receiving it. I don't have to be a slave to all those possessions."

He tried to explain that to his Atlanta attorney, Joel Katz, during a meeting in a Los Angeles hotel room where Willie fired him. Joel had scheduled a meeting, wanting to show Willie an estate plan he'd drawn up.

When Willie realized what Joel had done, he blew up.

"Why are you doing this? Who asked you to draw this up? I don't want an estate plan. I didn't ask for an estate plan. I never want to hear about an estate plan again," he fumed, stomping out of the room.

Visions of having lost his most important client swirled around Joel Katz's head when Willie returned a few minutes later in a calmer state of mind.

"I know you're really trying to help, so I apologize," he said, putting his arm around Joel. "You were trying to do what you thought was right for me, but you've got to understand my philosophy of life. I want the people around me to be happy, but I look at life as a roller coaster. When I'm up, I'm up. And when I'm down, I'm down. And I hope when it's all over, the money runs out just about the same time that I'm through with my life.

"Let's not plan. It's a lot more fun if we don't," he said, shooting Joel a wink.

Shortly after *Stardust* had been certified triple platinum in 1984, Ray Benson tried to use similar forethought, asking Willie about his corporate structure. "Nothing—it just goes in the Willie Nelson bank account," Willie told him, even though the income stream was reaching $30 million a year. "Do you have a will?" Ray asked. "Naw," Willie replied. "When I die, I just want to watch them all fight it out. May the best attorney win," he said, laughing.

It took a while but Ray finally figured out how Willie ticked. Driving down the golf course, Benson told him, "You should take some golf lessons." Willie stopped the cart and looked him in the eyes. "Let me tell you something, Ray. If there's a right way to do something, I'll do it the wrong way first."

Looking ahead instead of being in the moment got in the way of making music, doing shows, recording with everyone he ever wanted to record with, playing however he had a hankering to play. "A lot of people make money off of fear and negativity and any way they can feed it to you is to their benefit in a lot of ways," he said. "You can't avoid it completely; you have to be open enough that shit doesn't stick on you, it goes through, because you are gonna be hit and bombarded all the time with negativity. It's kind of like with martial arts when you go through a target instead of hitting a target. You just let things go on through without trying to stop them or block them."

Annie Nelson kept him thinking like that.

Marriage had been a constant throughout his adult life. As difficult as it had been staying married, he appreciated the institution, no matter how much he strayed. Like with reincarnation, he was determined to get marriage right. His first marriage, to Martha, provided all the conflict and friction he needed to inspire him to write great songs. Where finances and ambition denied Lana, Susie, and Billy a home life that was stable and nurturing, his second marriage, to Shirley, made him want to give his kids from his first marriage a better living situation than the one they'd had. Third wife Connie was a stunning, steadying presence by his side throughout his meteoric ascent while she went the extra mile to bring up their daughters Paula Carlene and Amy as normally as possible. And his fourth marriage, to Annie, gave him the opportunity to raise sons Lukas Autry and Jacob Micah under close to ideal conditions. Annie knew there would be long absences when she married him. "We have been blessed to be able to pay our bills and not have to try to raise children while holding down two and three jobs," Annie said. Whenever he took a break from the road, he had a wife and kids to go home to.

Annie had been married to Willie longer than his previous three wives. She was the strong, steely type, like Mamma Nelson and Bobbie and Connie, spoke her mind like Myrle and Martha, and didn't suffer layabouts. She did not hesitate to upbraid him for not doing his part as a father or to tell him to pick up his wet towel off the floor when he was home, reminding him he wasn't in some motel. Whatever Willie's ol' boy friends may have thought of her, she embodied ideals similar to the people who embraced Willie when he got to Austin thirty years before. The tree-hugging, animal-loving, tofu-eating, peace-agitating earth-mama hippie matched Willie's personal philosophy of the way things ought to be.

Annie didn't just talk the talk, she role-modeled, helping move her husband's activist sentiments from words to actions when she bought a brand-new 2003 Volkswagen Jetta wagon that ran on cooking grease. The Maui landfill had banned restaurant grease about the same time Bob King, a diesel mechanic, launched Pacific Biodiesel, the first biofuel plant on Maui. Annie got involved with the company out of her desire for "clean air, clean water, and clean food for my children" on the island where they lived.

Willie thought she was crazy at first. "She must have gotten in my stash" was the standard line he repeated again and again. But Willie saw the light and bought a Mercedes that ran on biodiesel. His three buses were refitted to run on biodiesel after Neil Young had rigged up his own fleet. Annie said the conversion was as much for the health of the drivers and the passengers on the buses as anything; they risked chronic respiratory ailments and even cancer by breathing the exhaust of conventional diesel over the years. In 2005, he rented his name to a branded biodiesel, BioWillie.

Annie Nelson saw biofuel as an extension of the mission of Farm Aid. "I thought of it as the answer to the farmers' problems if we could get them back on the land they've been foreclosed on and get them growing clean food and our fuel," she said.

Annie did the research and fed Willie the information. "All I had to do was help him to understand the actual potential of biodiesel for this country, how it would help farmers, how it would help the economy and national security," she said. "I keep him up on everything that's happening. There is no better spokesperson."

Willie's interest was initially piqued back in 1991 when he rode around Kentucky with Gatewood Galbraith in his Mercedes fueled by hemp oil. When

Gatewood stepped on Willie's bus thirteen years later while Willie and Family were touring minor league baseball parks with Bob Dylan, Willie greeted him saying, "I never forgot that day when you and I poured that hemp oil into the Mercedes. I've started WN Biodiesel, and you laid it out for me."

Willie saw it as a practical solution to several problems and set out to sell it. "It's a way for the farmers to work themselves out of the financial hole that they've been in for years and years," he reasoned. "They can grow corn for ethanol. They can grow cotton for biodiesel. It's like a community telling a farmer what they'd like to eat so he can grow food for the whole neighborhood."

His advocacy dovetailed onto his embrace of organic food, another cause that connected him to his hometown. Willie cited the case of Eldon Stafford, with whom he spent many nights on his family's farm when he was young, as one motivation. "I believe Eldon died because of the chemical poison he used on his crops," he said. "He had the best cotton. He was always out in the fields, applying the poison himself with the tractor, breathing all that stuff ten to twelve hours a day. Nobody told you chemicals were bad."

Mark Rothbaum viewed Willie's embrace of causes as natural. "Willie sees the plight of the farmer from a poet's eyes. He's almost like Steinbeck or Willa Cather—he's taken by the farming life. He sees himself as a farmer on the prairie, scratching out a meager existence. The fundamental struggle between the corporate and the personal, the encroachment of the monopolistic capitalistic private sector, and the genetically modified foods—he sees it as good against evil. It's not just for the farmer; selfishly he knows that the environment will be made better without all of the pesticides and chemicals, and that he will get better food."

Willie was determined to spread his message, and his activism extended to ex-wives. Willie helped Connie lobby Congress to ban horse slaughterhouses in the United States. In his seventies, he became the face of the Willie Nelson Peace Research Institute, promoting "The Promise of Peace on Earth in Our Lifetime as the Birthright of Our Global Human Family." The institute operated according to the following tenets: "Peace on Earth is possible NOW with Unconditional Love; Do unto others as you would have them do unto you is the Golden Rule from the Highest Order; Peace on Earth is possible NOW with Unyielding Hope; Replace negative thoughts with positive thoughts to create positive results; Peace on Earth is possible NOW with Unlimited Compassion; and Open your heart and make connections to people everywhere and to the world around us."

Home, 2006

YES, SUH! YES, SUH! 'You Ain't Woman Enough to Take My Man.' Sounds like Loretta, but that's Martina!" It was a May afternoon in the spring of 2006 and Bill Mack was on the air on Channel 171, the Open Road on XM satellite radio, talking Texas-style country to thousands of his faithful listeners, the vast majority of whom were driving trucks while tuned in to his daily show broadcast live from his home studio on the east side of Fort Worth, Texas. The house was a few blocks from the former studios of WBAP radio 820 AM, where for more than twenty years Bill was the Midnight Cowboy, the drawling late-night voice speaking to truckers coast-to-coast via the station's powerful 50,000-watt signal.

"When Willie made the transition, when he came

back home to Texas after his house burned down in Nashville and he killed Ray Price's prized fighting rooster, the people in Nashville were saying, 'He's lost his mind,' " Bill was telling his audience in his distinctive baritone as a lead-in to Willie Wednesday when Willie Nelson called to talk to the Satellite Cowboy on the air. For the next hour, Willie would shoot the bull with Bill and his wife, sweet Cindy, and Bill's talking duck, Truman, and field questions and requests from listeners.

On this particular day, Willie was calling from New York, where he reported he'd had "ninety-two-dollar pea soup" for lunch, leading Bill to ask what he was having for dinner? "Ninety-two-dollar pea soup."

Mormon Boy, Odie in New Mexico, Stargazer headed to Cleveland from Pennsylvania, the Rebel Kid somewhere in the south, John in Magnolia, Texas, Sherri from Tomball, Skeeter, Simple Cowboy, Big Mike, and Carolina Pepsi were all waiting on the phone lines. Several wanted to talk about Bio-Willie, the biodiesel fuel Nelson was endorsing and E85 ethanol fuel and other alternatives to gasoline. Biodiesel offered hope for economically depressed communities in America's farm belt, some callers said.

Fifty miles south of Bill Mack's studio, Carl Cornelius, owner of Carl's Corner, was fixing to host one of two Willie Nelson Fourth of July Picnics scheduled for 2006, this one the day before the official July Fourth version behind Billy Bob's, the World's Biggest Honky-tonk, in Fort Worth's Stockyards district.

Carl's version of the Fourth of July Picnic was a glorified "phone deal." Before the event was publicly announced, Willie gave away one thousand tickets to the family of Jimmy Giles, a Department of Public Safety trooper and fan who had recently passed away, to defray funeral expenses. Hill County firefighters received five thousand tickets for all eighteen fire departments in the county, which would raise well over $100,000. Another five hundred tickets went to Paw Pals, a group formed to establish a Humane Society for animals in the county. Since the give-aways were in the name of charity, it was hard for Billy Bob's to complain about the "competing" picnic.

Leon Russell, David Allan Coe, Ray Price, Johnny Bush, Johnny Gimble, Ray Wylie Hubbard, Noel Haggard (Merle's son), Shooter Jennings (Waylon's son), the Harmonic Tribe (Willie's own sons' world music/reggae band from Maui), daughter Paula Nelson and her country band, Pauline Reese's country band, the Latino band Del Castillo, honky-tonk singer James "Slim" Hand, and Dar Jamail's "way underground" band, Titty Bingo, all played the twelve-hour music marathon at Carl's on July 3. The real show was backstage, where buses were lined up in two long rows, their occupants mixing and mingling like carnival workers pausing for a visit before taking off in all directions to put on their own shows. Willie merchandise, including Willie braids for $10, T-shirts for $20, and Willie red bandannas for $5, moved briskly.

A FEW months before, Willie Hugh Nelson had been inducted into the Hill County Hall of Fame. Several church representatives indicated they wouldn't attend the ceremony due to the recipient's lifestyle, never mind his ability to quote from the Bible or his donation of $275,000 from two benefit concerts toward a $9 million restoration of the Hill County Courthouse, whose gingerbread architecture earned accolades as the most beautiful courthouse in Texas until it burned in a fire in 1993. Nor did the churches object when Willie donated $25,000 to the Hill County Cellblock Museum, where a display honors Willie. They said nothing about his keeping open the only grocery in Abbott, or raising money to help the hospital in Whitney in the northwest corner of the county, or bringing in $325,000 for the American Heart Association in Waco.

He shrugged off the disrespect. He'd been hearing the same hypocritical judgments ever since he was a kid. He was humble in his acceptance speech, telling the Hall of Fame gathering at the old train station, "When people ask me where I'm from, I say, Abbott, Hillsboro, and West. When I was growing up, you could get anything you want between Hillsboro, Abbott, and West. I imagine it still holds true." For all the miles racked up, all the faces he'd seen and places he'd been, he was still at home in the place where he came from.

"When I'm around him, it's just like it was fifty years ago," Jackie Clements, Abbott High Class of '50, said one Sunday morning in Abbott. "We're just buddies. Nothing's changed."

"He's one of my best friends," said Donald Reed, another member of the same graduating class. "He always will be, no matter what he does or I do."

"Willie's my inspiration," agreed Faye Dell Brown Clements, his one-time fiancé who was never able to get him out of her life, even after she married Jackie, one of Willie's best friends. "Not many gals my age get compliments, and he lays them on me. He called from Hawaii and said when he came back, he could come over so we could get in trouble. What would two people our age do to get in trouble? I don't smoke pot."

WILLIE had plenty of ways to get in trouble, or at least stir up some controversy. Booker T. Jones had tried to goad Willie into writing more songs and recorded six demos of originals in early 2005. But his proposed album of all new Willie Nelson material was shelved when another song Willie had recorded, a cover of Ned Sublette's humorous cowboy song "Cowboys Are Secretly, Frequently (Fond of Each Other)," gained traction in the wake of the success of the gay cowboy romance film *Brokeback Mountain*, on whose soundtrack Willie performed Bob Dylan's "He Was a Friend of Mine." The songs kept his name in the news and shored up his gay following, an audience he'd unwittingly tapped into when he wrote "Crazy" more than forty years earlier. Patsy Cline's sad rendition of "Crazy" had been a jukebox staple of lesbian bars across America ever since.

Of all the people Booker T. had worked with, he held Willie in highest regard. "He's more special," Booker T. said with a chuckle, "because he's a journeyman musician. Willie's a farmer that found out he was a musician. He comes from where I come from in the music, from making six dollars a night playing to four a.m. That's what we have in common. None of the other people that I've worked with have that blue-collar journeyman past."

No one else had made an album with Booker T. that stayed on the country charts for more than ten years, selling more than four million copies, either.

Booker T. had witnessed a change in Willie as he'd aged. Booker wondered if Willie had lost confidence in his songwriting, because he'd written so little in recent years. But Willie didn't see eye to eye with Booker T.'s assessment. He liked having his friends around, especially his gypsy pirate friends who kept life interesting. As for writing, "I don't have any discipline at all," he admitted. "I'm a lazy, lazy writer, and I'll put off doing it until a line or something comes along that just kills me and I feel really guilty if I don't go write the song. Didn't used to be that way—when I was hungrier, I wasn't that goddamn lazy." He still wrote, but the drive wasn't the same.

But he wasn't taking Fats Domino's path either; the New Orleans rock-and-roll pianist Fats Domino reasoned, "Why should I write any more songs? I can't play all the ones I wrote in a single show anyhow."

Willie used to think of material to write while driving, and riding in the back of a bus didn't stimulate ideas the same way. "Driving is still the best way for me to write, I believe—to get in a car and take off driving, head anywhere and start thinking about something," he said. "If I'm lucky, I'll write a song. But I have to get somewhere by myself to do it. There are a lot of things going on and a lot of interruptions that make it difficult to do that riding on the bus."

He did roll out two new numbers with a humorous bent: "I Ain't Superman" ("Too many pain pills/too much pot/Trying to be/something I'm not/Superman"), which was released on the iTunes music download site on the Internet, and "You Don't Think I'm Funny Anymore" ("Did you hear the one about the dirty whore?/Oh, I forgot/You don't think I'm funny anymore"), from *Momemt of Forever,* produced by Kenny Chesney and released on Lost Highway, Willie's label of record. A third new song built on a single riff without a bridge, "I Gotta Get Over You," was also on the Chesney album and played at live dates.

If there was a creative crisis of confidence, Willie wasn't letting it show. In early 2007 he ginned up rave reviews for his performance with jazz trumpeter Wynton Marsalis's quintet and Mickey Raphael at Lincoln Center.

Despite Willie's limited range, his talking blues vocals dragging behind the beat were the ensemble's signature. His guitar picking was the bigger surprise. The *New York Times'* Nate Chinen noted a "flinty and casually gripping guitar solo on 'Rainy Day Blues' when everything clicked into place. . . . Wynton Marsalis shot the saxophonist Walter Blanding, Jr. a knowing glance, one eyebrow appreciatively raised." Chinen observed that during the stop-time breaks of "Basin Street Blues," "Mr. Nelson's phrasing was almost perversely free of tempo, rustling like a breeze." With Marsalis's trumpet popping out front and his cool combo in back, "Stardust," "Georgia," "Don't Get Around Much Any More," and "Down By the River Side" were injected with a Second Line strut, making the ensemble sound as if they were marching down St. Charles Avenue arm in arm.

Two months later, Mac Randall of *Newsday* called the Last of the Breed tour, starring Willie Nelson, his mentor Ray Price, and his colleague Merle Haggard, along with Ray Benson and Asleep at the Wheel, Floyd Domino, and reliable Mickey Raphael, "historic," while *Rolling Stone's* Amanda Trimble described the triple bill as "a master class in classic country music."

Of course, not everyone loved Willie. The same voice hailed for its distinctive jazz qualities at Lincoln Center was derided by a Merle Haggard and Ray Price fan reacting to a review in the *Nashville*

Tennessean. "This dude has never been able to sing a note," read a message on the newspaper's Web site discussion board. "He couldn't carry a tune in a bucket."

OVER the course of Willie's career, the Bible Belt had transformed into the Sun Belt, and the technology of recorded music had evolved from 78 rpm discs to twelve-inch polyvinyl chloride phonograph records played at 33⅓ revolutions per minute and seven-inch 45 rpm singles to compact discs to MP3 files downloaded from the Internet and played on devices smaller than a pack of cigarettes.

Communications on the road had advanced from sending telegrams and talking on pay phones to CB radios, cell phones, BlackBerry personal digital assistants, global positioning satellite devices to tell you where you are, and televisions and computers with wireless connectivity.

"It's easier than it used to be," Paul English said, looking back. "We used to drive a station wagon pulling a trailer, and I worked the books with a crank calculator and had receipts scattered up and down the hall. Now I've got a fine bus and computers to work with. I do the books on an Excel spreadsheet. I can be on the Internet as we are driving down the road."

"The ride is a thousand percent better," Gates Moore said. "The old buses were like dump trucks. There was a reason to sedate yourself. Roads are four hundred percent better, despite congestion." Fuel worked the other way. A fill-up that once was eighty bucks is five hundred. The places to fill up changed too. "Truck stops used to be friendly places, but now they don't care," Gates said.

The road was Willie's calling. He had performed at church socials, revivals, community dance halls, beer joints, roadhouses, honky-tonks, ballrooms, living rooms, motel rooms, race tracks, nightclubs, dives, basketball arenas, football stadiums, opera houses, and open fields. It was all the same stage.

His Fourth of July picnics were a Texas tradition, the Farm Aid concerts a slice of heartland Americana. Ben Ratliff of the *New York Times* described the twenty-second Farm Aid, held in New York City in September 2007, as "circuslike: it included American Indian wisdom dancers, a few marines, a talented practitioner of the stumpf fiddle (a bouncing stick with noisemakers attached), two of his children and about a dozen guitarists onstage at the same time, including Neil Young and Derek Trucks." But to

Ratliff, the most striking thing about Farm Aid was "the novelty of going to a (more or less) rock festival focused not on outsiderness, fashion, derangement of the senses or even its own brand power, but on the survival of small businesses and the health of our species."

His March shows at the Backyard Amphitheater halfway between Austin and Spicewood, kicking off the six-thousand-seat amphitheater's warm-weather season, were an annual rite; it was a favor to the venue's owner, Tim O'Connor. When the Backyard opened in 1993, it was an idyllic Hill Country oasis shaded by four-hundred-year-old oaks. Since then, Austin had grown right up to its doorstep, and an upscale shopping mall surrounded the facility.

Willie remained a familiar face on the big and small screen. He appeared in an episode of the NBC-TV comedy *My Name Is Earl* as the character Uncle Jess and on an episode of *Myth Busters* on the Discovery Channel. He contributed songs to the "House of the Rising Sun" episode of the ABC-TV adventure series *Lost* and the "Script and the Sherpa" episode of the HBO series *Entourage*. He performed "Blue Eyes Crying in the Rain," "Old Five and Dimers Like Me," and "Funny How Time Slips Away" in the Tommy Lee Jones action-comedy *Man of the House*, set in Austin, and sang "Uncloudy Day," appearing as himself in the film *Broken Bridges,* a vehicle for country singer Toby Keith.

He made cameos in *It's Happiness: A Polka Documentary,* the movie comedy *Beerfest,* set around Munich, Germany's Oktoberfest, the marijuana documentary *The Hempsters: Plant the Seed,* the dope comedy *Half Baked,* two episodes of the cartoon comedy series *Space Ghost: Coast to Coast,* and the Disney family film *The Country Bears,* and performed at the Nobel Peace Prize concert in Sweden.

Outside the spotlight he was wheeling and dealing, partnering with nephew Freddy Fletcher and Stratus Properties on a new two-thousand-seat venue and studio for the Austin City Limits music series in downtown Austin, while Bobby Day, a developer friend who was managing Willie's golf course, built forty-one luxury homes in a sixty-three-acre subdivision by the highway on the Pedernales ranch.

FOUR thousand miles west of Willie World, the breezes off the Pacific blew soft and seductive. The low-slung ranch house hidden in the coastal vegetation on the island of Maui was unremarkable when viewed from the road. The interior was earthy, comfortable, and solar-powered, with a saline pool in back. Two wings extended from the main house, one wing with a beaded curtain entrance to Django's Lounge, Willie Nelson's own personal Shangri-la beer joint/casino/studio/party palace, with hand-cranked glass windows, Hank Williams on the sound system, and a view where you could see all the way to tomorrow.

In the center of the neon-lit room, Willie Nelson sat shirtless in his master's chair, his already furrowed brow creased deep as he twisted the end of a long strand of his unbraided hair, lost in concentration. Recording equipment and musical instruments were within arm's reach. A shuffleboard table was against the wall, the heavy metal discs set up on the slick-as-a-dance-floor surface, ready for play. His eyes darted from side to side, from the chessboard to the card table in front of him. Bills were piled high in the middle of the card table and to the side of the chessboard. One hand held five cards. The other nudged a pawn. Several old mountain men who'd descended from the surrounding hills sat across the tables from Willie, their eyes following his from one table to the other and back to Willie. Bets accompanied all of Willie's games—$100 a game for chess, $100 a hole for golf, whatever the players could bear around the poker table. "Usually at the end of the night we're about even," Willie said.

His concentration was broken when the beads

parted and Kris Kristofferson walked in, followed by Pat Simmons from the Doobie Brothers, pro basketball coach Don Nelson, and former Alice Cooper manager Shep Gordon—his Maui neighbors.

As the sun dipped into the west and Hank Williams warbled ". . . no matter how I struggle and strive, I'll never get out of this world alive," the games, the gambling, and the music went on.

"It's really a place to get away," Willie said of his Hawaii residence. He could rest, play golf, play music, play family man, or play poker. "I think of Maui as my hospital," he said. "It's where I go to heal up from the battle zone."

But he never got too serious about staying. During a three-month break in the fall of 2006, the longest stretch off since his carpal tunnel surgery, Willie spent quality time at Django's but also managed to record an album in Nashville, appear in a movie in Louisiana, work a jazz gig in New York, and lay down some country tracks in Texas.

Hawaii was nice—as a short break. "It's kind of like you stopped a big train for a minute," Willie said. "It gives everybody a time to stop and think, Whatever this is, it is not going to last forever. So we might as well enjoy the rest and take it as far as we can." The highway was home. His bus was like other tour buses—sofas, booth, toilet/shower, bunks, the back room for the star—with a few tricked-out extras. The hand-carved wooden pillars above the booth in the front of the bus were the kind of elaborate ornamentation fit for a gypsy king. The kitchen across the aisle from the booth was the envy of any celebrity chef, with all the essentials needed to cook and roll. There were flat-screen televisions, satellite hookups, video games, computers with Internet access, and phones to stay plugged in and connected. Often as not, though, the mobile cocoon he shared with Bobbie, Lana, David, L.G., Gator, and Tony Sizemore was shrouded in silence, a safe place like nowhere else on earth. "We know each other so well, we can sit on the bus for four hours without saying a word," Gates Moore said.

Gates the Gator was recognized among tour bus drivers as the ultimate road dog, the first driver in the modern era to surpass a million miles driving the same act. With well over three million road miles under their belts, Gates and Tony Sizemore both eclipsed Hoot Shaw, the driver for Ernest Tubb and the Texas Troubadours for several decades, as the kings of the road. Everyone else on board shared Willie's love of the highway.

"Billy Joe Shaver wrote, 'Moving is the closest thing to being free,' " Willie said. "I believe that. It's that old cowboy trail-riding thing." He reveled in the surprise factor that mobility brought to his life every day. "You lift the shades and you're looking at a new view and you didn't have to buy a home to appreciate the scenery," he said about the joys of peering out the tinted window. "The other night we were in Los Angeles and we went over to [Texas film actor] Matthew McConaughey's place on the ocean and had some steaks. He's got one of those Airstream trailers. He drove it in from somewhere and knows he can drive it out of there when he gets ready to leave. It's kinda like this bus."

Brother and sister were doing what they had been raised to do. "We had a lot of energy and we fortunately had instruments to work with," Willie said. "Sister Bobbie had a piano and I had a guitar and we had a place to act out our fantasies and put words to melodies. Nothing's changed."

Sister agreed. "I have tried so many times in my life to change something that I want to do so much," she said. "But you have to know it's just supposed to be that way. All I want to do is the best I can. My job is to assist him, and that's my desire. We just want to make sure every night's a great show. Once a show is over, we can't wait to do it again. We have the energy and we love the music. I'm at this spot right now where I'm going back and remembering. I'm going into the studio and playing this beautiful piano I've got out at Pedernales Studio that Freddy rebuilt, and I'm playing some things I remember from a long time ago, just the piano. But I want to learn more new things too. It's very hard when you get to the stage that everything you play is a performance. I want to still be learning, do some learning. There are many things to learn, many shows to play." In the fall of 2007, Bobbie finally got around to releasing an album of her own, *Audiobiography*. Her little brother joined her to sing and play guitar on the first and last songs on the album, "Back to Earth" and "Til Tomorrow," which he wrote. The other ten tracks were simply Bobbie playing the Bösendorfer piano.

Bobbie was as zealous as her brother when it came to playing for the sake of playing. She filled in at Abbott Methodist Church, where she first performed as a pianist, when the church's volunteer organist quit in protest of the well-publicized arrest of the Nelson siblings near Breaux Bridge, Louisiana, on September 18, 2006. Bobbie, Willie, David Anderson, Gates Moore, and Tony Sizemore were returning to Texas after Willie headlined a benefit concert with Ray Price, Don Helms, and Andy Norman at the Riverwalk Theatre in Montgomery, Alabama, celebrating Hank Williams's birthday. At a commercial vehicle checkpoint on Interstate 10, Louisiana state police detected a suspicious odor emanating from the bus. A search of Honeysuckle Rose yielded nearly one and a half pounds of high-quality marijuana and a baggie full of psychedelic mushrooms. The accused, all eligible for AARP membership, were issued misdemeanor drug-possession citations and released at the scene.

Willie joked about the incident. "It was like they busted an old folks home," he said. The cops didn't wake Ben Dorcy, eighty-three, the world's oldest band boy, who was asleep on the sofa. "I told them you were dead," Willie informed Ben afterwards. Willie considered himself fortunate. "It's a good thing I had a bag of marijuana instead of a bag of spinach—I'd be dead by now," he said, referring to a nationwide outbreak of E. coli–tainted spinach that had killed several people. Television comedian Jay Leno joked, "Willie was really worried he was going to have to spend the rest of 1969 in jail."

The stop prevented Willie, his sister, and his road manager and drivers from attending the funeral of former Texas governor Ann Richards, a Waco native and a kindred celebrity. They both stood tall in their chosen paths and shared a love of where they came from. Willie sang the cowboy lament, "Don't Fence Me In" for Ann's official biography film, which was adopted as the theme song for the 110th Congress of the United States by Nancy Pelosi, the first female Speaker of the House of Representatives.

Willie was philosophical about the bust. "Compared to other negative experiences it could have been, it was okay," he said.

While Willie didn't often share his beliefs with the audience when he was onstage (he was there to give a great show, not to tell the audience what he was thinking), he did offer comfort, bandannas, and whiskey to Democratic Party lawmakers from the Texas Legislature who fled the state to Oklahoma and New Mexico to avoid voting on redistricting mandated by Texas Republican congressman Tom DeLay, whose efforts were ultimately repudiated by the United States Supreme Court. Willie's support of the renegade Democrats, the dominant political party in Texas for all of Willie's life up until the 1990s, prompted several Republican legislators in Texas to shoot down efforts to name a road in Willie's honor (Republican presidents George H. W. Bush, George W. Bush, and Ronald Reagan all had Texas roadways named in their honor while they were still alive). Willie said he wouldn't have wanted a road named after him anyway, because people would be cussing him while stuck in traffic.

Willie leaned left and populist but otherwise was predictably unpredictable. He supported Republican Barry Goldwater when he was running against Texas Democrat Lyndon B. Johnson for president in 1964, according to Zeke Varnon, and recorded a radio spot for Texas Republican John Tower in one of his races for U.S. Senate. In 1989, he and Waylon campaigned for Houston mayor Fred Hofheinz. In 1992, he backed third-party presidential candidate H. Ross Perot. In 2004 and 2008 Willie endorsed Ohio congressman Dennis Kucinich, a Gandhi Peace Prize winner, in his unsuccessful bids for the Democratic Party nomination for president of the United States. Although Kucinich garnered few delegate votes, he positioned himself squarely as an antiwar, anticorporate candidate.

"Willie has always been to the left of me, and always a little higher than me," Kinky Friedman said. "Before the Iraq invasion [in 2003], we were arguing about the wisdom of it, and Willie was against it. He was where the country is now. I was for it. I thought, quite logically at the time, having a stake in the Middle East and Israel, let's knock off a bad guy. Willie was smoking a joint the size of a large Kosher salami on this occasion, and I felt I wasn't getting through to him, which was very frustrating. That's when I told him, 'Look, Willie, this guy is a tyrannical bully, and we've got to take him out.' Willie said, 'No, he's our president, and we've got to stand by him.' "

Kinky, whose best-selling detective novels earned him status as a White House guest during both the Clinton and Bush administrations, was still smarting from his unsuccessful run for governor of Texas. He garnered less than 15 percent of the vote—taking last place in the four-candidate race—despite his promise if elected to name Willie Texas's energy czar. Humbled in defeat, he credited Willie as the better politician. "His political instincts are very good. The beauty of Willie is that he can do a show and you don't know where he stands. He won't make an off-the-cuff political remark onstage or be flying an American flag or anything. But if you talk to him offstage, he'll give it to you."

But for all the ways he'd been able to spread whatever wealth and knowledge he'd gained through Farm Aid, through BioWillie, through singing the gospel and celebrating the secular, through being one of the few on earth to resolve the eternal contradiction of embracing the sacred and the profane with equal joy, at the end of the day it was all about the music.

"Some people feared movies would distract him," his daughter Lana said. "But I never thought it did.

He had so much fun playing cowboy, he was like a kid. Maybe some of the band had the fear that movies would become more important, because during the movie they wouldn't work unless Willie got them a part in the movie (which he did a lot of times). There might have been some hesitancy from the band, but if you really knew him, there was no comparison. He loved the music.

"He works all the time by choice—he's a workaholic."

"If he slowed down, he'd die," agreed Carl Cornelius, seven years his junior. "I asked him when he was going to retire, and he said, 'What do you want me to retire from? My music or my golf? That's all I do and I enjoy both of 'em.' "

Hank Cochran, Willie's long-ago partner in songwriting, wondered why Willie bothered. He didn't need the money. "Well, Hank, first of all, I like room service," Willie told him. "If I was home, I'd be pickin' in one of them bars downtown or somewhere around there for nothing. And as long as they are gonna pay me to sit on this two- or three-million-dollar bus with everything imaginable on it, I'm going to keep doin' it."

"He just wants to pick," Hank concluded. "He picks constantly. He's like Chet Atkins. Chet Atkins could never go an hour without pickin' up his guitar and pickin'. No matter where he was—on a boat, in the office, anywhere. He could talk on the phone, pick two or three songs at the same time on the guitar, and carry on a conversation with you."

To sing, to play guitar, to write songs, to lead a band, to lead a movement, to perform and entertain, to play wherever and whenever—that was living.

ON a cool, cloudy day in early January 2007, some of the crew showed up at Bobbie Nelson's house, less than a quarter mile from Pedernales Studio, led by stage manager Poodie Locke, Bobby "Flaco" Lemons, Budrock, aka Buddy Prewitt Jr., aka Peckerhead, Willie's lighting director since 1978, and a couple regulars from Poodie's Hilltop Bar down the road.

Flaco was orchestrating the teardown, packing, and moving of Bobbie's grand piano from her living room into a six-foot-tall anvil case, where it would be wheeled into a tractor-trailer and hauled to Miami. When the band arrived in Florida after a run through Europe, the piano would be waiting.

Bobbie Nelson's Persian rug was rolled up and then Flaco broke down the piano in less than fifteen minutes, removed the wheels and legs, and directed helpers as they tilted the instrument into the padded case. It was the same drill done every night following a performance before the piano was unpacked at the next tour stop.

"Did you have a good time off?" Bobbie asked the men, who'd all been on an extended break. Vacation stories were swapped and grumbles exchanged over the news that there would be a nineteen-city mini-tour in March with Willie, Merle Haggard, and Ray Price, backed by Asleep at the Wheel and without the Family Band, which meant without most of the crew. The three-month break had been long enough, the road crew agreed. Two months on and another month off was putting the hurt on their wallets.

Bobbie understood the situation. Merle and Ray probably needed the work worse than they did, she reasoned. Willie was just doing what he always did, trying to lend a hand to those who extended a hand to him when he needed it. "He wasn't thinking he was hurting anybody," she said. "He was thinking of helping Ray and Merle."

There was idle chatter about the band's semi-acoustic live sound. "His voice is as good as it's ever been," Poodie Locke reckoned. "I can hear myself better," Bobbie nodded. Budrock agreed: "When I listen to the *Willie and Family Live* album from Harrah's in 1978, it sounds like everybody was on speed. Every song is too fast. Everything's slowed down now."

Paul English had initially resisted the downsizing. "It was Willie's idea to cut me down to one snare drum, which I thought was ridiculous," he said later. "But he was right all along. We used to be a hot, smoking band. Now that we are in our seventies, we don't wanna be a hot, smoking band anymore." They don't have to be. As Paul put it, "The band just feels the music. You never know where he's going to go, but then he will hit a chord and it will bring it back to your memory, and you know where he is going. It just comes to your mind. I mainly just listen. Playing with Willie is like driving a car, you float along, and then you come to a red light, which is the end of a song. Then you stop, and you have to pay attention. Then the red light turns green, and then you are going and you can think of other things while you are driving. But then you come to another red light, and it's time to stop and look both ways before you take off again. It's similar to that."

Flaco Lemons heard it all. It took a special kind of soundman to understand Willie, and the lean West Texan did so more than anyone. "On the surface, Willie has a band that can't find One [the beat] with both hands," he said. "The beat is flexible. All these things people try to spend days, months, years, to avoid doing—everybody loves him for it. He'll forget the words or do something that's not supposed to be there, and he'll just stop and smile. The crowd just loves it. Usually, if the crowd sees that you're vulnerable, they'll turn on you. Not Willie. He just smiles and starts over."

Flaco factored everyone's age on stage when he miked the band. "Willie's voice is not as strong as it was," he said. "A lot of times you gotta have a lot of input and I don't care what kind of PA you have, you only have a certain amount of gain. When you don't have that, you can't turn a knob and get it. Basically, it's a pyramid. The vocal is at the top. At the bottom are kick drums and bass, but we've just got the bass and Bee plays it differently because he doesn't have drums to couple up with. He plays more of a melodic bass. A lot of times, I can tune out Willie's guitar from the PA and can't tell the difference. I get more out of his guitar with his vocal mic than I do out of the mic that's three inches away. Nobody else does anything like this. Nobody else could get away with it."

Flaco told Willie that keeping up with him was "like throwing up a ball and turning around real fast three times and being able to catch it."

"Well, yeah, most of the time," Willie replied.

Part of Flaco's job was to record every show. For the first couple of years he was doing sound, he spent hours on Willie's bus, listening to show tapes with the boss. "He hired me to get a feel of what he was trying to feel because standing up there you can't tell. His style is not as casual and lax as you might think. It's like an orchestra. They are all playing different things; it's how they fit together. That's a lot harder to do than with everyone up there playing on the beat."

He cited the night Phil Lesh, the Grateful Dead's bassist, asked to sit in. Bee handed him the bass and walked off. "Phil was lost," Flaco said. At the end of the song, Bee walked back on. As Phil handed back the instrument, Bee winked. "Ain't so easy playing nine and a half, is it?"

"He follows me," Bee explained of Willie and his behind-the-beat sense of timing. "That's my job. My job is to show him where One is, so he can go wherever he wants to but he's got a place to come back home to. I don't listen to him. I've gotten to the point where I can listen to him now, but you don't get too caught up in what he's doing because he'll take you up the creek and dump you. That's the fun of it. That's his style. I think Waylon had it right: Willie can't count. He did it last night where he broke meter a couple times; when he can do that and we can make it seem like the melody doesn't catch it—that's our job. Somebody will sit in for a song or two every now and then, and I tell guys, 'That was like four and a quarter but wait till five and an eighth comes up.' "

The road crew had to pay attention too, or at least most of them did most of the time, although they good-naturedly grumbled about how none of the other crew guys were the professionals they were, as road warriors tended to do.

The only instructions Willie gave Budrock when he joined up was not to use green lighting on-stage. "A psychic told me it made me weak," Willie told him.

"You don't have to worry about that because I don't use green anyway," Buddy replied.

"You can use it on the band," allowed Willie. "Just don't use it on me."

Budrock ran a self-contained lighting operation when he joined Willie in 1979, with his own tractor-trailer diesel rig and his own driver and crew. "You had to have somebody to take with you to hang every-thing to be safe because you'd have tons of equip-ment hanging over your head," he said. "There weren't any such things as riggers. Nobody in Columbus, Georgia, knew what to do. You had to be self-sufficient back in those days and carry everything with you. You couldn't count on anybody having anything. Today you have house riggers. You draw a circle and an *X* and say, 'I want the points there.' "

Budrock knew his boss man's ticks. "He doesn't want to be lit the whole time," he said. "When someone else is doing a solo, he'll go back and get a drink of water, adjust his guitar, wipe sweat off his brow, or change the hat. He's still lit, he's just not the primary spotlight."

In addition to no-green, Budrock practiced a no-babyshit-yellow-on-Willie-either policy. "I used to put a real strong yellow color downlight on Willie when he was doing 'Red Headed Stranger' and came to the line about 'the yellow-haired lady,' " he said. "He just didn't like that color, so he asked me not to use it again."

The approach was old-school show business all the way. "All the new technology is all about programming a show during rehearsals and hitting the cues during the performance," Budrock said. "But Willie doesn't follow a set list, so I can't do that. I can tell if he starts one song, it'll be three songs in a row. If he starts 'Funny How Time Slips Away,' I know 'Crazy' and 'Night Life' will follow. If he's limited to an hour and a half or less or he's coming up on curfew, he'll start slinging 'em at me. The band knows the same time I know—when Willie hits the first note. I was taught to follow the bass and the drums when doing lighting, but that's not true with Willie. We all follow Willie. He's the one who starts everything."

Above all, Budrock knew to avoid aiming lights

directly into Willie's eyes. Direct light thwarted him from making eye contact with the audience.

Eye contact was everything. "A long time ago I'd look for one friendly face in the audience, when I was first getting started and I didn't know anybody, so I'd try to find somebody that was looking at me and liking what I was doing," Willie said. "I'd sing to that person all night long. I still look for who's looking at me — I'll check the audience out and see who's got me zeroed in and try to make contact back with them. And that grows, that little-bitty spark of energy exchanged will pick up some more around you and you can see some other people getting off on that one exchange."

Feeding off the audience was a factor in why neither band nor crew members were particularly fond of private parties, a necessary evil of roadwork. "They're the gigs that pay the most, but they're the ones we like least," Budrock said. "People talk through the whole damn thing. Nobody's paying attention, but you don't tell them to shut up. It's sad. It's the only time most people attending don't have worn blue jeans; the soles on their boots are new. They're dressed in designer rope skirts, cowboy hats that have never been worn, and they don't even watch the show. They pay us double at least, but it's frustrating to

Willie. He doesn't like doing them, because he doesn't get any energy off the crowd. It distracts him."

No matter where they played, one thing the band leader made sure of was band and crew were not distracted. "He throws shit on you," Budrock said. "He used to pull one out from forty years ago, and Paul would know it and Bobbie would know it but nobody else would. If he's doing something the band doesn't know, I'm not going to know it, either. If he wants a solo in a situation like that, they're all looking at him anyway and I'm looking at him, trying to figure out where it's going. After thirty years, I know a lot of his tendencies, like he's getting ready to give something to Bobbie or Jody on that side of the stage. I knew his hand was hurting a long time before he said anything about carpal tunnel."

Budrock also knew, at the end of the day Willie would be just fine if lit with a single naked lightbulb above his head.

TOUR manager David Anderson and his bodyguard L.G. were constants by Willie's side in public. David was the precious child of the family, joining when he was eighteen after meeting him through Leon Russell. He had been riding with Willie for more than thirty-five years. "I'm Willie's assistant," he explained of his role, although no one had an official title. "I ride on the bus, live on the bus, smoke a lot of dope, work on getting the word out on biodiesel, Farm Aid, and other causes. These days it's become less about the music and more about the other twenty-two hours in a day to fill his time." David was Willie's go-to guy, checking into hotels, looking after Bobbie, making sure everything in Willie's immediate world was to his liking, setting up appointments, and screening interviews and visitors who stopped by to say hidy.

David and Willie had been around each other long enough to just as well be family. "We will both be as blunt and as honest and as vocal to the point of almost rudeness with each other," David said. "If we go too far, we apologize for hurting each other's feelings, maybe, sometimes. It's that honesty, I don't know any other way to be. I'm not going to change it for him or anyone else. But you do give in to the ego. He is your boss. He's ultimately in control. Whatever he wants to do, we'll ultimately do. But I'll say, 'Damn, is that a good idea?' It would be lying to do otherwise, and that's not what I do."

Like in many other families, a strong paternal streak ran through this one. "Not everyone likes Daddy on Friday but loves him on Sunday," David Anderson said. "It goes back and forth. When you first asked what I did, I wanted to say I'm a babysitter. The kids do grow up and become the parents. I've been around Willie, Bobbie, and Lana longer than my own family. I love them and I hate them."

Whatever his conflicted feelings, David was close enough to the Nelsons to be able to come out of the closet in 2006 and reveal his homosexuality. It came on the heels of publicity surrounding the Academy Award–nominated *Brokeback Mountain,* to which Willie contributed music for the soundtrack. Willie signaled his acceptance of David's decision by making a joke out of it, protesting to David, "And after all these years when I was in the back of the bus alone . . ." David and his boyfriend appeared in the video of "Cowboys Are Frequently, Secretly (Fond of Each Other)."

Family, more than ever, was defined as the people you surround yourself with. Daughter Lana Nelson, Willie and Martha's firstborn, had joined the rolling roadshow for good in 1995. Her brief marriage to country singer Johnny Rodriguez was headed for divorce, "so rather than leave me here and worry, Dad asked me to go on the road." Her children were grown up and out of the house. She'd had enough of the married life. The highway sounded pretty good.

Like the others before her, she had to figure out

her place in the show on wheels. "Paul did the money," she said. "I had to figure out what David did."

She started the WillieNelson.com Web site, posting photographs, reviews, and filing on-the-road reports in the *Pedernales Poo Poo* online newsletter.

This post from January 22, 2007:

Day off in Amsterdam

This was the proposed schedule . . .

DAY OFF—AMSTERDAM

10:00 A.M.—Band and Crew—Hotel arrival / check-in

NOON—Lunch / coffee shop across the street from hotel

13:00 P.M.—Take trolley to Museum—Van Gogh

14:30 P.M.—Walk from Van Gogh museum to Rijksmuseum

16:00 P.M.—Take trolley to city square to listen to street musicians

17:00 P.M.—Shopping in City Square. Take trolley back to hotel

19:00 P.M.—Dinner—Italian restaurant across from hotel

21:00 P.M. — Walk off dinner with a nice stroll through Red Light District

21:30 P.M. — Dessert at Dutch Chocolate Bar, walk back to hotel

22:00 P.M. — Nightcap at Hotel bar

This was the actual *schedule:*

DAY OFF — AMSTERDAM

10:00 A.M. — Hotel arrival / check-in

10:05 A.M. — Visit coffee shop across the street from hotel

13:00 P.M. — Walk next door to Italian restaurant for lunch. Eat fast.

14:30 P.M. — Walk back to coffee shop across street from hotel

16:00 P.M. — Still in coffee shop across street from hotel

17:00 P.M. — Coffee shop across the street from hotel

19:00 P.M. — Coffee shop across the street from hotel

21:00 P.M. — Dessert at coffee shop across street from hotel

22:00 P.M. — Coffee shop across street from hotel closes

22:15 P.M. — Reluctantly leave coffee shop. Last
patrons on premises

22:18 P.M. — Feel way back to hotel across street
from coffee shop, narrowly avoiding getting hit
by the trolley

22:25 P.M. — Asleep in hotel across street from
coffee shop

The most important role Lana created for herself was personal chef. "I figured out what Dad needed more, which was good cooking. They were stopping at restaurants and the food wasn't very good." So she became her father's cook, doing many of the same domestic chores she had done with her kids. Honeysuckle Rose was outfitted with a full kitchen, and Lana stood at the counter preparing three meals a day.

"He likes my cooking. He knows what he can eat — what upsets his stomach and what won't," she said. "You can't afford an upset stomach when you're about to go out there and sing."

During a couple of his highest-flying years, Willie had hired a cook for his entourage named "The Beast," who traveled in his own bus, the former Pauletta, Paul English's old bus he'd gotten from Porter Wagoner after a smaller bus he had outfitted with steel plates proved too heavy to be roadworthy. Beast's bus, the fourth in the entourage, was outfitted with a kitchen, booths up front, and a large back room. But the band and crew ultimately rejected his cooking, citing his Italian roots. "He was a Yankee and we weren't Yankees," Poodie Locke said. "I love veal parmigiana and I love pasta, but he baked everything. You got to have grease to make a turd, you know. I'm serious. Everybody was all plugged up from eating all this baked food. I almost went to blows with him, teaching him to make iced tea. The Beast was a good guy, but he just never fit in." A cowboy could stand only so much cannoli.

The band and crew ate meals provided by promoters, with menus including both green, leafy foods that were often organic and, per the needs of Poodie Locke and others, meat and taters with a little bit of grease. As the rider noted, there was no substitute for bacon.

There was no substitute for riding with her dad, as far as Lana was concerned. "I get to see the last half of the show and then he comes onto the bus," she said. "He and the band are real high, or not, if the show didn't go well, but usually he's real high. He's happy. He's hungry. Everything tastes real good to him. We're rolling. The phone isn't ringing. No one's asking him to do anything. He's got his bus clothes on, his real big T-shirt. He's comfortable. Eating his eggs. That's my favorite time. He doesn't eat much meat. I make a lot of vegetables. He loves cabbage. Thank God I don't have to please everybody. I just have to please Dad."

Lana stayed up into the early morning, looking after her father until David got up. "It takes both of us to handle that, plus Mark's office [financial manager Mark Rothbaum] to do all the legal stuff," Lana said. "Then there's the two other buses. He keeps so many people hopping."

Daddy's girl just wanted him to take better care of himself. "But I know where he's coming from and that's what he's going to do. I just try to figure out ways to make it easier on him, instead of trying to stand in his way."

In early 2007, Willie played a benefit for his tour manager David Anderson and David's partner, Darrin Davis, a Dallas choreographer and singer. The couple had created the AetheriA Foundation to promote art in schools and award college scholarships for the arts in the Dallas–Fort Worth area. The foundation made its public debut with "AetheriA: An Artclectic Evening," a gala fund-raiser, including a $1,000-a-plate VIP dinner at the Nokia Theatre in Grand Prairie, and featuring performances by ·the Dallas Black Dance Theatre and the Living Opera of

Dallas, a vignette by performers from Cirque du Soleil, and performances by the Fort Worth Symphony Orchestra and Willie Nelson and band.

"Yes, I sort of thought he was nuts when he first told me about it," Willie told the *Fort Worth Star-Telegram* of David's idea. "But I've seen a lot of nutty ideas turn out pretty good, so I didn't want to completely squelch it for him." Instead, he donated his services and those of the band and crew.

The band and crew had driven overnight from playing a gambling casino in Tunica, Mississippi, arriving early enough to indulge in that timeless road game called "Hurry Up and Wait."

Amid the chaos of a symphony orchestra and stage-hands at a rehearsal, Willie walked onto the stage to the applause of symphony musicians. The star-studded event, which attracted an audience of around two thousand, was a fancier-than-normal Willie Nelson and Family Show. His friends Kinky Friedman and Little Jewford, actors Morgan Fairchild and Larry Hagman (J.R. of television's *Dallas*), and stunt-freak Johnny Knoxville of MTV's *Jackass* fame shared the emcee podium. Johnny Knoxville tried to lead the crowd into a cheer for Poodie, but most of the audience had no clue who Poodie was. Backstage, Johnny Knoxville spoke admiringly of Poodie doing a pole dance at his home in California, while Willie and Kinky discussed Anna Nicole Smith, the buxom, bleached-blonde bombshell from Texas and the well-publicized paternity of her four-month-old daughter, while an effeminate cast performer from Cirque du Soleil walked past. "He sure isn't the father," Willie joshed.

Willie and Mickey Raphael performed six classics with the symphony, with arranger David Campbell as guest conductor — the trifecta of his early hits written for others ("Funny How Time Slips Away," "Night Life," and "Crazy") along with Darren Hayes's "I Can't Help Falling in Love with You," a cover of Jerome Kern's much-covered "All the Things You Are," and a stirring rendition of his own "Healing Hands of Time."

The strings, oboes, and cellos effectively conveyed the deep sadness of the melodies and the songs' lyrics. His vocals were strong and assertive.

Willie returned to the stage for a very loose and very rambling forty-five-minute set as Grandpa Nelson and His Extended Family, the band augmented by sons Luke on guitar and Micah on percussion (the boys had just finished recording an album at Pedernales by their new band, 40 Points) and, for the last three songs, Dallas actress-singer Jessica Simpson.

Lest anyone think the idea of Willie performing with a symphony behind him was a one-of-a-kind experience, Mickey Raphael put the show in perspective. "Yeah, this was a good gig. But you should have heard us with the Los Angeles Philharmonic at the Hollywood Bowl." He was referring to the four-night stand where Mrs. Gene Autry showed up to present Willie with another pair of her deceased husband's custom cowboy boots. "Willie didn't take them off the whole time we were California," Bobbie Nelson said.

ON a chilly April afternoon in 2007, forty years after the Summer of Love in San Francisco spawned the hippie phenomenon, three buses and a tractor-trailer bearing the Willie Nelson and Family Show rolled up to a side street by a park one block from the corner of Fillmore and Geary, signaling the beginning of a five-night run at the Fillmore Ballroom. The storied music venue dated back to the 1930s but was best known as the mother ship of psychedelic music in the late 1960s, where bands like Santana, the Jefferson Airplane, Big Brother and the Holding Company, Steve Miller, and the Grateful Dead, as well as concert promoter Bill Graham, got their start. The Fillmore had been one of the most enduring institutions of the counterculture ever since.

"It's not a very good payday," Paul English said of

the 1,250-capacity room, "but they're good people and the room's got a reputation. We play here for several nights every year."

Rick Moher drove the equipment truck. Neal Smidt was behind the wheel of the bus dubbed the Smoking Bus, which carried stage manager Poodie Locke, audio pro Kenny Koepke, house engineer Flaco Lemons, lighting director Buddy Prewitt Jr., aka Budrock, and guitarist Jody Payne.

The second bus, driven by Johnny Sizemore, was the no-smoking bus. It carried drummer and business manager Paul English, his brother Billy, the band's percussionist, harmonica player Mickey Raphael, bassist Bee Spears, L.G. — Larry Gorham — Willie's security, Tunin' Tom Hawkins, the piano tuner and guitar tech, and Josh Duke, the hired hand in charge of monitors.

The no-smoking bus was inspired by Paul's quitting smoking after a house fire. He had raced back into his home in Dallas to fetch his black hat with the gold bling and some of his guns, and suffered permanent lung damage. Whether marijuana qualified as smoking was a running debate among the Family.

The third bus, with the airbrushed painting of an Indian warrior on horseback on one side and a painting of an eagle's head morphing into Willie Nelson's face on the back, was Honeysuckle Rose IV, the 2004 Prevost known simply as the Bus, containing the boss, his sister, his eldest daughter, his right-hand man, and his drivers.

The crew did their usual afternoon load-in. Tunin' Tom invested close to an hour unpacking and tuning Sister Bobbie's Steinway B piano as Poodie oversaw the stage setup, backstage accommodations, and hospitality rider. In the back of the room, Flaco Lemons tweaked the knobs and pods on the huge audio console. Upstairs, Budrock conversed with the house lighting director, matching his ideal lighting chart with her lighting computer program. In a dressing room off to the side of the stage, Jody Payne was pulling out the pickup from the base of his guitar to fiddle with the electronics while Kenny Koepke positioned the microphones onstage and helped Billy English set up his array of percussion instruments.

The band and crew ate the dinner served by the Fillmore in the back bar, talked about the previous night's gig at the TV Land Awards show in Los Angeles, honoring classic television series, where Jerry Mathers and Tony Dow, who played Beaver and his brother, Wally, in the series *Leave It to Beaver*, showed up; planned group tours of Alcatraz; a medical marijuana clinic; and two golf excursions, and went through the familiar ritual of getting ready for the

show. Several individuals were invited to step inside
Honeysuckle Rose such as veteran *San Francisco
Chronicle* music writer Joel Selvin and the manager
of the reggae band Toots and the Maytals, bearing
an herbal gift to Willie from Toots.

By eight o'clock, the auditorium was packed with
a sold-out house of young and middle-aged hipsters
primed for the night. Tobacco smokers had to go
outside to a designated smoking area to indulge their
habit. But the ballroom was clouded with a thick
haze of smoke bearing the pungent scent of high-
quality marijuana.

Fifteen minutes later, Scooter Franks, all three
hundred pounds of him, scooted to the microphone.
Scooter, along with his brother Bo, had been following Willie Nelson and Family in their van and trailer
since the early 1970s, hawking Willie T-shirts, posters ("Willie Nelson For President, Paul English For
Vice"), records, tapes, CDs, and Willie braids.
Scooter had adopted a secondary role as Willie's
announcer, and his bullshit ran thick as a midway
carnival barker's as he hyped the five Willie albums
out this year, including the fifty-five-song four-CD
set ("sold only at the Fillmore tonight!"), cited Willie's
birthday ("He's been saying that for the past two
months," Budrock muttered in the lighting booth),
and told everyone that Paul English was celebrating

his forty-first year with Willie (Budrock weighed in on that one too), and that they could hear this kind of music on *Willie's Place* on XM satellite radio and could even call Willie on *Willie Wednesdays* on Bill Mack's XM show. With a final flourish extolling the virtues of an artist who's "played over six thousand stages" (greatly underestimating the real number), Scooter shouted, "Let's hear it for Willie Nelson!" as the band shuffled onto the stage and the lights hit the huge State of Texas flag hanging from the backdrop.

The cumulative experience of Willie Nelson's six-piece band exceeded four hundred years, a number unmatched by any group in popular music. Sister Bobbie Lee, seventy-six, wearing a black pantsuit with subtle sparkles and a black wide-brim felt hat that deliciously complemented her long mane of blonde hair, sat down in front of her piano. Helping seat Bobbie was Jody Payne, seventy-one and rock-star handsome after all these years with a full head of honey-colored hair and full mustache and fresh beard that tempered his crusty, grizzly countenance. On the opposite side of the stage, Mickey Raphael, fifty-five, stood tall, looking dark and cool in a black long-sleeved button-down shirt, shirttail out, jeans, and boots, one hand clutching a harmonica. Behind them, bunched together on a riser, were Paul English, seventy-five, the man in black and Willie's best friend, sitting on a stool and playing a snare drum with brushes, and, at the other end, Paul's little brother, Billy, fifty-six ("We don't know what he does," Willie says, introducing him to the audience), dressed casually, moving businesslike among bells, chimes, shakers, bongos, and sticks to embellish the percussive impact. Between Paul and Billy was Bee Spears, fifty-four, alternately sitting and standing while playing bass and keeping the beat.

The crew were the graybeards of roadies, with less turnover than even the Grateful Dead's. "We're all Texans and we grew up together," Kenny Koepke said during setup before one Fillmore show. "When I joined, my sister [Connie] warned me this was something that wasn't going to last long, and that was twenty-nine years ago."

Willie bounded onto the stage with his arms raised high like a boxing champion, wearing a black T-shirt advertising Poodie's Hilltop Bar, loose black jeans, dark tennis shoes, and a black felt cowboy hat over his long braids. He draped his familiar red-white-and-blue macramé guitar strap around his neck and strummed Trigger, his battered, beat-up, priceless Martin guitar. He looked older and grayer because he *was* older and grayer, his wild eyebrows and large ears accentuating his almost seventy-four years. He flashed a quick smile that seemed sincere while his piercing brown eyes scanned the crowd, trying to make eye contact. Cell phones with cameras raised high above heads in the audience captured the grand entry.

Without a cue, he strummed the chords to "Whiskey River" with his right hand, his left hand pressing strings onto the fret board. The lyrics rolled out of his mouth slurred in a talking blues. The race was on. The next two hours were spent thumbing through his own version of the Great American Songbook, introducing himself with the familiar "Well, hello, there," the first lines to "Funny How Time Slips Away," one of his first songwriting successes in 1961, and segueing into "Crazy" and "Night Life," his vocals warming up and gaining strength as he spoke both wisdom and poetry in lines like "life is just another scene / in this old world of broken dreams."

"Little sister" Bobbie cut loose on the instrumental breakdown "Down Yonder," her attack of the notes establishing the band's honky-tonk bona fides before the spotlight shifted to Jody, who croaked out Merle Haggard's "Working Man's Blues" in honor of his former employer and blue-collar folks everywhere, followed by Willie singing three Kris Kristofferson songs in a row—"Help Me Make It Through the

Night," "Me and Bobby McGee," and a new one, "Moment of Forever."

Over the course of the first few minutes, Willie the Showman, Willie the Songwriter, Willie the Bandleader, and Willie the Stylist all made appearances. The band was hardly warmed up. The music went stone country on Lefty Frizzell's "If You've Got the Money (I've Got the Time)" as Willie tossed his hat into the crowd and started twisting up a headband out of a Willie bandanna, using his guitar neck as an extra hand before putting it on. The band got to swinging on "All of Me," did a dramatic build with some serious rock and roll three-chord guitar riffing on the new Willie composition, "Gotta Get Over You," and shifted into a sweet groove for "Red Headed Stranger," "Blue Eyes Crying in the Rain," "Blue Skies," and "Stardust"—all singles from Willie's biggest hit-making period—before stomping their way through three Hank Williams songs in a row.

Elvis-worthy screams greeted the romantic ballad "To All the Girls I've Loved Before," made famous by his duet with Julio Iglesias. He sang Hoagy Carmichael's ballad "Georgia," popularized by Ray Charles, Steve Goodman's "City of New Orleans," made famous by Arlo Guthrie, and Townes Van

Zandt's "Pancho and Lefty" with so much familiarity that all the songs sounded like he'd written them. There were plenty of reasons for the perception. Willie's version of "Georgia" alternated with Brother Ray's on the sound system at the Stone Mountain Park historic site near Atlanta at sunset every day. Arlo may have had the hit single of Goodman's tune, but the lines "Good morning, America, how are ya? Don't you know me? I'm your native son/ I'm a train they call the City of New Orleans, I'll be gone five hundred miles when the day is done," with the crowd singing along and adding whoops, were autobiographical as far as Willie was concerned. And without Willie covering his song, Townes would have likely died unrecognized and unappreciated.

"Mammas, Don't Let Your Babies Grow Up to Be Cowboys" and "On the Road Again" got the sing-along treatment from the audience too, but it was the gospel numbers — "Will the Circle Be Unbroken?," "I'll Fly Away," and "I Saw the Light" — that roused them so much that the room felt like it was levitating. Agnostics may have outnumbered Christians in the crowd, but the man onstage holding his index finger high in the air for emphasis, preaching salvation through music, had them testifying, shouting, and raising beer cups and cellular telephones.

"Me and Paul" was a literal telling, with Paul

watching Willie's back like he'd done for more than forty years, moving the brushes over the snare and beaming every time the words made the audience cheer, especially the references to something illegal going on. The line "Nashville was the roughest" had become "Branson was the roughest" because it was. "Still Is Still Moving," his signature piece of the 1990s, was followed by two newer originals, "I Ain't Superman" and "You Don't Think I'm Funny Anymore." He was pure drama on his ballad "Angel Flying Too Close to the Ground" and pure rowdy on his own "I Gotta Get Drunk." The audience spontaneously sang along and swayed without any prompting whatsoever to "Always on My Mind" and stayed with him on "Good Hearted Woman" as the spirit of Waylon filled the room.

He did "Georgia on a Fast Train" as a shout-out to Billy Joe Shaver and played some nasty guitar riffs as he grooved through Bob Wills's "Milk Cow Blues." Willie's guitar was getting respect like it never had before for good reason. He wasn't playing second to anyone anymore.

"There used to be Jackie King over there, and before that, Grady Martin over there," Willie explained. "When it got to 'Stardust,' did I want to hear me play or did I want to hear Grady play? I'm enjoying playing, I'm enjoying getting to do Django stuff. Jody instinctively does it right, [invoking Merle] Travis, Chet [Atkins], bluegrass, or whatever that is in there, with an authentic sound. I've got a good rhythm section behind me and a good band and I can go for it," he said.

The musicianship ranged from sloppy (the musicians looking at one another to find the beat) to precise (Billy English donning headphones to ring a bell on cue) to hillbilly (Bobbie's piano) to urbane (Mickey's lonely notes on his Hohner) to jazzy (Willie and Bobbie's interplay on Django Reinhardt's "Nuages")—all clearly feeding off an audience that was giving back.

Budrock worked the lighting board upstairs like an extra instrument, making the lights sync with the music, calling up cues on a computer, chattering into his headset to hip the spotlight operators to what was coming up next, sliding knobs, and orchestrating the low-key visuals, gently leading the audience to focus on vocals and instrumental solos.

An hour and forty-five minutes into the set, Willie swung around and popped the question, "Anybody have any requests?" The band was clearly tuckered out, but Willie was feeling his oats, working the house. Jody leaned in to suggest "Why Do I Have to Choose," a Willie original the band hadn't performed in at least four years. They remembered it well enough to pull it off.

After positing a rhetorical "Y'all got time for a couple more?" Willie eventually returned to a verse of "Whiskey River" and the band's instrumental outro.

On cue, David Anderson and L.G. materialized by the side of the stage to walk Willie off as soon as he finished blowing kisses, shaking hands, tossing out guitar picks, signing books, and basking in the adoration. They escorted him past the side of the stage, where folk singer Ramblin' Jack Elliott, the daughter of late guitarist Sandy Bull, and several other FOWs were standing, down the alley, and onto the bus parked in front of the Fillmore. He signed fifteen posters advertising the concert that were laid out on a sofa of Honeysuckle Rose as Bobbie tossed onto another sofa a dozen roses that had been given to her. Five minutes later, the bus pulled away from the curb in a chilly rain, headed to the next town, while Lana Nelson started cooking eggs, hash browns, and toast for her father and aunt.

Outside on the crew bus, Jody Payne waxed philosophical, telling a visitor, "Music is the only thing that's never changed. G has always been G. It never runs away, never runs off with your old lady, never gets drunk. Music is just music. I can't imagine not hearing music. We're sitting here talking in northern California, but in the background, there's a doorbell, wind chimes — it's music."

Poodie and Bee toe-to-toe in the aisle argued good-naturedly about a piece of equipment. "They wanted four hundred dollars. I wouldn't spend that on two whores!" Poodie groused. "Poodie, I believe you spent more than that on one whore," corrected Bee.

SOONER or later, no matter where they'd been or where they were going, the road led back to Abbott. "It keeps calling me back," Willie said. "You go back to where you feel good. It's not really a big surprise to me that I can't wait to get back there again and hang out or ride my bike or run or take off on some of those little roads."

On the first Sunday morning of July in the year of our Lord 2006, just north of West and not too far from Bug Tussle, Honeysuckle Rose IV and four other buses found their way to the Abbott Methodist Church and surrounded the modest 107-year-old white clapboard church with its humble shake-shingled steeple like wagons around the campfire. The United Methodist congregation of the church that Bobbie Lee and Willie Hugh Nelson had grown up in had dwindled to the point where they had merged with the larger United Methodist congregation in Hillsboro. The small church building was put up for sale, with a likely fate of being torn down or moved to become a wedding chapel on the highway or a steakhouse in Dallas. Donald Reed, Willie's classmate from the class of '50, called him with a heads-up. The asking price for the prettiest building in all of Abbott was $72,000.

"See if they'll take twenty-five hundred more than they're asking," Willie instructed Donald.

An old-fashioned Sunday-morning gospel singing celebrated the church's rebirth. The chapel, which could seat a little more than one hundred worshippers, was packed. All two hundred folding chairs under tent awnings on the lawn outside the church were filled, its occupants cooling themselves with commemorative fans while watching two giant flatscreens showing what was going on inside. On the lawn by the tents, a Sunday community supper of fresh food along with free bottles of Willie Nelson Spring Water was being readied by members of the Texas Organic Farmers & Gardeners Association and the Austin Spice Company.

Inside, on the platform by the pulpit, was Sister Bobbie, with her long mane of honey blonde hair, seated behind the seven-foot Steinway B she played on the road, home again with her brother by her side, dressed in his Sunday best, with a dark suit jacket over a black oxford shirt, his hair pulled back in a ponytail down to the small of his back—as long as his sister's—playing the prelude to "What a Friend We Have in Jesus," she on piano, he on guitar.

"What a glorious day," preached Pastor Denise Rogers to open the service. "Let us pray." With the congregation bowing their heads she read from chapter 43, verse 19 of the Book of Isaiah, focusing on the line "I am about to do a new thing, now it springs forth, do you not perceive it? I will make a way in the wilderness and rivers in the desert."

"That is why we're here today," the pastor said. "God is doing a new thing here today in Abbott, Texas. These words were written for a group that had been in exile, a larger number who had dwindled down to a few, a remnant that had faith in God."

When it was Willie's turn, he brought it all back home and witnessed like he rarely did when he was the star of the Willie Nelson Show. "Sister Bobbie and I have been going to this church ever since we were born," he said to the gathering. "I don't know what persuasion y'all were when you entered this door, but now you're all members of the Abbott Methodist Church and will be, forever and ever. We're starting a Department of Peace here in Abbott; we've got departments of war everywhere, so go forth and spread the peace."

Holding a lyric sheet, he sang "Precious Memories" as Bobbie played piano and Leon Russell, tucked away in a corner, ever enigmatic with white hair, gray-and-black jacket, black Hawaiian shirt, and dark sunglasses, played chords on a small Yamaha. Willie didn't need a lyric sheet to forcefully sing the next song with the opening line, "There's a family Bible on the table, its pages worn and hard to read . . ."

Willie introduced a preacher friend from up near Dallas, Dave Rich, who told a story about Willie writing "It's Not for Me to Understand" back in the mid-1960s. Upon hearing the demo Rich had recorded of the song, Willie jumped from behind a desk and started beating the floor, saying to Pete Drake, "I don't care if I never get another song recorded, I'm satisfied now." The song of acceptance and redemption became part of the *Yesterday's Wine* song cycle.

He sang "What Happened to Peace on Earth?" solo, then was joined by Paul and Billy and Mickey and Bee for some up-tempo gospel with "Will the Circle Be Unbroken?" and "I'll Fly Away."

Daughter Susie Nelson read the closing statement from the Abbott United Methodist Church congregation, affirming "the end of an era is the beginning of another" and that a church is not "a place or building, but the people of God."

"That's where we all are today. Thank you for coming out and visiting with us today," Willie said, leading into "Amazing Grace," accompanied by piano, harmonica, and the whir of locusts in full summer song and the low rumble of five buses idling, punctuated by an occasional warning whistle from a Katy freight train passing through.

The service was captured by television cameras and microphones for the RFD cable television channel, local stations in Dallas–Fort Worth and Waco, and for KHBR 1560, "Radio for Your Hometown," the station where Willie Nelson first performed on the radio.

Outside town along Trlica Road, an expansive blue Texas sky laced with puffy clouds lorded over a landscape in full summer glory, with thickets of trees along property lines, clustered around houses, and in groves lining creek and river bottoms, wearing their richest greens. What little corn, wheat, and sorghum remained in the fields had dried up and withered, but tiny white cotton bolls were beginning to emerge on the cotton plants. Giant sunflowers dappled stretches of the rolling countryside with splotches of bright yellow.

The good, God-fearing church people along with other town citizens pressed up close to Honeysuckle Rose IV, trying to peer through the tinted windows of the touring bus belonging to the local boy made good, alongside representatives of the sheriff's department and fire department who were keeping the street clear. They all appeared to be oblivious to the putrid skunk aroma wafting out of the bus—the telltale sign that someone was burning Willie Weed on this fine Sunday morning. The firemen and the sheriff's deputies were too busy cheering the little man emerging from the church to mind the odor.

Instamatics, 35-mm film, and digital and cell phone cameras were held high in the air, all aimed at the man slowly making his way into the throng of the faithful who were crowding the twenty-yard path from church door to bus. A noble among his flock, he was one of them. He set off a round of cheers by simply signing the guitar that had been passed over heads in his direction, and another round as he sent it back over the sea of hands to its owner.

That Sunday morning, Abbott looked, sounded, and smelled liked Texas. The gathering attracted all shapes, sizes, and colors, an estuary of humanity where the sacred mingled with the profane, ebbing and flowing around a solitary man, a Texan's Texan.

Willie Hugh Nelson was living in the moment, "the only time," he said, "I can do anything about."

He had done what he'd set out to do. "I think I've about covered it," he said with satisfaction. And he was on to the next.

AUTHOR'S NOTE

The realization that Texans are different from everybody else hit me about an hour after I'd first set foot on Texas soil. I was only two years old, but I distinctly remember my father picking up my mother, my sister, and me at the Greater Fort Worth International Airport and driving us to our new home in Fort Worth, stopping along the way at the Big Apple Barbecue on Highway 183. The waitresses talked funny, and the smoked beef brisket covered in barbecue sauce that we were served tasted like nothing I'd experienced. It was familiar and strange and exotic all at once. Even as the hot spices set fire to my lips and scorched the inside of my mouth, I immediately wanted more.

I've been trying to figure out Texas and Texans ever since. Fifty-two years later, I realized the answer had been right in front of me for most of my life. I first encountered the smiling friendly face as a black-and-white image flickering on Channel 11, singing songs live from Panther Hall on *The Cowtown Jamboree* and on *The Ernest Tubb Show* in a voice that could have come only from Texas. I grew familiar with the voice by listening to KCUL, the country and western radio station, although versions of "Hello Walls" and "Crazy" sung by other people were Top 40 hits in Fort Worth. The first interview was in Austin in 1973 for *Zoo World* magazine. After thirty-five years of writing about him and many others, I can now safely say that no single public person living in the twentieth or twenty-first century defines Texas or Texans better than Willie Hugh Nelson.

Texans by nature are independent, freethinking, open, outgoing, and friendly. Iconoclasts, they respect tradition but are not beholden to it. Whether it's God or sin, they tend to embrace excess. The good ones have a whole lot of heart. They are creatures of geography and exude a sense of place in an increasingly homogenized world. They reflect the climate and sometimes are a little crazy from the heat. They are wanderers and explorers, keen to improvise, curious enough to go places they shouldn't. They are loud and boisterous when they need to be. They seem to go out of their way to make friends with strangers. They are great storytellers and some of the most distinctive music makers on earth. You know Texas music when you hear it, just like you know Willie's music.

A certain Red Headed Stranger was once said to say, "Don't let the truth get in the way of a good story." I tried my best to ignore that sage advice once I took on this project. On the back side, all I can say is that getting all the facts straight while piecing together the history of a culture once considered too low, too sordid, and too wild to be worth documenting in print was no sure thing. Many characters were too busy living life to the fullest, sometimes under the influence, and sometimes living proof of the adage "If you can remember the sixties, you weren't there." Others took their stories with them when they passed. Then there were those who were inclined to con for the pure sport of it.

Fortunately, my subject was accommodating and open — exactly the person I've always known him to be. He's the story. I'm just the teller.

In that spirit, my special thanks to Willie Hugh and his family for opening their lives to me; my wife, Kris, and sons, Jake and Andy, for their support and for putting up with me; my sister, Christina Patoski, especially for the stash of *Country Song Roundup*s and other vintage publications; Margaret Patoski for being the mother she is; and Lindy Barger and Johnny Reno for the all-star honkalicious support.

I thank my editor, John Parsley, my agent, Jim Fitzgerald, my copyeditor, Pamela Marshall, and my publisher, Michael Pietsch (don't give up your day job), for making this book happen; my assistants, Sarah McNeely and Joel Minor, for the support, heavy lifting, feedback, and safety net; photo editor Kathy Marcus for the images; Joe "King" Carrasco and the Crowns and Alejandro Escovedo and the True Believers for the on-the-job training; Nick Tosches for the sage advice; and Bill Crawford for the help, advice, and the Opry passes.

Many thanks to Mark Rothbaum; Miss Bobbie Lee Nelson; Lana Nelson; Connie Nelson; Annie Nelson; Freddy Fletcher; Paul, Billy, and Oliver English; Sibyl Neely; Evelyn Flood; Paula Carlene Nelson; Shirley Nelson; Gates and Pamela Moore; David E. Anderson; the fine citizens of Abbott, Texas, and Hill County; the volunteers at the Abbott Methodist Church, especially Donald Reed, Joyce Clements Reed, Jackie Clements, and Faye Dell Clements; Morris Russell; Jimmy Graves; Laurie Nichols Carrell; Mickey Raphael; Jody Payne; Flaco Lemons; Steve Davis and Connie Todd at the Southwestern Writers Collection at Texas State University, San Marcos, Texas; Bud Shrake; Tim O'Connor; Tim Hamblin and the Austin History Center; Jhon Case; Charlie Owens; Casey James Monahan and the governor's Texas Music Office; Elaine Shock and Shock, Inc.; Jurgen Koop and Rich Kienzle and Bear Family Records for the scholarship; Douglas Hanners and the Austin Record Convention; Lynda and Johnny Bush; Rick Crow; Kevin Connor; Billy Cooper; Poodie Locke and Poodie's Hilltop Bar & Grill; Brenda Colladay at the Grand Ole Opry archives; George Hamilton IV and George Hamilton V; John Lomax III; Buddy Prewitt Jr.; Linda Banks; Kenny Koepke; Tunin' Tom Hawkins; Billy Joe Shaver; Ray Benson; Jim Haber; Floyd Domino; Billy Cooper; Tracy Pitcox of the Heart of Texas Country Music Museum in Brady, Texas; Darrell and Mona McCall; Jeannie Seely; Hank Cochran; Aaron Allen and the fine folks at KCTI, Gonzales, Texas; Bill Mack, Cindy Mack, Truman, and the Open Road gang on XM Satellite Radio; Eddie Stubbs; Cowboy Jack Clement; Eddie Kilroy of Willie's Place on XM Satellite Radio; Freddy Powers; Sammy Allred at KVET-FM; Kevin Connor and Music & Entertainment Television, Austin, Texas; Jody Denberg and other friends at KGSR-FM, Austin, Texas; Coach Darrell K and Edith Royal; Larry and Pat Butler; Ronald Greer; Jerry Bradley; Herky Williams; Nick Hunter; Al Bianculli; Evelyn Shriver; Susan Nadler and Bandit Records; Kissy Black; Martha Moore; Susan Levy; Chet Flippo and CMT; Peter Blackstock; Grant Alden and the fine folks at *No Depression* magazine; Jerry Retzloff; Les Leverett; Jimmy

Moore; Jimmy C. Newman; Joe Gracey and Kimmie Rhodes; Bob Hedderman; Edwin O. Wilson; Jim Franklin; Micael Priest; Mike Tolleson; Cleve Hattersley; Kinky Friedman; Dave Rich; Bruce Lundvall; Tamara Saviano; John Kunz; John T. Davis; Steve Wynn; Alicia Villegas; Sylvie Simmons; Terri Minnick; Ed Melton; Tim and Andra Shepard; Roland Swenson, and Louis Black; Nick Barbaro and the *Austin Chronicle* and South by Southwest; Ed Ward; Jake Bernstein and the *Texas Observer;* Greg Curtis and *Texas Monthly* magazine; Robert Macias; Randy Brudnicki, Louie Bond, and Charles Lohrmann and *Texas Parks & Wildlife* magazine; Stoney Burns and *Buddy* magazine; Kirby Warnock; Mark Shimmel; Diann Bayes and the Hillsboro Chamber of Commerce; Ronnie Pugh and the Nashville Public Library; John Rumble and the Country Music Hall of Fame and Museum; Clark County Public Library, Washington; Oregon Historical Association; Searcy County Library, Arkansas; Bruce Tabb, special collections librarian, University of Oregon Library; Craig Adams and the Portland Radio Guide; Ed Dailey; Gene Breeden; Rick Crow; Herb Steiner; Mary Buelow; Fort Vancouver Regional Library District, Washington; Tom Kellam and the Fort Worth Public Library, Texas; Lee Woodward; Lawton Williams; Clark County Historical Museum,

Washington; Max Hall; Bobby Gibson; Leon Smith; Stephen Bruton; Sumter Bruton; Gene Kelton; John Young of the *Waco Tribune-Herald;* Beverly Moore; Bobby Earl Smith; Frank and Jeanie Oakley and the Willie Nelson General Store; Tracee Crump; Larry Gieschen, periodicals librarian, Texas State University; James Luther and Mary Lindsay Dickinson; George J. Emmel; Ed Enoch; Gary Burton; Booker T. Jones; Owen McFadden and the BBC; Carlyn Majer; Jack Kinslow; Logan Rogers; Phil York; Kandy Kicker; Carolyn Emanuel; Alison Beck; Jimmy Herrington; David Bartlett; Randy Meadows; Mark Fields; Ernie and Tracey Renn; Johnny Hughes; David Dennard; Gordon Perry; Bud Kennedy; Bob Bruton; Martha Moore; Curtis Potter; Felix Rejcek; Charlie Ryan; Fran Weatherholt; Wendy Goldstein; Delbert McClinton; Mel Tillis; Claude Gray; Bobby Bare; Leona Williams; Gerald Wexler; Luke Lewis; Lost Highway Records; and all the other good people who helped make this possible.

NOTES

Somewhere in America

Information taken from field notes.

Abbott

INTERVIEWS
Bobbie Nelson, Willie Nelson

ORAL HISTORIES
Wilcox, Mildred Turney. Oral history. Edwin (Bud) Shrake
    Papers. San Marcos, TX: Southwestern Writers Collec-
    tion.

BOOKS
Nelson, Willie, with Bud Shrake. *Willie: An Autobiography*.
    New York: Simon and Schuster, 1988.

WEB SITES
Willienelson.com

East of Western Grove on Pindall Ridge

INTERVIEWS
Laurie Nichols Carrell, Evelyn M. Flood, Jeff Henthorne,
    Sibyl Neely, Irene Nichols Young

Oral Histories

Wilcox, Mildred Turney. Oral history. Edwin (Bud) Shrake Papers. San Marcos, TX: Southwestern Writers Collection.

Young, Sybil Greenhaw. Oral history. Edwin (Bud) Shrake Papers. San Marcos, TX: Southwestern Writers Collection.

Books

Boone County Historical and Railroad Society. *History of Boone County.* Narrative by Roger V. Logan Jr. Turner, ME: Turner Publishing, 1998.

Grayson, Lisa. *A Beginner's Guide to Shape-Note Singing.* Chicago: Chicago Sacred Harp Singers, 2001.

Handbook of Texas. Austin: Texas State Historical Association, 2007.

Harrell, Mary Frances, ed. *History and Folklore of Searcy County, Arkansas.* Harrison, AR: New Leaf Press, 1977.

Lackey, Walter F. *History of Newton County.* Salem, MA: Higginson Books, 1984.

Lair, Jim, and the Carroll County Historical and Genealogical Society. *Carroll County Families: These Were the First.* Dallas: Taylor Publishing, 1991.

Niswonger, Thomas, ed. *Newton County Family History Vol. 2.* Jasper, AR: Newton County Historical Society, 1999.

Turney-McMindes, Helen Cavaness. *Marion County Arkansas in 1890.* Ozark, MO: Dogwood Printing, 1992.

Additional Sources

Holcomb, George. *Harrison Daily Times,* Harrison, AR.

McMurrin, Kathleen. Boone County genealogist, Boone County, AR.

Miller, Jim. Boone County Library, Harrison, AR.

Newton County Historical Society, Jasper, AR.
Sacred Harp Singing. Anniston, AL: Sacred Harp Musical
    Heritage Association.
"Sacred Harp Singing in Texas," TexasFaSoLa.org.
Smith, Marilyn. Boone County Museum, Harrison, AR.
Steel, Warren. University of Mississippi, Oxford, MS.
Whyte, Geraldine. Searcy County Library, Marshall, AR.

WEB SITES
Freepages.genealogy.rootsweb.com/~rkinfolks/ (Rkinfolks)
Stillisstillmoving.com
Willienelson.com

Abbott

INTERVIEWS
Faye Dell Clements, Jackie Clements, Jimmy Graves, James
    (Slim) Hand, Marie Urbanovsky Kershen, Helen
    Urbanovsky Lenart, Donald Reed, Joyce Clements Reed,
    Felix Rejcek, Morris Russell, Jerry Frank Ruzicka, Leo
    Ruzicka, Fran Weatherholt

ORAL HISTORIES
Nelson, Willie. Oral history. *American Routes* radio program.
    New Orleans: American Public Media, November 29, 2000.
Shelton, W. B. Oral history. Edwin (Bud) Shrake Papers.
    San Marcos, TX: Southwestern Writers Collection.
Varnon, Zeke. Oral history. Edwin (Bud) Shrake Papers.
    San Marcos, TX: Southwestern Writers Collection.
Wilcox, Mildred Turney. Oral history. Edwin (Bud) Shrake
    Papers. San Marcos, TX: Southwestern Writers Collection.
Young, Sybil Greenhaw. Oral history. Edwin (Bud) Shrake
    Papers. San Marcos, TX: Southwestern Writers Collection.

Books

Abbott Centennial Planning Committee. *Abbott, Texas, 1881–1981: A History*. Belton, TX: Centex Press, 1981.

Bailey, Ellis. *A History of Hill County, 1863–1965*. Waco, TX: Texian Press, 1966.

Cooper, Daniel. *Lefty Frizzell: The Honky-tonk Life of Country Music's Greatest Singer*. New York: Little, Brown, 1995.

George-Warren, Holly. *Public Cowboy No. 1: The Life and Times of Gene Autry*. New York: Oxford University Press, 2007.

Handbook of Texas. Austin: Texas State Historical Association, 2007.

Hillbilly Hit Parade of 1951. New York: Peer International.

Hillsboro Con Survey City Directory. Chillicothe, OH: Mullin-Kille Company, 1948.

Morrison and Fourmey's Waco City Directory, 1951.

Nelson, Willie. *Willie Nelson: The Facts of Life and Other Dirty Jokes*. New York: Random House, 2002.

Nelson, Willie, with Bud Shrake. *Willie: An Autobiography*. New York: Simon and Schuster, 1988.

Nelson, Willie, with Turk Pipkin. *The Tao of Willie: A Guide to Happiness in Your Heart*. New York: Gotham, 2006.

Pugh, Ronnie. *Ernest Tubb: The Texas Troubadour*. Durham, NC: Duke University Press, 1996.

Texas Almanac. Dallas: *Dallas Morning News*, 2005.

Willie Nelson Family Album. Compiled by Lana Nelson. Amarillo, TX: H. M. Poirot & Company, 1980.

Articles

Nelson, Susie. "Old-time Religion Was Genesis of Nelson's Love for Music." *Dallas Times Herald*, August 25, 1987.

ADDITIONAL SOURCES

Hill County Genealogical Society, Hillsboro, TX.

Hill County Library, Hillsboro, TX.

Kienzle, Rich. Liner notes. From *Legends of Country Music: Bob Wills and His Texas Playboys*. Sony Legacy, 2006.

McFadden, Owen. "Outlaw: The Willie Nelson Story." Broadcast on BBC2, London, November 14, 21, and 28, and December 5, 2006.

McLennan County Library, Waco, TX.

Nelson, Willie. Willie Nelson songbook. Texas Music Archives, San Marcos, TX: Southwestern Writers Collection.

Sacred Harp Singing. Anniston, AL: Sacred Harp Musical Heritage Association.

"Sacred Harp Singing in Texas," TexasFaSoLa.org.

WEB SITES

Stillisstillmoving.com

Willienelson.com

Waco

INTERVIEWS

Johnny Gimble, James (Slim) Hand, Bobbie Nelson, Lana Nelson, Willie Nelson, George Uptmor

ORAL HISTORIES

Nelson, Martha. Edwin (Bud) Shrake Papers. San Marcos, TX: Southwestern Writers Collection.

Varnon, Zeke. Edwin (Bud) Shrake Papers. San Marcos, TX: Southwestern Writers Collection.

Books

Cooper, Daniel. *Lefty Frizzell: The Honky-tonk Life of Country Music's Greatest Singer.* New York: Little, Brown, 1995.

Handbook of Texas. Austin: Texas State Historical Association, 2007.

Morrison and Fourmey's Waco City Directory, 1951.

Nelson, Willie, with Bud Shrake. *Willie: An Autobiography.* New York: Simon and Schuster, 1988.

Wallace, Patricia Ward. *Waco: A Sesquicentennial History.* Virginia Beach: Donning Company, 1999.

Willie Nelson Family Album. Compiled by Lana Nelson. Amarillo, TX: H. M. Poirot & Company, 1980.

Articles

Ferman, Dave. "Let's Go to Carl's Corner, Texas, with Willie and Carl and Zeke." *Dallas Morning News,* July 4, 1987.

Additional Sources

Country Song Roundup. Various issues, 1951–1954.

Harrison, Glen Bryer Jr. Associate professor of history. Baylor University, Waco, TX.

Hill County Library, Hillsboro, TX.

McFadden, Owen. "Outlaw: The Willie Nelson Story." Broadcast on BBC2, London, November 14, 21, and 28, and December 5, 2006.

McLennan County Library, Waco, TX.

Texas Collection. Baylor University, Waco, TX.

Waco Chamber of Commerce, Waco, TX.

Web Sites

Willienelson.com

San Antonio

INTERVIEWS
Aaron Allan, Johnny Bush, Ricky Davila, Dave Isbell, Willie Nelson, Mary Parker Pool

ORAL HISTORIES
Nelson, Martha. Edwin (Bud) Shrake Papers. San Marcos, TX: Southwestern Writers Collection.
Nelson, Willie. Oral history. *American Routes* radio program. New Orleans: American Public Media, November 29, 2000.

BOOKS
Bush, Johnny, with Rick Mitchell. *Whiskey River (Take My Mind): The True Story of Texas Honky-tonk*. Austin: University of Texas Press, 2007.
Handbook of Texas. Austin: Texas State Historical Association, 2007.
Nelson, Willie, with Edwin (Bud) Shrake. *Willie: An Autobiography*. New York: Simon and Schuster, 1988.
Texas Almanac. Dallas: *Dallas Morning News*, 2005.
Willie Nelson Family Album. Compiled by Lana Nelson. Amarillo, TX: H. M. Poirot & Company, 1980.

ADDITIONAL SOURCES
Country Song Roundup. Various issues, 1953–1954.
Kienzle, Rich. "It's Been Rough and Rocky Travelin'." From *Willie Nelson: It's Been Rough and Rocky Travelin'*. CD booklet. Bear Family, 2003.
McFadden, Owen. "Outlaw: The Willie Nelson Story." Broadcast on BBC2, London, November 14, 21, and 28, and December 5, 2006.

Web Sites
Willienelson.com

Fort Worth

Interviews
Bob Bruton, Stephen Bruton, Sumter Bruton, Jerry Case, Jhon Case, Billy English, Oliver English, Paul English, Mark Fields, Pat Kirkwood, Dandy Don Logan, Quentin McGown, Tommy Morrell, Bobbie Nelson, Charlie Owens, Freddy Powers, Dave Rich, Horace Lee Sewell, Bud Shrake, Leo Teel, Lee Woodward

Oral Histories
Nelson, Martha. Edwin (Bud) Shrake Papers. San Marcos, TX: Southwestern Writers Collection.

Books
Arnold, Ann. *Gamblers and Gangsters*. Austin: Eakin Press, 1998.

Bush, Johnny, with Rick Mitchell. *Whiskey River (Take My Mind): The True Story of Texas Honky-tonk*. Austin: University of Texas Press, 2007.

Cooper, Daniel. *Lefty Frizzell: The Honky-tonk Life of Country Music's Greatest Singer*. New York: Little, Brown, 1995.

George-Warren, Holly. *Public Cowboy No. 1: The Life and Times of Gene Autry*. New York: Oxford University Press, 2007.

Handbook of Texas. Austin: Texas State Historical Association, 2007.

Nelson, Willie, with Bud Shrake. *Willie: An Autobiography*. New York: Simon and Schuster, 1988.

Selcer, Richard F. *Hell's Half Acre.* Fort Worth: Texas Christian University Press, 1991.

Texas Almanac. Dallas: *Dallas Morning News,* 2005.

Willie Nelson Family Album. Compiled by Lana Nelson. Amarillo, TX: H. M. Poirot & Company, 1980.

ARTICLES

Case, Johnny. "Calling Me Back: The Doug Bragg Story." Hillbilly-music.com.

"Complete Television and Radio Log." *Fort Worth Press,* March 8, 1955.

"Complete Television and Radio Log." *Fort Worth Press,* March 18, 1955.

"Electric Flag Is Criticized." *Fort Worth Press,* March 9, 1955.

Jeansonne, Billy. "Paul English: On the Road . . . Again." *Classic Drummer,* January–February 2005.

"Metal Courthouse Flag May Be Hauled Down." *Fort Worth Star-Telegram,* January 20, 1957.

Moulder, John. "Paul English: Underworld Runaway Who Bangs the Drum for Willie Nelson." *Country Rambler,* January 13, 1977.

Peel, Mark. "Austin Country." *Daily Texan,* June 28, 1974.

Shurley, Traci. " 'People Person' Ran Many Bars, Eateries: Inez Mortenson, 1918–2006." *Fort Worth Star-Telegram,* July 2, 2006.

Wolfe, Charles K. "Honky-tonk Starts Here: The Jim Beck Dallas Studio." *Journal of Country Music* 11, no. 1.

ADDITIONAL SOURCES

Country Song Roundup. Various issues, 1954–1957.

Fort Worth Star-Telegram television and radio listings, January 1, January 12, January 24, and June 6, 1954; January 1 and January 3, 1955; January 1–3 and January 31, 1956; January 1, January 3–5, and January 18–19, 1957.

Kellam, Thomas, and the Fort Worth Public Library, Fort Worth, TX.

Kienzle, Rich. "It's Been Rough and Rocky Travelin'." From *Willie Nelson: It's Been Rough and Rocky Travelin'*. CD booklet. Bear Family, 2003.

Lynch, Patrick. Eugene Public Library, Eugene, OR.

McFadden, Owen. "Outlaw: The Willie Nelson Story." Broadcast on BBC2, London, November 14, 21, and 28, and December 5, 2006.

Shannon, Mike, KNUS99.com.

WEB SITES
Stillisstillmoving.com
Willienelson.com

Vancouver

INTERVIEWS
Craig Adams, Wes Bakken, Gene Breeden, Bobby Gibson, Max Hall, Dory Hylton, Lana Nelson, Willie Nelson, Leon Smith

ORAL HISTORIES
Axton, Mae Boren. Edwin (Bud) Shrake Papers. San Marcos, TX: Southwestern Writers Collection.

Harvey, Myrle. Edwin (Bud) Shrake Papers. San Marcos, TX: Southwestern Writers Collection.

Nelson, Martha. Edwin (Bud) Shrake Papers. San Marcos, TX: Southwestern Writers Collection.

Nelson, Willie. Oral history. *American Routes* radio program. New Orleans: American Public Media, November 29, 2000.

Young, Sybil Greenhaw. Edwin (Bud) Shrake Papers. San Marcos, TX: Southwestern Writers Collection.

BOOKS
City Directory, Vancouver, WA, 1956, 1957, 1958.
Johnson, Dr. Thomas S. *Willie Nelson: A Discographic Listing.* Danbury, CT: Mark Rothbaum and Associates, 1985.
Nelson, Willie, with Bud Shrake. *Willie: An Autobiography.* New York: Simon and Schuster, 1988.

ARTICLES
"Bar 27 Corral (Heck Harper's Bar 27 Corral)." Yesterday's KPTV. Home.comcast.net/~kptv/Shows/corral.htm.
"Country Artists Move from Spinning Records to Cutting Them." *Country Weekly,* August 1996.
Gordon, Jack. "Frantic Man and the Shrill Ring at Night." *Fort Worth Press,* March 14, 1955.
Jewett, Dave. "Local Folks Remember Nelson's Time Here." *Vancouver Columbian,* August 5, 1997.
————. "Local Legend Willie Nelson Returns." *Vancouver Columbian,* July 27, 1997.
————. "Vancouver on His Mind." *Vancouver Columbian,* August 3, 1997.
"Willie Nelson's Tale Truly the Write Stuff; His Life Runs from Old Tin Mandolins to Gold Record." *Portland Oregonian,* November 18, 1988.

ADDITIONAL SOURCES
Blecha, Peter. "Country Music in the Pacific Northwest." Essay 7441. In *The Online Encyclopedia of Washington State History,* 2005. Historylink.org.
Country Song Roundup. Various issues, 1956–1958.
Kienzle, Rich. "It's Been Rough and Rocky Travelin'." From

Willie Nelson: It's Been Rough and Rocky Travelin'. CD booklet. Bear Family, 2003.

Lynch, Patrick. Eugene Public Library, Eugene, OR.

McFadden, Owen. "Outlaw: The Willie Nelson Story." Broadcast on BBC2, London, November 14, 21, and 28, and December 5, 2006.

Oregon Historical Society.

Web Sites

Edscountry.com (Ed Dailey)

PDXradio.com

Pnwbands.com (Pacific Northwest Bands)

Willienelson.com

Fort Worth Again

Interviews

Stephen Bruton, Sumter Bruton, Johnny Bush, Jerry Case, Jhon Case, Richard Davis, Lynn Echols, Billy English, Oliver English, Paul English, Freddy Fletcher, Chuck Jennings, Dandy Don Logan, Delbert McClinton, Quentin McGown, Frankie Miller, Tommy Morrell, Bobbie Nelson, Lana Nelson, Willie Nelson, Joe Paul Nichols, Charlie Owens, Curtis Potter, Dave Rich, Homer Lee Sewell, Bud Shrake, Leo Teel, Lawton Williams

Oral Histories

Nelson, Martha. Edwin (Bud) Shrake Papers. San Marcos, TX: Southwestern Writers Collection.

Walker, Billy. Edwin (Bud) Shrake Papers. San Marcos, TX: Southwestern Writers Collection.

BOOKS

Arnold, Ann. *Gamblers and Gangsters*. Austin: Eakin Press, 1998.

Bush, Johnny, with Rick Mitchell. *Whiskey River (Take My Mind): The True Story of Texas Honky-tonk*. Austin: University of Texas Press, 2007.

Cooper, Daniel. *Lefty Frizzell: The Honky-tonk Life of Country Music's Greatest Singer*. New York: Little, Brown, 1995.

Handbook of Texas. Austin: Texas State Historical Association, 2007.

Johnson, Dr. Thomas S. *Willie Nelson: A Discographic Listing*. Danbury, CT: Mark Rothbaum and Associates, 1985.

Nelson, Willie, with Bud Shrake. *Willie: An Autobiography*. New York: Simon and Schuster, 1988.

Selcer, Richard F. *Hell's Half Acre*. Fort Worth: Texas Christian University Press, 1991.

Willie Nelson Family Album. Compiled by Lana Nelson. Amarillo, TX: H. M. Poirot & Company, 1980.

ARTICLES

Case, Johnny. "Calling Me Back: The Doug Bragg Story." Hillbilly-music.com.

Shurley, Traci. " 'People Person' Ran Many Bars, Eateries: Inez Mortenson, 1918–2006." *Fort Worth Star-Telegram*, July 2, 2006.

ADDITIONAL SOURCES

Country Song Roundup. Various issues, 1958–1959.

Escott, Colin. "South Coast Special." From *The Complete D Singles Collection, Volume 1*. CD booklet. Bear Family, 2000.

Kellam, Thomas, and the Fort Worth Public Library, Fort Worth, TX.

Kienzle, Rich. "It's Been Rough and Rocky Travelin'." From *Willie Nelson: It's Been Rough and Rocky Travelin'*. CD booklet. Bear Family, 2003.

McFadden, Owen. "Outlaw: The Willie Nelson Story." Broadcast on BBC2, London, November 14, 21, and 28, and December 5, 2006.

"Tommy Rosnosky Is Back, Mountaineer, Dancing, Western String Band Nightly, Jam Session Every Sunday, All Musicians Welcome, 1013 Main, Cool Refrigerated Air." Advertisement. *Fort Worth Press*, June 13, 1958.

WEB SITES
Willienelson.com

Houston

INTERVIEWS
Johnny Bush, Pat Butler, Claude Gray, Dave Isbell, Frankie Miller, Bobbie Nelson, Willie Nelson, Herb Remington

ORAL HISTORIES
Buskirk, Paul. Edwin (Bud) Shrake Papers. San Marcos, TX: Southwestern Writers Collection.

Butler, Larry. Edwin (Bud) Shrake Papers. San Marcos, TX: Southwestern Writers Collection.

Butler, Pat. Edwin (Bud) Shrake Papers. San Marcos, TX: Southwestern Writers Collection.

Nelson, Martha. Edwin (Bud) Shrake Papers. San Marcos, TX: Southwestern Writers Collection.

Nelson, Willie. Oral history. *American Routes* radio program. New Orleans: American Public Media, November 29, 2000.

Walker, Billy. Edwin (Bud) Shrake Papers. San Marcos, TX: Southwestern Writers Collection.

BOOKS

Bush, Johnny, with Rick Mitchell. *Whiskey River (Take My Mind): The True Story of Texas Honky-tonk.* Austin: University of Texas Press, 2007.

Cooper, Daniel. *Lefty Frizzell: The Honky-tonk Life of Country Music's Greatest Singer.* New York: Little, Brown, 1995.

Handbook of Texas. Austin: Texas State Historical Association, 2007.

Johnson, Dr. Thomas S. *Willie Nelson: A Discographic Listing.* Danbury, CT: Mark Rothbaum and Associates, 1985.

Nelson, Willie, with Bud Shrake. *Willie: An Autobiography.* New York: Simon and Schuster, 1988.

Texas Almanac. Dallas: *Dallas Morning News,* 2005.

Willie Nelson Family Album. Compiled by Lana Nelson. Amarillo, TX: H. M. Poirot & Company, 1980.

ARTICLES

Jeansonne, Billy. "Paul English: On the Road . . . Again." *Classic Drummer,* January–February 2005.

ADDITIONAL SOURCES

The Complete D Singles Collection, Volume 3. Bear Family, 2000.

Country Song Roundup. Various issues, 1959–1960.

Escott, Colin. "South Coast Special." From *The Complete D Singles Collection, Volume 1.* CD booklet. Bear Family, 2000.

Houston Collection. Houston Public Library, Houston, TX.

Kienzle, Rich. "It's Been Rough and Rocky Travelin'." From *Willie Nelson: It's Been Rough and Rocky Travelin'*. CD booklet. Bear Family, 2003.

McFadden, Owen. "Outlaw: The Willie Nelson Story." Broadcast on BBC2, London, November 14, 21, and 28, and December 5, 2006.

Pasadena and Houston directories. Southwestern Bell Telephone, 1959–1960.

WEB SITES
Willienelson.com

Nashville

INTERVIEWS
Bobby Bare, Pat Butler, Hank Cochran, Fred Foster, George Hamilton V, Dandy Don Logan, Bill Mack, Darrell McCall, Frankie Miller, Willie Nelson, Jimmy C. Newman, Frank Oakley, Ray Price, Mel Tillis, Pete Wade

ORAL HISTORIES
Atkins, Chet. Oral history. Edwin (Bud) Shrake Papers. San Marcos, TX: Southwestern Writers Collection.

Collie, Biff. Oral history. Edwin (Bud) Shrake Papers. San Marcos, TX: Southwestern Writers Collection.

Nelson, Martha. Oral history. Edwin (Bud) Shrake Papers. San Marcos, TX: Southwestern Writers Collection.

Nelson, Willie. Oral history. *American Routes* radio program. New Orleans: American Public Media, November 29, 2000.

Walker, Billy. Oral history. Edwin (Bud) Shrake Papers. San Marcos, TX: Southwestern Writers Collection.

BOOKS

Bush, Johnny, with Rick Mitchell. *Whiskey River (Take My Mind): The True Story of Texas Honky-tonk*. Austin: University of Texas Press, 2007.

Cooper, Daniel. *Lefty Frizzell: The Honky-tonk Life of Country Music's Greatest Singer*. New York: Little, Brown, 1995.

Johnson, Dr. Thomas S. *Willie Nelson: A Discographic Listing*. Danbury, CT: Mark Rothbaum and Associates, 1985.

Kosser, Michael. *How Nashville Became Music City USA: 50 Years of Music Row*. Milwaukee, WI: Hal Leonard, 2006.

Mack, Bill. *Bill Mack's Memories from the Trenches of Broadcasting*. Fort Worth, TX: Unit II, 2004.

Nelson, Willie, with Bud Shrake. *Willie: An Autobiography*. New York: Simon and Schuster, 1988.

Style, Lyle E. *Ain't Got No Cigarettes: Memories of Music Legend Roger Miller*. Winnipeg, MB: Great Plains Publications, 2005.

Willie Nelson Family Album. Compiled by Lana Nelson. Amarillo, TX: H. M. Poirot & Company, 1980.

ARTICLES

Dansby, Andrew. "Early Willie Demos Due." RollingStone.com, December 12, 2002.

Edwards, David, and Mike Callahan. "Liberty Records Discography, Part 1." Both Sides Now Publications. Bsnpubs.com, 2003.

Hurst, Jack. "The Last Call at Tootsie's." *Chicago Tribune*, March 26, 1985.

Nelson, Susie. "Nelson's Career Took Off in a Honky-tonk Named Tootsie's." *Dallas Times Herald*, August 23, 1987.

———. "Willie's Early Crooning Didn't Sing." *Dallas Times Herald*, August 24, 1987.

Patoski, Joe Nick. "Willie Nelson 1961." *Country Music,* 1979.

"Tootsie's Orchid Lounge: Where the Music Began." *White Star,* 2005.

Additional Sources

Colladay, Brenda. Curator, Grand Ole Opry Archives, Nashville, TN.

Country Song Roundup. Various issues, 1959–1962.

"Crazy." From "The 100 Most Important American Musical Works of the Twentieth Century." National Public Radio, September 4, 2000.

Kienzle, Rich. "It's Been Rough and Rocky Travelin'." From *Willie Nelson: It's Been Rough and Rocky Travelin'.* CD booklet. Bear Family, 2003.

McFadden, Owen. "Outlaw: The Willie Nelson Story." Broadcast on BBC2, London, November 14, 21, and 28, and December 5, 2006.

"Nashville: 'The Athens of the South.' " Publicity department. Nashville, TN: Nashville Chamber of Commerce, 1960.

Pitcox, Tracy. Heart of Texas Country Music Museum, Brady, TX.

Pugh, Ronnie. Nashville Room. Nashville City Library, Nashville, TN.

Ray Price Fan Club.

Rumble, John. Country Music Hall of Fame, Nashville, TN.

Web Sites

Stillisstillmoving.com

Willienelson.com

Los Angeles

INTERVIEWS

Tommy Allsup, Bobby Bruce, Johnny Bush, Jerry Case, Jhon Case, Lynn Echols, Mark Fields, Fred Foster, Tommy Morrell, Bobbie Nelson, Shirley Nelson, Curtis Potter, Ray Price, Jeannie Seely, Leo Teel, Pete Wade

ORAL HISTORIES

Collie, Biff. Oral history. Edwin (Bud) Shrake Papers. San Marcos, TX: Southwestern Writers Collection.

Cooper, Carl. "Lawton Memories." Oral history. Recorded for Jhon Case, 1997.

Nelson, Shirley. Oral history. Edwin (Bud) Shrake Papers. San Marcos, TX: Southwestern Writers Collection.

Nelson, Willie. Oral history. *American Routes* radio program. New Orleans: American Public Media, November 29, 2000.

BOOKS

Bush, Johnny, with Rick Mitchell. *Whiskey River (Take My Mind): The True Story of Texas Honky-tonk*. Austin: University of Texas Press, 2007.

Jennings, Waylon, with Lenny Kaye. *Waylon: An Autobiography*. New York: Grand Central, 1996.

Johnson, Dr. Thomas S. *Willie Nelson: A Discographic Listing*. Danbury, CT: Mark Rothbaum and Associates, 1985.

Kosser, Michael. *How Nashville Became Music City USA: 50 Years of Music Row*. Milwaukee, WI: Hal Leonard, 2006.

Mack, Bill. *Bill Mack's Memories from the Trenches of Broadcasting*. Fort Worth, TX: Unit II, 2004.

Moore, Thurston. *Who's Who of Country Music 1965*. Denver, CO: Heather Publications, 1964.

Nelson, Willie, with Bud Shrake. *Willie: An Autobiography.* New York: Simon and Schuster, 1988.

Oakley, Frank. *The Nashville "Sidekick" Had the World by the Tail . . . "Then I Woke Up": The Frank Oakley Story.* Nashville, TN: Willie Nelson General Store and Museum, 2007.

Opdyke, Steven. *Willie Nelson Sings America.* Austin: Eakin Press, 1998.

Style, Lyle E. *Ain't Got No Cigarettes: Memories of Music Legend Roger Miller.* Winnipeg, MB: Great Plains Publications, 2005.

Thompson, Graeme. *Willie Nelson: The Outlaw.* London: Virgin Books, 2006.

Willie Nelson Family Album. Compiled by Lana Nelson. Amarillo, TX: H. M. Poirot & Company, 1980.

ARTICLES

"Cowtown Jamboree." Channel Choices one-hour special. *Dallas Morning News,* September 2, 1963.

Edwards, David, and Mike Callahan. "Liberty Records Discography, Part 1." Both Sides Now Publications. Bsnpubs.com, 2003.

Moulder, John. "Paul English: Underworld Runaway Who Bangs the Drum for Willie Nelson." *Country Rambler,* January 13, 1977.

Zoppi, Tony. "Chalet Is Featuring the Songs of Liberty Recording Star Willie Nelson." *Dallas Morning News,* February 14, 1963.

ADDITIONAL SOURCES

Colladay, Brenda. Curator, Grand Ole Opry Archives, Nashville, TN.

Kienzle, Rich. "It's Been Rough and Rocky Travelin'." From

Willie Nelson: It's Been Rough and Rocky Travelin'. CD booklet. Bear Family, 2003.

McFadden, Owen. "Outlaw: The Willie Nelson Story." Broadcast on BBC2, London, November 14, 21, and 28, and December 5, 2006.

Pitcox, Tracy. Heart of Texas Country Music Museum, Brady, TX.

Ray Price Fan Club.

"Willie with Sonny James and Alex Houston on Big D Jamboree." Listing in "What's Going On in Dallas This Week." *Dallas Morning News,* June 1, 1963.

WEB SITES
Rogermiller.com
Willienelson.com

Ridgetop

INTERVIEWS
Bobby Bare, Bobby Bruce, Judy Budge, Jhon Case, Fred Foster, Ronald Greer, Bill Mack, Darrell McCall, Randy Moore, Tommy Morrell, Connie Nelson, Lana Nelson, Shirley Nelson, Pete Wade

ORAL HISTORIES
Nelson, Connie. Oral history. Edwin (Bud) Shrake Papers. San Marcos, TX: Southwestern Writers Collection.

Nelson, Shirley. Oral history. Edwin (Bud) Shrake Papers. San Marcos, TX: Southwestern Writers Collection.

Nelson, Willie. Oral history. *American Routes* radio program. New Orleans: American Public Media, November 29, 2000.

Books

Bush, Johnny, with Rick Mitchell. *Whiskey River (Take My Mind): The True Story of Texas Honky-tonk*. Austin: University of Texas Press, 2007.

Johnson, Dr. Thomas S. *Willie Nelson: A Discographic Listing*. Danbury, CT: Mark Rothbaum and Associates, 1985.

Kosser, Michael. *How Nashville Became Music City USA: 50 Years of Music Row*. Milwaukee, WI: Hal Leonard, 2006.

Mack, Bill. *Bill Mack's Memories from the Trenches of Broadcasting*. Fort Worth, TX: Unit II, 2004.

Moore, Thurston. *Who's Who of Country Music 1965*. Denver, CO: Heather Publications, 1964.

Nelson, Willie, with Bud Shrake. *Willie: An Autobiography*. New York: Simon and Schuster, 1988.

Nelson, Willie, with Turk Pipkin. *The Tao of Willie: A Guide to Happiness in Your Heart*. New York: Gotham, 2006.

Oakley, Frank. *The Nashville "Sidekick" Had the World by the Tail . . . "Then I Woke Up": The Frank Oakley Story*. Nashville, TN: Willie Nelson General Store and Museum, 2007.

Opdyke, Steven. *Willie Nelson Sings America*. Austin: Eakin Press, 1998.

Shaw, Arnold. *American Dictionary of Pop Rock*. New York: Schirmer, 1983.

Style, Lyle E. *Ain't Got No Cigarettes: Memories of Music Legend Roger Miller*. Winnipeg, MB: Great Plains Publications, 2005.

Thompson, Graeme. *Willie Nelson: The Outlaw*. London: Virgin Books, 2006.

Willie Nelson Family Album. Compiled by Lana Nelson. Amarillo, TX: H. M. Poirot & Company, 1980.

Articles

Edwards, David, and Mike Callahan. "Liberty Records Discography, Part 1." Both Sides Now Publications. Bsnpubs .com, 2003.

Hieronymous, Clara. "Opry Drops Twelve Top Stars." *Nashville Tennessean,* December 6, 1964.

Additional Sources

Colladay, Brenda. Curator, Grand Ole Opry Archives, Nashville, TN.

Kienzle, Rich. "Nashville Was the Roughest." From *Willie Nelson: Nashville Was the Roughest* . . . . CD booklet. Bear Family, 1998.

McFadden, Owen. "Outlaw: The Willie Nelson Story." Broadcast on BBC2, London, November 14, 21, and 28, and December 5, 2006.

TV Dial. *Fort Worth Press,* May 2, 1965.

WSM Radio. Press release, November 24, 1964.

Web Sites

Astara.org (Astara: A Place of Light)
Rogermiller.com
Willienelson.com

Tennessee to Texas

Interviews

Jerry Bradley, Johnny Bush, Cowboy Jack Clement, Billy Cooper, Paul English, Bill Mack, Jimmy Moore, Randy Moore, Tommy Morrell, Connie Nelson, Lana Nelson, Willie Nelson, Bo Powell, Bee Spears

Oral Histories

Atkins, Chet. Oral history. Edwin (Bud) Shrake Papers. San Marcos, TX: Southwestern Writers Collection.

Gresham, Tom. Oral history. Edwin (Bud) Shrake Papers. San Marcos, TX: Southwestern Writers Collection.

Jennings, Waylon. Oral history. Edwin (Bud) Shrake Papers. San Marcos, TX: Southwestern Writers Collection.

Nelson, Connie. Oral history. Edwin (Bud) Shrake Papers. San Marcos, TX: Southwestern Writers Collection.

Nelson, Shirley. Oral history. Edwin (Bud) Shrake Papers. San Marcos, TX: Southwestern Writers Collection.

Trader, Larry. Oral history. Edwin (Bud) Shrake Papers. San Marcos, TX: Southwestern Writers Collection.

Books

Arnold, Ann. *Gamblers and Gangsters*. Austin: Eakin Press, 1998.

Bush, Johnny, with Rick Mitchell. *Whiskey River (Take My Mind): The True Story of Texas Honky-tonk*. Austin: University of Texas Press, 2007.

Johnson, Dr. Thomas S. *Willie Nelson: A Discographic Listing*. Danbury, CT: Mark Rothbaum and Associates, 1985.

Kosser, Michael. *How Nashville Became Music City USA: 50 Years of Music Row*. Milwaukee, WI: Hal Leonard, 2006.

Mack, Bill. *Bill Mack's Memories from the Trenches of Broadcasting*. Fort Worth, TX: Unit II, 2004.

Moore, Thurston. *Who's Who of Country Music 1965*. Denver, CO: Heather Publications, 1964.

Nelson, Willie, with Bud Shrake. *Willie: An Autobiography*. New York: Simon and Schuster, 1988.

Opdyke, Steven. *Willie Nelson Sings America*. Austin: Eakin Press, 1998.

Style, Lyle E. *Ain't Got No Cigarettes: Memories of Music Leg-*

end Roger Miller. Winnipeg, MB: Great Plains Publications, 2005.

Thompson, Graeme. *Willie Nelson: The Outlaw.* London: Virgin Books, 2006.

Willie Nelson Family Album. Compiled by Lana Nelson. Amarillo, TX: H. M. Poirot & Company, 1980.

ARTICLES

"Annual Prison Rodeo Lively October Event." *Dallas Morning News,* September 1, 1970.

Blair, Sam. "East Makes Like Yeast: Willie Nelson Don Meredith's House Guest." *Dallas Morning News,* November 23, 1966.

Cartwright, Gary. "Pressure the Main Factor: Don Meredith Sings 'One Day at a Time' Before NFL Title Game." *Dallas Morning News,* December 30, 1966.

Jeansonne, Billy. "Paul English: On the Road . . . Again." *Classic Drummer,* January–February 2005.

Moulder, John. "Paul English: Underworld Runaway Who Bangs the Drum for Willie Nelson." *Country Rambler,* January 13, 1977.

Nelson, Susie. "Nelson's Second Marriage Was as Rocky as His First." *Dallas Times Herald,* August 26, 1987.

Raffetto, Francis. "Longhorn Performer: Writer-Performer Willie Nelson Plays Longhorn Ballroom." *Dallas Morning News,* April 11, 1969.

———. "Roger Miller to Star in Special Road Show with Don Meredith, Willie Nelson, and Others at Sportatorium." *Dallas Morning News,* May 6, 1965.

ADDITIONAL SOURCES

Colladay, Brenda. Curator, Grand Ole Opry Archives, Nashville, TN.

"Ernest Tubb: 1960s TV Shows." Southern Music Network, n.d.

"Jamboree Road Show: Grand Ole Opry Road Show with Willie Nelson, George Jones, Wade Ray, the Springfield Singers Joins Big D Jamboree." *Dallas Morning News,* November 20, 1965.

"Jamboree Road Show: Willie Nelson, Wade Ray, Hank Cochran, and Johnny Paycheck Top Stars at Big D Jamboree Road Show." *Dallas Morning News,* February 5, 1965.

Kienzle, Rich. "Nashville Was the Roughest." From *Willie Nelson: Nashville Was the Roughest . . . .* CD booklet. Bear Family, 1998.

McFadden, Owen. "Outlaw: The Willie Nelson Story." Broadcast on BBC2, London, November 14, 21, and 28, and December 5, 2006.

"What's Going On: Willie Nelson and Wade Ray on Big D Jamboree at Sportatorium and Longhorn Ballroom, Victor Borge at State Fair Music Hall." *Dallas Morning News,* April 16, 1966.

"Willie Nelson Hosts Cowtown Jamboree." Channel Choices for Saturday. *Dallas Morning News,* December 9, 1967.

"Willie Nelson Plays Cowtown Jamboree with Johnny Bush and the Record Men." Channel Choices for Saturday. *Dallas Morning News,* June 6, 1968.

"Willie Nelson and Wade Ray on Cowtown Jamboree." Channel Choices for Saturday, August 7. *Dallas Morning News,* August 7, 1965.

"Willie Nelson and Wade Ray on Cowtown Jamboree." Channel Choices for Saturday, November 6. *Dallas Morning News,* November 6, 1965.

WEB SITES
Rogermiller.com
Stillisstillmoving.com
Willienelson.com

Coast-to-Coast, Border-to-Border

INTERVIEWS
John Anders, Jerry Bradley, Johnny Bush, Cowboy Jack Clement, Billy English, Oliver English, Paul English, Kris Kristofferson, Bill Mack, Jimmy Moore, Tommy Morrell, Bobbie Nelson, Connie Nelson, Bo Powell, Neil Reshen, Bee Spears

ORAL HISTORIES
Allred, Sammy. Oral history. Edwin (Bud) Shrake Papers. San Marcos, TX: Southwestern Writers Collection.
Gresham, Tom. Oral history. Edwin (Bud) Shrake Papers. San Marcos, TX: Southwestern Writers Collection.
Jennings, Waylon. Oral history. Edwin (Bud) Shrake Papers. San Marcos, TX: Southwestern Writers Collection.
Nelson, Connie. Oral history. Edwin (Bud) Shrake Papers. San Marcos, TX: Southwestern Writers Collection.
Trader, Larry. Oral history. Edwin (Bud) Shrake Papers. San Marcos, TX: Southwestern Writers Collection.

BOOKS
Bush, Johnny, with Rick Mitchell. *Whiskey River (Take My Mind): The True Story of Texas Honky-tonk*. Austin: University of Texas Press, 2007.
Jennings, Waylon, with Lenny Kaye. *Waylon: An Autobiography*. New York: Grand Central, 1996.
Johnson, Dr. Thomas S. *Willie Nelson: A Discographic Listing*. Danbury, CT: Mark Rothbaum and Associates, 1985.

Kosser, Michael. *How Nashville Became Music City USA: 50 Years of Music Row*. Milwaukee, WI: Hal Leonard, 2006.

Mack, Bill. *Bill Mack's Memories from the Trenches of Broadcasting*. Fort Worth, TX: Unit II, 2004.

Opdyke, Steven. *Willie Nelson Sings America*. Austin: Eakin Press, 1998.

Style, Lyle E. *Ain't Got No Cigarettes: Memories of Music Legend Roger Miller*. Winnipeg, MB: Great Plains Publications, 2005.

Thompson, Graeme. *Willie Nelson: The Outlaw*. London: Virgin Books, 2006.

Willie Nelson Family Album. Compiled by Lana Nelson. Amarillo, TX: H. M. Poirot & Company, 1980.

Articles

Altgelt, Ernie. "Career Kept 'Band Boy' Close to Legends Like Willie." *Hill Country Sun,* January 2007.

Jeansonne, Billy. "Paul English: On the Road . . . Again." *Classic Drummer,* January–February 2005.

Moulder, John. "Paul English: Underworld Runaway Who Bangs the Drum for Willie Nelson." *Country Rambler,* January 13, 1977.

Patoski, Joe Nick. "With Strings Attached." *Texas Monthly,* February 1988.

Additional Sources

Colladay, Brenda. Curator, Grand Ole Opry Archives, Nashville, TN.

Kienzle, Rich. "Nashville Was the Roughest." From *Willie Nelson: Nashville Was the Roughest . . . .* CD booklet. Bear Family, 1998.

McFadden, Owen. "Outlaw: The Willie Nelson Story."

Broadcast on BBC2, London, November 14, 21, and 28, and December 5, 2006.

Moeller Talent. Flyer, circa 1966–1972.

Willie Nelson Museum. Willie Nelson General Store, Nashville, TN.

WEB SITES

Rogermiller.com

Willienelson.com

Lost Valley

INTERVIEWS

Aaron Allan, Jerry Bradley, Morgan Choat, Cowboy Jack Clement, Billy Cooper, Chet Flippo, Nick Hunter, Kris Kristofferson, Bill Mack, Darrell McCall, Jimmy Moore, Bobbie Nelson, Connie Nelson, Willie Nelson, Neil Reshen, Bee Spears, Jerry Wexler

ORAL HISTORIES

Allred, Sammy. Oral history. Edwin (Bud) Shrake Papers. San Marcos, TX: Southwestern Writers Collection.

Cooper, Billy. Oral history. Edwin (Bud) Shrake Papers. San Marcos, TX: Southwestern Writers Collection.

English, Paul. Oral history. Edwin (Bud) Shrake Papers. San Marcos, TX: Southwestern Writers Collection.

Gresham, Tom. Oral history. Edwin (Bud) Shrake Papers. San Marcos, TX: Southwestern Writers Collection.

O'Connor, Tim. Oral history. Edwin (Bud) Shrake Papers. San Marcos, TX: Southwestern Writers Collection.

Tolleson, Mike. Oral history. Edwin (Bud) Shrake Papers. San Marcos, TX: Southwestern Writers Collection.

Trader, Larry. Oral history. Edwin (Bud) Shrake Papers. San Marcos, TX: Southwestern Writers Collection.

BOOKS

Bush, Johnny, with Rick Mitchell. *Whiskey River (Take My Mind): The True Story of Texas Honky-tonk.* Austin: University of Texas Press, 2007.

Mack, Bill. *Bill Mack's Memories from the Trenches of Broadcasting.* Fort Worth, TX: Unit II, 2004.

Nelson, Willie, with Bud Shrake. *Willie: An Autobiography.* New York: Simon and Schuster, 1988.

Opdyke, Steven. *Willie Nelson Sings America.* Austin: Eakin Press, 1998.

Willie Nelson Family Album. Compiled by Lana Nelson. Amarillo, TX: H. M. Poirot & Company, 1980.

ARTICLES

Edwards, Roy. "Evening with DKR." *Dallas Morning News,* March 22, 1972.

Flippo, Chet. "Records: 'The Willie Way.'" *Rolling Stone* 122 (November 23, 1972).

Jeansonne, Billy. "Paul English: On the Road . . . Again." *Classic Drummer,* January–February 2005.

Knocke, Ed. "Toe-Tapping Great at Music Festival." *Dallas Morning News,* March 19, 1972.

Miller, Townsend. "Willie Changes His Label but Not His Musical Stripe." *Austin American-Statesman,* November 11, 1972.

Moulder, John. "Paul English: Underworld Runaway Who Bangs the Drum for Willie Nelson." *Country Rambler,* January 13, 1977.

"Smith, Ralph Attend 'Reunion.'" Dripping Springs Reunion coverage. Associated Press, March 20, 1972.

Tarradell, Mario. "Willie's Eager to Celebrate in Fort Worth." *Dallas Morning News,* July 4, 2004.

ADDITIONAL SOURCES
Hamblin, Tim. Austin History Center. Austin Public Library, Austin, TX.
Kienzle, Rich. "Nashville Was the Roughest." From *Willie Nelson: Nashville Was the Roughest . . . .* CD booklet. Bear Family, 1998.
McFadden, Owen. "Outlaw: The Willie Nelson Story." Broadcast on BBC2, London, November 14, 21, and 28, and December 5, 2006.
Miller, Townsend. Country Music column. *Austin American-Statesman,* August 17, 1972.
Willie Nelson Museum. Willie Nelson General Store, Nashville, TN.
Wuntch, Philip. Dallas After Dark column. *Dallas Morning News,* October 13, 1972.

WEB SITES
Stillisstillmoving.com
Willienelson.com

Austin

INTERVIEWS
David E. Anderson, Marc Benno, Ray Benson, Jerry Bradley, Steve Coffman, Rick Crow, Floyd Domino, Chet Flippo, Jim Franklin, Kinky Friedman, Joe Gracey, Cleve Hattersley, Bobby Hedderman, Nick Hunter, Kris Kristofferson, Poodie Locke, Carlyn Majer, Darrell McCall, Gates Moore, Bobbie Nelson, Connie Nelson, Lana Nelson, Tim O'Connor, Jody Payne, Mickey Raphael, Neil

Reshen, Jerry Retzloff, Mark Rothbaum, Darrell K Royal, Wallace Selman, Billy Joe Shaver, Bud Shrake, Bobby Earl Smith, Herb Steiner, Mike Tolleson, Jerry Wexler, Eddie Wilson

Oral Histories

Allred, Sammy. Oral history. Edwin (Bud) Shrake Papers. San Marcos, TX: Southwestern Writers Collection.

English, Paul. Oral history. Edwin (Bud) Shrake Papers. San Marcos, TX: Southwestern Writers Collection.

Gresham, Tom. Oral history. Edwin (Bud) Shrake Papers. San Marcos, TX: Southwestern Writers Collection.

Jennings, Waylon. Oral history. Edwin (Bud) Shrake Papers. San Marcos, TX: Southwestern Writers Collection.

Leverett, Sheryl. Oral history. Edwin (Bud) Shrake Papers. San Marcos, TX: Southwestern Writers Collection.

Nelson, Connie. Oral history. Edwin (Bud) Shrake Papers. San Marcos, TX: Southwestern Writers Collection.

O'Connor, Tim. Oral history. Edwin (Bud) Shrake Papers. San Marcos, TX: Southwestern Writers Collection.

Tolleson, Mike. Oral history. Edwin (Bud) Shrake Papers. San Marcos, TX: Southwestern Writers Collection.

Trader, Larry. Oral history. Edwin (Bud) Shrake Papers. San Marcos, TX: Southwestern Writers Collection.

Books

Bush, Johnny, with Rick Mitchell. *Whiskey River (Take My Mind): The True Story of Texas Honky-tonk.* Austin: University of Texas Press, 2007.

Johnson, Dr. Thomas S. *Willie Nelson: A Discographic Listing.* Danbury, CT: Mark Rothbaum and Associates, 1985.

Mack, Bill. *Bill Mack's Memories from the Trenches of Broadcasting.* Fort Worth, TX: Unit II, 2004.

Nelson, Willie, with Bud Shrake. *Willie: An Autobiography.* New York: Simon and Schuster, 1988.

Opdyke, Steven. *Willie Nelson Sings America.* Austin: Eakin Press, 1998.

Willie Nelson Family Album. Compiled by Lana Nelson. Amarillo, TX: H. M. Poirot & Company, 1980.

ARTICLES

Alterman, Loraine. "Shine On, Country Soul." *New York Times,* May 19, 1974.

Anders, John. "Godfather of Texas Country Music." *Dallas Morning News,* June 29, 1975.

Bowman, Harry. "Willie Nelson on Channel 13." *Dallas Morning News,* September 28, 1974.

"Country Music Benefit Planned." *Dallas Morning News,* October 28, 1972.

"Country Stars Will Attend Springs Fete." *Dallas Morning News,* June 21, 1973.

Dailey, David. "Nelson Headlines Musical Week." *Daily Texan,* December 4, 1973.

Ditlea, Steve. Review of *Shotgun Willie. Rolling Stone,* August 30, 1973.

Flippo, Chet. "Country Music: The R & R Influence." *Rolling Stone,* December 20, 1973.

———. "Matthew, Mark, Luke, and Willie." *Texas Monthly,* September 1975.

———. "Willie Nelson's New York Country Sessions." *Rolling Stone,* April 12, 1973.

Halberstadt, Alex. "Jerry Wexler." Salon.com, September 5, 2000.

Harris, Will. "Willie Nelson: The Complete Atlantic Sessions." Review on amazon.com, 2006.

Herschorn, Connie. "Austin Builds Country Rock Base." *Billboard,* September 8, 1973.

———. "Nelson Day Draws 10,000 to Abbott." *Dallas Morning News,* November 6, 1973.

Hickey, Dave. "In Defense of Telecaster Cowboy Outlaws." *Country Music,* March 1974.

Hilburn, Robert. "Phases and Stages of a Maverick." *Los Angeles Times,* November 30, 1975.

Jaxon. "You Gotta Have a Lotta Soul to Attend a Willie Nelson Fourth of July Picnic." *Austin Sun,* July 24–August 6, 1975.

Jeansonne, Billy. "Paul English: On the Road . . . Again." *Classic Drummer,* January–February 2005.

Martin, William C. "Growing Old at Willie Nelson's Picnic." *Texas Monthly,* September 1974.

McNeely, Dave. "Country and Rock Drawing Together: KPFT Tribute to Cosmic Cowboys." *Dallas Morning News,* February 12, 1974.

———. "His Music Speaks for Willie Nelson." *Dallas Morning News,* February 8, 1974.

———. "Willie Nelson, Et. Al., Appeal to Most Avid." *Dallas Morning News,* July 7, 1974.

Miller, Tom. "ShelterVision Captures Texas Music Scene." *Daily Texan,* February 2, 1975.

Miller, Townsend. "Weekend Filled with Sound." *Austin American-Statesman,* September 1, 1973.

———. "Willie's Fest 'Smash Success.' " *Austin American-Statesman,* July 7, 1973.

Moulder, John. "Paul English: Underworld Runaway Who Bangs the Drum for Willie Nelson." *Country Rambler,* January 13, 1977.

Nelson, Susie. "Country Fans and Hippie Folk Both Take a Liking to Willie." *Dallas Times Herald,* August 27, 1987.

"Singer Asks for License." *Daily Texan,* April 22, 1974.

Tarradell, Mario. "Willie's Eager to Celebrate in Fort Worth." *Dallas Morning News,* July 4, 2004.

Thomas, Patrick. "Leon Russell: Out-of-Town Boy Makes Good." *Country Music,* April 1974.

Tomlin, Janice. "Willie's 4th Bash." *Daily Texan,* June 28, 1973.

Weiss, Leighton. "All in the Family." *Austin Citizen,* July 6, 1973.

"Willie Nelson's Homecoming." *Nashville Tennessean,* November 18, 1973.

Wuntch, Philip. "Hit Trio Makes Spanish Oaks Debut: Willie Closes Out at Western Place." *Dallas Morning News,* October 13, 1972.

———. "Registration Concerts: Live from SMU Television Studio with Eric Quincy Tate, Greezy Wheels, Freda and the Firedogs, Willie Nelson, and Steelrail." *Dallas Morning News,* September 29, 1972.

———. "Triumvirate Set at Market Hall Eve." *Dallas Morning News,* December 16, 1973.

ADDITIONAL SOURCES

Flippo, Chet. Nashville Skyline column. CMT.com, May 11, 2006.

Hamblin, Tim. Austin History Center. Austin Public Library, Austin, TX.

McFadden, Owen. "Outlaw: The Willie Nelson Story." Broadcast on BBC2, London, November 14, 21, and 28, and December 5, 2006.

Retzloff, Jerry. "Lone Star Longnecks, Willie Nelson, and Armadillos: No Place but Texas." Personal paper, 1990.

"Unique Osibisa for the Majestic." Channel 13 live broadcast of Free Stage Voters.

Willie Nelson Museum. Willie Nelson General Store, Nashville, TN.

Web Sites
Stillisstillmoving.com
Willienelson.com

Orange to El Paso, Dalhart to Brownsville

Interviews
David E. Anderson, Bobby Bare, Ray Benson, Steve Coffman, Rick Crow, Floyd Domino, Chet Flippo, Kinky Friedman, Joe Gracey, Jimmy Graves, Cleve Hattersley, Bobby Hedderman, Nick Hunter, Kris Kristofferson, Poodie Locke, Carlyn Majer, Randy Meadows, Gates Moore, Bobbie Nelson, Connie Nelson, Tim O'Connor, Jody Payne, Buddy Prewitt Jr., Mickey Raphael, Neil Reshen, Jerry Retzloff, Mark Rothbaum, Wallace Selman, Bud Shrake, Bobby Earl Smith, Herb Steiner, Dave Thomas, Jerry Wexler, Eddie Wilson

Oral Histories
Allred, Sammy. Oral history. Edwin (Bud) Shrake Papers. San Marcos, TX: Southwestern Writers Collection.

English, Paul. Oral history. Edwin (Bud) Shrake Papers. San Marcos, TX: Southwestern Writers Collection.

Gresham, Tom. Oral history. Edwin (Bud) Shrake Papers. San Marcos, TX: Southwestern Writers Collection.

Jennings, Waylon. Oral history. Edwin (Bud) Shrake Papers. San Marcos, TX: Southwestern Writers Collection.

Nelson, Connie. Oral history. Edwin (Bud) Shrake Papers. San Marcos, TX: Southwestern Writers Collection.

Tolleson, Mike. Oral history. Edwin (Bud) Shrake Papers. San Marcos, TX: Southwestern Writers Collection.

Trader, Larry. Oral history. Edwin (Bud) Shrake Papers. San Marcos, TX: Southwestern Writers Collection.

BOOKS

Handbook of Texas. Austin: Texas State Historical Association, 2007.

Johnson, Dr. Thomas S. *Willie Nelson: A Discographic Listing.* Danbury, CT: Mark Rothbaum and Associates, 1985.

Mack, Bill. *Bill Mack's Memories from the Trenches of Broadcasting.* Forth Worth, TX: Unit II, 2004.

Nelson, Willie, with Bud Shrake. *Willie: An Autobiography.* New York: Simon and Schuster, 1988.

Opdyke, Steven. *Willie Nelson Sings America.* Austin: Eakin Press, 1998.

Texas Almanac. Dallas: *Dallas Morning News,* 2005.

Willie Nelson Family Album. Compiled by Lana Nelson. Amarillo, TX: H. M. Poirot & Company, 1980.

ARTICLES

Allen, Nelson. "Willie Nelson Talks." *Picking Up the Tempo,* May 1975.

Flippo, Chet. "Homecoming in Plains Is a Summit of Two Giants." CMT.com, December 2, 2004.

———. "Willie and Waylon and the Outlaw Thing." CMT.com, October 28, 2004.

King, Larry L. "The Great Willie Nelson Commando Hoo-Ha and Texas Brain Fry." *Playboy,* November 1976.

Moulder, John. "Paul English: Underworld Runaway Who

Bangs the Drum for Willie Nelson." *Country Rambler,* January 13, 1977.

Peel, Mark, and Debra Triplett. "A Grand Ole Picnic." *Daily Texan,* July 9, 1974.

Ward, Ed. "Troublemaker: My Contribution to Willie Nelson's Complete Atlantic Sessions." *Austin Chronicle,* December 29, 2006.

White, Susan, and Bob Doerschuk. "Parachutists Drop In to 'Say Hello to Willie.' " *Austin American-Statesman,* July 5, 1974.

ADDITIONAL SOURCES

Hamblin, Tim. Austin History Center. Austin Public Library, Austin, TX.

Hill County Library, Hillsboro, TX.

Hubbard, Ray Wylie, to Jerry Wexler. Personal letter, n.d.

Kienzle, Rich. "Nashville Was the Roughest." From *Willie Nelson: Nashville Was the Roughest. . . .* CD booklet. Bear Family, 1998.

McFadden, Owen. "Outlaw: The Willie Nelson Story." Broadcast on BBC2, London, November 14, 21, and 28, and December 5, 2006.

New York Public Library, New York.

Retzloff, Jerry. "Lone Star Longnecks, Willie Nelson, and Armadillos: No Place but Texas." Personal paper, 1990.

WEB SITES

Stillisstillmoving.com

Willienelson.com

Garland to Hollywood

INTERVIEWS

David E. Anderson, Bobby Bare, Ray Benson, Jerry Bradley, Hank Cochran, Floyd Domino, Billy English, Paul English, Chet Flippo, Kinky Friedman, Larry Gorham, Joe Gracey, James (Slim) Hand, Tunin' Tom Hawkins, Nick Hunter, Booker T. Jones, Kris Kristofferson, Poodie Locke, Bruce Lundvall, Bill Mack, Randy Meadows, Gates Moore, Tommy Morrell, Connie Nelson, Paula Nelson, Tim O'Connor, Jody Payne, Buddy Prewitt Jr., Mickey Raphael, Jerry Retzloff, Mark Rothbaum, Wallace Selman, Bud Shrake, Bobby Earl Smith, Herb Steiner, Mike Tolleson, Leona Williams, Steve Wynn, Phil York

ORAL HISTORIES

Blackburn, Rick. Oral history. Edwin (Bud) Shrake Papers. San Marcos, TX: Southwestern Writers Collection.

DuShay, Cookie. Oral history. Edwin (Bud) Shrake Papers. San Marcos, TX: Southwestern Writers Collection.

Glaser, Tompall. Oral history. Edwin (Bud) Shrake Papers. San Marcos, TX: Southwestern Writers Collection.

Jennings, Waylon. Oral history. Edwin (Bud) Shrake Papers. San Marcos, TX: Southwestern Writers Collection.

Katz, Joel. Oral history. Edwin (Bud) Shrake Papers. San Marcos, TX: Southwestern Writers Collection.

Nelson, Amy. Oral history. Edwin (Bud) Shrake Papers. San Marcos, TX: Southwestern Writers Collection.

Nelson, Connie. Oral history. Edwin (Bud) Shrake Papers. San Marcos, TX: Southwestern Writers Collection.

Nelson, Lana. Oral history. Edwin (Bud) Shrake Papers. San Marcos, TX: Southwestern Writers Collection.

Nelson, Paula. Oral history. Edwin (Bud) Shrake Papers. San Marcos, TX: Southwestern Writers Collection.

Pollack, Sydney. Oral history. Edwin (Bud) Shrake Papers. San Marcos, TX: Southwestern Writers Collection.

Rothbaum, Mark. Oral history. Edwin (Bud) Shrake Papers. San Marcos, TX: Southwestern Writers Collection.

Varnon, Zeke. Oral history. Edwin (Bud) Shrake Papers. San Marcos, TX: Southwestern Writers Collection.

BOOKS

Cooper, Daniel. *Lefty Frizzell: The Honky-tonk Life of Country Music's Greatest Singer.* New York: Little, Brown, 1995.

George-Warren, Holly. *Public Cowboy No. 1: The Life and Times of Gene Autry.* New York: Oxford University Press, 2007.

Johnson, Dr. Thomas S. *Willie Nelson: A Discographic Listing.* Danbury, CT: Mark Rothbaum and Associates, 1985.

Mack, Bill. *Bill Mack's Memories from the Trenches of Broadcasting.* Fort Worth, TX: Unit II, 2004.

Nelson, Willie. *Willie Nelson: The Facts of Life and Other Dirty Jokes.* New York: Random House, 2002.

Nelson, Willie, with Bud Shrake. *Willie: An Autobiography.* New York: Simon and Schuster, 1988.

Opdyke, Steven. *Willie Nelson Sings America.* Austin: Eakin Press, 1998.

Thompson, Graeme. *Willie Nelson: The Outlaw.* London: Virgin Books, 2006.

ARTICLES

Albrecht, James. "It's High Time: Willie Gathers His Disciples." *CountryStyle,* October 1979.

Allen, Nelson. "Further Adventures of the Gypsy Cowboy." *Country Music,* May 1979.

———. "Willie Nelson Talks." *Picking Up the Tempo,* May 1975.

Anders, John. "Case of the Willies." *Dallas Morning News,* August 26, 1976.

———. "Symphony Gets the Willies." *Dallas Morning News,* June 30, 1975.

———. "Symphony: 'Tell Them Willie-Boy Is Here.' " *Dallas Morning News,* June 29, 1975.

"As a Duo, They Weren't Bad." *Time,* September 24, 1978.

Axthelm, Pete. "King of Country Music." *Newsweek,* August 14, 1978.

Bane, Michael. "Willie Nelson: The Gypsy Cowboy Goes Hollywood." *Country Music,* May 1979.

Bettner, Jill, ed. "The Drawing Cards in the Capital of Texas." *Business Week,* May 26, 1980.

Biffle, Kent. "Getting Up for the Gig." *Dallas Morning News,* June 27, 1976.

Bishop, Nancy. "A Wait for Willie Is Worth It." *Dallas Morning News,* January 17, 1980.

Carr, Patrick. "The Outlaws of Country Music." *Village Voice,* July 28, 1975.

———. "Waylon and Willie Go to a Party." *New Times,* February 20, 1978.

Cochran, Mike. "Nelson, Friends Got Drugs Illegally." Associated Press. *Waco Tribune-Herald,* August 28, 1980.

"Convict, Country Singers Highlight Prison Rodeo." *Dallas Morning News,* September 22, 1974.

"Country's Platinum Outlaw." *Time,* September 18, 1978.

"Country Woodstock Attracts Top Artists." *Tonkawa Review,* July 4, 1975.

Eyre, Ruth. "Hicks Testifies He Owes Willie Nelson About $60,000." *Dallas Times Herald,* September 29, 1976.

Faber, Nancy. "Country Music's Shaggy Rebel, Willie Nelson, Makes Outlawing In." *People,* May 3, 1976.

Flippo, Chet. "Homecoming in Plains Is a Summit of Two Giants." CMT.com, December 2, 2004.

———. "Matthew, Mark, Luke, and Willie." *Texas Monthly,* September 1975.

———. "Review: *Willie and Family Live.*" *Rolling Stone,* April 19, 1979.

———. "Willie and Waylon and the Outlaw Thing." CMT. com, October 28, 2004.

———. "Willie Nelson: Holy Man of the Honky-tonks—The Saga of Willie Nelson, from the Night Life to the Good Life." *Rolling Stone* 269 (July 13, 1978).

"Former Sheriff Talks to Jury." *Dallas Morning News,* June 9, 1976.

Fort Worth Bureau. "Subpoena Issued to Willie Nelson in Narcotics Trial." *Dallas Morning News,* August 27, 1976.

"'Grammy Awards Are Bad News,' Willie Charges." *CountryStyle,* June 1976.

Guralnick, Peter. "Review: *The Sound in Your Mind.*" *Rolling Stone* 214 (June 3, 1976).

Heard, Robert. "'Willie's' Popularity Falling in Texas, Cresting on Coasts." *Dallas Times Herald,* October 31, 1977.

Henderson, Jim. "The Outlaw and the IRS." *Dallas Times Herald,* February 24, 1991.

Hershorn, Connie. "Message to the Faithful." *Dallas Morning News,* December 17, 1974.

———. "Nelson Packs Longhorn Again." *Dallas Morning News,* March 17, 1975.

Himes, Geoffrey. "Willie Nelson's Concert for Carter." *Washington Post,* September 15, 1980.

"The Hits and Misses of Atoka Music Fest." *Dallas Morning News,* September 1, 1975.

"It's Willie, Jimmy, and the Boys." Associated Press, April 26, 1978.

Jeansonne, Billy. "Paul English: On the Road . . . Again." *Classic Drummer,* January–February 2005.

King, Larry L. "The Great Willie Nelson Commando Hoo-Ha and Texas Brain Fry." *Playboy,* November 1976.

Lorange, Bruce. "Lone Star Beer: The 98 Percent Solution." *All About Beer* 4 (1979).

MacKenzie, Richard. "Willie Nelson Has No Comment About Grand Jury Appearance." *Dallas Times Herald,* June 10, 1976.

Martin, Douglas. "Willie Will Serve Up Redneck Rock Feast at Texas-Size Picnic." *Wall Street Journal,* July 1, 1976.

McDonald, Gary. "Willie Remains the Constant for Progressive Country Hordes." *Dallas Times Herald,* December 30, 1977.

Miller, Townsend. "Country Music: Another Local Gig for Willie." *Austin American-Statesman,* December 19, 1975.

Mitchell, Sean. "Beware of Getting Stuck with an Inferior Willie." *Dallas Times Herald,* August 14, 1977.

———. "Gang's All Here for 'Texas Music.' " *Dallas Times Herald,* March 29, 1976.

———. "The Phases and Stages of Bringing Up Willie." *Dallas Times Herald,* September 5, 1976.

Moulder, John. "Paul English: Underworld Runaway Who Bangs the Drum for Willie Nelson." *Country Rambler,* January 13, 1977.

Nelson, Pat. "Lone Star Label Launched in Texas." *Billboard,* July 1, 1978.

"Nelson Subpoenaed in Texas Drug Probe." *Rolling Stone,* June 17, 1976.

Nordhem, Randy. "Irate Willie Fans Denied Concert Seats." *Dallas Morning News,* January 16, 1980.

————. "Jury Selected in Trial of Joe Hicks, Two Others." *Dallas Morning News,* September 21, 1976.

————. "Two Singers Among Twenty Subpoenaed." *Dallas Morning News,* May 8, 1976.

————. "Willie Nelson Queried by Grand Jury." *Dallas Morning News,* June 10, 1976.

Nordhem, Randy, and Pat Svacina. "Seventh Person Held in Narcotics Investigation." *Dallas Morning News,* July 3, 1976.

Olderman, Murray. "Pickin' and Wailin' at Soap Creek Saloon." NEA (news service), May 21, 1976.

Oppel, Pete. "It's Nothing but Blue Skies Now for Willie." *Dallas Morning News,* September 17, 1978.

————. "Nelson to Keep Roots in Texas." *Dallas Morning News,* August 17, 1977.

————. "Texas' Altamont." *Dallas Morning News,* December 31, 1977.

Patoski, Joe Nick. "Hot Times in the Heart of Texas." *Rolling Stone,* August 24, 1978.

————. "It Was No Picnic." *Texas Monthly,* September 1976.

————. "Rednecks Frying in the Sun: Willie Nelson's Picnic Is On." *Rolling Stone,* July 15, 1976.

————. "Thunder Deep in the Heart of Texas: Dylan Meets Willie Nelson." *Rolling Stone,* June 17, 1976.

Perez, Raymundo. " 'Shotgun' Willie Isn't Slowing Down at All." United Press International, June 23, 1979.

"Picnic, TV, Concert, They're All Willie's." *Dallas Morning News,* June 21, 1975.

Reinert, Al. "Willie Nelson's Struggle to the Top Gets Him There." *New York Times Magazine,* March 26, 1978.

Rockwell, John. "The Pop Life: Willie Nelson on Stardom Trail." *New York Times,* August 8, 1975.

"70,000 Watch Willie at Liberty Hill Bash." *Marble Falls Highlander,* July 10, 1975.

St. John, Bob. "Willie Nelson—A Real Man and His Music." *Dallas Scene,* August 10, 1975.

"'Summertop': Symphony Meets Pop." *Dallas Morning News,* June 14, 1975.

Taggart, Patrick. "Willie's 4th Party's Over . . . ." *Austin American-Statesman,* July 6, 1976.

Trader, Larry. "Willie Nelson, as Seen Through Eyes of a Friend." *San Antonio Express-News,* circa 1976.

Walsh, Mary. "Rain, Exhaustion Mar Nelson Bash." *Daily Texan,* July 7, 1975.

West, Paul. "Nelson Sings for Rosalynn, Race Drivers." *Dallas Times Herald,* September 14, 1978.

————. "100,000 Expected at Picnic." *Dallas Times Herald,* July 2, 1976.

Willcott, Paul. "Cross-Country with Willie Nelson." *The Runner,* July 1980.

"Willie Nelson." *Current Biography,* February 1979.

"Willie Nelson Awarded Grammy." Associated Press, February 29, 1976.

"Willie's Pool Hall." In "The Reporter." *Texas Monthly,* April 1976.

Wood, Gerry. "Nelson's Picnic." *Billboard,* July 17, 1976.

Wuntch, Philip. "Nelson Reunion at Sportatorium." *Dallas Morning News,* October 25, 1974.

Yemma, Mark. "Masses and Music: Legal, Financial Hassles Plague Outdoor Festivals." *Dallas Morning News,* July 18, 1976.

York, Phil. "*Red Headed Stranger* Revisited." *Buddy,* February 1999.

Additional Sources

Advertisement for Sportatorium gig. *Dallas Morning News,* March 30, 1977.

Hamblin, Tim. Austin History Center. Austin Public Library, Austin, TX.

McFadden, Owen. "Outlaw: The Willie Nelson Story." Broadcast on BBC2, London, November 14, 21, and 28, and December 5, 2006.

New York Public Library, New York.

Retzloff, Jerry. "Lone Star Longnecks, Willie Nelson, and Armadillos: No Place but Texas." Personal paper, 1990.

Willie Nelson Museum. Willie Nelson General Store, Nashville, TN.

Web Sites

Stillisstillmoving.com

Willienelson.com

The Hill

Interviews

David E. Anderson, Bobby Arnold, Ray Benson, Kevin Connor, Floyd Domino, Fred Foster, Kinky Friedman, Larry Gorham, Joe Gracey, Booker T. Jones, Kenny Koepke, Poodie Locke, Gates Moore, Connie Nelson, Lana Nelson, Paula Nelson, Freddy Powers, Buddy Prewitt Jr., Mickey Raphael, Kimmie Rhodes, Mark Rothbaum, Bud Shrake, Steve Wynn

Oral Histories

Binion, Bennie. Oral history. Edwin (Bud) Shrake Papers. San Marcos, TX: Southwestern Writers Collection.

DuShay, Cookie. Oral history. Edwin (Bud) Shrake Papers. San Marcos, TX: Southwestern Writers Collection.

Katz, Joel. Oral history. Edwin (Bud) Shrake Papers. San Marcos, TX: Southwestern Writers Collection.

Nelson, Amy. Oral history. Edwin (Bud) Shrake Papers. San Marcos, TX: Southwestern Writers Collection.

Nelson, Connie. Oral history. Edwin (Bud) Shrake Papers. San Marcos, TX: Southwestern Writers Collection.

Nelson, Paula. Oral history. Edwin (Bud) Shrake Papers. San Marcos, TX: Southwestern Writers Collection.

Prewitt, Buddy Jr. Oral history. Edwin (Bud) Shrake Papers. San Marcos, TX: Southwestern Writers Collection.

BOOKS

Johnson, Dr. Thomas S. *Willie Nelson: A Discographic Listing*. Danbury, CT: Mark Rothbaum and Associates, 1985.

Nelson, Willie. *Willie Nelson: The Facts of Life and Other Dirty Jokes*. New York: Random House, 2002.

Nelson, Willie, with Bud Shrake. *Willie: An Autobiography*. New York: Simon and Schuster, 1988.

Oakley, Frank. *The Nashville "Sidekick" Had the World by the Tail . . . "Then I Woke Up": The Frank Oakley Story*. Nashville, TN: Willie Nelson General Store and Museum, 2007.

Opdyke, Steven. *Willie Nelson Sings America*. Austin: Eakin Press, 1998.

Thompson, Graeme. *Willie Nelson: The Outlaw*. London: Virgin Books, 2006.

ARTICLES

Bettner, Jill, ed. "The Drawing Cards in the Capital of Texas." *Business Week,* May 26, 1980.

Bryant, Debby. "Give Me Land, Lotsa Land . . . A Talk with

Willie Nelson." *Rumors, Gossip, Lies, and Dreams,* July 2, 1979.

Burchett, Chet. "Nelson's Picnic Attracts 20,000." *Waco Tribune-Herald,* July 5, 1979.

Cocks, Jay. "Forty-five Voices as One: U.S. Pop Stars Unite to Fight Famine with a Song." *Time,* March 25, 1985.

Coggins, Cheryl. "Heat Fails to Faze 4th's Revelers: 60,000 Bake at Willie's Final Fling." *Austin American-Statesman,* July 5, 1980.

Crewdson, John M. "The Last of the Best Little Picnics in Texas." *New York Times,* July 6, 1980.

Darden, Bob. "It's a Family Affair for Nelson Show." *Waco Tribune-Herald,* May 2, 1982.

Downing, Roger. "Willie Nelson Goes Outlaw." *San Antonio Express-News,* February 21, 1982.

"Fans Flock to Willie Nelson's Last Picnic." Associated Press. *Waco Tribune-Herald,* July 5, 1980.

Flippo, Chet. "King Willie Summons Good Ole Boy Kris Down Home to Texas for a Royal Send-up of the Music Biz." *People,* February 13, 1984.

Frolik, Joe. "Willie Draws Big Crowd, but Few Problems." *Austin American-Statesman,* July 5, 1979.

"From Pig Farmer to Superstar." *San Antonio Express-News,* June 15, 1980.

Gelder, Lawrence Van. "Screen: 'Hell's Angels' Forever—A Documentary Version." *New York Times,* October 9, 1983.

Graustark, Barbara. "The Style of Texas Is Upon Us." *Newsweek,* July 21, 1980.

Hailey, Mike. "Abbott Man Sells Souvenirs." *Waco Tribune-Herald,* June 14, 1982.

Hanauer, Joan. "What's Wealth?" United Press International, October 18, 1983.

Hart, Lianne. "Austin's Unsinkable Rock Master Proves You Can Come Home." *Time,* July 23, 1985.

Hassenpflug, Glenn. "Willie's Picnic Goes Outdoors Again." *Corpus Christi Caller-Times,* June 24, 1979.

Hawkins, Robert J. "Whee Willie." *San Diego Union-Tribune,* January 23, 1985.

Hendrickson, Paul. "Suburban Cowboy: Where the Beltway Meets the Western Sky, Where All the Dudes Buck for Glory at the End of the Beltway Trail." *Washington Post,* July 29, 1980.

Hilburn, Robert. "Another Note in the Gospel of Texas Chic." *Los Angeles Times,* August 10, 1980.

———. "Behind the Scenes of a Pop Miracle." *Los Angeles Times,* March 24, 1984.

Hilburn, Robert, and Dennis McDougal. "Farm Aid: Music, Political Harvest." *Los Angeles Times,* September 23, 1985.

Himes, Geoffrey. "Willie Nelson and a Year of Country." *Washington Post,* January 22, 1984.

Holden, Stephen. "A New Wave of Country Music." *New York Times,* September 7, 1980.

Holmes, Michael. "Singer to Premiere New Film in Austin." *Dallas Morning News,* February 19, 1987.

Hyde, Nina, and Henry Allen. "Which Side Are You On?: The List." *Washington Post,* December 31, 1980.

"Indian of the Year." United Press International, March 20, 1981.

Kelly, Lee. "Pop Nelson Dies at Age Sixty-five." *Austin American-Statesman,* December 5, 1978.

Klemesrud, Judy. "Dyan Cannon Gets to Sing—And Rewrite." *New York Times,* September 12, 1980.

Kreps, Mary Ann. "Fading Love: Owner Selling Nite Owl Club—Where Willie Got His Start." *Waco Tribune-Herald,* December 9, 1984.

————. "Red Head No Stranger: Willie Nelson Testifies for Lundy." *Waco Tribune-Herald,* September 16, 1982.

Lippman, Laura. "Abbott Names Week to Honor Willie Nelson." *Waco Tribune-Herald,* April 20, 1983.

Lowry, Bob. "Texas Horizons: Popular PBS Country Music Show Enters Tenth Season." United Press International, March 24, 1984.

Lyon, Pamela. "Reaching Willie's Picnic Was Half the Fun, and Took Most of the Time." *Corpus Christi Caller-Times,* July 6, 1980.

Mack, Toni. "Tell Them Willie Boy Is Here." *Forbes,* July 7, 1980.

Maslin, Janet. *"Honeysuckle Rose."* Review. *New York Times,* July 18, 1980.

McCall, Cheryl. *"Life* Visits Willie Nelson: The Colorado and Texas Retreats of the Private Willie." *Life,* August 1983.

McDonald, Mark. "Swingin' at Willie's Club." *Dallas Morning News,* September 28, 1990.

McNeely, Dave. "Balladeer Nelson Grabs Convention Spotlight." *Waco Tribune-Herald,* August 14, 1980.

Montgomery, Dave. " 'Laid Back' and Eighty-five — Willie's Way." *Dallas Times Herald,* January 15, 1980.

Novak, Ralph. "Songwriter: Willie Nelson and Kris Kristofferson." *People,* December 3, 1984.

Oppel, Pete. " 'Rose' Film Nelson's First Starring Role." *Dallas Morning News,* July 20, 1980.

Palmer, Robert. "In Pop It Was the Conservatives vs. the Progressives." *New York Times,* December 28, 1980.

————. "Singer: Willie Nelson at the Palladium." *New York Times,* December 13, 1980.

————. "Willie Nelson Likes to Keep on the Move." *New York Times,* December 5, 1980.

Patoski, Joe Nick. "With Strings Attached." *Texas Monthly,* February 1988.

"People." *Time,* May 28, 1979.

Phinney, Kevin. "Willie Left His Legend at Home, Brought His Magic to the Stage." *Austin American-Statesman,* April 24, 1981.

Powell, Ronald. "Good-bye, Pop Nelson." *Austin American-Statesman,* December 8, 1978.

"Progress Has Overtaken the Armadillo World Headquarters." United Press International, December 30, 1980.

Racine, Marty. "Willie Nelson: Days on the Road and Nights in Honky-tonks Gave Him a Style That Took a Long Time to Be Accepted." *Houston Chronicle,* December 18, 1983.

"Review: *Honeysuckle Rose.*" United Press International, December 21, 1980.

Rockwell, John. "Country Music Is No Small Town Affair." *New York Times,* July 17, 1983.

"Rollicking Texas Honky-tonk Hears Its Last Cord." Special report. *New York Times,* January 2, 1981.

Schwed, Mark. "The Big Bucks They Earn in Country Music Today." United Press International, April 17, 1981.

Smith, C. W. "Willie's 'Rose' Never Blossoms." *Dallas Times Herald,* July 18, 1980.

Smith, Rick. "The Fourth; Law and Disorder; Taming the Cowboys at Willie Nelson's Bash." *Washington Post,* July 5, 1980.

Stevens, William K. "Hollywood Comes to Texas with Lonestar Gusto." *New York Times,* June 5, 1980.

Szilagyi, Pete. "When He's Not on the Road Again, Willie Prefers Austin." *Austin American-Statesman,* July 26, 1981.

———. "Whiskey River Flows into Land of Casinos." *Austin American-Statesman,* July 26, 1981.

Trachtenberg, Jay. "Willie's Last Picnic: His Best." *Daily Texan,* July 7, 1980.

Trott, William C. "Bullish Loan." United Press International, December 13, 1984.

Ward, Ed, and others. "Chaos, Country Rule at Willie's Last Picnic." *Austin American-Statesman,* July 5, 1980.

"Weekend Memorable for Nelson, Guests." *San Antonio Express-News,* July 6, 1980.

"Willie Nelson Heads to Japan." *San Antonio Star,* January 8, 1984.

"Willie Nelson to Join Joggers in Singer's First Distance Classic." Associated Press, June 11, 1980.

"Willie Nelson and Just About Everybody." *Austin Chronicle,* September 10, 1987.

"Willie Nelson Will Entertain Special Athletes." Associated Press, May 4, 1983.

"Willie Owns Country Club." *Austin Citizen,* June 1979.

"Willie's Son Faces Drug Charge." United Press International, November 29, 1979.

Wilson, Jeff. "Willie Nelson Says His Music Crosses All Borders." United Press International, February 21, 1984.

ADDITIONAL SOURCES

Hamblin, Tim. Austin History Center. Austin Public Library, Austin, TX.

McFadden, Owen. "Outlaw: The Willie Nelson Story." Broadcast on BBC2, London, November 14, 21, and 28, and December 5, 2006.

McLennan County Library, Waco, TX.

WEB SITES

Rogermiller.com

Stillisstillmoving.com

Willienelson.com

The World

INTERVIEWS

Carl Cornelius, Fred Foster, Larry Gorham, Kris Kristofferson, Annie Nelson, Connie Nelson, Paula Nelson, Shirley Nelson

ORAL HISTORIES

Fletcher, Freddy. Oral history. Edwin (Bud) Shrake Papers. San Marcos, TX: Southwestern Writers Collection.

Locke, Poodie. Oral history. Edwin (Bud) Shrake Papers. San Marcos, TX: Southwestern Writers Collection.

Nelson, Shirley. Oral history. Edwin (Bud) Shrake Papers. San Marcos, TX: Southwestern Writers Collection.

Wynn, Steve. Oral history. Edwin (Bud) Shrake Papers. San Marcos, TX: Southwestern Writers Collection.

BOOKS

Johnson, Dr. Thomas S. *Willie Nelson: A Discographic Listing*. Danbury, CT: Mark Rothbaum and Associates, 1985.

Nelson, Willie. *Willie Nelson: The Facts of Life and Other Dirty Jokes*. New York: Random House, 2002.

Nelson, Willie, with Bud Shrake. *Willie: An Autobiography*. New York: Simon and Schuster, 1988.

Nelson, Willie, with Turk Pipkin. *The Tao of Willie: A Guide to Happiness in Your Heart*. New York: Gotham, 2006.

Opdyke, Steven. *Willie Nelson Sings America*. Austin: Eakin Press, 1998.

Preston, Amarillo Slim. *Amarillo Slim in a World Full of Fat People*. New York: Harper Paperbacks, 2005.

Thompson, Graeme. *Willie Nelson: The Outlaw*. London: Virgin Books, 2006.

ARTICLES

Atkins, Ken. "Sweltering Crowds Brave Sun for Willie." *Waco Tribune-Herald*, July 4, 1984.

"Back Home Again." *Dallas Morning News,* June 14, 1984.

Baker, Kathryn. "TV Special Brings Willie Back to Roots." Associated Press. *Waco Tribune-Herald*, March 5, 1988.

Booth, William, and Jerry White. "Willie Nelson's Picnic Packs Texas-Size Party." *Austin American-Statesman*, July 5, 1984.

Cadwallader, Robert. "Singer Not Comin' for 4th." *Waco Tribune-Herald,* June 16, 1988.

Carpenter, Sally. "Willie Nelson Whistling a Different Tune: Jeans." Associated Press. *Houston Post,* June 8, 1980.

Davis, John T. "Picnic Hotter Than Fourth of July." *Austin American-Statesman,* July 5, 1984.

Davis, John T., and Reggie Rivers. "Problem-Free Picnic Reminiscent of Willie Past." *Austin American-Statesman,* July 5, 1987.

Douthat, Bill. "UT Officials 'Outlaw' Willie Nelson Concert." *Waco Tribune-Herald*, April 28, 1983.

Edgar, Mark, and Suzanne Taylor. "Concert Becomes a Jammed Session." *Dallas Morning News,* July 5, 1986.

"Farms Get More Aid: Nelson Stages No. 3." Associated Press. *Waco Tribune-Herald*, September 20, 1987.

Ferman, Dave. "Let's Go to Carl's Corner, Texas, with Willie and Carl and Zeke." *Dallas Morning News,* July 4, 1987.

Frons, Marc. "The Jeaning of America." *Newsweek,* October 6, 1980.

Graham, Don. "Willie's Story: Nelson, Friends Review His Life from Redneck to Reincarnation." *Dallas Morning News,* October 30, 1988.

Holmes, Michael. "Willie Plans Austin 'Picnic.' " *New York Times* News Service. *Waco Tribune-Herald*, May 14, 1984.

Hoover, Carl. "Blue Skies and Willie: The Owner of Carl's Corner Says the Picnic Is 'A Total Success 'Cause Everybody's Happy.'" *Waco Herald-Tribune,* July 5, 1987.

———. "Food, Fun, and Fireworks: As Many as 50,000 Are Expected for Willie Nelson's Picnic." *Waco Tribune-Herald,* July 3, 1987.

———. "Willie and Leroy." *Waco Tribune-Herald,* November 11, 1988.

Kantor, Seth. "Singing Farmers' Blues." *Waco Tribune-Herald,* June 19, 1987.

Lipscombe, Derek. "Red Headed Friend: Willie Nelson Plays to a Packed House in Carl's Corner." *Waco Tribune-Herald,* April 29, 1987.

Logan, Joe. "Benefit Performance Backlash Has Willie Singing the Blues." *Dallas Morning News,* November 6, 1988.

Lowry, Bob. "Austin Live Music Scene Waning — Or Changing?" United Press International, July 23, 1984.

"Martha Scott, Willie Nelson's First Wife, Is Buried." Associated Press, December 5, 1989.

Mason, Julie. "Baylor Cancels Nelson Concert." *Dallas Morning News,* August 18, 1988.

"Nelson Benefit Canceled." Associated Press, April 28, 1983.

"Nelson Benefit Concert Raised $4,096." Associated Press, November 16, 1988.

"Nelson Sings for Church Dedication." Associated Press. *Waco Tribune-Herald,* April 23, 1985.

"Nelson Steamed by Concert Ban." Associated Press, August 21, 1988.

"Offspring Tells All About 'Red Headed Stranger.'" *Valley Morning Star,* November 8, 1987.

Patoski, Joe Nick. "This Is Jeans Country." *Texas Monthly,* September 1993.

———. "With Strings Attached." *Texas Monthly*, February 1988.

"Peltier Position Follows Nelson." Associated Press. *Valley Morning Star*, October 22, 1988.

"Police Ire Threatens Singer's Show." Associated Press. *Dallas Morning News*, October 28, 1988.

"Police Void Ban; Willie Apologizes." Associated Press. *Waco Tribune-Herald*, November 7, 1988.

Rhodes, Joe. "The Happy Days of Willie Nelson." *Dallas Times Herald*, December 23, 1984.

Schmook, Deborah. "Baylor Axes Nelson Concert Because of 'Health' Concern." *Waco Tribune-Herald*, August 17, 1988.

———. "Baylor Trustees Agree with Canceling Willie." *Waco Tribune-Herald*, September 3, 1988.

———. "Nelson to Perform at HOT Coliseum." *Waco Tribune-Herald*, August 18, 1988.

"Sinatra Cancels After One Show with Willie Nelson." United Press International, June 24, 1984.

"Singer Nelson Tells Senate Panel That Farmers 'Dropping Like Flies.' " Associated Press. *Valley Morning Star*, June 19, 1987.

"Singer Threatens to Sue U.S. Forest Service." Associated Press. *Valley Morning Star*, June 28, 1996.

Slater, Wayne. "40,000 Bake to Beat." *Dallas Morning News*, July 5, 1986.

Small, Michael. "Chatter." *Time*, November 19, 1984.

Smith, Russell. "Farm Aid II Promises Bumper Crop of Stars." *Dallas Morning News*, June 24, 1986.

———. "A Long, Hot Day of Diversity." *Dallas Morning News*, July 5, 1986.

———. "Willie's Picnic." *Dallas Morning News*, June 30, 1985.

———. "Willie's Picnic." *Dallas Morning News,* June 28, 1987.

Szilagyi, Pete. "Willie Fires Up the Fourth with a Picnic in the Park." *Austin American-Statesman,* July 1, 1990.

Taylor, Paul. "Development Boom Shakes Austin." *Washington Post,* November 25, 1984.

Trott, William C. "New Roost for Nite Owl." United Press International, December 29, 1984.

Vliet, Ann. "Bein' Willie's Daughter Was Sure No Picnic." *Dallas Morning News,* October 25, 1987.

"Willie 'Disappointed' Police Refuse Security." Associated Press. *Waco Tribune-Herald,* October 21, 1988.

"Willie Nelson Finds New Site for Bank Depositors Benefit." Associated Press, August 19, 1988.

Young, John. "Willie Doesn't Expect Us All to Hum His Tune." *Waco Tribune-Herald,* September 29, 1988.

ADDITIONAL SOURCES

McFadden, Owen. "Outlaw: The Willie Nelson Story." Broadcast on BBC2, London, November 14, 21, and 28, and December 5, 2006.

Texas Collection. Baylor University, Waco, TX.

WEB SITES

Farmaid.org
Stillisstillmoving.com
Willienelson.com

The Valley

INTERVIEWS

David E. Anderson, Ray Benson, Freddy Fletcher, Fred Foster, Kinky Friedman, Johnny Gimble, Joe Gracey, Ronald

Greer, Jimmy Herrington, Kenny Koepke, Poodie Locke, Gates Moore, Annie Nelson, Bobbie Nelson, Connie Nelson, Lana Nelson, Frank Oakley, Buddy Prewitt Jr., Mickey Raphael, Neil Reshen, Kimmie Rhodes, Mark Rothbaum, Darrell K Royal, Aaron Schechter, Bud Shrake, Evelyn Shriver, Mel Tillis, Mike Tolleson

Books

George-Warren, Holly. *Public Cowboy No. 1: The Life and Times of Gene Autry.* New York: Oxford University Press, 2007.

Johnson, Dr. Thomas S. *Willie Nelson: A Discographic Listing.* Danbury, CT: Mark Rothbaum and Associates, 1985.

Nelson, Willie. *Willie Nelson: The Facts of Life and Other Dirty Jokes.* New York: Random House, 2002.

Nelson, Willie, with Turk Pipkin. *The Tao of Willie: A Guide to Happiness in Your Heart.* New York: Gotham, 2006.

Oakley, Frank. *The Nashville "Sidekick" Had the World by the Tail . . . "Then I Woke Up": The Frank Oakley Story.* Nashville, TN: Willie Nelson General Store and Museum, 2007.

Opdyke, Steven. *Willie Nelson Sings America.* Austin: Eakin Press, 1998.

Thompson, Graeme. *Willie Nelson: The Outlaw.* London: Virgin Books, 2006.

Wildman, Sherman. *The Willie Nelson "Cooked Goose" Cookbook and IRS Financial Advisor.* Atlanta: Longstreet Press, 1992.

Articles

"AG Sues Country Willie for Taxes." *Austin American-Statesman,* April 24, 1974.

Chase, Marilyn Johnson. "Fans Responding to 'Willie Aid.' " *Dallas Morning News,* December 3, 1990.

———. "Willie Nelson Still Upbeat Despite Financial Problems." *Dallas Morning News,* February 1, 1991.

Corcoran, Michael. "Willie Nelson's Heart of Gold." *Dallas Morning News,* March 8, 1992.

"Country Singer Nelson Submits to State Audit." Associated Press, June 15, 1974.

Draper, Robert, and Katy Bee. "What, Me Worry?" *USA Weekend,* July 21, 1991.

"Drug Charges Against Singer Willie Nelson to Be Dropped." Associated Press, April 4, 1995.

Everbach, Tracy. "Willie Nelson, Manager Sue Firm." *Dallas Morning News,* August 16, 1990.

Henderson, Jim. "The Outlaw and the IRS." *Dallas Times Herald,* February 24, 1991.

Hightower, Susan. "Auctioneer's Gavel Fails to Fall." Associated Press, January 26, 1991.

Hoppe, Christy. "Looking for Auction: IRS Sale Disappoints Willie Nelson's Fans, Friends." *Dallas Morning News,* January 24, 1991.

"IRS Allows Release of Acoustic Nelson Music." Associated Press. *Valley Morning Star,* June 3, 1991.

"IRS to Buy Back Singer's Golf Course." *Dallas Times Herald,* April 24, 1991.

"IRS Seizes Property of Willie Nelson's." Associated Press, November 11, 1990.

"IRS Seizes Willie Nelson Holdings in $6.5 Million Tax Claim." Associated Press, November 11, 1990.

Irving, Rebecca. "Willie Nelson's Son Hero in Real Gunplay." *Austin Citizen,* March 19, 1979.

"It's Farmer Aid for Willie." *Dallas Times Herald,* February 1, 1991.

Johnson, Marilyn. "Willie Nelson Feels Free After Paying Off IRS Debt." *Dallas Morning News,* August 10, 1994.

Mason, Todd. "Mamma, Don't Let Your Babies Grow Up to Work for the Tax Boys." *Wall Street Journal,* January 29, 1991.

Minutaglio, Bill. "Red Headed Debtor." *Dallas Morning News,* May 12, 1991.

Nelson, Alan. "Lien on Me: Willie's Latest IRS Ballad." *Waco Tribune-Herald,* September 26, 1990.

"Nelson in No Hurry to Pay Taxes." Associated Press, March 15, 1990.

"Nelson No Longer an IRS Outlaw." *Waco Tribune-Herald,* February 3, 1993.

"Nelson Offers Fans Free Antiwar Song." United Press International. *Valley Morning Star,* January 3, 1991.

"Nelson Offspring Suicide Noted." Associated Press. *Valley Morning Star,* December 27, 1991.

"Nelson's Clothes Come from Hemp." Associated Press. *Valley Morning Star,* March 16, 1992.

"Nelson's Club Brings $230,000 at Auction." Associated Press. *Dallas Times Herald,* May 24, 1991.

"Saving the Farm." Associated Press. *Dallas Times Herald,* September 18, 1994.

Selby, Gardner. "Two Hundred Fans Bid on Treasures at IRS Auction." *Dallas Times Herald,* January 24, 1991.

"Stars Pack Willie's Birthday Bash." Associated Press. *Valley Morning Star,* May 2, 1991.

Stevens, Tara. "Willie Nelson and the Tax Man." *Washington Post,* February 9, 1985.

Szilagyi, Pete. "From Country to Country Club: Hassle with IRS Hits Sour Note." *Austin American-Statesman,* February 23, 1986.

————. "Nelson Rolls Along Despite Toll of IRS Debt." *Austin American-Statesman,* January 13, 1991.

Tate, Bret. "Nelson Arrested in Hewitt." *Waco Tribune-Herald,* May 11, 1994.

"Uncle Sam Puts Tax Lien on Willie Nelson's Property." Associated Press, September 26, 1990.

"Willie Gets Off the Road." Associated Press. *Valley Morning Star,* September 17, 1991.

"Willie Nelson Arrested on Drug Charge." Associated Press, May 11, 1994.

"Willie Nelson Belongings Set for IRS Auction." Associated Press, January 12, 1991.

"Willie's 'Memories' Interests Few." *Waco Tribune-Herald,* September 2, 1991.

"Willie's Son Faces Drug Charge." United Press International, November 29, 1979.

Witherspoon, Tommy. "Country Star's Court Date Off Again." *Waco Tribune-Herald,* January 13, 1995.

————. "County Wants Willie Off the Road Again." *Waco Tribune-Herald,* September 16, 1994.

————. "Judge Throws Out Willie's Pot: Ruling Suppresses Evidence Seized from Car by Hewitt Police." *Waco Tribune-Herald,* March 22, 1995.

————. "Nelson to Challenge Search." *Waco Tribune-Herald,* February 1, 1995.

————. "Nelson Court Date Reset, Again." *Waco Tribune-Herald,* December 9, 1994.

————. "Wild Willie in Harmony with the Law: Singer-Songwriter to Perform This Summer at Sheriffs' Conference." *Waco Tribune-Herald,* May 14, 1995.

————. "Willie Skips Grammys for Drug Hearing." *Waco Herald-Tribune,* March 2, 1995.

————. "Willie Urges Legalizing, Taxing of Pot." *Waco Tribune-Herald,* March 23, 1995.

Young, John. "Abbott's Prodigal Son." *Waco Tribune-Herald,* August 14, 1994.

Zelfden, Alan Van. "Willie Says Firm Steered Him Wrong." *Dallas Times Herald,* August 16, 1990.

ADDITIONAL SOURCES

Hamblin, Tim. Austin History Center. Austin Public Library, Austin, TX.

Lost Highway Records. Press releases. Nashville, TN, 2004–2007.

McFadden, Owen. "Outlaw: The Willie Nelson Story." Broadcast on BBC2, London, November 14, 21, and 28, and December 5, 2006.

McLennan County Library, Waco, TX.

People column. *Dallas Morning News,* June 29, 1983.

Texas Collection. Baylor University, Waco, TX.

WEB SITES

Farmaid.org
Stillisstillmoving.com
Willienelson.com

The New World

INTERVIEWS

David E. Anderson, Bobby Arnold, Ray Benson, Carl Cornelius, Floyd Domino, Oliver English, Fred Foster, Kinky Friedman, Gatewood Galbraith, Tunin' Tom Hawkins, Kenny Koepke, Kris Kristofferson, Bobby Lemons, Poodie Locke, Gates Moore, Bobbie Nelson, Tim O'Connor, Buddy Prewitt Jr., Mickey Raphael, Kimmie Rhodes, Darrell K Royal, Billy Joe Shaver, Herkie Williams

ORAL HISTORIES

Cherry, Don. Oral history. Edwin (Bud) Shrake Papers. San Marcos, TX: Southwestern Writers Collection.

BOOKS

George-Warren, Holly. *Public Cowboy No. 1: The Life and Times of Gene Autry.* New York: Oxford University Press, 2007.

Johnson, Dr. Thomas S. *Willie Nelson: A Discographic Listing.* Danbury, CT: Mark Rothbaum and Associates, 1985.

Nelson, Willie. *Willie Nelson: The Facts of Life and Other Dirty Jokes.* New York: Random House, 2002.

Nelson, Willie, with Turk Pipkin. *The Tao of Willie: A Guide to Happiness in Your Heart.* New York: Gotham, 2006.

Opdyke, Steven. *Willie Nelson Sings America.* Austin: Eakin Press, 1998.

Thompson, Graeme. *Willie Nelson: The Outlaw.* London: Virgin Books, 2006.

ARTICLES

Beal, Jim Jr. "Take It as It Comes." *San Antonio Express-News,* August 6, 1998.

Branom, Mike. "Willie Nelson Seeks to End Pork Check-offs." Associated Press. *Houston Chronicle,* May 14, 2000.

Brumley, Al. "Performance Honors Are up to Expectations." *Dallas Morning News,* December 30, 1998.

Christensen, Thor. "Willie's Unusual Guitar Style Dominates Show." *Dallas Morning News,* November 14, 2004.

"Farm Aid Show Moves from Dallas." *Waco Tribune-Herald,* September 18, 1997.

Fikac, Peggy. "Nelson's Spot Wins Antilitter Contest." Associated Press. *Valley Morning Star,* November 3, 1998.

Hancock, Lee. "A Poor Man's O.J." *Dallas Morning News*, February 1995.

Hoover, Carl. "Video Saves Nelson's Latest CD." *Waco Tribune-Herald*, June 23, 2000.

"Nelson Films Music Video in Austin." Associated Press. *Waco Tribune-Herald*, December 29, 2001.

"Nelson, Hootie and the Blowfish to Headline Farm Aid Concert." Associated Press. *Waco Tribune-Herald*, July 18, 1996.

"Nelson Wants to Keep Farms Strong." Associated Press. *Houston Chronicle*, September 30, 2001.

Patoski, Joe Nick. "Entertainer of the Century." *Texas Monthly*, December 1999.

————. "Gonna Catch Tomorrow Now." *No Depression*, September–October 2004.

Perry, Claudia. "Justice Becomes Him: Singer Says Recording 'Moonlight' on Local Label a Good Move." *Houston Post*, May 1, 1994.

Roura, Phil. "Red Headed Stranger Has a New Blues Album." *New York Daily News*, April 14, 2000.

"Sellout Crowd Attended Farm Aid." Associated Press. *Valley Morning Star*, September 13, 1999.

Shelton, Robert M. "Doing Theology with Willie Nelson." *Black Sacred Music: A Journal of Theomusicology* 8, no. 1 (spring 1994).

Shine, Dan. "Farm Aid Frolic—Benefit Concert Draws 40,000 Fans to Texas Stadium." *Dallas Morning News*, March 15, 1992.

Stegall, Tim. "Twisted Williemania." *Austin Chronicle*, February 9, 1996.

Tarradell, Mario. "Nelson Keeps on Evolving." *Dallas Morning News*, September 24, 1998.

————. "Nelson to the Rescue." *Dallas Morning News*, April 5, 2000.

————. "Willie Keeps It Simple." *Dallas Morning News*, October 24, 2004.

————. "Willie Pours On the Blues." *Dallas Morning News*, September 17, 2000.

Tarrant, David. "At Sixty, the Outlaw Slows to a Gallop, Pondering His Trail." *Dallas Morning News*, May 16, 1993.

"Willie Bringing Farm Aid Show Back to Texas." *Waco Tribune-Herald*, July 13, 1997.

"Willie Nelson Visits with Jimmy Carter." Associated Press. *Odessa American*, September 12, 2004.

"Willie's 4th Party Draws Thousands." *Waco Tribune-Herald*, July 5, 1998.

Wilonsky, Robert. "Bringin' It All Back Home." *Dallas Observer*, June 29, 1995.

"Woodstock Willie." Associated Press. *Waco Herald-Tribune*, July 26, 1999.

ADDITIONAL SOURCES

"Crazy." From "The 100 Most Important American Musical Works of the Twentieth Century." National Public Radio, September 4, 2000.

Hamblin, Tim. Austin History Center. Austin Public Library, Austin, TX.

Luckenbach Moon. Official souvenir program, July 1995.

McFadden, Owen. "Outlaw: The Willie Nelson Story." Broadcast on BBC2, London, November 14, 21, and 28, and December 5, 2006.

WEB SITES
Farmaid.org
Stillisstillmoving.com
Willienelson.com

Paradise

INTERVIEWS
David E. Anderson, Ray Benson, Kevin Connor, Carl Cor-
nelius, Rick Crow, Billy English, Paul English, Fred Fos-
ter, Kinky Friedman, Gatewood Galbraith, Larry Gorham,
Joe Gracey, Tunin' Tom Hawkins, Kenny Koepke, Kris
Kristofferson, Bobby Lemons, Gates Moore, Annie Nel-
son, Bobbie Nelson, Jody Payne, Curtis Potter, Buddy
Prewitt Jr., Mickey Raphael, Billy Joe Shaver, Bee Spears,
Kevin Wommack

BOOKS
Nelson, Willie. *Willie Nelson: The Facts of Life and Other
Dirty Jokes.* New York: Random House, 2002.
Nelson, Willie, with Turk Pipkin. *The Tao of Willie: A Guide
to Happiness in Your Heart.* New York: Gotham, 2006.
Opdyke, Steven. *Willie Nelson Sings America.* Austin: Eakin
Press, 1998.

ARTICLES
Bauder, David. "Bob Dylan and Willie Nelson Round the
Bases This Summer." Associated Press. *Austin American-
Statesman,* August 15, 2004.
Patoski, Joe Nick. "Entertainer of the Century." *Texas
Monthly,* December 1999.
———. "Gonna Catch Tomorrow Now." *No Depression,*
September–October 2004.

Starnes, Joe Samuel. "The Sweetest Fourth of July Memories Start with Willie." *New York Times,* July 2, 2007.
"Willie Plays for Troops Injured in Iraq." Associated Press, February 18, 2006.

ADDITIONAL SOURCES
Hamblin, Tim. Austin History Center. Austin Public Library, Austin, TX.
Hill County Library, Hillsboro, TX.
Lost Highway Records. Press releases. Nashville, TN, 1998– 2007.
McFadden, Owen. "Outlaw: The Willie Nelson Story." Broadcast on BBC2, London, November 14, 21, and 28, and December 5, 2006.
McLennan County Library, Waco, TX.

WEB SITES
Stillisstillmoving.com
Willienelson.com

Home

INTERVIEWS
David E. Anderson, Johnny Bush, Lynda Bush, Faye Dell Clements, Jackie Clements, Kevin Connor, Carl Cornelius, Floyd Domino, Billy English, Paul English, Fred Foster, Kinky Friedman, Gatewood Galbraith, Larry Gorham, Tunin' Tom Hawkins, Kenny Koepke, Kris Kristofferson, Bobby Lemons, Poodie Locke, Bill Mack, Gates Moore, Annie Nelson, Bobbie Nelson, Connie Nelson, Lana Nelson, Paula Nelson, Willie Nelson, Jody Payne, Curtis Potter, Buddy Prewitt Jr., Mickey Raphael, Donald Reed, Joyce Clements Reed, Dave Rich, Billy Joe Shaver, Bee Spears

BOOKS

Bush, Johnny, with Rick Mitchell. *Whiskey River (Take My Mind): The True Story of Texas Honky-tonk*. Austin: University of Texas Press, 2007.

George-Warren, Holly. *Public Cowboy No. 1: The Life and Times of Gene Autry*. New York: Oxford University Press, 2007.

Johnson, Dr. Thomas S. *Willie Nelson: A Discographic Listing*. Danbury, CT: Mark Rothbaum and Associates, 1985.

Mack, Bill. *Bill Mack's Memories from the Trenches of Broadcasting*. Fort Worth, TX: Unit II, 2004.

Nelson, Willie. *Willie Nelson: The Facts of Life and Other Dirty Jokes*. New York: Random House, 2002.

Nelson, Willie, with Turk Pipkin. *The Tao of Willie: A Guide to Happiness in Your Heart*. New York: Gotham, 2006.

ARTICLES

Anderson, Karin Shaw. "Hottest Ticket Around." *Dallas Morning News,* July 5, 2004.

Anderson, Mike. "Friends Gear Up for Bio Willie Plant." *Waco Tribune-Herald,* April 17, 2006.

Arend, Jennifer. "Going Crazy for Willie." *Dallas Morning News,* July 5, 2005.

"Austin Legends Pairing Up." Associated Press, December 5, 2006.

Bark, Ed. "Willie and Sister Share an Unrivaled Sibling Bond." *Dallas Morning News,* October 2, 2004.

Becker, Elizabeth. "Nelson Still Fielding Farmers' Calls for Aid." *New York Times,* September 13, 2002.

" 'BioWillie' Truck Stop Opens." *Austin Business Journal,* March 28, 2006.

Chase, Marilyn Johnson. "Hillsboro Benefit an Easy Decision for Willie Nelson." *Dallas Morning News,* March 21, 1993.

Chinen, Nate. "Just a Couple of Guys Dressed in the Blues." *New York Times,* January 15, 2007.

Cohen, Jonathan, ed. "Willie Readies Reggae Riddums." *Billboard,* May 12, 2005.

Cuellar, Dulcinea. "American Icon." *McAllen Monitor,* March 28, 2003.

Culp, Cindy V. "It's Time We Love Him Back." *Waco Tribune-Herald,* December 29, 2004.

Curry, Matt. "Nelson Hits Road to Pitch Biodiesel." Associated Press. *Waco Tribune-Herald,* January 15, 2005.

———. "Texas Due Bush, Willie Nelson on Road Again for Cleaner Fuels." Associated Press. *Waco Tribune-Herald,* February 5, 2006.

Edwards, Joe. "Nelson to Receive 'Overdue' Honor." Associated Press. *Valley Morning Star,* September 22, 1993.

Elliot, David, and Samuel Adams. "Nelson Concert a Start: County to Use $125,000 for Grants to Restore Courthouse." *Waco Tribune-Herald,* April 7, 1993.

Farber, Jim. "Willie Rides into Town with New Record, Book." *New York Daily News,* January 27, 2002.

"Farm Aid 2004 Choose Washington Site for Show." Associated Press. *Houston Chronicle,* August 4, 2004.

Granberry, Michael. "Aetheria Fund-raiser Taps Texas Talent." *Dallas Morning News,* February 11, 2007.

Gross, Joe, and others. "Smaller Crowd, Smoother Traffic Make for a Much Mellower Event." *Austin American-Statesman,* July 6, 2003.

Hoover, Carl. "Benefit Tickets Sell Like Wildfire." *Waco Tribune-Herald,* March 26, 1993.

———. "Fifteen Reasons Why Willie Beats Elvis." *Waco Tribune-Herald,* August 30, 2002.

———. "Why Nelson's Birthday Should Be a State Holiday." *Waco Tribune-Herald,* April 25, 2003.

"In Willie Nelson's Defense." In "Letters to the Editor." *Austin American-Statesman,* February 26, 2006.

Jeansonne, Billy. "Paul English: On the Road . . . Again." *Classic Drummer,* January–February 2005.

Jinkins, Shirley. "Small Church Born Again." *Fort Worth Star-Telegram,* July 3, 2006.

Langer, Andy. "Willie Isn't Finished Giving." *Dallas Morning News,* January 16, 2005.

Machan, Tibor. "Willie Nelson, Public Enemy?" *Odessa American,* October 1, 2006.

"Nelson Is a Hit with Researchers." Associated Press, June 15, 2005.

"Nelson Plays for Injured Soldiers." Associated Press. *Waco Tribune-Herald,* February 18, 2006.

"Nelson Rolls in Funds for Rockin' Heart." *Waco Tribune-Herald,* April 11, 2004.

Orshoski, Wes. "Young, Nelson, Mellencamp Help Farm Aid Turn Twenty-one." *Billboard,* October 4, 2006.

Patoski, Joe Nick. "Entertainer of the Century." *Texas Monthly,* December 1999.

———. "Gonna Catch Tomorrow Now." *No Depression,* September–October 2004.

———. "With Strings Attached." *Texas Monthly,* February 1988.

Ratliff, Ben. "Making Connections Between Town and Country." *New York Times,* September 11, 2007.

Ratliff, John. "Willie's 'Facts' Has Little Sense." *Waco Tribune-Herald,* January 20, 2002.

Rosenfeld, Steven. "Willie Returns for an Encore." Associated Press. *Waco Tribune-Herald,* April 18, 1993.

"Saving a Church." Editorial. *Waco Tribune-Herald,* July 4, 2006.

Shaw, Punch. "Variety Fund-raiser Benefiting Scholarship

Organizations Presents a Truly Eclectic Show." *Fort Worth Star-Telegram,* February 11, 2007.

Tarradell, Mario. "Downpour of Talent." *Dallas Morning News,* July 5, 2006.

———. "Most Wanted: Singer, Author, Whiskey Maker: Willie's the Toast of the Town." *Dallas Morning News,* February 10, 2002.

———. "Willie Joins Celebration of Twenty Years of Farm Aid." *Dallas Morning News,* July 12, 2005.

———. "Willie Opens Closet with 'Cowboys.' " *Dallas Morning News,* February 14, 2006.

———. "Willie's Eager to Celebrate in Fort Worth." *Dallas Morning News,* July 4, 2004.

Varga, George. "Performances Make Nelson Salute Special." *Valley Morning Star,* May 22, 1993.

Weitz, Matt. "Burstin' Fourth." *Dallas Morning News,* July 6, 2003.

Westfall, Michael. "Willie Nelson and the Decadent American Music Industry." Speroforum.com, February 27, 2006.

"Willie Holding July Fourth Picnic in Fort Worth." *Odessa American,* April 18, 2004.

"Willie Honored in Hillsboro." *Willie's World,* spring 2006.

"Willie Nelson Avoids Jail Time in Marijuana Case." *Dallas Morning News,* April 25, 2007.

"Willie Nelson to Be Inducted into Hillsboro Area Chamber Hall of Fame." *Clifton Record,* December 23, 2005.

"Willie Nelson Cited for Pot, Mushrooms." Associated Press. CNN.com, September 18, 2006.

"Willie Nelson Goes Above and Beyond." *Clifton Record,* June 2, 2006.

"Willie Nelson Releases Gay Cowboy Song." Associated Press, February 15, 2006.

"Willie's Fete." *Waco Tribune-Herald*, March 26, 1993.

"Willie's Picnic Off Again." *Waco Tribune-Herald*, July 2, 2002.

ADDITIONAL SOURCES

American Digest column. *Austin American-Statesman*, February 26, 2006.

"Crazy." From "The 100 Most Important American Musical Works of the Twentieth Century." National Public Radio, September 4, 2000.

Family Bible with Willie Nelson and Sister Bobbie. RFD-TV, 2006.

Hamblin, Tim. Austin History Center. Austin Public Library, Austin, TX.

Lost Highway Records. "Music Legends" and other press releases. Nashville, TN, January 2006–2007.

McFadden, Owen. "Outlaw: The Willie Nelson Story." Broadcast on BBC2, London, November 14, 21, and 28, and December 5, 2006.

New York Public Library, New York.

Pedernales Records. Press release, March 16, 2007.

WEB SITES

Stillisstillmoving.com

Willienelson.com

SELECTED
DISCOGRAPHY

There are more than three hundred records with Willie Nelson's name on the cover. Many are original recordings, many others are reissues, and some are bootlegs.

The complete compilation of known recordings by Willie Nelson between 1953 and 1972 can be found in two box sets issued by Bear Family Records in Germany.

It's Been Rough and Rocky Travelin', consisting of three CDs and a sixty-four-page booklet written by Rich Kienzle, contains Willie's earliest recordings, covering the period from 1953 to 1964, including his first demo tape, with "When I've Sang My Last Hillbilly Song" and "The Storm Has Just Begun," made for Sarg Records; his first single, "No Place for Me" b/w "Lumberjack," for Willie Nelson Records, including alternate versions; his "Attention, Songwriters" commercial aired on XEG radio; his singles for D Records; his "Nite Life" for Rx Records; and his two albums for Liberty Records.

Nashville Was the Roughest . . . , consisting of eight CDs and a seventy-two-page booklet written by Rich Kienzle, contains all of Willie's recordings for Monument Records and RCA Records between 1964 and 1972.

Willie Nelson: The Complete Atlantic Sessions (Atlantic Records) covers the pivotal period of 1973 to 1974, including the *Shotgun Willie* and *Phases and Stages* albums, plus outtakes from both sessions, and the 1974 live recording from the Texas Opry House in Austin. In addition, there is a forty-three-page booklet written by compilation producer James Austin, record producer Jerry Wexler, and music critic Bill Bentley.

Willie Nelson: A Classic and Unreleased Collection (Rhino) is a two-CD set with a thirty-page booklet written by Rich Kienzle. It features Nelson's first single, "No Place for Me" b/w "Lumberjack"; the fifteen-song demo he recorded for Pamper Music in Nashville in 1961; outtakes from his recording sessions for Atlantic Records in 1973 to 1974; his duet with Tracy Nelson on "After the Fire Is Gone"; the 1974 live recording from the Texas Opry House in Austin; and twenty-four mid-1980s vintage tracks from the unreleased albums *Sugar Moon* and *Willie Sings Hank Williams,* and from *The IRS Tapes: Who'll Buy My Memories?*

One Hell of a Ride (Columbia Legacy) features one hundred songs recorded by Willie between 1975 and 1995, when he was with Columbia Records.

Everyone has their Willie favorites. My forty must-have Willie Nelson albums are:

Crazy: The Demo Sessions (Sugar Hill)
And Then I Wrote (Liberty)
Here's Willie Nelson (Liberty)
Country Willie: His Own Songs (RCA)
Live Country Music Concert (live at Panther
    Hall) (RCA)
Texas in My Soul (RCA)
Yesterday's Wine (RCA)
Shotgun Willie (Atlantic)
Phases and Stages (Atlantic)
Red Headed Stranger (Columbia)
The Sound in Your Mind (Columbia)
The Troublemaker (Columbia)
To Lefty from Willie (Columbia)
Wanted! The Outlaws (with Waylon Jennings,
    Jessi Colter, Tompall Glaser) (RCA)
Stardust (Columbia)
Waylon and Willie (RCA)

Willie and Family Live (Columbia)

One for the Road (with Leon Russell)
  (Columbia)

Honeysuckle Rose (sound track) (Columbia)

Somewhere Over the Rainbow (Columbia)

Always on My Mind (Columbia)

Pancho and Lefty (with Merle Haggard)
  (Columbia)

Half Nelson (with various artists) (Columbia)

The Highwayman (with the
  Highwaymen—Johnny Cash, Kris
  Kristofferson, and Waylon Jennings)
  (Columbia)

Clean Shirt (with Waylon Jennings) (Sony)

A Horse Called Music (Sony)

The IRS Tapes: Who'll Buy My Memories?
  (Sony)

Across the Borderline (Sony)

Just One Love (with Kimmie Rhodes) (Justice)

Spirit (Island)

How Great Thou Art (Finer Arts)

Teatro (Island)

Night and Day (Finer Arts)

Milk Cow Blues (Lost Highway)

Rainbow Connection (Island)

Run That by Me One More Time (with Ray
  Price) (Lost Highway)

Countryman (Lost Highway)
It Will Always Be (Lost Highway)
You Don't Know Me: The Songs of Cindy Walker
  (Lost Highway)
Last of the Breed (with Ray Price and Merle
  Haggard) (Lost Highway)